W9-CAG-373

The Social Animal

Books by Elliot Aronson

Handbook of Social Psychology (with G. Lindzey), 2nd ed., 1968–1969

Theories of Cognitive Consistency (with R. Abelson et al.), 1968

Voices of Modern Psychology, 1969

The Social Animal, 1972, 1976, 1980, 1984, 1988, 1992, 1995, 1999

Readings About The Social Animal, 1972, 1976, 1980, 1984, 1988, 1992, 1995, 1999

Social Psychology (with R. Helmreich), 1973

Research Methods in Social Psychology (with Carlsmith & Ellsworth), 1976

The Jigsaw Classroom, 1978

Burnout: From Tedium to Personal Growth (with A. Pines & D. Kafry), 1981

Energy Use: The Human Dimension (with P. C. Stern), 1984

The Handbook of Social Psychology (with G. Lindzey), 3rd ed., 1985

Career Burnout (with A. Pines), 1988

Methods of Research in Social Psychology (with Ellsworth, Carlsmith, & Gonzales), 1990

Age of Propaganda (with A. R. Pratkanis), 1992, 2000

Social Psychology: Volumes 1, 2, & 3 (with A. R. Pratkanis), 1992

Social Psychology: The Heart and the Mind (with T. Wilson & R. Akert), 1994

Nobody Left to Hate: Teaching Compassion After Columbine, 2000

Social Psychology: An Introduction (with T. Wilson & R. Akert), 2002

Ninth Edition

The Social Animal

Elliot Aronson
University of California, Santa Cruz

WORTH PUBLISHERS

to Vera, of course

The Social Animal, Ninth Edition

Senior Sponsoring Editor: Laura Pople
Executive Marketing Manager: Renée Altier
Art Director: Babs Reingold
Project Management: Print Matters, Inc.
Production Manager: Sarah Segal
Permissions Manager: Nancy Walker
Composition: Compset, Inc.
Printing and Binding: R. R. Donnelley and Sons
Cover drawing by Tom Durfee

Library of Congress Control Number: 2003107776

ISBN: 0-7167-5715-X

© 2004, 1999 by Worth Publishers
© 1995, 1992, 1988, 1984, 1980, 1976, 1972 by W. H. Freeman & Company
All rights reserved.

Printed in the United States of America

First printing 2003

Worth Publishers
41 Madison Avenue
New York, NY 10010
www.worthpublishers.com

Contents

Saul Steinberg, *Untitled drawing*, ink on paper.
Originally published in *The New Yorker*, May 29, 1965.
© The Saul Steinberg Foundation / Artists Rights Society (ARS), New York

Why I Wrote
This Book

In 1970–1971, I was invited to spend the year in Stanford, California, at the Center for Advanced Study in the Behavioral Sciences. During that year, I was given all the support, encouragement, and freedom to do whatever I wanted, and I was assured that I was not responsible to anyone for anything. There, on a beautiful hill, roughly thirty miles from San Francisco (my favorite city), with a whole year in which to do anything my heart desired, I chose to write this book. Surrounded as I was by the beauty of the countryside, and close as I was to the excitement of San Francisco, why did I lock myself in a cubicle and write a book? It's not that I'm crazy and it's not that I needed the money. If there's a single reason why I wrote this book, it's that I once heard myself tell a large class of sophomores that social psychology is a young science—and it made me feel like a coward.

Let me explain: We social psychologists are fond of saying that social psychology is a young science—and it *is* a young science. Of course, astute observers have been making interesting pronouncements and proposing exciting hypotheses about social phenomena at least since the time of Aristotle, but these pronouncements and hypotheses were not seriously tested until well into the twentieth century. The first systematic social psychological experiment (to my knowledge) was conducted by Triplett in 1898 (he measured the effect of competition on performance), but it was not until the late 1930s that experimental social psychology really took off, primarily under the inspiration of Kurt Lewin and his talented students. By the same token it is interesting to note that, although Aristotle first asserted some of the basic principles of social influence and persuasion around 350 B.C., it was not until the middle of the twentieth century that those principles were put to the experimental test by Carl Hovland and his associates.

In another sense, however, to claim that social psychology is a young science is to be guilty of a gigantic cop-out: It's a way of pleading with people not to expect too much from us. Specifically, it can be our way of dodging the responsibility for, and avoiding the risks inherent in, applying our findings to the problems of the world we live in. In this sense, protesting that social psychology is a young science is akin to claiming that we are not yet ready to say anything important, useful, or (if the reader will forgive me for using an overused word) relevant.

The purpose of this volume is unashamedly (but with some trepidation) to spell out the relevance that sociopsychological research might have for some of the problems besetting contemporary society. Most of the data discussed in this volume are based on experiments; most of the illustrations and examples, however, are derived from current social problems—including prejudice, propaganda, war, alienation, aggression, unrest, and political upheaval. This duality reflects two of my own biases—biases that I cherish. The first is that the experimental method is the best way to understand a complex phenomenon. It is a truism of science that the only way to really know the world is to reconstruct it: That is, in order to truly understand what causes what, we must do more than simply observe—rather, we must be responsible for producing the first "what" so that we can be sure that it really caused the second "what." My second bias is that the only way to be certain that the causal relations uncovered in experiments are valid is to bring them out of the laboratory and into the real world. Thus, as a scientist, I like to work in a laboratory; as a citizen, however, I like to have windows through which I can look out upon the world. Windows, of course, work in both directions: We often derive hypotheses from everyday life. We can best test these hypotheses under the sterile conditions of the laboratory; and in order to try to keep our ideas from becoming sterile, we attempt to take our laboratory findings back out through the window to see if they hold up in the real world.

Implicit in all this is my belief that social psychology is extremely important—that social psychologists can play a vital role in making the world a better place. Indeed, in my more grandiose moments, I nurse the secret belief that social psychologists are in a unique position to have a profound and beneficial impact on our lives by providing an increased understanding of such important phenomena as conformity, persuasion, prejudice, love, and aggression. Now that my secret belief is no longer a secret, I can promise only to try not to force it down the readers' throats on the following pages. Rather, I'll leave it to the readers to decide, after they have finished this volume, whether social psychologists have discovered or can ever discover anything useful—much less anything uniquely important.

Compared to other texts in social psychology, this is a slim volume—and purposely so. It is meant to be a brief introduction to the world of social psychology, not an encyclopedic catalogue of research and theory. Because I opted to make it brief, I had to be selective. This means both that there are some traditional topics I chose not to cover and that I have not gone into exhaustive detail with those topics I did choose to cover. Because of my desire to keep the book compact and accessible, it was a difficult book to write. I have had to be more a "news analyst" than a "reporter." For example, there are many controversies that I did not fully describe. Rather, I exercised my own judgment, made an educated (and, I hope, honest) assessment of what is currently the most accurate description of the field, and stated it as clearly as I could.

This decision was made with the student in mind—this book was written for students, not for my colleagues. If I have learned one thing in almost forty years of college teaching, it is that, although a detailed presentation of all positions is useful (and sometimes even fascinating) to one's colleagues, it tends to leave students cold. Students, in effect, ask us what time it is, and we, in effect, present them with a chart showing the various time zones around the world, a history of time-telling from the sundial to the latest computerized creation, and a detailed description of the anatomy of the grandfather clock. By the time we've finished, they've lost interest in the question. Nothing is safer than to state all sides of all issues, but few things are more boring. Although I have discussed controversial issues, I have not hesitated to draw conclusions. In short, I have attempted to be brief without being unfair, and I have tried to present complex material simply and clearly without oversimplifying. Only the reader can determine how successful I have been in accomplishing either of these goals.

When I finished writing the first edition of this book in 1972, I thought I was done with it. How naive. Early in 1975, I decided, with some reluctance, to revise this book for the first time. A lot had happened in three years. Not only had new and exciting things been discovered in the field of social psychology, but, even more important, the world had taken a few major turns since the winter of 1972, when I put the final scrawl on my yellow pad for the first edition. To name just a few of the major events: A brutal, draining, and divisive war came to an end; a vice-president and a president of the United States were forced to resign in humiliation; and the women's liberation movement was beginning to have a significant impact on the consciousness of the nation. These were sociopsychological events of the greatest significance. The indolent slob who lives inside me was forced to acknowledge (with a long sigh) that any book that purports to be about our lives—yours and mine—must strive to stay abreast of the times.

Needless to say, it didn't end with one revision. As it turned out, the steady march of events has forced me to revise the book every three or four years. Again, not only do societal events change rapidly, but, social psychology, being a vibrant science, continues to produce interesting new concepts and findings. To fail to keep in touch with this research would be a disservice to the serious student. But here, an author must be careful. In our zeal to be thoroughly modern, there is a tendency for textbook writers to neglect perfectly respectable research just because it happens to be more than ten years old.

Here's how it happens: We writers want to retain the classics and we want to add the research that has come out since the last edition. But we don't want the book to get much fatter. Something has to go; and so, in most textbooks, a lot of good research gets swept into oblivion, not because it has been replaced by something better—only by something newer. This creates the illusion that the field lacks continuity—that is, there's the classic research and the modern research with very little in between. This is terribly misleading.

Over the past three decades, I have tried to deal with this problem by steadfastly refusing to replace a fine "middle-aged" study by a newer one unless the newer one added something important to our understanding of the phenomenon being discussed. In the ninth edition, I have described a great many new studies—studies that were performed during the past five years. But I hasten to add that, by and large, these studies really are *new*—not simply recent. My hope is that the revisions of *The Social Animal* retain the compact grace of the original and remain up to date without eliminating or short-changing the fine research of the recent past.

Acknowledgments

I am indicated on the title page as the sole author of this book, and it is certainly true that I wrote down all the words and did most of the thinking that produced them. Accordingly, if there are any stupidities in this book, they are mine, and if anything you read on these pages makes you angry, I'm the person you should yell at. At the same time, I want to confess that I never do anything entirely by myself: Many people contributed their knowledge and ideas to my word factory, and I would like to take this opportunity to thank them for their generous help.

For the first edition of this book, Vera Aronson (my wife) and Ellen Berscheid (one of my most distinguished former students) were particularly helpful. They painstakingly went over the original manuscript, page by page and line by line, making numerous suggestions and criticisms that had a significant impact on the final form of this book. Moreover, their enthusiasm for the project was infectious and helped me to climb out of frequent bouts of "writer's despair."

Several other people contributed valuable ideas and suggestions. I cannot possibly cite them all, but the most significant contributors were Nancy Aston, Leonard Berkowitz, David Bradford, John Darley, Richard Easterlin, Jonathan Freedman, James Freel, Robert Helmreich, Judy Hilton, Michael Kahn, John Kaplan, Judson Mills, and Jev Sikes.

Most of this book was written while I was a Fellow at the Center for Advanced Study in the Behavioral Studies at Stanford, California, and I am deeply grateful to the staff of that fine institution for providing me with the necessary leisure and facilities.

Finally, I am pleased to report that my friend and mentor, Leon Festinger, did not have anything to do with this manuscript—directly. He never read it, and, to my knowledge, he was not even aware that I was writing it. He is, however, responsible for its existence. Leon was a wonderful teacher and a demanding role model. I could say that he taught me all I know about social psychology, but that would be a gross understatement. He taught me something much more valuable than that: He taught me how to find out the things that neither I nor anybody else knew.

March 1972

This book is now in its ninth edition. One might say that I have grown old revising it. It is a bittersweet feeling to be able to trace the passage of time by watching the face on the back cover of this book (*my* face!) become increasingly wrinkled and gray-bearded. When I first wrote the book, I was moved to acknowledge my indebtedness to my friend and mentor, Leon Festinger. It goes without saying that I still feel gratitude and affection for that good and great man. If anything, these feelings intensified over the years. I loved being his student—and I guess I will never stop being his student. In 1989, Leon died, marking the end of an important era in social psychology. He is sorely missed—not only by those of us who knew and loved him, but also by anyone who has been influenced by his research and theories; this would include just about anyone who has ever been a student of social psychology.

In addition, as this book and I have grown older, I have become increasingly aware of my indebtedness to *my own* students. Every four years, as I begin revising the book, I am struck by the realization that these are not simply my own ideas—rather, they are ideas I have developed in collaboration with my students. Over the past four decades, I have been blessed with a great many outstanding students, starting with my very first research assistants in 1960 (Merrill Carlsmith, Tony Greenwald and John M. Darley) to the present moment. They have taught me a great deal, and it is a pleasure to acknowledge my debt to all of them. I have also enjoyed talking with and stealing ideas from some remarkably gifted colleagues. Two of them in particular, Anthony Pratkanis and Carol Tavris, have contributed a great deal to the development of this book. It is a pleasure to acknowledge their generosity.

There is also a sense in which this book is, in part, a family enterprise. This has been especially true in recent years when I have experienced the singular gratification of being deeply influenced by my grown children—each in his/her own fashion. My youngest son, Joshua Aronson (a brilliant experimental social psychologist in his own right), takes great delight in trying to keep me on my toes regarding recent methodological and theoretical innovations. More specifically, he has provided me with invaluable insights and suggestions about changes to be made in this, the ninth edition of this book—and has even done some of the writing. My eldest son, Hal Aronson (an environmental sociologist), helps to keep my focus broader than the confines of the laboratory. And my middle children, Neal Aronson (a firefighter for the city of Santa Cruz) and Julie Aronson (an educational researcher and evaluator), are in the trenches of human service on a day-to-day basis, reminding me by their example that, ultimately, social psychology must strive to be useful to people in their daily lives.

Finally, as you may have noticed, the dedication of this book reads, "To Vera, of course." The Vera in question is Vera Aronson, who has been my best friend and favorite consultant for almost fifty years and who (to my great good fortune) also happens to be my wife. To anyone who knows us well, the phrase, "of course" in the dedication is redundant. And, because redundancy is an occupational hazard in the teaching game, I must admit (with a blush) that it is almost certainly not the last redundancy you will need to put up with.

Elliot Aronson
March 2003

The Social Animal

Man is by nature a social animal; an individual who is unsocial naturally and not accidentally is either beneath our notice or more than human. Society is something in nature that precedes the individual. Anyone who either cannot lead the common life or is so self-sufficient as not to need to, and therefore does not partake of society, is either a beast or a god.

Aristotle
Politics, c. 328 B.C.

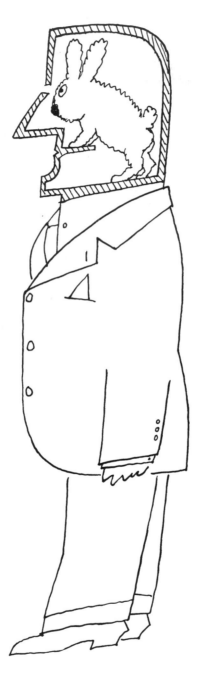

Saul Steinberg, *Untitled drawing*, ink on paper.
Originally published in *The New Yorker*, November 1, 1958.
© The Saul Steinberg Foundation / Artists Rights Society (ARS), New York

1
What Is Social Psychology?

As far as we know, Aristotle was the first serious thinker to formulate some of the basic principles of social influence and persuasion. However, although he did say that man is a social animal, it is unlikely that he was the first person to make that observation. Moreover, chances are he was not the first person to marvel at the truth of that statement while simultaneously puzzling over its triteness and insubstantiality. Although it is certainly true that humans are social animals, so are a host of other creatures, from ants and bees to monkeys and apes. What does it mean to say that humans are "social animals"? Let's look at some concrete examples:

A college student named Sam and four of his acquaintances are watching a presidential candidate make a speech on television. Sam is favorably impressed; he likes him better than the opposing candidate because of his sincerity. After the speech, one of the other students asserts that she was turned off by the candidate, that she considered him to be a complete phony, and that she prefers the opposing candidate. All of the others are quick to agree with her. Sam looks puzzled and a trifle distressed. Finally, he mumbles to his acquaintances, "I guess he didn't come across as sincere as I would have hoped."

A second-grade teacher stands before her class and asks, "What is the sum of six, nine, four, and eleven?" A girl in the third row puzzles over the question for several seconds, hesitates, raises her hand tentatively, and when called on, haltingly answers, "Thirty?" The teacher nods, smiles at her, says, "Nice work, Carol," and pastes a gold star on her forehead. She then asks the class, "What is the sum of seven, four, eight, three, and ten?" Without wasting a moment, Carol leaps to her feet and shouts, "Thirty-two!"

A 4-year-old boy is given a toy drum for his birthday. After pounding on it for a few minutes, he casts it aside and studiously ignores it for the next several weeks. One day a friend comes to visit, picks up the drum, and is about to play with it. Suddenly the young "owner" tears the drum from his friend's grasp and proceeds to play with it as if it had always been his favorite toy.

A 10-year-old girl avidly consumes two bowls of Wheaties daily because an Olympic gymnastics champion endorses the product and implies that she owes her athletic prowess, in part, to the consumption of that particular brand of cereal.

A shopkeeper who has lived his entire life in a small town in Montana has never had any contact with real, live black people, but he "knows" they are unintelligent, lazy, and oversexed.

Charlie, a high-school senior, has recently moved to a new city. He used to be quite popular, but not anymore. Although the kids at school are civil to him, they have not been particularly friendly. He is feeling lonely, insecure, and unattractive. One day, during lunch period, he finds himself at a table with two of his female classmates. One of them is warm, attractive, brilliant, and vivacious; he has been admiring her and daydreaming about her. For several weeks he has been longing for an opportunity to talk to her. The other young woman is not nearly as appealing. Charlie ignores the vivacious woman of his dreams and begins an earnest conversation with her companion.

A college student named Debbie, receives a "Dear Jane" letter from her longtime boyfriend. Although Debbie has always prided herself on keeping fit and eating sensibly, the rejection sets her on an eating binge, during which she consumes several boxes of Oreos, Mallomars and Chips Ahoy in the space of a weekend. Moreover, although a straight-A student, at or near the top in the Engineering major, she flunks an exam in calculus that she normally would have aced.

During the war in Vietnam, a few hundred Kent State University students were demonstrating against that war—a common occurrence on college campuses during that troubled time in our history. For some unexplained reason, the Ohio National Guard, assigned to keep the peace on that campus, opened fire, killing four of the students. Following the tragedy, a local high-school teacher asserted that the slain students deserved to die. She made this statement even though she was well aware of the fact that at least two of the victims were not participating in the demonstration but were peacefully walking across campus at the time of the shooting. Indeed, she went on to say, "Anyone who appears on the streets of a city like Kent with long hair, dirty clothes, or barefooted deserves to be shot."[1]

When the Reverend Jim Jones sounded the alert, over 900 members of the People's Temple settlement in Guyana gathered before him. He knew that some of the members of a congressional investigation party had been murdered and that the sanctity and isolation of Jonestown would soon be violated. Jones proclaimed that it was time for them to die. Vats of poison were prepared, and amid only scattered shouts of protest or acts of resistance, mothers and fathers administered the fatal mixture to their infants and children, drank it themselves, and lay down, arm in arm, waiting to die.

On April 20, 1999, the corridors and classrooms of Columbine High School in Littleton, Colorado, reverberated with the sound of gunshots. Two students, armed with assault weapons and explosives, had gone on a rampage, killing a teacher and several of their fellow students. They then turned their guns on themselves. After the smoke had cleared, fifteen people lay dead (including the shooters) and 23 were hospitalized—many with severe wounds.

Mary has just turned 9. For her birthday, she received a Suzie Homemaker baking and cooking set complete with "her own little oven." Her parents chose this present because she seems very interested in culinary things and is forever helping Mommy set the table, prepare the meals, and clean the house. "Isn't it wonderful," says Mary's father, "how at age nine she is already interested in being a housewife? Little girls must have housewifery built into their genes. Those feminists don't know what they're talking about."

My boyhood friend, George Woods, is an African American. When he and I were growing up together in Massachusetts in the 1940s, he thought of himself as a "colored boy" and felt inferior to his white friends.[2] There were many reasons for this feeling. That George was treated like an inferior by the white community had a direct influence upon him, of course; a number of other forces influenced him less directly. In those days, George could entertain himself by turning on the radio and listening to *Amos 'n Andy*, an enormously popular radio show in which black adults were portrayed as naive children, as stupid, lazy, and illiterate, but rather cute—not unlike friendly, domesticated animals. The black characters were, of course, played by white actors. In films, George could see the stereotyped "colored man," usually a chauffeur or some other menial. A standard plot would have the colored man accompany the white hero into a haunted house, where they heard a strange and ominous noise: The camera would pan in on the "colored man's" face; his eyes growing large with fright, he would scream, "Feets, do your stuff!" and dash through the door, not taking time to open it first. We can only guess what George experienced while viewing these films in the company of his white friends.

Things change. For example, although discrimination and unfairness are still very much a part of our society, George Woods's grandchildren, growing up in the 21st century, do not face exactly the same tribulations as George himself did. The mass media now depict blacks in roles that are not exclusively menial. In the latter part of the 20th century pride in being black began to emerge, along with an interest in, and enthusiasm about African American history and culture. The society is influencing George's grandchildren in a much different way than it influenced George.

Although things do change, we should not be complacent in the belief that all changes are in a linear, humanistic direction. On August 30, 1936, during the Spanish Civil War, a single plane bombed Madrid. There were several casualties, but no one was killed. The world was profoundly shocked by the idea of a congested city being attacked from the air. Newspaper editorials around the world expressed the general horror and indignation of the citizenry. Only 9 years later, U.S. planes dropped nuclear bombs on Hiroshima and Nagasaki. More than 100,000 people were killed and countless thousands suffered severe injuries. Shortly thereafter, a poll indicated that only 4.5 percent of the U.S. population felt we should not have used those weapons, and an astonishing 22.7 percent felt we should have used many more of them before Japan had a chance to surrender.[3] Clearly, something had happened during those 9 years to influence opinion.

A Definition

What is **social psychology**? There are almost as many definitions of social psychology as there are social psychologists. Instead of listing some of these definitions, it might be more informative to let the subject matter define the field. The examples presented on the preceding pages are all illustrations of sociopsychological situations. As diverse as these situations may be, they do contain one common factor: social influence. The opinion of Sam's friends on the merits of the presidential candidate influenced Sam's judgment (or at least his public statement regarding that judgment). The rewards emanating from the teacher influenced the speed and vigor of Carol's classroom responses. The 4-year-old seemed to find his toy drum more attractive because of the inadvertent influence of his friend's interest. The Olympic athlete's influence on our Wheaties-eating youngster, on the other hand, was far from inadvertent; rather, it was intentionally designed to motivate her to convince her parents to buy Wheaties. The Montana shopkeeper was certainly not born with an unflattering stereotype of black people in his head; somebody somehow put it there. Debbie's eating binge and poor performance had something to do with her having been rejected—but precisely how does that work? That Charlie ignored the woman of his dreams almost certainly has something to do with his fear of rejection, the way he was feeling about himself, and his implicit assumption about the relative likelihood of being rejected by either of the two women. Being rejected can have far-reaching consequences, as Debbie's behavior suggests. It may also be that rejection and humiliation played a role in the rampage killings at Columbine High School. Exactly how the high-school teacher in Kent, Ohio, came to believe that innocent people deserved to die is a fascinating and frightening question; for now, let us simply say that this belief was probably influenced by her own indirect complicity in the tragic events on campus. A still more disturbing question arises from Jonestown and Columbine: What forces could induce parents to poison their own children and then take their own lives? What is it that induces teenagers to kill their classmates? Again, these are complex questions to which I hope to provide some insights as this text unfolds.

Turning to little Mary and her Suzie Homemaker set, it is conceivable, as Mary's father says, that "housewifery" is genetic; it is far more likely that, from infancy on, Mary was rewarded and encouraged every time she expressed an interest in such traditionally feminine things as cooking, sewing, and dolls—to a far greater extent than if she expressed an interest in football, boxing, and chemistry. It is also reasonable to assume that, if Mary's kid brother had shown an interest in "housewifery," he would not have received a Suzie Homemaker set for his birthday. Also, as with young George Woods, who felt inferior to his playmates, Mary's self-image could have been shaped by the mass media, which tend to depict women in roles that the culture encourages them to play: housewife, secretary, nurse, schoolteacher; the mass media rarely depict women as biochemists, college professors, or business executives. If we compare the young George Woods with his grandchildren, we see that the self-images of minority-group members can change, and these changes can influence and be influenced by changes in the mass media and changes in the attitudes of the general population. This, of course, is graphically illustrated by the opinions of Americans about the use of nuclear weapons in 1945.

The key phrase in the preceding paragraph is **social influence**. And this becomes our working definition of *social psychology:* the influences that people have upon the beliefs or behavior of others. Using this as our definition, we will attempt to understand many of the phenomena described in the preceding illustrations. How are people influenced? Why do they accept influence—or, put another way, what's in it for them? What are the variables that increase or decrease the effectiveness of social influence? Does such influence have a permanent effect or is it merely transitory? What are the variables that increase or decrease the permanence of the effects of social influence? Can the same principles be applied equally to the attitudes of the high-school teacher in Kent, Ohio, and to the toy preferences of young children? How does one person come to like another person? Is it through these same processes that we come to like our new sports car or a box of Wheaties? How does a person develop prejudices against an ethnic or racial group? Is it akin to liking—but in reverse—or does it involve an entirely different set of psychological processes?

Most people are interested in questions of this sort. Because all human beings spend a good deal of our time interacting with other people—being influenced by them, influencing them, being delighted, amused, saddened and angered by them—it is natural that we develop hypotheses about social behavior. In that sense, we are all amateur social psychologists. Although most amateur social psychologists test these hypotheses to their own satisfaction, these "tests" lack the rigor and impartiality of careful scientific investigation. Often, the results of scientific research are identical with what most people "know" to be true. This is not surprising; conventional wisdom is usually based upon shrewd observation that has stood the test of time.

In fact, when you are reading the experiments in this volume, you may occasionally find yourself thinking: "That's obvious—why did they spend time and money to 'discover' that one?" There are several reasons why we do experiments, even though the results often seem unsurprising. For one thing, we are all susceptible to the **hindsight bias**, which refers to our tendency to overestimate our powers of prediction once we know the outcome of a given event. For example, research has shown that on the day after an election, when people are asked which candidates they would have picked to win, they almost always believe they would have picked the actual winners—even though the day *before* the election, their predictions wouldn't have been nearly as accurate.[4] Similarly, the outcome of an experiment almost always seems more predictable once we have the results in hand than if we had been asked to predict the results without the benefit of hindsight.

In addition, it is important to conduct research—even if the results seem obvious—because many of the things we "know" to be true turn out to be false when carefully investigated. Although it seems reasonable, for example, to assume that people who are threatened with severe punishment for engaging in a certain behavior might eventually learn to despise that behavior, it turns out that when this question is studied scientifically, just the reverse is true: People who are threatened with mild punishment develop a dislike for the forbidden behavior; people who are severely threatened show, if anything, a slight increase in liking for the forbidden behavior. Likewise, most of us, from our own experience, would guess that, if we overheard someone saying nice things about us (behind our backs), we would tend to like that person—all other things being equal. This turns out to be true. But what is equally true is that we tend to like that person even more if some of the remarks we overhear are anything but nice. More will be said about these phenomena in the following chapters.

In our attempt to understand human social behavior, professional social psychologists have a great advantage over most amateur social psychologists.

Although, like the amateurs, we professionals usually begin with careful observation, we can go far beyond that. We do not need to wait for things to happen so that we can observe how people respond; we can, in fact, *make* things happen. That is, social psychologists can conduct an experiment in which scores of people are subjected to particular events (for example, a severe threat or a mild threat; overhearing nice things or overhearing a combination of nice and nasty things). Moreover, we can do this in situations in which everything can be held constant except the particular events being investigated. Professional social psychologists can, therefore, draw conclusions based on data far more precise and numerous than those available to the amateur social psychologist, who must depend upon observations of events that occur randomly and under complex circumstances where many things are happening at once.

Nearly all the data presented in this book are based upon experimental evidence. It is important, for this reason, that the reader (1) understands what constitutes an experiment in social psychology and (2) understands the advantages, disadvantages, ethical problems, excitements, headaches, and heartaches that are associated with this adventure. Although an understanding of the experimental method is important, it is by no means essential to an understanding of the substantive material presented here. Therefore, the chapter "Social Psychology as a Science" is the final one in this book. As a reader, you can peruse this chapter before reading on (if you prefer to understand the technicalities before delving into the substantive material), or you can read it at any point on your journey through the book—whenever your interest is piqued.

People Who Do Crazy Things Are Not Necessarily Crazy

The social psychologist studies social situations that affect people's behavior. Occasionally, these natural situations become focused into pressures so great that they cause people to behave in ways easily classifiable as abnormal. When I say people, I mean very large numbers of people. To my mind, it does not increase our understanding of human behavior to classify these people as psychotic. It is much more useful to try to understand the nature of the situation and the processes that were operating to produce the behavior. This leads us to Aronson's first law:

People who do crazy things are not necessarily crazy.

Let us take, as an illustration, the Ohio schoolteacher who asserted that the four Kent State students deserved to die. I don't think she was alone in this belief—and although all the people who hold this belief may be insane, I seriously doubt it. Moreover, I doubt that classifying them as psychotic does much to enhance our understanding of the phenomenon. Similarly, in the aftermath of the Kent State slayings, the rumor spread that the slain girls were pregnant anyway—so that it was a blessing they died—and that all four of the students were so filthy and so covered with lice that the mortuary attendants became nauseated while examining the bodies. These rumors, of course, were totally false. But, according to James Michener,[5] they spread like wildfire. Were all the people who believed and spread these rumors insane? Later in this book, we will examine the processes that produce this kind of behavior, to which most of us are susceptible, under the right sociopsychological conditions.

One of my former students, Ellen Berscheid,[6] has observed that people have a tendency to explain unpleasant behavior by attaching a label to the perpetrator ("crazy," "sadistic," or whatever), thereby excluding that person from the rest of "us nice people." In that way, we need not worry about the unpleasant behavior because it has nothing to do with us nice folks. According to Berscheid, the danger in this kind of thinking is that it tends to make us smug about our own susceptibility to situational pressures producing unpleasant behavior, and it leads to a rather simple-minded approach to the solution of social problems. Specifically, such a simple-minded solution might include the development of a set of diagnostic tests to determine who is a liar, who is a sadist, who is corrupt, who is a maniac. Social action might then consist of identifying these people and relegating them to the appropriate institutions. Of course, this is not to say that psychosis does not exist or that psychotics should never be institutionalized. Nor am I saying that all people are the same and respond exactly as crazily to the same intense social pressures. To repeat, what I *am* saying is that some situational variables can move a great proportion of us "normal" adults to behave in very unappetizing ways. It is of paramount importance that we attempt to understand these variables and the processes producing unpleasant or destructive behavior.

An illustration might be useful. Think of a prison. Consider the guards. What are they like? Chances are that most people would imagine prison guards to be tough, callous, unfeeling people. Some might even consider them to be cruel, tyrannical, and sadistic. People who take this kind of **dispositional** view of the world might suggest that the reason people become guards is to have an opportunity to exercise their cruelty with relative impunity. Now picture the prisoners. What are they like? Rebellious? Docile? No matter what specific pictures exist inside our heads, the point is that there are pictures there—and most of us believe that the prisoners and the guards are quite different from us in character and personality.

This may be true, but it may be more complicated than that. In a dramatic demonstration, Philip Zimbardo and his colleagues created a simulated prison in the basement of the Psychology Department at Stanford University. Into this "prison" he brought a group of normal, mature, stable, intelligent young men. By flipping a coin, Zimbardo designated one-half of them prisoners and one-half of them guards, and they lived as such for several days. What happened? Let's allow Zimbardo to tell us in his own words:

> At the end of only six days we had to close down our mock prison because what we saw was frightening. It was no longer apparent to us or most of the subjects where they ended and their roles began. The majority had indeed become "prisoners" or "guards," no longer able to clearly differentiate between role-playing and self. There were dramatic changes in virtually every aspect of their behavior, thinking and feeling. In less than a week, the experience of imprisonment undid (temporarily) a lifetime of learning; human values were suspended, self-concepts were challenged, and the ugliest, most base, pathological side of human nature surfaced. We were horrified because we saw some boys ("guards") treat other boys as if they were despicable animals, taking pleasure in cruelty, while other boys ("prisoners") became servile, dehumanized robots who thought only of escape, of their own individual survival, and of their mounting hatred of the guards.[7]

Saul Steinberg, *Untitled drawing*, ink on paper.
Originally published in *The New Yorker*, April 24, 1965.
© The Saul Steinberg Foundation / Artists Rights Society (ARS), New York

2
Conformity

One consequence of the fact that we are social animals is that we live in a state of tension between values associated with individuality and values associated with conformity. James Thurber has captured the flavor of conformity in the following description:

Suddenly somebody began to run. It may be that he had simply remembered, all of a moment, an engagement to meet his wife, for which he was now frightfully late. Whatever it was, he ran east on Broad Street (probably toward the Maramor Restaurant, a favorite place for a man to meet his wife). Somebody else began to run, perhaps a newsboy in high spirits. Another man, a portly gentleman of affairs, broke into a trot. Inside of ten minutes, everybody on High Street, from the Union Depot to the Courthouse was running. A loud mumble gradually crystallized into the dread word "dam." "The dam has broke!" The fear was put into words by a little old lady in an electric car, or by a traffic cop, or by a small boy: nobody knows who, nor does it now really matter. Two thousand people were abruptly in full flight. "Go east!" was the cry that arose east away from the river, east to safety. "Go east! Go east!" A tall spare woman with grim eyes and a determined chin ran past me down the middle of the street. I was still uncertain as to what was the matter, in spite of all the shouting. I drew up alongside the woman with some effort, for although she was in her late fifties, she had a beautiful easy running form and seemed to be in excellent condition. "What is it?" I puffed. She gave a quick glance and then looked ahead again, stepping up her pace a trifle. "Don't ask me, ask God!" she said.[1]

This passage from Thurber, although comical, is an apt illustration of people conforming. One or two individuals began running for their own reasons; before long, everyone was running. Why? Because others were running. According to Thurber's story, when the running people realized that the dam hadn't given way after all, they felt pretty foolish. And yet, how much more foolish would they have felt if they hadn't conformed and the dam had, in fact, burst? Is conformity good or bad? In its simplest sense, this is an absurd question. But words do carry evaluative meaning. Thus, to be called an individualist or a nonconformist is to be designated, by connotation, as a "good" person. The label evokes an image of Daniel Boone standing on a mountaintop with a rifle slung over his shoulder, the breeze blowing through his hair, as the sun sets in the background. To be called a conformist, in our culture, is somehow to be designated as an "inadequate" person. It evokes an image of a row of bureaucratic men dressed in gray flannel suits, carrying identical attaché cases, looking as though they had been created by a cookie cutter.

But we can use synonymous words that convey very different images. For *individualist* or *nonconformist* we can substitute *deviate;* for *conformist* we can substitute *team player.* Somehow, *deviate* does not evoke Daniel Boone on the mountaintop, and *team player* does not evoke the cookie cutter–produced bureaucrat.

When we look a little closer, we see an inconsistency in the way our society seems to feel about conformity (team playing) and nonconformity (deviance). For example, one of the best-sellers of the 1950s was a book by John F. Kennedy called *Profiles in Courage,* wherein the author praised several politicians for their courage in resisting great pressure and refusing to conform. To put it another way, Kennedy was praising people who refused to be good team players, who refused to vote or act as their parties or constituents expected them to. Although their actions earned Kennedy's praise long after the deeds were done, the immediate reactions of their colleagues were generally far from positive. Nonconformists may be praised by historians or idolized in films or literature long after the fact of their nonconformity, but they are usually not held in high esteem at the time by those people to whose demands they refuse to conform. This observation receives strong support from a number of experiments in social psychology. For example, in a classic experiment by Stanley Schachter,[2] several groups of students met for a discussion of the case history of a juvenile delinquent named Johnny Rocco. After reading the case, each group was asked to discuss it and to suggest a treatment for Johnny on a scale that ranged from "very lenient treatment" on one end to "very hard treatment" on the other. A typical group consisted of approximately nine participants, six of whom were real participants and three of whom were paid confederates of the experimenter. The confederates took turns playing one of three roles that they had carefully rehearsed in advance: the *modal* person, who took a position that conformed to the average position of the real participants; the *deviate,* who took a position diametrically opposed to the general orientation of the group; and the *slider,* whose initial position was similar to the deviate's but who, in the course of the discussion, gradually "slid" into a modal, conforming position. The results clearly showed that the person who was liked most was the modal person who conformed to the group norm; the deviate was liked least. In a more recent experiment, Arie Kruglanski and Donna Webster[3] found that when nonconformists voiced a dissenting opinion close to the deadline (when groups were feeling the pinch to come to closure), they were rejected even more than when they voiced their dissenting opinion earlier in the discussion.

Thus, the data indicate that the "establishment" or modal group tends to like conformists better than nonconformists. Clearly, there are situations in which conformity is highly desirable and nonconformity constitutes an unmitigated disaster. Suppose, for example, that I suddenly decide that I am fed up with being a conformist. So I hop into my car and start driving down the left-hand side of the road—not a very adaptive way of displaying my rugged individualism and not very fair to you if you happen to be driving toward me (conformist-style) on the same street. Similarly, consider the rebellious teenager who smokes cigarettes, stays out late, gets tattooed, or dates a certain boy just because she knows that her parents disapprove. She is not manifesting independence so much as she is displaying anticonformity, not thinking for herself but automatically acting contrary to the desires or expectations of others.

On the other hand, I do not intend to suggest that conformity is always adaptive and nonconformity is always maladaptive. There are compelling situations in which conformity can be disastrous and tragic. Moreover, even knowledgeable and sophisticated decision makers can fall prey to special kinds of conformity pressures inherent in making group decisions. Consider the following examples: In his memoirs, Albert Speer, one of Adolf Hitler's top advisers, describes the circle around Hitler as one of total conformity—deviation was not permitted. In such an atmosphere, even the most barbarous activities seemed reasonable because the absence of dissent, which conveyed the illusion of unanimity, prevented any individual from entertaining the possibility that other options might exist.

> In normal circumstances people who turn their backs on reality are soon set straight by the mockery and criticism of those around them. In the Third Reich there were not such correctives. On the contrary, every self-deception was multiplied as in a hall of distorting mirrors, becoming a repeatedly confirmed picture of a fantastical dream world which no longer bore any relationship to the grim outside world. In those mirrors I could see nothing but my own face reproduced many times over.[4]

A more familiar but perhaps less dramatic example concerns some of the men involved with former president Richard Nixon and his "palace guard" in the Watergate cover-up. Here, men in high government office—many of whom were attorneys—perjured themselves, destroyed evidence, and offered bribes without an apparent second thought. This was due, at least in part, to the closed circle of single-mindedness that surrounded the president in the early 1970s. This single-mindedness made deviation virtually unthinkable until after the circle had been broken. Once the circle was broken, several people (for example, Jeb Stuart Magruder, Richard Kleindienst, and Patrick Grey) seemed to view their illegal behavior with astonishment, as if it were performed during some sort of bad dream. John Dean put it this way:

> Anyway, when you picked up the newspaper in the morning and read the new cover story that had replaced yesterday's cover story, you began to believe that today's news was the truth. This process created an atmosphere of unreality in the White House that prevailed to the very end. If you said it often enough, it would become true. When the press learned of the wiretaps on newsmen and White House staffers, for example, and flat denials failed, it was claimed that this was a national security matter. I'm sure many people believed that the taps were for national security; they weren't. That was concocted as a justification after the fact. But when they said it, you understand, they really *believed* it.[5]

On January 28, 1986, the space shuttle *Challenger* exploded seconds after launching. Seven astronauts, including a civilian schoolteacher, perished in a fireball of smoke and flames. The decision had been made to go ahead with the launch despite a near disaster on an earlier *Challenger* flight and despite strenuous objections and warnings from knowledgeable engineers about the defective O-rings at the joints of the booster rockets. Were key National Aeronautics and Space Administration (NASA) administrators ignorant of the danger or cavalier about the lives of the astronauts? I doubt it.

A more likely explanation involves a number of factors that contributed to flaws in NASA's decision-making process. First, NASA had already conducted two dozen successful launches with essentially the same equipment. With their confidence boosted by previous successes, NASA administrators were oriented toward a "go" decision. Second, NASA officials, like the general public, were caught up in the enthusiasm surrounding the launching of the first civilian (schoolteacher Christa McAuliffe) into space.

Further, according to a penetrating analysis by Arie Kruglanski,[6] there were additional, practical reasons for NASA administrators to be victimized by their own wishful thinking: Given NASA's need to secure congressional funding by displaying its efficiency and productivity, given the intense public interest in the "teacher in space" program, given NASA's wish to demonstrate its technological capabilities, "liftoff was clearly a more desirable decision than delay. Any mention of possible system failure would have suggested a need to spend more money, a conclusion NASA found distasteful in light of its commitment to cost-effectiveness and economy."

Finally, in this atmosphere of enthusiasm and external pressures, no one at NASA wanted to be reminded that any kind of accident was possible, and they weren't. Unlike NASA administrators, engineers at Morton Thiokol (the company that manufactured the solid rocket boosters) were not concerned about the political, economic, and public relations implications of a decision on whether or not to launch. All they cared about was whether or not the damn thing would work—and given the subfreezing temperatures at the launch site, they objected strenuously to the launch.

But the top executives at Morton Thiokol were not so fortunate. For them, more was at stake than a successful launch. They were in great conflict. On the one hand, as engineers, they were sensitive to the opinions of their fellow engineers. On the other hand, as executives, they were dependent on NASA for a contract worth approximately $400 million per year. Thus, in part, they tended to identify with the same concerns that NASA administrators did. According to his testimony before a presidential investigative commission, Robert Lund, Thiokol's vice president for engineering, at first opposed the launch but changed his position after he was advised to "take off his engineering hat and put on one representing management." How did the Morton Thiokol executives such as Lund deal with this conflict? Before their last conference with NASA administrators, they polled Thiokol employees but not the engineers—only other management personnel, who voted to "go" with the launch. Thus, in a conference between NASA officials and Thiokol executives the night before the fateful launch, participants reinforced one another's commitment to proceed.

Let's take stock. What do Hitler's inner circle, Nixon's "palace guard," and NASA administrators have in common, aside from the fact that they made tragic decisions? They were relatively cohesive groups isolated from dissenting points of view. When such groups are called upon to make decisions, they often fall prey to what social psychologist Irving Janis calls **groupthink**.[7] According to Janis, groupthink is "the mode of thinking that persons engage in when concurrence seeking becomes so dominant in a cohesive ingroup that it tends to override realistic appraisal of alternative courses of action." Groups engaging in this maladaptive decision-making strategy typically perceive themselves as invulnerable—they're blinded by optimism. And this optimism is perpetuated when dissent is discouraged. In the face of conformity pressures, individual group members come to doubt their own reservations and refrain from voicing dissenting opinions. Consensus seeking is so important that certain members of the group sometimes become *mindguards*—people who censor troublesome incoming information, as did the executives at Morton Thiokol.

By citing these examples, I do not mean to suggest that individuals who make foolish, disastrous decisions should not be held accountable. What I do intend to suggest is that it is a lot easier to conduct an inquiry and assign blame than it is to understand the psychological processes underlying faulty decision making. But it is only through digging deeper and trying to understand these processes that we can have any hope of improving the way people make decisions and thus of reducing the frequency of disastrous decisions in the future.

What Is Conformity?

Conformity can be defined as a change in a person's behavior or opinions as a result of real or imagined pressure from a person or group of people. Most situations are not as extreme as the examples cited above. We will attempt to zero in on the phenomenon of conformity by beginning with a less extreme (and perhaps simpler) illustration. Let's return to our friend Sam, the hypothetical college student we first encountered in Chapter 1. Recall that Sam watched a presidential candidate on television and was favorably impressed with his sincerity. However, in the face of the unanimous opinion of his friends that the candidate was insincere, Sam acceded—verbally, at least—to their opinion.

Several questions can be asked about this kind of situation: (1) What causes people to conform to group pressure? Specifically, what was in it for Sam? (2) What was the nature of the group pressure? Specifically, what were Sam's acquaintances doing to induce conformity? (3) Did Sam revise his opinion of the candidate during that brief but horrifying period when he learned that all his fellow students disagreed with him? Or was it the case that Sam maintained his original opinion but only modified what he said about the candidate? If there was a change in opinion, was it permanent or merely transient?

Unfortunately, we cannot say precisely and definitely what was going on in Sam's mind at the time because there are many factors in the situation that we don't know about. For example, we don't know how confident Sam was in his initial opinion; we don't know how much he liked the people with whom he watched the candidate; we don't know whether Sam considered himself to be a good judge of sincerity or whether he considered the others to be good judges of sincerity; we don't know whether Sam is generally a strong person or a wishy-washy person; and so on. What we can do is construct an experimental situation that is somewhat like the one in which Sam found himself, and we can control and vary the factors we think might be important. Such a basic situation was devised by Solomon Asch[8] in a classic set of experiments. Put yourself in the following situation: You have volunteered to participate in an experiment on perceptual judgment. You enter a room with four other participants. The experimenter shows all of you a straight line (line X). Simultaneously, he shows you three other lines for comparison (lines A, B, and C). Your job is to judge which of the three lines is closest in length to line X. The judgment strikes you as being a very easy one.

X   A B C

It is perfectly clear to you that line B is the correct answer, and when your turn comes, you will clearly say that B is the one. But it's not your turn to respond. The young man whose turn it is looks carefully at the lines and says, "Line A." Your mouth drops open and you look at him quizzically. "How can he believe it's A when any fool can see that it's B?" you ask yourself. "He must be either blind or crazy." Now it's the second person's turn to respond. He also chooses line A. You begin to feel like Alice in Wonderland. "How can it be?" you ask yourself. "Are *both* of these people blind or crazy?" But then the next person responds, and he also says, "Line A." You take another look at those lines. "Maybe I'm the only one who's crazy," you mutter inaudibly. Now it's the fourth person's turn, and he also judges the correct line to be A. Finally, it's your turn. "Why, it's line A, of course," you declare. "I knew it all the time."

This is the kind of conflict that the college students in Asch's experiment went through. As you might imagine, the individuals who answered first were in the employ of the experimenter and were instructed to agree on an incorrect answer. The perceptual judgment itself was an incredibly easy one. It was so easy that, when individuals were not subjected to group pressure but were allowed to make a series of judgments of various sizes of lines while alone, there was almost a complete absence of errors. Indeed, the task was so easy, and physical reality was so clear-cut, that Asch himself firmly believed that there would be little, if any, yielding to group pressure. But his prediction was wrong. When faced with a majority of their fellow students agreeing on the same incorrect responses in a series of 12 judgments, approximately three-quarters of the participants conformed at least once by responding incorrectly. When we look at the entire spectrum of judgments, we find that an average of 35 percent of the overall responses conformed to the incorrect judgments rendered by Asch's accomplices.

Solomon Asch performed his classic experiment over 50 years ago. Although the results were powerful, it is tempting to dismiss his findings on the grounds that American college students are quite different now. Specifically, with the advent of computers and the Internet we have grown more sophisticated and, therefore, much less susceptible to this kind of group pressure. Not so. Over the years, the Asch experiment has been successfully replicated a great many times. Just a few years ago, in a particularly striking demonstration on national television, Anthony Pratkanis[9] repeated the Asch experiment precisely as Asch did it fifty years earlier. The participants in Pratkanis's experiment were particularly sophisticated college students, most of whom considered themselves to be nonconformists. The striking results were almost identical to Asch's.

The situation created by these experiments is especially intriguing because, unlike many situations in which we may tend to conform, there were no explicit constraints against individuality. In many situations, the sanctions against nonconformity are clear and unequivocal. For example, I hate to wear a tie, and under most circumstances I can get away with this minor idiosyncrasy. On occasion, however, I can't. I often find myself stopped at the entrance to a restaurant and politely (but firmly) informed that if I refuse to don the tie offered me by the headwaiter, I cannot dine in the restaurant. I can either put on the tie and eat in the restaurant or leave, open-necked and comfortable but hungry. The negative consequences of nonconformity are made very explicit.

But in Asch's experiment (and in the hypothetical example of Sam watching the candidate on television), the situations were much more subtle. In these situations, there were no explicit rewards for conformity and no explicit punishments for deviance. Why, then, did Asch's participants and Sam conform? There are two major possibilities; either they became convinced, in the face of the judgment of the unanimous majority, that their own opinions were wrong, or they "went along with the crowd" (while inwardly believing their initial judgments were correct) in order to be accepted by the majority or to avoid being disliked by them for disagreeing.

In short, what I am suggesting is that these individuals had two important goals: the goal of being correct and the goal of staying in the good graces of other people by living up to their expectations. In many circumstances, both of these goals can be satisfied by a simple action. Driving on the right-hand side of the road is the correct thing to do, and it satisfies other people's expectations. So, too, are telephoning your mother on Mother's Day, giving proper directions to a visitor in town, and studying hard to perform well on an exam. Similarly, if others agreed with your judgment of the lengths of the lines, you could satisfy both goals by being true to your own estimate. But, in Asch's experiment, these two goals were placed in conflict. If you were a participant in that experiment and you initially believed that the correct answer was line B, then saying so might satisfy your desire to be correct—but it might also violate the expectations of your peers, and they might think you a bit odd. On the other hand, choosing line A might win you the acceptance of the others, but unless you became convinced that they were correct, it would violate your desire to be right.

Most people believe that *they* are motivated primarily by a desire to be correct but that *others* are motivated primarily by a desire to stay in the good graces of other people. For example, when people unobtrusively observe an Asch-like conformity experiment, they typically predict that the experimental participants will conform more than they actually do.[10] Interestingly enough, these same surreptitious observers predict that *they* will conform *less* than people like themselves actually do. That is, we know *other* people conform, but we underestimate the extent to which *we* can be induced to follow the group.

Was Sam convinced by his fellow college students that his preferred presidential candidate was a phony, or did he simply go along with their judgment in order to be accepted while continuing to believe in the sincerity of the candidate? Because Sam is a hypothetical person, we cannot answer that question definitively. Were the yielders in Asch's experiment convinced that their initial judgment was incorrect and the unanimous judgment of the others was right? We could ask them; indeed, in Asch's experiment, the yielders were asked afterward whether they really saw the lines differently or whether they merely said so. A few of the participants insisted that they really saw them that way. But how can we be certain that they were being truthful? Put yourself in a participant's place. Suppose you bowed to group pressure even though you remained certain that your initial judgment was correct. This might be embarrassing for you to admit because it would make you appear weak and wishy-washy. Moreover, you would be admitting that you were not following the experimenter's instruction to present your own judgment. Thus, it is quite possible that participants who said they actually saw it the way the group saw it might have been deceiving the experimenter in order to save face.

How, then, can we determine whether or not group pressure actually affects one's judgment? Let's speculate for a moment. If we could follow Sam into the voting booth and witness which candidate he chooses, we could discover whether he was actually convinced by his acquaintances that his original candidate was a phony or if he merely mumbled his agreement with them while still privately trusting the candidate. But we can't follow Sam into the voting booth. Fortunately, we can determine whether the public behavior exhibited by participants in the Asch experiment corresponds with their private acceptance of those judgments. Suppose we were to repeat the experiment, but although we would allow the real participants to see the responses of the accomplices as before, we would not require them to make their own judgments in the presence of the others. If the participants' private choices were identical with their public ones, then we would see that the responses of the others in the original experiment did actually convince the participants that their initial judgments were wrong. If, on the other hand, the participants were going against their own best judgment only in order to mollify the group, then there would be significantly less yielding to the judgments of others in decisions made in private. This proposition has been tested experimentally on several occasions. The results are consistent: The greater the privacy, the less the conformity. This finding has held up consistently whether the participants were judging lengths of lines,[11] the number of metronome clicks,[12] or the aesthetic value of a piece of modern art.[13] Thus, it appears that pressure to conform to the judgments of others has little (if any) effect on the *private* judgments of experimental participants.

Factors That Increase or Decrease Conformity

Unanimity In situations like the one investigated by Asch, one of the crucial factors that determines the likelihood that the participant's opinion will conform to that of the majority is whether or not the majority opinion is unanimous. If a participant is joined by even one ally who gives the correct response, his or her conformity to the erroneous judgment of the majority drops sharply.[14] In fact, even if unanimity is broken by a non-ally, the power of the group is seriously diminished.[15] That is, if one of the other group members gives an incorrect response that is *different* from the error of the majority (answering that the correct line is C as the rest of the group responds A), the presence of this fellow dissenter dramatically reduces the pressure to conform, and the participant is likely to give the correct response: line B. A fellow dissenter exerts a powerful freeing effect from the influence of the majority. If there is unanimity, however, the actual size of the majority need not be very great in order for it to elicit maximum conformity from a person. In fact, the tendency for someone to conform to group pressure is about as great when the unanimous majority consists of only 3 other people as it is when the unanimous majority is 16.

Commitment   One way conformity to group pressure can be decreased is by inducing the individual to make some sort of commitment to his or her initial judgment. Picture yourself as an umpire at a major-league baseball game. There is a close play at first base and you call the runner out—in the presence of 50,000 fans. After the game, the three other umpires approach you and each says that he thought the runner was safe. How likely are you to alter your judgment? Compare this with a situation (like the Asch situation) in which each of the three umpires calls the runner safe and then it is your turn to make a judgment. Such a comparison was made in an experiment by Morton Deutsch and Harold Gerard,[16] who used the Asch paradigm and found that where there was no prior commitment (as in the Asch experiment), some 25 percent of the responses conformed to the erroneous judgment of the majority. But, when the individuals had publicly committed themselves before hearing the judgment of the other "umpires," only less than 6 percent of their new responses were conformist.

Accountability   Suppose you found yourself being subjected to group pressure while trying to make a decision. In addition, suppose that you knew that, at the end of the session, you would need to justify your decision to the other members of the group. What effect do you think that might have on your decision-making? Research has shown that under most conditions, this kind of accountability to the group tends to increase conformity.[17] But what happens if you were also given instructions indicating that it is important for you to be as accurate as possible? In a recent experiment, Andrew Quinn and Barry Schlenker[18] put people through a procedure aimed at producing conformity to a poor decision. Before the conformity aspect of the experiment began, the experimenters did two things: 1) They got half of their participants thinking about the importance of being as accurate as possible while getting the other half thinking about the importance of cooperation. 2) They made it clear to half the subjects in each of those two conditions that, after they made a decision, they would need to talk to their partners about their decision and justify having made it. The results were clear. The people who showed the most independence and made the best decisions were those who were oriented toward being accurate *and* had to explain their non-conformity to the very people whose influence they resisted. It is interesting to note that the people in this condition behaved with greater independence than those people who were oriented toward being accurate but were not held accountable. What this suggests is that most people will go along in order to get along unless they know that they will be held accountable for a dumb, compliant decision.

The Person and the Culture Another important factor affecting conformity involves some of the characteristics of the target person. Specifically, individuals who have generally low **self-esteem** are far more likely to yield to group pressure than those with high self-esteem. Furthermore, task-specific self-esteem plays an important part in the process. If individuals are led to believe that they have little or no aptitude for the task at hand, their tendency to conform increases. Similarly, individuals who are given the opportunity to have prior success with a task like judging the lengths of lines are far less likely to conform than those who walk into the situation cold.[19]

There are also some important cultural differences in the tendency to go against the group. One of these cultural differences is nicely illustrated by the following pieces of folk wisdom: In America, "the squeaky wheel gets the grease"; in Japan, "the nail that stands out gets pounded down." This general impression was confirmed by Rod Bond and Peter Smith. In an analysis of some 133 experiments using the Asch procedure in 17 different countries, they found that conformity is more prevalent in collectivist societies (like Japan Norway, and China) than in individualistic societies (like the United States and France).[20] There also seems to be a small but consistent gender difference, with women conforming more than men.[21] It should be noted, however, that this gender difference greatest when the researcher was male or when the group task was male-oriented.[22]

The Group Exerting Pressure The other side of that issue, of course, has to do with the makeup of the group exerting the pressure. A group is more effective at inducing conformity if (1) it consists of experts, (2) the members (individually or collectively) are important to the individual, or (3) the members (individually or collectively) are comparable to the individual in some way. Thus, to go back to Sam, our hypothetical college student, I would speculate that it is more likely that Sam would conform to the pressure exerted by his acquaintances if he thought they were expert in politics and in making judgments about human relations. Similarly, he would be more likely to yield to those people if they were important potential friends than if they were of no consequence to him. And finally, their being fellow students gives the judgments of Sam's acquaintances more impact on his behavior than, say, the judgment of a group of 10-year-old children, a group of construction workers, or a group of Portuguese biochemists. There is at least one exception to the comparability phenomenon. Research has shown that, if the unanimous majority consists of white children, more conformity is induced in other children—both white *and* black.[23] Apparently, among children, whites are seen as having more power than blacks.[24] Thus, the power granted to whites by our culture is sufficient to overcome the tendency for people to be more influenced by comparable others, though this situation may be changing as blacks continue to gain power in our society.

The results for the black children may be due in part to a feeling of insecurity. For example, to return to our previous illustration, if Sam had felt sure that he was liked and accepted by his acquaintances, he would have been more likely to voice disagreement than if he felt insecure in his relationship with them. This assertion receives strong support from an experiment by James Dittes and Harold Kelley[25] in which college men were invited to join an attractive, prestigious group and subsequently were given information about how secure their position was in that group. Specifically, all members of the group were informed that, at any point during the lifetime of the group, the members could remove any member in the interest of efficiency. The group then engaged in a discussion of juvenile delinquency. Periodically, the discussion was interrupted and each member was asked to rate every other member's value to the group. After the discussion, each member was shown how the others rated him; in actuality, the members were given prearranged false feedback. Some members were led to believe they were well accepted, and others were led to believe they were not terribly popular. Each member's conformity was measured by the opinions he subsequently expressed in further discussion of juvenile delinquency and by his vulnerability to group pressure during the performance of a simple perceptual task. The results showed that, for the individuals who valued their membership in the group, those who were led to feel only moderately accepted were more likely to conform to the norms and standards set by the group than were those who were led to feel totally accepted. In other words, it's easier for an individual who is securely ensconced in a group to deviate from that group.

Factors associated with conformity are similar when the source of influence is an individual rather than a group. Thus, we are more likely to conform to the behavior or opinions of an individual who is similar or important to us, or who appears to have expertise or authority in a given situation. For example, research has shown that people are more willing to comply with a demand from a person wearing a uniform compared with someone in civilian clothes—even when it comes to relatively trivial matters. In one study,[26] pedestrians were asked to give spare change to a motorist (actually one of the experimenters) who was parked at an expired meter. When approached by a uniformed parking officer, participants complied with her request far more often than when she was wearing either sloppy clothes or professional, business attire. Thus, the appearance of authority—as potently symbolized by a uniform—can lend legitimacy to a demand, thereby generating high rates of compliance.

On a broader level, popular writer Malcolm Gladwell[27] suggests that major social trends often change dramatically and suddenly through the mechanism of conformity when certain kinds of respected people happen to be in the right place at the right time. He calls these sudden changes, when a major change reaches a critical mass, "the tipping point." And he calls the people who induce these changes "connectors." These connectors can, by word of mouth alone, turn a struggling restaurant into a popular, overflowing place within a matter of weeks or can take a small trend (say, the number of women requesting regular mammograms) and turn it into an epidemic. According to Gladwell, connectors do not have to be experts; they are simply people who seem to be "in the know" and are talking about appropriate topics in appropriate places. How can people who are not medical experts induce large numbers of women to get regular mammograms? The place is important. In this instance, the tipping point happened in places where women (and only women) gather informally and have the leisure to talk and listen to one another. The places were beauty salons, and the connectors were beauticians.

Rewards and Punishments Versus Information

As I suggested earlier, there are two possible reasons why people like us might conform. One is that the behavior of others might convince us that our initial judgment was erroneous. The other is that we may wish to avoid punishment (such as rejection or ridicule) or to gain a reward (such as love or acceptance) from the group. The behavior of the individuals in Asch's experiment and in similar other experiments seemed to be largely a matter of attempting to obtain a reward or to avoid punishment. This can be inferred from the fact that there was very little conformity when participants were allowed to respond privately.

At the same time, there are many situations in which we conform to the behavior of others because their behavior is our only guide to appropriate action. In short, we often rely on other people as a means of determining reality. The quotation from Thurber at the beginning of this chapter gives an example of this type of conformity. According to Leon Festinger,[28] when physical reality becomes increasingly uncertain, people rely more and more on "social reality"—that is, they are more likely to conform to what other people are doing, not because they fear punishment from the group but because the group's behavior supplies them with valuable **information** about what is expected of them. An example should help clarify this distinction: Suppose that you need to use the toilet in an unfamiliar classroom building. Under the sign "Rest Rooms" there are two doors, but unfortunately, a vandal has removed the specific designations from the doors; that is, you cannot be certain which is the men's room and which is the women's room. Quite a dilemma—you are afraid to open either door for fear of being embarrassed or embarrassing others. As you stand there in dismay and discomfort, hopping from one foot to the other, the door on your left opens and out strolls a distinguished-looking gentleman. With a sigh of relief, you are now willing to forge ahead, reasonably secure in the knowledge that left is for men and right is for women. Why are you so confident? As we have seen, research has shown that the more faith an individual has in the expertise and trustworthiness of the other person, the greater the tendency to follow his or her lead and conform to his or her behavior. Thus, the distinguished-looking gentleman would almost certainly be followed to a greater extent than, say, a seedy-looking fellow with wildly darting eyes.

Indeed, research on jaywalking indicates that people will conform more often to the behavior of a seemingly high-status person than to the behavior of someone who looks less respectable or less well-to-do. Across several studies, researchers have found that, when in the presence of a model who refrains from jaywalking, other pedestrians are more likely to curb the impulse to jaywalk compared with people who are not exposed to any model. This conformity effect is much stronger, however, when the person modeling the behavior is neat and well attired rather than disheveled and dressed in shabby clothes.[29]

On Wasting Water and Littering Let us take this one step further. Institutions frequently request us to perform certain behaviors without making an outright demand. For example, in the men's shower room at my university's field house, there is a sign asking us to practice conservation by turning off the water while soaping up. Since this behavior is slightly inconvenient, I was not surprised when our systematic observation revealed that only 6 percent of the students conformed to this request. Subsequently, Michael O'Leary and I conducted a simple experiment aimed at inducing a greater number of people to conserve water and the energy needed to heat it.[30] We reasoned that people would be more likely to turn off the shower while soaping up if they believed other students took the request seriously. Accordingly, we enlisted the aid of a few male students who simply acted as models for the desired behavior. But we didn't want people to conform out of a fear of disapproval or punishment, so we set up the experiment in the following way: Our model entered the shower room (an open space consisting of eight shower nozzles spaced at regular intervals) when it was empty, went to the far end, turned his back to the entrance, and turned on the shower. As soon as he heard someone enter, he turned off the shower, soaped up, turned it back on, briefly rinsed off, and left the room without so much as glancing at the student who had entered. As he left, another student (our observer) entered and surreptitiously noted whether the "participant" turned off the shower while soaping up. We found that 49 percent of the students followed suit! Moreover, when two students simultaneously modeled the appropriate behavior, the percentage of people obeying the sign zoomed to 67. Thus, in an ambiguous situation, other people can induce conformity by providing us with information suggestive of what people generally do in a given situation.

Let's look at the cultural norm against littering. Littering doesn't seem like a big deal to most people—and that's part of the problem: Most people think nothing of leaving a little trash around; but the little trash accumulates, polluting our environment and costing taxpayers a great deal of money. In California alone, the cost of cleaning up roadside litter now exceeds $100 million a year. Suppose, as you approach your car in the parking lot of the local library, you notice that someone has stuck one of those annoying fliers under your windshield wiper. So you remove it and, without thinking, crumple it up. The crucial question: Do you throw it on the ground or shove it into your pocket so that you can drop it in a trash can later? The answer: To a large extent, it depends on what other people are doing. In a clever experiment, Robert Cialdini and his associates[31] placed fliers under the windshield wipers of a number of cars and waited to observe what each driver did when he or she discovered them. For some people, when they first left the library, an accomplice of the experimenters walked past them, stooped down, picked up a discarded fast-food bag that was lying in the street, and placed it in a trash can. In the control condition, no bag was lying on the ground; the accomplice simply walked past the people who were headed toward their car. In the control condition, when the people got to their car and noticed the flier, 37 percent threw it on the ground. In the "modeling" condition only 7 percent threw the flier on the ground.

In a parallel experiment, Cialdini and his colleagues[32] used a more subtle technique of informational influence. They eliminated the human model and, instead, manipulated the appearance of the parking lot. Specifically, when the experimenters had previously littered the parking lot with fliers, the majority of the drivers simply followed suit—probably thinking, "After all, if no one cares about the cleanliness of the parking lot, why should I?" Interestingly enough, people were much less likely to litter if there was one piece of litter on the ground nearby than if the parking lot was completely free of litter. The reason is that seeing one piece of litter reminds us of litter—and shows us that the vast majority of people are subscribing to that norm. If the parking lot is free of litter, most people probably do not even think about the norm and, therefore, will be more likely to litter mindlessly.

In the experiments in the shower room and in the parking lot, conformity was induced by information rather than by fear. But it is not always easy to distinguish between the two types of conformity. Often the behavior is identical; the key element that differentiates the two processes is the presence or absence of a punitive agent. Imagine that, in the mythical nation of Freedonia, it is considered gracious for guests to belch after eating as a way of showing the host that they enjoyed the meal. Suppose you didn't know this, and you were visiting the home of a Freedonian dignitary in the company of some diplomats from the U.S. State Department. If, after the meal, these diplomats began to belch, chances are you would belch also. They were providing you with valuable information. On the other hand, suppose you were in the same home in the company of some rather rude and brawny young men who were introduced to you as members of the Freedonian Olympic heavyweight wrestling team. If these behemoths belched after their meal, my guess is that you might not go along with this behavior. That is, you would probably consider this an act of bad manners and would avoid belching. However, if they glared at you for your failure to follow suit, you might indeed belch too—not because of the information they supplied but because you feared rejection or reprisal for refusing to be a good sport by going along with their boorish behavior.

I would suggest that conformity resulting from the observation of others for the purpose of gaining information about proper behavior tends to have more powerful ramifications than conformity in the interest of being accepted or of avoiding punishment. I would argue that, if we find ourselves in an ambiguous situation wherein we must use the behavior of other people as a template for our own behavior, it is likely that we will repeat our newly learned behavior, without a cue, on subsequent similar occasions. This would be the case unless, of course, we later received clear evidence that our actions were inappropriate or incorrect. Thus, to go back to our example, suppose you are reinvited to the home of the Freedonian dignitary for dinner. But this time you are the only guest. The question is: Do you or don't you belch after the meal? A moment's reflection should make the answer perfectly clear: If you had belched after the first meal at his home because you realized it was the proper thing to do (as would have been the case had you dined in the company of the diplomats), you would be quite likely to belch when dining alone with the dignitary. However, if you had belched the first time out of fear of rejection or punishment (as would have been the case had you dined in the company of the wrestlers), you would almost certainly not belch when you are the lone guest. To go back to Sam and the political candidate on television, you can now readily understand one of the many reasons why it would be so difficult for us to predict how Sam would actually vote in the election. If he had been merely going along with the group to avoid punishment or to gain acceptance, he would be likely, in the privacy of the polling booth, to vote in opposition to the view expressed by his acquaintances. If, on the other hand, Sam had been using the group as a source of information, he would almost certainly vote against the candidate that he had initially preferred.

Social Influence and Emotion To repeat: When reality is unclear, other people become a major source of information. The generality of this phenomenon is nicely illustrated by some research performed by Stanley Schachter and Jerome Singer, who demonstrated that people conform to others even in assessing something as personal and idiosyncratic as the quality of their own emotions.[33] Before describing this research, it is useful to clarify what is meant by *emotions*. According to William James,[34] an emotion has both a "feeling" content and a cognitive content. His two-part conception of emotions can be likened to the process of playing a song on a jukebox: First, you need to activate the machine by inserting the coin; then you select the song you want to hear by pushing the right buttons. An emotion also requires both physiological arousal and a label. Specifically, if we are walking in the forest and bump into a hungry and ferocious bear, we undergo a physiological change. This change produces excitement. Physiologically, this is a response of the sympathetic nervous system similar to one that might be produced by coming across a person with whom we are angry. We interpret this response as fear (rather than anger, say, or euphoria) only when we cognitively become aware that we are in the presence of a fear-producing stimulus (a ferocious bear). But what if we experienced physiological arousal in the absence of an appropriate stimulus? For example, what if someone surreptitiously slipped into our drink a chemical that produced the same physiological response? Would we experience fear? William James would say that we wouldn't—not unless there was an appropriate stimulus around.

Here is where Schachter and Singer enter the picture. In one experiment, they injected volunteers either with epinephrine—a synthetic form of adrenaline, which causes physiological excitation—or with a harmless placebo. All the participants were told that this chemical was a vitamin supplement called "suproxin." They told some of those who received the drug that there would be side effects, including palpitations of the heart and hand tremors. These, indeed, are some of the effects of epinephrine. Accordingly, when these people experienced the epinephrine-produced symptoms, they had an appropriate explanation. In effect, when the symptoms appeared, they said to themselves, "My heart is pounding and my hands are shaking because of this injection I received and for no other reason." But other participants were not forewarned about these symptoms. Thus, when their hearts started pounding and their hands started trembling, what were they to make of it? The answer is that they made of it whatever the people around them made of it. Specifically, a stooge was introduced into the situation, and the participants were informed that he had also received an injection of "suproxin." In one situation, the stooge was programmed to behave in a euphoric manner; in another, he was programmed to express a great deal of anger. Picture yourself in this situation: You are alone in this room with a person who supposedly has just been injected with the same drug you received. He bounces around energetically, happily wads up paper into balls, and begins sinking hook shots into the wastebasket. His euphoria is obvious. Gradually, the chemical you were given begins to take effect, and you begin to feel your heart pounding, your hands trembling, and so on. What emotion do you feel? Most participants in this situation reported a feeling of euphoria—and behaved happily. On the other hand, imagine that instead of being placed in a room with a euphoric stooge, you were placed in a room with a stooge programmed to behave in an angry manner. He complains about a questionnaire you both are filling out, and eventually, in a fit of extreme annoyance, he rips up the questionnaire and angrily hurls it into the wastebasket. Meanwhile, the symptoms of epinephrine are becoming apparent; you feel your own heart pounding, and your hands begin to tremble. How do you feel? In this situation, the vast majority of the participants felt angry and behaved in an angry fashion.

It should be noted that, if the people were given a placebo (that is, an injection of a benign solution that produces no symptoms), or if they were forewarned about the symptoms of the drug that they had been given, they were relatively unaffected by the antics of the stooge. To sum up this experiment: When physical reality was clear and explainable, the participants' emotions were not greatly influenced by the behavior of other people. However, when they were experiencing a strong physiological response, the origins of which were not clear, they interpreted their own feelings as either anger or euphoria, depending on the behavior of other people who supposedly were in the same chemical boat.

Social Influence: Life and Death As we have seen, the influence of other people, whether intentional or not, can have an important effect on a person's behavior. Unless we understand how this process works, these effects can have major unwanted consequences for society as well. An investigation by Craig Haney into the *death qualification procedure* provides an interesting and instructive example.[35] Basically, the death qualification procedure refers to the process whereby, in selecting a jury for a murder trial, prospective jurors who are opposed to the death penalty are systematically excluded from the jury. This procedure takes place in the presence of those people who are eventually selected to serve on the jury. Haney, who is both an attorney and a social psychologist, reasoned that it is possible that when jurors who believe in capital punishment witness others being dismissed because they oppose the death penalty, this may subtly suggest to them that the law disapproves of people who oppose the death penalty. This conclusion may increase their tendency to impose the death penalty. To test this notion, Haney performed an experiment in which a random sample of adults was shown a videotape of a convincing jury selection procedure filmed in the moot courtroom of a law school—a highly realistic setting complete with all the courtroom accouterments. Experienced trial lawyers served as prosecutor, defense attorney, and judge on the videotape. In one condition, the procedure included a segment on death qualification; in the other condition (control), this segment did not appear. Compared to people in the control condition, those who viewed the death qualification segment were more convinced of the defendant's guilt, they believed it was more likely that he would receive the death penalty, and they also believed that the judge thought he was guilty. They themselves were also more likely to impose the death penalty if the defendant were convicted. Thus, the factors that influence our opinions and behavior can be subtle—and they may be a matter of life and death.

Responses to Social Influence

Thus far, I have been describing two kinds of conformity in more or less commonsensical terms. This distinction was based upon (1) whether the individual was being motivated by rewards and punishments or by a need to know and (2) the relative permanence of the conforming behavior. Let us move beyond this simple distinction to a more complex and useful classification that applies not only to conformity but to the entire spectrum of social influence. Instead of using the simple term *conformity*, I would like to distinguish among three kinds of responses to social influence: *compliance, identification,* and *internalization*.[36]

Compliance The term **compliance** best describes the behavior of a person who is motivated by a desire to gain reward or avoid punishment. Typically, the person's behavior is only as long-lived as the promise of reward or the threat of punishment. Thus, one can induce a rat to run a maze efficiently by making it hungry and placing food at the end of the maze. Chances are that a ruthless dictator could get a percentage of his citizens to indicate their allegiance by threatening them with torture if they don't comply or by promising to feed and enrich them if they do. On the level of compliance, most researchers see little difference between the behavior of humans and other animals because all organisms are responsive to concrete rewards and punishments. Thus, remove the food from the goal box and the rat will eventually stop running the maze; remove the food or the threat of punishment and the citizens will cease showing allegiance to the dictator.

Identification The term **identification** describes a response to social influence brought about by an individual's desire to be like the influencer. In identification, as in compliance, we do not behave in a particular way because such behavior is intrinsically satisfying; rather, we adopt a particular behavior because it puts us in a satisfying relationship to the person or persons with whom we are identifying. Identification differs from compliance in that we do come to believe in the opinions and values we adopt, although we do not believe in them very strongly. Thus, if we find a person or a group attractive or appealing in some way, we will be inclined to accept influence from that person or group and adopt similar values and attitudes—not in order to obtain a reward or avoid a punishment (as in compliance), but simply to be like that person or group. I refer to this as the good-old-Uncle-Charlie phenomenon. Suppose you have an uncle named Charlie who happens to be a warm, dynamic, exciting person; ever since you were a young child, you loved him and wanted to grow up to be like him. Uncle Charlie is a corporate executive who has a number of strong opinions, including a deep antipathy to social welfare legislation. That is, he is convinced that anyone who really tries can earn a decent wage and that, by handing money to people, the government only succeeds in eliminating their desire to work. As a young child, you heard Uncle

Charlie announce this position on several occasions, and it has become part of your system of beliefs—not because you thought it through and it seemed right to you or because Uncle Charlie rewarded you for adopting (or threatened to punish you for not adopting) this position. Rather, it has become part of your belief system because of your liking for Uncle Charlie, which has produced in you a tendency to incorporate into your life that which is his.

Internalization The **internalization** of a value or belief is the most permanent, most deeply rooted response to social influence. The motivation to internalize a particular belief is the desire to be right. Thus, the reward for the belief is intrinsic. If the person who provides the influence is perceived to be trustworthy and to have good judgment, we accept the belief he or she advocates and we integrate it into our system of values. Once it is part of our own system, it becomes independent of its source and will become extremely resistant to change.

Let us discuss some of the important distinguishing characteristics of these three responses to social influence. Compliance is the least enduring and has the least effect on the individual because people comply merely to gain reward or to avoid punishment. The complier understands the force of the circumstance and can easily change his or her behavior when the circumstance no longer prevails. At gunpoint, I could be made to say almost anything; but with the threat of death removed, I could quickly shrug off those statements and their implications. If a child is kind and generous to his younger brother in order to obtain a cookie from his mother, he will not necessarily become a generous person. He has not learned that generosity is a good thing in itself; what he has learned is that generosity is a good way to get cookies. When the cookie supply is exhausted, his generous behavior will eventually cease unless that behavior is bolstered by some other reward (or punishment). Rewards and punishments are important means of inducing people to learn and perform specific activities but they are very limited techniques of social influence because they must be ever present to be effective—unless the individual discovers some additional reason for continuing the behavior. This last point will be discussed shortly.

Continuous reward or punishment is not necessary for the response to social influence that I call identification. The person with whom the individual identifies need not be present at all; all that is needed is the individual's desire to be like that person. For example, if Uncle Charlie moves to a different city and months (or even years) go by without your seeing him, you will continue to hold beliefs similar to his as long as (1) he remains important to you, (2) he still holds the same beliefs, and (3) these beliefs are not challenged by counteropinions that are more convincing. But, by the same token, these beliefs can be changed if Uncle Charlie has a change of heart or if your love for Uncle Charlie begins to fade. They can also change if a person or group of people who are more important to you than Uncle Charlie profess a different set of beliefs. For example, suppose you are away at college and you find a group of new, exciting friends who, unlike Uncle Charlie, are strongly in favor of social welfare. If you admire them as much as (or more than) your uncle, you may change your beliefs in order to be more like them. Thus, a more important identification may supersede a previous identification.

The effect of social influence through identification can also be dissipated by a person's desire to be right. If you have taken on a belief through identification and you are subsequently presented with a convincing counterargument by an expert and trustworthy person, you will probably change your belief. Internalization is the most permanent response to social influence precisely because your motivation to be right is a powerful and self-sustaining force that does not depend upon constant surveillance in the form of agents of reward or punishment, as does compliance, or on your continued esteem for another person or group, as does identification.

It is important to realize that any specific action may be due to either compliance, identification, or internalization. For example, let us look at a simple piece of behavior: obedience to the laws pertaining to fast driving. Society employs highway patrol officers to enforce these laws, and as we all know, people tend to drive within the speed limit if they are forewarned that a certain stretch of highway is being carefully scrutinized by these officers. This is compliance. It is a clear case of obeying the law in order to avoid paying a penalty. Suppose you were to remove the highway patrol. As soon as people found out about it, many would increase their driving speed. But some people might continue to obey the speed limit; a person might continue to obey because Dad (or Uncle Charlie) always obeyed the speed limit or always stressed the importance of obeying traffic laws. This, of course, is identification. Finally, people might conform to the speed limit because they are convinced that speed laws are good, that obeying such laws helps to prevent accidents, and that driving at a moderate speed is a sane and reasonable form of behavior. This is internalization. And with internalization you would observe more flexibility in the behavior. For example, under certain conditions—at 6 o'clock on a Sunday morning, with perfect visibility and no traffic for miles around—the individual might exceed the speed limit. The compliant individual, however, might fear a radar trap, and the identifying individual might be identifying with a very rigid model; thus, both would be less responsive to important changes in the environment.

Let us look at the major component in each response to social influence. In compliance, the important component is *power*—the power of the influencer to dole out the reward for compliance and punishment for noncompliance. Parents have the power to praise, give love, provide cookies, scream, give spankings, withhold allowances, and so on; teachers have the power to paste gold stars on our foreheads or flunk us out of college; and employers have the power to praise, promote, humiliate, or discharge us. The U.S. government has the power to increase economic aid to or withhold it from a dependent nation. Thus, the government can use this technique to persuade a small country in Latin America to hold a more or less democratic election. Rewards and punishments are effective means for producing this kind of compliance, but we might ask whether or not mere compliance is desirable: To induce a nation to hold a democratic election is easier than to induce the rulers of that nation to think and rule democratically.

In identification, the crucial component is *attractiveness*—the attractiveness of the person with whom we identify. Because we identify with the model, we want to hold the same opinions that the model holds. Suppose a person you admire takes a particular stand on an issue. Unless you have strong feelings or solid information to the contrary, there will be a tendency for you to adopt this position. Incidentally, it is interesting to note that the reverse is also true: If a person or group that you dislike announces a position, there will be a tendency for you to reject that position or adopt the opposite position. Suppose, for example, that you dislike a particular group (say, the Nazi party in the United States), and that group speaks out against raising the minimum wage. If you know nothing about the issue, your tendency will be to favor raising the minimum wage—all other things being equal.

In internalization, the important component is *credibility*—the credibility of the person who supplies the information. For example, if you read a statement by a person who is highly credible—that is, someone who is both expert and trustworthy—you would tend to be influenced by it because of your desire to be correct. Recall our earlier example of the diplomats at the Freedonian dinner party. Your acceptance of their expertise made their behavior (belching after the meal) seem the right thing to do. Accordingly, my guess is that this behavior (your tendency to belch after a meal at the home of a Freedonian dignitary) would become internalized; you would do it, thereafter, because you believed it to be right.

Recall the experiment on conformity performed by Solomon Asch, in which social pressure induced many participants to conform to the erroneous statements of a group. Recall further that, when the participants were allowed to respond in private, the incidence of conformity dropped considerably. Clearly, then, internalization or identification was not involved. It seems obvious that the participants were *complying* with the unanimous opinion of the group in order to avoid the punishment of ridicule or rejection. If either identification or internalization had been involved, the conforming behavior would have persisted in private.

The trichotomy of compliance, identification, and internalization is a useful one. At the same time, like most ways of classifying the world, it is not perfect; there are some places where the categories overlap. Specifically, although it is true that compliance and identification are generally more temporary than internalization, there are circumstances that can increase their permanence. For example, permanence can be increased if an individual makes a firm commitment to continue to interact with the person or group of people that induced the original act of compliance. Thus, in an experiment by Charles Kiesler and his colleagues,[37] when participants believed that they were going to continue interacting with an unattractive discussion group, they not only complied publicly, but they also seemed to internalize their conformity—that is, they changed their private opinions as well as their public behavior. This kind of situation will be discussed in greater detail in Chapter 5.

Permanence can also result if, while complying, we discover something about our actions, or about the consequences of our actions, that makes it worthwhile to continue the behavior even after the original reason for compliance (the reward or punishment) is no longer forthcoming. This is called a **secondary gain.** For example, in behavior modification therapy, an attempt is made to eliminate unwanted or maladaptive behavior by systematically punishing that behavior, by rewarding alternative behaviors, or both. For example, various attempts have been made to use this technique as a way of helping people kick the cigarette habit.[38] Individuals might be given a series of painful electric shocks while performing the usual rituals of smoking—that is, while lighting a cigarette, bringing it up to their lips, inhaling, and so on. After several trials, the individual will refuse to smoke. Unfortunately, it is fairly easy for people to notice a difference between the experimental situation and the world outside: They realize they will not be shocked when smoking outside of the experimental situation. Consequently, a person may later experience a little residual anxiety when lighting a cigarette, but because electric shocks are clearly not forthcoming, the anxiety eventually fades. Thus, many people who temporarily cease smoking after this form of behavior modification will eventually smoke again after electric shock is no longer a threat. How about those who stay off cigarettes after behavior modification? Here is the point: Once we have been induced to comply, and therefore do not smoke for several days, it is possible for us to make a discovery. Over the years, we may have come to believe it was inevitable that we awaken every morning with a hacking cough and a hot, dry mouth, but after refraining from smoking for a few weeks, we may discover how delightful it feels to have a clear throat and a fresh, unparched mouth. This discovery may be enough to keep us from smoking again. Thus, although compliance, in and of itself, usually does not produce long-lasting behavior, it may set the stage for events that will lead to more permanent effects.

Obedience As a Form of Compliance

I indicated that acts of compliance are almost always ephemeral. This does not mean they are trivial. Impermanent behavior can be extremely important. This fact has been demonstrated dramatically by Stanley Milgram in a series of studies of obedience.[39] Picture the scene in his initial experiment: Forty men volunteer for an experiment advertised as a study of learning and memory. But this is just the cover story; actually, it is a study of the extent to which people will obey authority. When the volunteer appears at the lab for his appointment, he is paired with another man, and a somewhat stern experimenter in a technician's coat explains that they will be testing the effects of punishment on learning. The exercise requires one person, the learner, to memorize a list of word pairs on which the other person, the teacher, will test him. The two men draw slips to determine their roles; the actual participant draws the role of teacher. He is led to a "Shock Generator," which has an instrument panel with a row of 30 toggle switches, calibrated from a low point of 15 volts (labeled "Slight Shock") and extending through levels of moderate and severe shocks to a high of 450 volts (labeled "XXX"). By throwing the successive switches, the teacher will deliver an increasingly intense shock each time the learner fails to answer correctly. Then the teacher follows the experimenter and the other man (the learner) into the next room, where the learner is strapped into an electric chair apparatus and is attached by electrodes to the Shock Generator. In response to the learner's inquiry about his mild heart condition, the experimenter reassures him, "Although the shocks can be extremely painful, they cause no permanent tissue damage."

In actuality, the learner knows that he needn't worry. He is not a real participant but is an accomplice of the experimenter, and the drawing to assign roles has been rigged so that he will play the role of the learner and the real participant will be the teacher. The learner is not really wired to the electricity. But the teacher firmly believes that the victim in the next room is wired to the Shock Generator that he operates. He has even experienced a sample shock (from a 45-volt battery inside the machine), he hears the learner react as if he is really being hurt, and he is convinced that the shocks are extremely painful.

As the exercise begins, the learner responds correctly several times but makes mistakes on a few trials. With each error, the teacher throws the next switch, supposedly administering a shock of increasing intensity. With the fifth shock, at 75 volts, the victim begins to grunt and moan. At 150 volts, he asks to be let out of the experiment. At 180 volts, he cries out that he can't stand the pain. As the shock levels approach the point labeled "Danger: Extreme Shock," the teacher hears the victim pound the wall and beg to be let out of the room. But this, of course, does not constitute a correct response, so the experimenter instructs the teacher to increase the voltage and deliver the next shock by throwing the next switch.

The participants in this experiment were a random sample of businessmen, professional men, white-collar workers, and blue-collar workers. What percentage of these people continued to administer shocks to the very end of the experiment? How long would you have continued? Every year in my social psychology class, I pose these questions, and every year some 99 percent of the 240 students in the class indicate that they would not continue to administer shocks after the learner began to pound on the wall. The guesses made by my students are consistent with the results of Milgram's survey of 40 psychiatrists at a leading medical school. The psychiatrists predicted that most participants would quit at 150 volts, when the victim first asks to be freed. They also predicted that only about 4 percent of the participants would continue to shock the victim after he refused to respond (at 300 volts), and that less than 1 percent would administer the highest shock on the generator.

How do people respond when they are actually in the situation? Milgram found, in the typical study described above, that the great majority of participants—some 65 percent—continued to administer shocks to the very end of the experiment, although some of them required a degree of prodding from the experimenter. The obedient individuals did not continue administering shocks because they were particularly sadistic or cruel people. Indeed, when Milgram and Alan Elms compared participants' scores on a series of standardized personality tests, they discovered no differences between individuals who were fully obedient and those who successfully resisted the pressure to obey.[40] Nor were obedient people insensitive to the apparent plight of the victim. Some protested; many sweated, trembled, stuttered, and showed other signs of tension. Some burst out in fits of nervous laughter. But they continued to obey to the very end.

This behavior is not limited to American men living in Connecticut. Wherever the Milgram procedure has been tried, it has produced a significant degree of obedience. For example, several replications of the experiment[41] have demonstrated that people in Australia, Jordan, Spain, Germany, and the Netherlands react in much the same way as the people in Milgram's experiment. Similarly, women are just as obedient as men.[42]

Implications An astonishingly large proportion of people will cause pain to other people in obedience to authority. The research may have important counterparts in the world outside of the experimental laboratory. For example, it is difficult to read about these studies without noticing some similarity between the behavior of the teachers in Milgram's experiment and the blind obedience expressed by Adolf Eichmann, who attributed his responsibility for the murder of thousands of innocent civilians to the fact that he was a good bureaucrat merely obeying orders issued by his superiors in the Nazi regime.

More recently, during the war in Vietnam, Lieutenant William Calley, who was convicted of the deliberate and unprovoked murder of Vietnamese women and children at My Lai, freely admitted to these acts but said he felt this was justifiable obedience to the authority of his superior officers. Interestingly, one of Milgram's obedient participants, when questioned after the session, replied: "*I* stopped, but he [the experimenter] made me go on."

As provocative as these comparisons are, we should be cautious lest we overinterpret Milgram's results. Given that 65 percent of the participants in Milgram's experiment complied with the experimenter's command, some commentators have been tempted to suggest that perhaps most people would have behaved as Adolf Eichmann or Lieutenant Calley did if they found themselves in a similar situation. This may be true; but it should be emphasized that there are, in fact, some important factors in the situation encountered by Milgram's participants that tend to maximize obedience. Because he freely consented to participate, he had every reason to assume that his victim has also volunteered. Accordingly, it is likely that he felt that they were both obligated to avoid disrupting the experiment. Moreover, he faced the demands of the experimenter alone; a variation of the study demonstrated that the proportion of fully obedient people dropped to just 10 percent when they were joined by two fellow teachers who defied the experimenter.[43] Also, in most of Milgram's studies, the authority figure issuing the orders was a scientist in a prestigious laboratory at Yale University, and his cover story credits the experiment as being an investigation of an important scientific question. In our society, we have been conditioned to believe that scientists tend to be responsible, benevolent people of high integrity. This is especially true if the scientist is affiliated with a well-known and highly respected institution like Yale. The participants might reasonably assume, then, that no scientist would issue orders that would result in the death or injury of a human as a part of his experiment. This was clearly not true in either the Eichmann or the Calley example.

Some evidence in support of this conjecture comes from further research by Milgram. He conducted a separate study[44] comparing the obedience of people to the commands of a scientist at Yale University with obedience of people to the commands of a scientist working in a suite of offices in a rather rundown commercial building in the downtown shopping area of the industrial city of Bridgeport, Connecticut. In this study, the Yale scientist achieved an obedience rate of 65 percent compared to only 48 percent in Bridgeport. Thus, removing the prestige of Yale University did seem to reduce the degree of obedience somewhat.

Of course, 48 percent is still a high figure. Would even fewer people have obeyed if the person conducting the experiment were not a scientist or another legitimate authority figure? Milgram addressed this question in another version of the study, in which the scientist-experimenter was replaced at the last minute by a nonauthoritative "substitute." Here's how it worked: After making the usual preparations for the learning task, but without designating what shock levels were to be used, the experimenter was called away from the laboratory by a prearranged telephone call. Another "participant" (actually a confederate) assumed the experimenter's role. The substitute pretended to hit upon the idea of having the teacher raise the shock level every time the learner made a mistake. He also prodded the teacher to proceed with the shocks, just as the scientist-experimenter had done in previous versions of the experiments. Under these conditions, the proportion of fully obedient participants plummeted to 20 percent, demonstrating that, for most people, only legitimate authority can command high obedience, not just any person assuming the role of authority.

Another factor that reduces the extent of obedience is the physical absence of the authority figure. Milgram found that, when the experimenter was out of the room and issued his orders by telephone, the number of *fully* obedient participants dropped to below 25 percent. Moreover, several of the people who did continue with the experiment cheated; specifically, they administered shocks of lower intensity than they were supposed to—and never bothered to tell the experimenter that they deviated from the proper procedure. This last datum, I feel, represents a touching attempt by some individuals to respond to the demands of legitimate authority while at the same time minimizing the pain they inflict on others. It is reminiscent of the behavior of Dunbar, a character in Joseph Heller's classic war novel *Catch 22*. During World War II, Dunbar is ordered to bomb some villages in Italy. Unwilling either to rebel openly or to harm innocent civilians, he drops his bombs over empty fields close to the Italian villages designated as his targets.

Dunbar's sensitivity to the potential victims of his bombs is especially poignant, given the distance and anonymity afforded by his position high in the sky above the villagers. Indeed, Milgram found in subsequent studies that the farther teachers were from the learner, the more willing they were to obey the commands of authority. When teachers actually saw the learner, only 40 percent continued to deliver painful shocks compared to 62 percent who merely heard the victim's cries of agony. Similarly, when teachers were instructed to physically force the learner's arm down on the shock plate—instead of using the more remote Shock Generator to deliver shocks—the rate of obedience dropped to 30 percent. Thus, vividly witnessing the suffering of others makes it more difficult to continue inflicting pain upon them. Conversely, the weapons used in modern warfare preclude such close proximity to potential victims, making it easier for those who wield the instruments of death to be indifferent to the plight of innocent targets.

In a recent set of experiments in the Netherlands, Wim Meeus and Qutinten Raaijmakers[45] explored the issue of obedience and distance in a slightly different manner. In addition to successfully replicating the original Milgram procedure, they tried it a different way. In the new procedure, the experimenter asked people to obey them by making a series of increasingly negative remarks about an applicant's performance on a test that would determine whether he or she would be hired for a job. Thus, the participants were convinced that they were harming the person—but the harm was such that it would not be manifested until some future time, when the participants would not be present to witness the consequences of their obedience. As one might expect, obedience in these situations was much higher than in their direct replication of the Milgram experiment; in this version, over 90 percent of the participants continued to obey to the very end of the series.

Disobedience in the Milgram Experiments As you know, several people in the Milgram experiments chose to defy the experimenter and refused to continue with the experiment—in spite of the prodding of the experimenter. Human history, likewise, contains many inspiring examples of such courage. For example, there are "freedom museums" in Norway, Denmark, and other European countries that celebrate the efforts of a heroic few to resist the occupation of the Nazis or to attempt to help Jews escape the ravages of the Holocaust. But these acts of humanity and bravery, however encouraging, should not blind us to the pervasiveness of our tendency to obey authority. Many of us tour such museums and admire the displays, certain that we, too, would exhibit such courage. We harbor a myth of our personal invulnerability to obedience pressures. When participants were asked to predict their own performance in the Milgram study, their values and self-conceptions caused 100 percent of them to predict that they would discontinue the shocks at or below the moderate level.[46] But we have seen how the forces of the actual situation can override those values and self-conceptions. One year, when, as usual, I asked my social-psychology students whether they might continue delivering shocks until the end of the scale, only one hand slowly rose; everyone else in the class was confident that he or she would defy the experimenter's instructions. But the student who raised his hand was a Vietnam veteran who was in a position to know; he had experienced the impact of similar pressures, and he painfully and tragically came to recognize his own vulnerability in certain situations. Indeed, not only do we find it difficult to resist pressures to hurt people, we often avoid taking action when presented with opportunities to help others.

The Uninvolved Bystander As Conformist

In 1964, a young woman named Kitty Genovese was stabbed to death in New York City. This was a tragic event but not, in itself, a particularly novel occurrence. After all, in a major population center, brutal murders are not uncommon. What is interesting about this event is that no fewer than 38 of her neighbors came to their windows at 3:00 a.m. in response to the victim's screams of terror—and remained at their windows watching in fascination for the 30 minutes it took her assailant to complete his grisly deed, during which time he returned for three separate attacks. No one came to her assistance; no one so much as lifted the phone to call the police until it was too late.[47] Why?

Well, perhaps the onlookers were sleepy or dazed. After all, people are hardly in full control of their mental faculties at three o'clock in the morning. Perhaps. But it was in broad daylight that Eleanor Bradley, while shopping on Fifth Avenue in New York City, tripped, fell, and broke her leg. She lay there for 40 minutes in a state of shock while literally hundreds of passersby paused momentarily to gawk at her and then kept on walking.

Why did these bystanders fail to help? Are people impervious to the distress of others? Have they become so accustomed to disaster that they can be nonchalant in the face of pain and violence? Were the bystanders in these situations different from you and me in some way? The answer to all of these questions appears to be no. Interviews conducted with the bystanders in the

Genovese murder revealed that they were anything but nonchalant—they were horrified. Why, then, didn't they intervene? This is a difficult question to answer.

One possible explanation concerns the existence of different norms for helping in large cities as opposed to smaller towns. Several experiments[48] have found that the likelihood of receiving help is greater in nonurban than in urban locales. However, these studies examined small requests for help—change for a quarter, the correct time, and so forth. Whether or not these rural-urban differences occur in serious emergency situations, like those faced by Kitty Genovese and Eleanor Bradley, is unclear.

More convincing explanations have been suggested by a series of ingenious experiments conducted by John Darley, Bibb Latane, and their colleagues.[49] These investigators hypothesized that the large number of people witnessing the tragedies militated against anyone's helping—that is, a victim is less likely to get help if a large number of people are watching his or her distress. Thus, nonintervention can be viewed as an act of conformity. In this case it appears that, for each individual, the other people were defining the reasonableness and appropriateness of helping or not helping. As we have seen, it is often reasonable to take one's cue from others. Occasionally, however, it can be misleading, and it tends to be particularly misleading in critical situations. In our society, it is considered "uncool" to reveal strong emotions in public. When we are with others, most of us try to appear less fearful, less worried, less anxious, or less sexually aroused than we really are. For example, from the blasé looks on the faces of the patrons of topless nightclubs, one would never guess that they were turned on or even interested. Similarly, the proverbial visitor from Mars would never suspect the anxiety of the patients in a dentist's waiting room by observing the impassive looks on their faces.

With these things in mind, let us consider the case of the woman who fell and broke her leg on Fifth Avenue. Suppose you arrived at the scene 10 minutes after she fell. You see a woman lying on the ground in apparent discomfort. What else do you see? You see scores of people walking past the woman, glancing at her, and continuing on their way. How will you define the situation? You may conclude that it's inappropriate for you to intervene. Perhaps it's not serious; perhaps she's intoxicated; perhaps she is playacting; perhaps the whole thing is staged for "Candid Camera," and you will make a fool of yourself on national television if you intervene. "After all," you ask yourself, "if it's so damn important, why are none of these other people doing anything about it?" Thus, the fact that there are a lot of other people around, rather than increasing the likelihood that *someone* will help, actually decreases the likelihood that any *one* of them will help.[50]

This is an interesting conjecture, but is it true? To find out, Bibb Latane and Judith Rodin[51] conducted an experiment constructed around a "lady in distress." In this experiment, a female experimenter asked college students to fill out a questionnaire. The experimenter then retired to the next room through an unlocked collapsible curtain, saying she would return when they finished the questionnaire. A few minutes later, she staged an "accident." What the students actually heard was the sound (from a hidden tape recording) of the young woman climbing a chair, followed by a loud scream and a crash, as if the chair had collapsed and she had fallen to the floor. They then heard moaning and crying and the anguished statement, "Oh, my God, my foot, I . . . I can't move it. Oh . . . my ankle . . . I can't get this thing off me." The cries continued for about a minute and gradually subsided.

The experimenters were interested in determining whether or not the participants would come to the young woman's aid. The important variable in the experiment was whether or not the people were alone in the room. Of those who were alone, 70 percent offered to help the young woman; of those who were participating in pairs with strangers, only 20 percent offered help. Thus, it is clear that the presence of another bystander tends to inhibit action. This phenomenon has been dubbed the **bystander effect**. When interviewed subsequently, the unhelpful participants who had been in the room with another person said they had concluded that the accident probably wasn't serious, at least in part because of the inactivity of their partner.

In the Genovese murder, there was probably an additional reason the bystanders did not help. In such a situation it may be that, if people are aware that an event is being witnessed by others, the responsibility felt by any individual is diffused. Each witness to the Genovese slaying who noticed lights flick on and faces watching in several other windows might have felt no personal responsibility to act. Since others were watching, each bystander could have concluded that someone else was calling the police or that it was someone else's duty to do so. To test this idea, Darley and Latane[52] arranged an experimental situation in which people were placed in separate rooms but were able to communicate with each other by microphones and earphones. Thus, the participants could hear one another but couldn't see one another. The investigators then staged a simulated epileptic attack: They played a tape recording of a supposed epileptic seizure on the part of one of the participants. In one experimental condition, each person was led to believe that he or she was the only one whose intercom was tuned in during the seizure; in other conditions, each person was led to believe that one or more people were tuned in also. Those who thought they were the only listener were far more likely to leave their room and try to help than were those who thought others were listening, too. As the number of people listening increased, the likelihood of offering assistance decreased.

The behavior of the onlookers in the Genovese murder case and the participants in the Darley-Latane experiments projects a rather grim picture of the human condition. Is it true that people avoid helping each other if at all possible—that is, if someone provides a bad example by not intervening or if the responsibility for action seems the least bit diffuse? Perhaps not. Perhaps there are situations in which people are inspired to come to the aid of their fellows. An incident in my own experience may shed some light on this issue. I was backpacking in Yosemite National Park several years ago. It was late at night, and I was just dropping off to sleep when I heard a man's voice cry out. I couldn't be certain whether it was a cry of pain, surprise, or joy. I had no idea whether some people were just horsing around or whether one of my fellow campers was being attacked by a bear. I crawled out of my sleeping bag and looked around, trying to shake the cobwebs out of my head and trying to ascertain the place from which the scream had come, when I noticed a strange phenomenon. From all over the area, myriad flickering lights were converging on a single point. These were lanterns and flashlights being carried by dozens of campers running to the aid of the individual who had screamed. It turned out that his scream had been one of surprise caused by a relatively harmless flare-up in his gasoline stove. The other campers seemed almost disappointed when they learned that no help was needed. They trudged back to their tents and, I assume, dropped off to sleep immediately. Not so with me, however: I tossed and turned, unable to get back to sleep. As a social psychologist with a great deal of faith in scientific data, I spent the night puzzling over the fact that my fellow campers had behaved in a totally different manner from the participants in the Darley-Latane experiments.

Why had the campers behaved so differently? In what way were the situations different? There were at least two factors operating in the campground that were either not present or present only to a very small degree in the situations previously discussed. One of these factors is reflected in my use, in the preceding paragraph, of the term "my fellow campers." Specifically, a feeling of "common fate" or mutuality may be engendered among people sharing the same interests, pleasures, hardships, and environmental conditions of a closed environment like a campground, a feeling of mutuality that is stronger than among people who are merely residents of the same country, county, or city. A second, somewhat related factor is that there was no escape from the face-to-face aspect of the situation: The onlookers in the Genovese case could walk away from their windows into the relative protection and isolation of their own homes; the people on Fifth Avenue could walk past the woman lying on the sidewalk and keep on going, right out of her environment; the participants in the Darley-Latane experiments were not in a face-to-face relationship with the victim, and they knew they could escape from the environment in a very short time. In the campground, the events were occurring in a relatively restricted environment; whatever the campers allowed to happen that night they were going to have to face squarely the next morning. It seems that, under these circumstances, individuals are more willing to take responsibility for each other.

Of course, this is mere speculation. The behavior of the campers at Yosemite, while provocative, is not conclusive because it was not part of a controlled experiment. One of the major problems with observational data like these is that the observer has no control over who the people in the situation are. Thus, differences between people always loom as a possible explanation for the differences in their behavior. For example, one might argue that individuals who go camping are—by nature or experience—kinder, gentler, more thoughtful, and more humane than New Yorkers. Perhaps they were Boy Scouts and Girl Scouts as children—hence their interest in camping—and, in scouting, they were taught to be helpful to other people. One of the reasons for doing experiments is to control this kind of uncertainty. Indeed, a subsequent experiment lends support to my speculation about my campground experience. This was an experiment performed by Irving Piliavin and his associates[53] in one of the cars of a train in the New York City subway system. In this experiment, an accomplice of the experimenters staggered and collapsed in the presence of several individuals riding the subway. The "victim" remained stretched out on the floor of the train, staring at the ceiling. This scene was repeated 103 times under a variety of conditions. The most striking result was that, a large part of the time, people spontaneously rushed to the aid of the "stricken" individual. This was especially true when the victim was made to seem obviously ill; in more than 95 percent of the trials, someone offered help immediately. Even when the "victim" had been given a liquor bottle to carry and was made to reek of alcohol, he received immediate help from someone on 50 percent of the trials. Unlike the behavior of the participants that Darley and Latane dealt with, the helping behavior of the people on the subway train was not affected by the number of bystanders. People helped just as often and just as speedily on crowded trains (where there could be a diffusion of responsibility) as they did on virtually empty trains. Although the people doing the helping were New Yorkers (as in the Genovese case, the Fifth Avenue case, and the Darley-Latane experiments), they were also in an environment that, although very much unlike Yosemite National Park, did have two things in common with the campground: (1) people riding on the same subway car do have the feeling of sharing a common fate, and (2) they were in a face-to-face situation with the victim from which there was no immediate escape.

How can the tendency to help be increased? Consider the questions that would run through your mind should you confront a possible emergency: Is the situation really serious? Does it require my personal intervention? Will helping be difficult or costly for me? Will my help benefit the victim? Can I easily leave? Your response will depend on your answers to each of these questions.

The first prerequisite for helping is to define the situation as an emergency. We have seen that the clues provided by the presence of unresponsive bystanders can discourage other onlookers from concluding that an emergency exists. But the interpretations of bystanders can also influence perceptions in the opposite direction. In an experiment conducted by Leonard Bickman,[54] female students sitting in cubicles and listening over intercoms heard a crash and a victim's scream, followed by the reaction of a witness to the apparent accident. When the participants heard the witness interpret the event as a certain emergency, they helped more frequently and more quickly than when the interpretation was uncertain or when the event was labeled a nonemergency. The less ambiguous the emergency, the greater the likelihood of helping.

Defining the situation as an emergency is the first step; assuming personal responsibility for intervening is the next. Onlookers are more likely to help when they cannot reduce their sense of responsibility by assuming others will act. I have described an experiment by Darley and Latane demonstrating that people help more when they think they are the only ones aware of an emergency. In Bickman's experiments, although the participants thought others were aware of the situation, some were led to believe that the other participants were unable to respond. Specifically, some of the female students were informed that the other participants they would hear over the intercom were located in nearby cubicles, while others were told that one voice (turning out to be the victim's) was originating from a nearby cubicle but that the other participant was speaking from a different building. People responded significantly more speedily to the emergency in the latter condition when perceiving that the other bystander was unable to help. In fact, the people who could not diffuse their responsibility intervened as quickly as those who thought nobody else heard the accident.

Although an event might be a clear emergency that demands their aid, people help less when the costs of their assistance are high. In a variation of the Piliavins's subway experiments,[55] the "victim" sometimes bit a capsule of red dye as he collapsed, so that he appeared to be bleeding from the mouth. Though the "blood" made the emergency appear more serious, the bleeding victims were helped less frequently than those who collapsed without bleeding. Apparently, potential helpers were scared or repulsed by the blood, reducing their inclination to help. Other kinds of costs also can enter the calculation, including seemingly trivial ones, as John Darley and Daniel Batson[56] cleverly illustrated. They enlisted divinity students at Princeton Theological Seminary, ostensibly for the purpose of recording a speech. Each student practiced his talk in one room; then he was instructed to walk to another building, where his presentation would be taped. At this point, some of the students were told they were late for their appointment and were hurried out. Others were told they were on time, and the rest that they had time to spare. On their way to the recording session in the other building, the students encountered an apparent victim slumped in a doorway, with head down and eyes closed, coughing pathetically. Over half of these future ministers who were early or on time stopped to assist the victim, but only 10 percent of those who thought they were late for their appointment offered help, even when the speech they were to deliver involved the parable of the Good Samaritan!

In addition to assessing the costs of helping, people consider the benefits their assistance will provide. There is a good deal of evidence that people will help one another if they are certain they can do something truly useful.[57] For example, in one experiment, Robert Baron[58] showed that, when an individual was in obvious pain—and when the bystander knew his or her response could alleviate the suffering—then the greater the apparent pain, the more quickly the bystander responded. But when the bystander did not believe he or she could reduce the victim's pain, there was an inverse relationship between pain and speed of responding—that is, the greater the apparent pain, the more slowly the bystander responded. To make sense out of these results, we need to make use of the concept of empathy: in this case, our tendency to experience unpleasant physiological responses at the sight of another person in pain. The greater the victim's pain, the greater our unpleasant feeling. We can reduce this unpleasant feeling either by helping the victim or by removing ourselves psychologically from the situation. If there is clearly something we can do about it, we act quickly—especially when the victim is in great pain. If we believe there is nothing we can do about it, the greater is our tendency to turn away from it (in order to reduce our own feelings of unpleasantness), especially if the victim is in great pain.

Up to this point, we have been focusing on the considerations surrounding a decision to help a victim. As this discussion of empathy exemplifies, the bystander also considers the personal benefits and costs of not helping. The discomfort aroused by seeing a victim's plight can be assuaged if the witness can redefine the incident as a nonemergency or relinquish the responsibility for intervening. When it is easy to remove oneself from the situation, helping is reduced. Several factors, however, strengthen the connection the bystander feels with the victim and thereby discourage leaving. We have all heard anecdotes of people going to extraordinary lengths—entering burning buildings or stepping in front of moving cars—to save members of their family. We tend to feel more empathy and assume more responsibility when the victim is someone close to us. The connection can be more superficial than family ties; for instance, potential helpers render more assistance to those who exhibit attitudes similar to their own. In 1971, as protesters demonstrated in Washington against President Nixon's Vietnam policy, Peter Suedfeld and his colleagues[59] staged an experiment to test the relationship between similarity of attitudes and willingness to help. They trained a young woman to approach individual demonstrators with a request to help her male friend, who was ill. Her ailing friend carried a sign reading either "Dump Nixon" or "Support Nixon." Demonstrators offered more assistance to a fellow protester carrying the anti-Nixon placard than to a seeming supporter of Nixon. Finally, as I mentioned when discussing the Yosemite camping incident and the subway experiments, helping is more likely when people share a sense of common fate. This sense of interdependence is easily disregarded in our society; the predominant explanation given by the 38 onlookers to the Genovese murder was "I didn't want to get involved."

A Note on the Ethics of Experiments

In their quest for knowledge, experimental social psychologists occasionally subject people to some fairly intense experiences. In this chapter alone, I have discussed experiments in which people have been led into conflict between the evidence of their own eyes and the unanimous judgments of other people, in which they have been ordered to deliver intense electric shock to an apparently suffering victim, and in which scores of innocent people riding a subway have been forced to witness the apparent agony of a person in distress.

These procedures raise serious ethical problems. A more complete treatment of ethics is presented in Chapter 9; here, let it suffice to make two general points: First, it is the responsibility of all experimenters in this field to protect the experimental participant from all harm. The experimenter must take steps to ensure that participants leave the experimental situation in a frame of mind that is at least as sound as it was when they entered the experimental situation. This frequently requires postexperimental "**debriefing**" procedures that require more time and effort than the main body of the experiment.

Given the ethical thin ice that experimenters must skate upon, why bother with these kinds of experiments at all? This brings me to the second point of ethics I want to emphasize at this time: For social psychologists, the ethical issue is not a one-sided affair. In a real sense, they are obligated to use their research skills to advance our knowledge and understanding of human behavior for the ultimate aim of human betterment. In short, social psychologists have an ethical responsibility to the society as a whole; they would be remiss in fulfilling this responsibility if they failed to conduct research to the best of their ability. Social psychologists face a dilemma when their general ethical responsibility to society conflicts with their more specific ethical responsibility to each individual experimental participant; and to compound the situation, the conflict is greatest when investigating such important issues as conformity, obedience, helping, and the like because, in general, the more important the issue, (1) the greater the potential benefit for society and (2) the more likely it is that an individual participant will experience discomfort, anxiety, or upset. For a more complete treatment of this topic, the reader is directed to Chapter 9.

Saul Steinberg, *Untitled drawing*, ink on paper.
Published in Steinberg, *The Labyrinth*, 1960.
© The Saul Steinberg Foundation / Artists Rights Society (ARS), New York

3
Mass Communication, Propaganda, and Persuasion

During the past three decades, the predominance of mass communication has turned the world into a global village. This is particularly true in the United States, where almost every household has at least one TV set—and, as a result, virtually an entire population can be exposed to a similar diet of information as soon as it becomes available. Let me provide you with a few graphic examples of this phenomenon and some of its consequences: In 1977, American television presented its very first blockbuster miniseries. Over 130 million viewers tuned in to watch at least one of the segments of *Roots*, the ABC television network's production of Alex Haley's history of several generations of an African-American family in the United States. The show received widespread acclaim for promoting the awareness of black history and for inspiring blacks' pride in their heritage. Six years later, ABC aired *The Day After*, a made-for-TV movie that graphically depicted the aftermath of a nuclear attack on the United States. In November 1983, over 40 million U.S. households tuned in; the audience was far larger than our wildest predictions. Weeks before it was shown, *The Day After* was the subject of numerous cover stories in national news magazines. Movie stars, physicists, and political leaders (including the president) aired their views about the program and its potential impact.[1]

The Day After clearly did have an impact, even on those who had not actually watched the show but had merely heard some of the hype. After the movie aired, watchers and nonwatchers alike thought more about nuclear war, thought nuclear war was more likely, felt that surviving such a war was less likely, and viewed survival as less positive. Moreover, both groups reported that they intended to work toward preventing a nuclear war by supporting a nuclear-weapons freeze and engaging in other antinuclear activities. These effects were generally stronger for the watchers than the nonwatchers. Amazingly, just two hours of prime-time television had a major impact on most Americans, influencing both their attitudes and their intentions to do something constructive about the threat of nuclear war.[2]

A simple two hours of television can also have powerfully negative effects, preventing viewers from taking action. Some years ago, CBS aired a film called *Cry Rape*. Essentially, the story made it clear that a rape victim who chooses to press charges against her attacker runs the risk of undergoing an ordeal that may be as harrowing as the rape itself. In this case, the rapist, exuding boyish innocence, presented a convincing argument to the effect that the woman had seduced him. During the next few weeks, there was a sharp decrease in the number of rapes reported by victims to police—apparently because victims, taking their cue from the television movie, feared the police would not believe them.[3]

In 1995, tens of millions of viewers sat transfixed in front of their TV sets for several months, watching the murder trial of O. J. Simpson. During that period, lawyers of every stripe paraded in front of the video cameras offering their expert opinions on every nuance of the proceedings. Millions of viewers were insatiable—they couldn't seem to get enough of the trial. When the verdict was finally announced and Mr. Simpson was found not guilty, we witnessed a vivid example of a powerful racial division in this country: Most blacks felt it was a just verdict; most whites felt it was a miscarriage of justice. It was as if white people and black people had been watching two different trials.

And then, September 11. How many times did TV viewers see those towers collapse? The images of the collapsing towers, the shocked onlookers, the heroic rescue workers, and the grieving relatives remain embedded in the minds of most Americans and have had a major impact on our fear and anger at terrorists, our patriotism, our willingness to go to war and alas, in some people, unwarranted prejudice against Muslims.

Attempts at Persuasion. It is a truism to say that we live in an age of mass communication; indeed, it can even be said that we live in an age characterized by attempts at mass persuasion. Every time we turn on the radio or television set, every time we open a book, magazine, or newspaper, someone is trying to educate us, to convince us to buy a product, to persuade us to vote for a candidate or to subscribe to some version of what is right, true, or beautiful. This aim is most obvious in advertising: Manufacturers of nearly identical products (aspirin, for example, or toothpaste, or detergent) spend vast amounts of money to persuade us to buy the product in *their* package. But influence through the mass media need not be so blatant. The impact of *Roots, The Day After,* and the O. J. Simpson trial extended far beyond their most obvious effects as documentaries or court dramas. This influence can be very subtle indeed, even unintentional. As the example of the film about rape aptly illustrates, even when communicators are not making a direct attempt to sell us something, they can succeed in influencing the way we look at the world and the way we respond to important events in our lives.

Let's look at something supposedly objective—like the news. Are the newscasters *trying* to sell us anything? Probably not. But those who produce television news can exert a powerful influence on our opinions simply by determining which events are given exposure and how much exposure they are given.

Several years ago, a motorist named Rodney King was stopped for reckless driving. In the course of the arrest, he was savagely beaten by officers of the Los Angeles police department. By a fluke of luck, a resident of the neighborhood recorded the event on videotape; during the next several weeks, the tape was shown over and over again on TV screens across the nation. Subsequently, in the spring of 1992, when a jury found the police officers innocent of any wrongdoing, the inner city of Los Angeles erupted in the worst riot in American history. By the time peace was restored, 44 people had been killed, some 2,000 were seriously injured, and entire city blocks in South-Central Los Angeles were in flames—resulting in over a billion dollars in property damage. Needless to say, there were many causes of the riot. But certainly one of the triggers was the fact that people had seen that beating many times and were therefore in a position to be outraged by the verdict.

Given the power of TV newscasts, it is reasonable to ask what factors determine which news items are selected for television newscasts. The answer is not a simple one, but one major factor is the need to attract viewers. Indeed, it has been said by no less an expert than the director of the British Broadcasting Corporation that television news is a form of *entertainment*. Recent studies suggest[4] that when those in charge of news programming decide which news events to cover and which fraction of the miles of daily videotape to present to the public, they make their decisions, at least in part, on the basis of the entertainment value of their material. Film footage of a flooded metropolis has much more entertainment value than footage of a dam built to prevent such flooding: It is simply not very exciting to see a dam holding back a flood. And yet, the dam may be more important news.

Just as action events such as football games are more entertaining on television than quiet events such as chess matches, it is more likely that riots, bombings, earthquakes, massacres, and other violent acts will get more air time than stories about people working to prevent violence. Thus, news telecasts tend to focus on the violent behavior of individuals—terrorists, protesters, strikers, or police—because action makes for more exciting viewing than does a portrayal of people behaving in a peaceful, orderly manner. Such coverage does not present a balanced picture of what is happening in the nation or the world, not because the people who run the news media are evil and trying to manipulate us but simply because they are trying to entertain us. And, in trying to entertain us, they may unwittingly influence us to believe that people behave far more violently now than ever before. This may cause us to be unhappy and even depressed about the temper of the times or the state of the nation. Ultimately, it may affect our vote, our desire to visit major urban centers, our attitudes about other nations, and so on. As we shall see in Chapter 6, it may actually cause people to behave more violently.

Of course, some violent events are important and warrant a great deal of coverage. As I mentioned earlier, following the terrorist attack of September 11, most Americans sat glued to their TV sets because they wanted to know what was happening and they needed reassurance that the situation was under control. In the process, many of us saw the collapse of the Twin Towers dozens of times as the cable news channels gave that event round-the-clock coverage. How can we be sure that is what our citizens wanted at that time? In the two weeks following the attack, the number of people tuned into CNN jumped 667 percent and the *New York Times* sold a quarter of a million more newspapers on September 12 than it did on September 10.[5]

It is always good to be informed—and the media play an important role in keeping us informed. But there can be a downside to this kind of exposure, as well. Whether it is intentional or not, repeated vivid imagery of this sort shapes attitudes and opinions. The constant images of the Twin Towers' fall, as well as the repetition of bellicose slogans on cable news channels ("the war on terrorism," "America fights back," etc.), contributed to the arousal of intense emotions in viewers and doubtless served to reduce the possibility of any real debate about the wisdom of invading Afghanistan. Moreover, one year after September 11, when President Bush somehow managed to link Saddam Hussein with the al-Qaida terrorists, his request for the authority to invade Iraq sailed through Congress with hardly a murmur of opposition. It should be clear that I am not asserting that these policies were ill-conceived. What I am suggesting is that, in a democracy, important decisions, like whether to go to war, should be open to free, rational public debate. Strong emotions often impede debate or dissent. As Hermann Goering, one of Adolf Hitler's top aides, said before being sentenced to death at Nuremberg, "The people can always be brought to the bidding of the leaders. . . . All you have to do is tell them they are being attacked, and denounce the peacemakers for lack of patriotism and exposing the country to danger. It works the same in any country."[6]

Media Contagion

The power of the media is perhaps best illustrated by a phenomenon known as **emotional contagion.** For example, in October 1982, when seven people in the Chicago area died after taking Tylenol headache capsules laced with cyanide, the tragedy was widely publicized by the national news media. Indeed, for several days it was difficult to turn on the television or radio or to pick up a newspaper without learning about the Tylenol poisonings. Of course, it was both tragic and bizarre—and therefore very good copy. The effects of this prominent coverage were immediate: Similar poisonings were reported in cities across the country, involving the contamination of mouthwash, eyedrops, nasal spray, soda pop, and even hot dogs. Dramatically billed as "copycat poisonings," these poisonings, in turn, received widespread media attention. The public reaction took on all the properties of a spiral: Many people panicked, seeking medical aid for burns and poisonings when they suffered from no more than common sore throats and stomachaches. False alarms outnumbered actual cases of product tampering by seven to one.[7] Because these events occurred just prior to Halloween, worried officials in scores of communities banned trick-or-treating, fearing that many individuals might mimic the murders by contaminating children's candy.

The initial Chicago poisonings were almost certainly the work of one person. Subsequent events were caused by the publicity given to the Chicago poisonings. But the belief was spread that the wave of poisoning constituted "an epidemic without a cure," in the words of one news service,[8] and was itself the symptom of a "sick" society, a country going "crazy." Many newspapers found themselves in the ironic position of first sensationalizing the poisoning incidents and then sensationalizing the subsequent critical comments of media experts discussing the disastrous consequences of such publicity.

A few years later, four teenagers in New Jersey made a suicide pact and then carried out their plan. Within a week of this multiple suicide, two teenagers in the Midwest were found dead under similar circumstances. Media reports no doubt spotlighted the confusion and grief surrounding teenage suicide. But is it possible that the media's coverage of these tragedies actually inspired copycat suicides? According to sociologist David Phillips, the answer is a qualified "yes."

Phillips and his colleagues studied suicide rates among teenagers following network television news or feature stories about suicide. Their research tracked fluctuations in teenage suicides by comparing suicide rates before the stories with rates after the stories. Within a week of the broadcasts, the increase in teenage suicides was far greater than could be explained by chance alone. Furthermore, the more coverage devoted by major television networks to suicide, the greater the subsequent increase in suicides among teenagers. The increases held even when the researchers took other possible causes into account. Thus, the most likely explanation for the increase in teenage suicides following media publicity is that such publicity actually triggers subsequent copycat suicides.[9]

Copycat suicides are not something peculiar to teenagers. In another study on the effects of highly publicized suicides, Phillips chose to examine fatal car crashes.[10] Some people, trying to save family members from the trauma of a suicide, will choose to kill themselves in car crashes that may look like accidents. These suicides should show up on official records as single-car, one-passenger fatal accidents. Phillips reasoned that after a publicized suicide, there should be a dramatic increase in these types of accidents, and that the victims should be similar in some respect to the publicized suicide victim. This is exactly what he found after examining highway-patrol records both before and after highly publicized suicides. There were no changes in multiple-car accidents or single-car accidents with passengers, and the victims in these accidents did not resemble the publicized suicide victims. There was, however, an increase in suicide-type accidents, and the victims' ages were highly correlated with the age of the publicized suicide victim. Again, the most likely explanation for these findings is that the publicity of one suicide incited others to take their own lives.

The Tylenol poisonings and copycat suicides were newsworthy. I am not suggesting that the media created these events or that they should not have been reported. Rather, I am underlining the obvious fact that selective emphasis puts the media in the position of determining subsequent events—not simply reporting them.

As I stated earlier, this form of influence is probably unintentional; the news media are not *trying* to foster violence or create the illusion that most people are cruel. But the pervasiveness of electronic media cannot be overstated. In fact, sometimes the role of the media in reporting an event becomes more newsworthy than the event itself. For example, let's look at the Beirut hostage crisis of 1985, in which some 40 innocent U.S. passengers on a TWA jet were held captive by Shiite terrorists. Television cameras offered viewers back home around-the-clock coverage of all aspects of the crisis—important and trivial alike. There were press conferences held by the terrorists, press conferences held by the hostages, intimate shots of anguished families, demands, counterdemands, pistol wavings, outrageous statements, luncheon menus, and so on. The television camera crews did everything but follow the hostages into the restrooms!

At one point, it was suggested that the electronic media might be prolonging the ordeal by giving so much free publicity to the Shiite cause. So what did the television networks do? They televised a series of panel discussions by pundits about the role of the media in such a situation. The message became the media. In its endlessness, this series of events reminded me of a brand of table salt, popular when I was a kid; on the box was a picture of a little girl holding up a box of the table salt on which there was a picture of a little girl holding up a box of the table salt on which there was a picture of a little girl. . . . With the advent of 24-hour cable news, this kind of endlessness has become commonplace.

Politicians as Entertainers

In such cases, persuasion is usually incidental. Let's turn from these unintentional forms of media influence and take a look at a more conscious, direct attempt to persuade people by the judicious selection of material to be presented in the media. Imagine the following hypothetical situation: Two men are running for president. One of the candidates has far less money to spend on his campaign than the other. Accordingly, in order to get maximum free exposure, he consents to numerous interviews and appears frequently at news conferences and on panel-type programs on television. The interviewers on these occasions are seasoned reporters who are not always sympathetic to the candidate. Frequently, they ask him difficult questions—occasionally, questions that are downright hostile. The candidate finds himself forever on the defensive. Sometimes the camera catches him at an unflattering angle or in the act of scratching his nose, yawning, or fidgeting. While viewing at home, his mother is surprised at the bags under his eyes and at how tired and old he looks. Sometimes, when faced with a tough or unexpected question, he has difficulty finding the right response; he hems and haws and sounds inarticulate.

His opponent with the well-stocked campaign chest does not need to appear in these kinds of forums. Instead, he spends vast amounts of money videotaping spot commercials. Because he pays the camera crew and the director, his countenance is captured only from the most flattering angles. His personal makeup person works extra hard to conceal the bags under his eyes and to make him appear young and dynamic. His mother, watching him at home, never saw him looking so well. The interviewer asks him questions prepared and rehearsed in advance, so that his answers are reasonable, concise, and articulate. If the candidate does happen to stumble over a word or to draw a blank, the cameras are stopped and the scene is shot over and over again until it is letter perfect.

This example was hypothetical in the 1960s. Since then, it has become a reality.[11] Contemporary candidates (from those running for president to those running for dog catcher) must look good on television if they are to stand a chance of winning the election. Following TV presidential debates, pundits usually discuss which of the candidates acted "more presidential." One very successful candidate who did a great job acting presidential was a former film and TV actor named Ronald Reagan. In addition, most candidates now must spend increasingly more time and energy soliciting campaign contributions in order to cover the spiraling costs of paid TV commercials. In a given election year, the combined cost of congressional campaigns now exceeds a billion dollars.[12]

Effectiveness of Media Appeals

The broad question is this: How credible and effective are obvious attempts to package and sell products (toothpaste, aspirin, presidential candidates) through the mass media? The prima facie evidence suggests that they are extremely effective. Why else would corporations and political parties spend hundreds of millions of dollars a year trumpeting their products? Moreover, as parents, most of us have seen our children being seduced by toy commercials that artfully depict the most drab toys in an irresistible way. Similarly, a child watching cartoons on any Saturday morning is deluged by fast-paced ads for cereal, fast food, and candy. The aim is to get kids to demand that their parents buy them the products they have seen in the commercials, and it seems to work. Over 90 percent of preschool children asked for toys or food they saw advertised on television, according to a survey of their mothers.[13] In fact, almost two-thirds of the mothers reported hearing their children sing commercial jingles they learned from television, most by the age of three.

Most children do catch on after a time; I've seen my own children, after several disappointments, develop a healthy skepticism (alas, even a certain degree of cynicism) about the truthfulness of these commercials. Indeed, one survey[14] found that only 12 percent of 6th-graders believed television commercials told the truth all or most of the time; by the 10th grade, only 4 percent felt they were truthful even most of the time. This kind of skepticism is common among adults as well. A public opinion poll showed that the overwhelming majority of the adult respondents believed television commercials contain untruthful arguments. Moreover, the results indicate that the more educated the person, the greater the skepticism, and further, people who are skeptical believe their skepticism makes them immune to persuasion. This might lead us to conclude that the mere fact of knowing that a communicator is biased serves to protect us from being influenced by the message. This is not true. Simply because we *think* we are immune to persuasion does not necessarily mean we *are* immune. In the case of many consumer products, the public tends to buy a specific brand for no other reason than the fact that it is heavily advertised.

Let's look at the headache-remedy business. Daryl Bem[15] provides us with an interesting analysis of our susceptibility to television commercials even when we know they are biased. According to Bem, a well-known brand of aspirin (which we will call "Brand A") advertises itself as 100 percent pure aspirin; the commercial goes on to say that government tests have shown that no other pain remedy is stronger or more effective than Brand A. What the maker didn't bother to mention is that the government test actually showed that no brand was any weaker or less effective than any of the others. In other words, all tested brands were equal—except in price, that is. For the privilege of popping Brand A, consumers must pay approximately three times the price of an equally effective but unadvertised brand.

Another product proclaims it uses the special (unnamed) ingredient "that doctors recommend." By reading the label, we discover the "secret" ingredient to be good old inexpensive aspirin. Several pharmaceutical companies also market "extra strength" varieties of "arthritic pain" formulations. You will pay a premium price for these products, but are they worth it? Actually, their extra strength comes from extra aspirin (or acetaminophen, an aspirin substitute), along with a dose of caffeine. Taking additional aspirin would be less expensive, but it sounds great in the ads: "Not one, but a combination of medically proven ingredients in an extra-strength formula."

Such blatant attempts at mass persuasion seem pitifully obvious. Yet tremendous numbers of consumers apparently set aside their skepticism even though they know the message is an obvious attempt to sell a product. Of course, there may be a basic difference between susceptibility to aspirin commercials and susceptibility to commercials for presidential candidates. When we are dealing with identical or very similar products, mere familiarity may make a huge difference. Robert Zajonc[16] has shown that, all other things being equal, the more familiar an item is, the more attractive it is. Suppose I walk into a grocery store looking for a laundry detergent. I go to the detergent section, and I am staggered by the wide array of brand names. Because it doesn't matter too much to me which one I buy, I may simply reach for the most familiar one—and, chances are, it is familiar because I've heard and seen the name on television commercials over and over again. If this is the case, then sudden increases in television exposure should produce dramatic changes in familiarity and, perhaps, in sales. And that seems to be the case. For example, several years ago, the Northwest Mutual Life Insurance Company conducted a nationwide poll to find out how well the public recognized its name. It came out 34th among insurance companies. Two weeks later the company repeated the poll. This time it came out third in name familiarity. What caused this amazing leap from obscurity to fame? Two weeks and $1 million worth of advertising on television. Familiarity does not necessarily mean sales, but the two are frequently linked—as evidenced by the fact that A & W Root Beer boosted its share of the market from 15 percent to 50 percent after 6 months of television advertising.

But is voting for a presidential candidate the same kind of decision as choosing toothpaste or root beer? The answer is a qualified "yes." Several years ago, Joseph Grush and his colleagues[17] found that, by and large, the congressional candidates who spent the most money typically received the most votes. More recently, Michael Pfau and his colleagues[18] have shown that spot television commercials are by far the most effective determinants of how people vote. Moreover, spot commercials on TV are especially effective when the campaign centers on a highly charged issue that arouses strong emotions in voters. For a compelling illustration, let's go back to the 1988 presidential campaign between George Bush (the elder) and Michael Dukakis, former governor of Massachusetts. In the summer of 1988, Bush trailed far behind

Dukakis in the race for the presidency. Many observers were convinced that Dukakis's lead was insurmountable. Within a few short months, however, the lead had all but evaporated and, on election day, Bush won handily. A number of political analysts credit Willie Horton with playing a major role in this turnaround. Indeed, *Time* magazine went so far as to refer to Willie Horton as "George Bush's most valuable player."[19]

Who was Willie Horton? He was not one of Bush's advisors, nor was he a major financial contributor to the Bush campaign. Indeed, the two men had never met. Willie Horton was a convicted felon who had been released from a Massachusetts prison before the end of his term as part of a furlough program. While on furlough, Horton escaped to Maryland; there, he raped a woman in view of her male companion, whom he had wounded and tied to a chair. Michael Dukakis was governor of Massachusetts when Horton's furlough was granted. Claiming that Dukakis was soft on crime, Bush ran a series of television ads showing the mug shot of a scowling Willie Horton and depicting criminals going in and out of prison through a revolving door. These ads struck a chord with many Americans who had legitimate fears of street crime and who strongly suspected that the criminal justice system favored criminals at the expense of victims. Moreover, the fact that Willie Horton was black, and that his victims were white, was not lost on most viewers.[20]

How did Dukakis fight back? With an abundance of facts and figures: He pointed out that Massachusetts was only one of many states with furlough programs and that even the federal government (of which Bush was a member) furloughed inmates from its prisons. In addition, he noted, furlough programs were generally very effective. For example, in 1987, 53,000 inmates received over 200,000 furloughs and only a small percentage got into trouble.[21] Dukakis also pointed out that, typically, furloughs were granted to convicts who were near the end of their terms, and that the furloughs were intended to orient them to the outside world. He insisted that the whole issue was a contrivance—that, if elected, George Bush had no intention of changing the furlough system.

Are you getting bored yet? So were the voters. If Michael Dukakis had had a social psychologist on his staff, he would have received better advice. As Anthony Pratkanis and I have pointed out,[22] when people are scared and angry, facts and figures alone are not very convincing. They can be effective if they are tied to solutions to problems the voters are deeply concerned about. In the 1992 and 1996 presidential elections, candidate Bill Clinton (apparently having learned a lesson from the Dukakis campaign) kept the attention of the American people focused on one overriding issue—the state of the economy—and did not allow himself to be sidetracked by emotional issues on which there was no real difference between the candidates.[23] It has been argued that, in the presidential election of 2000, candidate Al Gore forgot the lesson taught by Mr. Clinton and lost a great many votes by losing focus, waffling on issues and occasionally changing his position.

Education or Propaganda?

Aspirin commercials are obvious attempts to sell something at a high price by intentionally misleading the audience. They can be considered propaganda. "Selling" a presidential candidate, however, is much more complicated. Thus, the devices used by spin doctors and speech writers to display their candidate in a favorable manner could conceivably be considered as education—an attempt to educate the public on the policies and virtues of the candidate by allowing him to present his views as clearly, efficiently, and articulately as possible. What is the difference between propaganda and education? *The American Heritage Dictionary of the English Language* defines *propaganda* as "the systematic propagation of a given doctrine" and *education* as "the act of imparting knowledge or skill." Again, we could all agree that aspirin ads are propaganda designed to promote the sale of certain brands. But what about television, which often depicts women, old people, and minorities in stereotyped roles? Or, more subtly, what about the vast majority of high-school history textbooks which until recently totally ignored the contributions made by blacks and other minorities—and now pay lip service to these contributions? Is this merely imparting knowledge?

The problem of distinguishing between education and propaganda can be more subtle still. Let us look at arithmetic as taught in the public schools. What could be more educational? By that I mean, what could be more pure, objective, factual, and untainted by doctrine? Watch out. Do you remember the examples used in your elementary-school arithmetic text? Most of the examples dealt with buying, selling, renting, working for wages, and computing interest. As Zimbardo, Ebbesen, and Maslach[24] point out, these examples do more than simply reflect the capitalistic system in which the education is occurring: They systematically endorse the system, legitimize it, and, by implication, suggest it is the natural and normal way. As a way of illustrating multiplication and percentages, the textbook might have Mr. Jones borrowing $15,000 at 9 percent interest in order to purchase a new car. Would this example be used in a society that felt it was sinful to charge interest, as early Christian societies believed? Would this example be used in a society that believed people shouldn't seek possessions they can't afford? I am not suggesting it is wrong or immoral to use these kinds of illustrations in arithmetic books; I am merely pointing out that they are a form of propaganda and that it might be useful to recognize them as such.

In practice, whether a person regards a particular course of instruction as educational or propagandistic depends, to a large extent, on his or her values. Reflect, for a moment, on a film about drug abuse my children were required to see in their high school. At one point, the film mentioned that many hard-core narcotics addicts began by sampling marijuana. I'm certain that most school officials would probably regard the presentation of this piece of factual knowledge as a case of "imparting knowledge," and most marijuana users would probably regard it as "the systematic propagation of a given doctrine"—that is, the implication that marijuana leads to the use of addictive drugs. By the same token, consider the topic of sex education in the schools as viewed by a member of the Christian Right, on the one hand, or by the editor of *Playboy* magazine, on the other hand. This is not to say that all communications are drastically slanted and one-sided. Rather, when we are dealing with an emotionally charged issue about which people's opinions differ greatly, it is probably impossible to construct a communication that people on both sides of the issue would agree is fair and impartial. I will present a more detailed discussion of communication as viewed through "the eye of the beholder" in the next chapter. For now, it is important to note that, whether we call it propaganda or education, persuasion is a reality. It won't go away if we ignore it. We should therefore attempt to understand it by analyzing the experimental literature on persuasion.

Two Major Routes to Persuasion

When we are in contact with a persuasive argument, do we think deeply about it or do we accept it without much thought? This question underlies much of our understanding of persuasion. According to the theorizing of Richard Petty and John Cacioppo,[25] we are inclined to think deeply about it if the issue is one that is relevant and important to us. In these circumstances, we are inclined to give the argument careful scrutiny. But sometimes, even if the issue is important, we may be distracted or busy—or if the communication is slickly presented, we may not give it close scrutiny.

Petty and Cacioppo theorize that there are essentially two ways that people are persuaded—**centrally** or **peripherally.** The **central route** involves weighing arguments and considering relevant facts and figures, thinking about issues in a systematic fashion and coming to a decision. In contrast, the **peripheral route** to persuasion is less judicious; rather than relying on a careful process of weighing and considering the strength of arguments, the person responds to simple, often irrelevant cues that suggest the rightness, wrongness, or attractiveness of an argument without giving it much thought. For example, considering arguments about how to remedy an ailing economy has to do with the central route; getting scared and angry by the image of Willie Horton has to do with the peripheral route. Likewise, when a man decides to buy a particular computer because the ad depicts it as having the kind of user-friendliness, processing speed, memory, and data storage capacity that he needs, he is being moved by the logic of the argument. This is the central route. But, if he decides to buy the computer because his favorite movie star owns the identical model, he is being moved by issues irrelevant to the product. This is the peripheral route.

It should be noted that few persuasive appeals are purely central or peripheral; most contain elements aimed at both routes to persuasion. A well-known ad campaign, for example, touts the low cost, great warrantee, and cutting edge components, of a popular brand of computer. But the brand's young pitchman, and his now familiar "dude, you're gettin' a Dell!" is clearly aimed at making the product appear cool to adolescents, even those who care little about processing speed or warrantees.

Lawyers and politicians often make great use of the combination of arguments and peripheral cues. Readers who watched the O. J. Simpson trial may recall the dramatic moment when the prosecutor asked Simpson to try on the bloodstained gloves worn by the murderer. The gloves fit Simpson very tightly. In his summation, which contained some very persuasive arguments, Simpson's attorney, Johnny Cochrane, added what some believe to be a highly persuasive peripheral cue. Repeatedly he told the jury, "If the glove doesn't fit, you must acquit." The statement was persuasive, not because of the argument's logic—after all, it is certainly possible to commit murder wearing tight gloves. Rather the statement had power because when people are evaluating the quality of an argument, they can be highly influenced by the way things are phrased. In Cochrane's case, his rhyme gave the statement a ring of truth. Recent research by Matthew McGlone reveals our susceptibility to such tactics. He found that college students were more persuaded by unfamiliar aphorisms that rhyme ("woes unite foes") than the same ideas presented in nonrhyming form ("woes unite enemies"). The peripheral route to persuasion can be surprisingly subtle—yet surprisingly effective—indeed.

Let us look at the issue in a bit more detail. What are the key factors that can increase the effectiveness of a communication? Basically, three classes of variables are important: (1) the source of the communication (who says it), (2) the nature of the communication (how he or she says it), and (3) characteristics of the audience (to whom he or she says it). Put most simply: Who says what to whom? We will look at each of these separately.

The Source of the Communication

Credibility Picture the following scene: Your doorbell rings, and when you answer it, you find a middle-aged man in a loud, checkered sports jacket. His tie is loose, his collar is frayed, his pants need ironing, he needs a shave, and his eyes keep looking off to the side and over your head as he talks to you. He is carrying a small can in his hand with a slot on the top, and he's trying to convince you to contribute a few dollars to a charitable organization you've never heard of. Although his actual pitch sounds fairly reasonable, what is the possibility of his succeeding in prying loose some of your money?

Now let's turn back the clock a few minutes: You open your door in response to the ringing of the doorbell, and standing there is a middle-aged man in a conservative business suit, well tailored and well pressed. He looks you squarely in the eye, introduces himself as a vice-president of the City National Bank, and asks you to contribute a few dollars to a charitable organization (that you've never heard of), using exactly the same words as the fellow in the loud, checkered jacket. Would you be more likely to contribute some money?

I was struck by this phenomenon several years ago when I saw the poet Allen Ginsberg on one of the late-night talk shows. Ginsberg was among the most popular poets of the so-called beat generation; his poem "Howl" had shocked and stimulated the literary establishment in the 1950s. On the talk show, Ginsberg was at it again: Having just finished boasting about his homosexuality, he was talking about the generation gap. The camera panned in. He was fat, bearded, and looked a trifle wild-eyed (was he stoned?); long hair grew in unruly patches from the sides of his otherwise bald head; he was wearing a tie-dyed T-shirt with a hole in it and a few strands of beads. Although he was talking earnestly—and, in my opinion, very sensibly—about the problems of the young, the studio audience was laughing. They seemed to be treating him like a clown. It dawned on me that, in all probability, the vast majority of the people at home, lying in bed watching the poet from between their feet, could not possibly take him seriously—no matter how sensible his message and no matter how earnestly he delivered it. His appearance was probably overdetermining the audience's reaction. The scientist in me longed to substitute the conservative-looking banker in the neatly pressed business suit for the wild-eyed poet and have him move his lips while Ginsberg said the same words off camera. My guess is that, under these circumstances, Ginsberg's message would have been well received.

No need. Similar experiments have already been done. Indeed, speculations about the effects of prestige on persuasion are ancient. More than 300 years B.C., Aristotle, the world's first published social psychologist, wrote:

> We believe good men more fully and more readily than others: this is true generally whatever the question is, and absolutely true where exact certainty is impossible and opinions are divided. . . . It is not true, as some writers assume in their treatises on rhetoric, that the personal goodness revealed by the speaker contributes nothing to his power of persuasion; on the contrary, his character may almost be called the most effective means of persuasion he possesses.[26]

It required more some 2,300 years for Aristotle's observation to be put to a rigorous scientific test. This was accomplished by Carl Hovland and Walter Weiss.[27] What these investigators did was very simple: They presented large numbers of people with a communication that argued a particular point of view—for example, that building atomic-powered submarines was a feasible undertaking (this experiment was performed in 1951, when harnessing atomic energy for such purposes was merely a dream). Some of the people were informed that the argument was made by a person possessing a great deal of **credibility**; for others, the same argument was attributed to a source with low credibility. Specifically, the argument that atomic-powered submarines could be built in the near future was attributed to J. Robert Oppenheimer, a nationally known and highly respected atomic physicist, or to *Pravda,* the official newspaper of the Communist Party in the Soviet Union—a publication not famous for its objectivity and truthfulness. A large percentage of the people who were told that the communication came from Oppenheimer changed their opinions; they then believed more strongly in the feasibility of atomic submarines. Very few of those who read the identical communication attributed to *Pravda* shifted their opinions in the direction of the communication.

This same phenomenon has received repeated confirmations by several different investigators using a wide variety of topics and attributing the communications to a wide variety of communicators. Careful experiments have shown that a judge of the juvenile court is better than most people at swaying opinion about juvenile delinquency, that a famous poet and critic can sway opinion about the merits of a poem, and that a medical journal can sway opinion about whether or not antihistamines should be dispensed without a prescription. What do the physicist, the judge, the poet, and the medical journal have that *Pravda* doesn't have? That is, what factor makes the difference in their effectiveness? Aristotle said we believe "good men," by which he meant people of high moral caliber. Hovland and Weiss use the term *credible,* which removes the moral connotations present in the Aristotelian definition. Oppenheimer, a juvenile court judge, and the poet are all credible—that is, they are not necessarily good, but they are both *expert* and *trustworthy*. It makes sense to allow yourself to be influenced by communicators who are trustworthy and who know what they are talking about. It makes sense for people to be influenced by J. Robert Oppenheimer when he is voicing an opinion about atomic power, and it makes sense for people to be influenced by T. S. Eliot when he is talking about poetry. These are expert, trustworthy people.

But not all people are equally influenced by the same communicator. Indeed, the same communicator may be regarded by some people as possessing high credibility and by others as possessing low credibility. Moreover, certain peripheral attributes of the communicator may loom large for some members of the audience; such attributes can serve to make a given communicator either remarkably effective or remarkably ineffective.

This phenomenon was forcefully demonstrated in an experiment I performed in collaboration with Burton Golden,[28] in which we presented 6th-graders with a speech extolling the usefulness and importance of arithmetic. The communicator was introduced either as a prize-winning engineer from a prestigious university or as someone who washed dishes for a living. As one might expect, the engineer was far more effective at influencing the youngsters' opinions than the dishwasher. This finding is consistent with previous research; in itself, it is obvious and not very interesting. But, in addition, we varied the race of the communicator: In some of the trials the communicator was white; in others, black. Several weeks prior to the experiment, the children (all of whom were white) had filled out a questionnaire designed to measure the degree of their prejudice against black people. The results were striking: Among those children who were most prejudiced against blacks, the black engineer was *less* influential than the white engineer, although both delivered the same speech. Moreover, among those children who were least prejudiced against blacks, the black engineer was *more* influential than the white engineer. It seems unreasonable that a peripheral attribute such as skin color would affect a person's credibility. It might be argued that, in a purely rational world, a prestigious engineer should be able to influence 6th-graders about the importance of arithmetic regardless of the color of his or her skin, but apparently this is not a purely rational world. Depending upon listeners' attitudes toward blacks, they were either *more* influenced or *less* influenced by a black communicator than by an otherwise identical white communicator.

This kind of behavior is not very adaptive. If the quality of your life depends on the extent to which you allow a communication about arithmetic to influence your opinion, the expertise of the communicator would seem to be the most reasonable factor to heed. To the extent that other factors (such as skin color) decrease or increase your susceptibility to persuasion on an issue irrelevant to such factors, you are behaving in a maladaptive manner. But advertisers bank on this kind of maladaptive behavior and often count on irrelevant factors to increase a spokesperson's credibility. For example, since television was in its infancy, actors who have played the role of doctors in TV dramas show up regularly on commercials peddling such products as aspirin and cold medicine.

Not only are such peripheral aspects of the communicator often emphasized in commercials, but frequently they are the only aspects of the communicator the viewer is able to perceive. Throughout the 1950s and 1960s, one of the most persistent peddlers of breakfast food was the former Olympic decathlon champion Bob Richards, who was probably far more effective at selling Wheaties than some learned professor of nutrition, no matter how expert he or she might have been. In the 1970s, Richards was replaced by another gold medal decathlon champion, Bruce Jenner. How effective are these people? We cannot be sure—but when Bruce Jenner was finally replaced in the 1980s, the Wheaties people again decided not to use a nutritionist and hired Mary Lou Retton, an Olympic gymnastics gold medalist. And there was no real surprise when the manufacturer of Wheaties subsequently hired such amazing athletes as Michael Jordan, Bret Favre, and Tiger Woods to appear on the cereal box and to induce Mr. Jordan to utter those famous words, "You better eat your Wheaties." Apparently, whoever is in charge of selling Wheaties to the masses is convinced that athletes are effective communicators.

Is this conviction justified? Will people be influenced by an ad just because a prominent sports personality is involved? Even if we admire the skill such athletes display on the playing field, can we really trust them to tell us the truth about the products they endorse? After all, we all know that the sports star peddling a particular brand of breakfast cereal or athletic shoes is getting paid handsomely for his or her endorsement. My guess is that most of us would be quick to say, "No way. I'm not going to eat Wheaties and buy Nikes just because Michael Jordan *says* that he eats Wheaties and favors Nikes. Maybe *other* people might be persuaded to run out and buy certain products just because a sports figure tells them to, but I certainly wouldn't trust even my favorite player's advice on how to spend my hard-earned cash." But can people really predict their own behavior? Before answering, let's take a closer look at the factor of trust.

Increasing Trustworthiness Clearly, trust is an important factor in determining whether or not a communicator will be effective. For example, it may be that the crucial reason the more prejudiced 6th-graders in the Aronson-Golden experiment were less influenced by the black engineer than by the white engineer was that they simply did not trust blacks. If this is true, then if we could offer the audience clear, independent evidence that a person is trustworthy, that person should be a very effective communicator.

How might communicators make themselves seem clearly trustworthy to us? One way is to argue against their own self-interest. If people have nothing to gain (and perhaps something to lose) by convincing us, we will trust them and they will be more effective. An illustration may be helpful. Suppose a habitual criminal, recently convicted as a smuggler and peddler of heroin, was delivering a communication on the abuses of the U.S. judicial system. Would he influence you? Probably not. Most people would probably regard him as unattractive and untrustworthy: He seems clearly outside of the Aristotelian definition of a good man. But suppose he was arguing that criminal justice was too lenient—that criminals almost always beat the rap if they have a smart lawyer, and that even if criminals are convicted, the sentences normally meted out are too soft. Would he influence you?

I'm certain he would; in fact, I performed this very experiment in collaboration with Elaine Walster and Darcy Abrahams,[29] and it confirmed our hypothesis. In the actual experiment, we presented our participants with a newspaper clipping of an interview between a news reporter and Joe "The Shoulder" Napolitano, who was identified in the manner described above. In one experimental condition, Joe "The Shoulder" argued for stricter courts and more severe sentences. In another condition, he argued that courts should be more lenient and sentences less severe. We also ran a parallel set of conditions in which the same statements were attributed to a respected public official. When Joe "The Shoulder" argued for more lenient courts, he was totally ineffective; indeed, he actually caused the participants' opinions to change slightly in the opposite direction. But when he argued for stricter, more powerful courts, he was extremely effective—as effective as the respected public official delivering the same argument. This study demonstrates that Aristotle was not completely correct. A communicator can be an unattractive, immoral person and still be effective, as long as it is clear that he or she has nothing to gain (and perhaps something to lose) by persuading us.

Why was Joe "The Shoulder" so effective in our experiment? Let's take a closer look. Most people would not be surprised to hear a known convict arguing in favor of a more lenient criminal justice system. Their knowledge of the criminal's background and self-interest would lead them to expect such a message. When they receive the opposite communication, however, these expectations are disconfirmed. To make sense of this contradiction, the members of the audience might conclude that the convict had reformed, or they could entertain the notion that the criminal is under some kind of pressure to make the anticrime statements. In the absence of any evidence to substantiate these suppositions, however, another explanation becomes more reasonable: Maybe the truth of the issue is so compelling that, even though it apparently contradicts his background and self-interest, the spokesman sincerely believes in the position he espouses.

Further evidence for this phenomenon comes from a more recent experiment. Alice Eagly and her colleagues[30] presented students with a description of a dispute between business interests and environmental groups over a company polluting a river. The students then read a statement about the issue. In some conditions, the spokesman was described as having a business background and was said to be speaking to a group of businessmen. In others, his background and audience were varied, thereby altering the participants' expectations about his message. The results supported the reasoning presented above; when the message conflicted with their expectations, listeners perceived the communicator as being more sincere, and they were more persuaded by his statement. For example, it's hard to imagine a more convincing spokesperson for an antismoking campaign than someone whose fortune was made off the habits of millions of U.S. smokers. In fact, Patrick Reynolds, who inherited millions of dollars from the R. J. Reynolds Tobacco Company, founded by his grandfather, has taken a strong public stand against smoking and has encouraged victims of smoking-related illnesses to file lawsuits against tobacco companies![31]

The trustworthiness of a person can also be increased if the audience is absolutely certain the person is not *trying* to influence them. Suppose a stockbroker calls you up and gives you a hot tip on a particular stock. Will you buy? It's hard to be sure. On the one hand, the broker is probably an expert, and this might influence you to buy. On the other hand, the broker has something to gain by giving you this tip (a commission), and this could lower her effectiveness. But suppose you happened to overhear her telling her close friend that a particular stock was about to rise. Because she was obviously not trying to influence you, you might be more readily influenced.

Several years ago, the nonhypothetical brokerage firm E. F. Hutton incorporated this very scenario into a series of highly successful television commercials. A typical commercial opened with a shot of two people engaged in private conversation in a noisy, crowded restaurant. When one person began to pass on some stock advice from E. F. Hutton, a sudden hush fell over the room and everyone—waiters, customers, busboys—strained toward the speaker to overhear the tip. "When E. F. Hutton talks," said the announcer, "people listen." The implication is clear: Everyone in the restaurant is getting in on advice that wasn't intended for them, and the information is all the more valuable as a result. When communicators are not *trying* to influence us, their potential to do so is increased.

This is exactly what Elaine Walster and Leon Festinger[32] discovered a few years before the Hutton commercial was invented. In their experiment, they staged a conversation between two graduate students in which one of them expressed his expert opinion on an issue. An undergraduate was allowed to overhear this conversation. In one experimental condition, it was clear to the participant that the graduate students were aware of his presence in the next room; therefore, the participant knew that anything being said could conceivably be directed at him with the intention of influencing his opinion. In the other condition, the situation was arranged so that the participant believed the graduate students were unaware of his presence in the next room. In this condition, the participant's opinion changed significantly more in the direction of the opinion expressed by the graduate students.

Attractiveness Where do these findings leave Michael Jordan or Tiger Woods urging us to eat Wheaties or wear Nikes? Clearly, they are *trying* to influence us. Moreover, they are operating in their own self-interest; when we take a close look at the situation, it's clear that Wheaties and Nike are paying these athletes a huge amount of money to hawk their products. We expect them to recommend these products, and we know they want us to see the commercial. These factors should make them less trustworthy. But does that make them less effective?

Not necessarily. Although most of us might not *trust* the sincerity of the endorsers, that does not mean we don't buy the products they endorse. Another crucial factor determining the effectiveness of communicators is how attractive or likable they are—regardless of their overall expertise or trustworthiness. Some years ago, Judson Mills and I did a simple laboratory experiment demonstrating that a beautiful woman—simply because she was beautiful—could have a major impact on the opinions of an audience on a topic wholly irrelevant to her beauty, and furthermore, that her impact was greatest when she openly expressed a desire to influence the audience.[33] More recently, Alice Eagly and Shelly Chaiken carried out an experiment that not only replicated the finding that more likable communicators are more persuasive but went on to show that attractive sources are expected to support desirable positions.[34]

It appears that we associate the attractiveness of the communicator with the desirability of the message. We are influenced by people we like. Where our liking for a communicator is involved (rather than his or her expertise), we behave as though we were trying to please that source. Accordingly, the more that communicator wants to change our opinions, the more we change them—but *only about trivial issues.* That is, it is true that football players can get us to use a particular shaving cream and beautiful women can get us to agree with them on an abstract topic, whether or not we are willing to admit it. At the same time, it is unlikely that they could influence us to vote for their presidential candidate or to adopt their position on the morality of abortion. To summarize this section, we might list these phenomena:

- Our opinions are influenced by individuals who are both expert and trustworthy.

- A communicator's trustworthiness (and effectiveness) can be increased if he or she argues a position apparently opposed to his or her self-interest.

- A communicator's trustworthiness (and effectiveness) can be increased if he or she does not seem to be trying to influence our opinion.

- At least where trivial opinions and behaviors are concerned, if we like and can identify with a person, his or her opinions and behaviors will influence our own more than their content would ordinarily warrant.

- Again, where trivial opinions and behaviors are concerned, if we like a person, we tend to be influenced even if it is clear that he or she is trying to influence us and stands to profit by doing so.

The Nature of the Communication

The manner in which a communication is stated plays an important role in determining its effectiveness. There are several ways in which communications can differ from one another. I have selected five I consider to be among the most important: (1) Is a communication more persuasive if it is designed to appeal to the audience's reasoning ability, or is it more persuasive if it is aimed at arousing the audience's emotions? (2) Are people more swayed by a communication if it is tied to a vivid personal experience or if it is bolstered by a great deal of clear and unimpeachable statistical evidence? (3) Should the communication present only one side of the argument, or should it also include an attempt to refute the opposing view? (4) If two sides are presented, as in a debate, does the order in which they are presented affect the relative impact of either side? (5) What is the relationship between the effectiveness of the communication and the discrepancy between the audience's original opinion and the opinion advocated by the communication?

Logical versus Emotional Appeals Several years ago, I was living in a community that was about to vote on whether or not to fluoridate the water supply as a means of combating tooth decay. An information campaign that seemed quite logical and reasonable was launched by the proponents of fluoridation. It consisted largely of statements by noted dentists describing the benefits of fluorides and discussing the evidence on the reduction of tooth decay in areas with fluoridated water, as well as statements by physicians and other health authorities that fluoridation has no harmful effects. The opponents used a much more emotional appeal. For example, one leaflet consisted of a picture of a rather ugly rat, along with the statement "Don't let them put rat poison in your drinking water." The referendum to fluoridate the water supply was soundly defeated. Of course, this incident doesn't prove conclusively that emotional appeals are superior, mainly because the incident was not a scientifically controlled study. We have no idea how the people would have voted on fluoridation if no publicity were circulated, nor do we know whether the antifluoridation circular reached more people, whether it was easier to read than the proponents' literature, and so forth. Although the actual research in this area is far from conclusive, there is some evidence favoring an appeal that is primarily emotional. In one early study, for example, George Hartmann[35] tried to measure the extent to which he could induce people to vote for a particular political candidate as a function of what kind of appeal he used. He demonstrated that individuals who received a *primarily* emotional message voted for the candidate endorsed by the message more often than did people who received a *primarily* logical message.

The word *primarily* is italicized for good reason; it defines the major problem with research in this area—namely, there are no foolproof, mutually exclusive definitions of *emotional* and *rational*. In the fluoridation illustration, for example, most people would probably agree the antifluoridation pamphlet was designed to arouse fear; yet, it is not entirely illogical because it is indeed true that the fluoride used in minute concentrations to prevent tooth decay is also used in massive concentrations as a rat poison. On the other side, to present the views of professional people is not entirely free from emotional appeal; it may be comforting (on an emotional level) to know that physicians and dentists endorse the use of fluorides.

Because, in practice, operational distinctions between *logical* and *emotional* are difficult to draw, some researchers have turned to an equally interesting and far more researchable problem: the problem of the effect of various levels of a specific emotion on opinion change. Suppose you wish to arouse fear in the hearts of your audience as a way of inducing opinion change. Would it be more effective to arouse just a little fear, or should you try to scare the hell out of them? For example, if your goal is to convince people to drive more carefully, would you be more effective if you showed them gory films of the broken and bloody bodies of the victims of highway accidents, or would you be more effective if you soft-pedaled your communication—showing crumpled fenders, discussing increased insurance rates due to careless driving, and pointing out the possibility that people who drive carelessly may have their driver's licenses suspended? Common sense argues on both sides of this street. On the one hand, it suggests that a good scare will motivate people to act; on the other hand, it argues that too much fear can be debilitating—that is, it might interfere with a person's ability to pay attention to the message, to comprehend it, and to act upon it. We've all believed, at one time or another, that "it only happens to the other guy—it can't happen to me." Thus, people continue to drive at very high speeds and to insist on driving after they've had a few drinks, even though they should know better. Perhaps this is because the possible negative consequences of these actions are so great that they try not to think about them. Thus, it has been argued that, if a communication arouses a great deal of fear, we tend *not* to pay close attention to it.

What does the evidence tell us? The overwhelming weight of experimental data suggests that, all other things being equal, the more frightened a person is by a communication, the more likely he or she is to take positive preventive action. The most prolific researchers in this area have been Howard Leventhal and his associates.[36] In one experiment, they tried to induce people to stop smoking and to take chest X rays. Some participants were exposed to a low-fear treatment: They were simply presented with a recommendation to stop smoking and get their chests X-rayed. Others were subjected to moderate fear: They were shown a film depicting a young man whose chest X rays revealed he had lung cancer. The people subjected to the high-fear condition saw the same film as those in the moderate-fear condition—and, in addition, they were treated to a gory film of a lung-cancer operation. The results showed that those people who were most frightened were also most eager to stop smoking and most likely to get chest X rays.

Is this true for all people? It is not. There is a reason why common sense leads some people to believe that a great deal of fear leads to inaction: It does—for certain people, under certain conditions. What Leventhal and his colleagues discovered is that people who had a reasonably good opinion of themselves (high self-esteem) were those who were most likely to be moved by high degrees of fear arousal. People with a low opinion of themselves were least likely to take immediate action when confronted with a communication arousing a great deal of fear—but (and here is the interesting part) after a delay, they behaved very much like the participants with high self-esteem. That is, if immediate action was not required but action could be taken later, people with low self-esteem were more likely to take that action if they were exposed to a communication arousing a great deal of fear. People who have a low opinion of themselves may have a great deal of difficulty coping with threats to themselves. A high-fear communication overwhelms them and makes them feel like crawling into bed and pulling the covers up over their heads. Low or moderate fear is something they can deal with more easily at the moment they experience it. But, if given time—that is, if it's not essential that they act immediately—they will be more likely to act if the message truly scares the hell out of them.

Subsequent research by Leventhal and his co-workers lends support to this analysis. In one study, participants were shown films of serious automobile accidents. Some participants watched the films on a large screen up close; others watched them from far away on a much smaller screen. Among the participants with high or moderate self-esteem, those who saw the films on the large screen were much more likely to take subsequent protective action than were those who saw the films on the small screen. Participants with low self-esteem were more likely to take action when they saw the films on a small screen; those who saw the films on a large screen reported a great deal of fatigue and stated that they had great difficulty even thinking of themselves as victims of automobile accidents. Thus, people with low self-esteem are apparently too overwhelmed by fear to take action when an immediate response is required.

It should be relatively easy to make people with high self-esteem behave like people with low self esteem. We can overwhelm them by making them feel there is nothing they can do to prevent or ameliorate a threatening situation. This will lead most people to bury their heads in the sand—even those who have high self-esteem. Conversely, suppose you wanted to reduce the automobile accident rate or to help people give up smoking, and you are faced with low self-esteem people. How would you proceed? If you construct a message containing clear, specific, and optimistic instructions, it might increase the feeling among the members of your audience that they could confront their fears and cope with the danger. These speculations have been confirmed; experiments by Leventhal and his associates show that fear-arousing messages containing specific instructions about how, when, and where to take action are much more effective than recommendations not including such instructions. For example, a campaign conducted on a college campus urging students to take tetanus shots included specific instructions about where and when they were available. The campaign materials included a map showing the location of the student health service and a suggestion that each student set aside a convenient time to stop by. The results showed high-fear appeals to be more effective than low-fear appeals in producing favorable *attitudes* toward tetanus shots among the students, and they also increased the students' stated intentions to take the shots. The highly specific instructions about how to get the shots did not in any way affect these opinions and intentions, but the instructions did have a big effect on the *actual behavior*: Of those participants who were instructed about how to proceed, 28 percent actually got the tetanus shots; but of those who received no specific instructions, only 3 percent went down to get them. In a control group exposed only to the action instructions—no fear-arousing message—no shots were taken. Thus, specific instructions alone are not enough to produce action. Fear is a necessary component for action in such situations.

Similar results were uncovered in Leventhal's cigarette experiment. Leventhal found that a high-fear communication produced a much greater *intention* to stop smoking. Unless it was accompanied by recommendations for specific behavior, however, it produced little behavior change. Similarly, specific instructions ("buy a magazine instead of a pack of cigarettes," "drink plenty of water when you have the urge to smoke," and so on) without a fear-arousing communication were relatively ineffective. The combination of fear arousal and specific instructions produced the best results; the students in this condition were smoking less 4 months after they were subjected to the experimental procedure.

So, in some situations, fear-arousing appeals accompanied by specific instructions for appropriate action can and *do* produce recommended behaviors. But as Leventhal and his colleagues[37] have indicated, the impact of fear appeals is context-specific. There are some situations in which fear appeals—even when coupled with specific instructions—will not produce the desired effect. Let's consider the most serious public health challenge in recent history: acquired immune deficiency syndrome (AIDS). AIDS has been described by the mass media as "The Plague of the 20th Century,"[38] and it appears to be gaining momentum in the 21st century. Public health officials have worked hard to educate the public about the hazards of unsafe sexual practices and intravenous drug use, and attempts have been made to teach sexually active people about the causes of AIDS and to convince them that the threat to life is real. Such information has been accompanied by specific recommendations for preventive action—such as celibacy, monogamy, or the use of condoms. Although celibacy and monogamy may be worthwhile goals, it has proved to be unrealistic to expect the great majority of teenagers and young adults to exercise these options. Even politically conservative experts like former Surgeon General C. Everett Koop eventually came to believe that for most sexually active young adults, the proper use of condoms may be the most realistic mode of AIDS prevention.[39]

Thus, the goal becomes to persuade sexually active people to use condoms. And what form have these persuasive appeals taken? They have typically involved vivid descriptions of the dangers of unsafe sex and the ravages of the disease. The implicit assumption of policymakers and educators seems to be that arousing a great deal of fear will induce people to change their sexual behavior. Condom manufacturers apparently share that assumption. For example, in one advertisement for condoms, an attractive woman is shown saying, "I love sex, but I'm not willing to die for it."[40] That sounds catchy. But there is some indication that, in the case of AIDS prevention, such an approach may be ineffective at best and perhaps even counterproductive. Why?

Most individuals, when contemplating having sex, do not want to think about death or disease. If the cognitive association between death and condoms is too powerful, the thought of using condoms may be so noxious as to diminish the pleasure associated with sex. Under these circumstances, many individuals will block all thoughts of death, disease, and condoms out of their minds, adopting a posture of denial. But they won't stop having sex. Thus, they will convince themselves that "It can't happen to me," or "I'm not attracted to the kind of person who would have AIDS," or "I can spot a person with AIDS just by looking at him." Others will defend against a fear-arousing message by refusing to believe the data presented in the communication; Akiva Liberman and Shelly Chaiken[41] have found that the more relevant the fearful message was for the behavior of any member of the audience (and hence the more threatening it was), the more these persons convinced themselves that the dangers contained in the message were overstated.

This analysis is supported by a host of findings in the AIDS literature. For example, research by Russell Clark[42] indicates that the AIDS epidemic has had little effect upon the general willingness of young adults to have casual sex; Katie Leishman[43] found that "many people at high risk nevertheless dispense with even minimal precautions"; research by Sunyna Williams and her colleagues[44] shows that college students justify their continued engagement in unsafe sex by the false belief that, if they know and like their partner, then he or she could not possibly be HIV positive. Similarly, surveys on college campuses across the country indicate that the majority of sexually active college students are not engaging in safe sex, are not discussing sexually transmitted diseases with their partners, and have never even purchased a condom.[45]

If fear arousal is ineffective because it leads to denial, must we simply sit back and brace ourselves for the onslaught of a major epidemic? Not necessarily. There is no simple solution to this problem. But if we believe that getting people to use condoms is the most realistic way to stem the spread of AIDS, one possibility is to design the message to overcome whatever it is that sexually active people find unattractive about condoms. For example, in our survey of sexually active college students, we found that the great majority see the putting on of condoms as a "turnoff," as "an antiseptic procedure" that detracts from the romantic sequence of a sexual encounter.[46] Accordingly, one possible approach to this problem might be to find a way to change people's mind-set—perhaps by convincing them that putting on the condom could become a mutual event that can be used as an erotic aspect of foreplay—a prelude to lovemaking rather than a burdensome interference.[47] Other strategies aimed at dealing with this important issue will be described in Chapter 5.

Fear and the Threat of Terrorism In the aftermath of the September 11 terrorist attack, most Americans were understandably shocked, angry, and frightened. Among other things, we wanted to know when we might expect the next attack and what we might do to minimize the danger. Into the breach stepped the Department of Homeland Security and the Attorney General of the United States. It is their job to gather data about terrorist intentions, sound the alarm, and tell us what to do. Most of us would be only too willing to comply with their recommendations.

As we have seen, to be effective, warnings and instructions should be based on reliable evidence, and should be presented by a credible communicator. The communicator must clearly state what the threat is and what specific actions people should take to avoid a catastrophe. When a hurricane is coming, we are told to board up our windows and even abandon our homes if they are in the path of the storm. When rivers are in danger of flooding, we are warned to head for the high ground. If I were told that terrorists were going to attack my shopping mall this weekend, I would refrain from shopping. If I were told that terrorists were about to attack planes, trains, and buses, I would be inclined to postpone my trip.

Any warning becomes ineffective if it is vague about what the danger is or where it is coming from or what people can do to avert the danger. In the eighteen months that have elapsed between the bombing of the World Trade Center and this writing, high-ranking government officials have issued seven separate warnings of a possible imminent terrorist attack. Each of these warnings has failed to meet even one of the necessary criteria to be effective. That is, each has been vague as to what the attack would consist of, vague about the time and place of the attack, and confusing about what people should do to avoid becoming victims. At one and the same time, the Director of Homeland Security has warned us to be vigilant but not to let that interfere with our day-to-day lives. What does that mean? I guess it means that I should not cancel my trip to New York, but after I board the airplane I should make sure that the guy sitting next to me doesn't try to set fire to his shoe!

If the situation were not so dangerous, one might see a comedic aspect to their warnings. Indeed, their public statements have provided material for the likes of Jay Leno and David Letterman. For example, during the February, 2003, alarm, government officials urged us to stock up on plastic sheeting and duct tape so that we could tape up our windows and doors against a possible poison gas or anthrax attack. But some experts warned that such an action might cause people to suffocate. In response to that warning, government officials responded by saying, in effect, "Well, we said to stock up on that stuff, but we didn't say to *use* it!"

But, of course, the situation *is* dangerous. The possibility of a serious terrorist attack is real. Moreover, the behavior of our government officials is not simply inept; rather, I would suggest that it has done far more harm than good. As we have seen, scaring people without offering them a sensible course of action leads to a heightened state of anxiety without producing appropriate action. Worse still, people cannot tolerate living in a state of constant anxiety. Thus, if vague warnings recur every few months (as they have since September 11) and prove to be false alarms, most of us will eventually drift into a state of denial and become bored and complacent and will eventually stop listening.[48]

Consensual Statistical Evidence versus a Single Personal Example Suppose you are in the market for a new car, and the two most important things you are looking for are reliability and longevity. That is, you don't care about looks, style, or mileage; what you *do* care about is the frequency of repair. As a reasonable and sensible person, you consult *Consumer Reports* and, let us say, you learn that the car with the best repair record is the Volvo. Naturally, you decide to buy a Volvo. But suppose that, the night before you are to make the purchase, you attend a dinner party and announce your intention to one of your friends. He is incredulous: "You can't be serious," he says. "My cousin bought a Volvo last year and has had nothing but trouble ever since. First, the fuel injection system broke down; then the transmission fell out; then strange, undiagnosable noises started to come from the engine; finally, oil started to drip from some unknown place. My poor cousin is literally afraid to drive the car for fear of what will happen next."

Let's suppose the ranking made by *Consumer Reports* was based on a sample of 1,000 Volvo owners. Your friend's cousin's unfortunate experience has increased the size of the sample to 1,001. It has added one negative case to your statistical bank. Logically, this should not affect your decision. But a large body of research by Richard Nisbett and his associates[49] (from whose work this example was borrowed) indicates that such occurrences, because of their vividness, assume far more importance than their logical statistical status would imply. Indeed, such occurrences are frequently decisive. Thus, with the example of the plight of your friend's cousin firmly fixed in your mind, it would be very difficult for you to rush out and purchase a Volvo.

In addition, the more vivid the examples are, the greater their persuasive power. A real-life demonstration of this comes from the area of energy conservation. Several years ago, my students and I set out to persuade homeowners to make the improvements necessary to have an energy-efficient house.[50] We worked with home auditors from local utility companies and taught them to use vivid examples when recommending home improvements. For example, most auditors, when left to their own devices, simply point to cracks around doors and recommend that the homeowner install weatherstripping. Instead, we trained several auditors to tell homeowners that if all the cracks around all the doors were added up, they would equal a hole the size of a basketball in their living room wall. "And if you had a hole that size in your wall, wouldn't you want to patch it up? That's what weather-stripping does." The results were striking. Auditors trained to use this kind of vivid language increased their effectiveness fourfold; whereas previously only 15 percent of the homeowners had the recommended work done, after the auditors began to use more vivid communication, this increased to 61 percent. Most people are more deeply influenced by one clear, vivid, personal example than by an abundance of statistical data. Thus, your friend's Volvo story or the thought of a basketball-sized hole in your living room will probably be extraordinarily powerful.

One-Sided versus Two-Sided Arguments
Suppose you are about to make a speech attempting to persuade your audience that capital punishment is necessary. Would you persuade more people if you simply stated your view and ignored the arguments against capital punishment, or would you be more persuasive if you discussed the opposing arguments and attempted to refute them? Before trying to answer this question, let us take a close look at what is involved. If a communicator mentions the opposition's arguments, it might indicate that he or she is an objective, fair-minded person; this could enhance the speaker's trustworthiness and thus increase his or her effectiveness. On the other hand, if a communicator so much as mentions the arguments on the other side of the issue, it might suggest to the audience that the issue is controversial; this could confuse members of the audience, make them vacillate, and ultimately reduce the persuasiveness of the communication. With these possibilities in mind, it should not come as a surprise to the reader that there is no simple relation between one-sided arguments and the effectiveness of the communication. It depends to some extent upon how well informed the audience is: The more well informed the members of the audience are, the less likely they are to be persuaded by a one-sided argument and the more likely they are to be persuaded by an argument that brings out the important opposing arguments and then proceeds to refute them. This makes sense: A well-informed person is more likely to know some of the counterarguments. When the communicator avoids mentioning these, the knowledgeable members of the audience are likely to conclude that the communicator is either unfair or unable to refute such arguments. On the other hand, an uninformed person is less apt to know of the existence of opposing arguments. If the counterargument is ignored, the less-informed members of the audience are persuaded; if the counterargument is presented, they may get confused.

Another factor playing a vital role is the initial position of the audience. As we might expect, if a member of the audience is already predisposed to believe the communicator's argument, a one-sided presentation has a greater impact on his or her opinion than a two-sided presentation. If, however, a member of the audience is leaning in the opposite direction, then a two-sided refutational argument is more persuasive.[51] Most politicians seem to be well aware of this phenomenon; they tend to present vastly different kinds of speeches, depending upon who constitutes the audience. When talking to the party faithful, they almost invariably deliver a hell-raising set of arguments favoring their own party platform and candidacy. If they do mention the opposition, it is in a derisive, mocking tone. On the other hand, when appearing on network television or when speaking to any audience of mixed loyalties, they tend to take a more diplomatic position, giving the opposing view a reasonably accurate airing before proceeding to demolish it.

The Order of Presentation Imagine you are running for the city council. You and your opponent are invited to address a large audience in the civic auditorium. It is a close election—many members of the audience are still undecided—and the outcome may hinge on your speech. You have worked hard on writing and rehearsing it. As you take your seat on the stage, the master of ceremonies asks you whether you would prefer to lead off or speak last. You ponder this for a moment. You think: *Speaking first may have an advantage because first impressions are crucial; if I can get the audience on my side early, then my opponent will not only have to sell himself, he'll also have to unsell the audience on me—he'll be bucking a trend. On the other hand, if I speak last, I may have an advantage because when the people leave the auditorium, they may remember the last thing they heard. The early statements made by my opponent, no matter how powerful, will be buried by my rhetoric simply because my speech will be more memorable.* You stammer: "I'd like to speak first . . . no, last . . . no, first . . . no, wait a minute." In confusion, you race off the stage, find a telephone booth, and call your friend the social psychologist. Surely, she must know which order has the advantage.

I'm afraid that if you expect a one-word answer, you are in for a disappointment. Moreover, if you wait to hear all of the social psychologist's elaborations and qualifying remarks, you might miss the opportunity of ever delivering your speech at all. Indeed, you might miss the election itself!

Needless to say, the issue is a complex one involving both learning and retention. I'll try to state it as simply as possible. The issues are similar to the commonsense issues that you, as our hypothetical politician, pondered alone. It is true that, all other things being equal, the audience's memory should be better for the speech made last, simply because it is closer in time to the election. On the other hand, the actual learning of the second material will not be as thorough as the learning of the first material, simply because the very existence of the first material disrupts and inhibits the learning process. Thus, from our knowledge of the phenomena of learning, it would appear that, all other things being equal, the first argument will be more effective; we'll call this the **primacy effect.** But from our knowledge of the phenomena of retention, on the other hand, it would appear that, all other things being equal, the last argument will be more effective; we'll call this the **recency effect.**

The fact that these two approaches seemingly involve opposite predictions does not mean that it doesn't matter which argument comes first; nor does it mean that it is hopeless to attempt to make a definitive prediction. What it does mean is that, by knowing something about the way both inhibition and retention work, we can predict the conditions under which either the primacy effect or the recency effect will prevail. The crucial variable is *time*—that is, the amount of time separating the events in the situation: (1) the amount of time between the first communication and the second communication and (2) the amount of time between the end of the second communication and the moment when the members of the audience must finally make up their minds. Here are the crucial points: (1) Inhibition (interference) is greatest if very little time elapses between the two communications; here, the first communication produces maximum interference with the learning of the second communication, and a primacy effect will occur—the first speaker will have the advantage. (2) Retention is greatest, and recency effects will therefore prevail, when the audience must make up its mind immediately after hearing the second communication.

Okay. Are you still on the phone? Here's the plan: If you and your opponent are to present your arguments back to back, and if the election is still several days away, you should speak first. The primacy of your speech will interfere with the audience's ability to learn your opponent's arguments; with the election several days away, differential effects due to memory are negligible. But if the election is going to be held immediately after the second speech, and there is to be a prolonged coffee break between the two speeches, you would do well to speak last. Because of the coffee break between speeches, the interference of the first speech with the learning of the second speech will be minimal; because the audience must make up its mind right after the second speech, as the second speaker you would have retention working for you. Therefore the recency effect would be dominant: All other things being equal, the last speech will be the more persuasive.

These speculations were confirmed in an experiment by Norman Miller and Donald Campbell.[52] In this experiment, a simulated jury trial was arranged, in which participants were presented with a condensed version of the transcript of an actual jury trial of a suit for damages brought against the manufacturers of an allegedly defective vaporizer. The pro side of the argument consisted of the testimony of witnesses for the plaintiff, cross-examination of defense witnesses by the plaintiff's lawyer, and the opening and closing speeches of the plaintiff's lawyer. The con side of the argument consisted of the testimony of witnesses for the defense, the defense lawyer's cross-examinations, and his opening and closing speeches. The condensed version of this transcript was arranged so that all of the pro arguments were placed in one block and all of the con arguments were placed in another block. The investigators varied the interval between the reading of the two arguments and between the reading of the last argument and the announcement of the verdict. A recency effect was obtained when there was a large interval between the first and second arguments and a small interval between the second argument and the verdict. A primacy effect was obtained when there was a small interval between the first and second arguments and a large interval between the second argument and the verdict. The topic of this experiment (a jury trial) serves to underscore the immense practical significance these two phenomena may have. Most jurisdictions allow the prosecution to go first (opening statement and presentation of evidence) and last (closing arguments), thus giving the state the advantage of both primacy and recency effects. Because the order of presentation may influence a jury's verdict of guilt or innocence, I would recommend that our trial procedures be modified to prevent any possible miscarriages of justice due to primacy or recency effects.

The Size of the Discrepancy Suppose you are talking to an audience that strongly disagrees with your point of view. Will you be more effective if you present your position in its most extreme form or if you modulate your position by presenting it in such a way that it does not seem terribly different from the audience's position? For example, suppose you believe people should exercise vigorously every day to stay healthy; any physical activity would be helpful, but at least an hour's worth would be preferable. Your audience consists of college professors who seem to believe that turning the pages of a book is sufficient exercise for the average person. Would you change their opinion to a greater extent by arguing that people should begin a rigorous daily program of running, swimming, and calisthenics or by suggesting a briefer, less-taxing regimen? In short, what is the most effective level of discrepancy between the opinion of the audience and the recommendation of the communicator? This is a vital issue for any propagandist or educator.

Let us look at this situation from the audience's point of view. As I mentioned in Chapter 2, most of us have a strong desire to be correct—to have the "right" opinions and to perform reasonable actions. When someone comes along and disagrees with us, it makes us feel uncomfortable because it suggests our opinions or actions may be wrong or based on misinformation. The greater the disagreement, the greater our discomfort. How can we reduce this discomfort? Simply by changing our opinions or actions. The greater the disagreement, the greater our opinion change will be. This line of reasoning, then, would suggest that the communicator should argue for the daily program of rigorous exercise; the greater the discrepancy, the more the opinion change. Indeed, several investigators have found that this linear relation holds true. A good example of this relation was provided by an experiment by Philip Zimbardo.[53] Each of the college women recruited as participants for the experiment was asked to bring a close friend with her to the laboratory. Each pair of friends was presented with a case study of juvenile delinquency, and then each of the participants was asked, separately and in private, to indicate her recommendations on the matter. Each participant was led to believe her close friend disagreed with her—either by a small margin or by an extremely large margin. Zimbardo found that the greater the apparent discrepancy, the more the participants changed their opinions toward what they supposed were the opinions of their friends.

However, a careful look at the research literature also turns up several experiments disconfirming the line of reasoning presented above. For example, James Whittaker[54] found a curvilinear relation between discrepancy and opinion change. By *curvilinear,* I mean that, as a small discrepancy increased somewhat, so did the degree of opinion change; but as the discrepancy continued to increase, opinion change began to slacken; and finally, as the discrepancy became large, the amount of opinion change became very small. When the discrepancy was very large, almost no opinion change was observed.

Building on Whittaker's finding, Carl Hovland, O. J. Harvey, and Muzafer Sherif[55] argued that, if a particular communication differs considerably from a person's own position, it is, in effect, outside of one's *latitude of acceptance,* and the individual will not be much influenced by it. In the experiment by Hovland and his colleagues, the communication was based on a red-hot issue—one the participants felt strongly about: whether their state should remain "dry" or "go wet"—that is, whether or not to change the law prohibiting the distribution and sale of alcoholic beverages. The voters of the state were virtually equally divided on this issue, and the participants were a representative sample: Some of the participants felt strongly that the state should remain dry, others felt strongly that it should go wet, and the rest took a moderate position. The participants were divided into groups of people reflecting all three positions. The members of each group were presented with communications supporting one of the three opinions, so that, in each group, there were participants who found the communication close to their own position, some who found it moderately discrepant from their own position, and some who found it extremely discrepant from their own position. Specifically, some groups were presented with a "wet" message, which argued for the unlimited and unrestricted sale of liquor; some groups were presented with a "dry" message, which argued for complete prohibition; and some groups were presented with a moderately "wet" message, which argued to allow some drinking but with certain controls and restrictions. The greatest opinion changes occurred when there was a *moderate* discrepancy between the actual message and the opinions of individual members of the groups.

For a scientist, this is an exciting state of affairs. When a substantial number of research findings point in one direction and a similarly substantial number of research findings point in a different direction, it doesn't necessarily mean someone has to be wrong; rather, it suggests there is a significant factor that hasn't been accounted for—and this is indeed exciting, for it gives the scientist an opportunity to play detective. I beg the reader's indulgence here, for I would like to dwell on this issue—not only for its substantive value, but also because it provides us with an opportunity to analyze one of the more adventurous aspects of social psychology as a science. Basically, there are two ways of proceeding with this game of detective. We can begin by assembling all the experiments that show one result and all those that show the other result and (imaginary magnifying glass in hand) painstakingly scrutinize them, looking for the one factor common to the experiments in group A and lacking in group B; then we can try to determine, conceptually, why this factor should make a difference. Or, conversely, we can begin by speculating conceptually about what factor or factors might make a difference; then we can glance through the existing literature, with this conceptual lantern in hand, to see if those in group A differ from those in group B on this dimension.

As a scientist, my personal preference is for the second mode. Accordingly, with two of my students—Judith Turner and Merrill Carlsmith—I began to speculate about what factor or factors might make such a difference. We began by accepting the notion discussed above: The greater the discrepancy, the greater the discomfort for the members of the audience. But we reasoned that this does not necessarily mean the members of an audience will change their opinion. There are at least four ways in which the members of an audience can reduce their discomfort: (1) they can change their opinion; (2) they can induce *the communicator* to change his or her opinion; (3) they can seek support for their original opinion by finding other people who share their views, in spite of what the communicator says; or (4) they can derogate the communicator—convince themselves the communicator is stupid or immoral—and thereby invalidate that person's opinion.

In many communication situations, including those in these experiments, the message is delivered either as a written statement (as a newspaper or magazine article, for example) or by a communicator who is not approachable by the audience (as on television, on the lecture platform, and so on). Also, the participant is often alone or part of an audience whose members have no opportunity to interact with each other. Thus, under these circumstances, it is virtually impossible for the recipients of the communication either to have immediate impact on the communicator's opinion or to seek immediate social support. This leaves the recipients two major ways of reducing this discomfort: They can change their opinion, or they can derogate the communicator.

Under what circumstances would an individual find it easy or difficult to derogate the communicator? It would be very difficult to derogate a liked and respected personal friend; it would also be difficult to derogate someone who is a highly trustworthy expert on the issue under discussion. But if the communicator's credibility were questionable, it would be difficult not to derogate him or her. Following this line of reasoning, we suggested that, if a communicator's credibility were high, the greater the discrepancy between the communicator's opinions and the audience's opinions, the greater the influence exerted on the opinions of the audience. However, if the communicator's credibility were not very high, he or she would be, by definition, subject to derogation. This is not to say that the communicator couldn't influence the opinions of the audience. The communicator would probably be able to influence people to change their opinions if his or her opinions were not too different from theirs. But the more discrepant such a communicator's position is from those of the audience, the more the audience might begin to question his or her wisdom, intelligence, and sanity. The more they question his or her wisdom, intelligence, and sanity, the less likely they are to be influenced.

Let's return to our example involving physical exercise: Imagine a 73-year-old man, with the body of a man half his age, who had just won the Boston Marathon. If he told me that a good way to stay in condition and live a long, healthy life was to exercise vigorously for at least 2 hours every day, I would believe him. Boy, would I believe him! He would get much more exercise out of me than if he suggested I should exercise for only 10 minutes a day. But suppose a person somewhat less credible, such as a high-school track coach, were delivering the communication. If he suggested I exercise 10 minutes a day, his suggestion would be within my own latitude of acceptance, and he might influence my opinion and behavior. But if he advised me to embark on a program of vigorous exercise requiring 2 hours every day, I would be inclined to write him off as a quack, a health freak, a monomaniac—and I could comfortably continue being indolent. Thus, I would agree with Hovland, Harvey, and Sherif: People will consider an extremely discrepant communication to be outside their latitude of acceptance—but only if the communicator is not highly credible.

Armed with these speculations, my students and I scrutinized the existing experiments on this issue, paying special attention to the ways in which the communicator was described. Lo and behold, we discovered that each of the experiments showing a direct linear relation between discrepancy and opinion change happened to describe the source of the communication as more credible than did those whose results showed a curvilinear relation. This confirmed our speculations about the role of credibility. But we didn't stop there: We constructed an experiment in which we systematically investigated the size of the discrepancy and the credibility of the communicator in one research design.[56] In this experiment, college women were asked to read several stanzas from obscure modern poetry and to rank them in terms of how good they were. Then each woman was given an essay to read purporting to be a criticism of modern poetry that specifically mentioned a stanza she had rated as poor. For some participants, the essayist described this particular stanza in glowing terms; this created a large discrepancy between the opinion of the communicator and the opinion voiced by the students in this experimental condition. For some participants, the essayist was only mildly favorable in the way he described the stanza; this set up a moderate discrepancy between the essayist and the students in this condition. In a third condition, the essayist was mildly scornful in his treatment of the stanza—which placed the recipients of this communication in a mild-discrepancy situation. Finally, to one-half of the women in the experiment, the writer of the essay was identified as the poet T. S. Eliot, a highly credible poetry critic; to the rest of the participants, the essay writer was identified as a college student. The participants were subsequently allowed to rank the stanzas once again. When T. S. Eliot was ostensibly the communicator, the essay had the most influence on the students when its evaluation of the stanza was most discrepant from theirs; when a fellow student of medium credibility was identified as the essayist, the essay produced a little opinion change when it was slightly discrepant from the opinion of the students, a great deal of change when it was moderately discrepant, and only a little opinion change when it was extremely discrepant.

To sum up this section, the conflicting results are accounted for: When a communicator has high credibility, the greater the discrepancy between the view he or she advocates and the view of the audience, the more the audience will be persuaded; on the other hand, when a communicator's credibility is doubtful or slim, he or she will produce maximum opinion change with moderate discrepancy.

Characteristics of the Audience

All listeners, readers, or viewers are not alike. Some people are more difficult to persuade. In addition, as we have seen, the kind of communication that appeals to one person may not appeal to another. For example, recall that the level of knowledge audience members possess and their prior opinions will play major roles in determining whether a two-sided communication will be more effective than a one-sided communication.

Self-Esteem What effect does an individual's personality have on his or her persuasibility? The one personality variable most consistently related to persuasibility is self-esteem. Individuals who feel inadequate are more easily influenced by a persuasive communication than individuals who think highly of themselves.[57] This seems reasonable enough, after all, if people don't like themselves, then it follows that they don't place a very high premium on their own ideas and have less confidence in their convictions. Consequently, if their ideas are challenged, they may be willing to give them up. Recall that people want to be right. If Sam, who has high self-esteem, listens to a communication at variance with his own opinion, he must make up his mind whether he stands a better chance of being right if he changes his opinion or if he stands pat. A person with high self-esteem may experience some conflict when he finds himself in disagreement with a highly credible communicator. He might resolve this conflict by changing his opinion, or he might remain firm. But if Sam had low self-esteem, there would be little or no conflict. Because he doesn't think very highly of himself, he probably believes he stands a better chance of being right if he goes along with the communicator.

Prior Experience of the Audience Another audience-related factor of considerable importance is the frame of mind the audience is in just prior to the communication. An audience can be made receptive to a communication if it has been well fed and is relaxed and happy. Indeed, as Irving Janis and his associates have discovered, people who have been allowed to eat desirable food while reading a persuasive communication are more influenced by what they read than are people in a control (noneating) group.[58] Similarly, research by Richard Petty and his colleagues suggests that being in a good mood can make people more vulnerable to persuasion.[59] Similarly, Geoffrey Cohen and his colleagues[60] found that people who have recently received self-esteem affirming feedback (such as learning they are well liked) are also more receptive to being persuaded by a communication.

Conversely, there are ways in which members of an audience can be made less receptive and less persuadable. As I noted, people predict they will be able to resist persuasive communications such as television commercials. Accordingly, one way of decreasing their persuasibility is by forewarning them that an attempt is going to be made to persuade them.[61] This is especially true if the content of the message differs from their own beliefs. I would argue that the phrase "And now, a message from our sponsor" renders that message less persuasive than it would have been if the communicator had simply glided into it without prologue. The forewarning seems to say, "Watch out, I'm going to try to persuade you," and people tend to respond by marshaling defenses against the message. This phenomenon was demonstrated in an experiment by Jonathan Freedman and David Sears.[62] Teenagers were told they would be hearing a talk entitled "Why Teenagers Should Not Be Allowed to Drive." Ten minutes later, the speaker presented them with a prepared communication. In a control condition, the same talk was given without the 10-minute forewarning. The participants in the control condition were more thoroughly convinced by the communication than were those who had been forewarned.

People tend to protect their sense of freedom. According to Jack Brehm's theory of reactance,[63] when our sense of freedom is threatened, we attempt to restore it. For example, I like to receive birthday presents. But if a borderline student (in danger of flunking my course) presented me with an expensive birthday present just as I was about to read term papers, I would feel uncomfortable. My sense of freedom or autonomy would be challenged. Similarly, persuasive communications, if blatant or coercive, can be perceived as intruding upon one's freedom of choice, activating one's defenses to resist the messages. For example, if an aggressive salesperson tells me I must buy something, my first reaction is to reassert my independence by leaving the store.

In an experiment by Lillian Bensley and Rui Wu,[64] college students watched one of two messages opposed to the drinking of alcoholic beverages. One was a heavy-handed, dogmatic message stating that there was no safe amount of alcohol and that all people should abstain all the time. The second message was a milder one that stressed the importance of controlling one's drinking. The second message was far more effective in getting people to reduce their consumption of alcohol. This was especially true for heavy drinkers—who almost certainly experienced the most reactance when confronted with the heavy-handed message.

Reactance can operate in a number of interesting ways. Suppose that, as I walk down the street, I am gently asked to sign a petition. I don't know much about the issue, and as it is being explained to me, another person accosts us and begins to pressure me not to sign. Reactance theory predicts that, to counteract this pressure and reassert my freedom of choice, I would be more likely to sign. This scenario was actually staged by Madeline Heilman,[65] and the results confirmed her prediction that, under most circumstances, the more intense the attempts to prevent participants from signing the petition, the more likely they were to sign. Of course, as we have seen in this chapter and the preceding one, people can be and are influenced and do comply with implicit social pressures, as in the Asch experiment. But when those pressures are so blatant that they threaten people's feeling of freedom, they not only resist them but tend to react in the opposite direction.

There is still another aspect of this need for freedom and autonomy that should be mentioned. All other things being equal, when faced with information that runs counter to important beliefs, people have a tendency, whenever feasible, to invent counterarguments on the spot.[66] In this way, they are able to prevent their opinions from being unduly influenced and protect their sense of autonomy. But it is possible to overcome some of this resistance. Leon Festinger and Nathan Maccoby[67] conducted an experiment in which they attempted to prevent members of their audience from inventing arguments to refute the message being presented to them. This was accomplished by simply distracting the audience somewhat while the communication was being presented. Two groups of students who belonged to a college fraternity were required to listen to a tape-recorded argument about the evils of college fraternities. The argument was erudite, powerful, and, as you might imagine, widely discrepant from their beliefs. During the presentation of the communication, one of the groups was distracted. Specifically, they were shown a highly entertaining silent film. Festinger and Maccoby reasoned that, because this group was engaged in two tasks simultaneously—listening to the tape-recorded argument against fraternities and watching an entertaining film—their minds would be so occupied they would have little or no opportunity to think up arguments to refute the tape-recorded message. The members of the control group, on the other hand, were not distracted by a film; therefore, they would be better able to devote some of their thoughts to resisting the communication by thinking up counterarguments. The results of the experiment confirmed this reasoning. The students who were distracted by watching the film underwent substantially more opinion change against fraternities than did those who were not distracted.

Let us take a closer look at the other side of the issue. How can we help people to resist attempts to influence them? An elaborate method for inducing such resistance has been developed by William McGuire and his associates. This method has been appropriately dubbed the **inoculation effect.** We have already seen that a two-sided (refutational) presentation is more effective for convincing most audiences than a one-sided presentation. Expanding on this phenomenon, McGuire suggested that, if people receive prior exposure to a brief communication that they are then able to refute, they tend to be "immunized" against a subsequent full-blown presentation of the same argument, in much the same way that a small amount of an attenuated virus immunizes people against a full-blown attack by that virus. In an experiment by McGuire and Dimitri Papageorgis,[68] a group of people stated their opinions; these opinions were then subjected to a mild attack—and the attack was refuted. These people were subsequently subjected to a powerful argument against their initial opinions. Members of this group showed a much smaller tendency to change their opinions than did the members of a control group whose opinions had not been previously subjected to the mild attack. In effect, they had been inoculated against opinion change and made relatively immune. Thus, not only is it often more effective as a propaganda technique to use a two-sided refutational presentation, but if it is used skillfully, such a presentation tends to increase the audience's resistance to subsequent counterpropaganda.

In an interesting field experiment, Alfred McAlister and his colleagues[69] inoculated 7th-grade students against existing peer pressure to smoke cigarettes. For example, the students were shown advertisements (popular at the time) implying that truly liberated women are smokers—"You've come a long way, baby!" They were then inoculated by being taught that a woman couldn't possibly be liberated if she were hooked on nicotine. Similarly, because many teenagers begin smoking, in part, because it seems "cool" or "tough" (like the Marlboro man), peer pressure took the form of being called "chicken" if one didn't smoke. Accordingly, McAlister set up a situation to counteract that process; the 7th-graders role-played a situation in which they practiced countering that argument by saying something like "I'd be a real chicken if I smoked just to impress you." This inoculation against peer pressure proved to be very effective. By the time the students were in the 9th grade, they were half as likely to smoke as those in a control group from a similar junior high school.

Research[70] has found that, in producing resistance, inoculation is most effective when the belief under attack is a cultural truism. A cultural truism is a belief accepted as unquestionably true by most members of a society, like "The United States is the most wonderful country in the world" or "If people are willing to work hard, they can succeed." Cultural truisms are rarely called into question; consequently, it is relatively easy for us to lose sight of why we hold those beliefs. Thus, if subjected to a severe attack, these beliefs may crumble. To motivate us to bolster our beliefs, we must be made aware of their vulnerability, and the best way to do this is to be exposed to a mild attack on those beliefs. Prior exposure, in the form of a watered-down attack on our beliefs, produces resistance to later persuasion because (1) we become motivated to defend our beliefs and (2) we gain some practice in defending these beliefs by being forced to examine why we hold them. We are then better equipped to resist a more serious attack.

This is an important point that was frequently ignored or misunderstood by policymakers during the height of the Cold War. For example, in the aftermath of the Korean War, when there was a great deal of fear about the possibility that our prisoners of war had been systematically "brainwashed" by the Chinese Communists, a Senate committee recommended that, in order to build resistance among our young people to brainwashing and other forms of Communist propaganda, courses on "patriotism and Americanism" should be instituted in our public school system. But my reading of the research on inoculation led me to an entirely different conclusion. Specifically, I asserted that the best way to help people resist antidemocratic propaganda would be to challenge their belief in democracy, and the best way to build resistance to one-sided Communist propaganda would be to teach fair, even-handed courses on Communism in high schools.[71] At the height of the Cold War, such a suggestion was undoubtedly considered subversive by those politicians who were terrified at the prospect of our young people learning anything positive about Communism. The fear was that this would make them more vulnerable to propaganda. But historical events have supported the social psychological research showing that, if one wants to mitigate against simplistic propaganda, there is no substitute for free inquiry into ideas of all kinds. The person who is easiest to brainwash is the person whose beliefs are based on slogans that have never been seriously challenged.

How Well Do the Principles Work?

Suppose you inherited controlling interest in a television network. Here is a golden opportunity to influence people's opinions on important issues. Let's say you are an enthusiastic proponent of national health insurance, and you would like to persuade others to agree with you. Having just finished reading this chapter, you know how to do it, and you are in control of a very powerful medium of communication. How do you set about achieving your goal? That's simple: You choose a time slot following a highly intellectual program (in order to be certain that well-informed people are watching), and accordingly, you present a two-sided argument (because two-sided arguments work best on well-informed people). You arrange your arguments in such a manner that the argument in favor of national health insurance is stronger and appears first (in order to take advantage of the primacy effect). You describe the plight of the poor, how they get sick and die for lack of affordable medical care. You use vivid personal examples of people you know. You discuss these events in a manner that inspires a great deal of fear; at the same time, you offer a specific plan of action because this combination produces the most opinion change and the most action in the most people. You present some of the arguments against your position and offer strong refutation of these arguments. You arrange for the speaker to be expert, trustworthy, and extremely likable. You make your argument as strongly as you can in order to maximize the discrepancy between the argument presented and the initial attitude of the audience. And then you sit back, relax, and wait for those opinions to start changing.

It's not that simple. Imagine a typical viewer: Let's say she is a 45-year-old middle-class real-estate broker who believes the government interferes too much in the private lives of individuals. She feels any form of social legislation undermines the spirit of individuality that is the essence of democracy. She comes across your program while looking for an evening's entertainment. She begins to hear your arguments in favor of national health insurance. As she listens, she becomes slightly less confident in her original convictions. She is not quite as certain as she had been that the government shouldn't intervene in matters of health. What does she do? If she is anything like the participants in Lance Canon's[72] experiment, she would most likely reach for her remote control "zapper" and switch channels to a rerun of *Wheel of Fortune*. Canon found that, as one's confidence is weakened, a person becomes less prone to listen to arguments against his or her beliefs. Thus, the very people you most want to convince, and whose opinions might be the most susceptible to change, are the ones *least* likely to continue to expose themselves to a communication designed for that purpose.

Must you resign yourself to broadcasting your message to an audience composed of viewers who already support national health insurance? That may be so—if you insist on airing a serious documentary devoted to the issue. After considering your alternatives, however, you might decide to take another approach. You call a meeting of your network executives. The programming director is instructed to commission a couple of scripts dramatizing the plight of families facing financial ruin due to the costs associated with serious illness. You order the news department to investigate the success of national health insurance in other countries. Finally, you provide the late-night talk-show host with a couple of jokes he might tell about his inept but affluent doctor. While none of these communications would match the documentary in terms of the information provided, their cumulative impact could be more significant. Embedded in dramas or news segments, they would not necessarily be labeled as arguments supporting national health insurance; they seem innocuous, but their message is clear. Not appearing to be explicit attempts at persuasion, they should arouse little resistance, avoiding an inoculation effect and inhibiting the formation of counterarguments by distracting the audience. Most important, people will probably *see* them; they would not switch channels.

I do not mean to imply that television executives conspire to disguise persuasive communications within other contexts, but as I stated near the beginning of this chapter, television plays a major role in shaping how we perceive the world. The sheer volume of television Americans see is staggering.[73] The typical household's television set is turned on for over 7 hours a day,[74] and the average American watches 30 hours of television a week—that's a little over 1,500 hours a year. At that rate, if you are an average viewer, you will see about 37,800 commercials a year, or more than 100 a day.[75] The average high-school graduate has spent much less time in the classroom than in front of the television.[76]

The medium has impact, and the view of reality it transmits seldom remains value-free. George Gerbner and his associates[77] have conducted the most extensive analysis of television yet. Since the late 1960s, these researchers have been videotaping and carefully analyzing thousands of prime-time television programs and characters. Their findings, taken as a whole, suggest that television's representation of reality is frequently misleading. In prime-time programming, males outnumber females by almost 3 to 1, and women are depicted as younger and less experienced than the men they encounter on television. Nonwhites (especially Latinos and Asian Americans) and the elderly are underrepresented, and members of minority groups are disproportionately cast in minor roles. Moreover, most prime-time characters are portrayed as professional and managerial workers: Although 67 percent of the workforce in the United States is employed in a blue collar or service job, only 25 percent of television characters hold such jobs. Finally, crime on television is at least 10 times as prevalent as in real life. Over half of television's characters are involved in a violent confrontation each week; in reality, less than 1 percent of Americans are victims of criminal violence in any given year, according to FBI statistics. During the past several years, FBI statistics reveal that the rate of violent crime has actually been decreasing in this country—but on TV, violent crime is on the increase. David Rintels, a television writer and former president of the Writers Guild of America, summed it up best when he said, "From 8 to 11 o'clock each night, television is one long lie."[78]

Gerbner and his associates have also compared the attitudes and beliefs of heavy viewers (those who watch more than 4 hours a day) and light viewers (those who watch less than 2 hours a day). They found that heavy viewers (1) express more racially prejudiced attitudes; (2) overestimate the number of people employed as physicians, lawyers, and athletes; (3) perceive women as having more limited abilities and interests than men; (4) hold exaggerated views about the prevalence of violence in society; and (5) believe old people are fewer in number and less healthy today than they were 20 years ago, even though, in actuality, the opposite is true. What's more, heavy viewers tend to see the world as a more sinister place than light viewers; they are likely to agree that most people are just looking out for themselves and would take advantage of you if they had a chance. Gerbner concludes that these attitudes and beliefs reflect the inaccurate portrayals of American life provided to us by television.*

Of course, each of us has had extensive personal contact with many people in myriad social contexts; the media are just one source of our knowledge about the sexes and about different ethnic or occupational groups. The information and impressions we receive through the media are probably less influential when we can also rely on firsthand experience. Thus, those of us who have been in close contact with several women in jobs outside of the home are probably less susceptible to the stereotypes of women portrayed on television. On the other hand, while each of us has formed conceptions about crime and violence, it is unlikely that many of those opinions developed from our personal experience. For most of us, television is virtually our only vivid source of information about crime. A major portion of television programming consists of crime shows—the average 15-year-old has viewed over 13,000 television killings. Moreover, several studies have shown that crime dramas dispense remarkably consistent images of both the police and criminals. For example, on TV, police officers are amazingly effective, solving almost every crime, and are infallible in one regard: The wrong person is almost never in jail at the end of a show. Television fosters an illusion of certainty in crime fighting. Television criminals generally turn to crime because of psychopathology or insatiable (and unnecessary) greed. Television emphasizes criminals' personal responsibility for their actions and largely ignores situational pressures correlated with crime, such as poverty and unemployment. This portrayal has important social consequences. People who watch a lot of television come to adopt this belief system, which affects their expectations and can cause them to take a hard-line stance when serving on juries. Heavy viewers are likely to reverse the presumption of innocence, believing that defendants must be guilty of *something;* otherwise, they wouldn't have been brought to trial.[79]

It has also been shown that the incidence of larceny (theft) increases when television is introduced into an area.[80] Why should this be the case? The most reasonable explanation is that television promotes the consumption of goods through advertisements; it also depicts upper- and middle-class lifestyles as the norm. This illusion of widespread wealth and consumption may frustrate and anger deprived viewers who compare their lifestyles with

---

*It should be noted that Gerbner's research is correlational, not experimental. It is therefore impossible to determine whether heavy viewing actually causes prejudiced attitudes and inaccurate beliefs or whether people already holding such attitudes and beliefs simply tend to watch more television. To bolster their conclusions, Gerbner and his associates sampled viewers from all age, education, income, and ethnic groups. After taking such viewer characteristics into account, they found that the relationship between heavy viewing and inaccurate beliefs still occurred in every category.

those portrayed on television, thereby motivating them to "share in the American dream" any way they can.

It is nearly impossible to specify the precise extent to which exposure to the media influences public opinion and behavior. Too many other factors are involved. Because the research described above is not experimental, it is difficult to separate the effects of mass communications from the impact of personal experiences and contact with family and friends. But experiments can be done. For example, let's suppose that, as the network executive, you went ahead with your original plan to televise the documentary on national health care. In this instance, it would be relatively easy for you to determine whether your message was persuasive. At the most basic level, both before and after the telecast, you could poll cross-sections of viewers about their opinions concerning national health insurance. If they changed in a favorable direction, you might conclude your program was effective. If you were interested in maximizing its effectiveness, you might tape several versions of the documentary to test different speakers, arguments, and styles of presentation. If you presented these versions to various test audiences, you could compare the effects of different combinations of factors. Indeed, this scenario approximates the way most of the research described earlier in this chapter was carried out. Communications about a variety of topics were prepared. Certain aspects of the presentation were systematically varied—the credibility of the speakers, for example, or the order of the arguments—and the resulting versions of the message were presented to audiences. When audience opinion is polled, the effects of the variables can be measured. This procedure allows great control over the message and is well suited for testing large numbers of participants. This method is so efficient, in fact, that it has been adapted to a computer controlled procedure for varying certain factors surrounding the messages and presenting them to people seated at computer consoles.[81] With the advent of cable television networks that have the technological capability for home viewers to communicate back to the station, it is now possible to instantaneously sample the responses of thousands of viewers to actual presentations.

Suppose that, instead of deciding to televise the documentary, you opted to broadcast the series of more subtle messages disguised within the regular programs and presented repeatedly. It would be much more difficult to measure and assess the impact of this approach, but it probably is more common. Rarely are we presented with explicit persuasive messages in favor of a given position immediately prior to deciding on an issue, except perhaps during political campaigns. Most of our beliefs develop more gradually, through repeated contacts with people and information over an extended period of time. In general, it is difficult to change important beliefs through direct communication. There appears to be a basic difference between an issue like national health insurance, on the one hand, and issues like the feasibility of atomic-powered submarines, whether antihistamines should be sold without a prescription, and the practical importance of arithmetic, on the other. What is the difference? One possible difference is that the medical-care issue feels more important. But what is the criterion for judging whether an issue is important or trivial?

To provide an answer to this question, we must first examine what we mean by the term **opinion,** which has been used throughout this chapter. On the simplest level, an opinion is what a person believes to be factually true. Thus, it is my opinion that there are fewer than 15,000 students enrolled at the University of California at Santa Cruz, that wearing seat belts reduces traffic fatalities, and that New York City is hot in the summer. Such opinions are primarily cognitive—that is, they take place in the head rather than in the gut. They are also transient—that is, they can be changed by good, clear evidence to the contrary. Thus, if longtime consumer advocate Ralph Nader (a highly credible source on automobile safety) presented me with data indicating that seat belts, as they are currently constructed, do not reduce fatalities significantly, it is likely that I would change my opinion on that issue.

On the other hand, suppose a person holds the opinion that Jews engage in "sharp" business practices, or that Asians are sneaky, or that old people are a drain on society, or that the United States of America is the greatest (or most awful) country in the history of the world, or that New York City is a jungle. How do these opinions differ from the ones stated in the preceding paragraph? They tend to be both emotional and evaluative—that is, they imply likes or dislikes. Believing Asians are sneaky implies that the person doesn't like Asians. The opinion that New York City is a jungle is different from the opinion that New York City is hot in the summer. The opinion that New York City is a jungle is not simply cognitive; it carries with it a negative evaluation and some degree of fear or anxiety. An opinion that includes an evaluative and an emotional component is called an **attitude.** Compared to opinions, attitudes are extremely difficult to change.

Suppose Sam is an ardent and careful consumer who is deeply concerned about matters of health. Over the years, he has come to trust Ralph Nader's research on many issues, including unsafe cars, cholesterol in hot dogs, hazardous electrical appliances, air pollution, and so on. But, further, suppose that Sam happens to be a white supremacist who believes that the white race is intellectually superior to all other races. What if Nader conducted an exhaustive study indicating that, when given culture-free intelligence tests, racial minorities score as high as whites? Would this information be likely to change Sam's attitude? Probably not. How come? Doesn't Sam regard Nader as a careful researcher? It is my guess that, because the issue is rooted in emotion, Nader's findings about intelligence testing would not influence Sam as easily or as thoroughly as Nader's findings about cars, cholesterol, or pollution. Attitudes are harder to change than simple opinions.

Human thinking is not always logical. Although we humans are capable of accurate and subtle thinking, we are equally capable of distortions and great sloppiness in our thought processes. In order to understand how to *change* attitudes, first it is essential to understand the complexities of human thinking as well as the motives that lead people to resist change. These are interesting and important issues that I will explore in the next two chapters. Chapter 4 is an attempt to understand how people construe and misconstrue social events; Chapter 5 is a description of the major motives underlying construal and misconstrual.

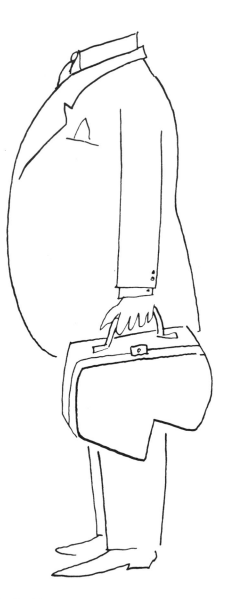

Saul Steinberg, *Untitled drawing*, ink on paper.
Published in Steinberg, *The Passport*, 1954.
© The Saul Steinberg Foundation / Artists Rights Society (ARS), New York

4
Social Cognition*

In his masterpiece, *Public Opinion,* the distinguished political analyst Walter Lippmann[1] recounts the story of a young girl, brought up in a small mining town, who one day went from cheerfulness into a deep spasm of grief. It seems that a gust of wind had suddenly cracked a kitchen windowpane. The young girl was inconsolable and spoke incomprehensibly for hours. When she was finally able to speak rationally, she explained that a broken pane of glass meant that a close relative had died. She was therefore mourning her father, whom she was convinced had just passed away. The young girl remained disconsolate until, days later, a telegram arrived verifying that her father was still very much alive. The girl had constructed a complete fiction based on a simple external fact (a broken window), a superstition (broken window means death), fear, and love for her father.

In the Middle Ages, it was common practice for Europeans to empty chamber pots—containers that stored a day's worth of urine and excrement—by throwing the contents out the window onto the street below. The waste matter would remain in the street, breeding pestilence and disease. To the modern mind, the practice seems primitive, barbaric, and downright stupid, especially when one considers that the ancient Romans had developed indoor plumbing. So how did the chamber pot come into being? During the Middle Ages, a belief arose that not only was nudity sinful but that an unclothed body was subject to attack by evil spirits. Because of that belief, the Roman practice of daily bathing was abandoned throughout Europe and replaced by a once-a-year bath. Eventually, the indoor baths fell into disrepair and society lost the plumbing skills needed to maintain indoor toilets. The chamber pot was born of necessity. It was centuries later that the "spirit" theory of disease was replaced by our modern theory based on viruses and bacteria.[2]

---

*I am indebted to my friend and colleague Anthony Pratkanis for drafting the initial version of this chapter.

My point here is not to explore the inner workings of the abnormal mind, nor to describe modern advances in health and hygiene. Instead, I tell these stories to raise a fundamental question: To what extent do *we moderns* behave like the young girl from the mining town and the users of the medieval chamber pot? How might *our* fictions guide our behavior and actions? It would not surprise me if the writer of a social psychology textbook in the twenty-second century began her chapter on *social cognition* not with a story about chamber pots, but with a tale of pesticide runoff or deaths due to the AIDS virus. The story might go something like this:

> During the twentieth and twenty-first centuries, millions died of famine—not from lack of food, but because their food had been poisoned by years of chemical runoff gradually building up in the food chain. A great many knowledgeable people suspected this was happening, but, unaccountably, little or nothing was done to prevent it.
>
> In addition, over a hundred and fifty million people died of the AIDS virus because they were unwilling to use condoms. The modern reader may be wondering how a culture that could place men and women on the moon and cure a plethora of dangerous diseases could behave so foolishly. Well, it seems that, in those days, many people apparently believed that talking frankly about the operation of their sexual parts was sinful and could cause harm. For example, at the turn of the twenty-first century, most parents of teenagers clung to the primitive belief that distributing condoms in high school would increase sexual promiscuity—in spite of the fact that careful research[3] demonstrated that this was not the case.
>
> My point in relating these stories is not, however, to point out how simpleminded most people were in the twentieth and twenty-first centuries, but to ask a more fundamental question: "How much are we like those heedless AIDS victims or those farmers who used pesticides so carelessly?"

We are forever trying to make sense of our social world; how we do it makes a difference. Whenever we meet a new person, we form a first impression. Every time we enter a supermarket, we walk down an aisle full of several brands for each of hundreds of products; we must attempt to discern which will best suit our needs. Occasionally, someone will ask us a question about ourselves, and we must think back over the bits and pieces of our lives to construct answers we believe to be accurate. Every day we make decisions— what clothes to wear, whom to lunch with, what to eat, which movie to see, whether or not to answer the telephone. Occasionally, our decisions are of vital importance: whom to trust, what to major in, what profession to follow, which social policy to support, which person to marry, whether or not to have children, and so on. How we make both trivial and important decisions depends on how we make sense of our social world.

How Do We Make Sense of the World?

We humans have powerful and efficient brains. But wonderful as they are, they are far from perfect. One consequence of this imperfection is that most of us end up "knowing" a lot of things that simply are not true. Let us take a common example: Many people harbor the belief that relatively infertile couples who adopt a baby are subsequently more likely to conceive a child of their own than relatively infertile couples who do not adopt. The reasoning goes something like this: After the adoption, the pressure is off; now that the couple is relaxed, this somehow makes conception easier. But according to Tom Gilovich,[4] this belief, while widespread, is simply not true; relatively infertile couples who adopt a baby are no more likely to conceive than relatively infertile couples who do not adopt. Why do most people believe it is so? Two reasons: (1) It is such a charming and comforting idea that we *want* it to be true; (2) we tend to focus our attention on those few instances when adoptive parents conceived a baby of their own and *not* on those instances when they failed to conceive or when nonadoptive parents conceived a baby. Thus, because of selective attention and selective memory, it sure *seems* to be true.

Are we rational animals or not? We sure try to be. One common view of human cognition is that it is completely rational; each individual attempts to do his or her best to be right and to hold correct opinions and beliefs. One of the primary proponents of this view of human thought was the eighteenth-century utilitarian philosopher Jeremy Bentham. According to Bentham, we engage in a *felicific calculus*, or happiness calculation, to determine what is good and what is bad.[5] To take a mundane example, suppose I wanted to purchase a new car. In determining the make and model to buy, I would add up the pleasures each brand would bring—sporty design, comfortable interior, powerful engine—and subtract the pain—the monthly payments that will mortgage my future, the high cost of frequent fill-ups at the pump, and so on. I then select the car that brings me the most pleasure with the least amount of pain. For Bentham, it was the role of governments and economic systems to ensure "the greatest happiness for the greatest number." Others agreed, for Bentham's concept of felicific calculus became a fundamental assumption underlying modern capitalism.

More recently, the social psychologist Harold Kelley has advanced a slightly more complex view of the rationality of human thought: People attempt to function as *naive scientists*.[6] In order to arrive at the best explanation for a given event or phenomenon, scientists look for covariation in their data—that is, they attempt to find cases where "X came before Y and always varied with Y and only with Y to conclude that X caused Y." Similarly, in explaining other people's behavior, people look for three pieces of information: the *consistency* of the person's action (Does he or she always behave in this manner in other situations and at other times?), *consensus* (Do others behave in the same way in the same situation?), and/or the *distinctiveness* of the action (Is he or she the only one to behave in this manner?).

For example, suppose Beth kisses Scott and someone asks you why. According to Kelley, before you could give a reasonable answer to that question, you would want to know a bit more about the situation: Does Beth go around kissing almost everyone at the drop of a hat? Beth's consistency would probably lead you to conclude that the reason Beth kissed Scott is that Beth is a very affectionate person. But suppose you found out that almost *everybody* kisses Scott. The consensus would suggest that the reason Beth kissed Scott is that Scott is a very kissable person who everybody likes. Finally, if Beth kisses only Scott and no one else kisses Scott, the distinctiveness of the kissing is due to some special relationship between Beth and Scott; either they are in love or Scott has done something especially deserving of a kiss.

Of course, the way we use information to make attributions can underlie far more important decisions than deciding why one person kisses another. Teachers must decide why students fail. Juries must decide innocence or guilt. Nations must decide how to respond to the provocations of other nations. In all such cases, a systematic weighing of consensus, consistency, and distinctiveness information can be highly valuable and extraordinarily important.

But do people really think this way? Are we as rational as Bentham and Kelley suggest we are?[7] There is little argument that we *are* capable of such behavior. For example, Benjamin Franklin reports that he routinely performed a felicific calculation by writing down the pros and cons for major decisions. There are times when many of us behave in the same way—as when purchasing a new car or deciding which college to attend. And the ease with which you could generate conclusions about Beth and Scott when given the appropriate covariation information indicates that it is at least possible to think like a naive scientist. However, rational thought requires at least two conditions: (1) the thinker has access to accurate, useful information, and (2) the thinker has the mental resources needed to process life's data. These conditions almost never hold in everyday life.

We do *not* possess a "God's-eye" view of the world—a perspective that is all-knowing and free from bias. Consider something as simple as my car purchase. I probably do not know all the facts. If it's a new model, long-term repair data simply do not exist. Furthermore, my view of the car is bounded by my own limited perspective; I hear about the car primarily from advertisers, who are motivated to exaggerate its positive features. I have limited experience with the car—a 10-minute dealer-supervised test drive as opposed to long-term driving in all kinds of hazardous road and weather conditions. If something as common as a new-car purchase can be fraught with missing and misleading information, imagine the difficulty when it comes to making more unusual decisions such as when to go to war, whom to marry, or how to spend tax money.

Moreover, even if the data were available, I simply do not have the leisure time or the motivation to devote to a full-scale analysis of every problem I encounter. Suppose I go ahead and make a felicific calculation on which car to purchase, and it takes about 5 hours of research and weighing of alternatives. In the meantime, a dozen other decisions need to be made: What shall I do for lunch? How should I revise my lecture notes? Which job candidate is best to hire? Does my daughter really need those expensive braces on her teeth (what's wrong with an overbite, anyway)?

Am I to spend several precious hours listing the pros and cons on each of these decisions while dozens of upcoming decisions are postponed? We live in a message-dense, decision-rich environment. The average American will see over 7 million advertisements in his or her lifetime and will need to make countless decisions every day—some important, some trivial, some seemingly trivial but with important consequences. It is impossible to think deeply about each and every piece of information that comes our way and about each and every decision that must be made.

What do we do? As you might guess, we try to use shortcuts whenever we can. According to Susan Fiske and Shelley Taylor, we human beings are **cognitive misers**—that is, we are forever trying to conserve our cognitive energy.[8] Given our limited capacity to process information, we attempt to adopt strategies that simplify complex problems. We accomplish this by ignoring some information to reduce our cognitive load; or we "overuse" other information to keep from having to search for more; or we may be willing to accept a less-than-perfect alternative because it is almost good enough. The strategies of the cognitive miser may be efficient—making fairly good use of our limited cognitive capacity to process a nearly infinite world of information— but these strategies can also lead to serious errors and biases, especially when we select an inappropriate shortcut or, in our rush to move on, we ignore a vital piece of information.[9]

Some readers may be disheartened to find that they are not as rational or as thorough in their thinking as they might have supposed. It is exciting to believe that the human mind has unlimited power or that we have a personal pipeline to absolute, objective truth. But, disheartened or not, it is critical to realize that our shortcuts can produce biases and prejudices that obscure the truth. Unless we recognize our cognitive limitations we will be enslaved by them. For example, if we fail to recognize that we often judge others on the basis of stereotypes or that the specific manner in which a piece of information is presented can bias our judgments, we will be unable to take steps to correct such errors. Worse yet, if we fail to understand the consequences of being cognitive misers, we are more prone to confuse our own interpretations of things with absolute truth and assume that those who don't share our perspective are misguided, stupid, crazy—or evil. As history demonstrates, it becomes easier for people to commit acts of hatred and cruelty to the extent that they are certain they are absolutely right.[10] Our propensity for bias and error, then, can be a significant barrier to interpersonal and intergroup understanding.

The fact that we are cognitive misers does not mean we are doomed to distort. Once we know some of the limitations and common biases of the human mind, we can begin to think a little better and make smarter decisions. It is my purpose in this chapter to do more than list some of these limitations of our thinking. Rather, by exploring these limitations, I hope that we can learn to think a little more clearly.

The Effects of Context on Social Judgment

Let's begin by looking at how the social context—the way things are presented and described—affects our judgments about people, including ourselves. We will take, in turn, four different aspects of the social context: the comparison of alternatives, the thoughts primed by a situation, how a decision is framed or posed, and the way information is presented. As we do so, a basic principle of social thinking should emerge: All judgment is relative; how we think about a person or thing is dependent on its surrounding context.

Reference Points and Contrast Effects An object can appear to be better or worse than it is, depending on what it is compared to. I suspect that most salespeople implicitly understand this phenomenon. Some act on it. Let me illustrate by taking you house shopping with a real estate agent. After determining your needs, the agent drives you to some homes "you might find interesting." The first stop is a tiny two-bedroom house sitting on a smallish lot. The house needs a new coat of paint; the interior is in disarray; the linoleum in the kitchen is buckling; the living room carpet is worn and smells bad; the master bedroom is so small that an average-sized bedroom suite simply won't fit. When the realtor tells you the asking price, you are stunned: "Holy cow! They want that much for this place? Who'd be dumb enough to pay so much for this shack?" Certainly not you and probably not anyone else. But how do you suppose viewing that dilapidated house might influence your evaluation of the average-looking house you are shown next?

In a sense, the dilapidated house is a decoy—and decoys can exercise a powerful impact on our decisions, by influencing the way the alternatives look. This process was nicely illustrated in an experiment by Anthony Pratkanis and his colleagues.[11] In this experiment, in the control condition, students were asked to make a series of decisions such as the following: Which would you select, (a) or (b)?

a. *Nutri-burger:* a burger made from tofu and other vegetables that is rated very good on nutrition but only average on taste.

b. *Tasti-burger:* a hamburger that is rated very good on taste but only average on nutrition.

So far, so good. The decision is a clear one: If you want good taste more than good nutrition, you will go for the Tasti-burger; if nutrition matters more, you will go for the Nutri-burger. And in this experiment, roughly half of the students selected the Tasti-burger and half selected the Nutri-burger.

But suppose we were working for the makers of Tasti-burger. How might we make it more attractive? We might insert a decoy. A **decoy** is an alternative that is clearly inferior to other possible selections—but serves the purpose of making one of the others—the one it's most similar to—look better by comparison. In the Pratkanis experiment, half of the students were given the following choice: Which would you prefer, (a), (b), or (c)?

a. *Nutri-burger:* a burger made from tofu and other vegetables that is rated very good on nutrition but only average on taste (exactly as described in the control condition).

b. *Tasti-burger:* a hamburger that is rated very good on taste but only average on nutrition (exactly as described in the control condition).

c. *Bummer-burger:* a hamburger that is rated only good on taste and only average on nutrition.

No reasonable person would select the Bummer-burger; it is neither as nutritious as the Nutri-burger nor as flavorful as the Tasti-burger. But even though no one chose it, putting the Bummer-burger on the menu had an effect; significantly more people in this condition chose the Tasti-burger over the Nutri-burger. How did a worthless burger create such a clear preference? The answer in a nutshell is: the **contrast effect.** In contrast to the Bummer-burger, the Tasti-burger looked great. When any object is contrasted with something similar but not as good (or pretty, or tall, etc.), that particular object is judged to be better, prettier, and taller than would normally be the case. For example, if a man of normal height (say, 5 feet 11 inches) is in the company of midgets, he seems very tall. If he is a member of a professional basketball team, he seems very short. Some of you may recall a young man who played basketball for the Boston Celtics several years ago named "Tiny" Archibald. Would it surprise you to learn that "Tiny" stood 6 feet 1 inch tall? In Jonathan Swift's classic novel *Gulliver's Travels,* the hero, a man of normal height, was considered a giant when traveling among the residents of Lilliput and a dwarf when traveling among the residents of Brobdingnag. This is the contrast effect.

One of my favorite examples of the contrast effect was produced in an experiment by Douglas Kenrick and Sara Gutierres,[12] who asked male college students to rate the attractiveness of a potential blind date before or after watching an episode of the popular television show *Charlie's Angels.* (As you may recall, the "angels" were extraordinarily attractive young women.) The males rated their blind date as far less attractive after they saw the show than before. The "angels" provided a stringent context for rating attractiveness; almost anyone would suffer by contrast.

Contrast effects can occur subtly and can have powerful effects. A used-car dealer may place an old clunker on the lot to "improve the appearance" of the autos in its immediate vicinity. A presidential candidate may select a vice-presidential running mate of lesser stature to enhance the positive perception of his or her own presidential qualities. And that dilapidated house the realtor showed you? You'll never buy it—but it's guaranteed to make all the other houses you see next look like better deals. The lesson to be learned from research on contrast effects is that the selection of comparisons makes a difference. Depending on the context, objects and alternatives can be made to look better or worse. Often we do not pay much attention to the influence of context, much less question the validity of the alternatives presented. This greatly enhances the power of "context makers" such as politicians, advertisers, journalists, and sales agents. The context they set can influence our perceptions and judgments, lulling us into decisions that we might not otherwise make.

Important judgments we make about ourselves can also be powerfully influenced by contrast effects. For example, many high school valedictorians experience a dip in self-esteem when they arrive at an elite college to find themselves surrounded by other former high school valedictorians. No longer the smartest kid around, they can feel stupid merely by being average.[13] Similarly, research has shown that, when people are exposed to images of beautiful people, they will rate themselves as less attractive than those shown images of more average-looking people.[14]

Priming and Construct Accessibility

One of the standard comedic devices on television sitcoms is the *double entendre*. A typical double entendre goes like this: Early in the show, the young teenage daughter tells everyone but her father that she made the school's coed softball team as the starting catcher. On the other hand, her father finds out about a big party sponsored by some of his daughter's classmates that promises to have "some wild goings-on" and just happens to be scheduled on the same night as the softball game. The climactic scene involves the father overhearing his "innocent" daughter telling her friend about a pitcher:

> "Boy, I can hardly wait for tonight—I am so excited. I've never played with Tommy before. I love his technique. If he tries, I know he can go all the way. Tommy has wonderful stuff." The father is outraged and storms out of the house to intercept his young daughter. The audience is "entertained" because they know what is happening; the father thinks his daughter is talking about sex when she is really discussing softball.

The double entendre of the sitcom illustrates an important principle of **social cognition**: How we interpret social events usually depends on what we are currently thinking about, as well as what beliefs and categories we typically use to make sense of things. The categories we use to interpret the world can vary with the individual; some people see the world through rose-colored glasses, whereas others see it in hostile or depressive terms. Our interpretation can also depend on what happens to be prominent in the situation. And what is prominent can be induced through **priming**—a procedure based on the notion that ideas that have been recently encountered or frequently activated are more likely to come to mind and thus will be used in interpreting social events.

A study by Tory Higgins, William Rholes, and Carl Jones illustrates the role of priming in the formation of impressions about other people.[15] In this experiment, subjects were asked to participate in two "different" research projects—one on perception and one on reading comprehension. The first experiment served to prime different trait categories; some of the subjects were asked to remember positive trait words (*adventurous, self-confident, independent,* and *persistent*), whereas the others were asked to remember negative trait words (*reckless, conceited, aloof,* and *stubborn*). Five minutes later, as part of the "reading comprehension" study, subjects then read an ambiguous paragraph about a fictitious person named Donald.

The paragraph described a number of behaviors performed by Donald that could be interpreted as either adventurous or reckless (e.g., skydiving), self-confident or conceited (e.g., believes in his abilities), independent or aloof (e.g., doesn't rely on anyone), and persistent or stubborn (e.g., doesn't change his mind often). The subjects then described Donald in their own words and rated how desirable they considered him to be. The results showed that how they were primed influenced their impressions of Donald. When negative trait categories had been primed, they characterized Donald in negative terms and saw him as less desirable than when positive categories had been primed.

Thus, cues too subtle for us to consciously notice can color our judgments about other people's behavior. But can such cues affect our own behavior? Apparently so. John Bargh and his associates have conducted studies showing surprisingly strong effects of exposure to words on behavior.[16] In one study, participants unscrambled jumbled-up words (anagrams) and were told to go get the experimenter in the next room when they were finished. Unbeknownst to the participants, the anagram task exposed them to different kinds of words; some participants saw words related to rudeness (intrude, disturb) whereas others saw more neutral words. Later when it was time to fetch the experimenter, the participants found him in the hallway deeply engaged in a conversation with another person. Compared to the participants primed with neutral words, those who had seen words associated with rudeness were far more likely to interrupt the conversation.

In a similar study, after being primed with words either consistent with the stereotype of old people (Florida, retirement) or with unrelated words, participants were observed walking down the hallway away from the experiment. Those primed with the elderly stereotype walked significantly more slowly—like the old people they were primed to think about. For brief periods of time, at least, we can "become" whomever or whatever pops into our mind.

Priming can and does have a major impact on the attitudes and behavior of many people—even of seasoned professionals in life-and-death situations in the real world. For example, consider experienced physicians who work with AIDS patients. One might imagine that they would have a clear, solid idea about their own risk of infection. Linda Heath and her colleagues[17] found that this is not necessarily the case. They asked several hundred physicians about their perceived risk of contracting HIV on the job. For one group of physicians, Heath primed their thoughts about the danger by getting them to imagine their being exposed to the virus while doing their work. The assessment of risk of these physicians was deeply affected by the priming. Specifically, those physicians who were instructed to imagine themselves being exposed to HIV on the job subsequently felt that there was a significantly higher risk of their being infected than did those who were not primed. This was true regardless of the extent of the physicians' actual experiences with HIV-infected patients.

Let us look at priming in the mass media. Several studies have shown that there is a link between which stories the media cover and what viewers consider to be the most important issues of the day.[18] In other words, the mass media make certain issues and concepts readily accessible and thereby set the public's political and social agendas. To take one example, in a pioneering study of an election in North Carolina, Maxwell McCombs and Donald Shaw[19] found that the issues voters came to consider to be most important in the campaign coincided precisely with the amount of coverage of those issues in the local media. In a similar vein, vast numbers of heterosexuals first became deeply concerned about the dangers of AIDS immediately following the extensive media coverage of basketball superstar Magic Johnson's announcement that he was HIV-positive.[20]

In an interesting series of experiments, the political psychologists Shanto Iyengar, Mark Peters, and Donald Kinder demonstrated the importance of priming to account for the relationship between repeated media exposure and issue importance.[21] In one experiment, the researchers edited the evening news so that participants received a steady dose of news reports about a specific problem facing the United States. For example, some participants watched reports of the weaknesses of U.S. defense capabilities; others watched reports emphasizing pollution concerns; a third group watched accounts of inflation and economic matters.

The results were clear. After a week of viewing the edited programs, participants emerged from the experiment convinced that the target problem—the one primed by extensive coverage in the programs they watched—was more important for the country to solve than they did before viewing the programs. What's more, the research participants acted on their newfound perceptions, evaluating the president's performance on the basis of how he handled the target problem, and were more positively disposed toward candidates who stated strong positions on those issues. As the political scientist Bernard Cohen observed:

The mass media may not be successful much of the time in telling people *what to think,* but it is stunningly successful in telling its readers *what to think about.* . . . The world will look different to different people, depending . . . on the map that is drawn for them by the writers, editors, and publishers of the papers they read.[22]

Framing the Decision Another factor influencing how we construct our social world is decision **framing**—whether a problem or decision is presented in a such a way that it appears to represent the potential for a loss or for a gain. To illustrate the power of decision framing, let's imagine that you are the president of the United States and the country is bracing itself for the outbreak of an unusual epidemic expected to kill 600 people. Your top advisors have prepared two alternative programs to combat the disease and have estimated, to the best of their ability, the likely consequences of adopting each program.

- If Program A is adopted, 200 people will be saved.
- If Program B is adopted, there is a one-third probability that 600 people will be saved and a two-thirds probability that no people will be saved.

Ms. or Mr. President, which program do you favor? Please think about this carefully and answer before you read on.

If you are like most of the subjects in an experiment performed by Daniel Kahneman and Amos Tversky, you would select Program A (72 percent of their subjects selected this option).[23] You might think to yourself, "Program A guarantees that 200 people will be saved, and Program B gambles the lives of these people for only a 1 in 3 chance that we could save more lives."

But suppose your advisors had asked for your judgment in a different manner. Suppose they presented the problem this way:

- If Program A is adopted, 400 people will die.
- If Program B is adopted, there is a one-third probability that nobody will die and a two-thirds probability that 600 people will die.

Which program would you favor? Please think about this carefully and answer the question before reading more.

The two options are functionally identical. In both versions, Program A means that 200 people will live and 400 will die; Program B results in a one-third chance that no one will die and 600 people will live and a two-thirds chance that no one will be saved and 600 people will die. But for most people, their thinking about the epidemic is quite different. They think, "If I go with Program A, 400 people will surely die. I might as well gamble on B." When asked in this second manner, 78 percent of Kahneman and Tversky's subjects favored Program B!

Why did such a simple rewording of the options produce such a drastic switch in answers? Kahneman and Tversky have noted that people dislike losses and seek to avoid them. It is more painful to give up $20 than it is pleasurable to gain $20. Your advisors framed the first policy decision so that Program B looked like the bigger loss; in the second version, your advisors framed it so that Program A looked like a sure loss. How the question is framed is of enormous importance.

But this is just an imaginary event. It is a hypothetical situation. Surely such a simple rewording of a request cannot influence real behavior. Don't bet on it. In an experiment I did in collaboration with two of my students, Marti Gonzales and Mark Costanzo, we showed that framing can play a major role in determining whether or not people are willing to commit several hundred dollars to insulate their homes in order to conserve energy.[24] In one condition, after examining each home, energy experts gave each homeowner a detailed, individualized description of how much money they could *save* each year on heating bills. In the other condition, auditors were trained to frame the description in terms of *loss;* that is, they provided the same information but informed the homeowners that they were losing money every day—that it was akin to throwing money out the window. Homeowners in the "loss" condition were twice as likely to invest the money to insulate their homes as those in the "save" condition.

Let's look at the prevention of breast cancer. Breast cancer poses a serious health threat for many women. Fortunately, early detection and diagnosis of breast cancer can greatly improve a woman's chances of surviving the disease. However, one of the best methods for detecting breast cancer, a monthly breast self-examination, is not performed regularly by the vast majority of women. Beth Meyerowitz and Shelly Chaiken developed and distributed three pamphlets designed to increase routine breast self-examination by women.[25] One pamphlet contained only information concerning the need to perform self-examinations plus how to do it. The second pamphlet contained this information plus arguments emphasizing the positive consequences of self-examination (e.g., women who perform such examinations have an *increased* chance of finding a tumor at the early, treatable stage). The third pamphlet stressed the negative consequences of failing to perform a self-examination (e.g., women who do not perform such examinations have a *decreased* chance of finding the tumor at the early, treatable stage). Meyerowitz and Chaiken found that, 4 months after reading the pamphlet, only those women who received the pamphlet stressing the negative consequences were significantly more likely to perform breast self-examination. How you frame a decision can make a big difference in a life-and-death situation.

The Ordering of Information Another factor influencing the way we organize and interpret the social world is the manner in which information is arranged and distributed. Let's look at two characteristics of the way information is presented and their effects on social judgment: (1) what comes first and (2) the amount of information given.

The Primacy Effect and Impression Formation

In the preceding chapter, we discussed the order of presentation for persuasive arguments—that is, in a debate, the conditions under which it is more effective to state one's arguments first (primacy effect) or last (recency effect). When it comes to forming impressions of other people, however, there is not much of a contest: With few exceptions, the old saw "Put your best foot forward" turns out to be accurate; the things we learn first about a person have a decisive impact on our judgment of that person. In a pioneering experiment, Solomon Asch demonstrated the power of the primacy effect in impression formation.[26] In Asch's study, subjects received descriptive sentences such as the following and then were asked to rate the person described in each sentence.

a. Steve is intelligent, industrious, impulsive, critical, stubborn, and envious.

b. Steve is envious, stubborn, critical, impulsive, industrious, and intelligent.

Note that the two sentences contain exactly the same information about Steve; however, sentence (a) puts the positive traits first, whereas sentence (b) puts them last. Asch found that Steve was rated more positively when he was described by sentence (a) compared to sentence (b)—a primacy effect.

Asch's original finding has been repeated many times in many ways. For example, in experiments by Edward Jones and his colleagues, research participants observed another individual performing on a series of 30 intelligence test items.[27] In each case, the person answered 15 of the 30 questions correctly. However, sometimes the person started out "hot"—that is, answering a lot of questions correctly at the beginning—and then declined in performance; at other times, the person started out slow, answering few questions correctly at first, and then finished with a bang, answering most of the final items. Who was perceived as most intelligent? As one might expect based on what we know about the primacy effect, the individual who started out "hot" was seen as more intelligent than the "late bloomer," despite the fact that both answered the same number of questions correctly.

An interesting exception to this rule was discovered in an experiment by Joshua Aronson and Edward Jones,[28] who motivated their subjects to try to improve the performance of a target person ("student") on a set of anagrams. Half of the subjects were instructed simply to try to raise their student's score; the remaining subjects were instructed to try to improve the *ability* of their student to solve anagrams. Within each of these conditions, after training their students, all subjects received information about their student's performance. This performance information was exactly like that in the Jones experiment cited above: That is, some received information that the earlier performance of their student was very good and the later performance was not so good; others received information that the early performance was not so good and the later performance was very good. The sum total was identical—only the order differed.

Those subjects who were motivated to improve the performance of their students rated them as more intelligent when their *early* performance was good. This is the primacy effect: They trained their students to do well and, after the first few trials, concluded that their students were intelligent—regardless of their later performance. But those subjects who were trying to improve the *ability* of their students to solve anagrams rated as more intelligent those who started poorly but ended up doing well. In other words, they were more impressed with *increases* in performance than with a fast start. Ability is something that develops. Thus, we like to see our students improve; it means they have real ability.

Although the results of the Aronson and Jones experiment demonstrate the complexity of the phenomenon, it is an interesting exception to the general rule. And with very few exceptions, in forming impressions of people, primacy predominates.

Why does the primacy effect in impression formation occur? Researchers have found evidence for two explanations—either of which can be true, depending on the circumstances. According to the *attention decrement* explanation, the later items in a list receive less attention as the observers tire and their minds start to wander; thus, these items have less impact on judgment. According to the *interpretive set* explanation, the first items serve to create an initial impression that then is used to interpret subsequent information, either through the discounting of incongruent facts (i.e., if Steve is intelligent, why should he be envious?) or by subtle changes in the meaning of the words further down the list (i.e., being critical is a positive attribute if Steve is intelligent but a negative one if he is stubborn). Regardless of the explanation, the primacy effect has an important impact on social judgment. Moreover, we usually have little control over the order in which we receive information—whether that information is from a television news show or from our everyday observations of friends and neighbors. Therefore, it is important to realize the existence of these effects so that we can try to correct for them.

The Amount of Information When pondering a difficult decision, a common plea is often heard: "If I only had more information." Although having more information may sometimes be helpful, it can also change how an object is perceived and evaluated through what is called the **dilution effect**— the tendency for neutral and irrelevant information to weaken a judgment or impression. Consider this example, taken from an experiment by Henry Zukier.[29] Which student has the higher grade point average?

- Tim spends about 31 hours studying outside of class in an average week.
- Tom spends about 31 hours studying outside of class in an average week. Tom has one brother and two sisters. He visits his grandparents about once every 3 months. He once went on a blind date and shoots pool about once every 2 months.

If you are similar to the students in Zukier's study, you would believe that Tim is smarter than Tom. Zukier found that including irrelevant and nondiagnostic information (such as information on siblings, family visits, and dating habits) that has nothing to do with the issue at hand can dilute—that is, make less potent—the impact of relevant information (that both Tim and Tom spend a lot of time studying).

The dilution effect has obvious practical value for persons interested in managing impressions, such as those in sales or politics. Advertisers know that including weak or irrelevant claims can reduce the impact of a strong sales appeal. A disliked politician can reduce the impact of his negative image by including irrelevant information—a story about his or her childhood or a description of the family house—in campaign advertisements. But why does the dilution effect occur? After all, it makes little sense to pay attention to nondiagnostic information in making a judgment. Why should information on dating habits make someone appear to be less intelligent or a story about the birthplace of a politician lessen the impact of his or her negative image? One answer is that irrelevant information about a person makes that person seem more similar to others, and thus more average and like everyone else. An average person is less likely to have an extremely high grade-point average or to be terribly negative.

Judgmental Heuristics

One way that we make sense of the buzzing, blooming array of information that comes our way is through the use of **judgmental heuristics.** A judgmental heuristic is a mental shortcut; it is a simple, often only approximate, rule or strategy for solving a problem.[30] Some examples include "If a man and a woman are walking down a street, the man walks on the outside." "If a particular food item is found in a health food store, it must be good for you." "If a person is from a rural town in Arkansas, he or she must be intellectually backward." Heuristics require very little thought—just the selection of the rule (which may not be the correct one to use) and a straightforward application to the issue at hand. It can be contrasted with more systematic thinking in which we may look at a problem from a number of angles, assemble and evaluate as much relevant information as possible, and work out in detail the implications of various solutions. Let's look at two of the most common classes of judgmental heuristics—the representative and the attitude heuristics.

The Representative Heuristic According to Daniel Kahneman and Amos Tversky,[31] when we use the **representative heuristic,** we focus on the similarity of one object to another to infer that the first object acts like the second one. For example, we know that high-quality products are expensive; therefore, if something is expensive, we might infer that it is really good. Thus, if I see two bottles of wine on the shelf and one has a higher price, I leap to the conclusion that it is the better wine. I select the one feature (price) from among the many others that I *might* have focused on—such as type of grape, vintner, vintage, wine-growing region—and I use that to make my decision. But, as most smart consumers know, high price does not always mean high quality. Let's look in more detail at the implications of the use of the representative heuristic by eavesdropping on a conversation between mother and child in the aisle of a local supermarket.

Picture the scene: Seven-year-old Rachel spots her favorite cereal, Lucky Charms, takes a box off the shelf, and quietly delivers it to the shopping cart. Her mom looks at the box in disgust. It is bright red. A leprechaun is sprinkling shining stars (must be sugar) over pink and purple marshmallow bits. On the back of the box, her mom finds a message informing her that an enclosed special pair of glasses are to be used to find hidden leprechauns.

Mom sternly announces, "Rachel, put that junk back on the shelf. It is loaded with sugar and nothing but empty calories."

Rachel replies, "But Mom, it tastes good."

Being a smart mom, she offers Rachel another choice and a little inducement. "Why not this one? It's called 100% Natural. It is good for you. Eat this and you'll grow up to be a big girl."

Rachel looks at the box. It is small but heavy. The picture on the front features a bowl of light brown cereal set against a wood-grain background and a couple of stalks of unprocessed grains. On the back of the box is a lot of small, hard-to-read writing.

Rachel exclaims, "Yukko! I don't want to be a big girl."

How would you resolve the great breakfast cereal standoff? Would you side with the mother and opt for nutrition even though Rachel may not like it? Or would you feel that Rachel, even at this tender age, should be making her own decisions, regardless of the consequences? My recommendation may surprise you: The fight is for naught. Tell Rachel and her mom to buy the Lucky Charms because, in actuality, it is more nutritious than the "natural" cereal. If Rachel's mom had bothered to read the fine print and conducted a systematic comparison between Lucky Charms and 100% Natural, she would have discovered that Lucky Charms is lower in calories and saturated fats than 100% Natural.[32] While it is also slightly higher in sugar, this difference is negligible and of little dietary importance. Indeed, in 1981 *Consumer Reports,* a highly respected source of consumer information, conducted a test of breakfast cereals.[33] Their researchers fed young rats, which have nutritional requirements remarkably similar to those of humans, a diet composed exclusively of water and one of 32 brands of breakfast cereal for a period of 14 to 18 weeks. They found that the rats grew and remained healthy on a diet of Lucky Charms. On the other hand, a diet of Quaker's 100% Natural actually stunted their growth!

What caused the disagreement between Rachel and her mom? It is clear that they used the cereal *package* (not the cereal) as a representative heuristic. In this case, the problem for Mom was to select a nutritious cereal; for Rachel the problem was to get a cereal that was fun and tasty. The box of Lucky Charms resembles a child's toy—bright colors, cartoon character, glistening sugar. We infer that this cereal is "childish," and since children eat junk food if not carefully supervised, this cereal must be junk. On the other hand, the 100% Natural box has the earth tones and a picture of unprocessed grains; it resembles nature itself. And, of course, the brand name is consistent; it is "natural" and, in our minds, the natural is equated with the good, the wholesome. The cereal must be nutritious.

The representative heuristic can be used in places other than the supermarket.[34] An analysis of folk remedies and early Western medicine shows that a common assumption is that the cure should resemble the cause of the disease. For example, in one culture, epilepsy is treated with a drug made from a monkey whose movements appear epileptic. Similarly, in Western culture, newspapers initially ridiculed Walter Reed's suggestion that yellow fever was carried by a mosquito, since there is little resemblance between the cause (mosquitoes) and the result (malaria). The representative heuristic is used to identify psychological causes as well. For example, in the 1960s and 1970s, many conservative adults clung to the belief that the political radicalism exhibited by the college students of that era was caused by permissive child-rearing practices. In early psychoanalytic theorizing, an obsessive-compulsive personality was known as anal-retentive and was believed to be the direct result of early and severe toilet-training practices. In the overwhelming majority of American presidential elections, the taller of the two major candidates has emerged victorious—suggesting the possibility that some Americans may implicitly believe that height may have something to do with the ability to lead.

The representative heuristic is often used to form impressions and to make judgments about other persons. The first information that we pick up about a person—information about gender, race, physical attractiveness, and social status—is usually associated with simple rules that guide thought and behavior. Gender and ethnic stereotypes tell us "just how men and women differ" and "what a particular member of an ethnic group is like." Much research has demonstrated that most people leap to the conclusion that beautiful people are more successful, sensitive, warmer, and of better character than less attractive people. Persons of high social stature, often inferred by dress and mannerisms, are respected and held in high esteem. Is it any wonder that "get ahead" self-help books often describe how to take advantage of these heuristics by urging their readers to "dress for success," that is, to wear the kinds of clothes that will create the image of a successful person? This is the representative heuristic in action.

The Availability Heuristic Suppose you go to a restaurant with some friends. Your friend Neal orders a steak with onion rings, but the waiter brings his steak with fries instead. "Oh, well," he says. "No big deal—I like fries almost as much as onion rings." This opens a discussion as to whether he should have sent back his order; Marlene accuses Neal of being unassertive. He turns to you and asks, "Do you think I'm an unassertive person?" How would you answer this question?

If you know Neal well and have already formed a picture of how assertive he is, you can recite your answer easily and quickly. Suppose, however, that you've never really thought about how assertive Neal is. In this kind of situation, most of us will rely on how quickly and easily an example might come to mind. If it is easy to think of one vivid occasion when Neal acted assertively (e.g., "that time he stopped someone from crashing in line in front of him at the movies"), you will conclude that Neal is a pretty assertive guy. If it is easier to think of an occasion when Neal acted unassertively (e.g., "that time he let a phone solicitor talk him into buying a Veg-O-Matic for $29.99"), you will conclude that he is pretty unassertive.

This mental rule of thumb is called the **availability heuristic,** which refers to judgments based on how easy it is for us to bring specific examples to mind. There are many situations in which the availability heuristic will prove accurate and useful. Specifically, if you can easily bring to mind several examples of Neal standing up for his rights, he probably is an assertive person; if you can easily bring to mind several examples of Neal letting people push him around, he probably is not. The main problem with employing the availability heuristic is that sometimes what is easiest to bring to mind is not typical of the overall picture. This will lead us to faulty conclusions.

Let's try something: Do you think more people in the United States die from shark attacks or from falling airplane parts? Do you think more people die from fires or from drowning? Think about it for a minute.

When asked those questions, the overwhelming majority of people report that deaths from shark attacks are more common than those from falling airplane parts and that deaths from fires are more common than those from drowning. In fact, both answers are wrong. Why do most people believe these things? As Scott Plous suggests, it is probably easier to bring to mind examples of deaths from sharks and fires because these events are more likely to be covered in a vivid manner on the 6:00 news and thus are more available in people's memories.[35]

Similarly, if you ask people to estimate the number of violent crimes committed each year in the United States, you will get very different answers, depending on how much prime-time television they watch, as we learned in Chapter 3. People who watch a great deal of television—and, hence, see a great deal of fictionalized violence—vastly overestimate the amount of real crime that occurs in our nation.[36]

The Attitude Heuristic

The Attitude Heuristic An attitude is a special type of belief that includes emotional and evaluative components; in a sense, an attitude is a stored evaluation—good or bad—of an object. According to Anthony Pratkanis and Anthony Greenwald, people tend to use the **attitude heuristic** as a way of making decisions and solving problems.[37] Attitudes can be used to assign objects to a favorable class (for which strategies of favoring, approaching, praising, cherishing, and protecting are appropriate) or to an unfavorable category (for which strategies of disfavoring, avoiding, blaming, neglecting, and harming are used). For example, if Sam dislikes former President Ronald Reagan, then, when Sam thinks about the current federal deficit, he is apt to attribute its cause to the "charge card" economic policies Reagan employed in the 1980s.

Much research has shown that attitudes can be used to make sense of our social world. For example, a study by Anthony Pratkanis found that a person's attitudes play a major role in determining what he or she "knows" to be true.[38] In this study, college students were asked to identify which of two possible statements—such as the following—was true:

a. Ronald Reagan maintained an A average at Eureka College.
b. Ronald Reagan never achieved above a C average at Eureka College.

What did Pratkanis find? Very few people actually know what Reagan's college grades were; their answer depended on their attitude toward him. Students who liked Reagan were more likely to believe statement (a); students who disliked him were more likely to believe statement (b). What is more, the more extreme the attitude toward Reagan, the more confidence the students had in their judgments. In other words, the students in this study used their attitudes as a heuristic to discern what is true and then believed that what they determined was correct. For those of you who are curious, statement (b) is correct. Reagan never achieved above a C average in college. (I hasten to add that this is an actual fact and has nothing to do with my personal attitude toward Mr. Reagan!)

The use of an attitude heuristic can influence our logic and ability to reason. For example, in the late 1940s, Donald Thistlewaite asked respondents to state whether syllogisms such as the following were valid:[39]

Premise 1: If production is important, then peaceful industrial relations are desirable.

Premise 2: If production is important, then it is a mistake to have Negroes for foremen and leaders over Whites.

Therefore: If peaceful industrial relations are desirable, then it is a mistake to have Negroes for foremen and leaders over Whites.

A moment's reflection shows that the syllogism, as stated, is fallacious; the conclusion does not logically follow from the premises. But Thistlewaite found that prejudiced individuals (who agree with the conclusion) are far more likely to indicate (incorrectly) that the logic is valid compared to less prejudiced people.

Another dimension of the attitude heuristic is the **halo effect,** a general bias in which a favorable or unfavorable general impression of a person affects our inferences and future expectations about that person. For example, if you really like George W. Bush, then you will be likely to discount or explain away any behavior on his part that might be considered negative while exaggerating the goodness of his positive actions. In your mind, it is almost as if he is wearing an angel's halo. Similarly, a disliked individual is assumed to possess negative traits, with their performance subsequently devalued. In one experiment, Richard Stein and Carol Nemeroff[40] demonstrated that college students gave a halo (both positive and negative) to women, depending upon the kinds of food they ate: All other things being equal, once they found out that a woman ate health food, they rated her as more feminine, more physically attractive, and more likable than junk-food eaters.

Still another dimension of the attitude heuristic is the **false-consensus effect.** Almost all of us have a tendency to overestimate the percentage of people who agree with us on any issue. If I believe something, then I will leap to the conclusion that most other people feel the same way. For example, in one experiment, Lee Ross and his colleagues[41] asked college students if they were willing to wear a sign around the campus that said "Eat at Joe's." Those who agreed to wear the sign thought that most other people would too; those who decided against wearing the sign estimated that few other students would wear it. In other words, we often make the (not necessarily true) assumption that others like what we like and do what we prefer to do.

When Do We Use Heuristics? Of course, decisions don't have to be based on heuristics. Rachel's mother might have carefully read the ingredients on the cereal box, subscribed to a consumer magazine, or consulted nutrition textbooks. Similarly, we could carefully reason about an issue or study the record and accomplishments of a politician; this would make us less likely to use our attitudes as a simple way to make sense of the world. And, occasionally, most of us do go through the decision-making process in a rational manner.

This raises an important question: What conditions are most likely to lead to heuristic employment rather than rational decision making? Research has identified at least five such conditions.[42] As you might expect from our earlier discussion of humans as cognitive misers, heuristics are most likely to be used when we don't have time to think carefully about an issue, or when we are so overloaded with information that it becomes impossible to process the information fully, or when the issues at stake are not very important, so that we do not care to think about it. Heuristics are also used when we have little solid knowledge or information to use in making a decision.

A moment's thought will reveal that the persuasion landscape faced by Rachel and her mother contains many of the features that lead to heuristic decision making. If she is like most Americans, Rachel's mother is feeling increasingly time-pressed since her leisure time has eroded considerably in the last 10 years. As a consumer, she faces a message-dense environment complete with a choice of over 300 different brands of cereal currently on the market. She probably has had little consumer education or training. At the same time, she has been the recipient of millions of advertisements, each repeating and repeating a brand image, so that this image will quickly come to mind in the aisles of the local supermarket. Given this state of affairs, it is a wonder that all decisions aren't made heuristically.

Categorization and Social Stereotypes

Before the Persian Gulf War of 1991, the U.S. Congress held a series of debates on the positive and negative consequences of going to war. Those who supported the war described Saddam Hussein as the "new Hitler"; they emphasized the parallels between Saddam's gassing of the Kurds and Hitler's gassing of the Jews, Iraq's invasion of Kuwait and Germany's invasion of Poland and the Baltics, and Saddam's and Hitler's buildup of armaments. Those who opposed the war saw the situation in Iraq as paralleling that of Vietnam; they saw both incidents as civil wars—a fight between North and South Vietnam and between various Arab factions; they worried about the U.S. military's ability to fight in foreign terrain of swamps and deserts; they characterized the war efforts as a war in support of "big business" and "big oil."

In a sense, the debate over whether or not to go to war with Iraq was really a debate over whose categorization of ambiguous events was correct. And with good reason. For once it is decided how an event or person should be categorized, it becomes clear what course of action should be taken. If Saddam is truly a "new Hitler," then the policy of economic sanctions (which some considered a form of appeasement) will only bring additional threats to peace and ultimately a much worse war. If Iraq is another Vietnam, then intervention would lead to a long and divisive war, becoming mired in a quagmire with no clear victors and losers.[43]

We "debate" over how to categorize persons and events hundreds of times a week, and although we often do not go to war over the results, the consequences of how we interpret and define events can be significant. For example, I know a social psychologist whom I consider one of the best researchers of his generation. He is also a thoughtful and considerate human being and a leading contributor to theory X. However, he is rarely described as "a leading light in the field who cares about people" or "a major proponent of theory X."

Instead, he is primarily described as a "very talented black social psychologist." What are the consequences for this person to be referred to constantly as black as opposed to any one of a number of other equally applicable attributes? Later in this book, we will look in detail at the nature and consequences of prejudice. For now, let us look at how we categorize events and persons and with what effect.

Stereotypic Knowledge and Expectations One of the most important consequences of categorization is that it can invoke specific data or *stereotypes* that then guide our expectations. For example, each of the following words probably invokes some very specific meanings: *yuppie, college professor, party girl, racist,* and *liberal democrat.* Once we categorize a person or an event using one of these terms (as opposed to others), we base our expectations about future interactions on the accompanying stereotypes. Suppose I go into a cafe that a friend of mine has categorized as a "bar" as opposed to a "fine dining establishment." I will probably think of the place in different terms and act in a different way—and, if the categorization is erroneous, my behavior might be foolish and might even get me into serious trouble.

An interesting study by John Darley and Paget Gross[44] demonstrates the power of expectations to influence the way we think and make judgments about people. In their experiment, they told four different stories about "Hannah"—a fourth-grade schoolgirl. After hearing one of the four stories, college students were asked to estimate Hannah's academic ability. In the first two stories, subjects merely saw a videotape of Hannah playing in either a high-class neighborhood or a poor, run-down neighborhood. This was designed to create stereotypic expectations about Hannah's background. In the second two stories, subjects saw one of these videotapes of Hannah playing and, in addition, viewed a film of Hannah completing 25 achievement-test problems. Hannah's performance on these tests was ambiguous; she sometimes answered tough questions and missed easy ones.

Darley and Gross found that when subjects saw just one of the two videotapes of Hannah playing in the park, they rated her ability as average; Hannah was just like everyone else in her class. In other words, subjects who saw these videos did not apply their stereotypes about rich kids and poor kids to their judgments of her ability. However, when subjects also watched the film of Hannah solving achievement-test problems, the effects of the stereotypes became apparent: Subjects rated Hannah as having less ability when she came from the low as opposed to the high socioeconomic background; they also interpreted her ambiguous performance as consistent with their judgments—evaluating the test as easier and estimating that Hannah solved fewer problems when she came from a poor background. Two lessons can be learned about stereotypes from this experiment. First, most people seem to have some understanding of stereotypes; they seem reluctant to apply them in the absence of solid data. Second, despite this understanding, our stereotypes still influence our perceptions and judgments when there is additional ambiguous information that lends a false sense of rationality to the judgment.

Often, in real face-to-face interactions, the process observed in the Darley and Gross experiment does not stop with mere judgments. In a classic experiment Robert Rosenthal and Lenore Jacobson[45] planted a false stereotype in the heads of school teachers, which had a dramatic impact on the performance of their students. In this study, the experimenters first gave an IQ test to all the children in an elementary school. After scoring the tests, 20 percent of the children from each class were chosen at random. The teachers were informed that the test had indicated that these students were "bloomers," on the verge of making significant intellectual gains over the coming year, thus giving the teachers a false expectancy about some of their students. Then the researchers simply sat back and watched. At the end of the year, they administered another IQ test.

What happened? Those students whom the teachers falsely believed to be bloomers had indeed gotten smarter, making significantly larger gains in IQ than the children not labeled bloomers. The process by which such expectations or stereotypes lead people to treat others in a way that makes them confirm their expectations is called a **self-fulfilling prophecy.** We will encounter this phenomenon several times in the following chapters. A self-fulfilling prophecy occurs when we act on our impressions of others. So how did the teachers' expectations turn into increased intelligence among the students labeled as bloomers? When teachers see potential in their students they create a warmer "climate" for them (both verbally and nonverbally); they give those students more attention, more critical feedback, and more opportunities to respond. These are conditions under which anyone would make gains in intellectual ability. In short, their belief in the student's potential for growth—whether true or false—leads them to create the optimal conditions for the student to grow.

Seeing Relationships Where There Are None: The Illusory Correlation
Still another effect of categorization is that we frequently perceive a relationship between two entities that we think should be related—but, in fact, they are not. Social psychologists have dubbed this the **illusory correlation.** Let me illustrate what I mean by describing an experiment by David Hamilton and his colleagues.[46] In this experiment, subjects read 24 statements that described different persons by their name, their occupation, and two prominent character traits. For example, subjects read statements such as "Tom, the salesman, is talkative and boring" or "Bill, the accountant, is timid and courteous." Occasionally, by chance, the trait words happened to be consistent with the common stereotype most people have of that occupation; that is, the salesman was occasionally described as enthusiastic and talkative or the accountant as perfectionist and timid. The data clearly showed that subjects overestimated the frequency with which stereotypic words were used

to describe each occupation. In other words, they succeeded in creating an illusory correlation between trait and occupation.

The illusory correlation shows up quite often in social judgments. Consider these two examples: In informal surveys, people consistently overestimate the extent to which lesbians are likely to contract the AIDS virus.[47] In fact, lesbians have the lowest rate of HIV infection compared to male homosexuals and male and female heterosexuals. However, the knowledge that male homosexuals have high rates of HIV infection coupled with the categorization of a woman as homosexual leads to the mistaken judgment that lesbians are likely to have AIDS. In clinical judgments, categorizing an individual into a certain diagnostic category (such as schizophrenic or manic-depressive) can lead to the perception of a relationship (even when none exists) between the individual and behavior consistent with that diagnosis.[48] Regardless of the setting, the illusory correlation does much to confirm our original stereotypes; our stereotype leads us to see a relationship that then seems to provide evidence that the original stereotype is true.

In-Group/Out-Group Effects One of the most common ways of categorizing people is to divide them into two groups: those in "my" group and the "out" group. For example, we often divide the world into us versus them, my school versus yours, my sports team versus the opponent, Americans versus foreigners, my ethnic group versus yours, or those who sit at my lunch table versus the rest of you. When we divide the world into two such realities, researchers have found considerable evidence for at least two consequences, which can be termed the **homogeneity effect** ("those people all look alike to me") and **in-group favoritism.**

In general, we tend to see members of **out-groups** as more similar to each other than the members of our own group—the **in-group.** For example, Bernadette Park and Myron Rothbart asked members of three different sororities to indicate how similar members of each sorority were to each other.[49] They found that the women perceived more similarity of members in other sororities compared to their own. One explanation for this effect is that when the subjects thought of members in their own group, they thought of them as individuals, each with a unique personality and lifestyle. When they thought of out-group members, they considered them in terms of a group label and thus saw them each as similar to this group identity.

In-group favoritism refers to the tendency to see one's own group as better on any number of dimensions and to allocate rewards to one's own group. In-group favoritism has been extensively studied using what has come to be known as the **minimum group paradigm.** In this procedure, originated by the British social psychologist Henri Tajfel,[50] complete strangers are formed into groups using the most trivial, inconsequential criteria imaginable. For example, in one study, subjects watched Tajfel flip a coin that randomly assigned them to either "Group X" or "Group W." In another study, Tajfel asked subjects to express their opinions about artists they had never heard of before and then randomly assigned them either to a group that appreciated "Klee" or one that appreciated "Kandinsky," ostensibly based on these mild picture preferences.

What makes Tajfel's research interesting is that significant results are often obtained on the basis of group identification that means very little. That is, the subjects are total strangers prior to the study and never interact with each other, and their actions are completely anonymous. Yet they behave as if those who share their meaningless label are their good friends or close kin. Subjects indicate that they like those who share their label. They rate others who share their label as likely to have a more pleasant personality and to have produced better output than the people who are assigned a different label. Most strikingly, subjects allocate more money and rewards to those who share their label. As we will see in Chapter 7, these tendencies can form the basis of racial and ethnic prejudice.

Re-constructive Memory

Memory plays an important role in our social interactions. It is, therefore, vital to grasp this: Remembering is a **re-constructive** process. By this I mean that we cannot tap into a literal translation of past events. It is not like playing back a tape recorder or a VCR; instead, we re-create our memories from bits and pieces of actual events filtered through and modified by our notions of what might have been, and what should have been, and we would like it to have been. Our memories are also profoundly influenced by what people might have told us about the specific events—long after they occurred. As Anthony Greenwald[51] has noted, if historians revised and distorted history to the same extent that we do in trying to recall events from our own lives, they'd lose their jobs! Of course, most of us would like to believe that our memories contain only the truth about the past.[52] To most people, the idea that their memory is fallible is unsettling. But consider how frightening it was to Timothy Hennis, who almost lost his life because the members of his jury believed that memory is infallible.

Let me explain. On July 4, 1986, Hennis was convicted of the triple murder of Kathryn, Kara, and Erin Eastburn and the rape of Kathryn Eastburn.[53] The crime was a particularly grisly one. Apparently, an intruder had broken into the Eastburn home, held a knife to Kathryn Eastburn, raped her, and then slit her throat and stabbed her 15 times. Three-year-old Erin and 5-year-old Kara were each stabbed almost a dozen times. The police followed a quick lead. Earlier in the week, Timothy Hennis had answered the Eastburns' newspaper ad requesting someone to adopt their black Labrador retriever. Hennis had taken the dog on a trial basis.

During the trial, two eyewitnesses placed Hennis at the scene of the crime. Chuck Barrett testified that he had seen Hennis walking in the area at

3:30 A.M. on the morning of the murders. Sandra Barnes testified that she had seen a man who looked like Hennis using a bank card that police had identified earlier as one stolen from the Eastburn residence. But Hennis had an airtight alibi for his whereabouts on the night of the murder. Moreover, there was no physical evidence (fingerprints, clothing fibers, footprints, bloodstains, hair) to link him to the scene. Nevertheless, the jury found the eyewitness testimony convincing and convicted Hennis—sentencing him to death by lethal injection.

Hennis spent 845 days on death row before a judge from the court of appeals ordered a new trial on the basis of a procedural technicality unrelated to the eyewitness testimony. Hennis's lawyers knew that if they had any chance of overturning his conviction, they would need to attack the eyewitness testimony placing him at the scene of the crime. On close scrutiny, it turned out to be very weak evidence. Chuck Barrett had originally told police 2 days after the murders that the man he saw had brown hair (Hennis is blond) and was 6 feet tall (Hennis is much taller). Furthermore, when asked to identify Hennis in a photo lineup, Barrett was uncertain of his judgment. When Sandra Barnes was first contacted by police a few weeks after the crime, she told them firmly and emphatically that she had not seen anyone at the bank machine that day. Why then at the trial had both of these witnesses so confidently placed Hennis at the scene of the crime? Were they both liars? No, they were just ordinary people like you and me; their memory of the events had been leveled and sharpened—constructed, shaped, and reconstructed—by over a year of questioning by police and lawyers.

Elizabeth Loftus, a prominent cognitive psychologist, served as an expert witness at the second Hennis trial. Loftus had previously conducted a fascinating program of research on reconstructive memory—investigating how such "suggestive" questioning can influence memory and subsequent eyewitness testimony.[54] In one of her experiments, Loftus showed subjects a film depicting a multiple-car accident. After the film, some of the subjects were asked, "About how fast were the cars going when they smashed into each other?" Other subjects were asked the same question, but the word *smashed* was replaced by the word *hit*. Subjects who were asked about smashing cars, as opposed to hitting cars, estimated that the cars were going significantly faster; moreover, a week after seeing the film, they were more likely to state (erroneously) that there was broken glass at the accident scene.

Leading questions can not only influence the judgment of facts (as in the case above), but also can affect the memory of what has happened. In one of her early studies, Loftus showed subjects a series of slides depicting an auto-pedestrian accident.[55] In a critical slide, a green car drove past the accident. Immediately after viewing the slides, half of the subjects were asked, "Did the *blue* car that drove past the accident have a ski rack on the roof?" The remaining subjects were asked this same question but with the word blue deleted. Those subjects who were asked about the "blue" car were more likely to claim incorrectly that they had seen a blue car. A simple question had altered their memories.

In her testimony at Hennis's second trial, Loftus discussed the nature of reconstructive memory and the way that an interrogation can lead an observer to construct an imaginary scenario and then believe that it really happened. Consider the earlier testimony of Sandra Barnes. At first, she could not recall the presence of anyone at the bank teller machine. However, after listening to months of television coverage and reading a year's worth of newspaper stories about the crime, coupled with the pressure stemming from the fact that she was the only one who might have seen the real murderer, Barnes reconstructed a memory of her visit to the bank machine that included someone who looked like Hennis—in a manner similar to the way the students recalled a blue rather than a green car in the Loftus experiment. By rehearsing this new construction repeatedly for lawyers and judges, Barnes came to accept it as fact. It is important to note that Sandra Barnes was not intentionally lying. She was simply reconstructing the event. She came to believe what she was saying. Chuck Barrett's testimony was tainted in much the same way. Subsequently, the man he saw the morning of the murder was conclusively identified as another man on his way to work—not Hennis.

Fortunately for Hennis, his story did not end on death row. On April 20, 1989, a second jury declared him to be innocent, noting the absence of physical evidence linking him to the scene and the weakness of the eyewitness testimony. In the first trial, Hennis had been victimized by mistaken identification coupled with the jury's assumption that memory is accurate.

Although the case remains unsolved, off the record, the local police have indicated that they now have good reason to believe that the crimes were actually committed by another person: A strikingly similar rape and murder were committed in a neighboring town while Hennis was on death row. Shortly after these crimes, both Hennis and the police received a convincing series of anonymous letters thanking Hennis for taking the rap for the Eastburn murders.

Autobiographical Memory

It is clear that memory can be reconstructive when it involves quick, snapshot-like events such as trying to recall the details of an automobile accident. But what about something more enduring, such as the recall of our own personal history? Here again, it's important to realize that we don't remember our past as accurately as we would like to believe. It is impossible to remember every detail of our lives. Serious revisions and important distortions occur over time. As you might imagine, these revisions of autobiographical memory are not random. Rather, we have a strong tendency to organize our personal history in terms of what Hazel Markus[56] calls **self-schemas**—coherent memories, feelings, and beliefs about ourselves that hang together and form an integrated whole. Thus, our memories get distorted in such a way that they fit the general picture we have of ourselves. For example, if we have a general picture of our childhood as having been unhappy, and our parents as having been cold and distant, any events from our childhood that violate that general picture will be more difficult to recall than events that support it. Thus, over the years, our memories become increasingly coherent and less accurate. In this manner, we rewrite our personal histories. It isn't that we are *lying* about our past; it is that we misremember in a way that fits with our schemas.

A simple experiment by Michael Ross, Cathy McFarland, and Garth Fletcher sheds considerable light on how this might come about.[57] In their experiment, college students received a persuasive message arguing the importance of frequent tooth brushing. After receiving the message, they changed their attitudes toward tooth brushing. Needless to say, this is not surprising. But here's what was surprising: Later that same day in a different situation, the students were asked, "How many times have you brushed your teeth in the past 2 weeks?" Those who received the message recalled that they brushed their teeth far more frequently than did students in the control condition. The students were not attempting to deceive the researcher; there was no reason for them to lie. They were simply using their new attitudes as a heuristic to help them remember. In a sense, they needed to believe that they had always behaved in a sensible and reasonable manner— even though they had just now discovered what that sensible behavior might be.

Elizabeth Loftus[58] has carried this line of research a step further. She has shown how easy it is to plant false memories of childhood experiences in the minds of young adults merely by instructing a close relative to talk about these events as fact. For example, if a young man's older sister said to him, "Remember the time when you were five years old and you got lost for several hours at the University City shopping mall? And you went into a panic—and an oldish man tried to help you? When we discovered you, you were holding the old man's hand and were crying." Within a few days of hearing such a story, most people will have incorporated that planted memory into their own history, will have embroidered it with details ("oh, yeah, the old man who helped me was wearing a flannel shirt"), and will be absolutely certain that it really happened—when, in fact, it didn't. This has been called the **false memory syndrome.**

The Recovered Memory Phenomenon

Loftus's research on the planting of false childhood memories has led her and many other cognitive scientists[59] to take a close and skeptical look at a recent societal phenomenon: the **recovered memory phenomenon.** During the 1980s and 1990s, thousands of adults seemed to remember horrifying childhood events that had been previously unavailable to them. Many of these memories involved sexual abuse, over a period of months or years, by their father or some other family member. Some memories even included (as part of the abuse) vivid accounts of forced participation in elaborate satanic rituals involving such bizarre and gruesome activities as the killing and devouring of infants.[60] Typically, these memories would surface during intensive psychotherapy—frequently under hypnosis—or after reading a vivid and highly suggestive self-help book.

Needless to say, sexual abuse does occur within families—and the consequences of such abuse can be tragic. Accordingly, all such revelations should be taken seriously. At the same time, most cognitive scientists who have made a systematic study of human memory are convinced that the majority of these reported memories do not reflect reality. They argue that just as police and lawyers can help witnesses "remember" incidents that never happened, many people can be led to "remember" such terrible things as childhood sexual abuse that never occurred.

According to the scientists who have done systematic research on the nature of memory, repeated instances of traumatic events occurring over a long stretch of time are not usually forgotten; they assert that, while this kind of thing might happen on rare occasions, it simply is not the way memory works.[61] Rather, they suggest that, in a manner parallel to the Loftus experiments, memories of abuse could have been unintentionally planted by the therapists themselves—not with any malevolent motive, of course, but in a sincere attempt to help the client. Here's how it might come about: Suppose a therapist holds the theory that certain fears or personality characteristics (e.g., low self-esteem, fear of being alone in the dark, fear of losing control)[62] are symptomatic of having been sexually abused. Into his or her office comes a person with some of these characteristics. Over the course of the therapy, with the best of intentions, the therapist might subtly suggest that these events might have taken place. The therapist might then invite the client to try to remember such instances and might unwittingly show increased interest—even excitement—when the client begins to explore these possibilities. Under these conditions, the client may begin to construct a coherent set of memories that may nonetheless be totally false.

Accordingly, memory researchers have criticized some self-help books— books that attempt to guide people to uncover dark secrets from their early childhood—on the grounds that the authors often grossly underestimate the power of suggestion and unwittingly lead people to recover false memories. For example, one best-selling self-help book actually encourages people to spend time trying to reconstruct their childhood story and goes on to list a variety of possibilities that allegedly are related to abuse. Here is a partial list; it is introduced in the following manner:

> There are common characteristics that exist in families where abuse takes place. You may not have experienced all of them, but you probably experienced several.

- "I felt ashamed of my family."
- "There were things I couldn't talk about."
- "There were always a lot of secrets in my family."
- "Along with the bad things, there was a lot of good in my family."
- "At least one of my parents took drugs or drank a lot."
- "I was often humiliated and put down."
- "A lot of my basic needs weren't taken care of."
- "Things were chaotic and unpredictable in my household."
- "There were a lot of broken promises."
- "I'm not sure if I was abused, but when I hear about sexual abuse and its effects, it all sounds creepy and familiar."[63]

Clearly, some of the items on this list would apply to most of us—whether or not we experienced anything resembling sexual abuse. Furthermore, as John Kihlstom[64] has recently pointed out, there is no scientific evidence of a specific link between child sexual abuse and any of these kinds of checklist items. What are we to make of a situation where thousands of adults assert that they were sexually abused as children, repressed the memory of abuse, and now, after reading this book, seem to remember the abuse? On the one hand, we have a desire to take each of these incidents seriously. If such a thing did take place, it is indeed tragic, and our hearts go out to the people who had such traumatic experiences. But what if the memory is false? In the absence of any corroborating evidence, should the person confront and prosecute the accused family member? Thousands of people have done just that—and many families have been torn apart by these accusations.[65] As you might imagine, when people are accused of such actions some 30 years after the alleged fact, it is usually impossible for them to prove their innocence.

It goes without saying that this has been a highly controversial issue in contemporary psychology. Some professional psychologists have been willing to take these accounts at face value. But most cognitive scientists, based on their research on memory, believe that, in the absence of any corroborating evidence to suggest abuse, it would be wrong to accuse the suspected family member of having committed this serious crime. In addition to the scientific research we have mentioned, researchers point to evidence from everyday life indicating that many of these recovered "memories" of abuse, when carefully examined, turn out to be either flat-out wrong or extremely unlikely. For example, in some instances, several siblings sleeping in the same room where the events allegedly occurred swore that they never took place; occasionally, the accused perpetrator was hundreds of miles away (e.g., serving in the military) when the series of events allegedly occurred; in many instances, people who acquire such memories in therapy have come to realize on their own, years later, that the events never actually occurred—and retract their accusations.[66] Sometimes, where there should be clear evidence, it is conspicuous by its absence. For example, as mentioned above, some people have recovered the vivid "memory" of having been forced to participate in a series of satanic rituals in which they killed and ate babies and buried their remains. Some of these memories are precise about where the bodies were buried. But thorough, systematic searches by law enforcement officers have never succeeded in turning up a single skeleton—and no coinciding kidnappings were reported that would have supported the veracity of these accounts.[67]

Many questions remain unanswered. For me, the most interesting one is, what's in it for the victim? It's one thing to falsely remember something relatively trivial, like having been lost in a shopping mall as a child, but recovering a memory of having been sexually abused would entail a lot of pain. If these events didn't, in fact, take place, why would anyone be willing to believe they did? I do not have a definitive answer to that question. I do have one case history that may or may not be typical. This involves a close friend of mine, a very bright, highly sophisticated middle-aged woman I will call "Madelaine." Here is what she wrote:

> I was at a very low point in life. I was feeling terribly unhappy and insecure. My marriage had recently fallen apart. I was having a lot of trouble relating to men. My professional life had taken a few terrible hits. My self-esteem was at an all-time low. I had the strong feeling that my life was out of control—and not what it should be. When I picked up a self-help book and began to read about dysfunctional families—and, more specifically, about characteristics of people who have been sexually abused as children—and characteristics of families where sexual abuse takes place—it was as if a flash bulb went off. In some strange way, I actually felt a sense of relief—it was a feeling of, "Oh, so that explains why I am so miserable!" The book told me that, if I didn't remember specifics, it probably meant I was repressing horrible memories. I felt like a detective. The more I began to think about my childhood, the more things began to fall into place. For several weeks, I vacillated between all kinds of emotions. I was feeling anger at my father, humiliation, hurt—and also a sense of relief. I now see that the relief came from the fact that, if I could blame my unhappiness on something terrible that was done to me when I was little, then I wouldn't have to take responsibility for my own failures as an adult.
>
> Luckily, I didn't ever confront my parents, because I came to realize that the memories probably weren't reliable—I started to have new "memories" in which the details of events were different. Both sets of memories couldn't have been correct. Also, I came to realize the events I'd "remembered" couldn't possibly have happened, for a whole host of reasons. It was incredibly hard giving up the idea that there was a clear,

identifiable reason for my daily sadness and hurt. I was very vulnerable and messed up when I read that book. I could have done untold damage to my family—and to myself—if I had ever made public my "memories." I still feel very angry—but not at my parents—at that damn book!

How Conservative Is Human Cognition?

Imagine that you are in a dark room looking at a photographic image so blurred that it is impossible to identify what is depicted. Gradually the picture is brought into focus until it is just slightly blurred. At this point, you are asked to guess what it is. If you are like most subjects who have participated in this study,[68] you will be correct about 25 percent of the time. But suppose you started by looking at the slightly blurred picture without the early gradual focusing. Will your hit rate be better or worse? At first, it might appear that your accuracy would decrease because you are spending less time looking at the picture. Not so. Even though you would now have a briefer period of exposure, without the gradual focusing, you would be correct almost 75 percent of the time—a threefold increase in accuracy. How come? The results of this experiment illustrate what is known as the **confirmation bias**—the tendency to seek confirmation of initial impressions or beliefs. When the picture is very blurred, most people will generate hypotheses about what it might be—it looks like an ice cream cone; no, a rearing horse; no, the Eiffel Tower. We have a tendency to cling to these preliminary guesses; these guesses then interfere with our ability to interpret the slightly blurred picture. Much evidence exists to suggest that the confirmation bias is a common tendency in human thought. For example, in an experiment by Mark Snyder and William Swann,[69] female college students were told that the person they were about to meet was either an extrovert (outgoing, warm, and friendly) or an introvert (reserved, cool, and aloof). They then prepared a set of questions that they would like to ask this person in order to get to know him or her. What types of questions did they wish to ask? In general, subjects sought to confirm their original hypotheses. Subjects who thought they would meet an extrovert were more likely to ask questions that confirmed their hypothesis, such as "What do you do to liven up a party?" and "In what situations are you most talkative?" Those expecting to meet an introvert were likely to ask questions like "In what situations do you wish you could be more outgoing?" and "What things do you dislike about loud parties?" Notice that, if the question is sincerely answered, the subjects' hypothesis about the person is likely to be confirmed. That is, a person who is neither extroverted nor introverted will look extroverted when he or she answers the first set of questions and introverted when he or she answers the second set of questions.

Not only do we tend to confirm our hypotheses, but we are often quite confident that they are true. This can be illustrated by what Baruch Fischhoff termed the **hindsight bias,** or the "I-knew-it-all-along" effect.[70] As you may recall from our discussion in Chapter 1, once we know the outcome of an event, we have a strong tendency to believe that we could have predicted it in advance. In the Fischhoff experiments, subjects were given a test assessing their knowledge of historical events. The subject's task was to indicate the likelihood that four possible outcomes of the event could have actually occurred. Some of the subjects were told that one of the four possibilities had actually happened but were asked to make the estimates that they would have made had they not first been told the "right" answers. The results showed that subjects could not ignore this information; they substantially overestimated their prior knowledge of correct answers. In other words, even though subjects really didn't know the answers to the test, once they were told an answer, they believed that they knew it all along and that their memories had not changed.

The confirmation and hindsight biases provide support for the proposition that *human cognition tends to be conservative.* That is, we try to preserve that which is already established—to maintain our preexisting knowledge, beliefs, attitudes, and stereotypes. Throughout this book we have seen numerous examples of cognitive conservatism: The first information received is almost always the most influential; easily accessible categories are overused in forming judgments; representative and attitude heuristics are sometimes misused; stereotypes distort information processing and confirm the apparent usefulness of the stereotype; and memory is reconstructed to fit with current perspectives.

In a provocative article, Anthony Greenwald[71] has argued that cognitive conservatism has at least one benefit: It allows us to perceive the social world as a coherent and stable place. For example, suppose that every time the library received some new books that didn't fit its previous cataloging system, a librarian renumbered and recataloged all the books in the library. The "HM251s" (social psychology books) were changed suddenly to "AP57s" and the "BFs" (psychology) were now divided into the "EAs" and the "DBs." It would probably take that librarian years to recatalog the books. When you show up to do your term paper on social cognition, you would find it nearly impossible to locate the books and articles you need; the library would be a place of utter confusion. To keep the library operating and coherent, it makes sense to modify only slightly the current cataloging system and fit the new books into the old system. Similarly, to keep our minds operating and coherent, it makes sense to practice cognitive conservatism and to modify only slightly our cognitive categories.

However, as we have seen throughout this chapter, cognitive conservatism has its costs. The misuse of inappropriate categories may cause a person to distort events or to miss important information. The misapplication of a heuristic can lead to poor decision making. The failure to update our conception of the world in the face of new and discrepant information can result in a mistaken picture of reality. The consequences are not just mental but can show their face in social problems that we call racism, sexism, prejudice, and just plain stupid thinking.

What can we do to avoid the negative consequences of cognitive conservatism? Here are four rules of thumb that might help. First, be wary of those who attempt to create your categories and definitions of the situations. There are many ways to define and label a person or event. Ask yourself, "Why is this particular label being suggested?" Second, try to use more than one way to categorize and describe a person or event. By seeing a person or event in a number of different ways, we do not rely on a single category that we then misemploy—bending and twisting the data so that they fit a preconceived notion. Third, try to think of persons and important events as unique; while they are members of a particular salient category (say, a given race or gender), they are also members of many other categories and have their own unique attributes. Individuation can help prevent the overuse of a given stereotype or heuristic. Finally, when forming an impression, consider the possibility that you might be mistaken—that you have fallen victim to one or more of the cognitive biases described in this chapter. In the next chapter, on self-justification, we will continue to explore cognitive conservatism and look at additional ways to protect ourselves from the adverse consequences of distorted thinking.

How Do Attitudes and Beliefs Guide Behavior?

In the last few sections, we have looked at how our beliefs and attitudes influence the way we think about the social world. A reasonable question to ask is: What is the relationship between our attitudes and our behavior? Can we use our attitudes to predict how we will behave? For example, suppose I like vanilla ice cream, but you dislike it. Would you and I behave differently toward vanilla ice cream? Our intuition says "yes." Most people would expect that I would purchase a lot of vanilla ice cream—choosing it over other flavors; you, on the other hand, would rarely buy it. This is usually true for simple preferences like vanilla ice cream. But we would be making a serious mistake if we assumed it was always the case. A long history of research suggests that in many situations, this intuition is wrong.

Let's take a closer look. One of the classic studies of the attitude-behavior relationship was conducted in the early 1930s by Richard LaPiere.[72] At the time, there was much more overt and blatant prejudice in the United States directed toward people of color than there is now. Often, Americans of Asian, Hispanic, or African descent were denied easy access to public rest rooms and the use of water fountains, restaurants, and hotel lodging. In 1933, LaPiere contacted 128 hotel and restaurant proprietors and assessed their attitude toward Chinese people by asking them, "Will you accept members of the Chinese race as guests in your establishment?" Over 90 percent of those contacted said, "No!" However, when a young Chinese couple actually made an appearance, LaPiere found that of these 128 establishments, only one refused them accommodations or service. The proprietors' attitudes concerning Chinese people did not predict their actual behavior.

La Piere's findings are not a fluke. In 1969, Alan Wicker undertook a scholarly review of over 40 studies that had explored the attitude-behavior relationship. These studies investigated a wide range of attitudes and opinions on such topics as job satisfaction, ethnic prejudice, consumer preferences, and political beliefs. Wicker found only weak support for the hypothesis that attitudes predict behavior. As he says, "Taken as a whole, these studies suggest that it is considerably more likely that attitudes will be unrelated or only slightly related to overt behaviors than that attitudes will be closely related to actions."[73]

The Attitude-Behavior Relationship in Our Heads   How can we reconcile this body of research with our intuition that a person's attitudes are strongly related to his or her behavior? One way is to conclude that there is no consistent relationship between attitudes and behavior. It is all in our heads; we just imagine that people act consistently with their beliefs and attitudes. There is some support for this proposition. In the previous two chapters, we saw the power of the social situation to induce conformity. LaPiere's innkeepers undoubtedly faced strong social pressures to say "no" to an inquiry about admitting Chinese people; at the same time, they faced contrary pressures (to avoid making a scene) to lodge the young Chinese couple once they appeared at the hotel. Perhaps they simply caved in to the most immediate pressures. Perhaps we are nothing more than creatures who succumb to whatever pressures happen to exist in our immediate social environment.

In support of the hypothesis that the perception of attitude behavior consistency is "all in our heads" is the common tendency to attribute the cause of an individual's behavior to characteristics of the individual, such as personality traits and attitudes, rather than to the power of the situation itself. For example, the inquiry "Why did little Johnny fail on his homework assignment?" is often answered with the statement "Because he is stupid or lazy"— ignoring such situational factors as overcrowded schools or a poor academic environment. In other words, as we learned in Chapter 1, when we see something happen to a person, most of us assume that the event is consistent with the kind of person he or she is. We would like to believe that people get what they deserve and deserve what they get. Edward Jones and his colleagues call this tendency to attribute the cause of a behavior to a corresponding characteristic of a person a **correspondent inference**:[74] The behavior of the person is explained in terms of an attribute or trait that is just like the behavior. Some examples include "Sam spilled wine on the carpet because he is clumsy" (not because of a momentary distraction), and "Amy snapped at Ted because she is a hostile person" (not because she momentarily lost her temper).

An experiment by Edward Jones and Victor Harris demonstrates that such inferences can be pervasive.[75] In this experiment, subjects read essays either favorable or unfavorable to Fidel Castro's regime in Cuba allegedly written by students in a political science course. Half of the subjects were told that the essay writers freely chose the position presented in their essays, whereas the others were told that the writers had been forced to take that position and were instructed to make the best case they could. Subjects then had to guess the essay writer's true attitude toward Castro. When the essay writers could choose a position freely, subjects assumed that the content of their essays reflected their attitudes: Those writing pro-Castro essays were believed to be pro-Castro, and those writing anti-Castro essays were assumed to be anti-Castro. This was not surprising. What *was* surprising is that the *same* results occurred even when it was made clear that the essay writer had been forced to argue an assigned position. In other words, essay writers forced to argue for Castro were assumed to be pro-Castro, and those forced to argue against Castro were assumed to be anti-Castro. In making their inferences, subjects discounted the situational pressure to take a position and assumed that the essayist's behavior was a result of a firmly held belief. In this case, the attitude-behavior relationship was located in the head of the observer.

When Do Attitudes Predict Behavior?   Just because attitudes don't always predict beliefs does not mean that attitudes never predict behavior. The role of scientists is to try to determine the conditions under which an event is more or less likely to occur. Russell Fazio[76] has identified one major factor that increases the likelihood that we will act on our attitude: accessibility. **Attitude accessibility** refers to the strength of the association between an object and your evaluation of it. For example, if I say "snake," most people will immediately think, "bad, dangerous." If I say "Renoir painting," most will quickly respond, "beautiful." We all know people about whom we immediately think, "Oh, no, not that jerk again," or conversely, "Wow! What a wonderful person." These are highly accessible attitudes.

Not all attitudes and beliefs are highly accessible. For example, we may have opinions on Puerto Rican statehood or the value of advertising, but for most of us, these opinions do not readily come to mind. Sometimes we have no *real* attitude, that is, no evaluation of the object stored in memory. Nevertheless, we might venture an opinion if asked. For example, survey researchers find that respondents are capable of giving their opinion about made-up issues such as a phony piece of legislation or foreign aid to a nonexistent country. In these latter two cases, our less accessible attitudes and nonattitudes are not likely to guide behavior.

How does attitude accessibility influence behavior? According to Fazio, attitudes are used to interpret and perceive an object selectively and to make sense of a complex situation. We have seen previously how attitudes can influence cognitive processing; an attitude serves as a heuristic to influence our interpretations, explanations, reasoning, and judgment of a situation. But any given attitude is only one of many factors that can be used to make sense of a situation. For example, to make sense of a complex situation, we may use the objective features of the situation, or what other people say about it, or our general attitude about similar situations. When an attitude is highly accessible, it is more likely to be the major thing we use for defining a situation. In those situations, we will act on the basis of that attitude.

There is considerable evidence to support the proposition that highly accessible attitudes guide behavior. One measure of attitude accessibility is the speed with which an individual can provide an evaluative response of an object or issue. Using this simple measure, Russell Fazio and Carol Williams[77] were able to make extraordinarily accurate predictions of who would vote for either Ronald Reagan or Walter Mondale in the presidential election of 1984. About 5 months before the election, Fazio and Williams took a microcomputer to a local shopping mall and asked passersby to give their opinions about various issues, including an evaluation of each of the two presidential candidates. The computer recorded the speed with which they evaluated the presidential candidates. This was their measure of attitude accessibility. Later, Fazio and Williams contacted the subjects and asked them about their perceptions of two presidential debates. After the election, they asked for whom they had voted. The results showed that those individuals with highly accessible attitudes (fast responses) 5 months before the election were more likely to vote for their favored candidate and to perceive the presidential debates in a manner consistent with their attitudes.

In a slightly different vein, Fazio and his colleagues[78] actually manipulated the accessibility of an attitude by having subjects repeatedly express their opinions or by giving subjects the opportunity to have direct experience with the attitude object. They consistently found that attitudes that are made accessible in this manner became predictive of subsequent behavior to a far greater extent than attitudes that are not made accessible. Fazio's concept of attitude accessibility provides us with several ways of interpreting the lack of an attitude-behavior relationship in the LaPiere study of innkeepers. The problem is that we do not know how accessible attitudes toward Chinese people were for each of the innkeepers. Moreover, it may be that different attitudes were activated by the questionnaire and by the actual visit of the Chinese couple. For example, a survey item mentioning only Chinese people may have reminded an innkeeper of his or her general prejudice, whereas the presence of a young, well-dressed Chinese couple may have invoked competing thoughts and feelings. Moreover, even if prejudiced attitudes were highly accessible and subsequently influenced perceptions of the situation, there is no guarantee that the innkeepers would or could have acted on those perceptions. Perhaps the presence of other guests made the innkeepers fearful of creating a scene. Perhaps the experience was a new one for the proprietors, and they simply did not know how to behave. These factors limit the extent to which a person will act on his or her beliefs.

Acting on Perceptions There is another way that attitudes and beliefs can influence behavior: The belief can come to create the social world in which we live. An experiment by Paul Herr illustrates how this can occur.[79] Using a word puzzle game, Herr intentionally increased the accessibility of the concept *hostility* in some of his subjects, using the technique of priming discussed earlier in the chapter. Specifically, Herr's subjects were required to find hidden names of persons in a matrix of letters. For half of the subjects, the hidden names were of persons associated with hostility—Charles Manson, Adolf Hitler, Ayatollah Khomeini, and Dracula. The other subjects sought and found the names of relatively gentle people—Peter Pan, Pope John Paul, Shirley Temple, and Santa Claus. The subjects then read an ambiguous description of a person named Donald, whose behavior could be seen as either hostile or gentle, and rated Donald's level of hostility. Consistent with our earlier discussion of contrast effects, we would expect the different puzzles to influence judgments about Donald. Compared to Hitler and Manson, almost everyone looks gentle—including Donald; compared to the Pope and Santa Claus, almost everyone appears hostile—including Donald. This is exactly what Herr found. Those subjects primed with the extremely hostile persons rated Donald as less hostile compared with those who received the gentle primes.*

But Herr's experiment didn't stop there. Next, the subjects played a bargaining game with a person whom they thought was Donald. In this game, participants were required to choose between one of two strategies—competing or cooperating. Herr found that when subjects expected to play against a hostile Donald, they played in a highly competitive manner; when they expected a gentle Donald, they played with far more cooperation. Interestingly, the subjects who were naively playing the role of Donald also perceived this competitiveness; they rated their opponent's level of hostility in a manner consistent with the way he or she played the game. In sum, a relatively subtle context had influenced attitudes and expectations that, in turn, affected behavior and subsequently affected the next round of perceptions.

*The reader should note the crucial difference between this experiment and one by Higgins et al., discussed earlier in this chapter. In the Higgins experiment, the researchers were priming a *category*—negativity. This influenced observers to see subsequent ambiguous stimuli (like Donald) more negatively—because that is what people are primed to look for. In the Herr experiment, the researchers were priming *exemplars* of hostility (like Hitler). Here, a contrast effect occurs: Compared to extremely hostile people, an ambiguous person (like Donald) comes off looking like a teddy bear. *Summary:* What then can we conclude from the considerable research on attitudes and behavior? First and foremost, the collective research on attitudes and behavior underscores a principle we will see quite often in this book: Subtle situational variables are often strong determinants of our behavior. Second, most people tend to overlook the importance of the situation in explaining behavior, preferring instead to explain other people's actions in terms of assumptions about their personalities and attitudes. In other words, most of us assume that people's attitudes do indeed forecast their behavior, and then we overapply this belief in interpreting the behavior of others. We see attitude-behavior relationships even when they may not exist in reality.

Carol Dweck and her colleagues have demonstrated the behavioral consequences of people's more enduring beliefs. According to Dweck, children develop implicit theories about the permanence of people's defining traits—like intelligence or goodness. These implicit theories exert a considerable influence upon a child's judgments and behavior. Let's take intelligence. Dweck has found that some people think that intelligence is fixed—that people can learn new things but they can't really get any smarter than they were when they were born. Others hold a different view, that intelligence is more malleable, that it can grow with hard work. In several studies, Dweck has shown how powerful this difference can be in the academic arena.[80]

The basic finding is that people who see intelligence as fixed are apprehensive about failure. Accordingly, they try to steer clear of real challenges which might reveal their limitations. In a way, this makes sense; if you can't improve your intelligence, you want to play it safe and foster the image that you are smart. Thus, relative to people who are equally smart but who see intelligence as malleable, people with the fixed view are more likely to choose easier tasks to do and give up when a task becomes too challenging. They frequently choke on hard tests, and will even lie to a stranger about their performance, reporting a higher score than they got. People who think intelligence is malleable behave differently. They tend to seek challenges and try to improve their abilities. Instead of giving up when they fail, they try harder or try a different strategy—they are more resilient.

The good news, as we will see in the next chapter, is that there are powerful ways to change this kind of behavior. For example, recent research shows that if you change people's attitudes about intelligence—getting them to believe in its malleability—they get better grades, enjoy academics more, accept challenges more eagerly, and perform better on standardized tests.[81]

Three Possible Biases in Social Explanation

Every day of our lives, we seek to explain a variety of events and happenings: Why are the North Koreans behaving so erratically? Why did that attractive person across the room ignore me? How come I did so poorly and you did so well on the recent essay assignment? Why did Mom not cook my favorite meal while I was home for Christmas? Our explanations are often rational and accurate. But they are also vulnerable to bias and inaccuracy. In studying how we interpret our social world, social psychologists have identified three general biases that often affect our attributions and explanations: the **fundamental attribution error,** the actor-observer bias, and self-biases.

The Fundamental Attribution Error
The term fundamental attribution error refers to a general human tendency to overestimate the importance of personality or dispositional factors relative to situational or environmental influences when describing and explaining the causes of social behavior.[82] We

have already seen one example of this tendency—correspondent inference. That is, when explaining why Sam took a specific political position or performed a specific behavior, we tend to favor personality explanations over situational ones. This may lead us to believe that there is more consistency of motive and behavior in the world than actually exists.

Another example of the fundamental attribution error is provided by an experiment conducted by Gunter Bierbrauer.[83] In this experiment, subjects witnessed a reenactment of a person's performance in Stanley Milgram's famous experiment on obedience to authority (described in Chapter 2). Recall that in this experiment, Milgram constructed a situation that elicited high rates of obedience; in this case, the behavior involved administering severe electric shocks to a "learner." Like most subjects in the original Milgram experiment, the person in Bierbrauer's reenactment showed a high level of obedience, administering the maximum level of electric shock. After showing the reenactment, Bierbrauer then asked his subjects to estimate how many of Milgram's subjects in general would be obedient in this situation. The results showed that subjects consistently underestimated the actual degree of obedience. Specifically, Bierbrauer's subjects estimated that only 10 to 20 percent of the people in this setting would give the maximum shock of 450 volts. In actuality, as you will recall, Milgram found that 65 percent of the subjects administered this level of shock. In other words, Bierbrauer's subjects assumed that this person was an aberration—that his behavior reflected distinguishing personal dispositions (i.e., that he was particularly aggressive or obedient). They failed to attribute his behavior to the power of the situation to produce this behavior in most people.

As observers, we frequently lose sight of the fact that each individual plays many social roles and that we might be observing only one of them. Thus, the importance of social roles can be easily overlooked in explaining a person's behavior. For example, I know a psychology professor whom I will call Dr. Mensch. The students adore Dr. Mensch. When they describe him on teacher evaluations and informally, they use words such as *warm, caring, concerned about students, approachable, charismatic, brilliant,* and *friendly*. However, Dr. Mensch's professional colleagues have a different image of him, especially those who have given professional talks when he was in the audience. Like the students, they see him as brilliant, but they also describe Dr. Mensch as *intense, critical, tough, argumentative,* and *relentless*.

Who has the right impression—the students or the professional colleagues? Is he really a tough, critical person who is simply putting on an act in order to appear to be warm and caring in front of his students? Or is he really a warm and caring individual who pretends to be tough when confronting other psychologists? These are the wrong questions. The fact is that my friend is capable of a wide range of behaviors. He is all these things—and more that we will never see. Some social roles tend to pull behavior from one part of the spectrum; other social roles tend to pull behavior from a different part of the spectrum. The students see Dr. Mensch in only one role—that of teacher. He is a very good teacher, and the job of a good teacher is to get the best out of the student; this usually requires warm and caring behavior. The students have accurately described my friend's behavior within this role.

On the other hand, the role of a useful professional colleague sometimes requires adversarial behavior. In order to discover the truth, a good professional often will strongly press an argument to see how far it will go. This frequently results in sharp, intense, and relentless criticism. Thus, Dr. Mensch's professional colleagues also accurately describe the behavior that they see. However, both students and professional colleagues make a fundamental attribution error when they assume that the behavior they observe is due entirely to some personality characteristic; rather, it is based largely on the way Dr. Mensch perceives the requirements of his social role. This is not to say that personality is irrelevant. Not everyone is capable of the wide array of behaviors manifested by Dr. Mensch. But to assume that he is either tough or warm is to ignore the power of the social role.

A clever experiment by Lee Ross, Teresa Amabile, and Julia Steinmetz illustrates how the impact of social roles can be underestimated in explaining behavior.[84] They set up a "quiz show" format in which they randomly assigned subjects to one of two roles: (1) a questioner, whose task it was to prepare difficult questions for (2) a contestant, whose task it was to answer them. An observer watched this simulated quiz show and then estimated the questioner's and the contestant's general knowledge. Try to put yourself in the role of the observer. What do you see? Well, unless you are very careful, you will see one very smart, knowledgeable person and one rather stupid person.

But take a closer look. Notice how these two roles constrain the behavior of the participants. The questioner is likely to come up with some fairly difficult questions based on esoteric knowledge: "In what baseball park did Babe Ruth hit his second-to-last home run?" "What is the capital city of Lithuania?" and "What is the date of Thomas Jefferson's death?"[85] By simply *asking* these questions, the questioner looks smart. On the other hand, the contestant is faced with answering these difficult questions and is likely to miss a few. This makes him or her look a little stupid. And this is exactly what Ross and his colleagues found. The observers felt that the questioners were far more knowledgeable than the contestants. However, since everyone was randomly assigned to their roles, it is extremely unlikely that all of the questioners were *actually* more knowledgeable than all of the contestants. What is most interesting is that the observers *knew* that the participants had been randomly assigned to these roles. Yet they failed to consider the impact of these social roles in making their judgments about the quiz-show participants and fell into the trap of attributing what they saw to personal dispositions.

If the fundamental attribution error were limited to judgments about college professors and quiz show participants, it probably would not be much of a cause for concern. However, its implications are far-reaching. Consider a common reaction of most Americans to a person using food stamps at a supermarket: "She is lazy; if she just tried harder, she could get a job." Or consider this characterization of a convicted burglar: "He is a terrible human being; what type of villain could commit such acts?" Both descriptions could conceivably be accurate, but what is more likely is that they represent the fundamental attribution error in action. Although this is not the place for a full discussion of the situational determinants of poverty and crime, there can be many factors other than personal characteristics that can explain why a person is poor or commits a crime. These include lack of job opportunities, illiteracy, economic recession, the lack of positive role models in one's neighborhood, and growing up in a dysfunctional family.

I do not mean to imply that a criminal should not be held accountable for his or her actions. Criminals are responsible for what they do and should be held accountable. But by focusing on personal rather than situational factors, we will endorse different policies for dealing with social problems such as poverty and crime. For example, the attribution "this criminal is a fiend" will result in a policy of spending more money on bigger and stronger prisons and doling out longer prison sentences. Perceiving the causes of crime as due largely to unemployment, poor role models, and illiteracy will result in policies like increased spending for better schools, better teachers, and tax credits to businesses that invest in poverty-stricken areas. Don't get me wrong. I am not suggesting that dispositional factors such as laziness, clumsiness, or viciousness do not exist. They do. But most of us, most of the time, are too prone to invoke a dispositional attribution when the cause of the behavior may well be situational. At the very least, our knowledge of the fundamental attribution error should alert us to the possibility that our attributions may not always be correct and that we should take seriously the motto of the novelist Samuel Butler: "There, but for the grace of God, go I."

The Actor-Observer Bias Another common bias in social judgment is known as the **actor-observer bias**—the tendency for actors to attribute their own actions to situational factors, whereas observers tend to attribute the same actions to stable personality dispositions of the actors.[86] For example, in my judgment, I go to the beach a lot because the weather is beautiful; but, in my judgment, you go to the beach a lot because you are probably a beach bum. Political leaders often describe wise moves and blunders as largely inescapable under the circumstances, whereas private citizens are likely to see both as a consequence of the leader's personal characteristics. Recall the Kitty Genovese murder discussed in Chapter 2. After Ms. Genovese was murdered in full view of 38 witnesses in New York City, the eyewitnesses claimed that the situation was ambiguous and that it was difficult to know what to do; newspaper reporters called it *bystander apathy*. In other words, I give myself the benefit of the doubt; I use situational causes to explain *myself*. But I don't give you the same benefit; when I try to explain your behavior, I make the fundamental attribution error.

There is considerable evidence that the actor-observer bias is pervasive. For example, studies have shown that (1) in explaining success and failure on an intelligence test, college students are likely to explain others' poor performance in terms of their ability, whereas they explain their own poor performance in terms of the difficulty of the test items; (2) college students who volunteered to participate in psychological research attributed their participation to the importance of the research, whereas observers viewed their participation as reflecting a personal inclination to participate in any and all research; (3) when observing a peer's behavior, college students leap to the conclusion that this person will continue to act in a similar manner in the future (thus implying an underlying disposition to behave in a particular way), whereas the "actors" indicated that they personally would probably act differently in the future; (4) students described their best friend's choice of girlfriends and a college major in terms of the qualities of their best friend but explained their own choices in terms of the qualities of their girlfriend or major; and (5) people ascribe more personality traits to others.[87]

What causes the actor-observer bias? An experiment by Michael Storms indicates that it is a function of where a person's attention is focused.[88] The actor's attention is usually focused on the environment and on past history; he or she may have special knowledge about the factors that led up to the behavior and how he or she felt about the behavior. On the other hand, the observer's attention is almost always focused on the actor; therefore, the observer may be unaware of historical or environmental reasons for why the actor did what he or she did.

In the Storms experiment, two subjects engaged in a conversation while two observers watched; each observer was instructed to monitor one of the conversationalists. After the conversation, the actors and the observers indicated to what extent behaviors such as friendliness, talkativeness, nervousness, and dominance were due either to personal characteristics or to the situation. As you might expect, the actors were more likely to explain their behavior in terms of the situation, whereas the observers explained the behavior in terms of the actor's personality dispositions. This was not surprising; it is consistent with what we know about the actor-observer bias. However, the study had an interesting twist. Some subjects viewed a videotape of the conversation that was played back either from the same angle at which they originally saw it (i.e., the actors saw a videotape of the other person, and the observers saw the person they were asked to monitor) or from a reverse angle (i.e., the actors saw themselves, and the observers saw the other person). When the camera angle was the same, the actor-observer bias occurred; however, when the camera angle was reversed, so was the actor-observer bias. Actors who saw themselves from the observer's point of view were more likely to explain their own behavior in terms of *dispositional* factors, whereas observers who saw the world from the point of view of the actors were more likely to explain behavior in *situational* terms. Often the actor-observer bias can lead to misunderstanding and conflict. For example, if Sam shows up late for a date with Susan, he (the actor) may explain his tardiness by noting that "all the traffic lights happened to be red," whereas Susan (the observer) may conclude that Sam "is losing interest in me." These differing perceptions and attributions might, in turn, serve as the basis for subsequent action that might serve to escalate feelings of hostility and conflict.

The Storms experiment points to one method for nipping this potential conflict in the bud before it happens: Change the actor's and the observer's perspectives. One tactic for doing this is to promote empathy by role-playing the other's point of view.[89] Another tactic, used on the international front, is cultural exchange programs in which citizens of one country live in another. Both tactics change both the perspective and the information available for making attributions.

The Self-Biases It is now time to turn our attention to what happens to our social cognitions when our most important social cognition—the self—is involved. As you will recall from our earlier discussion of self-schemas, psychologically, one of our major goals is to maintain and enhance our view of ourselves. In William James's view, this is especially true for our social and "spiritual" selves. As James put it:

> The social self . . . ranks higher than the material self. . . . We must care more for our honor, our friends, our human ties, than for a sound skin or wealth. And the spiritual self is so supremely precious that, rather than lose it, a man ought to be willing to give up friends and good fame, and property, and life itself.[90]

As a primary source of motivation, the way in which we conceive of the self greatly influences all of our social cognitions.[91] We will be discussing self-processes in more detail in the next chapter. For now, let us note two general ways that the self influences social cognition—*egocentric thought* and the *self-serving bias*.

Egocentric Thought Most people have a tendency to perceive themselves as more central to events than is actually the case.[92] We call this **egocentric thought**. People engaging in egocentric thought remember past events as if they were a leading player, influencing the course of events and the behavior of others. There are many examples of egocentric thought. Perhaps one of the most interesting is provided by the research of Robert Jervis, a political scientist.[93] He argues that important world leaders tend to believe, unreasonably, that an act of a foreign nation is either made in response to *their* prior decisions or made with the intent of eliciting a response from *them*. In other words, these world leaders perceive the world of foreign affairs to be revolving about themselves. For example, during World War II, Hitler attributed the fact that the British were not bombing German cities to the British desire to reciprocate German restraint rather than to the fact that the British were short on planes—which was actually the case.

Often world leaders believe that their action thwarts an adversary's evil intent when in fact no evil act was planned or it was aborted for other reasons. Such was the case with officials in the Nixon administration who predicted a massive North Vietnamese offensive during the visit of President Richard Nixon to China and then claimed to have prevented the attacks with massive bombing raids. After the war, it became clear that no such offensive was contemplated. In recent history, Ronald Reagan interpreted the sudden decline of the entity formerly known as the Soviet Union as primarily the result of his military spending program rather than economic and structural problems of the Soviet Union that had been festering for years. More recently, George W. Bush was criticized for having responded to North Korea's movement toward the development of nuclear weapons as if it were a personal affront.[94] Jervis draws a chilling conclusion about the effects of egocentric thought on heads of state: The (largely mistaken) belief that one has been the cause of the behavior of other nations leads to an enhanced faith in deterrence—the belief that one can prevent future events by punishment and threats of punishment.

It goes without saying that world leaders aren't the only ones who believe that they control events. It is a common phenomenon among us ordinary folks, as well. Ellen Langer demonstrated the power of the "illusion of control" in a simple experiment.[95] In this study, subjects bought lottery tickets, but here is the important twist: Some subjects chose their ticket, whereas others were assigned the ticket by the experimenter. Later, the subjects were given the opportunity to sell the ticket back to the experimenter. Langer found that those who had chosen their tickets demanded up to four times as much money for it as those who were assigned the tickets. The subjects in this experiment were under the illusion that their behavior of *choosing* a ticket could influence the outcome; therefore, they considered the ticket more valuable because they selected the numbers. Of course, as we all know, the winning ticket is determined by chance alone; no number has a greater chance of winning than any other number—regardless of who chose it. But the illusion of control fostered by egocentric thought is a powerful one. It is small wonder that most state lotteries allow us to select our own numbers.

The belief that one's self is the center of the universe helps explain a paradox that occurs every day in U.S. newspapers. Although many Americans are proud of their technological and scientific achievements, fewer than 10 percent of daily newspapers carry a regular column on science. In contrast, over 90 percent of these newspapers carry a daily feature on astrology—a means of attempting to predict the future using the position of the stars at birth. How come? The stock-in-trade of the newspaper horoscope is the Barnum statement—named after the showman P. T. Barnum, who once noted, "There is a sucker born every minute." A *Barnum statement* is a personality description composed of statements that are true of almost everyone. For example, suppose I were to study your astrological chart and tell you: "You are quite reserved in unfamiliar social situations. You view life with a mixture of optimism and pessimism. You have an open mind but can take a firm stand when the situation calls for it." Would you think me a particularly talented reader of the stars? A moment's reflection will tell you that this description applies to almost everyone. But, because of our tendency to think egocentrically, almost everyone believes that the Barnum statement is a bull's-eye statement about them; most of us do not stop to think that almost everyone else feels the same way. Thus, the newspaper horoscope is an appealing item for a great many people. Moreover, as Peter Glick, Deborah Gottesman, and Jeffrey Jolton[96] demonstrated, even those people who were initially skeptical of astrology could be swayed if the Barnum statement was both believable and very positive. That is, those skeptics who were given a phony astrological description of themselves that was generally true of most people (the Barnum statement) and was worded in a way so that it was very flattering came to reduce their skepticism and increase their confidence in astrology.

In another experiment designed to test the believability of Barnum statements, Richard Petty and Timothy Brock[97] gave subjects a phony personality test and then administered bogus personality feedback and results. Half of the subjects received a positively written Barnum statement describing them as "open-minded" (i.e., you can see many sides of an issue), whereas the other half received a positively written statement describing them as "closed-minded" (i.e., once you make up your mind, you take a firm stand). Although the personality feedback was bogus, almost all of the subjects believed it to be a very good description of their personality. What is more, Petty and Brock found that subjects' "new-found personality" influenced their subsequent behavior. Specifically, "open-minded" and "closed-minded" subjects were asked to list their thoughts on two controversial issues. Those subjects who had randomly received a Barnum statement describing them as open-minded listed thoughts on both sides of the issue, whereas those who had received a closed-minded personality statement tended to list arguments on only one side of the issue. This is still another example of how our beliefs and expectations can create social reality.

The tendency toward egocentric thought occurs in subtle ways that frequently include our memory for past events and information. One very common finding is that people have superior memory for information descriptive of the self.[98] Moreover, when working in groups, individuals tend to focus on and recall their own performance at the expense of retaining information about the performance of others. In addition, when a person plays an active role in generating information, that information is better recalled than when it was passively received. Finally, studies repeatedly show superior memory for information that is related to the self; that is, when people think about how a term or an object applies to themselves, they remember it better than when the same term or object applies to others. The role of egocentric thought in memory does have practical implications for the student: One of the best ways to recall material from this book is to relate it to your personal experiences—to think how it applies to you. This will help you do better on the next test.

The Self-Serving Bias

The **self-serving bias** refers to a tendency for individuals to make dispositional attributions for their successes and situational attributions for their failures. For example, in a basketball game, if Linda sinks a difficult shot, chances are she will attribute it to her great eye and leaping ability. On the other hand, if she misses, she might claim that she was fouled or that there was a soft spot in the floor that led to a mistiming of her jump. Automobile driving provides many opportunities for motorists to engage in the self-serving bias. For example, the following are actual written reports given by drivers involved in automobile accidents. As can be seen, the self-serving bias is much in evidence.[99]

- The telephone pole was approaching fast; I attempted to swerve out of its way, when it struck the front of my car.
- An invisible car came out of nowhere, struck my vehicle, and vanished.
- My car was legally parked as it backed into the other vehicle.
- As I reached an intersection, a hedge sprang up, obscuring my vision. I did not see the other car.
- A pedestrian hit me and went under my car.

Researchers have gathered a great deal of evidence in support of the informal observation that we take credit for the good and deny the bad. For example: (1) Students who do well on an exam tend to attribute their performance to ability and effort, whereas those who do poorly attribute it to an unfair exam or bad luck; (2) gamblers perceive their successes as based on skill and their failures as a fluke; (3) when married persons estimate how much of the housework each routinely did, their combined total of housework performed amounts to far more than 100 percent—in other words, each person thinks he or she did a greater proportion of the work than their partner thinks he or she did; (4) in general, people rate themselves more positively than others do, believing that they themselves are better than average; (5) two-person teams performing a skilled task accept credit for the good scores but assign most of the blame for the poor scores to their partner; and (6) when asked to explain why someone else dislikes them, college students take little responsibility for themselves (i.e., there must be something wrong with this other person), but when told that someone else likes them, the students attribute it to their own personality.[100] As Greenwald and Breckler note, "The presented self is (usually) too good to be true; the (too) good self is often genuinely believed."[101] An interesting question is: Why do people engage in the self-serving bias? One explanation that accounts for some of the data is purely cognitive; individuals are aware of different information as actors than as observers.[102] Consider the finding that couples' estimation of their contribution to housework totals more than 100 percent. This effect could easily be due to differential attention and memory. For example, every time I scrub the floor, clean the toilet, or wash the dishes, I am much more likely to keep track and recall my contributions than when you do it. It is very likely that I can recall doing the dishes four times last week, taking out the trash, cleaning up the garage, grooming the dog, and mowing the yard. I recall that you cleaned the oven, but I missed (or forgot) the fact that you cooked dinner and washed dishes on 3 nights, purchased the groceries, vacuumed the rugs, trimmed the hedges, and paid the bills. When I go to estimate the amount of housework each of us does, of course, I think I do more.

But a purely cognitive-informational explanation cannot account for all the examples of the self-serving bias. For example, the amount of information available to successful and unsuccessful test takers and gamblers is likely to be similar. Another explanation proposed for the self-serving bias is that we are *motivated* to engage in such attributions to protect and maintain our **self-concepts** and self-esteem. According to this perspective, if I have a positive self-view, it is easy for me to see and accept myself as accomplishing positive things; on the other hand, a threat to this positive self-view must be defended against—perhaps through denial or a good excuse. This is called **ego-defensive** behavior.

How can we be certain that some of this behavior is motivated by a desire to maintain high self-esteem? Let us look at the conditions under which we are most likely to engage in ego-defensive attributions. In a series of experiments, Gifford Weary and her colleagues[103] found that the likelihood of giving a self-serving explanation increases when (1) the person is highly involved in the behavior; (2) the person feels responsible for the outcome of his or her action; and (3) the person's behavior is publicly observed by others. Further, people are least likely to offer a self-serving attribution when they feel that they can't get away with it—that is, when the audience makes it clear that an excuse is not appropriate or that an excuse will set up unreasonable expectations about future performance. In other words, self-serving explanations occur most when the self is "on the line"—when the self is clearly threatened or when the person sees an opportunity to achieve a positive image.

Of What Value Are Self-Biases?

When we treat mental processes as objects and discover that the overwhelming majority of people engage in such behavior as egocentric thought and the self-serving bias, it would be easy to conclude that (1) humans are pathetic, irrational, silly organisms who blind themselves from seeing things as they are, and (2) self-biases should be eliminated at all cost. Such conclusions would be a gross oversimplification. First, as mentioned earlier, although we humans frequently engage in biased thinking, we are also capable of clear, rational thought. Moreover, self-biases can serve important purposes. The individual who believes that he or she is the cause of good things will try harder and persist longer to achieve difficult goals. Such efforts can result in new scientific discoveries, great works of art, or political agreements that can be of great benefit to millions of people.

An interesting example of this kind of process emerges from the results of a study of basketball players done by Robert Grove and his colleagues.[104] Grove found that winning teams attributed their success to stable causes, while teams that lost attributed their failure to unstable causes like flukes, bad breaks, and the like. This bias can be beneficial (at least in the short run) because it allows losing teams to avoid being psychologically devastated by setbacks, to hang in there and continue playing in the face of a string of defeats.

There may be even more important temporary benefits to self-biases as well. That's what Shelley Taylor found.[105] She interviewed hundreds of people who had faced tragic or near-tragic events. Her interviewees included rape victims, cancer patients, and others with life-threatening illnesses. She found that, far from destroying these individuals, the tragic event had given most of them a new lease on life. This was especially true if they held overly *optimistic* perceptions concerning their chances of recovery from disease or believed that they could control the likelihood of future victimization. The belief that one can overcome tragic obstacles—even if this belief was an illusion—led these people to adopt better health practices and to develop coping strategies for dealing with stress that had a salutary effect on their lives.

Similarly, Martin Seligman[106] has found across a variety of studies that an optimistic style of thinking—believing that a defeat is due to bad luck and can be overcome by effort and ability—leads to more achievement, better health, and an improved mental outlook. In brief, engaging in egocentric thought and self-serving attributions has an array of benefits. At the same time, it is important to bear in mind that these positive consequences are not without their price—and as you have undoubtedly gathered, the major price is a somewhat distorted picture of the self and the world in general.

Ironically, as we have seen, this distorted picture of the world is frequently caused by a motive to justify ourselves and our behavior—to interpret or distort the meaning of our actions so as to bring them in line with what we would regard as consistent with the actions of a morally good and sensible human being. For me, one of the most fascinating aspects of the social animal is our touching need to see ourselves as good and sensible people—and how this need frequently leads us to perform actions that are neither good nor sensible. The human tendency for self-justification is so important that it deserves a chapter all to itself; it is to this chapter that we now turn.

Saul Steinberg, *Untitled drawing*, ink on paper.
Published in Steinberg, *The New World*, 1965.
© The Saul Steinberg Foundation / Artists Rights Society (ARS), New York

5
Self-Justification

Picture the following scene: A young man named Sam is being hypnotized. The hypnotist gives Sam a posthypnotic suggestion, telling him that, when the clock strikes 4:00, he will (1) go to the closet, get his raincoat and galoshes, and put them on; (2) grab an umbrella; (3) walk eight blocks to the supermarket and purchase six bottles of bourbon; and (4) return home. Sam is told that, as soon as he reenters his apartment, he will "snap out of it" and be himself again.

When the clock strikes 4:00, Sam immediately heads for the closet, dons his raincoat and galoshes, grabs his umbrella, and trudges out the door on his quest for bourbon. There are a few strange things about this errand: (1) it is a clear, sunshiny day—there isn't a cloud in the sky; (2) there is a liquor store half a block away that sells bourbon for the same price as the supermarket eight blocks away; and (3) Sam doesn't drink.

Sam arrives home, opens the door, reenters his apartment, snaps out of his "trance," and discovers himself standing there in his raincoat and galoshes, with his umbrella in one hand and a huge sack of liquor bottles in the other. He looks momentarily confused. His friend, the hypnotist, says,

"Hey, Sam, where have you been?"

"Oh, just down to the store."

"What did you buy?"

"Um . . . um . . . it seems I bought this bourbon."

"But you don't drink, do you?"

"No, but . . . um . . . um . . . I'm going to do a lot of entertaining during the next several weeks, and some of my friends do."

"How come you're wearing all that rain gear on such a sunny day?"

"Well . . . actually, the weather is quite changeable this time of year, and I didn't want to take any chances."

"But there isn't a cloud in the sky."

"Well, you never can tell."

"By the way, where did you buy the liquor?"

"Oh, heh, heh. Well, um . . . down at the supermarket."

"How come you went that far?"

"Well, um . . . um . . . it was such a nice day, I thought it might be fun to take a long walk."

People are motivated to justify their own actions, beliefs, and feelings. When they do something, they will try, if at all possible, to convince themselves (and others) that it was a logical, reasonable thing to do. There *was* a good reason why Sam performed those silly actions—he was hypnotized. But because Sam didn't know he had been hypnotized, and because it was difficult for him to accept the fact that he was capable of behaving in a nonsensical manner, he went to great lengths to convince himself (and his friend) that there was a method to his madness, that his actions were actually quite sensible.

The experiment by Stanley Schachter and Jerry Singer discussed in Chapter 2 can also be understood in these terms. Recall that these investigators injected people with epinephrine. Those who were forewarned about the symptoms caused by this drug (palpitations of the heart, sweaty palms, and hand tremors) had a sensible explanation for the symptoms when they appeared. "Oh, yeah, that's just the drug affecting me." Those who were misled about the effects of the drug, however, had no such handy, logical explanation for their symptoms. But they couldn't leave the symptoms unjustified; they tried to account for them by convincing themselves that they were either deliriously happy or angry, depending on the social stimuli in the environment.

The concept of **self-justification** can be applied more broadly still. Suppose you are in the midst of a great natural disaster, such as an earthquake. All around you, buildings are toppling and people are getting killed and injured. Needless to say, you are frightened. Is there any need to seek justification for this fear? Certainly not. The evidence is all around you; the injured people and the devastated buildings are ample justification for your fear. But suppose, instead, the earthquake occurred in a neighboring town. You can feel the tremors, and you hear stories of the damage done to the other town. You are terribly frightened, but you are not in the midst of the devastated area; neither you nor the people around you have been hurt, and no buildings in your town have been damaged. Would you need to justify this fear? Yes. Much like the people in the Schachter-Singer experiment experiencing strong physical reactions to epinephrine but not knowing why, and much like our hypnotized friend in the raincoat and galoshes, you would be inclined to justify your own actions or feelings. In this situation, you see nothing to be afraid of in the immediate vicinity, so you would be inclined to seek justification for the fact that you are scared out of your wits.

These disaster situations are not hypothetical examples; they actually occurred in India. In the aftermath of an earthquake, investigators collected and analyzed the rumors being spread. What they discovered was rather startling: Jamuna Prasad,[1] an Indian psychologist, found that when the disaster occurred in a neighboring village such that the residents in question could feel the tremors but were not in imminent danger, there was an abundance of rumors forecasting impending doom. Specifically, the residents of this village believed, and helped spread rumors to the effect, that (1) a flood was rushing toward them; (2) February 26 would be a day of deluge and destruction; (3) there would be another severe earthquake on the day of the lunar eclipse; (4) there would be a cyclone within a few days; and (5) unforeseeable calamities were on the horizon.

Why in the world would people invent, believe, and communicate such stories? Were these people masochists? Were they paranoid? Certainly these rumors would not encourage the people to feel calm and secure. One rather compelling explanation is that the people were terribly frightened, and because there was not ample justification for this fear, they invented their own justification. Thus, they were not compelled to feel foolish. After all, if a cyclone is on the way, isn't it perfectly reasonable that I should be wild-eyed with fear? This explanation is bolstered by Durganand Sinha's study of rumors.[2] Sinha investigated the rumors being spread in an Indian village following a disaster of similar magnitude. The major difference between the situation in Prasad's study and the one in Sinha's study was that the people being investigated by Sinha had actually suffered the destruction and witnessed the damage. They were scared, but they had good reasons to be frightened; they had no need to seek additional justification for their fears. Thus, their rumors contained no prediction of impending disaster and no serious exaggeration. Indeed, if anything, the rumors were comforting. For example, one rumor predicted (falsely) that the water supply would be restored in a very short time.

Leon Festinger organized this array of findings and used them as the basis for a powerful theory of human motivation that he called the theory of *cognitive dissonance*.[3] It is a remarkably simple theory but, as we shall see, the range of its application is enormous. Basically, **cognitive dissonance** is a state of tension that occurs whenever an individual simultaneously holds two cognitions (ideas, attitudes, beliefs, opinions) that are psychologically inconsistent. Stated differently, two cognitions are dissonant if, when considered alone, the opposite of one follows from the other. Because the occurrence of cognitive dissonance is unpleasant, people are motivated to reduce it; this is roughly analogous to the processes involved in the induction and reduction of such drives as hunger or thirst—except that, here, the driving force arises from cognitive discomfort rather than physiological needs. To hold two ideas that contradict each other is to flirt with absurdity, and—as Albert Camus, the existentialist philosopher, has observed—humans are creatures who spend their lives trying to convince themselves that their existence is not absurd.

How do we convince ourselves that our lives are not absurd—that is, how do we reduce cognitive dissonance? By changing one or both cognitions in such a way as to render them more compatible (more consonant) with each other or by adding more cognitions that help bridge the gap between the original cognitions.*

Let me cite an example that is, alas, all too familiar to many people. Suppose a person smokes cigarettes and then reads a report of the medical evidence linking cigarette smoking to lung cancer and other respiratory diseases. The smoker experiences dissonance. The cognition "I smoke cigarettes" is dissonant with the cognition "cigarette smoking produces cancer." Clearly, the most efficient way for this person to reduce dissonance in such a situation is to give up smoking. The cognition "cigarette smoking produces cancer" is consonant with the cognition "I do not smoke."

But, for most people, it is not easy to give up smoking. Imagine Sally, a young woman who tried to stop smoking but failed. What will she do to reduce dissonance? In all probability, she will try to work on the other cognition: "Cigarette smoking produces cancer." Sally might attempt to make light of evidence linking cigarette smoking to cancer. For example, she might try to convince herself that the experimental evidence is inconclusive. In addition, she might seek out intelligent people who smoke and, by so doing, convince herself that if Debbie, Nicole, and Larry smoke, it can't be all that dangerous. Sally might switch to a filter-tipped brand and delude herself into believing that the filter traps the cancer-producing materials. Finally, she might add cognitions that are consonant with smoking in an attempt to make the behavior less absurd in spite of its danger. Thus, Sally might enhance the value placed on smoking; that is, she might come to believe smoking is an important and highly enjoyable activity that is essential for re-

---

*In the preceding chapter, we learned that beliefs and attitudes are not always good predictors of a person's behavior—that is to say, behavior is not always consistent with relevant beliefs and attitudes. Here we are making the point that most people feel that their beliefs and attitudes *should be* consistent with their behavior and, therefore, are motivated to justify their behavior when it is inconsistent with a preexisting attitude.

laxation: "I may lead a shorter life, but it will be a more enjoyable one." Similarly, she might try to make a virtue out of smoking by developing a romantic, devil-may-care self-image, flouting danger by smoking cigarettes. All such behavior reduces dissonance by reducing the absurdity of the notion of going out of one's way to contract cancer. Sally has justified her behavior by cognitively minimizing the danger or by exaggerating the importance of the action. In effect, she has succeeded either in constructing a new attitude or in changing an existing attitude.

Indeed, shortly after the publicity surrounding the original surgeon general's report in 1964, a survey was conducted[4] to assess people's reactions to the new evidence that smoking helps cause cancer. Nonsmokers overwhelmingly believed the health report, only 10 percent of those queried saying that the link between smoking and cancer had not been proven to exist; these respondents had no motivation to disbelieve the report. The smokers faced a more difficult quandary. Smoking is a difficult habit to break; only 9 percent of the smokers had been able to quit. To justify continuing the activity, smokers tended to debunk the report. They were more likely to deny the evidence: 40 percent of the heavy smokers said a link had not been proven to exist. They were also more apt to employ rationalizations: Over twice as many smokers as nonsmokers agreed that there are many hazards in life and that both smokers and nonsmokers get cancer.

Smokers who are painfully aware of the health hazards associated with smoking may reduce dissonance in yet another way—by minimizing the extent of their habit. One study[5] found that of 155 smokers who smoked between one and two packs of cigarettes a day, 60 percent considered themselves moderate smokers; the remaining 40 percent considered themselves heavy smokers. How can we explain these different self-perceptions? Not surprisingly, those who labeled themselves as moderates were more aware of the pathological long-term effects of smoking than were those who labeled themselves as heavy smokers. That is, these particular smokers apparently reduced dissonance by convincing themselves that smoking one or two packs a day isn't really all that much. *Moderate* and *heavy* are, after all, subjective terms.

Imagine a teenage girl who has not yet begun to smoke. After reading the Surgeon General's report, is she apt to believe it? Like most of the nonsmokers in the survey, she should. The evidence is objectively sound, the source is expert and trustworthy, and there is no reason not to believe the report. And this is the crux of the matter. Earlier in this book, I made the point that people strive to be right, and that values and beliefs become internalized when they appear to be correct. It is this striving to be right that motivates people to pay close attention to what other people are doing and to heed the advice of expert, trustworthy communicators. This is extremely rational behavior. There are forces, however, that can work against this rational behavior. The theory of cognitive dissonance does not picture people as rational beings; rather, it pictures them as rationalizing beings. According to the underlying assumptions of the theory, we humans are motivated not so much to *be* right as to believe we are right (and wise, and decent, and good).

Sometimes, our motivation to be right and our motivation to believe we are right work in the same direction. This is what is happening with the young woman who doesn't smoke and therefore finds it easy to accept the notion that smoking causes lung cancer. This would also be true for a smoker who encounters the evidence linking cigarette smoking to lung cancer and does succeed in giving up cigarettes. Occasionally, however, the need to reduce dissonance (the need to convince oneself that one is right or good) leads to behavior that is maladaptive and therefore irrational. For example, many people have tried to quit smoking and failed. What do these people do? It would be erroneous to assume that they simply swallow hard and prepare to die. They don't. Instead, they try to reduce their dissonance in a different way: namely, by convincing themselves that smoking isn't as bad as they thought. Thus, Rick Gibbons and his colleagues[6] recently found that heavy smokers who attended a smoking cessation clinic, quit smoking for a while and then relapsed into heavy smoking again, subsequently succeeded in lowering their perception of the dangers of smoking.

Why might this change of heart occur? If a person makes a serious commitment to a course of action, such as quitting smoking, and then fails to keep that commitment, his or her self-concept as a strong, self-controlled individual is threatened. This, of course, arouses dissonance. One way to reduce this dissonance and regain a healthy sense of self—if not a healthy set of lungs—is to trivialize the commitment by perceiving smoking as less dangerous. A more general study that tracked the progress of 135 students who made New Year's resolutions supports this observation.[7] Individuals who broke their resolutions—such as to quit smoking, lose weight, or exercise more—initially felt bad about themselves for failing but, after a short time, succeeded in downplaying the importance of the resolution. Ironically, making light of a commitment they failed to keep serves to restore their self-esteem but it also makes self-defeat a near certainty in the future. In the short run, they are able to feel better about themselves; in the long run, however, they have drastically reduced the chances that they'll ever succeed in achieving their goals.

Is this the only way to reduce the dissonance associated with failing to achieve a goal? No. An alternative response—and perhaps a less maladaptive one—would be to lower one's expectations for success. For example, a person who has been unable to give up smoking completely, but who has cut down on the number of cigarettes smoked daily, could interpret this outcome as a partial success rather than as a complete failure. This course of action would soften the blow to his or her self-esteem for having failed while still holding out the possibility of achieving success in future efforts to quit smoking altogether.

Let's stay with the topic of cigarette smoking for a moment and consider an extreme example: Suppose you are one of the top executives of a major cigarette company—and therefore in a situation of maximum commitment to the idea of cigarette smoking. Your job consists of producing, advertising, and selling cigarettes to millions of people. If it is true that cigarette smoking causes cancer, then, in a sense, you are partially responsible for the illness and death of a great many people. This would produce a painful degree of dissonance: Your cognition "I am a decent, kind human being" would be dissonant with your cognition "I am contributing to the early death of a great many people." In order to reduce this dissonance, you must try to convince yourself that cigarette smoking is not harmful; this would involve a refutation of the mountain of evidence suggesting a causal link between cigarettes and cancer. Moreover, in order to convince yourself further that you are a good, moral person, you might go so far as to demonstrate how much you disbelieve the evidence by smoking a great deal yourself. If your need is great enough, you might even succeed in convincing yourself that cigarettes are good for people. Thus, in order to see yourself as wise, good, and right, you take action that is stupid and detrimental to your health.

This analysis is so fantastic that it's almost beyond belief—almost. In 1994, Congress conducted hearings on the dangers of smoking. At these hearings, the top executives of most of the major tobacco companies admitted they were smokers and actually argued that cigarettes are no more harmful or addictive than playing video games or eating Twinkies! In a subsequent hearing, in 1997, James J. Morgan, president and chief executive officer of the leading U.S. cigarette maker, said that cigarettes are not pharmacologically addictive. "Look, I like gummy bears, and I eat gummy bears. And I don't like it when I don't eat gummy bears," Morgan said. "But I'm certainly not addicted to them."[8] This kind of public denial is nothing new, of course. Over a quarter of a century ago, the following news item was released by the *Washington Post*'s News Service:

> Jack Landry pulls what must be his 30th Marlboro of the day out of one of the two packs on his desk, lights a match to it and tells how he doesn't believe all those reports about smoking and cancer and emphysema. He has just begun to market yet another cigarette for Philip Morris U.S.A. and is brimming over with satisfaction over its prospects. But how does he square with his conscience the spending of $10 million in these United States over the next year to lure people into smoking his new brand? "It's not a matter of that," says Landry, Philip Morris' vice president for marketing. "Nearly half the adults in this country smoke. It's a basic commodity for them. I'm serving a need. . . . There are studies by pretty eminent medical and scientific authorities, one on a theory of stress, on how a heck of a lot of people, if they didn't have cigarette smoking to relieve stress, would be one hell of a lot worse off. And there are plenty of valid studies that indicate cigarette smoking and all those diseases are not related." His satisfaction, says Landry, comes from being very good at his job in a very competitive business, and he will point out

that Philip Morris and its big-selling Marlboro has just passed Ameri-can Tobacco as the No. 2 cigarette seller in America (R. J. Reynolds is still No. 1). Why a new cigarette now? Because it is there to be sold, says Landry. And therein lies the inspiration of the marketing of a new American cigarette, which Landry confidently predicts will have a 1 per-cent share of the American market within 12 months. That 1 percent will equal about five billion cigarettes and a healthy profit for Philip Morris U.S.A.[9]

It is possible that James Morgan and Jack Landry are simply lying. (Fancy that; executive officers of a tobacco company actually lying!) But it may be a bit more complicated than that; my guess is that, over the years, they may have succeeded in deceiving *themselves*. Near the close of Chapter 3, I dis-cussed the fact that information campaigns are relatively ineffective when they attempt to change deep-seated attitudes. We can now see precisely why. If people are committed to an attitude, the information the communicator presents arouses dissonance; frequently, the best way to reduce the dissonance is to reject or distort the evidence. The deeper a person's commitment to an attitude, the greater his or her tendency to reject dissonant evidence.

To mention one chilling example of this process, consider the Hale-Bopp suicides. In 1997, 39 members of Heaven's Gate, an obscure religious cult, were found dead at a luxury estate in Rancho Santa Fe, California—partici-pants in a mass suicide. Several weeks earlier, a few members of the cult had walked into a specialty store and purchased an expensive high-powered tele-scope so that they might get a clearer view of the Hale-Bopp comet and the spaceship they fervently believed was traveling behind it. Their belief was that, when the comet got close to Earth, it was time to rid themselves of their "Earthly containers" (their bodies) by killing themselves so that their essence could be picked up by the spaceship. A few days after buying the telescope, they came back to the store, returned the telescope, and politely asked for their money back. When the store manager asked them if they had had prob-lems with the scope, they indicated that it was defective: "We found the comet all right, but we can't find the spaceship that is following it." Needless to say, there was no spaceship. But, if you are so convinced of the existence of a spaceship to die for a ride on it, and your telescope doesn't reveal it, then, obviously, there must be something wrong with your telescope!

Juicy anecdotes are suggestive. But they do not constitute scientific evi-dence and, therefore, are not convincing in themselves. Again, taking the cig-arette example, it is always possible that Mr. Morgan and Mr. Landry know that cigarettes are harmful and are simply being cynical. Likewise, it is possi-ble that Landry always believed cigarettes were good for people even before he began to peddle them. Obviously, if either of these possibilities were true, his excitement about the benefits of cigarette smoking could hardly be attrib-uted to dissonance. Much more convincing would be a demonstration of a clear case of attitudinal distortion in a unique event. Such a demonstration was provided back in the 1950s by (of all things) a football game in the Ivy League. An important game between Princeton and Dartmouth, the contest was billed as a grudge match, and this soon became evident on the field: The game is remembered as the roughest and dirtiest in the history of either school. Princeton's star player was an All-American running back named Dick Kazmaier; as the game progressed, it became increasingly clear that the Dartmouth players were out to get him. Whenever he carried the ball, he was gang-tackled, piled on, and mauled. He was finally forced to leave the game with a broken nose. Meanwhile, the Princeton team was not exactly inactive: Soon after Kazmaier's injury, a Dartmouth player was carried off the field with a broken leg. Several fistfights broke out on the field in the course of the game, and many injuries were suffered on both sides.

Sometime after the game, a couple of psychologists—Albert Hastorf of Dartmouth and Hadley Cantril of Princeton[10]—visited both campuses and showed films of the game to a number of students on each campus. The students were instructed to be completely objective and, while watching the film, to take notes of each infraction of the rules, how it started, and who was responsible. As you might imagine, there was a huge difference in the way this game was viewed by the students at each university. There was a strong tendency for the students to see their own fellow students as victims of illegal infractions rather than as perpetrators of such acts of aggression. Moreover, this was no minor distortion: It was found that Princeton students saw fully twice as many violations on the part of the Dartmouth players as the Dartmouth students saw. Again, people are not passive receptacles for the deposition of information. The manner in which they view and interpret information depends on how deeply they are committed to a particular belief or course of action. Individuals will distort the objective world in order to reduce their dissonance. The manner in which they will distort and the intensity of their distortion are highly predictable.

A few years later, Lenny Bruce, a perceptive comedian and social commentator (who almost certainly never read about cognitive dissonance theory), had the following insight into the 1960 presidential election campaign between Richard Nixon and John Kennedy:

> I would be with a bunch of Kennedy fans watching the debate and their comment would be, "He's really slaughtering Nixon." Then we would all go to another apartment, and the Nixon fans would say, "How do you like the shellacking he gave Kennedy?" And then I realized that each group loved their candidate so that a guy would have to be this blatant— he would have to look into the camera and say: "I am a thief, a crook, do you hear me, I am the worst choice you could ever make for the Presidency!" And even then his following would say, "Now there's an honest man for you. It takes a big guy to admit that. There's the kind of guy we need for President."[11]

People don't like to see or hear things that conflict with their deeply held beliefs or wishes. An ancient response to such bad news was literally to kill the messenger. A modern-day figurative version of killing the messenger is to blame the media for the presentation of material that produces the pain of dissonance. For example, when Ronald Reagan was running for president in 1980, *Time* published an analysis of his campaign. Subsequent angry letters to the editor vividly illustrated the widely divergent responses of his supporters, on the one hand, and his detractors, on the other. Consider the following two letters:[12]

> Lawrence Barrett's pre-election piece on Candidate Ronald Reagan [October 20] was a slick hatchet job, and you know it. You ought to be ashamed of yourselves for printing it disguised as an objective look at the man.

> Your story on "The Real Ronald Reagan" did it. Why didn't you just editorially endorse him? Barrett glosses over Reagan's fatal flaws so handily that the "real" Ronald Reagan came across as the answer to all our problems.

The diversity of perception reflected in these letters is not unique to the 1980 campaign. It happened with Clinton supporters and detractors. It happened with G. W. Bush supporters and detractors. Indeed, it happens every 4 years. During the next presidential election, check out the letters to the editor of your favorite news magazine following a piece on one of the leading candidates. You will find a similar array of divergent perceptions.

Dissonance Reduction and Rational Behavior

I have referred to dissonance-reducing behavior as "irrational." By this I mean it is often maladaptive in that it can prevent people from learning important facts or from finding real solutions to their problems. On the other hand, it does serve a purpose: Dissonance-reducing behavior is ego-defensive behavior; by reducing dissonance, we maintain a positive image of ourselves—an image that depicts us as good, or smart, or worthwhile. Again, although this ego-defensive behavior can be considered useful, it can have disastrous consequences. In the laboratory, the irrationality of dissonance-reducing behavior has been amply demonstrated by Edward Jones and Rika Kohler.[13] These investigators selected individuals who were deeply committed to a position on the issue of racial segregation; some of the participants were in favor of segregation, and others were opposed to it. These individuals were allowed to read a series of arguments on both sides of the issue. Some of these arguments were extremely sensible and plausible, and others were so implausible that they bordered on the ridiculous. Jones and Kohler were interested in determining which of the arguments people would remember best. If people were purely rational, we would expect them to remember the plausible arguments best and the implausible arguments least; why in the world would people want to keep implausible arguments in their heads? Accordingly, the rational person would rehearse and remember all the arguments that made sense and would slough off all the ridiculous arguments. What does the theory of cognitive dissonance predict? It is comforting to have all the wise people on your side and all the fools on the other side: A silly argument in favor of one's own position arouses dissonance because it raises doubts about the wisdom of that position or the intelligence of the people who agree with it. Likewise, a plausible argument on the other side of the issue also arouses dissonance because it raises the possibility that the other side is right. Because these arguments arouse dissonance, one tries not to think about them—that is, one might not learn them very well, or one might simply forget about them. This is exactly what Jones and Kohler found. Their participants did not remember in a rational-functional manner. They tended to remember the plausible arguments agreeing with their own position and the implausible arguments agreeing with the opposing position.

In a conceptually similar experiment, Charles Lord, Lee Ross, and Mark Lepper[14] showed that we do not process information in an unbiased manner. Rather, we distort it in a way that fits our preconceived notions. These investigators selected several Stanford University students who opposed capital punishment and several who favored it. They showed the students two research articles that discussed whether or not the death penalty tends to deter violent crimes. One study confirmed and the other study disconfirmed the existing beliefs of the students. If these students were perfectly rational, they might conclude that the issue is a complex one, and accordingly, the two groups of students might move closer to each other in their beliefs about capital punishment. On the other hand, dissonance theory predicts that they would distort the two articles, clasping the confirming article to their bosoms and hailing it as clearly supportive of their belief while finding methodological or conceptual flaws in the disconfirming article and refusing to be influenced by it. This is precisely what happened. Indeed, rather than coming closer in their beliefs after being exposed to this two-sided presentation, the two groups of students disagreed more sharply than they did beforehand. This process probably accounts for the fact that, on issues like politics and religion, people who are deeply committed will almost never come to see things our way, no matter how powerful and balanced our arguments are.

Those of us who have worked extensively with the theory of cognitive dissonance do not deny that humans are capable of rational behavior. The theory merely suggests that a good deal of our behavior is not rational—although, from inside, it may seem very sensible indeed. If you ask the hypnotized young man why he wore a raincoat on a sunny day, he'll come up with an answer he feels is sensible; if you ask the vice president of Philip Morris why he smokes, he'll give you a reason that makes sense to him—he'll tell you how good it is for everyone's health; if you ask Jones and Kohler's participants why they remembered one particular set of arguments rather than others, they'll insist that the arguments they remembered were a fair and representative sample of those they read. Similarly, the students in the experiment on capital punishment will insist that the evidence against their position is flawed. It is important to note that the world is not divided into rational people on the one side and dissonance reducers on the other. People are not all the same, and some people are able to tolerate dissonance better than others, but we are all capable of rational behavior and we are all capable of dissonance-reducing behavior, depending on the circumstances. Occasionally, the same person can manifest both behaviors in rapid succession.

The rationality and irrationality of human behavior will be illustrated over and over again during the next several pages as we discuss some of the wide ramifications of our need for self-justification. These ramifications run virtually the entire gamut of human behavior, but for the sake of conserving time and space, I will sample only a few of these. Let us begin with the decision-making process, a process that shows humans at their most rational and their most irrational in quick succession.

Dissonance as a Consequence of Making a Decision

Suppose you are about to make a decision—about the purchase of a new car, for example. This involves a significant amount of money, so it is, by definition, an important decision. After looking around, you are torn between getting a van and purchasing a compact model. There are various advantages and disadvantages to each: The van would be convenient; you can haul things in it, sleep in it during long trips, and it has plenty of power, but it gets atrocious mileage and is not easy to park. The compact model is less roomy, and you are concerned about its safety, but it is less expensive to buy and operate, it is more fun to drive, and you've heard it has a pretty good repair record. My guess is that, *before* you make the decision, you will seek as much information as you can. Chances are you will read *Consumer Reports* to find out what this expert, unbiased source has to say. Perhaps you'll confer with friends who own a van or a compact car. You'll probably visit the automobile dealers to test-drive the vehicles to see how each one feels. All of this predecision behavior is perfectly rational. Let us assume you make a decision—you buy the compact car. What happens next? Your behavior will begin to change: No longer will you seek objective information about all makes of cars. Chances are you may begin to spend more time talking with the owners of small cars. You will begin to talk about the number of miles to the gallon as though it were the most important thing in the world. My guess is that you will not be prone to spend much time thinking about the fact that you can't sleep in your compact. Similarly, your mind will skim lightly over the fact that driving your new car can be particularly hazardous in a collision and that the brakes are not very responsive, although your failure to attend to these shortcomings could conceivably cost you your life.

How does this sort of thing come about? Following a decision—especially a difficult one, or one that involves a significant amount of time, effort, or money—people almost always experience dissonance. This is so because the chosen alternative is seldom entirely positive and the rejected alternatives are seldom entirely negative. In this example, your cognition that you bought a compact is dissonant with your cognition about any deficiencies the car may have. Similarly, all the positive aspects of the other cars that you considered buying but did not purchase are dissonant with your cognition that you did not buy one of them. A good way to reduce such dissonance is to seek out exclusively positive information about the car you chose and avoid negative information about it. One source of safe information is advertisements; it is a safe bet that an ad will not run down its own product. Accordingly, one might predict that a person who had recently purchased a new car will begin to read advertisements selectively, reading more ads about his or her car *after the purchase* than people who have *not* recently purchased the same model. Moreover, owners of new cars will tend to steer clear of ads for other makes of cars. This is exactly what Danuta Ehrlich and her colleagues[15] found in a well-known survey of advertising readership. In short, Ehrlich's data suggest that, *after* making decisions, people try to gain reassurance that their decisions were wise by seeking information that is certain to be reassuring.

People do not always need help from Madison Avenue to gain reassurance; they can do a pretty good job of reassuring themselves. An experiment by Jack Brehm[16] demonstrates how this can come about. Posing as a marketing researcher, Brehm showed several women eight different appliances (a toaster, an electric coffee maker, a sandwich grill, and the like) and asked that they rate them in terms of how attractive each appliance was. As a reward, each woman was told she could have one of the appliances as a gift—and she was given a choice between two of the products she had rated as being equally attractive. After she chose one, it was wrapped up and given to her. Several minutes later, she was asked to rate the products again. It was found that after receiving the appliance of her choice, each woman rated the attractiveness of that appliance somewhat higher and decreased the rating of the appliance she had a chance to own but rejected. Again, making a decision produces dissonance: Cognitions about any negative aspects of the preferred object are dissonant with having chosen it, and cognitions about the positive aspects of the unchosen object are dissonant with *not* having chosen it. To reduce dissonance, people cognitively spread apart the alternatives. That is, *after making their decision,* the women in Brehm's study emphasized the positive attributes of the appliance they decided to own while deemphasizing its negative attributes; for the appliance they decided *not* to own, they emphasized its negative attributes and deemphasized its positive attributes.

The tendency to justify one's choices is not limited to consumer decisions. In fact, research has demonstrated that similar processes can even affect our romantic relationships and our willingness to consider becoming involved with alternative partners. In a study conducted by Dennis Johnson and Caryl Rusbult,[17] college students were asked to evaluate the probable success of a new computer dating service on campus. Participants were shown pictures of individuals of the opposite sex, who they believed were applicants to the dating service. They were then asked to rate the attractiveness of these applicants, as well as how much they believed they would enjoy a potential date with him or her—a possibility that was presented in a realistic manner. The results of this study were remarkably similar to Brehm's findings about appliances: The more heavily committed the students were to their current romantic partners, the more negative were their ratings of the attractiveness of alternative partners presented in the study. In a subsequent experiment, Jeffry Simpson and his colleagues[18] also found that those in committed relationships saw opposite-sex persons as less physically and sexually attractive than did those who weren't in committed relationships. In addition, Simpson and his co-workers showed that this effect holds only for "available others"; when presented with individuals who were somewhat older or who were of the same sex, people in committed relationships did not derogate their attractiveness. In short, no threat, no dissonance; no dissonance, no derogation.

In sum, whether we are talking about appliances or romantic partners, once a firm commitment has been made, people tend to focus on the positive aspects of their choices and to downplay the attractive qualities of the unchosen alternatives.

Some Historical Examples of the Consequences of Decisions

Although some of the material discussed above is benign enough, it is impossible to overstate the potential dangers posed by our susceptibility to these tendencies. When I mentioned that ignoring potential danger in order to reduce dissonance could conceivably lead to a person's death, I meant that literally. Suppose a madman has taken over your country and has decided to eradicate all members of your religious group. But you don't know that for sure. What you do know is that your country is being occupied, that the leader of the occupation forces does not like your religious group, and that occasionally members of your faith are forced to move from their homes and are kept in detention camps. What do you do? You could try to flee from your country; you could try to pass as a member of a different religious group; or you could sit tight and hope for the best. Each of these options is extremely dangerous: It is difficult to escape or to pass and go undetected; and if you are caught trying to flee or disguising your identity, the penalty is immediate execution. On the other hand, deciding to sit tight could be a disastrous decision if it turns out that your religious group is being systematically annihilated. Let us suppose you decide not to take action. That is, you commit yourself to sit tight—turning your back on opportunities to try either to escape or to pass. Such an important decision naturally produces a great deal of dissonance. In order to reduce dissonance, you convince yourself that you made a wise decision—that is, you convince yourself that, although people of your religious sect are made to move and are being treated unfairly, they are not being killed unless they break the law. This position is not difficult to maintain because there is no unambiguous evidence to the contrary.

Suppose that, months later, a respected man from your town tells you that while hiding in the forest, he witnessed soldiers butchering all the men, women, and children who had recently been deported from the town. I would predict that you would try to dismiss this information as untrue—that you would attempt to convince yourself that the reporter was lying or hallucinating. If you had listened to the man who tried to warn you, you might have escaped. Instead, you and your family are slaughtered.

Fantastic? Impossible? How could anyone not take the respected man seriously? The events described above are an accurate account of what happened in 1944 to the Jews in Sighet, Hungary.[19]

The processes of cognitive distortion and selective exposure to information may have been an important factor in the senseless escalation of the war in Vietnam. In a thought-provoking analysis of the Pentagon Papers, Ralph White suggested that dissonance blinded our leaders to information incompatible with the decisions they had already made. As White put it, "There was a tendency, when actions were out of line with ideas, for decision makers to align their ideas with their actions." To take just one of many examples, the decision to continue to escalate the bombing of North Vietnam was made at the price of ignoring crucial evidence from the CIA and other sources that made it clear that bombing would not break the will of the North Vietnamese people but, quite the contrary, would only strengthen their resolve:

> It is instructive, for instance, to compare [Secretary of Defense Robert] McNamara's highly factual evidence-oriented summary of the case against bombing in 1966 (pages 555–63 of the Pentagon Papers) with the Joint Chiefs' memorandum that disputed his conclusion and called the bombing one of our two trump cards, while it apparently ignored all of the facts that showed the opposite. Yet it was the Joint Chiefs who prevailed.[20]

White surmises that the reason the Joint Chiefs prevailed was that their advice was consonant with decisions already made which, in turn, led to several important assumptions that proved to be erroneous.[21]

Escalation is self-perpetuating. Once a small commitment is made, it sets the stage for ever-increasing commitments. The behavior needs to be justified, so attitudes are changed; this change in attitudes influences future decisions and behavior. The flavor of this kind of cognitive escalation is nicely captured in an analysis of the Pentagon Papers by the editors of *Time* magazine:

> Yet the bureaucracy, the Pentagon Papers indicate, always demanded new options; each option was to apply more force. Each tightening of the screw created a position that must be defended; once committed, the military pressure must be maintained.[22]

The process underlying escalation has been explored, on a more individual level, under controlled experimental conditions. Suppose you would like to enlist someone's aid in a massive undertaking, but you know the job you have in mind for the person is so difficult, and will require so much time and effort, that the person will surely decline. What should you do? One possibility is to get the person involved in a much smaller aspect of the job, one so easy that he or she wouldn't dream of turning it down. This action serves to commit the individual to "the cause." Once people are thus committed, the likelihood of their complying with the larger request increases. This phenomenon was demonstrated by Jonathan Freedman and Scott Fraser.[23] They attempted to induce several homeowners to put up a huge sign in their front yards reading "Drive Carefully." Because of the ugliness and obtrusiveness of this sign, most residents refused to put it up; only 17 percent complied. A different group of residents, however, was first "softened up" by an experimenter who got them to sign a petition favoring safe driving. Because signing a petition is an easy thing to do, virtually all who were asked agreed to sign. A few weeks later, a different experimenter went to each resident with the obtrusive, ugly sign reading "Drive Carefully." More than 55 percent of these residents allowed the sign to be put up on their property. Thus, when individuals commit themselves in a small way, the likelihood that they will commit themselves further in that direction is increased. This process of using small favors to encourage people to accede to larger requests had been dubbed the **foot-in-the-door technique.** It is effective because having done the smaller favor sets up pressure toward agreeing to do the larger favor; in effect, it provides justification in advance for complying with the large request.

Similar results were obtained by Patricia Pliner and her associates.[24] These investigators found that 46 percent of their sample were willing to make a small donation to the Cancer Society when they were approached directly. A similar group of people were asked 1 day earlier to wear a lapel pin publicizing the fund-raising drive. When approached the next day, approximately twice as many of these people were willing to make a contribution.

Think back to Stanley Milgram's classic experiments on obedience discussed in Chapter 2. Suppose that, at the very beginning of the experiment, Milgram had instructed his participants to deliver a shock of 450 volts. Do you think many people would have obeyed? Probably not. My guess is that, in a sense, the mild shocks near the beginning of the experiment served as a foot-in-the-door induction to Milgram's participants. Because the increases in shock level are gradual, the participant is engaged in a series of self-justifications. If you are the participant, once you have justified step one, that justification makes it easier to go to step two; once you justify step two, it is easier to go to step three; and so on. By the time you get to 450 volts, well, heck, that's not much different from 435 volts, is it? In other words, once individuals start down that slippery slope of self-justification, it becomes increasingly difficult to draw a line in the sand—because in effect, they end up asking themselves, "Why draw the line here if I didn't draw it 15 volts ago?"

The Importance of Irrevocability

One of the important characteristics of the examples presented above is the relative irrevocability of the decision. This needs some explaining: Occasionally, we make tentative decisions. For example, if you had indicated you might buy an expensive house near San Francisco, but the decision was not finalized, chances are you would not expend any effort trying to convince yourself of the wisdom of the decision. Once you had put your money down, however, and you knew you couldn't easily get it back, you would probably start minimizing the importance of the dampness in the basement, the cracks in the foundation, or the fact that the house happened to be built on the San Andreas Fault. Similarly, once a European Jew had decided not to pass and had allowed himself to be identified as a Jew, the decision was irrevocable; he could not easily pretend to be a Gentile. By the same token, once Pentagon officials intensified the bombing of North Vietnam, they could not undo it. And once a homeowner had signed the petition, a commitment to safe driving was established.

Some direct evidence for the importance of irrevocability comes from a clever study of the cognitive gyrations of gamblers at a race track. The race track is an ideal place to scrutinize irrevocability because once you've placed your bet, you can't go back and tell the nice man behind the window you've changed your mind. Robert Knox and James Inkster[25] simply intercepted people who were on their way to place $2 bets. They had already decided on their horses and were about to place their bets when the investigators asked them how certain they were that their horses would win. Because they were on their way to the $2 window, their decisions were not irrevocable. The investigators collared other bettors just as they were leaving the $2 window, *after* having placed their bets, and asked them how certain they were that their horses would win. Typically, people who had just placed their bets gave their horses a much better chance of winning than did those who were about to place their bets. But, of course, nothing had changed except the finality of the decision. Similar results were obtained in a survey of Canadian voters.[26] Those voters interviewed immediately *after* voting were more certain their candidates would win and liked their candidates more than those voters interviewed immediately *before* they had cast their votes. In short, when a decision is irrevocable, more dissonance is aroused; to reduce this dissonance, people become more certain they are right *after* there is nothing they can do about it.

Although the irrevocability of a decision always increases dissonance and the motivation to reduce it, there are circumstances in which irrevocability is unnecessary. Let me explain with an example. Suppose you enter an automobile showroom intent on buying a new car. You've already priced the car you want at several dealers; you know you can purchase it for about $9,300. Lo and behold, the salesman tells you he can sell you one for $8,942. Excited by the bargain, you agree to the deal and write out a check for the down payment. While the salesman takes your check to the sales manager to consummate the deal, you rub your hands in glee as you imagine yourself driving home in your shiny new car. But alas, 10 minutes later, the salesman returns with a forlorn look on his face; it seems he made a calculation error, and the sales manager caught it. The price of the car is actually $9,384. You can get it cheaper elsewhere; moreover, the decision to buy is not irrevocable. And yet, far more people in this situation will go ahead with the deal than if the original asking price had been $9,384—even though the reason for purchasing the car from this dealer (the bargain price) no longer exists. Indeed, Robert Cialdini,[27] a social psychologist who temporarily joined the sales force of an automobile dealer, discovered that the strategy described above is a common and successful ploy called **lowballing,** or *throwing the customer a lowball.*

What is going on in this situation? There are at least three important things to notice. First, while the customer's decision to buy is certainly reversible, there is a commitment emphasized by the act of signing a check for a down payment. Second, this commitment triggered the anticipation of a pleasant or interesting experience: driving out with a new car. To have the anticipated event thwarted (by not going ahead with the deal) would have produced dissonance and disappointment. Third, although the final price is substantially higher than the customer thought it would be, it is only slightly higher than the price somewhere else. Under these circumstances, the customer in effect says, "Oh, what the hell. I'm already here; I've already filled out the forms—why wait?"[28] Clearly, such a ploy would not be effective if the consequences were somewhat higher as in matters of life and death.

The Decision to Behave Immorally How can an honest person become corrupt? Conversely, how can we get a person to be *more* honest? One way is through the dissonance that results from making a difficult decision. Suppose you are a college student enrolled in a biology course. Your grade will hinge on the final exam you are now taking. The key question on the exam involves some material you know fairly well—but, because of anxiety, you draw a blank. You are sitting there in a nervous sweat. You look up, and lo and behold, you happen to be sitting behind a woman who is the smartest person in the class (who also happens, fortunately, to be the person with the most legible handwriting in the class). You glance down and notice she is just completing her answer to the crucial question. You know you could easily read her answer if you chose to. What do you do? Your conscience tells you it's wrong to cheat—and yet, if you don't cheat, you are certain to get a poor grade. You wrestle with your conscience. Regardless of whether you decide to cheat or not to cheat, you are doomed to experience dissonance. If you cheat, your cognition "I am a decent moral person" is dissonant with your cognition "I have just committed an immoral act." If you decide to resist temptation, your cognition "I want to get a good grade" is dissonant with your cognition "I could have acted in a way that would have ensured a good grade, but I chose not to."

Suppose that, after a difficult struggle, you decide to cheat. How do you reduce the dissonance? Before you read on, think about it for a moment. One way to reduce dissonance is to minimize the negative aspects of the action you have chosen (and to maximize the positive aspects)—much the same way the women did after choosing an appliance in Jack Brehm's experiment. In this instance, an efficacious path of dissonance reduction would entail a change in your attitude about cheating. In short, you will adopt a more lenient attitude. Your reasoning might go something like this: "Cheating isn't so bad under some circumstances. As long as nobody gets hurt, it's really not very immoral. Anybody would do it. Therefore, it's a part of human nature—so how could it be bad? Since it is only human, those who get caught cheating should not be severely punished but should be treated with understanding."

Suppose that, after a difficult struggle, you decide not to cheat. How would you reduce dissonance? Once again, you could change your attitude about the morality of the act—but in the opposite direction. That is, in order to justify giving up a good grade, you must convince yourself that cheating is a heinous sin, that it's one of the lowest things a person can do, and that cheaters should be found out and severely punished.

The interesting and important thing to remember here is that two people acting in the two different ways described above could have started out with almost identical attitudes. Their decisions might have been a hair's breadth apart: One came within an ace of resisting but decided to cheat, while the other came within an ace of cheating but decided to resist. Once they have made their decisions, however, their attitudes toward cheating will diverge sharply as a consequence of their decisions.

These speculations were put to the test by Judson Mills[29] in an experiment with 6th-graders. Mills first measured their attitudes toward cheating. He then had them participate in a competitive exam with prizes being offered to the winners. The situation was arranged so that it was almost impossible to win without cheating; also, it was easy for the children to cheat, thinking they would not be detected. As one might expect, some of the students cheated and others did not. The next day, the 6th-graders were again asked to indicate how they felt about cheating. In general, those children who had cheated became more lenient toward cheating, and those who resisted the temptation to cheat adopted a harsher attitude toward cheating.

The data from Mills's experiment are provocative indeed. One thing they suggest is that the most zealous opponents of a given position are not those who have always been distant from that position. For example, one might hazard a guess that the people who are most angry at the apparent sexual freedom associated with the current generation of young people may not be those who have never been tempted to engage in casual sexual activity themselves. Indeed, Mills's data suggest the possibility that the people who have the strongest need to crack down hard on this sort of behavior are those who have been sorely tempted, who came dangerously close to giving in to this temptation, but who finally resisted. People who *almost* decide to live in glass houses are frequently the ones who are most prone to throw stones.

By the same token, it would follow that those individuals who fear that they may be sexually attracted to members of their own sex might be among those most prone to develop antigay attitudes. In an interesting experiment, Henry Adams and his colleagues[30] showed a group of men a series of sexually explicit erotic video tapes consisting of heterosexual, male homosexual, and lesbian encounters while measuring their sexual arousal (actual changes in their penile circumference). Although almost all of the men showed increases in sexual arousal while watching the heterosexual and lesbian videos, it was the men with the most negative attitudes toward male homosexuals who were the most aroused by the videos depicting male homosexual love-making.

Early in this chapter, I mentioned that the desire for self-justification is an important reason why people who are strongly committed to an attitude on an issue tend to resist any direct attempts to change that attitude. In effect, such people are invulnerable to the propaganda or education in question. We can now see that the same mechanism that enables a person to cling to an attitude can induce that individual to change an attitude. It depends on which course of action will serve most to reduce dissonance under the circumstances. A person who understands the theory can set up the proper conditions to induce attitude change in other people by making them vulnerable to certain kinds of beliefs. For example, if a modern Machiavelli were advising a contemporary ruler, he might suggest the following strategies based on the theory and data on the consequences of decisions:

1. If you want people to form more positive attitudes toward an object, get them to commit themselves to own that object.

2. If you want people to soften their moral attitudes toward some misdeed, tempt them so that they perform that deed; conversely, if you want people to harden their moral attitudes toward a misdeed, tempt them—but not enough to induce them to commit the deed.

The Psychology of Inadequate Justification

Attitude change as a means of reducing dissonance is not, of course, limited to postdecision situations. It can occur in countless other contexts, including every time a person says something he or she doesn't believe or does something stupid or immoral. The effects can be extremely powerful. Let us look at some of them.

In a complex society, we occasionally find ourselves saying or doing things we don't completely believe. Does this always lead to attitude change? No. To illustrate, I will choose a simple example. Joe Lawyer enters the office and sees that his law partner, Joyce, has hung a perfectly atrocious painting on the wall of the office they share. He is about to tell her how awful he thinks it is when she says proudly, "How do you like the painting? I did it myself—you know, in the art class I'm taking at night."

"Very nice, Joyce," Joe answers. Theoretically, Joe's cognition "I am a truthful person" is dissonant with the cognition "I said that painting was nice, although it really is disastrous." Whatever dissonance might be aroused by this inconsistency can easily and quickly be reduced by Joe's cognition that it is important not to hurt other people: "I lied so as not to hurt Joyce; why should I tell her it's an ugly painting? It serves no useful purpose." This is an effective way of reducing dissonance because it completely justifies Joe's action. In effect, the justification is situation-determined. I will call this **external justification**.

But what happens if there is not ample justification in the situation itself? For example, imagine that Joe Lawyer, who is politically conservative, finds himself at a cocktail party with many people he doesn't know very well. The conversation turns to politics. The people are talking with horror about the fact that the United States seems to be drastically escalating its friendly overtures toward Castro's regime in Cuba. Joe's belief is a complicated one; he has mixed feelings about the topic, but generally he is opposed to our forming an alliance with the Cuban dictatorship because he feels it is an evil regime and we should not compromise with evil. Partly because Joe's companions are sounding so pious and partly as a lark, he gradually finds himself taking a much more liberal-radical position than the one he really holds. As a matter of fact, Joe even goes so far as to assert that Fidel Castro is an extraordinarily gifted leader and that the Cuban people are better off with Communism than they've been in hundreds of years. Somebody counters Joe's argument by talking about the thousands of people that Castro is alleged to have murdered or imprisoned in order to achieve a unified government. In the heat of the argument, Joe replies that those figures are grossly exaggerated. Quite a performance for a man who does, in fact, believe that Castro killed thousands of innocent people during his rise to power.

When Joe awakens the next morning and thinks back on the previous evening's events, he gasps in horror. "Oh, my God, what have I done?" he says.

He is intensely uncomfortable. Put another way, he is experiencing a great deal of dissonance. His cognition "I misled a bunch of people; I told them a lot of things about Cuba that I don't really believe" is dissonant with his cognition "I am a reasonable, decent, and truthful person." What does he do to reduce dissonance? He searches around for *external justifications.* First, it occurs to Joe that he might have been drunk and therefore not responsible for what he said. But he remembers he had only one or two beers—no external justification there. Because Joe cannot find sufficient external justification for his behavior, it is necessary for him to attempt to explain his behavior by using **internal justification,** changing his attitude in the direction of his statements. That is, if Joe can succeed in convincing himself that his statements were not so very far from the truth, then he will have reduced dissonance; that is, his behavior of the preceding night will no longer be absurd in his own view. I do not mean to imply that Joe will suddenly become an avowed Communist revolutionary. What I do mean is that he might begin to feel a little less harsh about the Cuban regime than he felt before he made those statements. Most events and issues in our world are neither completely black nor completely white; there are many gray areas. Thus, Joe might begin to take a different look at some of the events that have taken place in Cuba during the past 50 years. He might start looking into Castro's politics and decisions and become more disposed toward seeing wisdom that he hadn't seen before. He might also begin to be more receptive to information that indicates the extent of the corruption, brutality, and ineptitude of the previous government. To repeat: If an individual states a belief that is difficult to justify *externally,* that person will attempt to justify it *internally* by making his or her attitudes more consistent with the statement.

I have mentioned a couple of forms of external justification. One is the idea that it's all right to tell a harmless lie in order to avoid hurting a person's feelings—as in the case of Joe Lawyer and his partner. Another is drunkenness as an excuse for one's actions. Still another form of external justification is reward. Put yourself in Joe's shoes for a moment, and suppose that you and I both were at that cocktail party and I am an eccentric millionaire. As the conversation turns to Cuba, I pull you aside and say, "Hey, I would like you to come out strongly in favor of Fidel Castro and Cuban Communism." What's more, suppose I hand you $5,000 for doing it. After counting the money, you gasp, put the $5,000 in your pocket, return to the discussion, and defend Fidel Castro to the hilt. The next morning when you wake up, would you experience any dissonance? I don't think so. Your cognition "I said some things about Fidel Castro and Cuban Communism that I don't believe" is dissonant with the cognition "I am a truthful and decent person." But, at the same time, you have adequate external justification for having made that statement: "I said those favorable things about Cuban communism in order to earn $5,000—and it was worth it." You don't have to soften your attitude toward

Castro in order to justify that statement because you know why you made those statements: You made them not because you think they are true but in order to get the $5,000. You're left with the knowledge you sold your soul for $5,000—and it was worth it.

This has been called the *"saying is believing" paradigm*. That is, dissonance theory predicts that we begin to believe our own lies—but only if there is not abundant external justification for making the statements that run counter to our original attitudes. Let's now elaborate on our earlier discussion of conformity. Recall in Chapter 2 we found that the greater the reward for compliance, the greater the probability that a person will comply. Now we can go one step further: When it comes to producing a *lasting* change in attitude, the greater the reward, the *less* likely any attitude change will occur. If all I want you to do is recite a speech favoring Fidel Castro, the Marx brothers, socialized medicine, or anything else, the most efficient thing for me to do would be to give you the largest possible reward. This would increase the probability of your complying by making that speech. But suppose I have a more ambitious goal: Suppose I want to effect a lasting change in your attitudes and beliefs. In that case, just the reverse is true. The smaller the external reward I give to induce you to recite the speech, the more likely it is that you will be forced to seek additional justification for delivering it by convincing yourself that the things you said were actually true. This would result in an actual change in attitude rather than mere compliance. The importance of this technique cannot be overstated. If we change our attitudes because we have made a public statement for minimal external justification, our attitude change will be relatively permanent; we are not changing our attitudes because of a reward (compliance) or because of the influence of an attractive person (identification). We are changing our attitudes because we have succeeded in *convincing ourselves* that our previous attitudes were incorrect. This is a very powerful form of attitude change.

Thus far, we have been dealing with highly speculative material. These speculations have been investigated scientifically in several experiments. Among these is a classic study by Leon Festinger and J. Merrill Carlsmith.[31] These investigators asked college students to perform a very boring and repetitive series of tasks—packing spools in a tray, dumping them out, and then refilling the tray over and over, or turning rows and rows of screws a quarter turn and then going back and turning them another quarter turn. The students engaged in these activities for a full hour. The experimenter then induced them to lie about the task; specifically, he employed them to tell a young woman (who was waiting to participate in the experiment) that the task she would be performing was interesting and enjoyable. Some of the students were offered $20 for telling the lie; others were offered only $1 for telling the lie. After the experiment was over, an interviewer asked the liars how much they enjoyed the tasks they had performed earlier in the experiment. The results were clear-cut: Those students who had been paid $20 for lying—that is, for saying the spool packing and screw turning had been enjoyable—rated the activity as dull. This is not surprising—it *was* dull. But what about the students who had been paid only $1 for lying? They rated the task as enjoyable. In other words, people who received abundant external justification for lying told the lie but didn't believe it, whereas those who told the lie *in the absence* of a great deal of external justification moved in the direction of believing that what they said was true.

Research support for the "saying is believing" phenomenon has extended beyond relatively unimportant attitudes like the dullness of a monotonous task. Attitude change has been shown on a variety of important issues. For example, in one experiment, Arthur R. Cohen[32] induced Yale college students to engage in a particularly difficult form of counterattitudinal behavior. Cohen conducted his experiment immediately after a student riot in which the New Haven police had over-reacted and behaved brutally toward the students. The students (who strongly believed the police had behaved badly) were asked to write a strong and forceful essay in support of the actions taken by the police. Before writing the essay, some students were paid $10; others, $5; still others, $1; and a fourth group, 50 cents. After writing his essay, each student was asked to indicate his own private attitudes about the police actions. The results were perfectly linear: The smaller the reward, the greater the attitude change. Thus, students who wrote in support of the New Haven police for the meager sum of 50 cents developed a more favorable attitude than did those who wrote the essay for $1; the students who wrote the essay for $1 developed a more favorable attitude toward the actions of the police than did those who wrote the essay for $5; and those who wrote the essay for $10 remained the least favorable.

Let's look at race relations and racial prejudice—surely one of our nation's most enduring problems. Would it be possible to get people to endorse a policy favoring a minority group—and then see if their attitudes become more favorable toward that group? In an important set of experiments, Mike Leippe and Donna Eisenstadt[33] induced white college students to write an essay demonstrating **counter-attitudinal advocacy:** publicly endorsing a controversial proposal at their university—to double the amount of funds available for academic scholarships for African-American students. Because the total amount of scholarship funds were limited, this meant cutting by half the amount of funds available for scholarships for white students. As you might imagine, this was a highly dissonant situation. How might the students reduce dissonance? The best way would be to convince themselves that they really believed deeply in that policy—that, taking the big picture into consideration, it was only fair to offer more financial aid to African-Americans. Moreover, it is reasonable to suggest that dissonance reduction might generalize beyond the specific policy—that is, the theory would predict that their general attitude toward African-Americans would become more favorable and much more supportive. And that is exactly what Leippe and Eisenstadt found.

What Constitutes External Justification?

As I mentioned a moment ago, external justification can and does come in a variety of forms. People can be persuaded to say things or do things that contradict their beliefs or preferences if they are threatened with punishment or enticed by rewards other than monetary gain—such as praise or the desire to please. Furthermore, most of us would consider doing something that we otherwise wouldn't do if a good friend asked us to do it as a favor. To take a farfetched example, suppose a friend asked you to eat an unusual food she or he had recently learned to prepare in an "exotic foods" cooking class. And just to make things interesting, let's say the food in question was a fried grasshopper. Now, imagine the reverse situation—that someone you didn't like very much asked you to sink your teeth into a fried grasshopper.

Okay, are you ready? Assuming you went ahead and ate the grasshopper, under which circumstance do you think you would enjoy the taste of it more—when asked to eat it by a good friend or by someone you didn't like? Common sense might suggest that the grasshopper would taste better when recommended by a friend. After all, a friend is someone you can trust and, hence, would be a far more credible source of information than someone you didn't like. But think about it for a moment: Which condition involves less external justification? Common sense notwithstanding, the theory of cognitive dissonance would predict that you would come to like eating grasshoppers more if you ate one at the request of someone you didn't like.

Here's how it works: Your cognition that eating a grasshopper is repulsive would be at odds with the fact that you just ate one. But if it was *your friend* who made the request, you would have a great deal of external justification for having eaten it—you did it as a favor for a good friend. On the other hand, you would not have as much external justification for munching on a grasshopper if you did it at the request of someone you didn't like. In this case, how could you justify your contradictory behavior to yourself? Simple. The way to reduce dissonance would be to change your attitude toward grasshoppers in the direction of liking them better—"Gee, they're pretty tasty critters after all."

While this may seem a rather bizarre example of dissonance-reducing behavior, it's not as farfetched as you might think. Philip Zimbardo and his colleagues conducted an analogous experiment in which army reservists were asked to try fried grasshoppers as part of a study allegedly about "survival" foods.[34] For half of the participants, the request was made by a warm, friendly officer; for the other half, it was made by a cold, unfriendly officer. The reservists' attitudes toward eating grasshoppers were measured before and after they ate them. The results were exactly as predicted above: Reservists who ate grasshoppers at the request of the unpleasant officer increased their liking for them far more than those who ate grasshoppers at the request of the pleasant officer. Thus, when sufficient external justification was present—when reservists complied with the friendly officer's request—they experienced little need to change their attitudes toward grasshoppers. They already had a convincing explanation for why they ate them—they did it to help a "nice guy." But reservists who complied with the unfriendly officer's request had little external justification for their action. As a result, they adopted a more positive attitude toward eating grasshoppers in order to rationalize their discrepant behavior.

What Is Inadequate Justification? Throughout this section, I have made reference to situations where there is *inadequate* external justification and to those with an *abundance* of external justification. These terms require some additional clarification. In the Festinger-Carlsmith experiment, all of the participants did, in fact, agree to tell the lie—including all of those paid only $1. In a sense, then, $1 was *adequate*—that is, adequate to induce the participants to tell the lie; but as it turns out, it wasn't sufficient to keep them from feeling foolish. In order to reduce their feeling of foolishness, they had to reduce the dissonance that resulted from telling a lie for so paltry a sum. This entailed additional bolstering in the form of convincing themselves that it wasn't completely a lie and the task wasn't quite as dull as it seemed at first; as a matter of fact, when looked at in a certain way, it was actually quite interesting.

It would be fruitful to compare these results with Judson Mills's data on the effects of cheating among 6th-graders.[35] Recall that, in Mills's experiment, the decision about whether or not to cheat was almost certainly a difficult one for most of the children. This is why they experienced dissonance, regardless of whether they cheated or resisted temptation. One could speculate about what would happen if the rewards to be gained by cheating were very large. For one thing, it would be more tempting to cheat; therefore, more children would actually cheat. But, more important, if the gains for cheating were astronomical, those who cheated would undergo very little attitude change. Much like the college students who lied in Festinger and Carlsmith's $20 condition, those children who cheated for a great reward would have less need to reduce dissonance, having been provided with an *abundance* of external justification for their behavior. In fact, Mills did include this refinement in his experiment, and his results are consistent with this reasoning: Those who cheated in order to obtain a small reward tended to soften their attitude about cheating more than those who cheated in order to obtain a large reward. Moreover, those who refrained from cheating in spite of the temptation of a large reward—a choice that would create a great deal of dissonance—hardened their attitude about cheating to a greater extent than those who refrained in the face of a small reward—just as one might expect.

Dissonance and the Self-Concept The analysis of the dissonance phenomenon presented in this section requires a departure from Festinger's original theory. In the experiment by Festinger and Carlsmith, for example, the original statement of dissonance went like this: The cognition "I believe the task is dull" is dissonant with the cognition "I said the task was interesting." Several years ago, I reformulated the theory in a way that focuses more attention on the way people conceive of themselves.[36] Basically, this reformulation suggests that dissonance is most powerful in situations in which the self-concept is threatened. Thus, for me, the important aspect of dissonance in the situation described above is not that the cognition "I said 'X'" is dissonant with the cognition "I believe 'not X.'" Rather, the crucial fact is that I have misled people: The cognition "I have told people something I don't believe" is dissonant with my self-concept; that is, it is dissonant with my cognition that "I am a person of integrity."

This formulation is based on the assumption that most individuals like to think of themselves as decent people who wouldn't ordinarily mislead someone. For example, consider Kathy, who believes marijuana is dangerous and should definitely not be legalized. Suppose she is induced to make a speech advocating the use of marijuana. Let us assume she makes the speech to an audience consisting of individuals whom she knows to be irrevocably opposed to the use of marijuana (e.g., the members of a police vice squad, the Daughters of the American Revolution, or prohibitionists). In this case, there is little likelihood that she will influence this audience because of the firmness of their convictions. According to my view of dissonance theory, Kathy would not change her attitude because she has not affected anyone's behavior. Similarly, if Kathy were asked to make the same statement to a group of individuals whom she knows to be irrevocably committed to the use of marijuana, there would be no possibility of impacting the audience. On the other hand, if Kathy were induced to make the identical speech to a group of individuals who have no prior information about marijuana, we would expect her to experience much more dissonance than in the other situations. Her cognition that she is a good and decent person is dissonant with her cognition that she has said something she doesn't believe that is likely to have serious *belief* or *behavioral consequences* for her audience. To reduce dissonance, she needs to convince herself that the position she advocated is correct. This would allow her to believe that she is a person of integrity. Moreover, in this situation, the smaller the incentive she receives for advocating the position, the greater the attitude change. I tested and confirmed this hypothesis in collaboration with Elizabeth Nel and Robert Helmreich.[37] We found an enormous change in attitude toward marijuana when participants were offered a small reward for making a videotape recording of a speech favoring the use of marijuana—but only when they were led to believe that the tape would be shown to an audience that was uncommitted on the issue. On the other hand, when participants were told that the tape would be played to people who were irrevocably committed on the subject of marijuana (one way or the other), there was relatively little attitude change on the part of the speaker. Thus, lying produces greater attitude change when the liar is undercompensated for lying, especially when the lie is likely to evoke a change in the audience's belief or behavior.*

A great deal of subsequent research[38] supports this reasoning and allows us to state a general principle about dissonance and the self-concept: Dissonance effects are greatest when (1) people feel personally responsible for their actions and (2) their actions have serious consequences. That is, the greater the consequence and the greater our responsibility for it, the greater the dissonance; the greater the dissonance, the greater our own attitude change.

My notion that dissonance is aroused whenever the self-concept is challenged has many interesting ramifications. Let us look at one in some detail. Suppose you are at home and someone knocks at your door, asking you to contribute to a worthy charity. If you didn't want to contribute, you probably wouldn't find it too difficult to come up with reasons for declining—you don't have much money, your contribution probably wouldn't help much anyway, and so on. But suppose that, after delivering a standard plea for a donation, the fundraiser adds that "even a penny will help." Refusing to donate after hearing this statement would undoubtedly stir up some dissonance by challenging your self-concept. After all, what kind of person is it who is too mean or stingy to come up with a penny? No longer would your previous rationalizations apply. Such a scenario was tested experimentally by Robert Cialdini and David Schroeder.[39] Students acting as fundraisers went door to door, sometimes just asking for donations and sometimes adding that "even a penny will help." As conjectured, the residents who were approached with the even-a-penny request gave contributions more often, donating almost twice as frequently as those getting just the standard plea. Furthermore, on the average, the even-a-penny contributors were likely to give as much money as the others; that is, the statement legitimizing the small donation did not reduce the size of the contributions. Why? Apparently, not only does the lack of external justification for refusing to donate encourage people to give money, but after they have decided *whether* to contribute, the desire to avoid appearing stingy affects their decision of *how much* to give. Once people reach into their pockets, emerging with a mere penny is self-demeaning; a larger donation is consistent with their self-perception of being reasonably kind and generous.

---

*It should be mentioned that, in this as well as in the other experiments discussed here, each participant was completely debriefed as soon as he or she had finished participating in the experiment. Every attempt was made to avoid causing a permanent change in the attitudes of the participants. It is always important to debrief participants after an experiment; it is especially important when the experiment induces a change in an important attitude or has important behavioral consequences.

Inadequate Rewards as Applied to Education A great deal of research has shown that the insufficient-reward phenomenon applies to all forms of behavior—not simply the making of counterattitudinal statements. Remember, it has been shown that if people actually perform a dull task for very little external justification, they rate the task as more enjoyable than if they have a great deal of external justification for performing it.[40] This does not mean people would rather receive low pay than high pay for doing a job. People prefer to receive high pay—and they often work harder for high pay. But if they are offered low pay for doing a job and still agree to do it, there is dissonance between the dullness of the task and the low pay. To reduce the dissonance, they attribute good qualities to the job and, hence, come to enjoy the mechanics of the job more if the salary is low than if it is high. This phenomenon may have far-reaching consequences. For example, let's look at the elementary-school classroom. If you want Johnny to recite multiplication tables, then you should reward him; gold stars, praise, high grades, presents, and the like are good external justifications. Will Johnny recite the tables just for the fun of it, long after the rewards are no longer forthcoming? In other words, will the high rewards make him enjoy the task? I doubt it. But if the external rewards are not too high, Johnny will add his own justification for performing the math drill; he may even make a game of it. In short, he is more likely to continue to memorize the multiplication tables long after school is out and the rewards have been withdrawn.

For certain rote tasks, educators probably do not care whether Johnny enjoys them or not, as long as he masters them. On the other hand, if Johnny can learn to enjoy them, he will perform them outside of the educational situation. Consequently, with such increased practice, he may come to gain greater mastery over the procedure and he may retain it indefinitely. Thus, it may be a mistake to dole out extensive rewards as an educational device. If students are provided with just barely enough incentive to perform the task, teachers may succeed in allowing them to maximize their enjoyment of the task. This may serve to improve long-range retention and performance. I am not suggesting that inadequate rewards are the only way people can be taught to enjoy material that lacks inherent attractiveness. What I am saying is that piling on excessive external justification inhibits one of the processes that can help set the stage for increased enjoyment.

Several experiments by Edward Deci[41] and his colleagues make this point very nicely. Indeed, Deci carries this analysis one step further by demonstrating that offering rewards to people for performing a pleasant activity actually decreases the intrinsic attractiveness of that activity. In one experiment, for example, college students worked individually on an interesting puzzle for an hour. The next day, the students in the experimental condition were paid $1 for each piece of the puzzle they completed. The students in the control group worked on the puzzle as before, without pay.

During the third session, neither group was paid. The question is: How much liking did each group have for the puzzle? Deci measured this during the third session by noting whether or not each student worked on the puzzle during a free break when they could do whatever they pleased. The unrewarded group spent more free time on the task than the rewarded group—whose interest waned when no rewards were forthcoming. Mark Lepper and his colleagues found the same kind of relationship with preschool children.[42] The researchers instructed half of the kids to work on a set of plastic jigsaw puzzles and promised them a more rewarding activity later. They instructed the remaining kids to play with the puzzles without promising them anything in return. After playing with the puzzles, all of the children were allowed to engage in the "more rewarding" activity (but recall that only half of them were led to believe this was a reward for having worked on the puzzles). A few weeks later, they turned all the youngsters loose on the puzzles. Those who had worked on the puzzles in order to earn the chance to engage in the more rewarding activity spent less of their free time playing with the puzzles. In short, by offering the children a reward for playing, the experimenters succeeded in turning play into work.

What happens if, instead of offering prizes or payments, we reward people by praising them. Most parents and teachers believe that praising a child's good performance is always a useful thing to do. Jennifer Henderlong and Mark Lepper[43] recently reviewed a host of studies in this area and found that it is not that simple. Praise can be beneficial but only if it is done in moderation and in a way that makes children feel competent. However if a parent or a teacher lavishes praise on children in such a way that it creates the illusion that the reason they performed the activity was to earn the praise, then children will not learn to enjoy the activity itself. By the same token, if the emphasis is placed on competition—that is, on doing better than most of the other kids in the class—the children's focus is on winning rather than on doing, and, consequently, they do not enjoy the thing they are doing. These findings parallel the results of the experiments on reward discussed above; causing a person to focus on the extrinsic reasons for performing well will reduce the attractiveness of the task itself. Moreover, as Carol Dweck[44] has shown, praise is most effective if it is focused on the child's effort rather than on the child's talent or ability. That is, if children are praised for their effort on a difficult task, they learn an important lesson: "When the going gets tough, I will work harder because hard work will result in a better performance." But if they are praised for being smart—then, if a situation arises where they are failing, they frequently draw the conclusion that "I am not as smart as people thought I was." This can have devastating consequences.

Insufficient Punishment In our everyday lives, we are continually faced with situations wherein those who are charged with the duty of maintaining law and order threaten to punish us if we do not comply with the demands of society. As adults, we know that if we exceed the speed limit and get caught, we will end up paying a substantial fine. If it happens too often, we will lose our licenses. So we learn to obey the speed limit when there are patrol cars in the vicinity. Youngsters in school know that if they cheat on an exam and get caught, they could be humiliated by the teacher and severely punished. So they learn not to cheat while the teacher is in the room watching them. But does harsh punishment teach them not to cheat? I don't think so. I think it teaches them to try to avoid getting caught. In short, the use of threats of harsh punishment as a means of getting someone to refrain from doing something he or she enjoys doing necessitates constant harassment and vigilance. It would be much more efficient and would require much less noxious restraint if, somehow, people could enjoy doing those things that contribute to their own health and welfare—and to the health and welfare of others. If children enjoyed *not* beating up smaller kids or *not* cheating or *not* stealing from others, then society could relax its vigilance and curtail its punitiveness. It is extremely difficult to persuade people (especially young children) that it's not enjoyable to beat up smaller people. But it is conceivable that, under certain conditions, they will persuade *themselves* that such behavior is not enjoyable.

Let's take a closer look. Picture the scene: You are the parent of a 5-year-old boy who enjoys beating up his 3-year-old sister. You've tried to reason with him, but to no avail. So, to protect the welfare of your daughter and to make a nicer person out of your son, you begin to punish him for his aggressiveness. As a parent, you have at your disposal a number of punishments that range from extremely mild (a stern look) to extremely severe (a hard spanking, forcing the child to stand in the corner for 2 hours, and depriving him of television privileges for a month). The more severe the threat, the greater the likelihood that the youngster will mend his ways while you are watching him. But he may very well hit his sister again as soon as you turn your back.

Suppose instead you threaten him with a very mild punishment. In either case (under the threat of severe or mild punishment), the child experiences dissonance. He is aware that he is not beating up his little sister and he is also aware that he would very much like to beat her up. When he has the urge to hit his sister and doesn't, he asks himself, in effect, "How come I'm not beating up my little sister?" Under a severe threat, he has a ready-made answer in the form of sufficient external justification: "I'm not beating her up because, if I do, that giant over there (my father) is going to spank me, stand me in the corner, and keep me from watching TV for a month." The severe threat has provided the child ample external justification for not hitting his sister while he's being watched.

The child in the mild-threat situation experiences dissonance, too. But when he asks himself, "How come I'm not beating up my little sister?" he doesn't have a good answer because the threat is so mild that it does not provide abundant justification. The child is not doing something he wants to do—and while he does have some justification for not doing it, he lacks complete justification. In this situation, he continues to experience dissonance. He is unable to reduce the dissonance by simply blaming his inaction on a severe threat. The child must find a way to justify the fact that he is not aggressing against his little sister. The best way is to try to convince himself that he really doesn't like to beat his sister up, that he didn't want to do it in the first place, and that beating up little kids is not fun. The less severe the threat, the less external justification; the less external justification, the greater the need for internal justification. Allowing people the opportunity to construct their own internal justification can be a large step toward helping them develop a permanent set of values.

To test this idea, I performed an experiment at the Harvard University nursery school in collaboration with J. Merrill Carlsmith.[45] For ethical reasons, we did not try to change basic values like aggression; parents, understandably, might not approve of our changing important values. Instead, we chose a trivial aspect of behavior—toy preference.

We first asked 5-year-old children to rate the attractiveness of several toys; then, in each instance, we chose one toy that the children considered quite attractive and told them they couldn't play with it. We threatened half of the children with mild punishment for transgression—"I would be a little angry"; we threatened the other half with more severe punishment—"I would be very angry; I would have to take all of the toys and go home and never come back again; I would think you were just a baby." After that, we left the room and allowed the children to play with the other toys—and to resist the temptation of playing with the forbidden one. All the children resisted the temptation; none played with the forbidden toy.

On returning to the room, we asked the children again to rate the attractiveness of all the toys. The results were both striking and exciting. Those children who underwent a mild threat now found the forbidden toy less attractive than before. In short, lacking adequate external justification for refraining from playing with the toy, they succeeded in convincing themselves that they hadn't played with it because they didn't really like it. On the other hand, the toy did not become less attractive for those who were severely threatened. These children continued to rate the forbidden toy as highly desirable; indeed, some even found it more desirable than they had before the threat. The children in the severe-threat condition had good external reasons for not playing with the toy—and they therefore had no need to find additional reasons; consequently, they continued to like the toy.

Jonathan Freedman[46] extended our findings and dramatically illustrated the permanence of the phenomenon. He used as his "crucial toy" an extremely attractive battery-powered robot that scurries around, hurling objects at a child's enemies. The other toys were sickly by comparison. Naturally, all of the children preferred the robot. He then asked them not to play with that toy, threatening some children with mild punishment and others with severe punishment. Then he left the school and never returned. Several weeks later, a young woman came to the school to administer some paper-and-pencil tests to the children. The children were unaware of the fact that she was working for Freedman or that her presence was in any way related to the toys or the threats that had occurred earlier. But it just so happened that she was administering her test in the same room Freedman had used for his experiment—the room where the same toys were casually scattered about. After she administered the test to the children, she asked them to hang around while she scored it—and suggested, offhandedly, that they might want to amuse themselves with those toys someone had left in the room.

Freedman's results are highly consistent with our own. The overwhelming majority of the children who had been mildly threatened weeks earlier refused to play with the robot; they played with the other toys instead. On the other hand, the great majority of the children who had been severely threatened did, in fact, play with the robot. In sum, a severe threat was not effective in inhibiting subsequent behavior—but the effect of one mild threat inhibited behavior as much as 9 weeks later. Again, the power of this phenomenon rests on the fact that the children did not come to devalue this behavior (playing with the toy) because an adult told them it was undesirable; they convinced *themselves* that it was undesirable. My guess is that this process may well apply beyond mere toy preference to more basic and important areas, such as the control of aggression. Partial support for this guess can be derived from some correlational studies performed in the area of child development indicating that parents who use severe punishment to stop a child's aggression tend to have children who, while not very aggressive at home, display a great deal of aggression at school and at play away from *home*.[47] This is precisely what we would expect from the compliance model discussed in Chapter 2.

The Justification of Effort

Dissonance theory leads to the prediction that, if a person works hard to attain a goal, that goal will be more attractive to the individual than it will be to someone who achieves the same goal with little or no effort. An illustration might be useful: Suppose you are a college student who decides to join a fraternity. In order to be admitted, you must pass an initiation; let us assume it is a rather severe one that involves a great deal of effort, pain, or embarrassment. After successfully completing the ordeal, you are admitted to the fraternity. When you move into the fraternity house, you find that your new roommate has some peculiar habits: For example, he plays his stereo loudly after midnight, borrows money without returning it, and occasionally leaves his dirty laundry on your bed. In short, an objective person might consider him to be an inconsiderate slob. But you are not an objective person any longer: Your cognition that you went through hell and high water to get into the fraternity is dissonant with any cognitions about your life in the fraternity that are negative, unpleasant, or undesirable. In order to reduce dissonance, you will try to see your roommate in the most favorable light possible. Again, there are constraints imposed by reality—no matter how much pain and effort you went through, there is no way an inconsiderate slob can be made to look much like Prince Charming—but, with a little ingenuity, you can convince yourself that he isn't so bad. What some people might call sloppy, for example, you might consider casual. Thus, his playing the stereo loudly at night and his leaving his dirty laundry around only serve to demonstrate what an easygoing fellow he is—and because he's so nice and casual about material things, it's certainly understandable that he would forget about the money he owes you.

Prince Charming he isn't, but he's certainly tolerable. Contrast this viewpoint with what your attitude would have been had you made no investment of effort: Suppose you had moved into a regular campus dormitory and encountered the same roommate. Because there was no investment of effort in obtaining this room, there is no dissonance; because there is no dissonance, there is no need for you to see your roommate in the best possible light. My guess is that you would quickly write him off as an inconsiderate slob and try to make arrangements to move to a different room.

These speculations were tested in an experiment I performed more than three decades ago in collaboration with my friend Judson Mills.[48] In this study, college women volunteered to join a group that would be meeting regularly to discuss various aspects of the psychology of sex. The women were told that, if they wanted to join, they would first have to go through a screening test designed to ensure that all people admitted to the group could discuss sex freely and openly. This instruction served to set the stage for the initiation procedure. One-third of the women were assigned to a severe initiation procedure, which required them to recite aloud a list of obscene words. One-third of the students underwent a mild procedure, in which they recited a list of words that were sexual but not obscene. The final one-third of the participants were admitted to the group without undergoing an initiation. Each participant was then allowed to listen in on a discussion being conducted by the members of the group she had just joined. Although the women were led to believe the discussion was a live, ongoing one, what they actually heard was a prerecorded tape. The taped discussion was arranged so that it was as dull and as bombastic as possible. After it was over, each participant was asked to rate the discussion in terms of how much she liked it, how interesting it was, how intelligent the participants were, and so forth.

The results supported the predictions: Those participants who made little or no effort to get into the group did not enjoy the discussion very much. They were able to see it for what it was—a dull and boring waste of time. Those participants who went through a severe initiation, however, succeeded in convincing themselves that the same discussion was interesting and worthwhile.

The same pattern of results has been shown by other investigators using different kinds of unpleasant initiations. For example, Harold Gerard and Grover Mathewson[49] conducted an experiment similar in concept to the Aronson-Mills study, except that the participants in the severe-initiation condition were given painful electric shocks instead of a list of obscene words to read aloud. The results paralleled those of Aronson and Mills: Those who underwent a series of severe electric shocks in order to become members of a group liked that group better than those who underwent a series of mild electric shocks.

It should be clear I am not asserting that people enjoy painful experiences—they do not; nor am I asserting that people enjoy things because they are associated with painful experiences. What I am stating is that, if a person goes through a difficult or a painful experience in order to attain some goal or object, that goal or object becomes more attractive—a process called **justification of effort**. Thus, if on your way to a discussion group you got hit on the head by a brick, you would not like that group any better; but if you volunteered to get hit on the head by a brick in order to join the group, you would definitely like the group better. The importance of volunteering to go through the unpleasant experience was nicely demonstrated in an experiment by Joel Cooper.[50] The participants in this experiment were people who had serious snake phobias. The extent of their fear of snakes was first measured unobtrusively by seeing how closely they would approach a 6-foot boa constrictor that was housed in a glass tank. They then were put through either a highly stressful or a highly effortful set of experiences that they were informed might have some therapeutic value in helping reduce their fear of snakes. But—and this is the crucial point—half were simply told about the procedure and then put through it. The others were induced to volunteer; they were told that they were not obliged to go through the procedure and were free to leave whenever they wished. After going through the therapeutic procedure, each participant was then brought back into the presence of the boa constrictor and asked to approach it as closely as they could. Only those who had been induced to volunteer for the unpleasant therapeutic procedure showed improvement; they were able to come much closer to the boa constrictor than they had before. Those who were simply put through the unpleasant therapeutic procedure (without actually volunteering) showed very little improvement.

In most dissonant situations, there is more than one way to reduce dissonance. In the initiation experiment, for example, we found that people who make a strong effort to get into a dull group convince themselves that the group is interesting. Is this the only way they could have reduced dissonance? No. Another way of making sense of the effort we've expended is to revise our memory of the past—that is, to misremember what things were like before we suffered or worked hard. In an experiment by Michael Conway and Michael Ross,[51] one group of students participated in a study-skills course that promised more than it actually delivered; another group of students signed up but did not participate. Whether or not they took the course, all students were asked to evaluate their study skills. After 3 weeks of useless training, the students who participated wanted to believe that their skills had improved, but the objective data showed that they were not doing well in their coursework. How could they reduce dissonance? What they did was misremember how bad they were before taking the course. That is, they underestimated the skills they had before they enrolled in the course. Students who signed up but did not participate showed no such self-justifying behavior; their recollections of earlier self-evaluations were accurate. These results may explain why people who spend time and money to get in shape may feel satisfied even if they don't fully succeed. They may not be able to convince themselves that they actually reached their goals, but they may be able to overestimate the progress they did make by distorting their memories of how out of shape they were before they went into training. As Conway and Ross pointed out, one way for people to get what they want is to revise what they had.*

The Justification of Cruelty

I have repeatedly made the point that we need to convince ourselves that we are decent, reasonable people. We have seen how this can cause us to change our attitudes on issues important to us. We have seen, for example, that if a person makes a counterattitudinal speech favoring the use and legalization of marijuana for little external justification, and learns that the videotape of the speech will be shown to a group of persuadable youngsters, the individual tends to convince him or herself that marijuana isn't so bad—as a means of feeling less like an evil person. In this section, I will discuss a variation on this theme: Suppose you performed an action that caused a great deal of harm to an innocent young man. Further, suppose that the harm was real and unambiguous. Your cognition "I am a decent, fair, and reasonable person" would be dissonant with your cognition "I have hurt another person." If the harm is clear, then you cannot reduce the dissonance by changing your opinion on the

---

*The astute reader may have noticed a connection between this study and one discussed earlier in this chapter, in which people who broke their New Year's resolutions felt bad about themselves for failing and later played down the importance of the resolutions. I suggested that an alternative method of reducing the dissonance associated with failure might involve making one's definition of success less stringent—such as settling for partial success. The study by Conway and Ross suggests yet another alternative: If, for example, an individual trying to give up smoking has not succeeded in either cutting down or quitting completely, the dissonance aroused by failure can still be reduced if the person misremembers how much he or she smoked prior to making the effort to quit.

issue, thus convincing yourself that you've done no harm, as the people in the marijuana experiment did. In this situation, the most effective way to reduce dissonance would be to maximize the culpability of the victim of your action—to convince yourself that the victim deserved what he got, either because he did something to bring it on himself or because he was a bad or reprehensible person.

This mechanism might operate even if you did not directly cause the harm that befell the victim, but if you only disliked him (prior to his victimization) and were hoping that harm would befall him. For example, after four students at Kent State University were shot and killed by members of the Ohio National Guard, several rumors quickly spread: (1) both of the women who were slain were pregnant (and therefore, by implication, were oversexed and wanton); (2) the bodies of all four students were crawling with lice; and (3) the victims were so ridden with syphilis that they would have been dead in 2 weeks anyway.[52] As I mentioned in Chapter 1, these rumors were totally untrue. The slain students were all clean, decent, bright people. Indeed, two of them were not even involved in the demonstrations that resulted in the tragedy but were peacefully walking across campus when they were gunned down. Why were the townspeople so eager to believe and spread these rumors? It is impossible to know for sure, but my guess is that it was for reasons similar to the reasons rumors were spread among the people in India studied by Prasad and Sinha—that is, because the rumors were comforting. Picture the situation: Kent is a conservative small town in Ohio. Many of the townspeople were infuriated at the radical behavior of some of the students. Some were probably hoping the students would get their comeuppance, but death was more than they deserved. In such circumstances, any information putting the victims in a bad light helped to reduce dissonance by implying that it was, in fact, a good thing that they died. In addition, this eagerness to believe that the victims were sinful and deserved their fate was expressed in ways that were more direct: Several members of the Ohio National Guard stoutly maintained that the victims deserved to die, and a Kent high-school teacher, whom James Michener interviewed, even went so far as to state that "anyone who appears on the streets of a city like Kent with long hair, dirty clothes or barefooted deserves to be shot." She went on to say that this dictum applied even to her own children.[53]

It is tempting simply to write such people off as crazy—but we should not make such judgments lightly. Although it's certainly true that few people are as extreme as the high-school teacher, it is also true that just about everyone can be influenced in this direction. To illustrate this point, let's look at some history. In his memoirs, Nikita Khrushchev, who was premier of the Soviet Union in the 1960s, described himself as a tough and skeptical person, boasting that he wasn't in the habit of believing everything he was told. In particular, he cited several examples of his reluctance to believe scandalous stories about powerful people. But let's look at Khrushchev's credulity when it suited his own needs. Soon after Stalin's death, there was a struggle for power. The head of the secret police, Lavrenty Beria, was on the verge of assuming leadership of the Communist Party. Fearing Beria, Khrushchev convinced the other members of the presidium that, because of the knowledge he had gained as head of the secret police, Beria posed a real danger to them. As a result of Khrushchev's maneuvering, Beria was arrested, imprisoned, and eventually executed. Dissonance theory would lead to the prediction that, because of his central role in Beria's downfall and demise, Khrushchev might put his general skepticism aside and become more willing to believe derogatory rumors about Beria—no matter how absurd they might be—as a way of bolstering his own attitudes and behavior. Let's check it out by allowing Khrushchev to tell us about it in his own words:

> After it was all over [Beria's arrest], Malenkov took me aside and said, "Listen to what my chief bodyguard has to say." The man came over to me and said, "I have only just heard that Beria has been arrested. I want to inform you that he raped my stepdaughter, a seventh grader. A year or so ago her grandmother died and my wife had to go the hospital, leaving the girl at home alone. One evening she went out to buy some bread near the building where Beria lives. There she came across an old man who watched her intently. She was frightened. Someone came and took her to Beria's home. Beria had her sit down with him for supper. She drank something, fell asleep, and he raped her. . . ." Later we were given a list of more than a hundred girls and women who had been raped by Beria. He had used the same routine on all of them. He gave them some dinner and offered them wine with a sleeping potion in it.[54]

It seems fantastic that anyone would believe that Beria had actually perpetrated this deed on more than 100 women. And yet, Khrushchev apparently believed it—perhaps because he had a strong need to believe it.

These examples fit my analysis based on dissonance theory, but they offer nothing resembling definitive proof. For example, it might be that the National Guardsmen at Kent State believed that the students deserved to die even *before* they fired at them. Perhaps Khrushchev would have believed those fantastic stories about Beria even *before* he had caused Beria's demise; it might even be true that Khrushchev didn't believe those rumors at all—but merely repeated them, cynically, in order to further discredit Beria.

To be more certain that the justification of cruelty can occur in such situations, it is essential for the social psychologist to step back from the helter-skelter of the real world (temporarily) and test predictions in the more controlled world of the experimental laboratory. Ideally, if we want to measure attitude change as a result of dissonant cognitions, we should know what the attitudes were *before* the dissonance-arousing event occurred. Such a situation was produced in an experiment performed by Keith Davis and Edward

Jones.[55] They persuaded students to volunteer to help with an experiment: Each student's participation consisted of watching another student being interviewed and then, on the basis of this observation, telling the other student he believed him to be shallow, untrustworthy, and dull. The major finding in this experiment was that participants who volunteered for this assignment succeeded in convincing themselves that they didn't like the victim of their cruelty. In short, after saying things certain to hurt the other student, they convinced themselves he deserved it—that is, they found him less attractive than they did before they hurt him. This shift occurred in spite of the fact that the participants were aware that the other student had done nothing to merit their criticism and that their victimizing him was merely in response to the experimenter's instructions.

An experiment by David Glass[56] had a similar result. In this study, when induced to deliver a series of electric shocks to other people, individuals who considered themselves good and decent people derogated their victims as a result of having caused them this pain. This result is clearest among people with high self-esteem. If I consider myself to be a scoundrel, then causing others to suffer does not introduce as much dissonance; therefore, I have less of a need to convince myself that they deserved their fate. Consider the irony: It is precisely because I think I am such a nice person that, if I do something that causes you pain, I must convince myself you are a rat. In other words, because nice guys like me don't go around hurting innocent people, you must have deserved every nasty thing I did to you.

There are circumstances that limit the generality of this phenomenon. One of those was mentioned above: Namely, people with low self-esteem have less need to derogate their victims. Another factor limiting the derogation phenomenon is the capacity of the victim to retaliate. If the victim is able and willing to retaliate at some future time, then a harm-doer feels that equity will be restored and thus has no need to justify the action by derogating the victim. In an ingenious experiment by Ellen Berscheid and her associates,[57] college students volunteered for an experiment in which each of them delivered a painful electric shock to a fellow student; as expected, each participant derogated the victim as a result of having delivered the shock. But half of the students were told there would be a turnabout—that is, the other students would be given the opportunity to shock *them*. Those who were led to believe their victims would be able to retaliate did *not* derogate them. In short, because the victims were able to retaliate, dissonance was reduced. The harm-doers had no need to belittle their victims in order to convince themselves that the victims deserved it.

These results suggest that, during a war, soldiers might have a greater need to derogate civilian victims (because they can't retaliate) than military victims. During the court-martial of Lieutenant William Calley for his role in the slaughter of innocent civilians at My Lai, his psychiatrist reported that the lieutenant came to regard the Vietnamese people as less than human.

Perhaps the research reported in this section helps to shed some light on this phenomenon. Social psychologists have learned that people do not perform acts of cruelty and come out unscathed. I do not know for sure how Lieutenant Calley (and thousands of others) came to regard the Vietnamese as subhuman, but it seems reasonable to assume that when we are engaged in a war in which, through our actions, a great number of innocent people are being killed, we might try to derogate the victims in order to justify our complicity in the outcome. We might poke fun at them, refer to them as "gooks," and **dehumanize** them; but, once we have succeeded in doing that, watch out—because it becomes easier to hurt and kill "subhumans" than to hurt and kill fellow human beings. Thus, reducing dissonance in this way has terrible future consequences; it increases the likelihood that the atrocities we are willing to commit will become greater and greater. I will elaborate on this theme in the next chapter. For now, I would like to enlarge on a point I made in Chapters 1 and 2: In the final analysis, people are accountable for their own actions. Not everyone behaved as Lieutenant Calley behaved. At the same time, it should be noted that Lieutenant Calley was not alone in his behavior; he stands as a striking example of a rather common phenomenon. With this in mind, it is important to acknowledge that certain situational factors can exert a very powerful impact upon human actions. Accordingly, before we can write off such behavior as merely bizarre, or merely crazy, or merely villainous, it would be wise to examine the situation that sets up the mechanism for this kind of behavior. We can then begin to understand the terrible price we are paying for allowing certain conditions to exist. Perhaps, eventually, we can do something to avoid these conditions. Dissonance theory helps to shed some light on this mechanism.

Of course, this kind of situation is not limited to wars. Many violent acts can be perpetrated on innocent victims and can lead to justifications that, in turn, can lead to more violence. Imagine you live in a society that is unfair to minority groups like blacks and Latinos. Just to take a wild example, let us pretend that, for several decades, the white majority did not allow blacks and Latinos to attend first-rate public schools but instead provided them with a second-rate and stultifying education. As a consequence of this "benign neglect," the average black child and the average Latino child are less well educated and less motivated than the average white child at the same grade level. They demonstrate this by doing poorly on achievement tests. Such a situation provides a golden opportunity for civic leaders to justify their discriminatory behavior and, hence, to reduce dissonance. "You see," they might say, "those people are stupid (because they perform poorly on the achievement test); see how clever we were when we decided against wasting our resources by trying to provide them with a high-quality education. These people are unteachable." This self-fulfilling prophecy provides a perfect justification for cruelty and neglect. So, too, is the attribution of moral inferiority to blacks and Chicanos. We imprison racial minorities in overcrowded ghettos, and we set up a situation in which skin color almost inevitably unleashes forces preventing people from participating in the opportunities for growth and success existing for most white Americans. Through the magic of television, minorities see people succeeding and living in the luxury of middle-class respectability. They become painfully aware of the opportunities, comforts, and luxuries unavailable to them. If their frustration leads them to violence or if their despair leads them to drugs, it is fairly easy for their white brothers and sisters to sit back complacently, shake their heads knowingly, and attribute this behavior to some kind of moral inferiority. As Edward Jones and Richard Nisbett[58] point out, when some misfortune befalls us, we tend to attribute the cause to something in the environment; but when we see the same misfortune befalling *another person,* we tend to attribute the cause to some weakness inherent in that person's character.

The Psychology of Inevitability

George Bernard Shaw was hard hit by his father's alcoholism, but he tried to make light of it. He once wrote: "If you cannot get rid of the family skeleton, you may as well make it dance."[59] In a sense, dissonance theory describes the ways people have of making their skeletons dance—of trying to live with unpleasant outcomes. This is particularly true when a situation arises that is both negative and inevitable. Here people attempt to make the best of things by cognitively minimizing the unpleasantness of the situation. In one experiment, Jack Brehm[60] got children to volunteer to eat a vegetable they had previously said they disliked a lot. After they had eaten the vegetable, the experimenter led half of the children to believe they could expect to eat much more of that vegetable in the future; the remaining children were not so informed. The children who were led to believe it was inevitable that they would be eating the vegetable in the future succeeded in convincing themselves that the vegetable was not so bad. In short, the cognition "I dislike that vegetable" is dissonant with the cognition "I will be eating that vegetable in the future." In order to reduce the dissonance, the children came to believe the vegetable was really not as noxious as they had previously thought. John Darley and Ellen Berscheid[61] showed that the same phenomenon works with people as well as vegetables. In their experiment, college women volunteered to participate in a series of meetings in which each student would be discussing her sexual behavior and sexual standards with another woman whom she didn't know. Before beginning these discussion sessions, each participant was given two folders. Each folder contained a personality description of a young woman who had supposedly volunteered for the same experience; the descriptions contained a mixture of pleasant and unpleasant characteristics. Half of the participants were led to believe they were going to interact with the young women described in folder A, and the remaining participants were led to believe they were going to interact with the one described in folder B. Before actually meeting these women, the participants were asked to evaluate each of them on the basis of the personality descriptions they had read. Those who felt it was inevitable that they were going to share their intimate secrets with the young woman described in folder A found her much more appealing than the one described in folder B, whereas those who believed they had to interact with the young woman described in folder B found *her* much more appealing. Just as with vegetables, inevitability makes the heart grow fonder. The knowledge that one is inevitably going to be spending time with another person enhances the positive aspects of that person—or at least deemphasizes his or her negative aspects. In short, people tend to make the best of something they know is bound to happen.

The same kind of phenomenon occurs during a presidential election. Think about it: The idea of having your nation (the most powerful nation on Earth) being led by someone you considered a complete jerk would be unbearable. So what do people do about it? They try to make the best of it, of course. A week before the 2000 presidential election, Aaron Kay[62] and his colleagues gave several hundred people an article that presented a convincing analysis of the election's likely outcome. Some participants read that most respected experts expected Bush to win by a landslide; others read that these same experts predicted that he would have a narrow victory. Still others read predictions of either a Gore landslide or narrow victory. These people were then asked to rate the desirability of both Gore and Bush presidencies.

The results showed a strong relationship between a candidate's perceived likelihood of winning and his desirability to voters. That is, both Republicans and Democrats tended to rate Gore as more desirable as the likelihood of his victory increased and to rate Bush as more desirable as the likelihood of *his* victory increased.

Deemphasizing the negative can be an adaptive strategy when what's in store is a disliked vegetable, a discussion with someone whom we've never met, or even learning to live with a president you didn't vote for. There are situations, however, when such a strategy can prove disastrous. Consider the case of students at UCLA. Geological studies conducted in the mid-1980s indicated that there was a 90 percent probability of at least one major earthquake in Los Angeles during the next 20 years. In the face of such an impending disaster, rational people would no doubt acknowledge the danger and work to prepare by learning all they can about it and by taking safety precautions. In 1987, two social psychologists at UCLA, Darrin Lehman and Shelley Taylor, conducted interviews with 120 undergraduates at their university and determined that such was not the case.[63] Their findings were unsettling: Only 5 percent had taken any safety precautions (such as locating the nearest fire extinguisher); only one-third knew that the best action to take during a quake is to crawl under a heavy piece of furniture or to stand in a doorway; and not one respondent had taken preparatory measures recommended by experts. It seems that even among well-educated people, a typical response to an inevitable catastrophe is to do nothing to prepare for it.

It's noteworthy that coping styles varied as a function of the students' living situation. Those students living in seismically unsafe residence halls were more likely than those living in relatively safe residence halls to cope with the impending disaster by refusing to think about it or by minimizing the expected damage. That is, those who were most at risk in the event of a quake were the very ones who refused to think about the imminent catastrophe or who underestimated its ultimate severity. In short, if I'm pretty sure that there's going to be an earthquake, how can I justify continuing to live in an unsafe residence hall? Easy: I deny that there's going to be an earthquake and refuse to think about it. Self-justifying responses to dangerous and inevitable events can be comforting in the short run. But when they keep us from taking steps to enhance our safety, such responses can, in the long run, prove deadly.

Needless to say, the geological predictions of the mid-1980s proved to be correct. In the winter of 1994 there *was* a major earthquake in the Los Angeles area, resulting in a great deal of property damage and the destruction of freeways, which disrupted transportation for several months. Fortunately, because the quake took place at 4:30 A.M. during a holiday, there was relatively little loss of life. While this was a major earthquake, most experts agree that "the big one" is still pending. Do you think that the earthquake of 1994 will lead people to be better prepared for the next one?

As you may have noticed, there is a curious difference between the responses of children facing a disliked vegetable or college students facing an inevitable interaction with another person, on the one hand, and the responses of UCLA students to the threat of an impending earthquake, on the other hand. In the former situations, the inevitable is accepted and attitudes stressing the positive aspects of the unavoidable event are embraced. The latter situation, however, involves confronting a highly probable event that is life-threatening and largely uncontrollable. It would be stretching the limits of the human imagination to redefine a major earthquake as desirable—or as anything less than a catastrophe. And we can't prevent earthquakes; the best we can hope for is to respond adaptively to one, with no guarantee that safety measures will really save us. Thus, the nature of our response may very well depend on whether we believe preventive steps will genuinely increase our sense of control over the inevitable. If such steps seem largely futile, then the prospect of expending energy on them will only serve to increase our feeling of dissonance even further. Under such circumstances, we are likely to justify not taking safety measures by denying the probability of the potential disaster or vastly underestimating its magnitude.

The Importance of Self-Esteem

Throughout this chapter, we have seen how our commitment to a particular course of action can freeze or change our attitudes, distort our perceptions, and determine the kind of information we seek out. In addition, we have seen that a person can become committed to a situation in a number of different ways—by making a decision, by working hard in order to attain a goal, by believing something is inevitable, by engaging in any action having serious consequences (such as hurting someone), and so on. As I have mentioned before, the deepest form of commitment takes place in those situations in which a person's self-esteem is at stake. Thus, if I perform a cruel or stupid action, this threatens my self-esteem because it turns my mind to the possibility that I am a cruel or stupid person. In the hundreds of experiments inspired by the theory of cognitive dissonance, the clearest results were obtained in those situations in which a person's self-esteem was involved. Moreover, as one might expect, we have seen that those individuals with the highest self-esteem experience the most dissonance when they behave in a stupid or cruel manner.

What happens when an individual has low self-esteem? Theoretically, if such a person were to commit a stupid or immoral action, he or she would not experience much dissonance. The cognition "I have done an immoral thing" is consonant with the cognition "I am a schlunk." In short, people who believe themselves to be schlunks expect to do schlunky things. In other words, people with low self-esteem will not find it terribly difficult to commit immoral acts—because committing immoral acts is not dissonant with their self-concept. On the other hand, people with high self-esteem are more likely to resist the temptation to commit immoral acts because to behave immorally would produce a great deal of dissonance.

I tested this proposition in collaboration with David Mettee.[64] We predicted that individuals who had a low opinion of themselves would be more likely to cheat (if given the opportunity) than individuals who had a high opinion of themselves. It should be made clear that we were not making the simple prediction that people who believe themselves to be dishonest will cheat more than people who believe themselves to be honest. Our prediction was a little more daring; it was based on the assumption that, if normal people receive a temporary blow to their self-esteem (e.g., if they are jilted by their lover or flunk an exam) and thus feel low and worthless, they are more likely to cheat at cards, kick their dog, or do any number of things consistent with a low opinion of themselves. As a function of feeling they are low people, individuals will commit low acts.

In our experiment, we temporarily modified the self-esteem of college students by giving them false information about their personalities. After taking a personality test, one-third of the students were given positive feedback; specifically, they were told the test indicated that they were mature, interesting, deep, and so forth. Another one-third of the students were given negative feedback; they were told the test indicated that they were relatively immature, uninteresting, rather shallow, and the like. The remaining one-third of the students were not given any information about the results of the test.

Immediately afterward, the students were scheduled to participate in an experiment, conducted by a different psychologist, that had no apparent relation to the personality inventory. As part of this second experiment, the participants played a game of cards against some of their fellow students. This was a gambling game in which the students were allowed to bet money and were told they could keep whatever they won. In the course of the game, they were presented with a few opportunities to cheat in a situation where it seemed impossible to be detected. The situation was arranged so that if a student decided *not* to cheat, she would certainly lose, whereas if she decided to cheat, she would be certain to win a sizable sum of money.

The results clearly showed that those students who had previously received information designed to lower their self-esteem cheated to a far greater extent than those who had received the high self-esteem information. The control group—those receiving no information—fell exactly in between. These findings suggest that it would be well worth the effort of parents and teachers to alert themselves to the potentially far-reaching consequences of their own behavior as it affects the self-esteem of their children and students. Specifically, if high self-esteem can serve as a buffer against dishonest behavior, then it might seem reasonable to do everything possible to help individuals learn to respect and love themselves.

But here, we must proceed with caution. High self-esteem is generally a good thing to have—but it is hardly a universal panacea. If a person's self-esteem is not grounded in reality[65] or if it is narcissistic—based on a false sense of superiority to others, this can produce a plethora of negative effects. For example, in a series of experiments, Roy Baumeister, Brad Bushman and Keith Campbell[66] found that when a person's narcissistic self-esteem is threatened by criticism, the person will aggress against his critic in an attempt to get even and restore his threatened self image. In one experiment, they asked participants to write an essay. Their essay was subsequently criticized by their partner. After receiving the criticism, the participants were given the opportunity to express hostility against their partners by blasting them with an unpleasant noise. The participants were in control of the decibel level. The people who turned the noise-maker up to the highest decibel levels turned out to be those who had scored high on measures of both self-esteem and narcissism. In short, when their inflated opinion of themselves is threatened, narcissistic people get angry and behave more aggressively than the average person. Christina Salmivalli and her colleagues suggest that this syndrome, high narcissistic self-esteem, is not genuine high self-esteem at all, but rather, it is paper-thin, self-aggrandizing, and based on feelings of insecurity. They found that this form of self-esteem is present in schoolyard bullies while those youngsters with genuinely high self-esteem are more secure and do not engage in bullying. Indeed, such individuals are more likely to try to defend the victims of bullying.[67]

Discomfort or Self-Perception?

The theory of cognitive dissonance is a motivational theory. According to the theory, it is the discomfort caused by a threat to the self-concept that motivates people to change their beliefs or behavior. But how do we know that people going through these experiments actually experience discomfort? Perhaps it is simply a matter of self-perception. This possibility is nicely captured by the humorous expression: "How do I know what I think until I see what I do?" Several years ago, Daryl Bem[68] developed the notion of self-perception and applied it to some of the research on dissonance theory. Bem suggested that the people who are undergoing attitude and behavior change in these situations may not be experiencing discomfort and may not be motivated to justify themselves. Rather, they may simply be observing their own behavior in a cool, calm and dispassionate way, and drawing a conclusion from their observations. Bem's suggestion makes a lot of sense. As you know, we all have a strong tendency to make these kinds of attributions—both about other people and ourselves. For example, suppose there were a huge array of desserts on display in a cafeteria and, after looking at all of them, you chose a wedge of rhubarb pie. If I were observing you in the cafeteria, I would guess that you like rhubarb pie. Bem suggests that, by observing your *own* behavior, you would draw the same conclusion: You would say: "Hey, I freely chose the rhubarb pie, therefore, I guess I must like it!"

So far there is no disagreement between Bem and me. But here is where it gets interesting: Suppose you were a Yale student and you found yourself writing an essay excusing the brutality of the New Haven police (as in Cohen's experiment described earlier). According to Bem, you would dispassionately observe your own behavior, shrug your shoulders and say, "Hmmm, because I wrote that essay (for only 50 cents!), I guess I must believe what I wrote . . . or else I wouldn't have written it." No dissonance, no discomfort, no self-justification; merely self-perception.

Bem's notion is elegant in its simplicity. If attitude change in this kind of situation is simply a matter of cool self-perception, then we do not need all this theorizing about discomfort, the self-concept, self-justification, and the like.

It turns out that Bem is partly right. Self-perception does play a role; but it seems to be operative only in those situations where a person doesn't have a clear, unambiguous belief to begin with. On the other hand, where a person has a fairly clear initial belief (e.g., the New Haven Police behaved badly; packing spools is a boring task; I am a decent, sensible person), then discomfort and threats to the self-concept do come into play.[69]

How can I be sure that discomfort plays a major role in these dissonant situations? Well, one reason is that people in these situations say so. For example, Patricia Devine and her colleagues[70] found that when people are put in a dissonance-arousing situation, they do indeed report feeling more agitated and more uncomfortable than people in the control condition.

Participants reporting their own discomfort is convincing. In addition, there is independent behavioral evidence of discomfort. For example, we know that discomfort is distracting. In a clever experiment, Michael Pallak and Thane Pittman[71] demonstrated that people experiencing dissonance perform a complex task more poorly than people not experiencing dissonance. The people experiencing dissonance show the same decrement in performance as people in other uncomfortable drive states like extreme hunger and thirst.

In addition, several investigators[72] have shown some striking behavioral evidence for the motivating qualities of dissonance. In one experiment, Mark Zanna and Joel Cooper gave participants a placebo pill. Some were told that the pill would arouse them and make them feel tense. Others were told that the pill would make them feel calm and relaxed. Participants in the control condition were told that the pill would not affect them in any way. After ingesting the pill, each person was induced to write a counterattitudinal essay, thus creating dissonance. Again, dissonance theory predicts that such participants will change their attitudes, bringing them in line with their essays in order to reduce their uncomfortable arousal state. However, if some of the participants think the arousal they are experiencing is due to the pill, they won't need to alter their attitudes to feel better about themselves. At the opposite end of the spectrum, if some of the participants think they should be feeling relaxed due to the pill, any arousal they experience should be particularly powerful for them because it is taking place in spite of the pill. Accordingly, these people should change their attitudes a great deal. Thus the theory predicts that attitude change will come or go across conditions, depending on whether the arousal due to dissonance is masked by an alternative explanation ("Oh, right—I took a pill that's supposed to make me feel tense; that's why I'm feeling this way") or magnified by an alternative explanation ("Oh, no—I took a pill that's supposed to make me feel relaxed and I feel tense").

And that is exactly what Zanna and Cooper found. Participants in the control condition underwent considerable attitude change, as would be expected in a typical dissonance experiment. Participants in the aroused condition, however, did not change their attitudes—they attributed their discomfort to the pill, not their counterattitudinal essay. Finally, participants in the relaxed condition changed their attitudes even *more* than the control participants did. They inferred that writing the counterattitudinal essay had made them *very* tense, since they were feeling aroused despite administration of a relaxing drug. Thus they inferred that their behavior was very inconsistent with their perception of themselves as decent and reasonable people, and they changed their attitude to bring it into line with their essay contents.

Physiological and Motivational Effects of Dissonance

How far can the effects of dissonance extend? In the past several years, researchers have shown that it can go beyond attitudes; it can modify the way we experience basic physiological drives. Under certain well-specified conditions, dissonance reduction can lead hungry people to experience less hunger, thirsty people to experience less thirst, and people undergoing intensive electric shock to experience less pain. Here's how it works: Imagine that Vic Volunteer is induced to *commit himself* to a situation in which he will be deprived of food or water for a long time or in which he will experience electric shock. If Vic *has low external justification* for doing this, he will experience dissonance. His cognitions concerning his hunger pangs, his parched throat, or the pain of electric shock are each dissonant with his cognition that he volunteered to go through these experiences and is not getting very much in return. In order to reduce this dissonance, Vic convinces himself that the hunger isn't so intense, or the thirst isn't so bad, or the pain isn't so great. This should not be astonishing. Although hunger, thirst, and pain all have physiological bases, they also have a strong psychological component. For example, through suggestion, meditation, hypnosis, placebo pills, the bedside manner of a skillful physician, or some combination of these, perceived pain can be reduced. Experimental social psychologists have shown that, under conditions of high dissonance arousal, ordinary people, with no special skills in hypnosis or meditation, can accomplish the same things for themselves.

Thus, Philip Zimbardo and his colleagues[73] subjected many people to intense electric shocks. Half of these people were in a high-dissonance condition—that is, they were induced to commit themselves to volunteer for the experience and were given very little external justification—and the other half were in a low-dissonance condition—that is, they had no choice in the matter and had a great deal of external justification. The results showed that the people in the high-dissonance condition reported experiencing less pain than those in the low-dissonance condition. Moreover, this phenomenon extended beyond their subjective reports. There is clear evidence that the physiological response to pain (as measured by the galvanic skin response) was somewhat less intense in the high-dissonance condition. In addition, the pain of those in the high-dissonance condition interfered less with the tasks they were performing. Thus, not only did they report less pain, but, objectively, they were less bothered by it.

Similar results have been shown for hunger and thirst. Jack Brehm[74] reported a series of experiments in which people were deprived of either food or water for long periods of time. In addition to experiencing hunger or thirst, these individuals experienced high or low dissonance for much the same reasons as Zimbardo's participants. Specifically, some had low external justification for undergoing the hunger or thirst, whereas others had high external justification. For the participants experiencing great dissonance, the best available way to reduce it was to minimize the experience of hunger or thirst. In separate experiments on hunger and thirst, Brehm found that high-dissonance participants said they were less hungry (or thirsty) than low-dissonance participants who were deprived of food (or water) for the same length of time. Again, this was no mere verbal report: After the experiment, when all of the participants were allowed to eat (or drink) freely, those in the high dissonance condition actually consumed less food (or water) than those in the low-dissonance condition.

Practical Applications of Dissonance Theory

One of the reasons the theory of cognitive dissonance has attracted such great interest and inspired so much research is its ability to explain and predict phenomena not readily explainable in commonsense terms. Furthermore, as the reader has seen, dissonance theory has been applied to account for a great many phenomena, ranging from how rumors are spread to major changes in important attitudes and behaviors—from practicing safer sex to the reduction of racial prejudice.

Understanding Responses to Disaster
It is exciting to use the theory as a way of understanding a number of events in contemporary society that otherwise might be puzzling indeed. For example, consider the Three Mile Island crisis in 1979, when an accident at the nuclear power plant caused an unstable condition in the reactor that lasted for several days, posing the threat of a meltdown that would result in catastrophic contamination of the surrounding area and endanger hundreds of thousands of people living in the vicinity. Common sense would suggest that the people living closest to the power plant would be the most frightened and, therefore, the most likely to take action. Dissonance theory makes a different prediction. Suppose you were living within a few miles of the plant at the time of the incident. Since radioactive steam escaped from the reactor during the initial stages of the accident, it is possible that you and your loved ones have already been contaminated. How will you respond? You can evacuate the area, but leaving your job and finding temporary lodging would be costly and difficult. Besides, even if you do evacuate, there is the likelihood that you have already been exposed to the radiation. Many contradictory reports are circulating about the extent of the danger. Some of your neighbors have decided to leave; others are downplaying the magnitude of the threat. After a time, the authorities from the

Nuclear Regulatory Commission (NRC) arrive on the scene, issuing reassuring statements that the danger of radiation leakage is minor and the probability of a serious disaster is minimal. How likely are you to believe these statements?

My guess at the time was that people living closest to the power plant would be most likely to latch on to these pronouncements and believe them, grasping at whatever reassurance they could find. If you were living near Three Mile Island, your cognition that you chose to live close enough to the nuclear power plant to absorb harmful radiation in case of an accident would be dissonant with your self-concept as smart, reasonable, prudent, and caring for your family. Therefore, regardless of whether or not you evacuated, you would be eager to believe these reassurances. Even when the authorities changed their stance a couple of days later, advising pregnant women to evacuate, those living near the plant would tend to trust the NRC spokesman when he said they were merely being cautious and the danger still is minimal. Contrast this with the reaction of those living just outside the immediate danger zone. These people were also worried and scared, though they were threatened less directly and had not already been contaminated. Since they were not as deeply committed as those living in the immediate danger zone, they should have been more able to express their skepticism and anger; indeed, it would have been in their self-interest to do so because they would have been imperiled if the situation in the nuclear power plant deteriorated or if the crisis was more serious than what was being publicized. My speculation—that residents nearest the Three Mile Island reactor would attribute more credibility to the pronouncements of the NRC than would those living farther away—was confirmed by an extensive survey conducted shortly after the incident.[75] The data reveal that respondents closest to the plant were significantly more likely to say that the information conveyed by the NRC was extremely useful: Those living more than 15 miles away were more inclined to say that the information was totally useless.*

Anecdotal evidence also supports this conclusion: It was reported that the most dire rumors about the crisis came from as far away as California, and while the national media were filled with reports of the NRC's incompetence and inadequacy, the populace near Three Mile Island was said to have greeted the NRC "like cavalry riding to a nick-of-time rescue."[76]

---

*It should be noted, however, that these findings are open to alternative explanations. Those who lived closest to the nuclear power plant at Three Mile Island may have differed in important ways from those who lived farther away. For example, the very fact that they chose to live close to the nuclear plant could conceivably reflect a more positive attitude about the nuclear power industry. Thus, even before the accident, those living closest to the plant might have perceived the NRC as more credible than those living farther away.

Reducing Weight by Reducing Dissonance

Beyond its power to help us understand and predict a variety of phenomena, a theory is of particular value if it can be practically applied in ways that benefit people. Earlier in this chapter, I pointed out cognitive dissonance theory's relevance for educators wishing to instill intrinsic motivation for learning in their students or for parents looking for a more effective means than severe punishment for helping their children learn moral and humane values. Institutions like the Marine Corps and college fraternities have long employed severe initiation to increase their members' commitment to the group. An experiment by Danny Axsom and Joel Cooper[77] provides a particularly compelling example of how dissonance theory can be used to help solve a difficult personal problem—obesity. Hypothesizing that expending a great deal of effort to reach an objective would increase a person's commitment to that goal, they induced a number of overweight women to volunteer for a weight-control program and engaged them in intellectual activities requiring either a large or a small amount of effort—that was *unrelated* to losing weight. Over the 4 weeks of the program, only slight weight losses were observed in either group. But 6 months and 12 months later, when the experimenters contacted the women again, they discovered major differences: The women who had expended a great amount of effort had lost an average of 8 pounds, while those who had performed tasks requiring little effort in the program had not lost any weight. Changing one's attitudes in order to justify one's behavior not only can have powerful effects but can also initiate processes that are remarkably persistent over long periods of time.

Dissonance and AIDS Prevention

As you know, dissonance makes people uncomfortable. Thus, not only do we strive to reduce dissonance whenever we experience it, but in addition, we try to defend ourselves against experiencing dissonance in the first place. One way of remaining oblivious to dissonance is by steadfastly refusing to pay close attention to what we are doing. A good example of this "mindless" behavior can be found in the sexual behavior of millions of young adults in the face of the AIDS epidemic. You will recall that I discussed this issue briefly in Chapter 3. Bear with me as I expand on it here. As you know, hundreds of millions of dollars have been spent on AIDS information and prevention campaigns in the mass media. While these campaigns have been reasonably effective in conveying information, they have not been nearly as successful in preventing people from engaging in risky sexual behavior. For example, although sexually active college students are aware of AIDS as a serious problem, only a surprisingly small percentage use condoms regularly. The reason for this seems to be that condoms are inconvenient and unromantic, and remind them of disease—something they do not want to be reminded of when getting ready to make love. Rather, as researchers have consistently discovered, there is a strong tendency for people to go into denial—in this case, to come to believe that, while AIDS is a problem for other people, they themselves are not at risk.[78] If the mass media have been ineffective, is there anything that can be done?

During the past several years, my students and I have had considerable success in convincing people to use condoms by employing a variation of the "saying is believing" paradigm discussed earlier in this chapter. As you will recall, in the typical "saying is believing" experiment, individuals are asked to make a speech advocating a point of view that runs counter to their own opinion. This arouses dissonance; dissonance is then reduced by changing their attitude to bring it more into line with the position they advocated. How can this paradigm be applied to the AIDS epidemic?

As researchers, here is the problem we faced: When it comes to practicing safe sex, almost everybody believes in the message—that is, almost everybody believes that AIDS is a danger and that, if people are going to be sexually active, using condoms is a good idea—it's just that very few of these people who profess these beliefs actually use condoms regularly. So how do you get a person to experience dissonance by making an argument favoring the use of condoms when they already believe that using condoms is a good idea? It's a dilemma. Our solution was actually quite simple: Because people were insulating themselves from dissonance via the mechanism of denial, we attempted to cut through this denial by confronting people with their own **hypocrisy**.

In our experiments,[79] we began by asking college students to compose a speech describing the dangers of AIDS and advocating the use of condoms "every single time you have sex." Every student was more than willing to do it—because every one of them believed it was a good idea for sexually active people to use condoms. In one condition, the students merely composed the arguments. In another condition, after composing the arguments, the students recited them in front of a video camera after being informed that the resulting videotape would be played to an audience of high-school students as part of a sex-education class. In addition, prior to making the speech, half of the students in each condition were made mindful of their own past failures to use condoms by making a list of the circumstances in their own lives when they found it particularly difficult, awkward, or "impossible" to use condoms.

Essentially then, the participants in one condition—those who made a video for high-school students after having been made mindful of their own failure to use condoms—were in a state of high dissonance. This was caused by being made aware of their own hypocrisy; that is, they were fully aware of the fact that they were preaching behavior to high school students that they themselves were not practicing. In order to remove the hypocrisy and maintain their self-esteem, they would need to start practicing what they were preaching. And that is exactly what we found. At the close of the experiment, students in the hypocrisy condition were far more likely to purchase condoms (on display on a table outside the experimental room) than in any of the other conditions. Furthermore, several months later, a large proportion of the students in this condition reported that they were using condoms regularly.

Dissonance and Water Conservation

A few years ago, while central California was suffering through one of its chronic water shortages, water was being rationed in the city of Santa Cruz—where my university is located. On my campus, the administration was trying desperately to find ways to induce students to conserve water by taking shorter showers. Direct appeals to the students' values regarding conservation had an effect—but a small one. As mentioned in Chapter 2, several years earlier, we had obtained a somewhat larger effect by inducing students to conform to the behavior of appropriate role models. In order to have a still greater impact on water conservation, we set about to induce a feeling of dissonance by utilizing the hypocrisy model—in much the same way as we did in the condom experiment discussed above.

In the shower experiment,[80] my research assistant intercepted students on their way to take a shower at the university field house. As in the condom experiment, we varied both commitment and mindfulness. In the commitment condition, each student was asked if she would be willing to sign a poster encouraging people to conserve water. The flyer read: "Take shorter showers. If I can do it, so can you!" In the mindful condition we also asked the students to respond to a water conservation "survey," which consisted of items designed to make them aware of their pro-conservation attitudes and the fact that their showering behavior was sometimes wasteful.

The students then proceeded to the shower room, where a second research assistant was unobtrusively waiting (with a hidden waterproof stopwatch) to time their showers. Exactly as in the condom experiment, we had a major impact on the students' behavior only in the high-dissonance condition—that is, where the students were induced to advocate short showers and also were made mindful of their own past behavior. In this condition, students became aware that they were not practicing what they were preaching: The length of the average shower was just over $3\frac{1}{2}$ minutes (that's short!) and was far shorter than in the control conditions.

Shedding Light on the Power of Cult Leaders

Dissonance theory has shown itself to be useful as a way of increasing our understanding of events that totally confound our imagination—like the enormous power certain cult leaders like Jim Jones (the massacre at Jonestown, Guyana), David

Koresh (the conflagration at Waco, Texas), and Marshall Herff Applewhite (the group suicide of the Heaven's Gate cult) have had over the hearts and minds of their followers. Let us focus on the Jonestown massacre. It goes without saying that the event was tragic in the extreme. It seems beyond comprehension that a single individual could have such power that, at his command, hundreds of people would kill their own children and themselves. How could this happen? The tragedy at Jonestown is far too complex to be understood fully by a simple and sovereign analysis. But one clue does emanate from the foot-in-the-door phenomenon discussed earlier in this chapter. Jim Jones extracted great trust from his followers one step at a time. Indeed, close scrutiny reveals a chain of ever-increasing commitments on the part of his followers. While it is almost impossible to comprehend fully the final event, it becomes slightly more comprehensible if we look at it as part of a series. As I mentioned earlier in this chapter, once a small commitment is made, the stage is set for ever-increasing commitments.

Let us start at the beginning. It is easy to understand how a charismatic leader like Jones might extract money from the members of his church. Once they have committed themselves to donating a small amount of money in response to his message of peace and universal brotherhood, he is able to request and receive a great deal more. Next, he induces people to sell their homes and turn over the money to the church. Soon, at his request, several of his followers pull up stakes, leaving their families and friends, to start life anew in the strange and difficult environment of Guyana. There, not only do they work hard (thus increasing their commitment), but they also are cut off from potential dissenting opinion, inasmuch as they are surrounded by true believers. The chain of events continues. Jones takes sexual liberties with several married women among his followers, who acquiesce, if reluctantly; Jones claims to be the father of their children. Finally, as a prelude to the climactic event, Jones induces his followers to perform a series of mock ritual suicides as a test of their loyalty and obedience. Thus, in a step-by-step fashion, the commitment to Jim Jones increases. Each step in itself is not a huge, ludicrous leap from the one preceding it.

Again, this is an admittedly oversimplified analysis. A great many events occurred among Jones's followers in addition to the gradual increases in commitment I have described. These contributed to the tragic outcome. At the same time, viewing the final outcome in the context of increasing commitment brought about by preceding events does shed a ray of light on a phenomenon that at first seems impossible to understand.

Was Osama bin Laden Capitalizing on Dissonance? Following the catastrophic destruction of the World Trade Center by suicide bombers on September 11, 2001, a wide range of political analysts have struggled to understand how hatred can be so strong that people would destroy themselves in order to destroy thousands of innocent people—when they must have known that their action could not possibly produce any direct political advantage. Most analysts have explained the behavior of the suicide bombers in terms of religious fanaticism. But this explanation does not add much to our understanding. Thomas Friedman, a Pulitzer Prize–winning journalist and one of our nation's most astute observers of the Middle East, has taken a different approach. He has offered a partial answer to this most difficult question based on the theory of cognitive dissonance. Friedman[81] suggests that there are thousands of young Muslim men all over the Middle East and Europe who are suffering from a loss of dignity. According to Friedman, these young men were

> taught from youth in the mosque that theirs is the most complete and advanced form of the three monotheistic faiths—superior to both Christianity and Judaism—yet who become aware that the Islamic world has fallen behind both the Christian West and the Jewish state in education, science, democracy, and development. This produces a cognitive dissonance in these young men—a cognitive dissonance that is the original spark for all their rage. . . . They reconcile this by concluding that the Islamic world has fallen behind the rest of the world either because the Europeans, Americans, and Israelis stole something from the Muslims, or because the Europeans, Americans, and Israelis are deliberately retarding the progress of Muslims, or because those who are leading the Muslim world have drifted away from the true faith and are behaving in un Islamic ways, but are being kept in power by America. . . . They see America as the most powerful lethal weapon destroying their religious universe, or at least the universe they would like to build. And that is why they transform America into the ultimate evil, even more than Western Europe, an evil that needs to be weakened and, if possible, destroyed. Even by suicide? Why not? If America is destroying the source of meaning in their lives, then it needs to be destroyed back.

Dissonance Reduction and Culture

How universal is the experience of cognitive dissonance? Is it something that is experienced mostly by Americans or is it part and parcel of the human condition? It is impossible to answer that question definitively—because dissonance experiments have not been done everywhere. But I can say this: Although most of the research has been done in North America, the effects have been shown to exist in every part of the world where research has been done.[82] It should be noted that the specific effects do not always take precisely the same form in some other cultures that they do in North America. For example, in less individualistic societies than ours, dissonance-reducing behavior might take a more communal form. Consider the classic experiment by

Festinger and Carlsmith discussed earlier in this chapter. When asked to tell a lie for either $1 or $20, would Japanese students behave the same way that American students behave? In a striking set of experiments, Japanese social psychologist Haruki Sakai[83] replicated the Festinger-Carlsmith experiment—and then some! First, Sakai found that, in Japan, those people who told another person that a boring task was interesting for minimal reward, actually came to believe the task was interesting. In addition, Sakai found that, if a person merely observes someone he knows and likes saying that a boring task is interesting, that causes the observer to experience dissonance. Consequently, in that situation, the observers come to believe that the task is interesting. In short, in a communal culture like Japan, the observers tend to bring their evaluation in line with a lie *their friend* has told!

"Man" Cannot Live by Consonance Alone

Near the beginning of this chapter, I made the point that people are capable of rational, adaptive behavior as well as dissonance-reducing behavior. Let's return to that issue. If individuals concentrate their time and effort on protecting their egos, they will never grow. In order to grow, we must learn from our mistakes. But if we are intent on reducing dissonance, we will not admit to our mistakes. Instead, we will sweep them under the rug or, worse still, we will turn them into virtues. The memoirs of former presidents are full of the kind of self-serving, self-justifying statements that are best summarized in the words of former President Lyndon Johnson: "If I had it all to do over again, I would not change a thing."[84]

On the other hand, people do frequently grow and learn from their mistakes. How? Under what conditions? Ideally, when I make a mistake, it would be useful for me to look at that mistake in a nondefensive manner and, in effect, say to myself, "Okay, I blew it. What can I learn from the experience so that I will not end up in this position again?" I can increase the probability of this kind of reaction in the following ways:

- Through a greater understanding of my own defensiveness and dissonance-reducing tendencies.

- Through the realization that performing stupid or immoral actions does not necessarily mean I am an irrevocably stupid or immoral person.

- Through the development of enough ego strength to tolerate errors in myself.

- Through increasing my ability to recognize the benefits of admitting my errors in terms of my own growth and learning as well as my ability to form close, meaningful relationships with other people.

Of course, it is far easier to list these procedures than it is to accomplish them. How do we get in touch with our defensiveness and dissonance-reducing tendencies? How can we come to realize that bright, moral people like ourselves can occasionally perform a stupid or immoral action? It is not enough to know it abstractly or superficially; in order to fully utilize this knowledge, a person must consciously practice it. We will take a closer look at this process in Chapter 8, where we will examine the advantage of authenticity and nondefensive communication in our relationships with other people.

Saul Steinberg, *Untitled drawing*, ink on paper.
Originally published in *The New Yorker*, January 18, 1964.
© The Saul Steinberg Foundation / Artists Rights Society (ARS), New York

6
Human Aggression

Over 35 years ago, at the height of the disastrous war our country was waging in Southeast Asia, I was watching the news on television. The anchorman (the inimitable Walter Cronkite) was reporting an incident in which U.S. planes dropped napalm on a village in South Vietnam believed to be a Vietcong stronghold. My son Hal, who was about 10 years old at the time, asked brightly, "Hey, Dad, what's napalm?"

"Oh," I answered casually, "as I understand it, it's a chemical that burns people; it also sticks so that if it gets on your skin, you can't remove it." And I continued to watch the news.

A few minutes later, I happened to glance at Hal and saw tears streaming down his face. Struck by his pain and grief, I grew dismayed as I began to wonder what had happened to me. Had I become so brutalized that I could answer my son's question so matter-of-factly—as if he had asked me how a baseball is made or how a leaf functions? Had I become so accustomed to human brutality that I could be casual in its presence?

In a sense, it is not surprising. The people of my generation have lived through an era of unspeakable horrors—the Holocaust in Europe, the dropping of atomic bombs on Hiroshima and Nagasaki, the Korean War, and the war in Southeast Asia—to name a few. In the ensuing years, we have also borne witness to several brutal civil wars in Central America; the slaughter of over a million civilians in the killing fields of Cambodia; "ethnic cleansing" in Bosnia; the bloodbaths in Rwanda, Sudan, and Algeria; the suicide bombings of September 11 on our own soil; and on and on and on. As horrifying as these events are, mass killings of this kind are certainly not peculiar to the present era. Many years ago, a friend showed me a very thin book—only 10 or 15 pages long—that purported to be a capsule history of the world. It was a chronological list of the important events in recorded history. Can you guess how it read? Of course—one war after another, interrupted every now and then by a few nonviolent events, such as the birth of Jesus and the invention of the printing press. What kind of species are we if the most important events in the brief history of humankind are situations in which people kill one another en masse?

Moreover, we Americans display a chilling acceptance of violence that at times seems utterly absurd and mindless. Let me give you one rather poignant example. In 1986, U.S. warplanes bombed Libya in retaliation for an upsurge in that country's acts of terrorism. When our citizens were later asked whether they approved of this military action, a whopping 71 percent responded "yes," even though only 31 percent believed the raid would actually be effective in curbing future terrorism.[1] What else can we conclude but that a substantial number of U.S. citizens find acts of pure vengeance an acceptable part of U.S. foreign policy?

On a broader scale, we humans have shown ourselves to be a particularly aggressive species. With the exception of certain rodents, no other vertebrates so consistently and wantonly kill members of their own kind. This prompts me to raise the following questions: Is aggression inborn—is it part of our very nature as human beings? Can it be modified? What are the social and situational factors that increase or decrease aggression?

Aggression Defined

Social psychologists define **aggressive action** as intentional behavior aimed at causing either physical or psychological pain. It is not to be confused with assertiveness—even though most people often loosely refer to others as "aggressive" if they stand up for their rights, write letters to the editor complaining about real or imagined injustices, work extra hard, display a great deal of ambition, or are real go-getters. Similarly, in a sexist society, a woman who simply speaks her mind or makes the first move by inviting a male acquaintance to dinner might be called aggressive by some. My definition is clear: Aggression is an intentional action aimed at doing harm or causing pain. The action might be physical or verbal. Whether it succeeds in its goal or not, it is still aggression. Thus, if an angry acquaintance throws a beer bottle at your head and you duck, so that the bottle misses its mark, it is still an aggressive act. The important thing is the intention. By the same token, if a drunk driver unintentionally runs you down while you're attempting to cross the street, that is not an act of aggression, even though the damage is far greater than that caused by the beer bottle that missed.

It is also useful to distinguish between hostile aggression and instrumental aggression.[2] **Hostile aggression** is an act of aggression stemming from a feeling of anger and aimed at inflicting pain or injury. In **instrumental aggression** there is an intention to hurt the other person, but the hurting takes place as a means to some goal other than causing pain. For example, in a professional football game, a defensive lineman will usually do whatever it takes to thwart his opponent (the blocker) and tackle the ball carrier. This typically includes intentionally inflicting pain on his opponent if doing so is useful in helping him get the blocker out of the way so that he can get to the ball carrier. This is instrumental aggression. On the other hand, if he believes his opponent has been playing dirty, he might become angry and go out of his way to hurt his opponent, even if doing so does not increase his opportunity to tackle the ball carrier. This is hostile aggression.

Is Aggression Instinctive?

Scientists, philosophers, and other serious thinkers are not in complete agreement with one another about whether aggression is an inborn, instinctive phenomenon or whether such behavior must be learned.[3] This controversy is not new; it has been raging for centuries. For example, Thomas Hobbes, in his classic work *Leviathan* (first published in 1651), took the view that we human beings, in our natural state, are brutes and that only by enforcing the law and order of society can we curb what to Hobbes was a natural instinct toward aggression. On the other hand, Jean-Jacques Rousseau's concept of the noble savage (a theory he developed in 1762) suggested that we human beings, in our natural state, are gentle creatures and that it is a restrictive society that forces us to become hostile and aggressive.[4]

Hobbes's more pessimistic view was elaborated in the 20th century by Sigmund Freud,[5] who theorized that human beings are born with an instinct toward life, which he called **Eros,** and an equally powerful death instinct, **Thanatos,** an instinctual drive toward death, leading to aggressive actions. About the death instinct, Freud wrote: "It is at work in every living being and is striving to bring it to ruin and to reduce life to its original condition of inanimate matter." Freud believed that aggressive energy must come out somehow, lest it continue to build up and produce illness. Freud's notion can best be characterized as a **hydraulic theory.** The analogy is one of water pressure building up in a container: Unless aggression is allowed to drain off, it will produce some sort of explosion. According to Freud,[6] society performs an essential function in regulating this instinct and in helping people to sublimate it—that is, to turn the destructive energy into acceptable or useful behavior.

Taking the notion of innate aggression one step further, some scholars believe not only that humans in their natural state are killers, but also that their wanton destructiveness is unique among animals. Consequently, these scholars suggest that to call human behavior "brutal" is to libel nonhuman species. This point of view has been expressed eloquently by Anthony Storr:

> We generally describe the most repulsive examples of man's cruelty as brutal or bestial, implying by these adjectives that such behavior is characteristic of less highly developed animals than ourselves. In truth, however, the extremes of "brutal" behavior are confined to man; and there is

no parallel in nature to our savage treatment of each other. The sombre fact is that we are the most cruel and most ruthless species that has ever walked the earth; and that although we may recoil in horror when we read in the newspaper or history book of the atrocities committed by man upon man, we know in our hearts that each one of us harbours within himself those same savage impulses which lead to murder, to torture, and to war.[7]

There is a lack of definitive or even clear evidence on the subject of whether or not aggression is instinctive in humans. I suppose that is why the controversy still rages. Much of the evidence, such as it is, stems from the observation of, and experimentation with, species other than humans. In one such study, for example, Zing Yang Kuo[8] attempted to explode the myth that cats will instinctively stalk and kill rats. His experiment was a simple one. He raised a kitten in the same cage with a rat. Not only did the cat refrain from attacking the rat, the two became close companions. Moreover, the cat refused either to chase or to kill other rats. It should be noted, however, that this experiment does not prove that aggressive behavior is not instinctive; it merely demonstrates that aggressive behavior can be inhibited by early experience. Thus, in an experiment reported by Irenaus Eibl-Eibesfeldt,[9] it was shown that rats raised in isolation (i.e., without any experience in fighting other rats) will attack a fellow rat when one is introduced into the cage; moreover, the isolated rat uses the same pattern of threat and attack experienced rats use. Thus, although aggressive behavior can be modified by experience (as shown by Kuo's experiment), Eibl-Eibesfeldt showed that aggression apparently does not need to be learned. On the other hand, one should not conclude from this study that aggression is necessarily instinctive, for as John Paul Scott[10] has pointed out, in order to draw this conclusion, there must be physiological evidence of a spontaneous stimulation for fighting that arises from within the body alone. The stimulus in the above experiment came from the outside—that is, the sight of a new rat stimulated the isolated rat to fight. Scott concluded from his survey of the evidence that there is no inborn need for fighting: If an organism can arrange its life so that there is no outside stimulation to fight, then it will not experience any physiological or mental damage as a result of not expressing aggression. This view contradicts Freud's contention and, in effect, asserts that there is no instinct of aggression.

The argument goes back and forth. Scott's conclusion has been called into question by Konrad Lorenz,[11] who observed the behavior of a species of highly aggressive tropical fish called cichlids. To defend their territory, male cichlids will attack other male cichlids. In its natural environment, the male cichlid does not attack female cichlids, nor does he attack males of a different species; he only attacks males of his own species. What happens if all other male cichlids are removed from an aquarium, leaving only one male alone with no appropriate sparring partner? According to the hydraulic theory of instinct, the need to aggress will build up to the point where the cichlid will attack a fish that doesn't usually serve as an appropriate stimulus for attack. That is exactly what happens. In the absence of his fellow male cichlids, he attacks males of other species—males he previously ignored. If all males are removed, the male cichlid will eventually attack and kill females.

More recently, Richard Lore and Lori Schultz[12] report that the universality of aggression among vertebrates strongly suggests that aggressiveness has evolved and has been maintained because it has survival value. At the same time, these researchers underscore the fact that nearly all organisms also seem to have evolved strong inhibitory mechanisms that enable them to suppress aggression when it is in their best interests to do so. Thus, even in the most violence-prone species, aggression is an optional strategy. Whether or not it is expressed is determined by the animal's previous social experiences, as well as by the specific social context in which the animal finds itself.

Social psychologists are in general agreement with the interpretation of the animal research of Lore and Schultz. Moreover, where humans are concerned, because of the complexity of our social interactions, the social situation takes on even greater importance than it does among the lower organisms. As Leonard Berkowitz[13] has suggested, we humans seem to have an inborn tendency to respond to certain provocative stimuli by striking out against the perpetrator. Whether or not the aggressive tendency is actually expressed in overt action is a function of a complex interplay between these innate propensities, a variety of learned inhibitory responses, and the precise nature of the social situation. For example, although it is true that many organisms, from insects to apes, will attack an animal that invades their territory, it is a gross oversimplification to imply, as some popular writers have, that humans are likewise programmed to protect their territory and behave aggressively in response to specific stimuli.

There is much evidence to support Berkowitz's contention that, among humans, innate patterns of behavior are infinitely modifiable and flexible. Human cultures vary dramatically on this dimension. For example, there are many so-called primitive tribes, like the Lepchas of Sikkim, the Pygmies of Central Africa, and the Arapesh of New Guinea, that manage to live in cooperative friendliness, both within their own tribe and in their relations with others. Among these people, acts of aggression are extremely rare.[14] Meanwhile, in a more "civilized" society like our own, our elected leaders choose to spend a huge percentage of our resources on military hardware and personnel, family violence is commonplace, drive-by shootings have become a tragic aspect of urban life, and rampage killings take place in our high schools.

The infinite variety of ways in which humans can modify their aggressive tendencies is highlighted by the fact that, within a given culture, changing social conditions can lead to dramatic changes in aggressive behavior. For example, the Iroquois Indians lived in peace for hundreds of years as a hunting nation. But in the 17th century, growing trade with the newly arrived

Europeans brought the Iroquois into direct competition with the neighboring Hurons over furs (to trade for manufactured goods). A series of wars developed—and the Iroquois became ferocious and successful warriors, not because of uncontrollable aggressive instincts, but because a *social* change produced increases in competition.[15]

In our own society, there are some striking regional differences in aggressive behavior and in the kinds of events that trigger violence. For example, Richard Nisbett has shown that homicide rates for white southern males are substantially higher than those for white northern males, especially in rural areas.[16] But this is true only for "argument-related" homicides. Nisbett's research shows that southerners do not endorse violence more than northerners *in general;* rather, southerners are more inclined to endorse violence only for the protection of property and in response to insults. This pattern suggests that the "culture of honor" that is the hallmark of the southern gentleman may be characteristic of particular economic and occupational circumstances—specifically those involving portable (and, therefore, stealable) wealth, as in the herding society of the early South and West, where one's entire wealth could be stolen away. That is, if you are a farmer in Iowa, chances are no one is going to steal your entire crop; therefore, it's not as necessary to establish the reputation of being a person who will stand up and fight to protect his property. But if you are a cattle rancher, it is important to establish a "don't mess with me" reputation so that rustlers will think twice before trying to take your property.

What is particularly interesting about this phenomenon is that the culture of honor persists long after the conditions that established it have disappeared. Thus, following up on their original findings, Nisbett and his colleagues[17] conducted a series of experiments in which they demonstrated that these norms characteristic of a culture of honor manifest themselves in the cognitions, emotions, behaviors, and physiological reactions of contemporary southern white male college students enrolled at the University of Michigan—young men whose families have not herded cattle for many generations. In these experiments, each study participant was "accidentally" bumped into by the experimenter's confederate, who then insulted him by calling him a denigrating name. Compared with northern white males (who tended to simply shrug off the insult), southerners were more likely to think their masculine reputation was threatened, became more upset (as shown by a rise in the cortisone level in their bloodstream), were more physiologically primed for aggression (as shown by a rise in the **testosterone** level in their bloodstream), became more cognitively primed for aggression, and, ultimately, were more likely to engage in aggressive and dominant behavior following the incident. In a subsequent experiment, Cohen and Nisbett[18] sent job application letters to companies across the United States allegedly from people who had killed someone in an honor-related conflict. Companies located in the South and

West were far more likely to respond in a receptive and understanding manner than those located in the North.

Taking these findings into account, we would conclude that, although an instinctual component of aggression is almost certainly present in human beings, aggression is not caused entirely by instinct. There are clear examples of situational and social events that can produce aggressive behavior. Even more important, we know that in human beings, such behavior can be modified by situational and social factors. In short, aggressive behavior can be reduced.

Is Aggression Useful?

The Survival of the Fittest

Okay, aggression in humans can be reduced, but should it be? Some investigators have suggested that aggression might be useful and perhaps even necessary. Konrad Lorenz,[19] for example, has argued that aggression is "an essential part of the life-preserving organization of instincts." Basing his argument on his observation of nonhumans, he sees aggression as being of prime evolutionary importance, allowing the young animals to have the strongest and smartest mothers and fathers and enabling the group to be led by the best possible leaders. From their study of Old World monkeys, anthropologist Sherwood Washburn and psychiatrist David Hamburg concur.[20] They find that aggression within the same group of monkeys plays an important role in feeding, reproduction, and determining dominance patterns. The strongest and most aggressive male in a colony will assume a dominant position through an initial display of aggressive behavior. Ironically, as Steven Pinker[21] has observed, this serves to reduce subsequent serious fighting within the colony because the other males know who's boss and simply back off. Furthermore, because the dominant male is responsible for a large proportion of reproduction, the colony increases its chances of survival as the strong male passes on his vigor to subsequent generations.

The pattern of behavior among elephant seals is similar—but a bit more bloody. According to psychobiologist Burney LeBoeuf,[22] every year before mating season, pairs of males square off against each other in order to establish dominance. The strongest, most aggressive, and shrewdest male is not only number one in the dominance hierarchy among his fellows, but also becomes number-one lovemaker in the group. For example, in one observation, the number-one or "alpha" male in a particular rookery of 185 females and 120 males was responsible for half of the observed copulations. In smaller rookeries of 40 or fewer females, the alpha male is typically responsible for 100 percent of the copulations.

With these data in mind, many observers urge caution in attempting to control aggression in humans, suggesting that, as in lower animals, aggression may be necessary for survival. This reasoning is based in part on the assumption that the same mechanism that drives one man to kill his neighbor drives another to "conquer" outer space, "sink his teeth" into a difficult mathematical equation, "attack" a logical problem, or "master" the universe.

But, as I argued earlier, this reasoning is based on an exaggerated definition of aggression. To equate high achievement and advancement with hostility and aggression is to confuse the issue. A problem or skill can be mastered without harming other people or even without attempting to conquer them. This is a difficult distinction for us to grasp because the Western mind—and perhaps the American mind in particular—has been trained to equate success with victory, to equate doing well with beating someone. M. F. Ashley Montagu[23] feels that an oversimplification and a misinterpretation of Darwin's theory has provided the average person with the mistaken idea that conflict is necessarily the law of life. Ashley Montagu states that it was convenient, during the Industrial Revolution, for the wealthy industrialists, who were exploiting the workers, to justify their exploitation by talking about life being a struggle and its being natural for the fittest (and only the fittest) to survive. The danger is that this kind of reasoning becomes a self-fulfilling prophecy and can cause us to ignore or play down the survival value of nonaggressive and noncompetitive behavior. For example, over a hundred years ago, Peter Kropotkin[24] concluded that cooperative behavior and mutual aid have great survival value for many forms of life. There is ample evidence to support this conclusion. The cooperative behavior of certain social insects, such as termites, ants, and bees, is well known. Perhaps not so well known is a form of behavior in the chimpanzee that can only be described as **altruistic.** It goes something like this: Two chimpanzees are in adjoining cages. One chimp has food and the other doesn't. The foodless chimpanzee begins to beg. Reluctantly, the "wealthy" chimp hands over some of his food. In a sense, the very reluctance with which he does so makes the gift all the more significant. It indicates he likes the food and would dearly enjoy keeping it for himself. Accordingly, it suggests that the urge to share may have deep roots, indeed.[25] But Kropotkin's work was largely ignored, perhaps because it did not fit the temper of the times or the needs of those who were profiting from the Industrial Revolution.

Let us look at our own society. As a culture, we Americans seem to thrive on competition; we reward winners and are disdainful of losers. For two centuries, our educational system has been based on competitiveness and the laws of survival. With very few exceptions, we do not teach our kids to love learning—we teach them to strive for high grades and great scores on the S.A.T. When sportswriter Grantland Rice said that what's important is not whether you win or lose but how you play the game, he certainly was not *describing* the dominant theme in U.S. life. If anything, he was expressing a hope that we might somehow rid ourselves of our morbid preoccupation with winning at all costs—a preoccupation that dominates life in this country. From the Little League ballplayer who bursts into tears after his team is defeated to the college students in the football stadium chanting "We're number one!"; from former President Lyndon Johnson, whose judgment during the Vietnam war was almost certainly distorted by his oft-stated desire not to be the first U.S. president to lose a war, to the third-grader who despises her classmate for a superior performance on an arithmetic test, we manifest a staggering cultural obsession with victory. Vince Lombardi, the legendary coach of the Green Bay Packers football team, may have summed it all up with the simple statement "Winning isn't the most important thing, it's the *only* thing." What is frightening about the acceptance of this philosophy is that it implies that the goal of victory justifies whatever means we use to win, even if it's only a football game—which, after all, was first conceived of as a recreational activity.

It may be true that, in the early history of human evolution, highly competitive and aggressive behaviors were adaptive. Some writers have traced human aggression to the time when our ancestors were hunters and gatherers who had to kill animals and forage widely to survive. On the other hand, more recent archaeological evidence unearthed by Richard Leakey and his associates[26] indicates that this assumption may be invalid—that human aggression grew much later, as people became increasingly concerned with ownership and protecting their possessions. In any case, as I look about and see a world full of international, interracial, and intertribal hatred and distrust, of senseless slaughter, of terrorism, of anthrax and smallpox being manufactured as weapons, of enough nuclear warheads floating around to destroy the world's population many times over, I feel justified in questioning the current survival value of this behavior. Anthropologist Loren Eiseley paid tribute to our ancient ancestors but warned against imitating them when he wrote: "The need is now for a gentler, a more tolerant people than those who won for us against the ice, the tiger, and the bear."[27]

Catharsis—Does It Work?

There is another sense in which it has been argued that aggressive behavior can serve a useful and perhaps a necessary function. I refer here to the psychoanalytic concept of **catharsis**—the release of energy. Specifically, as mentioned earlier, Sigmund Freud believed that unless people were allowed to express themselves aggressively, the aggressive energy would be dammed up, pressure would build, and the energy would seek an outlet, either exploding into acts of extreme violence or manifesting itself as symptoms of mental illness. In our own country, the distinguished psychiatrist William Menninger has asserted that "competitive games provide an unusually satisfactory outlet for the instinctive aggressive drive."[28]

This belief has become part of our cultural mythology. For example, a few years ago, in the excellent, highly popular film *Analyze This*, a psychiatrist (played by Billy Crystal) is forced into a therapeutic relationship with a Mafia boss and murderer played by Robert De Niro. The De Niro character is suffering from hypertension brought on by excessive anger and anxiety. During one of their therapy sessions, the Billy Crystal character says, "You know what

I do when I'm angry? I hit a pillow. Try that." In the mind of the gangster, "hit" means "kill." So De Niro promptly whips out his gun, and fires several bullets into a pillow. Billy Crystal gulps, forces a smile, and says, "Feel better?" "Yeah, I do!" says De Niro.

Charming? Yes. Accurate? Nope. There is a plethora of evidence indicating that the Billy Crystal solution simply does not work. In a recent experiment, Brad Bushman[29] made his participants angry by having his accomplice (a fellow student) insult them. Immediately afterward, the participants were assigned to one of three experimental conditions: In one condition, they were allowed to spend a few minutes slugging away at a punching bag while being encouraged to think about the student who had made them angry. In a second condition, the students hitting the punching bag were encouraged to think of this activity as physical exercise. In the third condition, the participants simply were allowed to sit still for a few minutes without punching anything. At the end of the experiment, which students felt the least angry? Those who had sat still without punching anything.

In addition, Bushman subsequently gave the participants a chance to express aggression against the person who had insulted them by blasting him with a loud, unpleasant noise. The students who had hit the punching bag while thinking about their "enemy" were the most aggressive—blasting him the loudest and the longest. Those who had just sat still after the insult were the least aggressive. Thus, the message is clear. Physical activity—like punching a punching bag—seems neither to dissipate anger nor to reduce subsequent aggression against the person who provoked our anger. In fact, the data lead us in precisely the opposite direction. Bushman's laboratory experiment is supported by a field study of high-school football players. Arthur Patterson[30] measured the general hostility of these football players, rating them before, during, and after the football season. If intense physical activity and aggressive behavior that are part of playing football serve to reduce the tension caused by pent-up aggression, we would expect the players to exhibit a decline in hostility over the course of the season. Instead, there was a significant *increase* in hostility among the players as the football season wore on.

What happens when acts of aggression are targeted directly against the person who provoked us? Does this satiate our need to aggress and therefore reduce our tendency to hurt that person further? Again, systematic research demonstrates that, as in the punching-bag experiment, exactly the opposite occurs. A good example of this research is found in an experiment by Russell Geen and his associates.[31] In this experiment, each participant was paired with another student, who (as you might imagine, by this time!) was actually a confederate of the experimenters. First, the confederate angered the participant. During this phase of the experiment, which involved the exchanging of opinions on various issues, the participant was given electric shocks when his partner disagreed with his opinion. Next, during a study of "the effects of punishment on learning," the participant acted as a teacher while the confederate served as learner. On the first learning task, some of the participants were required to shock the confederate each time he made a mistake; other participants merely recorded his errors. On the next task, all the participants were given the opportunity to deliver shocks to the confederate. If a cathartic effect were operating, we would expect those people who had previously shocked the confederate to administer fewer and less intense shocks the second time. This didn't happen; in fact, the people who had previously shocked the confederate were even more aggressive the second time around.

The same kind of behavior has also been observed systematically in naturally occurring events in the real world, where verbal acts of aggression served to facilitate further attacks. In this "natural experiment," several technicians who had recently been laid off, understandably, were angry at their employers. Several were then provided with a chance to verbalize their hostility against their ex-bosses. Later, all the technicians were asked to describe their bosses. Those who previously had been allowed to vent their feelings were *much* nastier in their subsequent descriptions than those who had not.[32] Venting anger against a target increases our nastiness toward that target.

In summary, the overwhelming weight of the evidence runs counter to the catharsis hypothesis. At first glance, this may strike you as odd because, on some level, the notion of catharsis does seem to make sense. I guess, by that, I mean that it is consistent with folk wisdom about what to do when we are angry. "Go blow off a little steam," you need to "vent" your anger, and so on. Why the contradiction between folk wisdom and science here? I think it stems from the fact that we humans are cognitive animals. Accordingly, for us, aggression is not merely dependent on tension—what a person feels—but also on what the person *thinks*. Put yourself in the place of a participant in the situation described by the two previous experiments: Once you've shocked another person or said nasty thing things about your boss, it becomes easier to do so a second time. In a sense, your initial hostile act provides you with a need to justify it. Why? As we have seen in the preceding chapter, when a person does harm to another person, it sets cognitive processes in motion aimed at justifying that act of cruelty. Specifically, when we hurt another person, we experience cognitive dissonance. The cognition "I have hurt Sam" is dissonant with the cognition "I am a decent, reasonable, good person who doesn't go around wantonly hurting people." A good way for me to reduce dissonance is somehow to convince myself that hurting Sam was not an indecent, unreasonable, bad thing to do. I can accomplish this by blinding myself to Sam's virtues and by emphasizing his faults, by convincing myself that Sam is a terrible human being who deserved to be hurt. This reduces dissonance, all right, and it also sets the stage for further aggression. For the sad fact is, once you have derogated a person, it makes it easier for you to hurt that person in the future.

Retaliation as Overkill Retaliation is blind. That is, when we retaliate, we often do far more harm to the person who hurt us than he had done to us. This was nicely illustrated in an experiment by Michael Kahn.[33] In Kahn's experiment, a medical technician, taking physiological measurements from college students, made derogatory remarks about these students. In one experimental condition, the students were allowed to vent their hostility by expressing their feelings about the technician to his employer—an action that they knew would get the technician into serious trouble, probably costing him his job. In another condition, they were not provided with the opportunity to express any aggression against him. The results were clear—and consistent with the research previously discussed: Those who were allowed to express their aggression subsequently felt greater dislike and hostility toward the technician than did those who were inhibited from expressing their aggression.

In comparison with the technician's offense, costing him his job can be considered overkill. Overkill maximizes dissonance. The greater the discrepancy between what the perpetrator did to you and your retaliation, the greater the dissonance. The greater the dissonance, the greater your need to derogate him. Given a particular level of retaliation on your part, the size of the discrepancy will be greatest if it turns out that the victim is completely innocent—i.e., if the victim of your aggression had not previously harmed you at all. Thus, ironically, when the victim of your aggression is innocent, your need to derogate him will be greatest. You may recall that this is precisely what happened in the experiments by David Glass and by Davis & Jones[34] (discussed in the preceding chapter). The participant inflicted either psychological or physical harm on an innocent person who had done the participant no prior harm. The participants then proceeded to flagrantly derogate the victim, convincing themselves that he deserved what he got—and more.

Let us go back to the "overkill" of someone who has harmed you. What happens if we can somehow arrange it so that retaliation is not allowed to run roughshod over the target? That is, what if the degree of retaliation is reasonably controlled so that it is not significantly more intense than the action that precipitated it? In such a circumstance, I would predict that there would be little or no dissonance. "Sam has insulted me; I've paid him back exactly in kind; we are even. I have no need to retaliate further." This is precisely what Anthony Doob and Larraine Wood found.[35] As in Kahn's experiment, Doob and Wood arranged things so that their subjects were insulted by an accomplice. In one condition, they were given the opportunity to retaliate in a way that settled the score. In this situation, once the score was evened, they had no further need to punish their tormentor. But those subjects who had not been given the opportunity to retaliate *did* subsequently choose to punish their tormentor. Thus, we have seen that retaliation can reduce the need for further aggression if something akin to equity has been restored.

There is a major point here that must be underscored: Most situations in the real world are not as neat as the Doob and Wood situation, where retaliation can be made functionally similar to the original act. In my opinion, the world is usually closer to the situation in Michael Kahn's experiment: Retaliation typically outstrips the original act by a great deal. For example, recall the example I gave in Chapter 1 that involved the shooting of students at Kent State University while they were protesting the war in Vietnam. Whatever those students might have been doing to the members of the Ohio National Guard (shouting obscenities, teasing, taunting), it hardly merited being shot and killed. Moreover, most victims of massive aggression are totally innocent. In all these situations, the opposite of catharsis takes place. Thus, to go back to some of the examples mentioned in previous chapters, once I have shot dissenting students at Kent State, I will convince myself they *really* deserved it, and I will hate dissenting students even more than I did before I shot them; once I have denied African Americans a decent education, I will become even more convinced that they are stupid and couldn't have profited from a good education to begin with. And how do you think members of anti-American terrorist groups and their sympathizers felt about Americans *after* the senseless slaughter of September 11? Do you think they felt sorrow and compassion for the thousands of innocent victims, rescue workers, and their families? Do you think they decided that Americans had suffered enough? In most situations, committing or condoning violence does not reduce the tendency toward violence. Committing acts of violence increases our negative feelings about the victims. Ultimately, this is why violence almost always breeds more violence.

Causes of Aggression

As we have seen, one major cause of violence—in addition to obvious causes like intergroup hatred, revenge, or war—is violence itself. When a person commits an act of aggression, especially with a force that exceeds what the victim may have done to elicit it, this sets up cognitive and motivational forces aimed at justifying that aggression, which open the door to increased aggression. Let us look at some of the other major causes of aggression.

Neurological and Chemical Causes
There is an area in the core of the brain called the **amygdala**, which is associated with aggressive behaviors in human beings as well as in the lower animals. When that area is electrically stimulated, docile organisms become violent; similarly, when neural activity in that area is blocked, violent organisms become docile.[36] But it should be noted that there is flexibility here also: The impact of neural mechanisms can be

modified by social factors, even in subhumans. For example, if a male monkey is in the presence of other, less dominant monkeys, he will indeed attack the other monkeys when the amygdala is stimulated. But if the amygdala is stimulated while the monkey is in the presence of more dominant monkeys, he will not attack but will run away instead.

Testosterone Certain chemicals have been shown to influence aggression. For example, the injection of testosterone, a male sex hormone, will increase aggression in animals.[37] Among human beings, there is a parallel finding: James Dabbs and his colleagues found that naturally occurring testosterone levels are significantly higher among prisoners convicted of violent crimes than among those convicted of nonviolent crimes. Also, once incarcerated, prisoners with higher testosterone levels violated more prison rules—especially those involving overt confrontation.[38] Dabbs and his colleagues also found that juvenile delinquents have higher testosterone levels than college students.[39] When fraternities within a given college were compared, those generally considered more rambunctious, less socially responsible, and more crude were found to have the highest average testosterone levels.[40] It is clear that testosterone affects aggressiveness. The reverse also seems to be true: Behaving aggressively increases the release of testosterone.[41]

If the testosterone level affects aggressiveness, does that mean men are more aggressive than women? When it comes to physical aggression, the answer appears to be yes. In a wide-ranging survey of research on children, Eleanor Maccoby and Carol Jacklin[42] found that boys are consistently more aggressive than girls. For example, in one study, the investigators closely observed children at play in a variety of different countries, including the United States, Switzerland, and Ethiopia. Among boys, there was far more nonplayful pushing, shoving, and hitting than among girls. Similarly, among adults worldwide, the overwhelming majority of persons arrested for violent crimes are men. When women are arrested, it is usually for property crimes (like shoplifting, forgery, fraud, and larceny) rather than for violent crimes (like murder and aggravated assault).

But when we consider nonphysical forms of aggression, the picture gets more complicated. Although research suggests that boys tend to be more physically aggressive, girls are more prone to engaging in a more social form of aggression, which Nikki Crick and her associates call **relational aggression.** Specifically, girls are more likely to engage in activity aimed at hurting others by sabotaging their relationships with peers. Exclusion, spreading false rumors, and gossip are prime examples, and their effects can have devastating consequences, as we shall soon see.

Is the gender difference in physical aggression biological or social in origin? We cannot be sure, but some evidence points to biology. Specifically, in our own country, the enormous social changes affecting women during the past 40 years have not produced increases in the incidence of violent crimes committed by women relative to those committed by men. At the same time, when we look at the comparative data between men and women involving nonviolent crimes, women have shown a far greater increase relative to that shown by men.[43]

The near universality of gender differences is bolstered by the results of a cross-cultural study by Dane Archer and Patricia McDaniel,[44] who asked teenagers from 11 countries to read stories involving interpersonal conflict. The stories were interrupted prior to their resolution, and the teenagers were instructed to complete the stories on their own. Archer and McDaniel found that, within each of the countries, young men showed a greater tendency toward violent solutions to conflict than young women did.

The near universality of these differences makes it reasonably clear that biochemical differences between men and women are involved in these findings. At the same time, it is also apparent that these findings are not due *solely* to biochemical differences. Archer and McDaniel found that, although within a given culture men showed evidence of consistently higher levels of tendencies toward physical aggression than women, culture also played a major role. For example, women from Australia and New Zealand showed greater evidence of physical aggressiveness than men from Sweden and Korea did.

Alcohol   One chemical that many people throughout the world happily ingest is alcohol. As most socially active college students know, alcohol tends to lower our inhibitions against committing acts sometimes frowned on by society, including acts of aggression.[45] Casual observation suggests that fistfights frequently break out in bars and nightclubs and that family violence is often associated with the abuse of alcohol. A wealth of hard data supports these casual observations. For example, crime statistics reveal that 75 percent of individuals arrested for murder, assault, and other crimes of violence were legally drunk at the time of their arrests.[46] In addition, controlled laboratory experiments demonstrate that when individuals ingest enough alcohol to make them legally drunk, they tend to respond more violently to provocations than those who have ingested little or no alcohol.[47]

This does not mean that alcohol automatically increases aggression; people who have ingested alcohol are not necessarily driven to go around picking fights. Rather, the results of laboratory and field experiments indicate that alcohol serves as a disinhibitor; that is, drinking reduces social inhibitions, making us less cautious than we usually are. But it is more than that. Recent experiments have shown that alcohol tends to disrupt the way we usually process information.[48] What this means is that intoxicated people often respond to the earliest and most obvious aspects of a social situation and tend to miss the subtleties. For example, in practical terms, if you are sober and someone accidentally steps on your toe, chances are you would know the person didn't do it on purpose. But, if you were drunk, you might miss the subtlety of the situation and respond as if he stomped on your foot with full intent. Accordingly (especially if you are a male), you might retaliate with physical aggression. This is precisely the kind of ambiguous situation that males might interpret as provocative if they are not thinking clearly.

Pain and Discomfort Pain and discomfort are major precursors of aggression. If an organism experiences pain and cannot flee the scene, it will almost invariably attack; this is true of rats, mice, hamsters, foxes, monkeys, crayfish, snakes, raccoons, alligators, and a host of other animals.[49] Such animals will attack members of their own species, members of different species, or anything else in sight, including stuffed dolls and tennis balls. Do you think this is true of human beings as well? A moment's reflection might help you guess that it may very well be. Most of us become irritable when subjected to a sharp, unexpected pain (e.g., when we stub our toe) and hence are prone to lash out at the nearest available target. In a series of experiments, Leonard Berkowitz[50] showed that students who underwent the pain of having their hand immersed in very cold water showed a sharp increase in actually committing aggressive acts against other students.

By the same token, observers have speculated that other forms of bodily discomfort, such as heat, humidity, air pollution, and offensive odors, might act to lower the threshold for aggressive behavior.[51] For example, during the late 1960s and early 1970s, when a great deal of tension existed in the United States concerning the war in Vietnam, racial injustice, and the like, national leaders worried a lot about a phenomenon they referred to as "the long, hot summer." That is, they suggested that the tendency for riots and other forms of civic unrest might occur with greater frequency in the heat of summer than in the fall, winter, or spring. Was this actually true or mere speculation? It turns out to be true. In a systematic analysis of disturbances occurring in 79 cities between 1967 and 1971, J. Merrill Carlsmith and Craig Anderson[52] found that riots were far more likely to occur during hot days than during cold days. Similarly, in a more recent study, Anderson and his colleagues have shown that, the hotter it is on a given day, the greater the likelihood that people will commit violent crimes. Moreover, they also showed that heat did not increase the incidence of burglary and other property crimes—thus strengthening the linkage between heat and violence (not simply general criminality).[53]

But, as you know by now, we have to be cautious about interpreting events that take place in natural settings. For example, the scientist in you might be tempted to ask whether increases in aggression are due to the temperature itself or merely to the fact that more people are apt to be outside (getting in one another's way!) on hot days than on cool or rainy days. So how might we determine that it's the heat itself that caused the aggression and not merely the greater opportunity for contact? We can bring the phenomenon into the laboratory. This is remarkably easy to do. For example, in one such experiment, William Griffitt and Roberta Veitch[54] simply administered a test to students, some of whom took it in a room with normal temperature, while others took it in a room where the temperature was allowed to soar to 90°F. The students in the hot room not only reported feeling more aggressive but also expressed more hostility to a stranger whom they were asked to describe and rate. Additional evidence from the natural world helps bolster our belief in the cause of this phenomenon. For example, it has been shown that in major league baseball games, significantly more batters are hit by pitched balls when the temperature is above 90° than when it is below 90°.[55] And in the desert city of Phoenix, Arizona, drivers without air-conditioned cars are more likely to honk their horns in traffic jams than are drivers with air-conditioned cars.[56]

Frustration and Aggression As we have seen, aggression can be prompted by any unpleasant or aversive situation, such as anger, pain, excessive high temperatures, and the like. Of all these aversive situations, the major instigator of aggression is frustration. Imagine the following situation: You must drive across town for an important job interview. On your way to the parking lot, you realize you are a bit late for your appointment, so you break into a fast trot. When you find your car you notice, to your dismay, that you have a flat tire. "Okay, I'll be twenty minutes late; that's not too bad," you say as you take the jack and lug wrench out of the trunk. After much tugging and hauling, you remove the old tire, put on the spare tire, tighten the lugs—and, lo and behold, the spare tire also is flat! Seething with frustration, you trudge back to your dorm and enter your room. Your roommate sees you standing there, resume in hand, sweaty, dirty, and rumpled. Immediately sizing up the situation, he asks humorously, "How did the interview go?" Shouldn't he be prepared to duck?

If an individual is thwarted on the way to a goal, the resulting frustration will increase the probability of an aggressive response. A clear picture of **frustration-aggression** relationships emerges from a classic experiment by Roger Barker, Tamara Dembo, and Kurt Lewin.[57] These psychologists frustrated young children by showing them a roomful of very attractive toys, which were then kept out of reach. The children stood outside a wire screen looking at the toys, hoping to play with them—even expecting to play with them—but were unable to reach them. After a painfully long wait, the children were finally allowed to play with the toys. In this experiment, a separate group of children was allowed to play with the toys directly without first being frustrated. This second group of children played joyfully with the toys. But the frustrated group, when finally given access to the toys, were extremely destructive. They tended to smash the toys, throw them against the wall, step on them, and so forth. Thus, frustration can lead to aggression.

Several factors can accentuate this frustration. Suppose you were about to bite into a Big Mac and somebody snatched it away. This would be more likely to frustrate you—and lead to an aggressive response—than if someone had stopped you if you were merely on your way to McDonald's to buy a Big Mac. An analogue of this situation was demonstrated in a field study by Mary Harris.[58] She had students cut in front of people waiting in line for tickets, outside of restaurants, or to check out of a grocery store; sometimes they cut in front of the 2nd person in line, other times in front of the 12th person. As we would expect, the responses of the people standing behind the intruder were much more aggressive when the student cut into the second place in line. Frustration is increased when a goal is near and your progress toward it is interrupted.

When the interruption is unexpected or when it seems illegitimate, the frustration is increased still further, as an experiment by James Kulik and Roger Brown points out.[59] Subjects were told they could earn money by telephoning for donations to charity and obtaining pledges. Some of them were led to expect a high rate of contributions, being informed that previous calls had been successful almost two-thirds of the time; others were led to expect far less success. When the potential donor refused to contribute, as all of them did (the subjects were actually calling confederates of the experimenters), the callers with the high expectations exhibited more aggression, speaking more harshly and slamming down the phone with more force. The experimenters also varied the reasons the confederates gave for refusing to contribute, sometimes making them sound legitimate ("I can't afford to contribute") and sometimes having them sound arbitrary and illegitimate ("Charities are a waste of time and a ripoff"). The subjects who heard refusals that seemed unjustified displayed more aggression.

In sum, as these experiments demonstrate, frustration is most pronounced when the goal is becoming palpable and drawing within reach, when expectations are high, and when the goal is blocked unjustifiably. These factors help to point out the important distinction between frustration and deprivation. Children who simply don't have toys do not necessarily aggress. Rather, as the earlier experiment indicates, it was those children who had every reason to expect to play with the toys who experienced frustration when that expectancy was thwarted; this thwarting was what caused the children to behave destructively. Similarly, in the 1960s, the most intense riots by African Americans did not take place in the geographical areas of greatest poverty; rather, they took place in Los Angeles (Watts) and Detroit, where things were not nearly so bad for blacks as they were in many other sections of the country. The point is that things were bad relative to what white people had. Revolutions usually are not started by people whose faces are in the mud. They are most frequently started by people who have recently lifted their faces out of the mud, looked around, and noticed that other people are doing better than they are and that the system is treating them unfairly. Thus, frustration is not the result of simple deprivation; it is the result of **relative deprivation**.

Suppose, after graduating from high school, I choose not to pursue a higher education and you choose to be educated. Ten years later, if I notice that you have a better job than I do, I may be unhappy with my job but I will not experience frustration. After all, I made a free choice, and this outcome is the reasonable consequence of my choice. But if we've both been educated, and you have a white-collar job and I (because I'm African American or Hispanic) am handed a broom, I will feel frustrated. Similarly, if you find it easy to get an education but because I grew up in an impoverished ghetto an education is denied me, I will also feel frustrated. This frustration will be exacerbated every time I turn on the television and see all those beautiful houses white people live in, and all those lovely appliances for sale to other people, and all that gracious living and leisure I cannot share. When you consider all the economic and social frustrations faced by members of underprivileged minority groups in this affluent society, it is surprising that there are so few riots. As Alexis de Tocqueville wrote more than 150 years ago, "Evils which are patiently endured when they seem inevitable, become intolerable once the idea of escape from them is suggested."[60]

As long as there is hope that is unsatisfied, there will be frustrations that can result in aggression. Aggression can be reduced by satisfying that hope, or it can be minimized by eliminating it. Hopeless people are apathetic people. The Ugandans, when they were under the tyrannical, repressive, and wantonly violent dictatorship of Idi Amin, dared not dream of improving conditions or rebelling against Amin's rule. The South African blacks, and to some extent the blacks in the United States, did not revolt as long as they were prevented from hoping for anything better. Clearly, eliminating people's hope is an undesirable means of reducing aggression. The saving grace of our nation is that—theoretically, at least—this is a land of promise. We teach our children, explicitly and implicitly, to hope, to expect, and to work to improve their lives. But unless this hope stands a reasonable chance of being fulfilled, turmoil will be inevitable.

Rejection, Exclusion, and Taunting

A few years ago, at Columbine High School in Littleton, Colorado, two students (Eric Harris and Dylan Klebold), armed to the teeth and very angry, went on a rampage, killing a teacher and 14 students (including themselves). It was the most lethal school shooting in our nation's history. But it was not unique. It was merely the most dramatic and most devastating of eleven such incidents that took place in our schools in less than three years.

What drove these kids over the edge? After an intensive study of the situation, I have come to the conclusion[61] that the rampage killings are just the pathological tip of an enormous iceberg: the poisonous social atmosphere prevalent at most high schools in this country—an atmosphere fraught with exclusion, rejection, taunting, and humiliation. In high school, there is an iron-clad hierarchy of cliques with athletes, class officers, cheerleaders, and "preppies" at the top. At the bottom are kids who those at the top refer to as nerds, goths, geeks, loners, homos—kids who are too fat, too thin, too short, too tall, wear the wrong clothes, or whatever. The teenagers near the top of the hierarchy are constantly rejecting, taunting, and ridiculing those near the bottom.

Recent experimental research by Jean Twenge and her colleagues[62] demonstrates that being rejected has a plethora of negative effects, not the least of which is a dramatic increase in aggressiveness. What Twenge was able to do to participants in her laboratory was, of course, much more pallid than the day-to-day rejections faced by teenagers in high school. For example, in one of Twenge's experiments, college students met in a group and became acquainted. They were then asked to indicate which of their fellow students they would want to collaborate with in the future. A random sample of the participants received information that nobody wanted to work with them. When subsequently provided with an opportunity to aggress, the "rejects" expressed far more intense hostility (against those who rejected them as well as against neutral individuals) than those who had not been excluded.

Back in the helter-skelter world of high school, my own research reveals that rejection and the accompanying humiliation were the dominant issues underlying every one of the rampage killings. At Columbine, for example, Harris and Klebold made this graphically clear. In a videotape they made just prior to the rampage, they specifically railed against the in-group who had rejected and humiliated them. This was confirmed by a student in the Columbine in-group, who, when interviewed a few weeks after the tragedy, justified his own behavior by saying:

> Most kids didn't want them there. They were into witchcraft. They were into voodoo. Sure we teased them. But what do you expect with kids who come to school with weird hairdos and horns on their hats? If you want to get rid of someone, usually you tease 'em. So the whole school would call them homos. . . .[63]

Of course, not all students who are rejected and taunted go on a murderous rampage. The behavior of the shooters was pathological in the extreme—but certainly not unfathomable. My best guess is that there are hundreds of thousands of students undergoing similarly stressful experiences who suffer in silence—but they do suffer. In the weeks following the Columbine massacre, Internet chatrooms were flooded with postings from unhappy teenagers. Although not condoning the behavior of the shooters, the overwhelming majority certainly understood it. They expressed their own hurt and anger about being rejected and taunted. A great many of these students made statements that can best be summarized as: "Of course, I would never shoot anybody, but I sure have had fantasies about doing it!" That kind of statement should make us sit up and take notice. Is there anything we can do to change the social atmosphere in our schools? Yes. I will discuss some tried-and-true interventions near the end of this chapter as well as in the following chapter.

Social Learning and Aggression

Social learning plays an important role in determining whether or not a person will aggress in a given situation. We have already seen how social learning can inhibit an aggressive response. Recall that, when the area of a monkey's brain that characteristically produces aggressive behavior is stimulated, the monkey will not aggress while in the presence of a monkey whom it has learned to fear.

Another qualification based upon social learning is the intention attributed to an agent of pain or frustration. One aspect of behavior that seems to distinguish human beings from other animals is our ability to take the intentions of others into account. Consider the following situations: (1) a considerate person accidentally steps on your toe; (2) a thoughtless person whom you know doesn't care about you steps on your toe. Let us assume the amount of pressure and pain is exactly the same in both cases. My guess is that the latter situation would evoke an aggressive response, but the former would produce little or no aggression.

This phenomenon was demonstrated in an experiment by Shabaz Mallick and Boyd McCandless[64] in which they frustrated third-grade children by having another child's clumsiness prevent them from achieving a goal that would have resulted in a cash prize. Some of these children were subsequently provided with a reasonable and unspiteful explanation for the behavior of the child who fouled them up. Specifically, they were told he had been "sleepy and upset." The children in this condition directed much less aggression against the thwarting child than did children who were not given this explanation. Moreover, later research[65] using adult subjects indicates that we are less apt to retaliate against someone who has provoked our anger when we hear a good excuse for their behavior *before* it occurs rather than after the fact.

On the other side of the coin, the tendency for frustration to provoke aggression can be strengthened if the experience of frustration is combined with exposure to certain provocative stimuli. Leonard Berkowitz and his colleagues have shown that, if an individual is angered or frustrated, the mere mention of a word or name associated with the provocation will increase that person's level of aggression. In one experiment,[66] subjects were paired with another student (an accomplice of the experimenter) who was introduced either as a "college boxer" or as a "speech major." This accomplice provoked the subjects by shocking them; then half of the angered subjects viewed a violent prizefighting scene from a movie while the others watched an exciting but nonaggressive film clip. When subsequently given the chance to shock the confederate, the subject who had seen the violent movie segment administered more and longer shocks, as we would expect from the preceding discussion. Interestingly, however, among the subjects who had seen the prizefighting film, those paired with the "boxer" delivered more shocks to that target than those paired with the "speech major." In a similar experiment,[67] the accomplice was introduced to some subjects as *"Kirk* Anderson" and to others as *"Bob* Anderson." Again, the subjects watched one of the two film segments, and those watching the boxing sequence delivered greater shocks. But among those watching the fight scene, which was taken from the then-popular movie *The Champion*, which starred Kirk Douglas, those subjects who had been introduced to *"Kirk* Anderson" administered more shocks than those paired with *"Bob* Anderson." Apparently, the description or the name of a person can act as a cue to increase the aggression directed against that target, even if it has nothing to do with what that person actually *did*.

Similarly, the mere presence of an object associated with aggression can serve as a cue for an aggressive response. In an experiment,[68] college students were made angry: Some of them were made angry in a room in which a rifle was left lying around (ostensibly from a previous experiment) and others in a room in which a neutral object (a badminton racket) was substituted for the rifle. The students were then given the opportunity to administer some electric shocks to a fellow college student. Those individuals who had been made angry in the presence of the **aggressive stimulus** administered more electric shocks than did those made angry in the presence of the badminton racket. This is another example of priming, first encountered in Chapter 4; in this instance, certain cues associated with aggression act to increase a person's tendency to aggress. These studies point to an opposite conclusion from the slogan often seen on bumper stickers—"Guns don't kill people, people do." As Berkowitz puts it, "An angry person can pull the trigger of his gun if he wants to commit violence; but the trigger can also pull the finger or otherwise elicit aggressive reactions from him, if he is ready to aggress and does not have strong inhibitions against such behavior."[69]

One aspect of social learning that tends to *inhibit* aggression is the tendency most people have to take responsibility for their actions. But what happens if this sense of responsibility is weakened? Philip Zimbardo[70] has demonstrated that persons who are anonymous and unidentifiable tend to act more aggressively than persons who are not anonymous. In Zimbardo's experiment, female students were required to shock another student (actually a confederate) as part of a "study of empathy." Some students were made anonymous; they were seated in a dimly lit room, dressed in loose-fitting robes and large hoods, and never referred to by name. Others were easily identifiable; their room was brightly lit, no robes or hoods were used, and each woman wore a name tag. As expected, those students who were anonymous administered longer and more severe shocks. Zimbardo suggests that anonymity induces **deindividuation,** a state of lessened self-awareness, reduced concern over social evaluation, and weakened restraints against prohibited forms of behavior.

Because it was part of a controlled laboratory experiment, the kind of aggression displayed by subjects in Zimbardo's research pales in comparison with the wild, impulsive acts of violence typically associated with riots, gang rapes, and vigilante justice. Nevertheless, there is reason to believe that the same kind of deindividuation takes place outside the laboratory. Brian Mullen[71] analyzed newspaper reports of 60 lynchings perpetrated between 1899 and 1946 and found a powerful relationship between mob size and violence; the larger the mob, the more heinous the atrocities committed. Mullen's research suggests that when people are part of a crowd, they are "faceless," less self-aware, and less mindful of prohibitions against aggressive, destructive actions. They are therefore less likely to take responsibility for aggressive acts.

Social Learning, Violence, and the Mass Media Several years ago, Albert Bandura and his colleagues conducted a series of classic experiments.[72] The basic procedure in these studies was to have an adult knock around a plastic, air-filled "Bobo" doll (the kind that bounces back after it has been knocked down). Sometimes the adult accompanied her physical aggression with verbal abuse against the doll. Children who watched the adult were then allowed to play with the doll. In these experiments, not only did the children imitate the aggressive models, they also engaged in other forms of aggressive behavior after having witnessed the aggressive behavior of the adult. In short, the children did more than copy the behavior of an adult; seeing a person behave aggressively served as an impetus for them to engage in innovative aggressive behavior. We call this process **social learning.** Why are these experiments considered so important? Who cares what happens to a Bobo doll, anyway? Stay tuned.

One particularly powerful set of agents of social learning is the mass media—especially television. There is no doubt that television plays a major role in the socialization of children.[73] There is also no doubt that TV remains steeped in violence. According to a recent study, 58 percent of all TV programs contain violence—and, of those, 78 percent are without remorse, criticism, or penalty for that violence.[74] Indeed, some 40 percent of the violent incidents seen on TV were initiated by characters portrayed as heroes or other attractive role models for children.[75]

Exactly what do children learn from watching violence on TV? A number of long-term studies indicates that the more violence individuals watch on TV as children, the more violence they exhibit years later as teenagers and young adults.[76] In a typical study of this kind, (1) teenagers are asked to recall which shows they watched on TV when they were kids and how frequently they watched them. (2) The shows are rated independently by judges for level of violence. (3) The general aggressiveness of the teenagers is rated independently by their teachers and classmates. Not only is there a high correlation between the amount of violent TV watched and the viewer's subsequent aggressiveness, but the impact also accumulates over time; that is, the strength of the correlation increases with age. While these are fairly powerful data, they do not definitively prove that watching a lot of violence on TV causes children to become violent teenagers. After all, it is at least conceivable that the aggressive kids were born with a tendency to enjoy violence and that this enjoyment manifests itself in both their aggressive behavior and their liking to watch violence on TV. Once again, we see the value of the controlled experiment in helping us to understand what causes what. In order to demonstrate conclusively that watching violence on TV actually causes violent behavior, the relationship must be shown experimentally.

Because this is an issue of great importance to society, it has been well researched. The overwhelming thrust of the experimental evidence demonstrates that watching violence does indeed increase the frequency of aggressive behavior in children.[77] For example, in an early experiment on this issue, Robert Liebert and Robert Baron[78] exposed a group of children to an extremely violent TV episode of a police drama. In a control condition, a similar group of children was exposed to an exciting but nonviolent TV sporting event for the same length of time. Each child was then allowed to play in another room with a group of other children. Those who had watched the violent police drama showed far more aggression against their playmates than those who had watched the sporting event.

A subsequent experiment by Wendy Josephson[79] showed, as one might expect, that watching TV violence has the greatest impact on youngsters who are somewhat prone to violence to begin with. In this experiment, youngsters were exposed to either a film depicting a great deal of police violence or an exciting nonviolent film about bike racing. The youngsters then played a game of floor hockey. Watching the violent film had the effect of increasing the number of aggressive acts committed during the hockey game—primarily by those youngsters who had previously been rated as highly aggressive by their teachers. These kids hit others with their sticks, threw elbows, and yelled aggressively at their opponents to a much greater extent than either the kids rated as nonaggressive who had also watched the violent film or those rated as aggressive who had watched the nonviolent film. Thus, it may be that watching media violence gives aggressive kids permission to express their aggression. Josephson's experiment suggests that youngsters who do not have aggressive tendencies to begin with do not necessarily act aggressively—at least, not on the basis of seeing only one violent film.

That last phrase is an important one because it may be that even youngsters who are not prone toward aggression will become more aggressive if exposed to a steady diet of violent films over a long period. That is exactly what was found in a set of field experiments performed by Ross Parke and his colleagues.[80] In these experiments, different groups of children were exposed to differing amounts of media violence over an extended period of time. In these experiments, the great majority of the kids (even those without strong aggressive tendencies) who were exposed to a high degree of media violence over a long period were more aggressive than those who watched more benign shows.

We might mention, in passing, that at a recent congressional hearing on TV violence, it was estimated that the average 12-year-old has witnessed more than 100,000 acts of violence on television.[81] We mention this because we believe that one of the crucial factors involved in the above findings (in addition to social learning and imitation) is the simple phenomenon of priming. That is, just as exposing children to rifles and other weapons left lying around the house or the laboratory tends to increase the probability of an aggressive response when children subsequently experience pain or frustration, so too might exposing them to an endless supply of violence in films and on TV.

Thus far, in discussing the effects of media violence, we have focused much of our attention on children—and for good reason. Youngsters are, by definition, much more malleable than adults; that is, it is generally assumed that their attitudes and behaviors can be more deeply influenced by the things they view. But the effect of media violence on violent behavior is not limited to children; media violence has a major impact on the aggressive behavior of adolescents and young adults as well. Recently, Jeffrey Johnson and his colleagues[82] published a study in which he monitored the behavior of more than 700 families over a period of 17 years. Their findings are striking: There was a significant association between the amount of time spent watching television during adolescence and early adulthood and the likelihood of subsequent violent acts against others. This association was significant regardless of parental education, family income, and neighborhood violence. Moreover, unlike most laboratory experiments on aggression which, understandably, must use rather pallid measures of aggression (like administering electric shocks or loud noises to the victim), this study, because it took place in the real world over a long period of time, was able to examine severe aggressive behavior like assault and armed robbery.

On numerous occasions, adult violence seems to be a case of life imitating art. For example, several years ago, a man drove his truck through the window of a crowded cafeteria in Killeen, Texas, and began shooting people at random. By the time the police arrived, he had killed 22 people, making this the most destructive shooting spree in American history. He then turned the gun on himself. In his pocket, police found a ticket stub to *Fisher King*, a film depicting a deranged man firing a shotgun into a crowded bar, killing several people.

Did seeing the film influence the violent act? We cannot be sure. But we do know that violence in the media can and does have a profound impact on the behavior of adults. Several years ago, David Phillips[83] scrutinized the daily homicide rates in the United States and found that they almost always increased during the week following a heavyweight boxing match. Moreover, the more publicity surrounding the fight, the greater the subsequent increase in homicides. Still more striking, the race of prizefight losers was related to the race of murder victims after the fights: After white boxers lost fights, there was a corresponding increase in the murder of white men but not of black men; after black boxers lost fights, there was a corresponding increase in the murder of black men but not of white men. Phillips's results are convincing; they are far too consistent to be dismissed as merely a fluke. Again, this should not be construed as indicating that all people or even a sizable percentage of people are motivated to commit violence after watching media violence. But the fact that some people are influenced—and that the results can be tragic—cannot be denied.

The Numbing Effect of TV Violence It seems to be the case that repeated exposure to painful or unpleasant events tends to have a numbing effect on our sensitivity to those events. Recall the example with which I opened this chapter: How I had become so accustomed to the wanton killing in Vietnam that I found myself actually being casual about it when I described it to my young son. There is good evidence that this is a general phenomenon. In one experiment, Victor Cline and his colleagues[84] measured the physiological responses of several young men while they were watching a rather brutal and bloody boxing match. Those who watched a lot of TV daily seemed relatively indifferent to the mayhem in the ring; they showed little physiological evidence of excitement, anxiety, or the like. They treated the violence in a lackadaisical manner. On the other hand, those who typically watched relatively little TV underwent major physiological arousal. The violence really got to them.

In a related vein, Margaret Hanratty Thomas and her colleagues[85] demonstrated that viewing television violence can subsequently numb people's reactions when they are faced with real-life aggression. Thomas had her subjects watch either a violent police drama or an exciting but nonviolent volleyball game. After a short break, they were allowed to observe a verbally and physically aggressive interaction between two preschoolers. Those who had watched the police show responded less emotionally than those who had watched the volleyball game. It seems that viewing the initial violence served to desensitize them to further acts of violence; they were not upset by an incident that should have upset them. While such a reaction may protect us psychologically from upset, it may also have the unintended effect of increasing our indifference to victims of violence and perhaps rendering us more accepting of violence as a necessary aspect of modern life. In a follow-up experiment, Thomas[86] took this reasoning a step further. She demonstrated that college students exposed to a great deal of TV violence not only showed physiological evidence of greater acceptance of violence but, in addition, when subsequently given the opportunity to administer electric shocks to a fellow student, administered more powerful electric shocks than those in the control condition.

Why Does Media Violence Affect Viewers' Aggression? Let me summarize what we have been saying in this section: There are four distinct reasons that exposure to violence via the media might increase aggression:

1. *"If they can do it, so can I."* When people watch characters on TV expressing violence, it might simply weaken their previously learned inhibition against violent behavior.

2. *"Oh, so that's how you do it!"* When people watch characters on TV expressing violence, it might trigger imitation, providing ideas as to how they might go about it.

3. *"I think it must be aggressive feelings that I'm experiencing."* There is a sense in which watching violence makes the feeling of anger more easily available and makes an aggressive response more likely simply through priming. Thus, an individual might erroneously construe his or her own feeling of mild irritation as anger and might be more likely to lash out.

4. *"Ho-hum, another brutal beating; what's on the other channel?"* Watching a lot of mayhem seems to reduce both our sense of horror about violence and our sympathy for the victims, thereby making it easier for us to live with violence and perhaps easier for us to act aggressively.

The Media, Pornography, and Violence against Women An important and troubling aspect of aggression in this country involves violence expressed by some men against women in the form of rape. According to national surveys during the past 25 years, almost half of all rapes or attempted rapes do not involve assaults by a stranger but rather are so-called date rapes in which the victim is acquainted with the assailant. What are we to make of this phenomenon?

It appears that many date rapes take place because the male refuses to take the word "no" at face value, in part because of some confusion about the "sexual scripts" adolescents learn as they gain sexual maturity. **Scripts** are ways of behaving socially that we learn implicitly from the culture. The sexual scripts adolescents are exposed to suggest that the traditional female role is to resist the male's sexual advances and the male's role is to be persistent.[87] Thus, in one survey of high school students, although 95 percent of the males and 97 percent of the females agreed that the man should stop his sexual advances as soon as the woman says "no," nearly half of those same students also believed that when a woman says "no" she doesn't always mean it.[88] This confusion has prompted several colleges to enact firm rules specifying that dating couples negotiate an explicit contract about their sexual conduct and limitations at the very beginning of the date. Given the problems associated with sexual scripts and the unpleasant (and occasionally tragic) consequences of misreadings of desires and intentions, it is understandable that college administrators would resort to this extreme precaution. At the same time, it should be noted that more than a few social critics have deplored this measure on the grounds that it encourages excessive fear and paranoia, destroys the spontaneity of romance, and reduces the excitement of dating to the point where it resembles a field trip to a lawyer's office.[89]

Coincidental with the increase in rape during the past few decades is an increase in the availability of the depiction of vivid, explicit sexual behavior in magazines and on film and videocassettes. For better or worse, in recent years, our society has become increasingly freer and more tolerant of pornography. If, as we've seen, the viewing of violence in films and on television contributes to violence, shouldn't it follow that viewing pornographic material would increase the incidence of rape? While this has been argued from both pulpit and lecture, it is much too simplistic an assumption. Indeed, after studying the available evidence, the President's Commission on Obscenity and Pornography concluded that explicit sexual material *in itself* did not contribute to sexual crimes, violence against women, or other antisocial acts.

The key phrase in the preceding sentence is "in itself." During the past several years, Neil Malamuth, Edward Donnerstein, and their colleagues have conducted a series of careful studies to determine the effects, if any, of pornography. Taken together, these studies indicate that exposure to pornography is harmless—but that exposure to *violent* pornography—which combines pornographic sex with violence—promotes greater acceptance of sexual violence toward women and is one factor associated with actually aggressive behavior toward women.[90] In one experiment,[91] Donnerstein showed men one of three films—an aggressive-erotic one involving rape, a purely erotic one without aggression, or a neutral film that was neither aggressive nor erotic. After viewing one of these films, the men took part in a supposedly unrelated study that involved teaching either a male or a female confederate some nonsense syllables. The men were instructed to administer electric shocks to the confederate when he or she gave incorrect answers; they were also allowed to choose whatever level of shock they wished to use. (Unknown to the subjects, no shocks were actually delivered.) Those men who had earlier seen the rape film subsequently administered the most intense shocks—but only to the *female* confederate.

Similarly, Malamuth conducted an experiment[92] in which male college students viewed one of two erotic films. One version portrayed two mutually consenting adults engaged in lovemaking; the other version portrayed a rape incident. After viewing the film, the men were asked to engage in sexual fantasy. The men who had watched the rape version of the film created more violent sexual fantasies than those who had watched the mutual consent version. In another experiment,[93] Malamuth and Check arranged for college students to watch either a violent, sexually explicit film or a film with no violent or sexual acts. Several days later, the students filled out a Sexual Attitude Survey. For the male students, exposure to the violent, sexually explicit film increased their acceptance of violence against women. In addition, these males came to believe certain myths about rape—for example, that women provoke rape and actually enjoy being raped.

I should point out that, in general, the belief in the rape myth is not limited to men. In a survey of university women, Malamuth and his colleagues found that, while not a single woman felt that she personally would derive any pleasure from being overpowered sexually, a substantial percentage believed that some other women might.[94] Again, exposure to aggressive pornography tends to increase the tendency of men to believe the rape myth. There is some evidence indicating that this myth is not necessarily part of a deep-seated belief system. For example, in one study, when college men were shown a pornographically aggressive film, their belief in the rape myth increased as predicted. But after the film, when they were provided with an explanation of the experimental procedure, they became less accepting of the rape myth than a control group that neither viewed the film nor received the explanation.[95]

Although this finding is encouraging, it should not lull us into complacency, for the data also suggest that a steady diet of violent pornography can lead to emotional desensitization and callused attitudes regarding violence against women. Moreover, there is reason to believe that repeated exposure to X-rated "slasher" films—which are extremely violent but less sexually explicit than pornographic films—has more damaging effects than nonviolent X-rated films. In one study,[96] Daniel Linz and his colleagues found desensitization effects after exposing male subjects to as few as two slasher films spaced 2 days apart. That is, when their reactions to the first and second films were compared, the men showed a reduced emotional response to the violent content of the film and found the treatment of the women in the film less degrading. In addition, the researchers compared the effects of X-rated slasher movies, X-rated soft-porn movies, and teen-sex movies on men's attitudes toward rape victims. Two days after watching the films, subjects participated in a supposedly unrelated study in which they viewed a reenactment of a rape trial and were asked to make judgments about the victim and defendant. Once again, the slasher films had a powerful impact on the attitudes of male viewers. Compared to subjects who watched the nonviolent pornography or teen-sex films, men exposed to the slasher films expressed less sympathy for the rape victim in the trial, as well as less empathy for rape victims in general. These findings suggest that our society's rating system for movies is off-target and misleading: Sexually explicit but nonviolent films are given more restrictive X ratings, while graphically violent slasher movies earn only an R rating—and thus are more widely seen—despite evidence of their negative impact.

To sum up, the combination of sex and violence—whether in pornographic films or slasher films—has effects remarkably similar to those associated with other violence in the media: The level of aggression is increased and, in many instances, attitudes condoning violence are strengthened. Viewing violence (pornographic or otherwise) does not serve a cathartic function but seems, rather, to stimulate aggressive behavior. These data raise complex policy issues involving censorship and First Amendment rights that extend beyond the scope of this book. While I personally am opposed to the imposition of censorship, I would think that an impartial reading of the research would lead those decision makers within the media to exercise some prudent self-restraint.

Does Violence Sell? As we noted earlier in this chapter, some 58 percent of all TV shows contain acts of violence. The reason for this is obvious: TV producers and advertising agencies believe that violence sells products. The cosmic joke is that this is probably not the case. Don't get me wrong. I am not suggesting that violent shows are unpopular. The average American might complain about all that violence on TV, but he also seems to enjoy watching it. True enough. But that does not necessarily mean that violence sells. After all, the goal of advertising is not simply to get a lot of people to tune in to the ad; the ultimate goal of advertising is to present the product in such a way that the public will end up purchasing that product over a prolonged period of time. What if it turns out that certain kinds of shows produce so much mental turmoil that the sponsor's product is soon forgotten? If people cannot remember the name of the product, seeing the show will not lead them to buy it. And recent research has shown that both sex and violence can be so distracting, that they cause viewers to be less attentive to the product being advertised.

In a recent experiment, Brad Bushman and Angelica Bonacci[97] got people to watch TV shows that were either violent, sexually explicit, or neutral. Each of the shows contained the same nine ads. Immediately after seeing the show, the viewers were asked to recall the brands and to pick them out from photos of supermarket shelves. Twenty-four hours later, they were telephoned and asked to recall the brands they had seen during the viewing. It turns out that the people who saw the ads during the viewing of a neutral (nonviolent, non-sexually explicit) show were able to recall the advertised brands better than the people who saw the violent show or the sexually explicit show. This was true both immediately after viewing and 24 hours after viewing and was true for both men and women of all ages. It seems that violence and sex impair the memory of viewers. In terms of sales, advertisers might be well advised to sponsor nonviolent shows.

Aggression to Attract Public Attention After the 1992 riots in south central Los Angeles, the president of the United States indicated that he was deeply concerned and that he would provide federal aid and create jobs for the unemployed. Do you think he would have placed such a high priority on the jobless in that area if there had been no riot? In a complex and apathetic society like ours, aggressive behavior may be the most dramatic way for an oppressed minority to attract the attention of the powerful majority. No one can deny that, over the years, the effects of riots in Watts, Detroit, and south central Los Angeles served to alert a large number of decent but apathetic people to the plight of ethnic and racial minorities in the United States. No one can doubt that the bloodshed in the state prison at Attica, New York, has led to increased attempts at prison reform. Are such outcomes worth the dreadful price in human lives? I cannot answer that question. But, as a social psychologist, what I can say (again and again) is that violence almost never ends simply with a rectification of the conditions that brought it about. Violence breeds violence, not only in the simple sense of the victim striking back against his or her enemy, but also in the infinitely more complex and insidious sense of the attackers seeking to justify their violence by exaggerating the evil they see in their enemies and thereby increasing the probability that they will attack again (and again, and again).

There will never be a war to end all wars or a riot to end all injustice—quite the contrary: Bellicose behaviors strengthen bellicose attitudes, which increase the probability of bellicose behaviors. We must search for alternative solutions. A less aggressive form of instrumental behavior might serve to redress social ills without producing an irreconcilable cycle of conflict. Consider Gandhi's success against the British in India during the 1930s. Strikes, boycotts, and other forms of civil disobedience eventually led to the end of British rule without fostering a rapid escalation of hatred between the citizens of the two countries. Such nonviolent strategies as sit-ins and boycotts also have been used effectively by Martin Luther King, Cesar Chavez, and others to awaken our own nation to real grievances. Accordingly, I would echo Loren Eiseley's call for a gentler people but, in addition, I would call for a people more tolerant of differences between one another—but not a people tolerant of injustice: a people who will love and trust one another but who will yell, scream, strike, boycott, march, sit in (and even vote!) to eliminate injustice and cruelty. Again, as we have seen in countless experiments, violence cannot be turned on and off like a faucet. Research has shown over and over again that the only solution is to find ways of reducing violence as we continue to try to reduce the injustice that produces the frustrations that frequently erupt in violent aggression.

Toward the Reduction of Violence

So far, we have focused our discussion primarily on factors that serve to increase aggressive behavior. If we believe, however, that reducing our propensity toward aggression is a worthwhile goal, how should we proceed? It is tempting to search for simple solutions. In the early 1970s, no less an expert than a former president of the American Psychological Association suggested that we develop an anticruelty drug to be fed to people (especially national leaders) as a way of reducing violence on a universal scale.[98] The quest for such a solution is understandable and even somewhat touching, but it is extremely unlikely that a drug could be developed that would reduce cruelty without completely tranquilizing the motivational systems of its users. Chemicals cannot make the fine distinction that psychological processes can. Gentle, peace-loving people (like Albert Einstein) who are also energetic, creative, courageous, and resourceful are produced by a subtle combination of physiological and psychological forces, of inherited capacities and learned values. It is difficult to conceive of a chemical that could perform as subtly. Moreover, chemical control of human behavior has the quality of an Orwellian nightmare. Whom could we trust to use such methods?

There are probably no simple, foolproof solutions. But let's speculate about some complex and less foolproof possibilities based upon what we've learned so far.

Pure Reason I am certain we could construct a logical, reasonable set of arguments depicting the dangers of aggression and the misery produced (not only in victims but also in aggressors) by aggressive acts. I'm even fairly certain we could convince most people that the arguments were sound; clearly, most people would agree that war is hell and violence in the streets is undesirable. But such arguments, no matter how sound, no matter how convincing, probably would not significantly curtail aggressive behavior. Even if convinced that aggression, in general, is undesirable, individuals will behave aggressively unless they firmly believe aggression is undesirable for them. As Aristotle observed more than 2,000 years ago, many people cannot be persuaded by rational behavior: "For argument based on knowledge implies instruction, and there are people whom one cannot instruct."[99] Moreover, because the problem of the control of aggression is one that first occurs in early childhood—that is, at a time when the individual is too young to be reasoned with—logical arguments are of little value. For these reasons, social psychologists have searched for alternative techniques of persuasion. Many of these have been developed with young children in mind but are adaptable to adults as well.

Punishment To the average citizen, an obvious way of reducing aggression is to punish it. If one man robs, batters, or kills another, the simple solution is to put him in prison or, in extreme cases, to kill him. If a young girl aggresses against her parents, siblings, or peers, we can spank her, scream at her, remove her privileges, or make her feel guilty. The assumption here is that this punishment "will teach them a lesson," that they will "think twice" before they perform that activity again, and that the more severe the punishment, the better. But it is not that simple. Severe punishment has been shown to be effective temporarily, but unless used with extreme caution, it can have the opposite effect in the long run. Observations of parents and children in the real world have demonstrated time and again that parents who use severe punishment tend to produce children who are extremely aggressive or who, as adults, favor violent means of obtaining personal and political ends.[100] This aggression usually takes place outside the home, where the child is distant from the punishing agent. But these naturalistic studies are inconclusive. They don't necessarily prove that punishment for aggression, in itself, produces aggressive children. Parents who resort to harsh punishment probably do a lot of other things as well—that is, they are probably harsh and aggressive people. Accordingly, it may be that the children are simply copying the aggressive behavior of their parents. Indeed, it has been shown that, if children are physically punished by an adult who has previously treated them in a warm and nurturant manner, they tend to comply with the adult's wishes when the adult is absent from the scene. On the other hand, children who are physically punished by an impersonal, cold adult are far less likely to comply with the adult's wishes once the adult has left the room. Thus, there is some reason to believe that punishment can be useful if it is applied judiciously in the context of a warm relationship.

One other factor of great significance to the efficacy of punishment is its severity or restrictiveness. A severe or restrictive punishment can be extremely frustrating; because frustration is one of the primary causes of aggression, it would seem wise to avoid using frustrating tactics when trying to curb aggression. This point was demonstrated very nicely in a study by Robert Hamblin and his colleagues.[101] In this study, hyperactive boys were punished by their teacher by having privileges taken away from them. Specifically, the boys had earned some tokens exchangeable for a wide variety of enjoyable things, but each time a boy aggressed, he was deprived of some of the tokens. During and after the application of this technique, the frequency of aggressive actions among these boys practically doubled. This was almost certainly the result of an increase in frustration.

What about the prisons in our own country—institutions of punishment that are quite severe and restrictive? Though it may seem intuitively correct to think that putting a criminal in such a harsh environment would deter that person from committing crimes in the future, there is precious little evidence to support such an assumption.[102] In fact, as this analysis would predict, imprisonment may have the opposite effect. Determining its specific consequences is difficult, however; in most instances, it is impossible to isolate the effects of being incarcerated because too many other factors influence the person in that situation. Does the harshness of prisons actually promote future criminality or do former inmates wind up returning to prison simply because they are criminal types? While these possibilities usually are hard to test in the real world, evidence from a natural experiment suggests that prisons fail to deter crime among the inmates who are released. A Supreme Court decision made the experiment possible,[103] isolating the effects of imprisonment on recidivism. In 1963, after the *Gideon* v. *Wainwright* ruling that people could not be convicted of a felony without being provided with a lawyer, a number of the inmates of Florida prisons were released early—way before they served their full sentence. The only systematic difference between these prisoners and those remaining in prison was that the released prisoners had not previously been represented by counsel. Thus, researchers could compare two groups of convicts that were nearly identical; some had been prematurely released, and others had been punished and "rehabilitated" to the full extent of their sentences. A startling difference emerged between the two groups: The prisoners who served their complete term were twice as likely to return to prison as those who were released early.

Does this mean that harsh punishment does not reduce crime? Not necessarily. While this study does offer persuasive evidence that lengthy prison terms do not deter the future criminal behavior of released inmates, it does not completely rule out the possibility that the mere prospect of harsh punishment might curb the criminal tendencies of those who have never been convicted. It is certainly possible that the threat of punishment deters many would-be criminals from ever breaking the law in the first place.

Although this is possible, I consider it unlikely. What I *do* know is that, while severe punishment frequently results in compliance, it rarely produces internalization. In order to establish long-term nonaggressive behavior patterns, it is important to induce people, when they are still children, to internalize a set of values that denigrates aggressive behavior. In two separate experiments discussed more fully in Chapter 5, both Merrill Carlsmith and I and Jonathan Freedman[104] demonstrated that, with young children, threats of mild punishment are far more effective than threats of severe punishment. Although these highly controlled experiments dealt only with toy preference in children, they strongly suggest that threats of mild (rather than severe) punishment would curb aggression in the same way.

Here's how it works. Suppose a mother threatens to punish her young son in order to induce him to refrain, momentarily, from aggressing against his little sister. If she is successful, her son will experience dissonance. The cognition "I like to wallop my little sister" is dissonant with the cognition "I am refraining from walloping my little sister." If he were severely threatened, he would have an abundantly good reason for refraining; he would be able to reduce dissonance by saying, "The reason I'm not hitting my sister is that I'd get the daylights beaten out of me if I did—but I sure would like to." However, suppose his mother threatens to use a punishment that is mild rather than severe—a punishment just barely strong enough to get the child to stop his aggression. In this instance, when he asks himself why he's not hitting his infinitely hittable little sister at the moment, he can't use the threat as a way of reducing dissonance—that is, he can't easily convince himself that he would be walloped if he hit his sister simply because it's not true—yet he must justify the fact that he's not hitting his sister. In other words, his external justification (in terms of the severity of the threat) is minimal; therefore, he must add his own in order to justify his restraint. He might, for example, convince himself that he no longer enjoys hitting his little sister. This would not only explain, justify, and make sensible his momentarily peaceful behavior, but more important, *it would decrease the probability of his hitting his little sister in the future.* In short, a counteraggressive value would have been internalized. He would have convinced *himself* that, for *him*, hitting someone is neither desirable nor fun.

This general notion has been applied with some success in the real world of the schoolyard. Dan Olweus,[105] working in the Norwegian school system, was able to curtail the frequency of bullying behavior by as much as 50 percent by training teachers and administrators to be vigilant to the problem and to take swift but moderate punitive action. Taken as a whole, this research indicates that children who have not yet formed their values are more apt to develop a distaste for aggression if the punishment for aggressive actions is both timely and not terribly severe.

Punishment of Aggressive Models A variation on the theme of punishment involves punishing someone else. Specifically, it has been argued that it might be possible to reduce aggression by presenting the child with the sight of an aggressive model who comes to a bad end. The theory here is that individuals who are exposed to this sight will in effect be vicariously punished for their own aggression and accordingly will become less aggressive. It is probable that, in our nation's past, public hangings and floggings were arranged by people who held this theory. Does it work? Gross data from the real world do not support the theory. For example, according to the President's Commission on Law Enforcement,[106] the existence and use of the death penalty does not decrease the homicide rate. Moreover, on the level of casual data, the mass media frequently depict aggressive people as highly attractive even though they are eventually punished. This tends to induce individuals to identify with these violent characters.

The evidence from controlled experiments presents a more precise picture. Typically, in these experiments, children watch a film of an aggressive person who subsequently is either rewarded or punished for acting aggressively. Later, the children are given an opportunity to be aggressive under circumstances similar to the ones shown in the film. The consistent finding is that the children who watched the film in which the aggressive person was punished display significantly less aggressive behavior than the children who watched the film of the person being rewarded.[107] As mentioned previously, there is also some evidence to indicate that the kids who watched an aggressive film character being punished displayed less aggressive behavior than did children who watched an aggressive film character who was neither rewarded nor punished. On the other hand—and this is crucial to our discussion—seeing a model being punished for aggression did not decrease the general level of aggression below that of a group of children who were never exposed to an aggressive model. In other words, the major thrust of the research seems to indicate that seeing an aggressor rewarded will increase aggressive behavior in a child and that seeing an aggressor punished will not increase the child's aggressive behavior, but it's not clear that seeing an aggressor punished will decrease the child's aggressive behavior. It might be just as effective not to expose the child to aggressive models at all. The implications of this research for the portrayal of violence in the mass media have already been discussed.

Rewarding Alternative Behavior Patterns Another possibility that has been investigated is to ignore a child when he or she behaves aggressively and to reward the child for nonaggressive behavior. This strategy is based in part on the assumption that young children (and perhaps adults as well) frequently behave aggressively as a way of attracting attention. For them, being punished is preferable to being ignored. Paradoxically, then, punishing aggressive behavior may actually be interpreted as a reward—"Hey, look, gang! Mommy pays attention to me every time I slug my little brother. I think I'll do it again." This idea was tested in an experiment conducted at a nursery school by Paul Brown and Rogers Elliot.[108] The nursery-school teachers were instructed to ignore all aggressive behavior on the part of the kids. At the same time, they were asked to be very attentive to the children and especially to give them a lot of attention when they were doing things incompatible with aggression—such as playing in a friendly manner, sharing toys, and cooperating with others. After a few weeks, there was a noticeable decline in aggressive behavior. In a more elaborate experiment, Joel Davitz[109] demonstrated that frustration need not necessarily result in aggression; rather, it can lead to constructive behavior if such behavior has been made attractive and appealing by prior training. In this study, children were allowed to play in groups of four. Some of these groups were rewarded for constructive behavior, while others were rewarded for aggressive or competitive behavior. Then the kids were deliberately frustrated. This was accomplished by building up the expectation that they would be shown a series of entertaining movies and be allowed to have fun. Indeed, the experimenter went so far as to begin to show a movie and to hand out candy bars to be eaten later. But then the frustration was administered. The experimenter abruptly terminated the movie at the point of highest interest and took the candy bars away. The children were then allowed to play freely. As you have learned, this is a setup for the occurrence of aggressive behavior. But the children who had been trained for constructive behavior displayed far more constructive activity and far less aggressive activity than those in the other group.

This research is encouraging indeed. Here I find it necessary to state my firm belief that it would be naive to expect many children in our society to spontaneously choose constructive rather than aggressive solutions to interpersonal conflicts and frustrating circumstances. The society at large presents us with all kinds of evidence to the effect that violent solutions to conflict and frustration are not only predominant but also valued. The Arnold

Schwarzenegger/James Bond–type hero has become a cultural icon. Explicitly or implicitly, whether in the guise of the avenging cowboy, the urban cop, the prizefighter, the Terminator or the suave secret agent who blows people away in exotic and entertaining ways, these movie heroes demonstrate to young kids what is valued by society and what might be expected of them.

Needless to say, our exposure to violent solutions to problems is not confined to films and videos; these events dominate the nightly news as well. Accordingly, it should come as no surprise that children learn that adults often solve their conflicts by resorting to violence. Moreover, many children are not even aware that alternative solutions are feasible or appropriate. If we would prefer our children to grow up favoring nonviolent strategies, it might be a good idea to offer them specific training in these techniques, as well as encouragement to use them. There is no reason why such training cannot be provided both in the home and in school.

The Presence of Nonaggressive Models An important curb to aggressive behavior is the clear indication that such behavior is inappropriate. And the most effective indicator is social—that is, the presence of other people in the same circumstances who are restrained and relatively unaggressive. For example, in a study by Robert Baron and Richard Kepner,[110] subjects were insulted by an individual and then observed that individual receiving electric shocks at the hands of a third person. The third person delivered either intense or very mild shocks. There also was a control group in which subjects did not observe a model administering shocks. Subjects were then given the opportunity to shock their tormentor. Those who had witnessed a person delivering intense shocks delivered more intense shocks than those in the control condition; those who had witnessed a person delivering mild shocks delivered milder shocks than those in the control condition. Does this paradigm seem familiar? The reader can readily see that the expression of aggressive behavior, like the expression of any behavior, can be viewed as an act of conformity. Specifically, in an ambiguous situation, people look to other people for a definition of what is appropriate. Recall that in Chapter 2, I described the conditions under which you might belch at the dinner table of a Freedonian dignitary. Here I am suggesting that, if you and your friends are frustrated or made angry, and all around you people in your group are throwing snowballs at your tormentors, it will increase the probability that you will throw snowballs; if they are merely talking forcefully, it will increase the probability that you will talk forcefully; and, alas, if the people in your group are swinging clubs at the heads of their tormentors, it will increase the probability that you will pick up a club and start swinging.

Building Empathy Toward Others Picture the following scene: There is a long line of cars stopped at a traffic light at a busy intersection. The light turns green. The lead driver hesitates for 15 seconds. What happens? Of course, there is an eruption of horn-honking. Not simply a little toot designed to supply the lead driver with the information that the light has changed, but prolonged and persistent blasting indicative of a frustrated group of people venting their annoyance. Indeed, in a controlled experiment, it was found that, in this kind of situation, approximately 90 percent of the drivers of the second car honked their horns in an aggressive manner. As part of the same experiment, a pedestrian who crossed the street between the first and second cars *while the light was still red* was out of the intersection by the time the light turned green. Still, almost 90 percent of the second-car drivers tooted their horns when the light turned green. But what happened when the pedestrian was on crutches? Apparently, seeing a person on crutches evoked an empathic response; the feeling of empathy overwhelmed the desire to be aggressive, and the percentage of people honking their horns decreased dramatically.[111]

Empathy is an important phenomenon. Seymour Feshbach[112] notes that most people find it difficult to inflict pain purposely on another human being unless they can find some way of dehumanizing their victim. Thus, when our nation was fighting wars against Asians (Japanese in the 1940s, Koreans in the 1950s, Vietnamese in the 1960s), our military personnel frequently referred to them as "gooks." We see this use of dehumanization as a way of justifying acts of cruelty. It is easier to commit violent acts against a "gook" than it is to commit violent acts against a fellow human being. As I have noted time and again in this book, this kind of self-justification not only makes it possible for us to aggress against another person, but it also guarantees that we will continue to aggress against that person. Recall the example of the schoolteacher living in Kent, Ohio, who, after the killing of four Kent State students by Ohio National Guardsmen, told author James Michener[113] that anyone who walks on the street barefoot deserves to die. This kind of statement is bizarre on the face of it; we begin to understand it only when we realize that it was made by someone who had already succeeded in dehumanizing the victims of this tragedy.

We can deplore the process of dehumanization, but at the same time, an understanding of the process can help us to reverse it. Specifically, if it is true that most individuals must dehumanize their victims in order to commit an extreme act of aggression, then, by building empathy among people, aggressive acts will become more difficult to commit. Indeed, Norma and Seymour Feshbach[114] have demonstrated a negative correlation between empathy and aggression in children: The more empathy a person has, the less he or she resorts to aggressive actions. Subsequently, Norma Feshbach developed a method of teaching empathy and successfully tested its effects on aggression.[115] Briefly, she taught primary-school children how to take the perspective of another. The children were trained to identify different emotions in people, they played the role of other people in various emotionally laden situations, and they explored (in a group) their own feelings. These "empathy training activities" led to significant decreases in aggressive behavior. Similarly, Georgina Hammock and Deborah Richardson[116] demonstrated that empathy is an important buffer against committing acts of extreme aggression. When they placed college students in a situation where they were instructed to deliver electric shocks to a fellow student, those who had learned to experience empathic concern for the feelings of others delivered less severe shocks than those who were less empathic. Ken-ichi Obuchi and his colleagues,[117] working with Japanese students, found similar results. Obuchi instructed students to deliver electric shocks to another student as part of a learning experiment. In one condition, prior to receiving the shocks, the victims first disclosed something personal about themselves—thus opening the door to the formation of empathy; in the control condition, the victims were not afforded an opportunity for self-disclosure. Subjects in the disclosure condition administered much milder shocks than subjects in the nondisclosure condition.

The research on building empathy has encouraging implications for the possible elimination of tragedies such as the Columbine massacre described earlier. In the following chapter, I will elaborate on this and other strategies for coping with aggression and prejudice.

Saul Steinberg, *Untitled drawing*, ink on paper.
Published in Steinberg, *The Art of Living*, 1949.
© The Saul Steinberg Foundation / Artists Rights Society (ARS), New York

7
Prejudice

> A white policeman yelled, "Hey boy! Come here!" Somewhat bothered, I retorted: "I'm no boy!" He then rushed at me, inflamed, and stood towering over me, snorting, "What d'ja say, boy?" Quickly he frisked me and demanded, "What's your name, boy?" Frightened, I replied, "Dr. Poussaint, I'm a physician." He angrily chuckled and hissed, "What's your first name, boy?" When I hesitated he assumed a threatening stance and clenched his fists. As my heart palpitated, I muttered in profound humiliation, "Alvin." He continued his psychological brutality, bellowing, "Alvin, the next time I call you, you come right away, you hear? You hear?" I hesitated. "You hear me, boy?"[1]

Hollywood would have had the hero lash out at his oppressor and emerge victorious. But in the real world, Dr. Poussaint simply slunk away, humiliated—or, in his own words, "psychologically castrated." The feeling of helplessness and powerlessness that is the harvest of the oppressed almost inevitably leads to a diminution of self-esteem that begins even in early childhood. Many years ago, Kenneth and Mamie Clark[2] demonstrated that black children, some of whom were only 3 years old, were already convinced that being black was not a good thing; they rejected black dolls, feeling that white dolls were prettier and generally superior. This experiment suggests that educational facilities that are "separate but equal" are never equal since the separation itself implies to the minority children that they are being segregated because there is something wrong with them. Indeed, this experiment was specifically cited in the landmark Supreme Court decision (*Brown* v. *Board of Education*, 1954) that declared segregated schools to be unconstitutional.

This diminution of self-esteem is not limited to African Americans; it affects other oppressed groups as well. In a study similar to the Clark and Clark experiment, Philip Goldberg[3] demonstrated that women have been taught to consider themselves the intellectual inferiors of men. In his experiment,

Goldberg asked a number of female college students to read scholarly articles and to evaluate them in terms of their competence, style, and so on. For some students, specific articles were signed by male authors (e.g., John T. McKay); and for others, the same articles were signed by female authors (e.g., Joan T. McKay). The female students rated the articles much higher if they were "written" by a male author than if they were "written" by a female author. In other words, these women had "learned their place"; they regarded the output of other women as necessarily inferior to that of men, just as the black youngsters learned to regard black dolls as inferior to white dolls. This is the legacy of a prejudiced society.

But things do change. After all, the Clark and Clark experiment was conducted in the 1940s; the Goldberg experiment was conducted in the 1960s. Significant changes have taken place in American society since then. Legislation on affirmative action has opened the door of opportunity for women and minorities, giving them greater access to higher education as well as to the more prestigious professions like law and medicine. Increasing numbers of women and minorities are being elected to Congress. Colin Powell, an African American, has held the important and highly visible office of Secretary of State. Respected African-American athletes like Michael Jordan and Tiger Woods have made frequent appearances on TV and, as a result, have become household names. Denzel Washington and Halle Berry have taken their place as major motion picture actors. As one might expect, these changes produced an increase in self-esteem among members of these groups. For example, in recent years, research indicates that African-American children have become more content with black dolls than they were in 1947.[4] Moreover, as Janet Swim and her colleagues[5] have shown, women (and men) no longer discriminate against a piece of writing simply because it is attributed to a woman.

While this progress is important and encouraging, it would be a mistake to conclude that prejudice and discrimination have ceased to be serious problems in our country. Even though most overt manifestations of prejudice tend to be both less frequent and less flagrant than they used to be, prejudice still exists and continues to exact a heavy toll on its victims. Every year we must still bear witness to numerous hate crimes, the burning of synagogues and African-American churches,[6] and countless miscellaneous acts of prejudice-induced violence, as well as lesser outrages—like the futility of trying to get a cab to stop for you late at night in an American metropolis if you happen to be a black man.[7] What is prejudice? How does it come about? How can it be reduced?

Stereotypes and Prejudice

Social psychologists have defined prejudice in a variety of ways. Technically, there are positive and negative prejudices; I can be prejudiced against modern artists or prejudiced in favor of modern artists. This means that, before I am introduced to Sam Smear (who I've been told is a modern artist), I will be inclined to like or dislike him—and I will be inclined to expect to see certain characteristics in him. Thus, if I associate the concept *modern artist* with effeminate behavior, I would be astonished if Sam Smear were to swagger through the door looking as though he could play middle linebacker for the Green Bay Packers. If I associate the concept of *modern artist* with the radical end of the political spectrum, I would be astonished if Sam Smear were wearing a George W. Bush political button.

In this chapter, I will not be discussing situations that concern prejudice "in favor" of people; accordingly, my working definition of prejudice will be limited to negative attitudes. I will define **prejudice** as a hostile or negative attitude toward a distinguishable group based on generalizations derived from faulty or incomplete information. For example, when we say an individual is prejudiced against blacks, we mean he or she is oriented toward behaving with hostility toward blacks; the person feels that, with perhaps one or two exceptions, all blacks are pretty much the same. The characteristics he or she assigns to blacks are either totally inaccurate or, at best, based on a germ of truth the person zealously applies to the group as a whole.

In his classic book *The Nature of Prejudice*, Gordon Allport reported the following dialogue:

> *Mr. X:* The trouble with the Jews is that they only take care of their own group.
>
> *Mr. Y:* But the record of the Community Chest campaign shows that they gave more generously, in proportion to their numbers, to the general charities of the community, than did non-Jews.
>
> *Mr. X:* That shows they are always trying to buy favor and intrude into Christian affairs. They think of nothing but money; that is why there are so many Jewish bankers.
>
> *Mr. Y:* But a recent study shows that the percentage of Jews in the banking business is negligible, far smaller than the percentage of non-Jews.
>
> *Mr. X:* That's just it; they don't go in for respectable business; they are only in the movie business or run night clubs.[8]

This dialogue illustrates the insidious nature of prejudice far better than a mountain of definitions. In effect, the prejudiced Mr. X is saying, "Don't trouble me with facts; my mind is made up." He makes no attempt to dispute the data presented by Mr. Y. He either distorts the facts in order to make them support his hatred of Jews or he bounces off them, undaunted, to a new area of attack. A deeply prejudiced person is virtually immune to information at variance with his or her cherished stereotypes. As famed jurist Oliver Wendell Holmes, Jr., once said, "Trying to educate a bigot is like shining light into the pupil of an eye—it constricts." A great deal of experimental evidence supports Allport's observations, demonstrating that bombarding people with facts running counter to their prejudices fails to get them to modify those prejudices. A typical response is one that involves "subtyping," where people convince themselves that what they have learned, while probably true, is a rare exception to the stereotype.[9] Thus, people often respond to counterstereotypic cases by mentally creating a new category—such as "aggressive female," "honest lawyer," or "well-educated African American." They may even label that exception as "the exception that proves the rule." Such responses make stereotypes hard, if not impossible, to eliminate.

It is reasonably safe to assume that all of us have some degree of prejudice—whether it is against an ethnic, national, or racial group, against people with different sexual preferences, against specific geographical areas as places to live, or against certain kinds of food. Let's take food as an example: In this culture, most people do not eat insects. Suppose someone (like Mr. Y) were to tell you that caterpillars or earwigs were a great source of protein and, when carefully prepared, extremely tasty. Would you rush home and fry up a batch? Probably not. Like Mr. X, you would probably find some other reason for your prejudice, such as the fact that most insects are ugly. After all, in this culture, we eat only aesthetically beautiful creatures—like lobsters!

Gordon Allport wrote his book in 1954; the dialogue between Mr. X and Mr. Y might seem somewhat dated to the modern reader. Do people really think that way? Is there anyone so simpleminded as to believe that old, inaccurate stereotype about Jewish bankers? Perhaps not. But some 20 years after Allport's dialogue, a similar statement was made—not by an ordinary citizen but by the person who, at that time, was the single most powerful military officer in the United States. General George S. Brown, chairman of the Joint Chiefs of Staff, in a public speech referring to "Jewish influence in Congress," said, "it is so strong you wouldn't believe, now. . . . They own, you know, the banks in this country, the newspapers. Just look at where the Jewish money is."[10] In 1997 when the Nixon Watergate tapes were released, we had the dubious privilege of overhearing a conversation between Mr. Nixon and his chief of staff, H. R. Haldeman, in which our former president expressed a similar set of erroneous opinions and negative feelings about Jews.

The kind of generalization of characteristics or motives to a group of people expressed by General Brown and President Nixon is called *stereotyping*. To **stereotype** is to assign identical characteristics to any person in a group, regardless of the actual variation among members of that group. Thus, to believe blacks have a natural sense of rhythm, or Jews are materialistic, is to assume that virtually all blacks are rhythmic or that virtually all Jews go around collecting possessions. We learn to assign identical characteristics at a very young age. In one study[11] fifth-grade and sixth-grade children were asked to rate their classmates in terms of a number of characteristics: popularity, leadership, fairness, and the like. The children of upper-class families were rated more positively than the children of lower-class families on every desirable quality. It seems the youngsters were unable to judge their classmates on an individual basis; instead, they had stereotyped them according to their social class.

As we have seen in Chapter 4, stereotyping is not necessarily an intentional act of abuse; it is frequently merely a way we humans have of simplifying our view of the world, and we all do it. Most of us have a specific picture in mind when we hear the words "New York cab driver" or "Italian barber" or "high-school cheerleader." To the extent that the stereotype is based on experience and is at all accurate, it can be an adaptive, shorthand way of dealing with complex events. On the other hand, if the stereotype blinds us to individual differences within a class of people, it is maladaptive and potentially dangerous.

For example, many white people in our society tend to associate black people with violent behavior. How might this stereotype lead to inequitable and oppressive actions against blacks? Charles Bond and his colleagues addressed this issue in a study comparing the treatment of black versus white patients in a psychiatric hospital run by an all-white staff.[12] In their research, they looked at the two most common methods staff members used to handle incidents of violent behavior by patients: secluding the individual in a "time-out" room or restraining the individual in a straitjacket, followed by the administration of a sedative drug. An examination of hospital records over an 85-day period revealed that the harsher method—physical restraint and sedation—was used against black patients nearly four times as often as against white patients, despite the fact that there was virtually no difference in the number of violent incidents committed by blacks and whites. Moreover, this discriminatory treatment occurred even though the black patients, on average, had been diagnosed as less violent than the white patients when they were first admitted to the hospital. Over time, however, the staff came to treat black and white patients equally, with the use of restraint against blacks declining dramatically after the first month of residence in the hospital. Evidently, stereotyping and prejudice against blacks as a group was in operation when black patients were relative newcomers to the hospital; then, as familiarity between white staff members and a particular black patient increased, prejudiced behavior against that individual diminished. Thus, this study suggests that the familiarity that comes with prolonged interracial contact can potentially reduce unfair stereotyping and pave the way for recognition of individual characteristics. But, as we shall see later in this chapter, contact between the races, in itself, is usually insufficient to break down well-entrenched stereotypes and bigotry.

To illustrate further the insidious effects of racial or ethnic stereotypes, consider the case of minority-group members who are convicted of crimes and sent to prison. When they come up for parole, will their racial or ethnic status outweigh other information—such as life circumstances or good behavior while in prison—used to make a parole decision? Research indicates that such a cognitive bias exists. Galen Bodenhausen and Robert Wyer[13] asked college students to read fictionalized files on prisoners who were up for parole and to use the information contained in the files to make a parole decision. Sometimes the crimes "fit" the offenders—for example, when a Latino, Carlos Ramirez, committed assault and battery or when an upper-class Anglo-Saxon, Ashley Chamberlaine, committed embezzlement. In other instances, the crimes were inconsistent with the stereotypes. When prisoners' crimes were consistent with the students' stereotypes, the students tended to ignore other relevant information—such as good behavior in prison—and were harsher in their recommendations for parole. Thus, when persons behave in a way that conforms to our stereotypes, we tend to blind ourselves to information that provides clues about why they *really* behaved as they did. Instead, we assume that it must be something about *them*, not their life circumstances, that caused their behaviors.*

How many of Bodenhausen and Wyer's subjects had ever been assaulted by a Latino or lost money to an Anglo-Saxon embezzler? Few if any—for most stereotypes are based not on valid experience but rather on hearsay or images concocted by the mass media or generated within our heads as ways of justifying our own prejudices and cruelty. Like the self-fulfilling prophecy discussed earlier in this book, it is helpful to think of blacks or Latinos as stupid or dangerous if it justifies depriving them of an education or denying them parole, and it is helpful to think of women as being biologically predisposed toward domestic drudgery if a male-dominated society wants to keep them tied to a vacuum cleaner. Likewise, it is useful to think that individuals from the lower classes are unambitious, stupid, and prone to criminal behavior if we want to pay them as little as possible for doing menial work or keep them out of our neighborhoods. In such cases, stereotyping is, indeed, abusive. In the early 1990s, President Clinton's attempt to remove the restrictions against homosexuals serving in the military was met with sturdy opposition. Ancient stereotypes were invoked as some military leaders and politicians predicted dire consequences and a lowering of morale if these citizens were allowed to wear a uniform. The cosmic joke, of course, is that, over the years, thousands of gays and lesbians had been quietly and skillfully performing their patriotic duty in the armed forces without causing trouble or lowering morale.

The quality of the stereotype is not always insulting per se. But it should be clear that stereotyping is harmful to the target, even if the stereotype seems to be neutral or even positive. For example, it is not necessarily negative to at-

---

*I hasten to add that these data are derived from college students in a hypothetical situation; accordingly, taken by themselves, they do not demonstrate that parole officers behave the same way. It is likely that parole officers are more experienced and more sophisticated than the subjects in this experiment. What the experiment does demonstrate is a cognitive bias that exists even in intelligent, well-meaning people—and, unless we are vigilant, any of us might make the same kind of error.

tribute "ambitiousness" to Jews, "a natural sense of rhythm" to blacks, or an "artistic temperament" to homosexuals.[14] But these generalizations are abusive, if only because they rob the person of the right to be perceived and treated as an individual with his or her own individual traits, whether positive or negative.

Stereotype Threat In most cases, stereotyping is not benign; it is directly insulting and can have a debilitating effect on the members of the targeted group. Let us highlight one striking example: Put simply, among college students, there is an academic performance gap between blacks and whites; moreover, the dropout rate for blacks is nearly twice that of whites. While there are many possible historical and societal explanations for this phenomenon, Claude Steele[15] argued that they fall short; they cannot account for the fact that the gap in school achievement between blacks and whites is as great for students with high preparation (as measured by earlier grades) as it is for those with low preparation. In other words, something seems to be happening that keeps even bright, motivated, and well-prepared black students from performing as well as white students with the same level of ability and preparation.

In researching this problem, Steele and Joshua Aronson[16] reasoned that a major contributing factor might involve apprehensiveness among black students (in highly evaluative educational contexts) about confirming the existing negative stereotype of "intellectual inferiority." Steele and Aronson dubbed this apprehension **stereotype threat.** They reasoned that the extra burden of apprehensiveness, in turn, might actually interfere with students' ability to perform well on standardized tests. In a remarkable experiment, Steele and Aronson administered a difficult verbal test (the Graduate Record Examination), individually to black and white Stanford University students. Half of the students were led to believe that the investigator was interested in measuring their intellectual ability; the other half were led to believe that the investigator was merely testing the test—and that the investigators were not interested in evaluating their intellectual ability.

The results were clear: White students performed equally well regardless of whether or not they believed the test was being used to evaluate their intellectual ability. However, black students were highly affected by the way the test was described: They performed about twice as well when they believed that the test was not being used to measure their intelligence. Such is the power of stereotypes; when people think their behavior may confirm a negative reputation about themselves or their group their anxiety can interfere with their performance.

The effects of stereotype threat are not limited to African Americans. A number of researchers have found similar results for other groups such as women working on math problems and Latinos working on verbal tests of ability—because the stereotype is that women are inferior to men at math and

Latinos are inferior to Anglos on verbal ability. Indeed, Steele and Aronson argue that any group that has some negative reputation as being inferior to some other group can experience stereotype threat to a meaningful degree. This can happen to a group even if, by all objective standards, that group excels in the relevant domain. Thus, in a striking experiment, Aronson and his associates[17] gave white male engineering majors (all with near-perfect scores on their math SATs) a difficult math test. Before the test, all of them were told that the test was a measure of their math ability. In addition half of them were confronted with a stereotype threat: The experimenter informed them that he was trying to understand why Asians appear to have superior math ability. This group performed significantly worse on the test. This finding underscores the situational nature of stereotype threat. The exotic situation imposed upon the white engineering majors—an unflattering comparison with a supposedly superior group—is commonplace for blacks and Latinos; they contend daily with such comparisons in any integrated academic setting. That such obviously bright and accomplished students can falter on a test when faced with stereotype threat should make us think twice about casually assuming that the low performance of blacks and Latinos reflects a lack of ability. And there is good news in this research. Namely, because processes like stereotype threat can be significantly reduced by changing the details of the situation, as in the Steele and Aronson experiment, there is reason to believe that, if we pay attention to these details, the achievement gap between minorities and whites can be reduced.

Stereotypes and Attributions

Stereotyping is a special form of attribution. As we saw in Chapter 4, if a person performs an action, observers will make inferences about the cause. For example, if the tight end on your favorite football team drops an easy pass, there are many possible explanations: Perhaps the sun got in his eyes; maybe he was distracted by worry over the ill health of his child; maybe he dropped the ball on purpose because he bet on the other team; or perhaps he just happens to be an untalented player. Note that each of these above attributions about the cause of the tight end's bobble has a very different set of ramifications. You would feel differently about him if he were worried about his child's illness than if he had bet on the other team.

As you know, our need to find a cause for another person's behavior is part of the human tendency to go beyond the information given. It is often functional. For example, suppose you have just moved into a strange town where you have no friends and you are feeling lonely. There is a knock on the door; it is Joe, a neighbor, who shakes your hand and welcomes you to the neighborhood. You invite him in. He stays for about 20 minutes, during which time you and he have an interesting conversation. You feel really good about the possibility of having discovered a new friend. As he gets up to leave, he says, "Oh, by the way, if you ever need some insurance, I happen to be in the business and I'd be happy to discuss it with you," and he leaves his card. Is he your friend who happens to be selling insurance, or is he pretending to be your friend in order to sell you insurance? It is important to know because you must decide whether or not to pursue a relationship with him. To repeat, in making attributions, the individual must go beyond the information given. We do not know why the tight end dropped the pass; we do not know Joe's motivation for friendly behavior. We are guessing. Thus, the attributer's causal interpretations may be accurate or erroneous, functional or dysfunctional.

In an ambiguous situation, people tend to make attributions consistent with their prejudices. Thomas Pettigrew has dubbed this **the ultimate attribution error.**[18] If Mr. Bigot sees a well-dressed white Anglo-Saxon Protestant sitting on a park bench sunning himself at three o'clock on a Wednesday afternoon, he thinks nothing of it. If he sees a well-dressed black man doing the same thing, he is liable to leap to the conclusion that the man is unemployed—and Mr. Bigot is apt to become infuriated because he assumes his own hard-earned money is being taxed to pay that shiftless, good-for-nothing enough in welfare subsidies to keep him in fancy clothes. If Mr. Bigot passes Mr. Anglo's house and notices that a trash can is overturned and garbage is strewn about, he is apt to conclude that a stray dog has been searching for food. If he passes Mr. Latino's house and notices the same thing, he is inclined to become annoyed and to assert that "those people live like pigs." Not only does prejudice influence his attributions and conclusions, his erroneous conclusions justify and intensify his negative feelings. Thus, the entire attribution process can spiral. Prejudice causes particular kinds of negative attributions or stereotypes that can, in turn, intensify the prejudice.[19]

Gender Stereotypes A particularly interesting manifestation of stereotyping takes place in the perception of gender differences. Kay Deaux and her associates have shown that it is almost universal for women to be seen as more nurturant and less assertive than men. It is possible that this perception may be entirely role related—that is, traditionally women have been assigned the role of homemaker and thus, may be seen as more nurturant.[20] At the other end of the continuum, evolutionary social psychologists[21] suggest that female behavior and male behavior differ in precisely those domains in which the sexes have faced different adaptive problems. From a Darwinian perspective, there are powerful biological reasons why women might have evolved as more nurturant than men. For example, among our ancient ancestors, for anatomical reasons, women were always the early caregivers of infants; those women who were not nurturant were less likely to have had many babies who survived.

Although there is no clear way of determining whether or not caregiving is more likely to be part of a woman's genetic nature than a man's, it does turn out that the cultural stereotype is not far from reality. As Alice Eagly, Wendy Wood, and Janet Swim[22] have shown, compared to men, women do tend to act in ways that can best be described as more socially sensitive, friendlier, and more concerned with the welfare of others, while men tend to act in ways that are more dominant, controlling, and independent. It goes without saying that there is a great deal of overlap between men and women on these characteristics; all of us have been around some men who are socially sensitive and some women who are not. And that's precisely the issue. Whether the reality underlying the stereotype is social or biological, the application of the stereotype to all women or all men deprives the individual of her and his right to be treated as an individual with specific characteristics and talents.

Of course, gender stereotyping often *does* depart from reality and can therefore be particularly harmful. For example, in an experiment performed in 1974 by Shirley Feldman-Summers and Sara Kiesler,[23] when confronted with a successful female physician, male college students perceived her as being less competent than a successful male physician. In a similar study, Kay Deaux and Tim Emsweiler[24] found that, if the sexual stereotype is strong enough, even members of the stereotyped group tend to buy it. Specifically, male and female students were shown a successful performance on a complex task by a fellow student and were asked how it came about. When it was a man who succeeded, both male and female students attributed his achievement to his ability; when it was a woman who succeeded, students of both genders concluded that her achievement was largely a matter of luck.

But this research was done more than a quarter of a century ago. As we have noted, American society has undergone many changes since then. Have these changes impacted the stereotypes held of women? Not as much as one might imagine. In 1996, Janet Swim and Lawrence Sanna[25] did a careful analysis of over 50 relatively recent experiments on this topic and discovered that the results are remarkably consistent with those of the earlier experiments. Swim and Sanna found that, although the gender effects are not large, they are remarkably consistent: If a man was successful on a given task, observers tended to attribute his success to ability; if a woman was successful on that same task, observers tended to attribute her success to hard work. If a man failed on a given task, observers tended to attribute his failure either to bad luck or to lower effort; if a woman failed, observers felt the task was simply too hard for her ability level.

Research has also shown that young girls have a tendency to downplay *their own* abilities. John Nicholls[26] found that, while fourth-grade boys attributed their own successful outcomes on a difficult intellectual task to their abilities, girls tended to derogate their own successful performances. Moreover, this experiment showed that while boys had learned to protect their egos by attributing their own failures to bad luck, girls tended to blame themselves for failures. In a more recent experiment, Deborah Stipek and Heidi Gralinski[27] showed that the tendency girls have to downplay their own abilities may be most prevalent in traditionally male domains—like math. Specifically Stipek and Galinski found that junior high-school girls attributed their success on a math exam to luck, while boys attributed their success to ability. Girls also showed less pride than boys following success on a math exam.

Where do these self-defeating beliefs come from? In general, they are almost certainly influenced by the prevailing attitudes of our society—but they are most powerfully influenced by the attitudes of the most important people in the young girl's life: her parents. In one study, Janis Jacobs and Jacquelynne Eccles[28] explored the influence of mothers' gender stereotypic beliefs on the way these same mothers perceived the abilities of their 11- and 12-year-old sons and daughters. Jacobs and Eccles then looked further to see what impact this might have on the children's perceptions of their own abilities. Those mothers who held the strongest stereotypic gender beliefs also believed that their own daughters had relatively low math ability and that their sons had relatively high math ability. Those mothers who did not hold generally stereotypic beliefs did not see their daughters as less able in math than their sons. These beliefs, in turn, had an impact on the beliefs of their children. The daughters of women with strong gender stereotypes believed that they did not have much math ability. The daughters of women who did not hold strong gender stereotypes showed no such self-defeating belief.

This phenomenon of self-attribution may have some interesting ramifications. Suppose a male tennis player loses the first set in a best-of-three-sets match by the score of 6–2. What does he conclude? Probably that he didn't try hard enough or that he was unlucky—after all, his opponent did have that incredible string of lucky shots. Now suppose a female tennis player loses the first set. What does she conclude? Given Nicholls's data, she might think she is not as skilled a player as her opponent—after all, she did lose 6–2. Here comes the interesting part: The attributions players make about their failure in the first set may, in part, determine their success in subsequent sets. That is, men may try harder to come from behind and win the next two sets and the match. However, women may give up, thus losing the second set and the match. This is, in fact, what seems to happen. In a systematic investigation of this phenomenon,[29] the outcomes of 19,300 tennis matches were examined. In those matches where a player lost the first set, men were more likely than women to come back and win the second and third sets. Women were more likely to lose a match in straight sets. This phenomenon occurs even among professional tennis players—who surely regard themselves as talented and able.

Marlene Turner and Anthony Pratkanis[30] carried the notion of debilitating self-attributions a step further by demonstrating that negative self-attributions generated by the manner in which women are selected for a job can impede their actual performance on the job. Specifically, Turner and Pratkanis were interested in investigating some possible unfortunate side effects of affirmative action programs. As you know, affirmative action programs have been generally beneficial inasmuch as they created employment opportunities for talented women who had been previously overlooked when applying for these positions. Unfortunately, there can be a downside as well: Some of these programs unintentionally stigmatized talented women by creating the illusion that they were selected primarily because of their gender rather than their talent. What effect does this have on the women involved? In a well-controlled experiment, Turner and Pratkanis led some women to believe that they were selected for a job because of their gender, while others were given a difficult test and were then told they were selected for that job on the basis of their meritorious performance on the test. Those women who were told they were selected because of their gender (not their merit) derogated their own abilities. In addition, they tended to engage in self-handicapping behaviors; specifically, when the task required a great deal of effort, the women who believed they were preferentially selected simply did not try as hard as the women who believed they were selected on the basis of merit.

Blaming the Victim

It is not always easy for people who have never experienced prejudice to understand fully what it is like to be a target of prejudice. For relatively secure members of the dominant majority, empathy does not come easily. They may sympathize and wish that it weren't so, but frequently a hint of self-righteousness may nevertheless creep into their attitudes, producing a tendency to lay the blame on the victim. This may take the form of the "well-deserved reputation." It goes something like this: "If the Jews have been victimized throughout their history, they must have been doing *something* wrong" or "If that woman got raped, she *must* have been doing something provocative" or "If those people [African Americans, Latinos, Native Americans, homosexuals] don't *want* to get into trouble, why don't they just . . ." (stay out of the headlines, keep their mouths shut, don't go where they're not wanted, or whatever). Such a suggestion constitutes a demand that the outgroup conform to demands more stringent than those set for the majority.

Ironically, this tendency to blame victims for their victimization, attributing their predicaments to their own personalities and disabilities, is often motivated by a desire to see the world as a just place. As Melvin Lerner and his colleagues have shown,[31] people tend to assign personal responsibility for any inequitable outcome that is otherwise difficult to explain. For example, if two people work equally hard on the same task and, by a flip of a coin, one receives a sizable reward and the other receives nothing, most observers will rate the unlucky person as having worked less hard. Similarly, negative attitudes toward the poor—including blaming them for their own plight—are more prevalent among individuals who believe most strongly that the world is a just place.[32] Apparently, we find it frightening to think about living in a world where people, through no fault of their own, can be deprived of what they deserve or need, be it equal pay for equal work or the basic necessities of life. By the same token, if 6 million Jews are exterminated for no apparent reason, it is somehow comforting to believe they might have done something to warrant such treatment.*

Further understanding of the phenomenon of **blaming the victim** comes from Baruch Fischhoff's work on the *hindsight bias*,[33] a phenomenon we discussed in Chapters 1 and 4. As you may recall, Fischoff's experiments reveal that most of us are terrific Monday-morning quarterbacks: After we know the outcome of an event, the complex circumstances surrounding its occurrence suddenly seem crystal clear; it seems as if we knew it all along, and if asked to predict the outcome, we could have done so without difficulty. But this is an illusion.

In an interesting set of experiments, Ronnie Janoff-Bulman and her co-workers demonstrated the power of the hindsight bias in increasing subjects' beliefs that rape victims were responsible for their own victimization.[34] Participants in this experiment read accounts of a date between a man and a woman who had met earlier in a college class. The accounts were identical except for the concluding sentence, which for half of the participants read, "The next thing I knew, he raped me," but for the other half read, "The next thing I knew, he took me home." After being advised to disregard their knowledge of the actual outcome of the date, participants were then asked to predict the likelihood of several possible outcomes, including the one they had read. Even though the events leading up to the outcome were exactly the same in both versions of the story, participants who read the rape outcome were more likely to predict that the rape would occur than were those who read the "take home" outcome. What's more, participants exposed to the rape scenario tended to blame the woman's behavior—such as letting the man kiss her—for the negative outcome of the date. The implications of these findings are unsettling. To understand and empathize with a victim's plight, we must be able to reconstruct events leading up to the victimization from the victim's point of view. But, as we have seen, it is all too easy to forget that—unlike us—victims did not have the benefit of hindsight to guide their behavior.

Prejudice and Science

Scientists are trained to be objective and fair-minded. But even they can be influenced by the prevailing atmosphere. Louis Agassiz, one of the great U.S. biologists of the 19th century, argued that God had created blacks and

---

*The astute reader may have noticed that this is a milder form of our tendency to derogate a person we have victimized. In Chapters 5 and 6, we saw that, when one person hurts another, the aggressor tends to derogate the target, turn the victim into a nonperson, and hurt that other person again. Now we see that, if one person notices that another person has gotten the short end of the stick, he or she somehow feels the victim must have done something to deserve it.

whites as separate species.[35] In a similar vein, in 1925, Karl Pearson, a distinguished British scientist and mathematician, concluded his study of ethnic differences by stating: "Taken on the average and regarding both sexes, this alien Jewish population is somewhat inferior physically and mentally to the native [British] population."[36] On the basis of his findings, Pearson argued against allowing the immigration of Eastern European Jews into Great Britain. Most contemporary scientists would demand more valid arguments than those put forward by Agassiz and Pearson. For example, some two or three decades ago, most psychologists were sophisticated enough to scrutinize IQ tests as possibly biased instruments that unintentionally discriminated in favor of white, middle-class suburbanites by stating examples in terms and phrases more familiar to children reared in the suburbs than to children reared in the ghetto or on the farm. Thus, before we were willing to conclude that it was stupidity that caused a black person, a Latino, or the resident of a rural community to do poorly on an IQ test, we demanded to know whether or not the IQ test was culture-free.

But such sophistication does not guarantee immunity. The traps that well-intentioned people can fall into in a prejudiced society can be very subtle. Let me offer a personal example involving sexism. In the first edition of this book, while discussing individual differences in persuasibility, I made the point that women seem to be more persuasible than men. This statement was based on an experiment conducted in the late 1950s by Irving Janis and Peter Field.[37] A close inspection of this experiment, however, suggests that it was weighted unintentionally against women in much the same way IQ tests were weighted against rural and ghetto residents. The topics of the persuasive arguments included civil defense, cancer research, von Hindenberg, and so on—topics the culture of the 1950s had trained men and boys to take a greater interest in than women and girls. Thus, the results may simply indicate that people are more persuasible on topics they don't care about or don't know about. Indeed, these speculations were confirmed by a subsequent series of experiments by Frank Sistrunk and John McDavid.[38] In their studies, they used a variety of topics, some of typically greater interest to men and others applying more to the traditional interests and expertise of women. Their results were clear: While women were more persuasible on the masculine-oriented topics, men were more persuasible on the topics that traditionally have appealed to women. Of course, the mere fact that women and men were raised not to be interested in different topics is itself an unfortunate consequence of sex discrimination.

In 1970, when I was writing the first edition of this book, I was unaware of the possible weakness in the experiment by Janis and Field until it was called to my attention (gently but firmly) by one of my former students. The lesson to be gained from this example is clear: When we are reared in a prejudiced society, we often accept those prejudices uncritically. It is easy to believe women are gullible because that is the stereotype held by the society. Thus, we tend not to look at supporting scientific data critically, and without realizing it, we use the data as scientific support for our own prejudice.

Some Subtle Effects of Prejudice

There is no doubt about it. Our society is a lot less prejudiced against women and minorities than it was some forty or fifty years ago. To mention just one indicator of this trend, in 1963 almost 80 percent of our white citizens said that they would move out of their own neighborhood if African Americans began moving in. But by 1997, that figure had declined to about 20 percent. That's progress, all right. At the same time, it cannot be denied that we live in a society with racist and sexist undercurrents. This can have subtle but important effects on the behavior of the dominant majority as well as on the behavior of women and minority-group members. Much of this behavior occurs without awareness. In an important set of experiments, Carl Word and his associates[39] first trained white Princeton students to interview applicants for a job. Their observations revealed huge differences in the way interviewers interacted with black and white applicants: When the applicant was black, the interviewer unwittingly sat slightly farther away, made more speech errors, and terminated the interview 25 percent sooner than when the applicant was white. Do you suppose this had an effect on the performance of the job applicants? Let's take a look. In a second experiment, Word and his colleagues trained their interviewers to treat white students in the same manner that the interviewers had treated either the white applicants or the black applicants in the previous experiment. The experimenters videotaped the students being interviewed. Independent judges rated those who had been treated like the black applicants as being more nervous and less effective than those treated like the white applicants. The results of this experiment lead us to suspect strongly that when women or minority-group members are being interviewed by a white Anglo-Saxon male, their performance may suffer, not because there is anything wrong with them but because, without necessarily intending it, the interviewer is likely to behave in a way that makes them uncomfortable.

Even if we never find ourselves in the position of the interviewers in the study above, we interact with people every day—men, women, young people, old people, blacks, whites, Asians, Latinos, homosexuals, and so on. And our preconceptions about what they're like often influence our behaviors in such a way as to elicit from them the very characteristics and behaviors we expected in the first place. I have referred to the phenomenon elsewhere as the self-fulfilling prophecy. For example, imagine that you and I had never met, but a mutual acquaintance had warned me that you are a cold, aloof, reserved person. When we finally meet, I would likely keep my distance and not try very hard to engage you in a lively conversation. Suppose that, in reality, you are generally warm and outgoing. My behavior would not afford you the opportunity to show me what a warm, outgoing person you really are. In response to my behavior, you would probably keep your distance from me, and my expectation that you're less than a warm, friendly person would have been confirmed.

This is but one of many situations in which "belief creates reality."[40] When we hold erroneous beliefs or stereotypes about other people, our responses to them often cause them to behave in ways that validate these erroneous beliefs. As sociologist Robert Merton wrote, this self-fulfilling prophecy generates and perpetuates a "reign of error."[41] If people hold stereotypes of women as passive and dependent, or of blacks as lazy and stupid, they may treat them as such and inadvertently create the very behaviors or characteristics associated with these stereotypes. "See," they say to themselves, "I was right all along about those people."

Of course, not all of us hold rigid stereotypes about members of other groups. We often embrace social beliefs only tentatively and work to determine whether or not they are accurate. Frequently we use social interactions to test our hypotheses about what other people are like. But there are pitfalls inherent in our hypothesis-testing strategies. That is, the strategies we use to test our hypotheses about other people can produce confirming evidence, even when the hypotheses themselves are incorrect. Recall (from Chapter 4) the experiments by Mark Snyder and William Swann. In one of those experiments, when individuals were asked to test the hypothesis that a person might fit the profile of an extrovert, they chose "extroverted" questions (e.g., "What would you do if you wanted to liven things up at a party?"). When they were asked to test the hypothesis that the person might fit the profile of an introvert, they chose "introverted" questions (e.g., "What factors make it hard for you to really open up to people?"). As you know, Snyder and Swann[42] found that the nature of the question helps determine the response. That is, people who were neither particularly extroverted nor introverted will look extroverted when they answer the first type of question and will look introverted when they answer the second type of question.

Taken together, results of the above studies make it easy to understand why stereotypes are resistant to change. When we hold beliefs about others, the self-fulfilling prophecy ensures that we create a social reality in line with our expectations. And even when we're open-minded enough to test the accuracy of our beliefs, we often unknowingly use "testing" strategies that confirm those beliefs—even when the beliefs are erroneous.

Despite their best efforts to be open-minded, many otherwise decent people are still capable of subtle acts of prejudice. Indeed, many investigators, like Thomas Pettigrew and his colleagues[43] believe that indirect—and perhaps more insidious—forms of prejudice have largely replaced the blatant kinds of racial bigotry expressed by many white Americans in the past. Today, most people probably think of themselves as unprejudiced, even though they may continue to discriminate against minority-group members in less obvious ways.

The kind of subtle racism I'm describing is exactly what David Frey and Samuel Gaertner discovered when they looked at the helping behavior of whites toward a black individual. In their study,[44] they found that white subjects were just as willing to help a black student as a white student, but only when the person needing help had demonstrated sufficient effort. When white students were led to believe that the student had not worked hard enough at the task, they were more likely to refuse a black student's request for help than a white student's. These findings suggest that subtle racism tends to emerge when it can be easily rationalized: It would be hard to justify refusing to help a minority person whose need for help stemmed from circumstances beyond his or her control—without feeling and looking like a bigot. But when withholding help seems more reasonable—such as when the person asking for help is "lazy"—people can continue to act in prejudiced ways while protecting an image of themselves as unprejudiced.

We can also find subtle examples of prejudice in overt behavior. For example, Ian Ayers and his colleagues[45] visited 90 automobile dealerships in the Chicago area and, using a carefully rehearsed, uniform strategy to negotiate the lowest possible price on a car (one that cost the dealer approximately $11,000), found that white males were given a final price that averaged $11,362; white females, $11,504; African-American males, $11,783; and African-American females, $12,237. Thus, all other things being equal, when it comes to buying a car, being African American or female puts a person at a disadvantage.

If you were applying for a job, how would you be treated by your potential employers if they had prior information that you were a homosexual? Would they refuse to hire you? Would they treat you with less warmth than they treated heterosexuals? The answer, in 2002, is no and yes. In a field experiment, Michelle Hebl and her colleagues[46] trained sixteen college students (eight males and eight females), to apply for jobs at local stores. In some of their interviews, they indicated that they were homosexual; in others they did not. In order to standardize the interactions, the applicants were all dressed similarly in jeans and pullover jackets and behaved identically whether they were in the "homosexual" or the "heterosexual" role.

The investigators found no evidence of blatant discrimination against those who indicated that they were homosexuals. For example, the "homosexual" students were allowed to fill out job applications, were allowed to use the employer's private bathroom, and received callbacks with the same frequency as when they were "heterosexual." On the other hand, there were strong indications of more subtle discrimination against those portrayed as homosexuals. The interviewers were less verbally positive, spent less time interviewing them, used fewer words while chatting with them, and made less eye contact with them. In other words, it was clear from their behavior that the potential employers were either uncomfortable or more standoffish with people they believed to be homosexual. The astute reader can readily see that the treatment of homosexuals was very similar to the manner in which African Americans were treated by interviewers in the experiments by Carl Word and his colleagues that we discussed previously.

Subtle Sexism and Gender-Role Socialization Subtle forms of prejudice are also directed toward women. As we mentioned earlier, not all prejudice consists of feelings of antipathy toward the target group. Because we live in a patriarchal society, many men have feelings of ambivalence toward women. Peter Glick and Susan Fiske[47] have shown that this ambivalence can take one of two forms: **hostile sexism** or **benevolent sexism**. Hostile sexists hold stereotypic views of women that suggest that women are inferior to men (e.g., that they are less intelligent, less competent, and so on). Benevolent sexists hold stereotypically positive views of women. Indeed, their views are actually chivalrous in nature. As we suggested earlier, harboring stereotypically positive feelings about a group (as is true of benevolent sexists) can be damaging to the target because it is limiting. But benevolent sexism goes a bit further. According to Glick and Fiske, underneath it all, benevolent sexists (like hostile sexists) assume that women are the weaker sex. Benevolent sexists tend to idealize women romantically, may admire them as wonderful cooks and mothers and want to protect them when they do not need protection. Thus, in the final analysis, both hostile sexism and benevolent sexism—for different reasons—serve to justify relegating women to traditional stereotyped roles in society.

Daryl and Sandra Bem[48] suggest that sexism is an example of a nonconscious ideology—that is, a set of beliefs many people accept implicitly because they cannot conceive of alternative conceptions of the world. In this culture, for example, most people over 50 have been socialized in such a way that it becomes difficult for them to imagine a woman going out to work as a truck driver or a physician while her husband stays home taking care of the kids, mending socks, and cleaning house. If they were to hear of such a situation, they would be prone to leap to the conclusion that something was wrong with that couple. Why? Because, until recently, such an arrangement was not held to be a real option in our society. Much as a fish is unaware that its environment is wet, most people who hold this ideology don't even see it as an ideology because it is so prevalent in their direct experience.

Recall the example in Chapter 1 in which little Mary received a Suzie Homemaker set ("complete with her own little oven") for her 9th birthday. If Mary was born in the 1960s, by the time she reached age 9, she would have been conditioned to know that her place was in the kitchen. This conditioning was so thorough that her father was convinced that "housewifery" was completely genetic in origin. This is no mere fantasy. Until recently, the first picture books very young children read tended to transmit these role stereotypes.[49] Indeed, in the middle of the last century, studies by Ruth Hartley[50] indicated that, by age 5, children had already developed clearly defined notions of what constitutes appropriate behavior for women and men. This nonconscious ideology had important consequences for society. For example, Jean Lipman-Blumen[51] reports that the vast majority of women who, in early childhood, acquired a traditional view of their gender role (that is, "a woman's place is in the home") opted not to seek advanced education; on the other hand, those women who acquired a more egalitarian view of gender roles showed a much stronger tendency to aspire to advanced education.

Things are changing. Current trends in the direction of raising women's consciousness are proving to be beneficial to women. Extrapolating from Lipman-Blumen's findings, as traditional gender-role stereotypes continue to crumble, one would expect to see an increase in the number of women who seek advanced education. In fact, this has already begun to happen: In 1980, for the first time in our history, women outnumbered men on our nation's college campuses—a trend that has continued into the 21st century. Looking at professional training, although at this writing men still outnumber women in traditionally male domains like engineering, in more gender-neutral fields like psychology, the majority of graduate students are women[52] and, in 2002 more than half of the students admitted to medical schools were women. The elevation of women's consciousness also is proving beneficial to men. As women widen their interests and enter new occupations, the role prescriptions for men are becoming less restrictive as well.

Let us broaden this example. In recent years, our society has become increasingly aware of the discrimination and stereotyping that occur as a result of differential gender roles. The notion of gender roles, or roles appropriate to one's biological sexual identity, is useful in understanding the pressures society places on both men and women. Traditionally, males have been expected to be the breadwinners, the initiators, and the aggressors, all the while hiding their softer emotions and their vulnerabilities. Traditionally, femininity has consistently been correlated with high anxiety, low self-esteem, and low social acceptance.[53] As mentioned previously, women are seen as warmer, more sensitive, and more expressive but less competent and decisive.[54] The female role has been centered on the home, children, and marriage, with limited access to higher status or more differentiated jobs.

This gender-role stereotyping has serious consequences. In an interesting experiment, Natalie Porter and Florence Geis[55] showed that, compared to their male counterparts, even female graduate students were not given much credit for intellectual leadership. College students were shown a picture of either a group of men or a group of women sitting around a table. The picture was described as a group of graduate students working on a research project. They were asked to guess which member contributed most to the group. Their strong tendency was to choose the person sitting at the head of the table. In another condition, college students were shown a picture of a mixed-gender group (two men and three women) sitting around a table. When a man was at the head of the table, the subjects overwhelmingly named him as the greatest contributor. When a woman was at the head of the table, she was hardly chosen at all. Indeed, each of the men in the picture received more "votes" than all three of the women combined. The results of this experiment provide an excellent example of what is meant by a nonconscious ideology inasmuch as the results were similar for male and female subjects; moreover, the women were underchosen by feminists as well as nonfeminists.

There is some evidence that women are being accepted more readily as leaders than they were in the past. For example, in a Gallup poll conducted in 1953, 57 percent of the women and 75 percent of the men preferred a man as a boss. But in 2000, the biases had virtually disappeared: Only 50 percent of the women and 45 percent of the men preferred a man as a boss. This does not mean that all is a bed of roses for women in leadership roles, however. When women become leaders they frequently find themselves in a double bind. According to Alice Eagly and Steven Karau's[56] analysis of the existing research, here is how it works: If female leaders behave in accordance with the usual societal norms (more caring, more sensitive, more communal than men), people perceive them as having less leadership ability. This is because most people expect successful leaders to be more forceful, decisive, and assertive than caring, sensitive, and communal. At the same time, when female leaders behave more forcefully, the people they work with evaluate them more negatively than men—precisely because these behaviors are contrary to how people believe that women are "supposed" to behave.

This research suggests that, if attitudes are going to change, it is important for both men and women to escape from the box of gender stereotyping—to act in ways that utilize a wide range of behaviors, depending on what the situation calls for. To illustrate, when asking for a pay raise, a degree of assertiveness is an adaptive, desirable action—for men and women alike. In this situation, behaving in a nondecisive or overly sensitive manner probably will not get you your raise. However, when two people are attempting to reconcile after an argument, caring, sensitivity, and other communal activites are highly effective—for both men and women. In this situation, assertiveness will serve only to increase the tension. The good news is that there is reason to believe that popular conceptions of appropriate behavior for men and women are slowly becoming more flexible. For example, Linda Jackson and Thomas Cash[57] found that men and women who were able to break out of the box of gender-stereotypical behavior were actually perceived as more likable and better adjusted than those who acted only in ways consistent with traditional gender roles.

One of the important lessons of this research involves the realization that all of us—men, women, boys, girls, blacks, Latinos, Asians, whites, rich, poor, homosexuals, heterosexuals—are the victims of confining stereotyped roles. It would be naive to miss the obvious fact that some roles are more restricting and debilitating than others. However, it would also be foolish to fail to realize that one group's effort to free itself from the chains of prejudice indirectly benefits all of us. As we learn to accept another person's out-of-role behavior, our own out-of-role behavior will also become increasingly accepted—and we will become freer to fulfill our potential as human beings.

Prejudice and the Media

The media play an important institutional role in sustaining prejudice. Not too long ago, newspapers tended to identify the race of a nonwhite criminal or suspect but never bothered to mention the wrongdoer's race if he or she happened to be white. This undoubtedly contributed to a distorted picture of the amount of crime committed by nonwhites. And until the door was opened wide by Bill Cosby, Michael Jordan, and Tiger Woods, it was rare to see a black face on television in a nonstereotypic role or in a commercial. Several years ago, when African Americans were limited to roles like the characters in *Amos 'n Andy* or the song-and-dance man on a variety show, the stereotype that blacks are stupid, shiftless, lazy, and have a natural sense of rhythm was reinforced.

During the past 30 years, this situation has changed—but how much? Given the tremendous popularity enjoyed by the groundbreaking *Bill Cosby Show* in the 1980s and the ubiquitous, graceful presence of such cultural icons as Oprah Winfrey, Tiger Woods, and Michael Jordan, it is tempting to assume that the changes have been dramatic. But although African Americans *have* appeared with greater frequency in the media in recent years (endorsing products or hosting talk shows), where drama is concerned, they tend to be concentrated in virtually all-black situation comedies or are featured as token characters in otherwise all-white shows. Let's look at prime-time dramas— the bellwether of American television fare. As I mentioned in Chapter 3, George Gerbner,[58] a distinguished scholar, conducts periodic, exhaustive surveys of the media. According to Gerbner's findings, during the past 20 years, the percentage of African-Americans appearing in prime-time dramas has fluctuated between 6 percent and 16 percent, with no clear upward trend during that period.

The situation is even more extreme in other forms of communication and entertainment. Let's look at something simple and common—like the humorous cartoon. Several years ago, one of my students, Ruth Thibodeau,[59] performed a thorough analysis of all of the cartoons appearing in *The New Yorker* magazine between 1946 and 1987. She found that the appearance of African-American characters was extremely rare. Moreover, in the early years of her study (the 1940s and 1950s), every time an African American appeared in a cartoon, he or she was presented in a highly stereotypical role. Accordingly, the frequency of African American characters actually decreased over the years as it became less acceptable to depict racial minorities in a stereotypical manner. Thibodeau was startled to find that, in the entire 42-year period, only a single African American appeared as a central character in a cartoon in which race was completely irrelevant. That's once in 35,874 cartoons! Thibodeau concluded that, in cartoons, a black person is simply not depicted as a representative of an ordinary citizen.

Going back to prime-time TV, the overall picture for other recognizable minorities is even bleaker. Gerbner found that, in the 1990s, slightly more than 1 percent of the characters in prime-time dramas were Latino and less than 1 percent were either Asian or Native American. The presence of gays and lesbians is extremely rare—and, when they do appear, it is most frequently in stereotypic roles. This is not inconsequential. For most of us, television provides an important source of information about the world. Accordingly, the infrequent and unrealistic portrayal of racial or sexual minorities is misleading and almost certainly harmful because it promotes the illusion that these are inconsequential members of our society—people who don't experience real adventures, ordinary problems, or human emotions.* Moreover, the dearth of positive role models in the media undoubtedly fosters feelings of inferiority and estrangement among minority-group members—especially children.

Similar problems have affected the portrayal of women. For many years, when the media did show women in prime-time TV dramas, advertisements, or children's books, they were almost never portrayed as authority figures, intellectuals, or adventurous people. Instead, they were typically viewed as attractive but simpleminded "girls" who worried excessively about which laundry detergent to use and who depended on men for guidance on important issues. In the 1990s, with the advent of such powerful, competent characters as Murphy Brown and the televising of sports events like women's basketball, this trend began to shift. However, although this change is encouraging, there is still a drastic imbalance. According to George Gerbner's analysis, in prime-time dramas, male characters outnumber women by almost two to one, and women are portrayed as victims of violent crime far more frequently than men. Similarly, newspaper comic strips, which are widely read by children, tend to perpetuate gender stereotypes. An analysis of 14 widely syndicated comic strips—such as *Peanuts, Spiderman,* and *The Wizard of Id*—found that women were represented as main characters only 15 percent of the time. In addition, only 4 percent of female characters were shown in working roles, even though roughly 69 percent of women in the United States are actually employed outside of the home.[60]

What are the implications of widespread stereotyping of women in the media? On a subtle level, we tend to believe or accept things we see with great frequency—unless there are powerful reasons against doing so. Moreover, it is very difficult for us to account for what is not represented. Thus, if we hardly ever see women in powerful roles, it is easy to conclude that they are incapable of using power effectively or that they prefer the laundry room to the boardroom.

Let's take this a step further. When internalized, such stereotypes may have debilitating effects on women's perceptions of their own life possibili-

*A noteworthy exception to this general trend involved the "coming out" of Ellen DeGeneres on television in 1997, in which the actress (as well as the character she portrayed) revealed herself as a lesbian. Interestingly enough, this was one of the most widely viewed episodes in TV sit-com history—and, although a number of conservative groups threatened boycotts, the revelation was generally accepted by the American public.

ties. Florence Geis and her colleagues suggest that traditional portrayals of women in television commercials provide implicit scripts for women's behavior that may inhibit their achievement aspirations. In one study,[61] these researchers showed some viewers stereotyped commercials with women portrayed as sex objects or subservient homemakers catering to the needs of men. Other viewers saw commercials in which the roles were reversed: with, for example, a husband proudly serving a delicious meal to his wife who has just come home after a hard day's work. When asked to imagine their lives "ten years from now," female viewers who saw commercials depicting women as subservient homemakers and sex objects were more likely to deemphasize careers and other achievement themes. Viewing stereotyped commercials did not simply depress women's aspirations temporarily during the experiment. On the contrary, women in the control condition (who saw no commercials) expressed the same low level of achievement aspiration as women exposed to the traditional commercials. Women who saw role-reversed commercials, however, aspired to the same high level of achievement as men. Interestingly enough, the aspirations of male viewers were unaffected by either traditional or nontraditional commercials. These findings suggest that sex-stereotyped commercials reflect a cultural image of women as second-class citizens and that a steady diet of such commercials serves to restrict women's conceptions of goals available to them. Moreover, repeated exposure to nonsexist alternatives would presumably enhance women's expectations for achievement and career success.

Causes of Prejudice

What makes people prejudiced? Is prejudice natural or unnatural? Evolutionary psychologists have suggested that animals have a strong tendency to act more favorably toward genetically similar others and to express fear and loathing toward genetically dissimilar organisms, even if the latter have never done them any harm.[62] Thus, prejudice may be built in—an essential part of our biological survival mechanism inducing us to favor our own family, tribe, or race and to express hostility toward outsiders. On the other hand, it is conceivable that, as humans, we are different from the lower animals; perhaps our natural inclination is to be friendly, open, and cooperative. If this is the case, then prejudice does not come naturally. Rather, the culture (parents, the community, the media) may, intentionally or unintentionally, instruct us to assign negative qualities and attributes to people who are different from us.

Although we human beings may have inherited biological tendencies that predispose us toward prejudicial behavior, no one knows for sure whether or not prejudice is a vital and necessary part of our biological makeup. In any case, most social psychologists would agree that the specifics of prejudice must be learned—either through imitating the attitudes and behavior of others or through the ways in which we construct our own psychological reality.

In this chapter, we will look at five basic causes of prejudice: (1) economic and political competition or conflict, (2) displaced aggression, (3) maintenance of status or self-image, (4) dispositional prejudice, and (5) conformity to existing social norms. These five causes are not mutually exclusive—indeed, they may all operate at once—but it would be helpful to determine how important each one is because any action we are apt to recommend in an attempt to reduce prejudice will depend on what we believe to be the major cause of prejudice. Thus, for example, if I believe bigotry is dispositional and, as such, is deeply ingrained in the human personality, I might throw my hands up in despair and conclude that, in the absence of deep psychotherapy, the majority of prejudiced people will always be prejudiced. This would lead me to scoff at attempts to reduce prejudice by reducing competitiveness or by attempting to counteract the pressures of conformity. Let us take a close look at each of the five causes.

Economic and Political Competition

Prejudice can be considered to be the result of economic and political forces. According to this view, given that resources are limited, the dominant group might attempt to exploit or derogate a minority group in order to gain some material advantage. Prejudiced attitudes tend to increase when times are tense and there is conflict over mutually exclusive goals. This is true whether the goals are economic, political, or ideological. Thus, prejudice has existed between Anglo and Mexican-American migrant workers as a function of a limited number of jobs, between Arabs and Israelis over disputed territory, and between northerners and southerners over the abolition of slavery. The economic advantages of discrimination are all too clear when one looks at the success certain craft unions have had, over the years, in denying membership to women and members of ethnic minorities, thus keeping them out of the relatively high-paying occupations the unions control. For example, the period between the mid-1950s and the mid-1960s was one of great political and legal advancement for the civil rights movement. Yet in 1966 only 2.7 percent of union-controlled apprenticeships were held by black workers—an increase of only 1 percent over the preceding 10 years. Moreover, in the mid-1960s, the U.S. Department of Labor surveyed four major cities in search of minority-group members serving as apprentices among union plumbers, steamfitters, sheetmetal workers, stonemasons, lathers, painters, glaziers, and operating engineers. In the four cities, they failed to find a single black person thus employed. Clearly, prejudice pays off for some people.[63] While enlightened legislation and social action over the past three decades have produced significant changes in these statistics, the situation remains far from equitable for minority groups.

Discrimination, prejudice, and negative stereotyping increase sharply as competition for scarce jobs increases. In one of his classic early studies of prejudice in a small industrial town, John Dollard documented the fact that, although there was initially no discernible prejudice against Germans in the town, it came about as jobs became scarce:

Local whites largely drawn from the surrounding farms manifested considerable direct aggression toward the newcomers. Scornful and derogatory opinions were expressed about these Germans, and the native whites had a satisfying sense of superiority toward them. . . . The chief element in the permission to be aggressive against the Germans was rivalry for jobs and status in the local wooden ware plants. The native whites felt definitely crowded for their jobs by the entering German groups and in case of bad times had a chance to blame the Germans who by their presence provided more competitors for the scarcer jobs. There seemed to be no traditional pattern of prejudice against Germans unless the skeletal suspicion against all outgroupers (always present) can be invoked in its place.[64]

Similarly, the prejudice, violence, and negative stereotyping directed against Chinese immigrants in the United States fluctuated wildly throughout the 19th century—spurred largely by changes in economic competition. For example, when the Chinese were attempting to mine gold in California, they were described as "depraved and vicious . . . gross gluttons . . . bloodthirsty and inhuman."[65] However, just a decade later, when they were willing to accept dangerous and arduous work building the transcontinental railroad—work that white Americans were unwilling to undertake—they were generally regarded as sober, industrious, and law-abiding. Indeed, Charles Crocker, one of the western railroad tycoons, wrote: "They are equal to the best white men. . . . They are very trusty, very intelligent and they live up to their contracts."[66] After the completion of the railroad, however, jobs became more scarce; moreover, when the Civil War ended, there was an influx of former soldiers into an already tight job market. This was immediately followed by a dramatic increase in negative attitudes toward the Chinese: The stereotype changed to "criminal," "conniving," "crafty," and "stupid."

These data suggest that competition and conflict breed prejudice. Moreover, this phenomenon transcends mere historical significance; it seems to have enduring psychological effects as well. In a survey conducted in the 1970s, most antiblack prejudice was found in groups that were just one rung above the blacks socioeconomically. And, as we might expect, this tendency was most pronounced in situations in which whites and blacks were in close competition for jobs.[67] At the same time, there is some ambiguity in interpreting the data because, in some instances, the variable of competition is intertwined with such variables as educational level and family background.

In order to determine whether competition itself causes prejudice, an experiment is needed. But how can we proceed? Well, if conflict and competition lead to prejudice, it should be possible to produce prejudice in the laboratory. This can be done by the simple device of (1) randomly assigning people of differing backgrounds to one of two groups, (2) making those two groups distinguishable in some arbitrary way, (3) putting those groups into a situation in which they are in competition with each other, and (4) looking for evidence of prejudice. Such an experiment was conducted by Muzafer Sherif and his colleagues[68] in the natural environment of a Boy Scout camp. The subjects were normal, well-adjusted, 12-year-old boys who were randomly assigned to one of two groups, the Eagles and the Rattlers. Within each group, the youngsters were taught to cooperate. This was done largely by arranging activities that made the members of each group highly interdependent. For example, within each group, individuals cooperated in building a diving board for the swimming facility, preparing group meals, building a rope bridge, and so on.

After a strong feeling of cohesiveness developed within each group, the stage was set for conflict. The researchers arranged this by setting up a series of competitive activities in which the two groups were pitted against each other in such games as football, baseball, and tug-of-war. In order to increase the tension, prizes were awarded to the winning team. This resulted in some hostility and ill will during the games. In addition, the investigators devised rather diabolical devices for putting the groups into situations specifically designed to promote conflict. In one such situation, a camp party was arranged. The investigators set it up so that the Eagles were allowed to arrive a good deal earlier than the Rattlers. In addition, the refreshments consisted of two vastly different kinds of food: About half of the food was fresh, appealing, and appetizing; the other half was squashed, ugly, and unappetizing. Perhaps because of the general competitiveness that already existed, the early arrivers confiscated most of the appealing refreshments, leaving only the less interesting, less appetizing, squashed, and damaged food for their adversaries. When the Rattlers finally arrived and saw how they had been taken advantage of, they were understandably annoyed—so annoyed that they began to call the exploitive group rather uncomplimentary names. Because the Eagles believed they deserved what they got (first come, first served), they resented this treatment and responded in kind. Name calling escalated into food throwing, and within a very short time a full-scale riot was in progress.

Following this incident, competitive games were eliminated and a great deal of social contact was initiated. Once hostility had been aroused, however, simply eliminating the competition did not eliminate the hostility. Indeed, hostility continued to escalate, even when the two groups were engaged in such benign activities as sitting around watching movies. Eventually, the investigators succeeded in reducing the hostility. Exactly how this was accomplished will be discussed later in this chapter.

Displaced Aggression: The Scapegoat Theory In the preceding chapter, I made the point that aggression is caused, in part, by frustration and such other unpleasant or aversive conditions as pain or boredom. In that chapter, we saw that there is a strong tendency for a frustrated individual to lash out at the cause of his or her frustration. Frequently, however, the cause of a person's frustration is either too big or too vague for direct retaliation. For example, if a 6-year-old boy is humiliated by his teacher, how can he fight back? The teacher has too much power. But this frustration may increase the probability of his aggressing against a less powerful bystander—even if the bystander had nothing to do with his pain. By the same token, if there is mass unemployment, who is the frustrated, unemployed worker going to strike out against—the economic system? The system is much too big and much too vague. It would be more convenient if the unemployed worker could find something or someone less vague and more concrete to blame. The president? He's concrete, all right, but also much too powerful to strike at with impunity.

The ancient Hebrews had a custom that is noteworthy in this context. During the days of atonement, a priest placed his hands on the head of a goat while reciting the sins of the people. This symbolically transferred the sin and evil from the people to the goat. The goat was then allowed to escape into the wilderness, thus cleansing the community of sin. The animal was called a *scapegoat*. In modern times the term **scapegoating** has been used to describe the process of blaming a relatively powerless innocent person for something that is not his or her fault. Unfortunately, the individual is not allowed to escape into the wilderness but is usually subjected to cruelty or even death. Thus, if people are unemployed or if inflation has depleted their savings, they can't very easily beat up on the economic system—but they can find a scapegoat. In Nazi Germany, it was the Jews; in 19th-century California, it was Chinese immigrants; in the rural South, it was black people. Some years ago, Carl Hovland and Robert Sears[69] found that, in the period between 1882 and 1930, they could predict the frequency of lynchings in the South in a given year from a knowledge of the price of cotton during that year. As the price of cotton dropped, the number of lynchings increased. In short, as people experienced an economic depression, they probably experienced a great many frustrations. The frustrations apparently resulted in an increase in lynchings and other crimes of violence.

Otto Klineberg[70] describes a unique scapegoating situation in Japan. The Burakumin are a group of 2 million outcasts scattered throughout Japan. Although there are no inherited racial or physical differences between the Burakumin and other Japanese, they are considered unclean and fit only for certain undesirable occupations. As you might imagine, the Burakumin usually lived in poor, slum areas. Their IQ scores were, on average, some 16 points lower than that of other Japanese. Burakumin children were absent from school more often, and their delinquency rate was three times higher than that of other Japanese children. According to Klineberg, it was considered taboo for a member of the Burakumin to marry outside of his or her group. They are an invisible race—an out-group defined more by social class than by any physical characteristics. They can be identified only by their distinctive speech pattern (which has developed from years of nonassociation with other Japanese) and their identity papers. Although their historical origins are unclear, they probably occupied the lower rungs of the socioeconomic ladder until an economic depression led to their complete expulsion from Japanese society. Now the Japanese consider the Burakumin to be innately inferior, thus justifying further scapegoating and discrimination.

It is difficult to understand how the lynching of blacks or the mistreatment of the Burakumin could be due only to economic competition. There is a great deal of emotion in these actions that suggests the presence of deeper psychological factors in addition to economics. Similarly, the zeal with which the Nazis carried out their attempt to erase all members of the Jewish ethnic group (regardless of economic status) strongly suggests that the phenomenon was not exclusively economic or political, but was (at least in part) psychological.[71] Firmer evidence for the existence of psychological processes comes from a well-controlled experiment by Neal Miller and Richard Bugelski.[72] Individuals were asked to state their feelings about various minority groups. Some of the subjects were then frustrated by being deprived of an opportunity to attend a film and were given a difficult series of tests instead. They were then asked to restate their feelings about the minority groups. These subjects showed some evidence of increased prejudicial responses following the frustrating experience. A control group that did not go through the frustrating experience did not undergo any change in prejudice.

Additional research has helped to pin down the phenomenon even more precisely. In one experiment,[73] white students were instructed to administer a series of electric shocks to another student as part of a learning experiment. The subjects had the prerogative to adjust the intensity of the shocks. In actuality, the learner was an accomplice of the experimenter who (of course) was not really connected to the apparatus. There were four conditions: The accomplice was either black or white; he was trained to be either friendly or insulting to the subject. When he was friendly, the subjects administered slightly less intense shocks to the black student; when he insulted them, they administered far more intense shocks to the black student than to the white student. In another experiment,[74] college students were subjected to a great deal of frustration. Some of these students were highly anti-Semitic; others were not. The subjects were then asked to write stories based on pictures they were shown. For some subjects, the characters in these pictures were assigned Jewish names; for others, they were not. There were two major findings: (1) After being frustrated, anti-Semitic subjects wrote stories that directed more aggression toward the Jewish characters than did subjects who were not anti-Semitic, and (2) there was no difference between the anti-Semitic students and the others when the characters they were writing about were not identified as Jewish. In short, frustration or anger leads to a specific aggression—aggression against an out-group member.

The laboratory experiments help to clarify factors that seem to exist in the real world. The general picture of scapegoating that emerges is that individuals tend to displace aggression onto groups that are disliked, that are visible, and that are relatively powerless. Moreover, the form the aggression takes depends on what is allowed or approved by the in-group in question: In society, lynchings of blacks and pogroms against Jews were not frequent occurrences unless they were deemed appropriate by the dominant culture or subculture.

I used the past tense in the preceding sentence because it is comforting to believe that extreme forms of scapegoating are a thing of the past. But, in the past two decades, events have taken place that have caused many of us a great deal of consternation. For example, when the Soviet Union fell apart, we were momentarily encouraged as all of Eastern Europe gained its freedom. Unfortunately, in much of the region, this new freedom was accompanied by increased feelings of nationalism, which have, in turn, produced additional prejudice and hostility against out-groups. Thus, in the Balkans, for example, intense nationalism led to eruptions of hostility throughout the region—most notably, in Bosnia. In addition, economic hardship and frustrated expectations in Eastern Europe have resulted in anti-Semitism throughout the region. Economic and political frustrations have also led to terrorist attacks against the United States—in part, because of its role as the most visible nation on Earth and, therefore, a most attractive target.

The Maintenance of Self-Image and Status
As we have seen, a powerful determinant of prejudice is embedded in our need to justify our behavior and sense of self. In the previous two chapters, for example, we have seen that, if we have done something cruel to a person or a group of people, most of us will try to derogate that person or group in order to justify our cruelty. If we can convince ourselves that a group is unworthy, subhuman, stupid, or immoral, it helps us to keep from feeling immoral if we enslave members of that group, deprive them of a decent education, or aggress against them. We can then continue to go to church and to feel like good Christians because it isn't a decent fellow human we've hurt. Indeed, if we're skillful enough, we can even convince ourselves that the barbaric slaying of old men, women, and children is a Christian virtue—as the crusaders did when, on the way to the holy land, they butchered European Jews in the name of the Prince of Peace. Again, as we have seen, this form of self-justification serves to intensify subsequent brutality. Although this may preserve the self-image, it leads to increased hostility against the target person or group.

By the same token, whether or not we have inflicted harm upon others, if our status is low on the socioeconomic hierarchy, may need the presence of a downtrodden minority group in order to be able to feel superior to somebody. Several studies indicate that a good predictor of prejudice is whether or not a person's social status is low or declining. For example, Jennifer Crocker and her colleagues[75] found that college women who belonged to low-status sororities expressed more prejudice and disparagement of other sororities than members of higher-status sororities did. Similarly, when researchers investigated the prejudice of whites against blacks[76] or of Gentiles against Jews,[77] they found that those whose social status is low or declining are apt to be more prejudiced than those whose social status is high or rising. Moreover, it has been found that white people who are at or near the bottom in terms of education, income, and occupation not only were the highest in their dislike of blacks but also were most likely to resort to violence in order to prevent the desegregation of schools.[78] Recently, Steven Fein and Stephen Spencer[79] found that even minor setbacks can increase prejudicial responses. In their experiment, anti-Semitic students became still more biased against Jews after receiving a low score on an exam.

The Prejudiced Personality There is some evidence to support the notion of individual differences in a general tendency to hate. In other words, there are people who are predisposed toward being prejudiced, not solely because of immediate external influences, but also because of the kind of people they are. Theodor Adorno and his associates[80] refer to these individuals as authoritarian personalities. Basically, authoritarian personalities have the following characteristics: They tend to be rigid in their beliefs; they tend to possess conventional values; they are intolerant of weakness (in themselves as well as in others); they tend to be highly punitive; they are suspicious; and they are respectful of authority to an unusual degree. The instrument developed to determine authoritarianism (called the *F* scale) measures the extent to which each person agrees or disagrees with such items as these:

> Sex crimes such as rape and attacks on children deserve more than mere imprisonment; such criminals ought to be publicly whipped, or worse.

> Most people don't realize how much our lives are controlled by plots hatched in secret places.

> Obedience and respect for authority are the most important virtues children should learn.

A high degree of agreement with such items indicates authoritarianism. The major finding is that people who are high on authoritarianism do not simply dislike Jews or blacks; rather, they show a consistently high degree of prejudice against *all* minority groups.

Through an intensive clinical interview of people high and low on the *F* scale, Adorno and his colleagues have traced the development of this cluster of attitudes and values to early childhood experiences in families characterized by harsh, threatening parental discipline. Moreover, people high on the *F* scale tend to have parents who use love and its withdrawal as their major way of producing obedience. In general, authoritarian personalities, as children, tend to be both insecure and highly dependent on their parents; they fear their parents and feel unconscious hostility toward them. This combination sets the stage for the emergence of an adult with a high degree of anger, which, because of fear and insecurity, takes the form of displaced aggression against powerless groups, while the individual maintains outward respect for authority.

It is instructive to note that, in a study of authoritarianism in the former Soviet Union, Sam McFarland and his colleagues[81] found that people high on the *F* scale tend to be in favor of overthrowing their newly acquired democracy and restoring the former Communist regime. Ideologically, this is quite different from American authoritarians, who tend to be anti-Communist. The common link, of course, is not a specific ideological belief but rather a kind of conventionalism and respect for authority. In other words, both American and Russian authoritarians are linked by their need to conform to the traditional values of their culture and by a tendency to be suspicious of new ideas and of people who are different from themselves.

Although research on the authoritarian personality has added to our understanding of the possible dynamics of prejudice, it should be noted that the bulk of the data are correlational. That is, we know only that two variables are related; we cannot be certain what causes what. Consider, for example, the correlation between a person's score on the *F* scale and the specific socialization practices he or she was subjected to as a child. Although it is true that adults who are authoritarian and highly prejudiced had parents who tended to be harsh and to use conditional love as a socialization technique, it is not necessarily true that this is what caused them to develop into prejudiced people. It turns out that the parents of these people tend themselves to be highly prejudiced against minority groups. Accordingly, it may be that the development of prejudice in some people is due to conformity through the process of identification, as described in Chapter 2. That is, a child might consciously pick up beliefs about minorities from his or her parents because the child identifies with them. This is quite different from, and much simpler than, the explanation offered by Adorno and his colleagues, which is based on the child's unconscious hostility to and repressed fear of his or her parents.

This is not to imply that, for some people, prejudice is not rooted in unconscious childhood conflicts. Rather, it is to suggest that many people may have learned a wide array of prejudices on Mommy's or Daddy's knee. Moreover, some people may conform to prejudices that are limited and highly specific, depending upon the norms of their subculture. Let's take a closer look at the phenomenon of prejudice as an act of conformity.

Prejudice through Conformity
It is frequently observed that there is more prejudice against blacks in the South than in the North. This prejudice manifested itself in stronger attitudes against racial integration. For example, in 1942, only 4 percent of southerners were in favor of the desegregation of transportation facilities, while 56 percent of northerners were in favor of it.[82] Why? Was it because of economic competition? Probably not; there is more prejudice against blacks in southern communities where economic competition is low than in northern communities where economic competition is

great. Are there relatively more authoritarian personalities in the South than in the North? No. Thomas Pettigrew[83] administered the *F* scale widely in the North and in the South and found the scores for northerners and southerners to be about equal. In addition, although there is more prejudice against blacks in the South, there is less prejudice against Jews in the South than there is in the nation as a whole; the prejudiced personality should be prejudiced against everybody—the southerner isn't.

How then do we account for the animosity toward blacks that exists in the South? It could be due to historical causes: The blacks were slaves, the Civil War was fought over the issue of slavery, and so on. This could have created the climate for greater prejudice. But what sustains this climate? One possible clue comes from the observation of some rather strange patterns of racial segregation in the South. One example, concerning a group of coal miners in a small mining town in West Virginia, should suffice.[84] The black miners and the white miners developed a pattern of living that consisted of complete integration while they were underground and complete segregation while they were above ground. How can we account for this inconsistency? If you truly hate someone, you want to keep away from him; why associate with him below ground and not above ground?

Pettigrew has suggested that the explanation for these phenomena is conformity. In this case, the white miners are simply conforming to the norm that exists in their society (above the ground!). The historical events of the South set the stage for greater prejudice against blacks, but it is conformity that keeps it going. Indeed, Pettigrew believes that, although economic competition, frustration, and personality needs account for some prejudice, the greatest proportion of prejudiced behavior is a function of slavish conformity to social norms.

How can we be certain that conformity is responsible? One way is to determine the relation between a person's prejudice and that person's general pattern of conformity. For example, a study of interracial tension in South Africa[85] showed that those individuals who were most likely to conform to a great variety of social norms also showed a higher degree of prejudice against blacks. In other words, if conformists are more prejudiced, prejudice may be just another thing to conform to. Another way to determine the role of conformity is to see what happens to people's prejudice when they move to a different area of the country. If conformity is a factor in prejudice, we would expect individuals to show dramatic increases in prejudice when they move into areas where the norm is more prejudicial and to show dramatic decreases when they are affected by a less prejudicial norm. And that is what happens. In one study, Jeanne Watson[86] found that individuals who had recently moved to New York City and had come into direct contact with anti-Semitic people became more anti-Semitic themselves. In another study, Pettigrew found that, as southerners entered the army and came into contact with a less discriminatory set of social norms, they became less prejudiced against blacks.

The pressure to conform can be relatively overt, as in the Asch experiment. On the other hand, conformity to a prejudicial norm might simply be due to the unavailability of accurate evidence and a preponderance of misleading information. This can lead people to adopt negative attitudes on the basis of hearsay. Examples of this kind of stereotyping behavior abound in the literature. For example, consider Christopher Marlowe's play *The Jew of Malta* or William Shakespeare's play *The Merchant of Venice*. Both of these works depict the Jew as a conniving, money-hungry, cringing coward. We might be tempted to conclude that Marlowe and Shakespeare had some unfortunate experiences with unsavory Jews, which resulted in these bitter and unflattering portraits—except for one thing: The Jews had been expelled from England some 300 years before these works were written. Thus, it would seem that the only thing with which Marlowe and Shakespeare came into contact was a lingering stereotype. Tragically, their works not only reflected the stereotype but undoubtedly contributed to it as well.

Even casual exposure to bigotry can affect our attitudes and behavior toward a group that is the victim of prejudice. For example, research has demonstrated that merely overhearing someone use a derogatory label—such as a racial or ethnic epithet—toward a given group can increase our likelihood of viewing someone from that group—or someone merely associated with that group—in a negative light. In one experiment,[87] Shari Kirkland and her co-researchers asked subjects to read a transcript of a criminal trial in which a white defendant was represented by a black attorney, whose picture was attached to the trial transcript. While reading the transcript, the subject "overheard" a brief exchange between two experimental confederates, who were posing as subjects. Some subjects heard the first confederate call the black lawyer a "nigger," while other subjects heard the confederate call him a "shyster." In both conditions, the second confederate expressed agreement with the first confederate's derogatory opinion of the black lawyer. With this conformity dynamic in place, the experimenters then asked the subject to evaluate the attorney and the defendant. An analysis of these ratings revealed that subjects who overheard the racial slur rated the black lawyer more negatively than those who overheard a derisive comment unrelated to the lawyer's race. Moreover, the white defendant received particularly harsh verdicts and highly negative evaluations from subjects who heard the racial slur against the black attorney. This latter finding indicates that conformity to the prejudiced norms can have damaging effects that extend beyond the initial target of racism.

Bigoted attitudes can also be fostered intentionally by a bigoted society that institutionally supports these attitudes. For example, a society that supports the notion of segregation through law and custom is supporting the notion that one group is inferior to another. Thus, in the days of apartheid, one investigator[88] interviewed white South Africans in an attempt to find reasons for their negative attitudes toward blacks. He found that the typical white South African was convinced that the great majority of crimes were committed by blacks. This was erroneous. How did such a misconception develop? The individuals reported that they saw many black convicts working in public places; they never saw any white convicts. Didn't this prove blacks were convicted of more crimes than whites? No. In fact, the rules forbade white convicts from working in public places! In short, a society can create prejudiced beliefs by its very institutions. In our own society, forcing blacks to ride in the back of the bus, keeping women out of prestigious clubs, and preventing Jews from staying at exclusive hotels are all part of our recent history—and create the illusion of inferiority or unacceptability.

Stateways Can Change Folkways

In 1954, the U.S. Supreme Court declared that separate but equal schools were, by definition, unequal. In the words of Chief Justice Earl Warren, when black children are separated from white children on the basis of race alone, it "generates a feeling of inferiority as to their status in the community that may affect their hearts and minds in a way unlikely ever to be undone." Without our quite realizing it, this decision launched our nation into one of the most exciting, large-scale social experiments ever conducted.

In the aftermath of this historic decision, many people were opposed to integrating the schools on "humanitarian" grounds. They predicted a holocaust if the races were forced to mingle in schools. They argued that laws cannot force people to get along with each other. This echoed the sentiments of the distinguished sociologist William Graham Sumner, who, years earlier, had stated, "Stateways don't change folkways." What Sumner meant, of course, is that you can't legislate morality or tolerance. Many people urged that desegregation be delayed until attitudes could be changed.

Social psychologists at that time, of course, believed that the way to change behavior is to change attitudes. Thus, if you can get bigoted white adults to become less prejudiced against blacks, then they will not hesitate to allow their children to attend school with blacks. Although they should have known better, many social scientists were relatively confident that they could change bigoted attitudes by launching information campaigns. They took a "sixteen-millimeter" approach to the reduction of prejudice: If prejudiced people believe blacks are shiftless and lazy, then all you have to do is show them a movie depicting that blacks are industrious, decent people. The idea is that you can combat misinformation with information. If Shakespeare believes Jews are conniving bloodsuckers because he has been exposed to misinformation about Jews, expose him to a more accurate range of information about Jews and his prejudice will fade away. If most white South Africans believe blacks commit virtually all the crimes, show them the white convicts and they'll change their beliefs. Unfortunately, it is not quite that simple. Whether prejudice is largely a function of economic conflict, conformity to social norms, or deeply rooted personality needs, it is not easily changed by an information campaign. Over the years, most people become deeply committed to their prejudicial behavior. To develop an open, accepting attitude toward minorities when all of your friends and associates are still prejudiced is no easy task. A mere movie cannot undo a way of thinking and a way of behaving that has persisted over the years.

As the reader of this book has learned, where important issues are involved, information campaigns fail because people are inclined not to sit still and take in information that is dissonant with their beliefs. Paul Lazarsfeld,[89] for example, described a series of radio broadcasts in the early 1940s designed to reduce ethnic prejudice by presenting information about various ethnic groups in a warm, sympathetic manner. One program was devoted to a description of Polish-Americans, another to Italian-Americans, and so forth. Who was listening? The major part of the audience for the program about Polish-Americans consisted of Polish-Americans. And guess who made up most of the audience for the program on Italian-Americans? Right. Moreover, as we have seen, if people are compelled to listen to information uncongenial to their deep-seated attitudes, they will reject it, distort it, or ignore it—in much the same way Mr. X maintained his negative attitude against Jews despite Mr. Y's information campaign and in much the same way the Dartmouth and Princeton students distorted the film of the football game they watched. For most people, prejudice is too deeply rooted in their own belief systems, is too consistent with their day-to-day behavior, and receives too much support and encouragement from the people around them to be reduced by a book, a film, or a radio broadcast.

The Effects of Equal-Status Contact Although changes in attitude might induce changes in behavior, as we have seen, it is often difficult to change attitudes through education. What social psychologists have long known, but have only recently begun to understand, is that changes in behavior can affect changes in attitudes. On the simplest level, it has been argued that, if blacks and whites could be brought into direct contact, prejudiced individuals would come into contact with the reality of their own experience, not simply a stereotype; eventually, this would lead to greater understanding. Of course, the contact must take place in a situation in which blacks and whites have equal status; throughout history many whites have always had a great deal of contact with blacks, but typically in situations in which the blacks played such menial roles as slaves, porters, dishwashers, shoe-shine boys, washroom attendants, and domestics. This kind of contact only serves to increase stereotyping by whites and thus adds fuel to their prejudice against blacks. It also serves to increase the resentment and anger of blacks. Until recently, equal-status contact has been rare, both because of educational and occupational inequities in our society and because of residential segregation. The 1954 Supreme Court decision was the beginning of a gradual change in the frequency of equal-status contact.

Occasionally, even before 1954, isolated instances of equal-status integration had taken place. The effects tended to support the notion that behavior change will produce attitude change. In a pioneering study, Morton Deutsch and Mary Ellen Collins[90] examined the attitudes of whites toward blacks in public housing projects in 1951. Specifically, in one housing project, black and white families were assigned to buildings in a segregated manner; that is, they were assigned to separate buildings in the same project. In another project, the assignment was integrated; black and white families were assigned to the same building. Residents in the integrated project reported a greater positive change in their attitudes toward blacks after moving into the project than did residents of the segregated project. From these findings, it would appear that stateways can change folkways, that you can legislate morality—not directly, of course, but through the medium of equal-status contact. If diverse racial groups can be brought together under conditions of equal status, they stand a chance of getting to know each other better. As Pettigrew[91] has recently found, this can increase understanding and decrease tension, all other things being equal. It should be noted that the Deutsch and Collins study took place in public housing projects rather than in private residential areas. This is a crucial factor that will be discussed in a moment.

The Vicarious Effects of Desegregation

It wasn't until much later that social psychologists began to entertain the notion that desegregation can affect the values of people who do not even have the opportunity to have direct contact with minority groups. This can occur through the mechanism referred to in Chapter 5 as the psychology of inevitability. Specifically, if I know that you and I will inevitably be in close contact, and I don't like you, I will experience dissonance. In order to reduce dissonance, I will try to convince myself that you are not as bad as I had previously thought. I will set about looking for your positive characteristics and will try to ignore, or minimize the importance of, your negative characteristics. Accordingly, the mere fact that I know I must at some point be in close contact with you will force me to change my prejudiced attitudes about you, all other things being equal. As we saw earlier, laboratory experiments have confirmed this prediction: For example, children who believed they must inevitably eat a previously disliked vegetable began to convince themselves that it wasn't as bad as they had previously thought.[92] Similarly, college women who knew they were going to spend several weeks working intimately with a woman who had several positive and negative qualities developed a great fondness for that woman before they even met her; this did not occur when they were not led to anticipate working with her in the future.[93]

Admittedly, it's a far cry from a bowl of vegetables to relations between blacks, Latinos, and whites. Few social psychologists are so naive as to believe that deep-seated racial intolerance can be eliminated if people reduce their dissonance simply by coming to terms with what they believe to be inevitable events. I would suggest that, under ideal conditions, such events can begin to unfreeze prejudiced attitudes and produce a diminution of hostile feelings in most individuals. I will discuss what I mean by "ideal conditions" in a moment; but first, let us put a little more meat on those theoretical bones. How might the process of dissonance reduction take place?

Turn the clock back to the late 1950s. Imagine a 45-year-old white male whose 16-year-old daughter attends a segregated school. Let us assume he has a negative attitude toward blacks, based in part on his belief that blacks are shiftless and lazy and that all black males are oversexed and potential rapists. Suddenly, the edict is handed down by the Justice Department: The following autumn, his fair-haired young daughter must go to an integrated school. State and local officials, while perhaps not liking the idea, clearly convey the fact that nothing can be done to prevent it; it's the law of the land, and it must be obeyed. The father might, of course, refuse to allow his child to obtain an education or he could send her to an expensive private school. But such measures are either terribly drastic or terribly costly. So he decides he must send her to an integrated school. His cognition that his fair-haired young daughter must inevitably attend the same school with blacks is dissonant with his cognition that blacks are shiftless rapists. What does he do? My guess is that he will begin to reexamine his beliefs about blacks. Are they really all that shiftless? Do they really go around raping people? He may take another look—this time, with a strong inclination to look for the good qualities in blacks rather than to concoct and exaggerate bad, unacceptable qualities. I would guess that, by the time September rolls around, his attitude toward blacks would have become unfrozen and would have shifted in a positive direction. If this shift can be bolstered by positive events after desegregation—for example, if his daughter has pleasant and peaceful interactions with her black schoolmates—a major change in the father's attitudes is likely to result. Again, this analysis is admittedly oversimplified. But the basic process holds. And look at the advantages this process has over an information campaign. A mechanism has been triggered that motivated the father to alter his negative stereotype of blacks.

My analysis strongly suggests that a particular kind of public policy would be potentially most beneficial to society—a policy exactly the opposite of what has been generally recommended. As mentioned previously, following the 1954 Supreme Court decision, there was a general feeling that integration must proceed slowly. Most public officials and many social scientists believed that, in order to achieve harmonious racial relations, integration should be delayed until people could be reeducated to become less prejudiced. In short, the general belief in 1954 was that the behavior (integration) must follow a cognitive change. My analysis suggests that the best way to produce eventual interracial harmony would be to start with behavioral change. Moreover, and most important, the sooner the individuals realize integration is inevitable, the sooner their prejudiced attitudes will begin to change. On the other hand, this process can be (and has been) sabotaged by public officials by fostering the belief that integration can be circumvented or delayed. This serves to create the illusion that the event is not inevitable. In such circumstances, there will be no attitude change; the result will be an increase in turmoil and disharmony. Let's go back to our previous example: If the father of the fair-haired daughter is led (by the statements and tactics of a governor, a mayor, a school-board chairman, or a local sheriff) to believe there's a way out of integration, he will feel no need to reexamine his negative beliefs about blacks. The result is apt to be violent opposition to integration.

Consistent with this reasoning is the fact that, as desegregation has spread, favorable attitudes toward desegregation have increased. In 1942, only 30 percent of the whites in this country favored desegregated schools; by 1956, the figure rose to 49 percent; in 1970, to 75 percent. Finally, in 1980, as it became increasingly clear that school desegregation was inevitable, the figure approached 90 percent.[94] The change in the South (taken by itself) is even more dramatic. In 1942, only 2 percent of the whites in the South favored integrated schools; in 1956, while most southerners still believed the ruling could be circumvented, only 14 percent favored desegregation; but by 1970, as desegregation continued, just under 50 percent favored desegregation—and the figures continued to climb in the 1980s. Of course, such statistical data do not constitute absolute proof that the reason people are changing their attitudes toward school desegregation is that they are coming to terms with what is inevitable—but the data are highly suggestive.

In a careful analysis of the process and effects of school desegregation, Thomas Pettigrew raised the question of why, in the early years of desegregation, violence occurred in some communities, such as Little Rock, Arkansas, and not in others, such as Norfolk, Virginia, and Winston-Salem, North Carolina. His conclusion, which lends further support to my reasoning, was that "violence has generally resulted in localities where at least some of the authorities give prior hints that they would gladly return to segregation if disturbances occurred; peaceful integration has generally followed firm and forceful leadership."[95] In other words, if people were not given the opportunity to reduce dissonance, there was violence. As early as 1953, Kenneth B. Clark[96] observed the same phenomenon during desegregation in some of the border states. He discovered that immediate desegregation was far more effective than gradual desegregation. Moreover, violence occurred in those places where ambiguous or inconsistent policies were employed or where community leaders tended to vacillate. The same kind of thing happened when military units began to desegregate during World War II: Trouble was greatest where policies were ambiguous.[97]

But All Other Things Are Not Always Equal In the preceding section, I presented an admittedly oversimplified view of a very complex phenomenon. I did this intentionally as a way of indicating how things can proceed theoretically under ideal conditions. But conditions are seldom ideal. There are almost always some complicating circumstances. Let us now look at some of the complications and then proceed to discuss how they might be eliminated or reduced.

When I stated that prejudice was reduced in an integrated housing project, I made special note of the fact that it was a *public* housing project. Some complications are introduced if integration involves privately owned houses. Primarily, there is a strong belief among whites that, when blacks move into a neighborhood, real estate values decrease. This belief introduces economic conflict and competition, which militate against the reduction of prejudiced attitudes. Indeed, systematic investigations in integrated *private* housing show an increase in prejudiced attitudes among the white residents.[98]

Moreover, as I mentioned, the experiments on the psychology of inevitability were done in the laboratory, where the dislikes involved in the studies were almost certainly not as intense or deep-seated as racial prejudice is in the real world. Although it is encouraging to note that these findings were paralleled by the data from actual desegregation efforts, it would be naive and misleading to conclude that the road to desegregation will always be smooth as long as individuals are given the opportunity to come to terms with inevitability. Frequently, trouble begins once desegregation starts. This is often due, in part, to the fact that the contact between white and minority-group children (especially if it is not begun until high school) is usually not equal status contact. Picture the scene: A 10th grade boy from a poor black or Latino family, after being subjected to a second-rate education, is suddenly dropped into a learning situation in a predominantly white, middle-class school taught by white, middle-class teachers, where he finds he must compete with white, middle-class students who have been reared to hold white, middle-class values. In effect, he is thrust into a highly competitive situation for which he is unprepared, a situation in which the rules are not his rules and payoffs are made for abilities he has not yet developed. He is competing in a situation that, psychologically, is far removed from his home turf. Ironically enough, these factors tend to produce a diminution of his self-esteem—the very factor that influenced the Supreme Court decision in the first place.[99] In his analysis of the research on desegregation, Walter Stephan[100] found no studies indicating significant increases in self-esteem among black children, while 25 percent of the studies he researched showed a significant drop in their self-esteem following desegregation. In addition, prejudice was not substantially reduced. Stephan found that it increased in almost as many cases as it decreased.

With these data in mind, it is not surprising to learn that a newly integrated high school is typically a tense place. It is natural for minority-group students to attempt to raise their self-esteem. One way of raising self-esteem is to stick together, lash out at whites, assert their individuality, reject white values and white leadership, and so on.[101]

Let me sum up the discussion thus far: (1) Equal-status contact under the ideal conditions of no economic conflict can and does produce increased understanding and a diminution of prejudice.[102] (2) The psychology of inevitability can and does set up pressures to reduce prejudiced attitudes and can set the stage for smooth, nonviolent school desegregation under ideal conditions. (3) Where economic conflict is present (as in integrated neighborhoods of private domiciles), there is often an increase in prejudiced attitudes. (4) Where school desegregation results in a competitive situation, especially if there are serious inequities for the minority groups, there is often an increase in hostility of blacks or Latinos toward whites that is at least partially due to an attempt to regain some lost self-esteem.

Interdependence—A Possible Solution

School desegregation can open the door to increased understanding among students but, by itself, it is not the ultimate solution. The issue is not simply getting youngsters of various races and ethnic backgrounds into the same school; it's what happens after they get there that is crucial. As we have seen, if the atmosphere is a highly competitive one, whatever tensions exist initially might actually be increased as a result of contact. The tension that is frequently the initial result of school desegregation reminds me somewhat of the behavior of the young boys in the summer camp experiment by Muzafer Sherif and his colleagues.[103] Recall that hostility was produced between two groups by placing them in situations of conflict and competition. Once the hostility was established, it could no longer be reduced simply by removing the conflicts and the competition. As a matter of fact, once distrust was firmly established, bringing the groups together in equal-status, noncompetitive situations served to *increase* the hostility and distrust. For example, the children in these groups had trouble with each other even when they were simply sitting near each other watching a movie.

How did Sherif eventually succeed in reducing the hostility? By placing the two groups of boys in situations in which they were mutually interdependent—situations in which they had to cooperate with each other in order to accomplish their goal. For example, the investigators set up an emergency situation by damaging the water-supply system. The only way the system could be repaired was if all the children cooperated immediately. On another occasion, the camp truck broke down while the boys were on a camping trip. In order to get the truck going again, it was necessary to pull it up a rather steep hill. This could be accomplished only if all the youngsters pulled together—regardless of whether they were Eagles or Rattlers. Eventually, there was a diminution of hostile feelings and negative stereotyping. The boys made friends across groups, began to get along better, and began to cooperate spontaneously.

The key factor seems to be *mutual interdependence*—a situation wherein individuals need one another in order to accomplish their goal. Several researchers have demonstrated the benefits of cooperation in well-controlled laboratory experiments. Morton Deutsch,[104] for example, has shown that problem-solving groups are both friendlier and more attentive when a cooperative atmosphere is introduced than when a competitive atmosphere prevails. Similarly, research by Patricia Keenan and Peter Carnevale has shown that cooperation within groups can also foster cooperation between groups.[105] That is, cooperative relations that are established in one group often carry over when that group is later called upon to interact with a different group. In their study, groups that engaged in a cooperative task were more cooperative in a subsequent negotiation with another group compared to groups that had initially worked in a competitive fashion.

Unfortunately, cooperation and interdependence are not characteristic of the process that exists in most school classrooms, even at the elementary level. On the contrary, intense competition reigns in most classrooms in this country. I got a chance to observe this phenomenon up close when I was asked to intervene during a major crisis in the Austin, Texas, public schools. The year was 1971. Desegregation had just taken place and had precipitated some ugly incidents. Because Austin had been residentially segregated, youngsters of various ethnic and racial groups encountered one another for the first time. There was a lot of suspicion and stereotyping prior to this contact. The contact seems to have exacerbated the problem. In any case, taunting frequently escalated into fistfights. The situation was both ugly and dangerous, shattering our illusions that desegregation would automatically reduce prejudice.

When the school superintendent asked for my help, my colleagues and I entered the system, not to smooth over the unpleasantness but rather, to see if there was anything we might do to help desegregation achieve some of the positive goals envisioned for it. The first thing we did was to systematically observe the dynamics of taking place in various classrooms. By far, the most common process we observed was typified by this scenario in a 6th-grade class: The teacher stands in front of the room, asks a question, and waits for the students to indicate that they know the answer. Most frequently, 6 to 10 youngsters strain in their seats and raise their hands—some waving them vigorously in an attempt to attract the teacher's attention. Several other students sit quietly with their eyes averted, as if trying to make themselves invisible.

When the teacher calls on one of the students, there are looks of disappointment, dismay, and unhappiness on the faces of those students who were eagerly raising their hands but were not called on. If the student comes up with the right answer, the teacher smiles, nods approvingly, and goes on to the next question. This is a great reward for that student. At that moment, however, an audible groan can be heard coming from the youngsters who were striving to be called on but were ignored. It is obvious they are upset because they missed an opportunity to show the teacher how smart they are.

Through this process, students learn several things in addition to the material being covered. First, they learn there is only one expert in the classroom: the teacher. The students also learn that the payoff comes from pleasing the teacher by actively displaying how smart they are. There is no payoff for consulting with their peers. Indeed, many learn that their peers are their enemies—to be defeated. Moreover, collaboration is frowned upon by most teachers; if it occurs during class time it is seen as disruptive, and if it takes place during an exam, it is called *cheating*.

In this highly competitive dynamic, if you are a student who knows the correct answer and the teacher calls on one of your peers, chances are you will hope that he or she will come up with the wrong answer so you will have a chance to show the teacher how smart you are. Those who fail when called on, or those who do not even raise their hands and compete, have a tendency to resent those who succeed. The successful students, for their part, often hold the unsuccessful students in contempt; they consider them to be stupid and uninteresting. This process discourages friendliness and understanding. It tends to create enmity, even among students of the same racial group. When this competitive classroom dynamic is added to a situation already strained by interracial distrust, it sets the stage for the kind of turmoil we encountered in Austin.

Although, at that time, competitiveness in the classroom was nearly universal, as social psychologists, we realized that it didn't have to be that way. Based, in part, on the experiment by Muzafer Sherif, described above, we reasoned that a cooperative process might be precisely what was needed in this situation. But how to do it? Actually, it wasn't that difficult. Within a few days, my students and I succeeded in developing a simple cooperative method designed specifically for the classroom. As it turned out, our method was virtually foolproof. We designed it so that, in order to learn the material and do well on the upcoming exam, students had to work *with* each other and cooperate. Trying to win became dysfunctional. We called our method the jigsaw classroom because it works very much like a jigsaw puzzle.[106]

An example will clarify: In a 5th-grade classroom, the children were studying biographies of famous Americans. The upcoming lesson happened to be a biography of Joseph Pulitzer, the famous journalist. First, we divided the students into groups of six—making certain that each group was as diverse (in terms of race and gender) as possible. We then constructed a biography of Pulitzer consisting of six paragraphs. Paragraph one was about Pulitzer's ancestors and how they came to this country; paragraph two was about Pulitzer as a little boy and how he grew up; paragraph three was about Pulitzer as a young man, his education, and his early employment; paragraph four was about his middle age and how he founded his first newspaper; and so forth.

Each major aspect of Joseph Pulitzer's life was contained in a separate paragraph. We mimeographed our biography of Joseph Pulitzer, cut each copy of the biography into six one-paragraph sections, and gave every child in each of the six-person learning groups one paragraph about Pulitzer's life. Thus, each learning group had within it the entire biography of Joseph Pulitzer but each student had no more than one-sixth of the story. In order to get the whole picture, each student needed to listen carefully to the other students in the group as they recited.

The teacher informed the students that they had a certain amount of time to communicate their knowledge to one another. She also informed them that they would be tested on their knowledge at the end of that time frame.

Within a few days, the students learned that none of them could do well without the aid of each person in the group. They learned to respect the fact that each member (regardless of race, gender, or ethnicity) had a unique and essential contribution to make to their own understanding and subsequent test performance. Now, instead of only one expert (the teacher), each student was an expert on his or her own segment. Instead of taunting each other, they began encouraging each other—because it was in each student's own best interest to make sure that the youngster reciting was able to communicate his or her material in the best possible way.

As I said, it took a few days; cooperative behavior doesn't happen all at once. The students in our experimental group had grown accustomed to competing during all of their years in school. For the first few days, most of them tried to compete against each other—even though competitiveness was dysfunctional. Let me illustrate with an actual example, typical of the way the children stumbled toward the learning of the cooperative process. In one of our groups there was a Mexican-American boy, whom I will call Carlos. Carlos's task was to report on Joseph Pulitzer's young manhood. He knew the material, but he was very nervous and was having a very hard time. During the past few weeks, some of the Anglo students had taunted him about his accent, and he was afraid that this might happen again.

He stammered, hesitated, and fidgeted. Sure enough, the other kids in the circle were not very helpful. They were well versed in the rough-and-tumble tactics of the competitive classroom. They knew what to do when a kid stumbled—especially a kid whom they believed to be stupid. They ridiculed him. During our experiment, it was Mary who was observed to say: "Aw, you don't know it, you're dumb, you're stupid. You don't know what you're doing." In our initial experiment, the groups were being loosely monitored by a research assistant who was floating from group to group. When this incident occurred, our assistant made one brief intervention: "Okay, you can do that if you want to. It might even be fun for you. But it's *not* going to help you learn about Joseph Pulitzer's young adulthood. By the way, the exam will take place in less than an hour." Notice how the reinforcement contingencies had shifted. No longer did Mary gain much from rattling Carlos; in fact, she now stood to lose a great deal.

After a few similar experiences, it dawned on the students in Carlos's group that the *only* way they could learn about the segment Carlos was trying to teach them was by paying attention to what Carlos had to say. Gradually, they began to develop into good listeners. Some even became pretty good interviewers. Instead of ignoring or ridiculing Carlos when he was having a little trouble communicating what he knew, they began asking gentle, probing questions—the kinds of questions that made it easier for Carlos to communicate what was in his mind. Carlos began to respond to this treatment by becoming more relaxed; with increased relaxation came an improvement in his ability to communicate. After a couple of weeks, the other children realized that Carlos was a lot smarter than they had thought he was. Because they were paying attention, they began to see things in him they had never seen before. They began to like him. For his part, Carlos began to enjoy school more and began to see the Anglo students in his group not as tormentors but as helpful and responsible people. Moreover, as he began to feel increasingly comfortable in class and started to gain more confidence in himself, his academic performance began to improve. The vicious cycle had been reversed; the elements that had been causing a downward spiral were changed—the spiral now began to move upward. Within a few weeks, the entire atmosphere in that classroom had changed dramatically.

We then randomly assigned several classrooms in Austin to the jigsaw condition and compared them with classrooms using the traditional competitive method. The results are clear and consistent. Children in jigsaw classrooms performed better on objective exams, grew to like each other better, developed a greater liking for school and greater self-esteem than children in traditional classrooms. The increase in liking among children in the jigsaw classroom crossed ethnic and racial barriers, resulting in a sharp decrease in prejudice and stereotyping. We replicated the same experiment in dozens of classrooms in several cities—always getting similar results.[107]

Over the years, research has shown that the jigsaw method's effectiveness is not limited to either Americans or to young children. Jigsaw has been used with great success in Europe, Africa, the Middle East, and Australia—with students at all levels, from elementary schools to universities.[108] In addition, researchers have applied jigsaw to a variety of prejudices including those that many people harbor toward people with physical and emotional disabilities. In one such experiment,[109] college students interacted with a fellow student who had been portrayed as a former mental patient. The interactions were part of a structured learning situation, with some of the students interacting with the "former mental patient" in a jigsaw group, while others interacted with him in a more traditional learning climate. The results are striking: Those in the jigsaw group quickly let go of their stereotypical expectations; they liked him better and enjoyed interacting with him more than did those who encountered him in the more traditional learning situation. Moreover, those people who went through the jigsaw session with the "former mental patient" subsequently described mental patients, in general, far more positively.

Underlying Mechanisms

Why does the jigsaw method produce such positive results? One reason for its effectiveness is that this cooperative strategy places people in a favor-doing situation. That is, each individual in a group, by sharing his or her knowledge with the other members, is doing them a favor. You will recall that, in Chapter 5, we discussed an experiment by Mike Leippe and Donna Eisenstadt[110] that demonstrated that people who acted in a way that benefited others subsequently came to feel more favorably toward the people they helped.

A different but complementary mechanism was illustrated in an experiment by Samuel Gaertner and his colleagues,[111] demonstrating that what seems to happen is that the process of cooperation lowers barriers between groups by changing the cognitive categories people use. In other words, cooperation changes our tendency to categorize the out-group from "those people" to "us people." But how does this change from "those people" to "us people" actually come about? I believe that the mediating process is **empathy**—the ability to experience what your group member is experiencing. In the competitive classroom, the primary goal is simply to show the teacher how smart you are. You don't have to pay much attention to the other students. But the jigsaw situation is different. In order to participate effectively in the jigsaw classroom, each student needs to pay close attention to whichever member of the group is reciting. In the process, the participants begin to learn that great results can accrue if each of their classmates is approached in a way that is tailored to fit his or her special needs. For example, Alice may learn that Carlos is a bit shy and needs to be prodded gently, while Phyllis is so talkative that she might need to be reigned in occasionally. Peter can be joked with, while Serena responds only to serious suggestions.

If our analysis is sound, then it should follow that working in jigsaw groups would lead to the sharpening of a youngster's general empathic ability. To test this notion, Diane Bridgeman[112] conducted a clever experiment with 10-year-old children. Prior to her experiment, half of the children had spent two months participating in jigsaw classes; the others spent that time in traditional classrooms. In her experiment, Bridgeman showed the children a series of cartoons aimed at testing a child's ability to empathize—to put themselves in the shoes of the cartoon characters. For example, in one cartoon, the first panel shows a little boy looking sad as he waves good-bye to his father at the airport. In the next panel, a letter carrier delivers a package to the boy. In the third panel, the boy opens the package, finds a toy airplane inside, and bursts into tears. Bridgeman asked the children why they thought the little boy burst into tears at the sight of the airplane. Nearly all of the children could answer correctly—because the toy airplane reminded him of how much he missed his father. Then Bridgeman asked the crucial question: "What did the letter carrier think when he saw the boy open the package and start to cry?"

Most children of this age make a consistent error; they assume that everyone knows what they know. Thus, the youngsters in the control group thought that the *letter carrier* would know the boy was sad because the gift reminded him of his father leaving. But the children who had participated in the jigsaw classroom responded differently. Because of their experience with jigsaw they had developed the ability to take the perspective of the letter carrier—to put themselves in his shoes—therefore, they realized that he would be *confused* at seeing the boy cry over receiving a nice present because the letter carrier hadn't witnessed the farewell scene at the airport.

At first glance, this might not seem very important. After all, who cares whether kids have the ability to figure out what is in the mind of a cartoon character? In point of fact, we should all care—a great deal. Recall our discussion of the Columbine tragedy in the preceding chapter. In that chapter we suggested how important empathy is in curbing aggression. The extent to which youngsters can develop the ability to see the world from the perspective of another human being has profound implications for interpersonal relations in general. When we develop the ability to understand what another person is going through, it increases the probability that our heart will open to that person. Once our heart opens to another person, it becomes virtually impossible to feel prejudice against that person, to bully that person, to taunt that person, to humiliate that person. My guess is that, if the jigsaw strategy had been used in Columbine High School (or in the elementary and middle schools that feed into Columbine), the tragedy could have been avoided and those youngsters would be alive today.

My students and I invented the **jigsaw technique** in 1971. Subsequently, similar cooperative techniques were developed by others.[113] Using both the jigsaw method and these other cooperative strategies, the striking results described in this chapter have been repeated in thousands of classrooms in all regions of the country.[114] John McConahay,[115] a leading expert on race relations, has called cooperative learning the single most effective practice for improving race relations in desegregated schools. What began as a simple experiment in one school system is slowly becoming an important force within the field of public education Unfortunately, the operative word in the preceding sentence is "slowly." The educational system, like all bureaucratic systems, tends to resist change. As the Columbine massacre illustrates, this slowness can have tragic consequences.[116]

The Challenge of Diversity

Diversity in a nation, in a city, in a neighborhood, or in a school can be an exciting thing—or a source of turmoil. Desegregation has given us the opportunity to benefit from that diversity. But in order to maximize those benefits, it is vital for us to learn to relate to one another across racial and ethnic lines in as harmonious a way as possible. It goes without saying that we have a long way to go before achieving anything re-sembling racial and ethnic harmony in this country. The introduction of co-operative learning into our classrooms has helped move us toward this goal. The challenges presented to an ethnically diverse nation have been graphi-cally depicted by the Pulitzer Prize–winning reporter David Shipler. A few years ago, Shipler traveled the length and breadth of this country interview-ing a wide variety of people about their racial feelings and attitudes. His rather bleak conclusion is summed up in the title of his book, *A Country of Strangers*.[117] Shipler observed that most Americans simply do not have close relationships with people of other races; therefore, a great deal of suspicion and misunderstanding prevail. Reading Shipler's book reminded me of a statement made to me by a Texas school principal in 1971, when desegrega-tion was causing problems in his school: "Look, professor, the government can force black kids and white kids to go to the same school," he said, "but no one can force them to enjoy hanging out with each other." (The astute reader will recognize this as a variation on the theme struck by William Graham Sumner, described earlier in this chapter.)

As if to underscore his point, that same day, during lunchtime, as I wan-dered around the schoolyard, what I saw was not an integrated school—far from it. What I saw were several clusters of self-segregated groups: Black youngsters clustered together in one group; Latino youngsters clustered to-gether in another group; white youngsters clustered together in still another group. Needless to say, it is not surprising to find that people of the same race and ethnicity might prefer one another's company. And, by itself, there is cer-tainly nothing wrong with that—unless such preferences become rigidified into exclusionary behavior. A few months after initiating the jigsaw technique in that same school, when I happened to walk through the schoolyard, I was suddenly (and quite unexpectedly) struck by the realization that virtually all of these clusters of students were fully integrated. No one "forced" the young-sters to like one another; they were actually *choosing* to relate to one another across racial and ethnic boundaries. The jigsaw experience was clearly easing some of the earlier distrust and suspicion. I recall thinking, "This is how it's *supposed* to be!"

Two centuries of de facto segregation may have turned most of our na-tion's adults into "a country of strangers," but those tens of thousands of chil-dren who have experienced learning together cooperatively give us hope for the future—a hope that they will eventually grow into adults who have learned to enjoy and benefit from diversity—who have learned to like and re-spect one another and who will continue to learn from one another.

Saul Steinberg, *Untitled drawing*, ink on paper.
Published in Steinberg, *The New World*, 1965.
© The Saul Steinberg Foundation / Artists Rights Society (ARS), New York

8
Liking, Loving, and Interpersonal Sensitivity

As social animals, we are capable of a wide range of behaviors toward one another. In previous chapters, we wrote mostly about some of the bleaker aspects of our behavior like obedience, aggression and prejudice. In this chapter, I will discuss the softer, more exciting, happier side of our social behavior, interpersonal attraction: What makes people like one another? More mysteriously, what makes people fall in love with each other?

The word "attraction" covers a lot of ground: from people we find appealing to work with, to those we simply enjoy hanging out with, to those who become our friends and confidants, to the deep, serious attachments of love. Why do we like some people and not others? Why, of all the people we like, do we fall in love with someone "special"? How does love change over the years? And, finally, what makes our love for another person increase or fade?

The question of attraction is almost certainly an ancient one. The first amateur social psychologist, who lived in a cave, undoubtedly wondered what he could do to make the fellow in a neighboring cave like him more or dislike him less—or, at least, to make him refrain from clubbing him on the head. Perhaps he brought him some saber-tooth tiger meat as a gift, hoping that would do the trick. Maybe he tried a new way of showing his teeth—not in a snarling, threatening grimace but in a softer, more submissive way—a way that eventually evolved into that gesture that we now call a smile.[1]

After several thousand years, people are still speculating about the antecedents of attraction—how to behave so that the person at the next desk, in the next house, or in the next country likes us more, or at least refrains from insulting us or trying to destroy us. What do we know about the causes of attraction? When I ask my friends why they like some of their acquaintances better than others, I get a wide variety of responses. The most typical responses are that people like most (1) those whose beliefs and interests are similar to their own; (2) those who have some skills, abilities, or competencies; (3) those with some pleasant or admirable qualities, such as loyalty, reasonableness, honesty, and kindness; and (4) those who like them in return.

These reasons make good sense. They are also consistent with the advice given by Dale Carnegie in a book with the chillingly manipulative title *How to Win Friends and Influence People.*[2] Manipulative title notwithstanding, this recipe book for interpersonal relations seems to have been exactly what people were looking for; it proved to be one of the greatest best-sellers of all time. That's not surprising. Americans seem to be deeply concerned with being liked and making a good impression. Polls taken of high school students[3] indicate that their most important concern is the way others react to them—and their overwhelming desire is for people to like them more. Such concerns may be greatest during adolescence, when the peer group assumes enormous importance, but the desire to be liked is certainly not limited to U.S. adolescents. The search for a simple formula to attract others seems universal. After all, Dale Carnegie's book was translated into 35 languages and was avidly read around the globe.

Carnegie's advice is deceptively simple: If you want people to like you, be pleasant, pretend you like them, feign an interest in things they're interested in, "dole out praise lavishly," and be agreeable. Is it true? Are these tactics effective? To a limited extent they are effective, at least in the early stages of the acquaintance process. Data from well-controlled laboratory experiments indicate that we like people with pleasant characteristics more than those with unpleasant characteristics;[4] we like people who agree with us more than people who disagree with us; we like people who like us more than people who dislike us; we like people who cooperate with us more than people who compete with us; we like people who praise us more than people who criticize us; and so on. These aspects of interpersonal attraction can be gathered under one sweeping generalization: We like people whose behavior provides us with maximum reward at minimum cost.[5]

A general reward theory of attraction covers a great deal of ground. It allows us to explain why we like people who are physically appealing more than people who are homely—because good-looking people bring us "aesthetic" rewards.[6] At the same time, it allows us to predict that we will like people with opinions similar to ours[7] because, when we run into such people, they reward us by providing us with consensual validation for our beliefs—that is, by helping us to believe our opinions are correct. Moreover, as we learned in the preceding chapter, one way prejudice and hostility can be reduced is by changing the environment in such a way that individuals cooperate with each other rather than compete. Another way of stating this relation is that cooperation leads to attraction. Thus, whether the environment is a summer camp, as in Muzafer Sherif's experiments,[8] or a classroom situation, as in the experiments I performed with my colleagues,[9] there is an increase in mutual attraction if people spend some time cooperating with each other. Cooperative behavior is clearly rewarding by definition. A person who cooperates with us is giving us aid, listening to our ideas, making suggestions, and sharing our load.

A general reward-cost theory can explain a great deal of human attraction but not all of it; the world is not that simple. For example, a reward-cost theory would lead us to suspect that, all other things being equal, we will like people who live in close proximity to us because we can get the same reward at less cost by traveling a short distance than we can by traveling a great distance. Indeed, it is true that people have more friends who live close by than friends who live far away; but this does not necessarily mean it is their physical proximity that makes them attractive. Their physical proximity may simply make it easier to get to know them, and once we get to know them, we tend to like them. Moreover, as I pointed out earlier in this book, individuals also like things or people for which or for whom they have suffered. For example, recall the experiment I did in collaboration with Judson Mills[10] in which we found that people who went through an unpleasant initiation in order to become members of a group liked that group better than did those who became members by paying a smaller price in terms of time and effort. Where is the reward? The reduction of suffering? The reduction of dissonance? How does the reward become attached to the group? It is not clear.

Moreover, simply knowing that something is rewarding does not necessarily help us to predict or understand a person's behavior. For example, recall that in chapters 2, 3, and 5, I analyzed why people conform and why they change their attitudes, and I discussed several reasons: out of a desire to win praise, to be liked, to avoid ridicule; out of a desire to identify with someone whom they respect or admire; out of a desire to be right; or out of a desire to justify their own behavior. In some way, all of these behaviors make sense, or feel good, or both, and therefore can be considered rewards. But simply to label them as rewards tends to obscure the important differences between them. Although both the desire to be right and the desire to avoid ridicule produce a state of satisfaction when gratified, the behaviors a person must employ to gratify these needs are frequently opposite in kind. For example, in judging the size of a line, a person might conform to group pressure out of a desire to avoid ridicule, but that same person might deviate from the unanimous opinion of the other group members out of a desire to be right. Little understanding is gained by covering both behaviors with the blanket term *reward*. For the social psychologist, a far more important task is to determine the conditions under which one or the other course of action will be taken. This point will become clearer as we address some of the research on interpersonal attraction.

The Effects of Praise and Favors

Recall that Dale Carnegie advised us to "dole out praise lavishly." This seems like good old-fashioned common sense: Surely we can "win friends" by praising our teachers' ideas or our employees' efforts. Indeed, several experiments have shown, in general, that we like people who evaluate us positively far more than those who evaluate us negatively.[11] But does it always work? Let's take a closer look. Common sense also suggests that there are situations in which criticism might be more useful than praise. For example, suppose you are a brand-new college instructor lecturing to a class of graduate students and presenting a theory you are developing. In the rear of the classroom are two students. One of them is nodding and smiling and looks as though he is in rapture. At the close of your presentation, he comes up and tells you that you are a genius and your ideas are the most brilliant he's ever heard. It feels good to hear that, of course. In contrast, the other student shakes her head and scowls occasionally during your presentation, and afterward, she comes up and tells you that there are several aspects of your theory that don't make sense. Moreover, she points these out in some detail and with a note of disdain in her voice. That evening, while ruminating on what was said, you realize that the remarks made by the second student, although somewhat extreme and not completely accurate, did contain some valid points and forced you to rethink a few of your assumptions. This eventually leads you to a significant modification of your theory. Which of these two people will you like better? I don't know. Although praise is clearly rewarding, disagreement that leads to improvement may carry its own rewards. Because I am, at this point, unable to predict which of these behaviors is more rewarding, it is impossible to be sure which of the two students you will like better.

The relative impact of praise and criticism is even more complicated—and more interesting. Some research shows that, all other things being equal, a negative evaluation generally increases the admiration we feel for the evaluator so long as he or she is not evaluating us! In one experiment, Theresa Amabile[12] asked college students to read excerpts from two reviews of novels that had appeared in the *New York Times* Book Review section. Both reviews were similar in style and quality of writing—but one was extremely favorable and the other extremely unfavorable. Students considered the negative reviewer to be considerably more intelligent, competent, and expert than the positive reviewer—but less likable!

Let us take a different example, one involving the attribution of ulterior motives to the praiser. Suppose Nancy is an engineer, and she produces an excellent set of blueprints. Her boss says, "Nice work, Nancy." That phrase will almost certainly function as a reward, and Nancy's liking for her boss will probably increase. But suppose Nancy is having an off day and produces a sloppy set of blueprints—and knows it. The boss comes along and uses the same phrase in exactly the same tone of voice. Will that phrase function as a reward in this situation? I am not sure. Nancy *may* interpret the statement as her boss's attempt to be encouraging and nice, even in the face of a poor performance; because of the boss's display of thoughtfulness, Nancy may come to like him even more than she would have had she, in fact, done a good job. On the other hand, Nancy may attribute all kinds of characteristics or ulterior motives to her boss: She may conclude that her boss is being sarcastic, manipulative, dishonest, nondiscriminating, patronizing, seductive, or stupid—any one of which could reduce Nancy's liking for him. A general reward-cost theory loses a good deal of its value if our definition of what constitutes a reward is not clear. As situations become complex, we find that such general notions decrease in value because a slight change in the social context in which the reward is provided can change a reward into a punishment. *Praise and*

Research in this area indicates that, although people like to be praised *favors* and tend to like the praiser,[13] they also dislike being manipulated. If the praise is too lavish, it seems unwarranted, or (most important) if the praiser is in a position to benefit from the ingratiating behavior, then he or she is not liked very much. In an experiment by Edward Jones[14] an accomplice observed a young woman being interviewed and then proceeded to evaluate her. The evaluations were prearranged so that some women heard a positive evaluation, some heard a negative evaluation, and some heard a neutral evaluation. In one experimental condition, the evaluator might have had an ulterior motive. In this condition, participants were informed in advance that the evaluator was a graduate student who needed participants for her own experiment and would be asking the students to volunteer. The results showed that the students liked the evaluators who praised them better than those who provided them with a negative evaluation—but there was a sharp drop in their liking for the praiser with the possible ulterior motive. Thus the old adage "flattery will get you nowhere" is clearly wrong. As Jones puts it, "flattery will get you *somewhere*"—but not everywhere.

By the same token, we like people who do us favors. Favors can be considered rewards, and we tend to like people who provide us with this kind of reward. For example, in a classic study of inmates in a women's reformatory, Helen Hall Jennings[15] found that the most popular women were those who initiated new and interesting activities and helped others become a part of those activities. Our liking for people who do us favors extends even to situations in which these favors are not intentional. This was demonstrated by Bernice and Albert Lott[16] in an experiment with young children. The researchers organized children into groups of three for the purpose of playing a game that consisted of choosing various pathways on a board. Those who were lucky enough to choose the safe pathways won the game; making the wrong choice led to disaster. The children were, in effect, walking single file in an imaginary mine field, whose mines remained active even after they exploded. If the child at the front of the line chose the wrong path, that player was "blown up" (out of the game), and the child next in line would, of course, choose a different path. Leaders who happened to choose correctly led the others to a successful completion of the game. The results indicated that those children who were rewarded (by arriving safely at the goal) showed a greater liking for their teammates (who, of course, had been instrumental in helping them achieve the reward) than did those children who did not reach the final goal. In short, we like people who contribute to our victory more than those who do not—even if they had no intention of doing us a favor.

But, as with those who praise us, we do not always like people who do favors for us; specifically, we do not like people whose favors seem to have strings attached to them. Such strings constitute a threat to the freedom of the receiver. People do not like to receive a gift if a gift is expected in return; moreover, people do not like to receive favors from individuals who are in a position to benefit from those favors. Recall the example I mentioned in a previous chapter: If you were a teacher, you might enjoy receiving gifts from your students. On the other hand, you might be made pretty uncomfortable if a borderline student presented you with an expensive gift just before you were about to grade his or her term paper. Strong support for this reasoning comes from an experiment by Jack Brehm and Ann Cole.[17] In this experiment, college students were asked to participate in a study (characterized by the experimenters as important) in which they would be giving their first impressions of another person. As each student was waiting for the experiment to begin, the "other person" (actually a stooge) asked permission to leave the room for a few moments. In one condition, he simply returned after a while and resumed his seat. In the other condition, he returned carrying a soft drink, which he immediately gave to the participant. Subsequently, each participant was asked to help the stooge perform a dull task. Interestingly enough, those students who had *not* been given the drink by the stooge were more likely to help him than those who *had* been given the drink.

The upshot of this research is that favors and praise are not universal rewards. For a starving rat or a starving person, a bowl of dry cereal is a reward—it is a reward during the day or during the night, in winter or in summer, if offered by a man or by a woman, and so on. Similarly, for a drowning person, a rescue launch is a reward under all circumstances. That is, such rewards are *transsituational.*

But praise, favors, and the like are not transsituational; whether or not they function as rewards depends on minor situational variations, some of which can be extremely subtle. Indeed, as we have seen, praise and favors can even function to make praisers or favor-doers less attractive than they would have been had they kept their mouths shut or their hands in their pockets. Thus, Dale Carnegie's advice is not always sound. If you want someone to like you, doing a favor as a technique of ingratiation is indeed risky.

If you want someone to like you, instead of doing her a favor, try to get her to do *you* a favor. It turns out that getting someone to do you a favor is a more certain way of using favors to increase your attractiveness. Recall that, in Chapter 5, I described a phenomenon called *justification of cruelty.* Briefly, I pointed out that, if individuals cause harm to a person, they will attempt to justify their behavior by derogating the victim. I also analyzed how the justification process could work in the opposite direction. If I do someone a favor, I will try to justify this action by convincing myself that the recipient of this favor is an attractive, likable, deserving person. In effect, I will say to myself, "Why in the world did I go to all of this effort (or spend all of this money, or whatever) for Sam? Because Sam is a wonderful person, that's why!"

This notion is not new—indeed, it seems to be a part of folk wisdom. One of the world's greatest novelists, Leo Tolstoy,[18] in 1869 wrote: "We do not love people so much for the good they have done us, as for the good we have done them." A century before Tolstoy's observation, Benjamin Franklin utilized strategy as a political ploy—with apparent success. Disturbed by the political opposition and animosity of a member of the Pennsylvania state legislature, Franklin set out to win him over:

> I did not . . . aim at gaining his favour by paying any servile respect to him but, after some time, took this other method. Having heard that he had in his library a certain very scarce and curious book I wrote a note to him expressing my desire of perusing that book and requesting he would do me the favour of lending it to me for a few days. He sent it immediately and I returned it in about a week with another note expressing strongly my sense of the favour. When we next met in the House he spoke to me (which he had never done before), and with great civility; and he ever after manifested a readiness to serve me on all occasions, so that we became great friends and our friendship continued to his death. This is another instance of the truth of an old maxim I had learned, which says, "He that has once done you a kindness will be more ready to do you another than he whom you yourself have obliged."[19]

While Benjamin Franklin was clearly pleased with the success of his maneuver, as a scientist I am not totally convinced. It is not entirely clear whether Franklin's success was due to this strategy or to any one of many charming aspects of his personality. In order to be certain, a well-controlled experiment is necessary. Some 230 years after Franklin borrowed the book, just such an experiment was conducted by Jon Jecker and David Landy.[20] In this experiment, students participated in a concept-formation task that enabled them to win a rather substantial sum of money. After the experiment was over, one-third of the participants were approached by the experimenter, who explained that he was using his own funds for the experiment and was running short—which would mean he might be forced to stop the experiment. He asked, "As a special favor to me, would you mind returning the money you won?" Another one-third of the participants were approached, not by the experimenter, but by the departmental secretary, who asked them if they would return the money as a special favor to the psychology department's research fund, which was running low. The remaining participants were not asked to return their winnings. Finally, all of the participants were asked to fill out a questionnaire, which included an opportunity to state their feelings about the experimenter. Those participants who had been cajoled into doing a special favor for the experimenter liked him best; that is, because they did him a favor, they succeeded in convincing themselves that he was a decent, deserving fellow.

Similar results were obtained in an experiment by Melvin Lerner and Carolyn Simmons[21] in which groups of participants were allowed to observe a student who appeared to be receiving a series of electric shocks as part of an experiment in learning. After watching for a while, some participants were allowed to vote (by private ballot) on whether or not the "victim" should continue to receive electric shocks. Others were not allowed to vote on this procedure. All those who were allowed to vote did, indeed, vote for the termination of the shocks; some of the voting participants succeeded in terminating the shocks, while others did not. Those people who succeeded in terminating the shocks came to like the victim the most. The people who tried but failed to terminate the shocks liked him about as much as those who didn't vote at all.

Personal Attributes

As I have already mentioned, there are several personal characteristics that play an important role in determining the extent to which a person will be liked.[22] Thus, people tend to like others who are sincere, competent, intelligent, energetic, and so on. Most of these studies involved a public opinion poll; people were simply asked to describe the attributes of people they like and those of people they dislike. In studies of this sort, it is difficult to establish the direction of causality: Do we like people who have pleasant attributes or do we convince ourselves that our friends have pleasant attributes? Chances are that causality flows in both directions. In order to be sure that people with certain positive personal attributes are liked better than others, however, it is necessary to examine this relation under more controlled conditions than exist in the opinion poll. In this section, we will closely examine two of the most important personal attributes: competence and physical attractiveness.

Competence It would seem obvious that, all other things being equal, the more competent an individual is, the more we will like that person. This is probably because we have a need to be right; we stand a better chance of being right if we surround ourselves with highly able, highly competent people. But as we continue to learn in this chapter, factors that determine interpersonal attraction are often complex; they cannot always be spelled out in simple terms. As for competence, there is a great deal of apparently paradoxical evidence in the research literature demonstrating that, in problem-solving groups, the participants who are considered to be the most competent and to have the best ideas tend not to be the ones who are best liked.[23] How can we explain this paradox? One possibility is that, although we like to be around competent people, a person who has a great deal of ability may make us uncomfortable. That person may seem unapproachable, distant, superhuman—and make us look bad by comparison. If this were true, we might like the person more were he or she to show some evidence of fallibility. For example, if Sam were a brilliant mathematician as well as a great basketball player and a fastidious dresser, I might like him better if, every once in a while, he added a column of numbers incorrectly, blew an easy layup, or appeared in public with a gravy stain on his tie.

Almost 45 years ago, I was speculating about this phenomenon when I chanced upon some startling data from a Gallup poll: When John Kennedy was president, his personal popularity actually increased immediately after his abortive attempt to invade Cuba at the Bay of Pigs in 1961. This was startling in view of the fact that this attempted invasion was such a phenomenal blunder that it was immediately dubbed (and is still commonly known as) "the Bay of Pigs fiasco." What can we make of it? This was a situation in which a president committed one of our country's greatest blunders (up until that time, that is), and miraculously, people came to like him more for it. Why? One possibility is that Kennedy may have been "too perfect." What does that mean? How can a person be too perfect?

In 1961, John Kennedy stood very high in personal popularity. He was a character of almost storybook proportions. Indeed, his regime was referred to as Camelot. Kennedy was young, handsome, bright, witty, charming, and athletic. He was a voracious reader, the author of a best-seller, a master political strategist, a war hero, and an uncomplaining endurer of physical pain. He was married to a talented and beautiful woman (who spoke several foreign languages), had two cute kids (one boy and one girl), and was part of a highly successful, close-knit family. Some evidence of fallibility (like being responsible for a major blunder) could have served to make him more human in the public eye and, hence, more likable.

Alas, this is only one of several possible explanations, and (as the reader knows all too well by now) the real world is no place to test such a hypothesis. In the real world, too many things are happening simultaneously, any one of which could have increased Kennedy's popularity. For example, after the fiasco occurred, President Kennedy did not try to make excuses or to pass the buck; rather, he bravely accepted full responsibility for the blunder. This selfless action could have done much to make him more attractive in the eyes of the populace. In order to test the proposition that evidence of fallibility in a highly competent person may make that person better liked, an experiment was needed. One of the great advantages of an experiment is that it eliminates or controls extraneous variables (such as the selfless assumption of responsibility) and allows us, therefore, to assess more accurately the effect of one variable on another. I performed such an experiment in collaboration with Ben Willerman and Joanne Floyd.[24] The participants were college men at the University of Minnesota. Each student listened to a simple audio tape recording featuring one of four stimulus persons: (1) a nearly perfect person, (2) a nearly perfect person who commits a blunder, (3) a mediocre person, and (4) a mediocre person who commits a blunder. In preparation, each student was told he would be listening to a person who was a candidate for the then-popular "College Bowl" quiz show, and that he would be asked to rate one of the candidates by the kind of impression he made, by how likable he seemed, and so forth. Each tape consisted of an interview between a young man (stimulus person) and an interviewer and contained a set of extremely difficult questions posed by the interviewer; the questions were like those generally asked on "College Bowl." On one tape, the stimulus person showed a high degree of competence—indeed, he seemed to be virtually perfect, answering 92 percent of the questions correctly—and in the body of the interview, when asked about his activities in high school, he modestly admitted he had been an honor student, the editor of the yearbook, and a member of the track team. On another tape, the stimulus person (actually the same actor using the same tone of voice) was presented as a person of average ability: He answered only 30 percent of the questions correctly, and during the interview he admitted he had received average grades in high school, had been a proofreader on the yearbook staff, and had tried out for the track team but had failed to make it. On the other two recordings (one of the "superior" young man and one of the "average" young man), the stimulus person committed an embarrassing blunder. Near the end of the interview, he clumsily spilled a cup of coffee all over himself. This "pratfall" was created by making a tape recording that included sounds of commotion and clatter, the scraping of a chair, and the anguished voice of the stimulus person saying, "Oh, my goodness, I've spilled coffee all over my new suit." To achieve maximum control, the tape of the incident was reproduced, and one copy was spliced onto a copy of the tape of the superior person, while the other copy was spliced onto a tape of the average person.

The results were striking: The superior person who committed a blunder was rated most attractive; the average person who committed the same blunder was rated least attractive. The perfect person (no blunder) was second in attractiveness, and the mediocre person (no blunder) finished third. Clearly, there was nothing inherently attractive about the simple act of spilling a cup of coffee. Although it did serve to add an endearing dimension to the perfect person, making him more attractive, the same action served to make the mediocre person appear that much more mediocre and, hence, less attractive. This experiment presents stronger evidence to support our contention that, although a high degree of competence does make us appear more attractive, some evidence of fallibility increases our attractiveness still further. This phenomenon has been dubbed the **pratfall effect.**

More complex experiments have since produced some interesting refinements of this general finding. Basically, the pratfall effect holds most clearly when, in the mind of the observer, there is an implicit threat of competition with the stimulus person. Thus, an experiment by Kay Deaux[25] demonstrates that the pratfall effect applies most strongly to males. She found that, although most males in her study preferred the highly competent man who committed a blunder, women showed a tendency to prefer the highly competent nonblunderer, regardless of whether the stimulus person was male or female. Similarly, my colleagues and I found that males with a moderate degree of self-esteem are most likely to prefer the highly competent person who commits a blunder, while males with low self-esteem (who apparently feel little competitiveness with the stimulus person) prefer the highly competent person who doesn't blunder.[26]

It should be emphasized that no sizable proportion of people—regardless of their own level of self-esteem—preferred the mediocre person. I want to take special pains to make this point because of a bizarre political event. In the early 1970s, when former President Richard Nixon was at the height of his popularity, he tried in vain to appoint to the Supreme Court two strikingly mediocre lower-court judges. In defending these nominees, Senator Roman Hruska argued (seriously, I'm afraid!) that while it was true that these men were mediocre, the mediocre citizens of the country needed someone on the Supreme Court to represent them, too! Our data do not support that argument.

Physical Attractiveness Imagine you are on a blind date. It is near the end of the evening, and you are wondering whether or not you want to go out with this person again. Which of your partner's characteristics will weigh most heavily: Warmth? Sensitivity? Intelligence? Compassion? *How about good looks?* You guessed it!

Most of us tend to be both incredulous and appalled by such a suggestion. We don't want this to be true. We would like to believe that beauty is only skin deep and, therefore, a trivial determinant of liking. Also, it seems so unfair; why should something like physical attractiveness—which is largely beyond a person's control—play an important role? Indeed, when asked what they looked for in a potential date, most college students put "physical attractiveness" at the very bottom of the list.[27] But I'm afraid this reflects only what students think they *ought* to believe—for, in study after study of their actual behavior, college students (as well as the population at large) are overwhelmingly influenced by another person's physical attractiveness.[28] In one study, for example, Elaine Walster (Hatfield) and her associates[29] randomly matched incoming students at the University of Minnesota for a blind date. The students previously had been given a battery of personality tests. Which of their many characteristics determined whether or not they liked each other? It was not their intelligence, masculinity, femininity, dominance, submission, dependence, independence, sensitivity, sincerity, or the like. The *one* determinant of whether or not a couple liked each other and actually repeated their date was their physical attractiveness. If a handsome man was paired with a beautiful woman, they were most likely to desire to see each other again.

This general phenomenon is not limited to a blind date. Gregory White[30] studied relatively long-term relationships among young couples at UCLA. Like Walster (Hatfield) and her colleagues, White found that physical attractiveness was an important factor; but in this situation it was the *similarity* of the attractiveness of the members of the couple that was crucial in determining whether or not a relationship had staying power. Specifically, some 9 months after the couples started dating, those who were well matched in terms of rated physical attractiveness were more deeply involved with each other than those who differed from each other in physical attractiveness.

What is clear from these studies of dating couples is that, in one way or another, physical attractiveness plays an important role in determining who likes whom in both the short run and the long run. Moreover, these studies indicate that there are clear cultural standards for physical attractiveness—at least in the United States, where most of this research has been done. Raters had no difficulty judging people on physical attractiveness. And the raters agreed with one another—that is, the ratings were highly *reliable*. Moreover, all other things being equal, people's physical attractiveness not only helps us predict whether or not others will want to date them, but also influences a wide range of attributions. For example, in one study, Karen Dion and her colleagues[31] showed college students photographs of three college-age people. The photos were especially selected for differing degrees of attractiveness: One was attractive, one average, and one unattractive. The participants were asked to rate each of the people depicted in these photographs on 27 different personality traits and to predict their future happiness. The physically attractive people were assigned by far the most desirable traits and the greatest prognosis for happiness. This was true whether men were rating men, men rating women, women rating men, or women rating women.

Does it surprise you to learn that most people seem to agree on both the physical characteristics and the concomitant personality traits of so-called beautiful people? Perhaps it shouldn't. From early childhood experiences we learn that a specific definition of beauty is associated with goodness. Walt Disney's movies and the illustrators of children's books have taught us that gentle and charming heroines like Snow White, Cinderella, and Sleeping Beauty—as well as the princes who charm and win them—all look alike. They all have regular features, small pert noses, big eyes, shapely lips, blemish-free complexions, and slim athletic bodies. They all look like Barbie and Ken dolls. Indeed, so do Barbie and Ken dolls! And how are the wicked stepmothers, stepsisters, giants, trolls, and queens depicted?

In addition, television sustains these cultural standards; actors who fit the U.S. stereotype of beauty are carefully selected to play the heroines and heroes of popular TV soap operas and prime-time sitcoms. And then there are the commercials. Anyone who watches a fair amount of television is subjected to a continuous flow of propaganda aimed at selling the idea of beauty in a bottle. Shampoo, skin lotion, deodorant, toothpaste, and exercise machines—all are peddled by promoting the conviction that these products will make us beautiful, desirable, and ultimately successful. And exposure to this kind of thing *does* have an impact. For example, in one experiment,[32] young women between the ages of 16 and 18 were systematically exposed to some 15 TV commercials extolling the virtues of beauty preparations. A control group of teenagers was shown 15 commercials unrelated to beauty products. Sometime later, all of the young women were asked to rank the relative importance of 10 attributes—sex appeal, intelligence, a pretty face, industriousness, and so on. The young women who had been shown the beauty ads were more likely than the control group to consider beauty-oriented attributes more important than other qualities.

One of the implications of our discussion is that cultural standards of beauty are learned early. If we learn about beauty by looking at the pictures in storybooks, or from Disney movies, or from watching television, then it should follow that even young children are influenced by these norms. And so they are. In a striking study, Karen Dion and Ellen Berscheid[33] found that, even as early as nursery school, children are responsive to the physical attractiveness of their peers. In their study, Dion and Berscheid first had several independent judges (graduate students) rate the physical attractiveness of nursery-school children. Then they determined who liked whom among the children themselves. They found that physical attractiveness was very important. The clearest results were obtained for the males: The physically attractive boys were liked better than the physically unattractive boys. Moreover, unattractive boys were considered to be more aggressive than their attractive counterparts, and when the children were asked to name the classmates that "scared them," they tended to nominate the unattractive children. Of course, it might have been the case that the less attractive children actually *behaved* more aggressively. In this study, the researchers did not observe the actual behavior of the children in the nursery school, so they could not test that possibility.

But we have independent evidence that people tend to attribute less blame to physically attractive children, regardless of the facts. This finding emerges from a subsequent experiment by Karen Dion.[34] Dion asked several women to examine reports of rather severe classroom disturbances, apparently written by a teacher. Attached to each report was a photo of the child who was said to have initiated the disturbance. In some instances, the photo was that of a physically attractive boy or girl; in others, the photo was that of a less attractive boy or girl. The women tended to place more blame on the less attractive children and to infer that this incident was typical of their everyday behavior. When the child was pictured as physically attractive, however, they tended to excuse the disruptive behavior. As one of the women put it, "She plays well with everyone, but like anyone else, a bad day can occur. Her cruelty . . . need not be taken seriously." When a physically unattractive girl was pictured as the culprit in exactly the same situation described in exactly the same way, a typical respondent said, "I think the child would be quite bratty and would probably be a problem to teachers. She would probably try to pick a fight with other children her own age . . . . All in all, she would be a real problem." Thus, it seems that we tend to give attractive children the benefit of the doubt. Their misbehaviors are seen as forgivable aberrations caused by special aspects of the situation, other people, or an unfortunate accident. Less attractive children, on the other hand, are not let off the hook so easily; their misdeeds are attributed *internally*—to stable negative personality dispositions.

It probably won't surprise anyone to learn that physical attractiveness plays an important role among early adolescents as well as in children and adults. For example, Richard Lerner and his colleagues[35] found that over the course of the school year, 6th-graders tended to rate their physically attractive classmates as being more competent than their less attractive classmates. Moreover, in that study, the teachers fell into the same trap. Speaking of teachers, all other things being equal, physically attractive teachers may also have an edge over their less attractive colleagues. In one study, Bruce Hunsberger and Brenda Cavanagh[36] found that 6th-graders rated physically attractive potential teachers as nicer, happier, less punitive, and more effective than their less attractive counterparts.

Physical attractiveness has important consequences in the business world as well. Irene Frieze and her associates[37] rated the attractiveness of over 700 young adults and tracked their employment histories—starting just after they attained masters degrees in business administration and continuing for a 10-year period. The results are clear. For men, being physically attractive resulted in a higher starting salary. Moreover, this effect did not fade over time as employers got to know them. Rather, attractive men continued to out-earn their less attractive counterparts over the entire 10-year period. For women, being attractive did not affect their starting salaries, but attractiveness began to influence salaries after they had been on the job a while and continued to the conclusion of the study. Attractiveness was rated on a 5-point scale. The researchers were able to calculate that each point on the scale was worth about $2,150; thus, theoretically, if you underwent plastic surgery and it improved your looks from a rating of 2 to a rating of 4, that would be worth exactly $4,300 per year!

Physical attractiveness is not necessarily a one-way street. Several years ago, I performed an experiment in collaboration with Harold Sigall[38] in which we demonstrated that attractive women have more impact on men than less attractive women—for better or for worse. In this experiment, a woman was made to appear either physically attractive or unattractive. This was accomplished by taking a naturally beautiful woman and, in the unattractive condition, providing her with loose, baggy, unflattering clothing, fitting her with a frizzy blond wig that did not quite match her skin coloring, and making her complexion look oily and unhealthy. Then, posing as a graduate student in clinical psychology, she interviewed several college men. At the close of the interview, she gave each student her own clinical evaluation of him. Half of the students received highly favorable evaluations and half received unfavorable evaluations. We found that, when the evaluator was made to look unattractive, the men didn't seem to care much whether they received a good evaluation or a poor one from her; in both situations, they liked her a fair amount. When she was beautiful, however, they liked her a great deal when she gave them a favorable evaluation but, when she gave them an unfavorable evaluation, they disliked her more than in any of the other conditions. Interestingly enough, although the men who were evaluated negatively by the attractive woman said they didn't like her, they did express a great desire to return in order to interact with her in a future experiment. Our guess is that the negative evaluations from the beautiful woman were so important to the men that they wanted the opportunity to return so as to induce her to change her mind about them.

In a subsequent experiment, Harold Sigall and Nancy Ostrove[39] showed that people tend to favor a beautiful woman unless they suspect her of misusing her beauty. Both male and female college students were asked to read an account of a criminal case in which the defendant was clearly guilty of a crime. Each participant then "sentenced" the defendant to a prison term he or she considered appropriate. The results showed that, when the crime was unrelated to attractiveness (burglary), the sentences were much more lenient when the defendant was physically attractive. When the crime was related to her attractiveness (a swindle in which the defendant induced a middle-aged bachelor to invest some money in a nonexistent corporation), the sentences were much harsher for the physically attractive defendant.

Let's pause for a second and take a deep breath. The Sigall–Ostrove experiment is an important one, in itself, because it demonstrates the power of physical attractiveness in influencing our decisions. But, when thinking of our legal system, how seriously should we take these data? After all, Sigall and Ostrove were not dealing with trained jurists; the participants in their experiment were only college students. Can we conclude from this experiment that our legal system is so biased that physical attractiveness plays a role in the sentencing of actual criminals? Are judges as susceptible to physical beauty as college students? Chris Downs and Phillip Lyons[40] decided to find out. They scrutinized the fines and bails set by real judges in actual court cases involving 915 female and 1,320 male defendants being charged with either misdemeanors or more serious felonies. What they found was interesting and somewhat comforting. Where misdemeanors were involved, the judges were much more lenient with physically attractive male and female defendants, assessing both lower bail and lower fines than they did for relatively unattractive defendants. But, when it came to actual felonies, the physical attractiveness of the defendant made no difference. Thus, the answer is that even trained judges are in danger of being influenced—but, when the crime is a serious one, their good judgment overrides the potential impact of this irrelevant variable.

The effects of a person's physical attractiveness go beyond how we evaluate or how much we are influenced by *that* person; it can also change our perceptions of the people with whom he or she is associated. An experiment by Harold Sigall and David Landy[41] demonstrated that, when seen in the company of a beautiful woman, a man is perceived differently from when he is seen with an unattractive woman. In their study, participants who met a man seated next to an extremely attractive woman tended to like him more, and to rate him as friendlier and more self-confident, than did those people who met the same man when he was seated beside an unattractive woman.

Taking all of this research into consideration, it is clear that beauty is more than skin deep. We are affected by physically attractive people, and unless we are specifically abused by them, we tend to like them better and we reward them more than less attractive people. Moreover, in ambiguous situations involving trouble and turmoil, beautiful people tend to be given the benefit of the doubt; they receive more favorable treatment than less attractive people. This begins at a very young age. The disconcerting aspect of these data is the strong possibility that such preferential treatment contains the seeds of a self-fulfilling prophecy: We know that the way people are treated affects the way they come to think of themselves. Some evidence for this phenomenon comes from a classic experiment conducted by Mark Snyder, Elizabeth Decker Tanke, and Ellen Berscheid.[42] Put yourself in the place of a typical male undergraduate in their experiment: You have volunteered to participate in an investigation of "how people become acquainted with each other," and you have been paired with a female student who is located in another room, ostensibly because the two of you are assigned to the "no nonverbal communication" condition of the study. Though you haven't seen your partner, you have been given a packet of information, which contains her photo. When you proceed to have a conversation with this woman over an intercom, do you think the physical attractiveness of the woman in the photo will influence your impressions of her?

As the reader might suspect, the photo viewed by the male participant did not depict his actual partner. For half of them, it pictured a very attractive woman; for the others, it pictured a relatively unattractive woman. But the photo did have an effect. The men who thought they were talking with an attractive partner rated her as more poised, humorous, and socially adept than did those who thought they were talking with a less attractive woman. This is not very surprising. But what was startling was this: When independent observers were allowed to listen to a tape recording of only the woman's half of the conversation (without looking at a photograph), they were far more impressed by the woman whose male partner thought she was physically attractive. In short, since the male partner thought he was talking to an attractive woman, he spoke to her in a way that brought out her best qualities. When these independent observers listened to her conversation, they rated her as more attractive, more confident, more animated, and warmer than the woman whose partner thought her to be less beautiful. Thus, physically attractive people may come to think of themselves as good or lovable because they are continually treated that way. Conversely, homely people may begin to think of themselves as bad or unlovable because they are continually treated that way—even as children. Ultimately, people may begin to behave in a way that is consistent with this self-concept—a way that is consistent with how they were treated to begin with.

Please note that, for the most part, our discussion of beauty has focused on visual beauty. But there are other kinds of beauty. Our visual perceptual mechanisms exercise a terribly conservative influence on our feelings and behavior. We are wedded to our eyes—especially as a means of determining attractiveness. And, as we have seen, once we have categorized a person as good looking or homely, we tend to attribute other qualities to that person; for example, good-looking people are likely to strike us as being warmer, sexier, more exciting, and more delightful than homely people. In the 1960s and 1970s, when sensitivity-training groups were at the height of their popularity, a great many people volunteered to engage in non-visual sensory experiences. For example, in one such experience, some 50 people were blindfolded and invited to wander around the room and become acquainted with each other solely through the sense of touch and by talking to one another. After participating in one of these exercises, group members typically reported a dramatic diminution of their prior stereotypes. Basically, individuals found that there is little "homeliness" in a nonvisual situation. Moreover, when they subsequently opened their eyes, participants were frequently astonished to learn that, for example, the funny-looking guy with the big nose and pimples standing in front of them was the very same person who, five minutes ago (when their eyes were closed) had impressed them as an incredibly warm, gentle, sensitive, charming human being. It is an experience that many of the participants never forgot.

Similarity and Attraction

Lynne goes to a cocktail party and is introduced to Suzanne. While they chat for only a few moments, it turns out that they agree completely on several issues, including the inequity of the income-tax structure, the eventual status of Richard Nixon in world history, and the importance of a liberal arts education. Upon returning home, Lynne tells her husband that she likes Suzanne a great deal and considers her a wonderful and intelligent person. Literally dozens of tightly controlled experiments by Donn Byrne and his associates[43] have shown that, if all you know about a person are his or her opinions on several issues, the more similar those opinions are to yours, the more you like the person.

Why is agreement attractive? There are at least two major reasons. First, it is obvious to most of us that people who share our attitudes and opinions on important issues are uncommonly intelligent, thoughtful individuals. It is always rewarding and interesting to hang out with and chat with intelligent and thoughtful people. Second, they provide us with a kind of social validation for our beliefs—that is, they provide us with the feeling that we are right. This is rewarding; hence, we like those who agree with us.

One additional factor must be mentioned here: We humans are so certain of the relationship between attitude similarity and liking that if we happen to like someone for some irrelevant reason, we will assume that his or her attitudes must be similar to ours. Thus, causality works in both directions: All other things being equal, we like people whose attitudes are similar to ours, and if we like someone, we attribute attitudes to him or her that are similar to ours.[44]

Liking, Being Liked, and Self-Esteem

There is still another reason why we tend to like people who hold opinions similar to ours. Research has shown that when we learn that someone shares our opinions, we are likely to believe he or she will really like us if and when that person gets to know us.[45] This assumes importance because, as it turns out, one of the most powerful determinants of whether we will like another person is whether the other person indicates that he or she likes us.[46]

What's more, merely believing someone likes you can initiate a spiraling series of events that promotes increasingly positive feelings between you and the other person. How does this work? To illustrate, imagine that you and I engaged in a brief, rather uneventful conversation at a party after a mutual friend introduced us to each other. A few days later, you run into our friend on campus, and she informs you that, following the party, I had some very complimentary things to say about you. How do you suppose you might act the next time you and I happened to meet? My hunch is that your knowledge that I liked you would probably lead you to like me and to act in ways that let me know that you liked me, too. You'd probably smile more, disclose more about yourself, and generally behave in a warmer, more interested, more likable manner than if you hadn't already learned that I liked you. And what effect do you think your actions would have on my behavior? Faced with your warm and likable behavior, my fondness for you would undoubtedly grow, and I, in turn, would convey my liking for you in ways that made me even more likable to you.

But, consider this: What if our mutual friend hadn't exactly been telling the truth? What if she had figured that you and I really would like each other a great deal once we got to know each other and, to get the ball rolling, had told you that I liked you, even though I hadn't ever expressed such feelings? What are the chances that her well-intentioned plan would work? Well, if you and I were like the participants in an experiment by Rebecca Curtis and Kim Miller,[47] her scheme would have worked like a charm! These researchers led some people to believe that another person liked them and led others to believe that that same person disliked them. In a subsequent interaction, those individuals who thought they were liked behaved in more likable ways; they disclosed more about themselves, disagreed less, and generally behaved in a warmer, more pleasant manner toward the other person than did those individuals who thought they were disliked. Moreover, the people who believed they were liked were, in fact, subsequently liked by the other person, while those who believed they were disliked were disliked by the other person. In other words, the misinformation produced a self-fulfilling prophecy. The behaviors of people who thought they were either liked or disliked led to reciprocal behaviors from their partners who—remember—had never actually expressed a liking or disliking for the other them. Our beliefs—whether right or wrong—play a potent role in shaping reality.

As we have seen, being liked indeed makes the heart grow fonder. Furthermore, the greater our insecurity and self-doubt, the fonder we will grow of the person who likes us. In a fascinating experiment by Elaine Walster (Hatfield),[48] female college students, while waiting to receive the results of personality tests they had taken previously, were approached by a rather smooth, good-looking, well-dressed young man who was, in fact, an accomplice of the experimenter. He struck up a conversation with each student, indicated he liked her, and proceeded to make a date. At this point, the experimenter entered and led the student into an office to inform her of the results of her tests. In the course of this procedure, the student was allowed to read an evaluation of her own personality. Half of them received highly positive descriptions designed expressly to raise their self esteem temporarily. The others received somewhat negative descriptions designed to lower their self-esteem temporarily. Finally, as part of the experiment, the students were asked to rate how much they liked a wide variety of people—a teacher, a friend, "and since we have one space left, why don't you rate that fellow you were waiting with?" The students who received unfavorable information about themselves (from the personality test) showed far more liking for their male admirer than did those who received favorable information about themselves. In short, we like to be liked—and the more insecure we feel, the more we like someone who likes us.

One of the implications of this experiment is that people who are secure about themselves are less "needy"—that is, they are less likely to accept overtures from just any person who comes along. Just as a starving person will accept almost any kind of food and a well-fed person can be more selective, an insecure person will accept almost anyone who expresses interest, while a secure person will be more selective. Moreover, a person who feels insecure may even seek out a less attractive person in order to diminish the possibility of being rejected. This implication was tested in an interesting experiment by Sara Kiesler and Roberta Baral,[49] who led male college students to believe they had done either very well or very poorly on a test of intellectual achievement. They then took a break, and the experimenter joined the student for a cup of coffee. As they entered the coffee shop, the experimenter "recognized" a female student seated alone at a table, joined her, and introduced the male participant to her. Of course, the female student was a confederate, intentionally planted there. Half of the time, the confederate was made up to look attractive; the other half of the time, she was made to look somewhat less attractive. The investigators observed the degree of romantic interest displayed by the male participants—whether they asked to see her again, offered to pay for her coffee, asked for her phone number, tried to get her to stay longer, and so on. As we would expect, those induced to feel secure about themselves (i.e., led to believe they had performed well on the test) showed more romantic interest toward the "attractive" woman; those induced to feel insecure showed more romantic interest toward the "unattractive" woman.

The Kiesler/Baral experiment suggests that most people fear rejection. They do, and for good reason. As we saw in Chapter 6, rejection produces an increase in aggression and was almost certainly one of the root causes of the Columbine High School shootings. Moreover, in a striking series of experiments, Roy Baumeister and his associates[50] demonstrated that rejection can be disruptive in a number of different ways. In one experiment, college students took a standard IQ test. Shortly before taking the test, they had been given bogus feedback based on a personality test they had taken earlier. By random assignment, some received the good news that their personality would lead them to be liked by others in the future. Others received the bad news that they would probably end up lonely because they had personalities that would lead them to be rejected in the future. A third group received bad news as well—but of a different sort. They were told that they had the kind of personalities associated with being accident prone and thus, they should anticipate a future of broken bones and hospital visits. The results were clear. Those young men and women who were led to anticipate future social rejection scored significantly lower on the IQ test than those in the other two conditions. This experiment demonstrates that, to social animals, even the *anticipation* of rejection can have a major impact on intellectual performance. In similar experiments, Baumeister and his associates found that anticipating social rejection also results in people choosing unhealthy versus healthy food (loading up on the Oreos!), procrastinating, and making unwise decisions.[51]

The Gain and Loss of Esteem

We have seen that being liked by a person increases the likelihood that we will like him or her. Let us take a closer look at this relationship. Imagine that, at a cocktail party, you meet a young woman for the first time and have an animated conversation with her. After a while, you excuse yourself to refill your glass. You return and find her back to you, deep in conversation with another person—and she's talking about you. So, naturally, you pause to listen. Clearly, the things she says about you will have an impact on how you feel about her. It is obvious that she has no ulterior motives; indeed, she doesn't even know you are eavesdropping. Thus, if she tells her partner that she was impressed by you, that she liked you, that she found you bright, witty, charming, gracious, honest, and exciting, my guess is that this disclosure will increase your liking for her. On the other hand, if she indicates that she was unimpressed, that she disliked you, that she found you dull, boring, dishonest, stupid, and vulgar, my guess is that this revelation will decrease your liking for her.

So far, so good. But I'm sure that's not very interesting to you; you've always known that the more good things we hear about ourselves, the better we like the speaker (unless that speaker is trying to con us), and the more bad things we hear about ourselves, the more we dislike the person who says them. Everybody knows that—but *it happens to be untrue*. Imagine this: You have attended seven consecutive cocktail parties, and miracle of miracles, the same general event has occurred each time. You chat with a person for several minutes, you leave, and when you come back, you overhear her talking about you. It's the same person each time. Her responses might remain constant throughout her seven encounters with you, or they might vary. There are four possibilities that are particularly interesting to me: (1) You overhear the person saying exclusively positive things about you on all seven occasions; (2) you overhear her saying exclusively negative things about you on all seven occasions; (3) her first couple of evaluations are negative, but they gradually become increasingly positive until they equal her statements in the exclusively positive situation and then level off; and (4) her first couple of evaluations are positive, but they gradually become more negative until they equal her statements in the exclusively negative situation and then level off. Which situation would render the person most attractive to you?

According to a simple reward-cost idea of liking, you should like the person most in the first situation, in which she says exclusively positive things, and you should like her least (or dislike her most) in the second situation, in which she says exclusively negative things. This seems obvious. Because positive statements are rewarding, the more the better; because negative statements are punishing, the more the worse.

A few years ago, I developed a theory of interpersonal attraction, called the gain-loss theory, that makes a rather different prediction.[52] My theory is a very simple one. It suggests that *increases* in positive, rewarding behavior from another person have more impact on an individual than constant, invariant positive, rewarding behavior from that person. Thus, if we take being liked as a reward, a person whose liking for us increases over time will be liked better than one who has always liked us. This will be true even if the number of rewards was greater from the latter person. Similarly, *losses* in positive behavior have more impact than constant negative behavior from another person. Thus, a person whose esteem for us decreases over time will be disliked more than someone who has always disliked us even if the number of negative actions were greater from the latter person. To return to the cocktail party for a moment, I would predict you will like the individual most in the gain situation (where she begins by disliking you and gradually increases her liking), and you will like her least in the loss condition (where she begins by liking you and gradually decreases her liking).

In order to test my theory, I needed an experimental analogue of the cocktail-party situation—but for reasons of control, I felt it would be essential to collapse the several events into a single long session. In such an experiment, it is important that the subject be absolutely certain that the evaluator is totally unaware that she (the evaluator) is being overheard. This eliminates the possibility of the subject's suspecting the evaluator of intentionally flattering him when she says positive things. This situation presents a difficult challenge for the experimentalist. The central problem in devising a way to perform the experiment was one of credibility: How can I provide a believable situation in which, in a relatively brief period of time, the subject (1) interacts with a preprogrammed confederate, (2) eavesdrops while the confederate evaluates him or her to a third party, (3) engages in another conversation with the confederate, (4) eavesdrops again, (5) converses again, (6) eavesdrops again, and so on, through several pairs of trials. To provide any kind of a cover story would indeed be difficult; to provide a sensible cover story that would prevent subjects from becoming suspicious would seem impossible. But, in collaboration with Darwyn Linder, I did devise such a situation.[53] The devices we used to solve these problems are intricate, and they provide a rare opportunity to look behind the scenes of an unusually fascinating experimental procedure. Accordingly, I would like to describe this experiment in some detail, in the hope that it will provide the reader with an understanding of some of the difficulties and excitements involved in conducting experiments in social psychology.

When the subject (a female college student) arrived, the experimenter greeted her and led her to an observation room connected to the main experimental room by a one-way window and an audio-amplification system. The experimenter told the subject that two women were scheduled for that hour: One would be the subject and the other would help perform the experiment—and because she had arrived first, she would be the helper. The experimenter asked her to wait while he left the room to see if the other woman had arrived. A few minutes later, through the one-way window, the subject was able to see the experimenter enter the experimental room with another female student (a paid confederate). The experimenter told the confederate to be seated for a moment and said that he would return shortly to explain the experiment to her. He then reentered the observation room and began the instructions to the real subject (who believed herself to be the confederate). The experimenter told her she was going to assist him in performing a verbal conditioning experiment on the other student; that is, he was going to reward the other student for certain words she used in conversation. He told the subject these rewards would increase the frequency with which the other woman would use these words. He went on to say that his particular interest was "not simply in increasing the output of those words that I reward; that's already been done. In this experiment, we want to see if the use of rewarded words generalizes to a new situation from the person giving the reward when the person is talking to a different person who does not reward those specific words." Specifically, the experimenter explained that he would try to condition the other woman to increase her output of plural nouns by subtly rewarding her with an "mmmm hmmm" every time she said a plural noun. "The important question is: Will she continue to use an abundance of plural nouns when she talks to you, even though you will not be rewarding her?" The real subject was then told that her tasks were (1) to listen in and record the number of plural nouns used by the woman while the latter was talking to the experimenter and (2) to engage her in a series of conversations (in which the use of plural nouns would not be rewarded) so that the experimenter could listen and determine whether generalization had occurred. The experimenter then told the subject they would alternate in talking to the woman (first the subject, then the experimenter, then the subject) until each had spent seven sessions with her.

The experimenter made it clear to the subject that the other woman must not know the purpose of the experiment, lest the results be contaminated. He explained that, in order to accomplish this, some deception must be used. The experimenter said that, as much as he regretted the use of deception, it would be necessary for him to tell the "subject" that the experiment was about interpersonal attraction. ("Don't laugh, some psychologists are actually interested in that stuff.") He said the woman would be told she was to carry on a series of seven short conversations with the subject and that, between each of these conversations, both she and the subject would be interviewed—the woman by the experimenter and the subject by an assistant in another room—to find out what impressions they had formed. The experimenter told the subject that this cover story would enable the experimenter and the subject to perform their experiment on verbal behavior because it provided the woman with a credible explanation for the procedure they would follow.

The major variable was introduced during the seven meetings the experimenter had with the confederate. During their meetings, the subject was in the observation room, listening to the conversation and dutifully counting the number of plural nouns used by the confederate. Because she had been led to believe the confederate thought the experiment involved impressions of people, it was quite natural for the experimenter to ask the confederate to express her feelings about the subject. Thus, the subject heard herself being evaluated by a fellow student on seven successive occasions.

Note how, by using a cover story that *contains* a cover story involving "interpersonal attraction," we were able to accomplish our aim without arousing much suspicion; only 4 of 84 subjects were suspicious of this procedure.

There were four major experimental conditions: (1) positive—the successive evaluations of the subject made by the confederate were all highly positive; (2) negative—the successive evaluations were all highly negative; (3) gain—the first few evaluations were negative, but they gradually became more positive, reaching a level equal to the level of the positive evaluations in the positive condition; and (4) loss—the first few evaluations were positive, but they gradually became negative, leveling off at a point equal to the negative evaluations in the negative condition.

The results confirmed our predictions: The subjects in the gain condition liked the confederate significantly better than those in the positive condition. By the same token, the subjects in the loss condition disliked the confederate more than those in the negative condition. Recall that a general reward-cost theory would lead us to a simple algebraic summation of rewards and punishments and, accordingly, would lead to somewhat different predictions. The results are in line with our general theoretical position: A gain has more impact on liking than a set of events that are all positive, and a loss has more impact than a set of events that are all negative. The philosopher Baruch de Spinoza may have had something like this in mind when, about 300 years ago, he observed:

> Hatred which is completely vanquished by love passes into love, and love is thereupon greater than if hatred had not preceded it. For he who begins to love a thing which he was wont to hate or regard with pain, from the very fact of loving, feels pleasure. To this pleasure involved in love is added the pleasure arising from aid given to the endeavor to remove the pain involved in hatred accompanied by the idea of the former object of hatred as cause.[54]

Two important conditions are necessary for the **gain-loss effect** to be operative. First, it is not just any sequence of positive or negative statements that constitutes a gain or loss; there must be an integrated sequence implying a change of heart. In other words, if you indicate that you think I'm stupid and insincere, and later you indicate that you think I'm generous and athletic, this does not constitute a gain according to my definition—or Spinoza's. On the other hand, if you suggest that you think I'm stupid or insincere and subsequently indicate you've changed your mind—that you now believe me to be smart and sincere—this is a true gain because it indicates a reversal, a replacement of a negative attitude with its opposite. David Mettee and his colleagues[55] performed an experiment that demonstrated this distinction. A gain effect occurred only when a change of heart was made explicit. Second, the change in attitude must be gradual. The reason for this should be clear: An abrupt about-face is viewed by the stimulus person with confusion and suspicion—especially if it occurs on the basis of scant evidence. If Mary thinks Sam is stupid after three encounters but brilliant after the fourth encounter, such a dramatic shift is bound to arouse suspicion on Sam's part. A gradual change, on the other hand, makes sense; it does not produce suspicion and hence produces an intensification of the person's liking for his or her evaluator.[56]

The Quest for Communal Relationships Suppose you are sharing an apartment with a casual friend—we'll call him Sam. Sam almost never washes the dishes, empties the trash, or straightens up the living room. If you want a tidy house, you usually need to do these things yourself. My guess is that, after a while, you might become upset and feel ripped off. Ah, but suppose Sam was a very special friend. Would you still feel ripped off? Perhaps, but perhaps not. It depends on what we mean by "very special."

Margaret Clark and Judson Mills[57] make an important distinction between exchange relationships and communal relationships. In **exchange relationships** the people involved are concerned about making sure that some sort of equity is achieved—that there is fairness in the distribution of the rewards and costs to each of the partners. In this kind of relationship, if there is a major imbalance, both people become unhappy; the person on the short end usually feels angry or depressed, and the person on the long end usually feels guilty.[58] In contrast, a **communal relationship** is one in which neither of the partners is keeping score. Rather, a person will be inclined to give of herself or himself in response to the other's need and will readily receive the same kind of care when he or she is feeling needy.

Although the partners in a communal relationship are not totally unconcerned about achieving a rough kind of equity, they are relaxed about it and have faith that, over the long haul, some semblance of equity will fall into place. The closer and more intimate the relationship, the more communal it becomes. Clark and Mills suggest that prenuptial agreements, in which people about to be married specify precisely what they expect from their partner, are more likely to undermine than enhance the intensity of their feelings for each other.

These issues are difficult to study scientifically. Nevertheless, Clark and Mills along with David Corcoran have done some clever experiments that succeed in capturing the essence of this important distinction. In one experiment, for example,[59] each participant was paired with either a very close friend or a stranger. The partner was then taken to another room to work on a complex task. Half of the participants were told that, if their partner needed help, that person would signal by flicking a switch that changed the pattern of some of the lights in the participant's room; the other half were told that the signal meant only that their partner was doing well, didn't need any help, and would soon complete the task for a reward that they would both share. The experimenters then observed how frequently the participants looked at the lights to see if their partner was signaling them. If the partner was a stranger (exchange relationship), they spent far more time looking at the lights when they were told that it meant they might be getting a reward; if the partner was a close friend (communal relationship), they spent far more time looking at the lights when they thought it meant their partner might need help. In short, even in this rather sterile scientific setting, the investigators were able to show that people in communal relationships are eager to be responsive to the needs of their partners.

Love and Intimacy

Until now, my discussion has focused primarily on factors that influence our initial feeling of liking or disliking early in the process of becoming acquainted. This does not mean that they are unimportant. Because first impressions are often lasting ones, they can be very important indeed.

With the discussion of research on communal relationships (above) we are beginning to edge into a more complex realm. We now turn to the topic of close relationships, paying special attention to that complex and delicious experience we call love.

What Do We Know About Love? Most of us grew up immersed in Hollywood love stories. The basic plot is simple: Boy and girl meet; they are immediately attracted to each other and (either swiftly or slowly) fall in love. Then there is a misunderstanding, one or both of them is hurt and angry, they break it off, they are both miserable; but then, through a happy accident, they find each other again, they resolve the misunderstanding, they get married, and live happily ever after. When they get married, the movie ends. But, of course, in real life, getting married is not the end of the story; indeed, I would say that's when the problems really begin. We will come back to that issue in a moment. But first, let us start with the most basic of questions: How do you meet the person with whom you will try to live happily ever after?

When I was a teenager, my friends and I clung to the romantic notion that there was one and only one true love with whom we were meant to spend our lives in passionate, romantic bliss. This belief was nourished by the popular songs of the day. So I knew that "some enchanted evening," I would "see a stranger, across a crowded room," and "once I had found her, [I would] never let her go." I could then dance with her, hold her close, and croon in her ear, "I was meant for you, you were meant for me; I'm content, the angels must have sent you, and they meant you just for me."

My friends and I were not unusual; a lot of young people had that belief then and many have it now. When you hold that belief, the major task at hand is to find the person who was meant for you. But think about it: There are nearly 6 billion people on the planet; the odds against finding your "one and only love," the "mate that fate had you created for" are enormous. Just imagine that you live in Fargo, North Dakota and your true love lives in Yazoo City,

Mississippi (or, more problematic yet, in Sofia, Bulgaria). Chances are slim-to-nonexistent that you will ever bump into each other. And if, against all odds, some enchanted evening your eyes happened to meet across a crowded room, how would you know that this was really love and not merely a fleeting infatuation?

How, and with whom, do people fall in love? Well, it turns out that people love one another for some of the same reasons that they come to like one another. A ton of research shows that the major factor is **proximity.** These findings make a shambles of the romantic myth that there is one and only one person (perhaps in Yazoo City!) waiting out there "for the right one to come along." The incontrovertible fact is that the people who live and work far away from each other are unlikely to fall in love with each other. Rather, those who are geographically nearest to you are most likely to become dearest to you, as well. From ancient times to the present, people have been and are most likely to love with and live with those who are in a nearby cave, a nearby home, or who study nearby or work in the same store, office, or factory. The second most important factor is **similarity.** Most of us fall in love with people who are similar to us in a great many ways: We fall in love with people who look like us and who have similar values, attitudes, beliefs, and personalities.[60]

Defining Love Given that liking and loving share some of the same major antecedents, does this mean that love is simply a more intense version of liking? Isn't there something special about love? Are there many types of love or is all love basically the same?

Although poets and philosophers have been struggling with these questions for centuries, they have yet to be answered in a fashion that all can agree on. The difficulty in defining love seems to lie, at least in part, with the fact that love is not a unitary, one-dimensional state but, rather, is a complex, multifaceted phenomenon experienced in a broad variety of relationships. Indeed, we use the word love to describe such diverse relationships as those between passionate teenagers (like Romeo and Juliet), newlyweds, elderly couples, and close friends.

Social psychologists have developed various approaches to categorizing and describing love in its many forms. For example, Zick Rubin, developed questionnaires to measure the various nuances of liking and loving.[61] Rubin's major finding is that loving does not appear to be simply a greater quantity of liking but typically involves a qualitatively different set of feelings and concerns regarding the loved one. Liking, in this view, is marked by admiration and friendly affection, reflected in such items as "_____is the sort of person I would like to be." Loving, in contrast, generally includes feelings of strong attachment, intimacy, and a deep concern for the beloved's welfare. Examples from Rubin's Loving Scale are "If I could never be with _____, I would be miserable" (attachment), and "I feel that I can confide in _____ about virtually everything" (intimacy).

Rubin administered his Loving and Liking scales to college students who were dating steadily but not engaged. They filled out both the liking and loving scales regarding their partner and also regarding a close friend. On the Liking Scale, their feelings about a close friend were similar to their feelings about their partner; but on the Loving Scale, their feelings about their partner were far more intense than their feelings about a close friend.

In addition, Rubin found that the higher the couple's scores on the Loving Scale, the more likely they were to believe they would get married some day. Is their degree of loving reflected in their everyday behavior? To test this, Rubin brought each of the dating couples into the laboratory and gave them a task to do. Unbeknownst to them, through a one-way mirror, he observed how frequently and for how long they gazed into each other's eyes. Couples with high scores on the Loving Scale gazed into each other's eyes with greater intensity and for longer periods of time than couples who scored somewhat lower that scale.[62]

Rubin's research strongly suggests that loving someone is a decidedly different experience from liking someone; other researchers have called attention to variations within the experience of love itself. Elaine Hatfield and Richard Rapson[63] draw an important distinction between two basic types of love: passionate and companionate. **Passionate love** is characterized by strong emotions, sexual desire, and intense preoccupation with the beloved. Its onset is usually rapid rather than gradual, and, alas, almost inevitably, its fiery intensity cools over time. In some relationships, passionate love may be a prelude to the eventual development of **companionate love**—a milder, more stable experience marked by feelings of mutual trust, dependability, and warmth. Compared to the typically short-lived intensity of romantic passion, companionate love generally lasts longer and deepens over time.

Robert Sternberg and his colleagues[64] have added a third element in a theory they call the **triangle of love.** Sternberg suggests that the three ingredients of love are passion (euphoria and sexual excitement), intimacy (feeling free to talk about anything, feeling close to and understood by the loved one), and commitment (needing to be with the other person, feeling loyal). Love can consist of one component alone or of any combination of these three parts. For example, a person may feel a great deal of passion or physical attraction for another (mere infatuation) but may not be experiencing anything approaching true intimacy. Romantic films tend to depict the love relationship as one primarily of passion. As I mentioned earlier, the film usually ends as the young couple, deeply in the throes of a passionate attraction, decides to marry. But this may not be the best moment to make that decision. As Roy Baumeister[65] puts it, passionate love is, in many respects, an altered state of consciousness (like that produced by marijuana or alcohol). Although this state is certainly exciting, it does not qualify as the best state to be in when one is making decisions with long-range, far-reaching consequences.

According to Sternberg, as the relationship develops, it often moves from pure passion and blossoms into a combination of passion and intimacy that Sternberg calls **romantic love.** As the relationship matures further, it becomes **companionate;** Sternberg uses this term to describe love characterized by the combination of intimacy and commitment—without a lot of passion. In Sternberg's system, the ultimate goal is **consummate love**—the blending of all three components. But this is achieved only rarely. The implication of this triangle is that, as a loving couple becomes increasingly accustomed to one another, there is the strong possibility that passion is likely to become the victim of routine and they may get stuck in a companionate state. It's not a terrible place to be stuck, but it falls short of the ideal—consummate love.

Gain-Loss Theory: Implications for Close Relationships In addition to enormous benefits, there is a potential dark side to being in a long-term, close, communal relationship.[66] In order to explore one of these less attractive dark sides, let us first take another look at the distinction between passionate love and companionate love. Compared with the ups and downs of a passionate love affair, the steadier, predictable rhythm of a companionate relationship offers its own special rewards. The benefits of a thriving, long-term relationship include emotional security and the priceless comfort of being accepted by someone who knows your shortcomings as well as your strengths.

What seems to be inherent in the nature of close relationships, however, is a fundamental irony, aptly expressed in the words of the classic old ballad "You Always Hurt the One You Love." Why might this be so? Recall from our earlier discussion of gain-loss theory the rather surprising fact that we find it more rewarding when someone's initially negative feelings toward us gradually become positive than if that person's feelings for us were entirely positive all along. Conversely, we tend to find it more noxious when a person who once evaluated us positively slowly comes to view us in a negative light than if he or she expressed uniformly negative feelings toward us. Although research testing the gain-loss theory has been limited to short-term liking relationships, it would be interesting to explore the possible implications of these findings for long-term relationships.

One possibility is that, once we have grown certain of the rewarding behavior of our long-term partner, that person may become less powerful as a source of reward than a stranger. We know that gains are important; but a long-term lover or spouse is probably behaving near ceiling level and, therefore, cannot provide us with much of a gain. To put it another way, once we have learned to expect love, support, and praise from a mate, such behavior is not likely to represent a gain in that person's esteem for us. By the same token, a loved one has great potential to hurt us. The closer the relationship and the greater the past history of invariant esteem and reward, the more devastating is the withdrawal of that person's esteem. In effect, then, the long-term lover has power to hurt the one he or she loves—but very little power to offer an important reward.

An example may help to clarify this point. After 20 years of marriage, a doting husband and his wife are getting dressed to attend a formal dinner party. He compliments her on her appearance: "Gee, honey, you look great." She hears his words, and they are nice but they may not fill her with delight. She already knows her husband thinks she's attractive; chances are she will not turn cartwheels at hearing about it for the thousandth time. On the other hand, if the doting husband (who in the past was always full of compliments) told his wife that she was losing her looks and he found her downright unattractive, this would cause her a great deal of pain because it represents a loss in his positive feelings about her.

Is she doomed to experience either boredom or pain? No, because there are other people in the world. Suppose Mr. and Mrs. Doting arrive at a party and a total stranger engages Mrs. Doting in a lively conversation. After a while, he begins looking at her with intense warmth and interest and says, with sincerity, that he finds her intelligent, witty, and attractive. My guess is that she would not find this at all boring. It represents a distinct gain for her—it makes her feel good about herself—and because of this it increases her positive feelings about the stranger as well.

This reasoning is consistent with existing research. For example, O. J. Harvey[67] found that people react more positively to strangers than to friends when each was designated as the person who evaluated them positively. Moreover, they tended to react more negatively to friends than to strangers when each was designated as the person who evaluated them negatively. Similarly, several experiments have shown that strangers have more impact on the behavior of young children than either parents or other familiar adults.[68] Most children are accustomed to receiving approval from parents and other adults with whom they are familiar. Therefore, additional approval from them does not represent much of a gain. However, approval from a stranger is a gain and, according to gain-loss theory, should result in more positive behavior.

These results and speculations suggest a rather bleak picture of the human condition; we seem to be forever seeking favor in the eyes of strangers while, at the same time, we are being hurt by our most intimate friends and lovers. Before we jump to this conclusion, however, let us take a few steps backward and look at the impact that gain or loss has on how individuals respond to close friends or strangers. One study is highly pertinent in this respect. Joanne Floyd[69] divided a group of young children into pairs so that each child was either with a close friend or with a stranger. One child in each pair was then allowed to play a game in which he or she earned several trinkets. The child was then instructed to share these with the assigned partner. The perceived stinginess of the sharer was manipulated by the experimenter. Some children were led to believe that the friend (or stranger) was treating them generously, and others were led to believe that the friend (or stranger) was treating them in a stingy manner. Each "receiving" child was then allowed to earn several trinkets and was instructed to share them with his or her partner. As expected, the children showed the most generosity in the gain and loss conditions—that is, they gave more trinkets to generous strangers and stingy friends. In short, they were relatively stingy to stingy strangers (and why not? The strangers behaved as they might have been expected to behave) and to generous friends ("Ho-hum, my friend likes me—so what else is new?"). But when it looked as though they might be gaining a friend (the generous stranger), they reacted with generosity; likewise, when it looked as though they might be losing one (the stingy friend), they also responded with generosity. Although it appears true that "you always hurt the one you love," the hurt person appears to be inspired to react kindly—rather than "in kind"—in an attempt to reestablish the positive intensity of the relationship. This suggests the comforting possibility that individuals are inclined to behave in a way that will preserve stability in their relations with others.

Along these lines, as far back as the year 46 B.C., and as recently as 1990, commentators from Cicero[70] to John Harvey and his colleagues[71] have suggested that, in a communal relationship, hurt feelings and conflict can produce healthy and exciting new understandings. How might these understandings come about? A clue comes from taking another look at the Dotings. Although Mr. Doting has great power to hurt his wife by criticizing her, because of the importance of the relationship, Mrs. Doting is apt to listen closely and be responsive to such criticism and will be inclined to make some changes in order to regain his interest. The reverse is also true: If Mrs. Doting were to suddenly change her high opinion of Mr. Doting, he would be likely to pay close attention and eventually take action to regain her approval. A relationship becomes truly creative and continues to grow when both partners resolve conflicts—not by papering them over, but by striving to grow and change in creative ways. In this process, **authenticity** assumes great importance.

Carrying this reasoning a step further, I would guess that the more honest and authentic a relationship is, the less the likelihood of its stagnating on a dull and deadening plateau like the one on which the Dotings appear to be stuck. What I am suggesting is that a close relationship in which the partners do not provide each other with gains in esteem is almost certain to be a relationship in which the partners are not open and honest with each other. In a closed relationship, people tend to suppress their annoyances and to keep their negative feelings to themselves. This results in a fragile plateau that appears stable and positive but that can be devastated by a sudden shift in sentiment. Unfortunately, this may be a common kind of relationship in this country.

In an open, honest, authentic relationship, one in which people are able to share their true feelings and impressions (even their negative ones), no such plateau is reached. Rather, there is a continuous zigzagging of sentiment around a point of relatively high mutual regard. These speculations receive support by research[72] showing that marriage partners who use an intimate, nonaggressive, yet *confrontational* method of conflict resolution report higher levels of marital satisfaction. In a relationship of this sort, the partners are reasonably close to the gain condition of the gain-loss experiment. By the same token, an exchange of intimate and important aspects of *oneself*—both positive and negative—is beneficial for the development of close relationships. That is, all other things being equal, we like a person better after we have disclosed something important about ourselves—even if it is unsavory. In addition, studies of people in close relations indicate that we tend to like other people better when they honor us by revealing something intimate and negative about themselves.[73]

Art Aron and his colleagues[74] have been studying this phenomenon in the laboratory by developing a conversational technique that encouraged self-disclosure among strangers. In this experiment, they divided college students into pairs for a conversation; the students had never met before. The conversational technique was structured in such a way that the students were obliged to reveal important information about themselves—with each new revelation escalating in intensity and intimacy. The results were clear: First of all, the students thoroughly enjoyed the procedure. Moreover, following the session, students who went through this procedure felt a good deal closer to each other than students in a control condition who engaged in friendly but non-self-revealing small talk. The increase in closeness took place even when the conversation revealed differences in important attitudes.

Incidentally, self-revelation seems to have a wide array of positive benefits in addition to feelings of interpersonal closeness. For example, in a striking series of studies, Jamie Pennebaker and his colleagues[75] demonstrated that when people disclose difficult or painful emotions, it brings about a strong feeling of relief, a general feeling of well-being, and even a diminution in symptoms of physical illness.

To summarize this section, the data indicate that, as a relationship moves toward greater intimacy, what becomes increasingly important is *authenticity*—our ability to give up trying to make a good impression and begin to reveal things about ourselves that are honest, even if unsavory. In addition, authenticity implies a willingness to communicate a wide range of interpersonal feelings to our friends and loved ones, under appropriate circumstances and in ways that reflect our caring. Thus, to return to the plight of Mr. and Mrs. Doting, the research data suggest that if two people are genuinely fond of each other, they will have a more satisfying and exciting relationship over a longer period of time if they are able to express both positive and negative feelings about each other as well as about themselves.

Intimacy, Authenticity, and Communication

Although honest communication with loved ones has beneficial effects, the process is not as easy as it might sound. Honest communication entails sharing negative feelings and unappetizing things about ourselves; these things increase our vulnerability—and most of us usually try to avoid making ourselves vulnerable—even to the people we love the most. How might we accomplish this in a real relationship? Imagine, if you will, the following scenario:

Phil and Alice Henshaw are washing the dishes. They have had several friends over for dinner, the friends have left, and Phil and Alice are cleaning up. During the evening Alice was her usual charming, witty, vivacious self. But Phil, who is usually delighted by her charm, is feeling hurt and a little angry. It seems that, during a political discussion, Alice had disagreed with his position and sided with Tom. Moreover, she seemed to express a great deal of warmth toward Tom in the course of the evening. In fact, her behavior could be considered mildly flirtatious.

Phil is thinking: "I love her so much. I wish she wouldn't do things like that. Maybe she's losing interest in me. God, if she ever left me, I don't know what I'd do. Is she really attracted to Tom?" But Phil is reluctant to share his vulnerability so he actually says: "You sure were throwing yourself at Tom tonight. Everybody noticed it. You really made a fool of yourself."

Alice cares a great deal about Phil. She felt that she had said some very bright things that evening—especially during the political discussion—and felt that Phil didn't acknowledge her intellectual contribution. "He thinks I'm just an uninteresting housewife. He is probably bored with me."

Alice: I don't know what you're talking about. You're just mad because I happened to disagree with you about the president's tax proposal. Tom saw it my way. I think I was right.

Phil: He saw it *your* way! Are you kidding? What else could he do? You were practically sitting in his lap. The other guests were embarrassed.

Alice (teasing): Why, Phil, I do believe you're jealous!

Phil: I'm not jealous! I really don't give a damn. If you want to act like a slut, that's your business.

Alice (angrily): Boy, are you old-fashioned. You're talking like some Victorian, for God's sake! You're always doing that!

Phil (coldly): That just shows how little you know about me. Other people find me up-to-date—even dashing.

Alice (sarcastically): Yes, I'm sure you cut quite a figure with all the secretaries at your office!

Phil: Now, what's *that* supposed to mean?

Alice falls into a stony silence. Phil makes several attempts to get a response from her, fails, then storms out of the room, slamming the door. What is going on? Here are two people who love each other. How did they get into such a vicious, hurtful, spiteful argument?

One of the major characteristics of humans that separates us from other organisms is our unique ability to communicate complex information through the use of a highly sophisticated language. The subtlety of communication that is possible among humans compared to that among other animals is truly awesome. And yet, misunderstandings among people are frequent. Moreover, misunderstandings typify even those relationships that are close and caring. Though hypothetical, the argument between the Henshaws is not at all unrealistic; rather, it is typical of hundreds of such conversations I have heard as a consultant trying to help straighten out dyadic communications that are garbled, indirect, and misleading.

It would be relatively easy to analyze the argument between Phil and Alice. Each had a major concern that was being threatened. Neither was able or willing to state in a clear, straightforward way what that concern was. For Alice, the major concern seemed to be her intellectual competence. She was afraid Phil thought she was dumb or boring; her major *implicit* complaint in this argument was that Phil didn't acknowledge the cogency of her statements during the political discussion, and he seemed to be implying that the only reason Tom paid attention to her or seemed to be interested in her statements was lust or sexual flirtation. This hurt her, threatened her self-esteem, and made her angry. She didn't express the hurt. She expressed the anger, but not simply by revealing it; rather, she took the offensive and attacked Phil by implying that he is stodgy and uninteresting.

Phil's major concerns seemed to stem from a feeling of insecurity. While he enjoys Alice's vivacity, he appears to be afraid of the possibility that, with increasing age, he may be losing his own attractiveness as a man. Thus, he assumed that Alice's agreeing with Tom is akin to her siding with Tom against him—and he attached sexual connotations to it because of his own insecurities. When Alice called him "old-fashioned," he seemed mostly to hear the "old"—and he quickly defended his masculinity and sex appeal, which Alice, driven by her *own* anger, promptly ridiculed.

This kind of argument is a familiar one among people living in close relationships. Important feelings and concerns are present. But instead of being discussed openly and honestly, the feelings are allowed to escalate into hostility, which only exacerbates the hurt and insecurity that initiated the discussion in the first place. As the divorce rate remains high in the United States, it seems reasonable to ask seriously why this happens. It would be silly to proclaim that all anger, disagreement, hurt, and hostility between people who supposedly care about each other are a function of poor or inadequate communication. Often there are conflicts between the needs, values, desires, and goals of people in close relationships. These produce stresses and tensions, which must either be lived with or resolved by compromise, yielding, or the dissolution of the relationship.

But frequently, the problem is largely one of communication. How might Phil have communicated differently? Pretend for the moment that you are Phil. And Alice, a person you care about, approaches you and makes the following statement in a tone of voice that was nonblaming and nonjudgmental:

> I'm feeling insecure about my intelligence—or at least the way people view me on that dimension. Since you are the most important person in my world, it would be particularly gratifying to me if you would acknowledge statements of mine that you think are intelligent or worthwhile. When we disagree on a substantive issue and you speak harshly or become impatient with me, it tends to increase my feeling of insecurity. Earlier this evening, during our political discussion, I would have been delighted if you had complimented me on some of my ideas and insights.

Imagine, now, that you are Alice, and Phil had opened the after-dinner discussion in the following way:

> This is difficult to talk about, but I'd like to try. I don't know what it is with me lately, but I was feeling some jealousy tonight. This isn't easy to say, but here goes: You and Tom seemed kind of close—both intellectually and physically—and I was feeling hurt and lonely. I've been worried lately about middle age. This may seem silly, but I've been slowing down, feeling tired, developing a paunch. I need some reassurance; do you still find me attractive? I would love it if you'd look at me the way you seemed to be looking at Tom this evening.

My guess is that most people would be receptive and responsive to that kind of **straight talk** from a loved one. By straight talk, I mean a person's clear statement of his or her feelings and concerns without accusing, blaming, judging, or ridiculing the other person. Straight talk is effective precisely because it enables the recipient to listen nondefensively.

Straight talk seems so simple, and it obviously is effective. Why don't people use it as a matter of course? The main reason is that it is not as easy as it appears. In the course of growing up in a competitive society, most of us have learned how to protect ourselves by making ourselves relatively invulnerable. Thus, when we are hurt, we have learned not to show it. Rather, we have learned either to avoid the person who hurt us or to lash out at him or her with anger, judgment, or ridicule. As we have seen, this will usually result in either a defensive response or a counterattack, and the argument escalates.

In short, the general lesson of our society is never to reveal your vulnerabilities. This strategy may be useful and in some situations even essential, but in many circumstances it is inappropriate, dysfunctional, and counterproductive. It is probably wise not to reveal your vulnerability to someone who is your sworn enemy. But it is almost certainly unwise to conceal your vulnerability from someone who is your loving friend and cares about you. Thus, if Alice and Phil had known about the other's insecurity, they each could have acted in ways that would have made the other feel more secure. Because each of them had overlearned the societal lesson of "attack rather than reveal," they inadvertently placed themselves on a collision course.

Often, the problem is even more complicated than the one described in this example. Alice and Phil seem to have some idea of what their concerns and feelings are. They got into serious conflict primarily because they had difficulty communicating their insecurity and hurt feelings with each other. But, in many situations, people are not fully aware of their own needs, wants, and feelings. Instead, there may be a vague feeling of discomfort or unhappiness that the person can't easily pinpoint. Often there is misattribution; that is, Phil may feel uncomfortable, and he could attribute the discomfort to embarrassment over Alice's allegedly flirtatious behavior rather than to his own underlying insecurities about advancing middle age. Thus, if we are not in touch with our own feelings and cannot articulate them clearly to ourselves, we cannot communicate them to another person. The key issue is sensitivity. Can we learn to be more sensitive to our own feelings? Can we learn to be sensitive to others so that, when people *do* make themselves vulnerable, we treat that vulnerability with care and respect?

Characteristics of Effective Communication

The Importance of Immediacy For communication to be effective in a close relationship, feelings must be expressed directly and openly. When this strategy is followed, we are able to receive immediate feedback on how our words and behavior are interpreted. With immediate feedback, we are better able to gain insight into the impact of our actions and statements and to consider our options for meeting our own needs as well as our partner's. To illustrate, suppose I perform an act that angers my best friend (who also happens to be my wife). If she doesn't express this anger, I may never become aware of the fact that my action makes her angry. On the other hand, suppose she gives me immediate feedback; suppose she tells me how my action makes me feel angry. Then I have at least two options: I can continue to behave in that way, or I can stop behaving in that way—the choice is mine. The behavior may be so important that I don't want to give it up. Conversely, my wife's feelings may be so important that I choose to give up the behavior. In the absence of any knowledge of how my behavior makes her feel, I don't have a choice. Moreover, knowing exactly how she feels about a particular action may allow me to explore a different action that may satisfy my needs as well as her needs.

The value of immediate feedback is not limited to the recipient. Frequently, in providing feedback, people discover something about themselves and their own needs. If Sharon feels, for example, that it's always destructive to express anger, she may block out her awareness of this feeling. When the expression of this feeling is legitimized, she has a chance to bring it out in the open, to look at it, and to become aware that her expression of anger has not caused the world to come to an end. Moreover, the direct expression of a feeling keeps the encounter on the up-and-up and thus helps to prevent the escalation of negative feelings. For example, if my wife has learned to express her anger directly, it keeps our discussion on the issue at hand. If she suppresses the anger but it leaks out in other ways—at different times and in different situations—I do not know where her hostility is coming from and I become confused, hurt, or angry.

Feelings versus Judgment People are often unaware of how to provide constructive feedback. We frequently do it in a way that angers or upsets the recipient, thereby leading to escalation and causing more problems than we solve. This point is better illustrated than described in the abstract. I will do this by providing an example of dysfunctional feedback and of how people can learn to modify their method of providing feedback (without diluting its content) in order to maximize communication and understanding. This example is an actual event that took place in a communication workshop I conducted for corporation executives.

In the course of the workshop, one of the members (Sam) looked squarely at another member (Harry) and said, "Harry, I've been listening to you and watching you for a day and a half, and I want to give you some feedback: I think you're a phony." Now that's quite an accusation. How can Harry respond? He has several options: He can (1) agree with Sam; (2) deny the accusation and say he's not a phony; (3) express anger by retaliating telling Sam what he thinks is wrong with *him;* or (4) feel sorry for himself and go into a sulk. None of these responses is particularly productive. But doesn't Sam have the right to express this judgment? After all, he's only being open. Don't we value openness and authenticity?

This sounds like a dilemma: Effective communication requires openness, but openness can hurt people. The solution to this apparent dilemma is rather simple: It is possible to be open and, at the same time, to express oneself in a manner that causes a minimum of pain and maximizes understanding. The key to effective communication rests on our willingness to express *feelings* rather than judgments. In this instance Sam was not expressing a feeling, he was interpreting Harry's behavior and judging it. The word *feeling* has several meanings. In this context I don't mean "hunch" or "hypothesis." By *feeling* I mean, specifically, anger or joy, sadness or happiness, annoyance, fear, discomfort, warmth, hurt, envy, excitement, and the like.

In the workshop, my intervention was a basic one: I simply asked Sam if he had any feelings about Harry. Sam thought for a moment and then said, "Well, I feel that Harry is a phony." Needless to say, this is not a feeling, as defined above. This is an opinion or a judgment expressed in the terminology of feelings. A judgment is nothing more or less than a feeling that is inadequately understood or inadequately expressed. Accordingly, I probed further by asking Sam what his feelings were. Sam still insisted that he felt Harry was a phony. "And what does that do to you?" "It annoys the hell out of me," answered Sam. "What kinds of things has Harry done that annoyed you, Sam?"

Sam eventually admitted that he got annoyed whenever Harry expressed warmth and understanding to other members of the group. On further probing, it turned out that Sam perceived Harry as being attractive—especially to women. What eventually emerged was that Sam owned up to a feeling of envy: Sam wished he had Harry's easy charm and popularity.

Note that Sam had initially masked this feeling of envy; instead, he had discharged his feelings by expressing disdain, by saying Harry was a phony. This kind of expression is ego-protecting: Because we live in a competitive society, Sam had learned over the years that, if he had admitted to feeling envious, it might have put him "one down" and put Harry "one up." This would have made Sam vulnerable—that is, it would have made him feel weak in relation to Harry. By expressing disdain, however, Sam succeeded in putting himself "one up."

Although his behavior was successful as an ego-protecting device, it didn't contribute to Sam's understanding of his own feelings and of the kinds of events that caused those feelings; and it certainly didn't contribute to Sam's understanding of Harry or to Harry's understanding of Sam. In short, Sam was communicating ineffectively. As an ego-defensive measure, his behavior was adaptive; as a form of communication, it was extremely maladaptive. Thus, although it made Sam vulnerable to admit he envied Harry, it opened the door to communication; eventually, it helped them to understand each other.

It's easier for all of us to hear feedback that is expressed in terms of feelings—"I'm upset"—than feedback expressed as a judgment or accusation—"You are a callous jerk!" A person's judgments about another person almost always take the form of dispositional attributions (attributing the cause of a person's behavior to a flaw in their personalities or dispositions). In this case, Sam was telling Harry what kind of person he (Harry) is. Generally, people resent being told what kind of person they are—and for good reason, because such attributions are purely a matter of conjecture. Sam's dispositional attribution about Harry's behavior may reflect reality or, just as likely, it may not—it is merely Sam's theory about Harry. Only Harry knows for sure whether he's an insincere phony; Sam is only guessing. But Sam's statement that he is feeling envious or angry is not a guess or a theory; it is an absolute fact. Sam is not guessing about his own feelings—he knows them. Harry may or may not care about Sam's intellectual theories or judgments, but if he wants to be Sam's friend, he might want to know Sam's feelings and what he (Harry) did to trigger them.[76]

Communication and Consummate Love Sam and Harry were not lovers. They were merely two guys in a workshop trying to improve their communication skills. Effective communication is useful for everyone. But it is particularly valuable in a close relationship. When lovers do not state their negative feelings (hurt, anger, upset) directly but conceal them and, instead, resort to judgments and dispositional attributions, minor disagreements will almost invariably escalate into major disputes—as in the argument that Phil and Alice were having earlier in this chapter. When lovers express their feeling without judging the other as wrong, insensitive, or uncaring, escalation rarely follows. Research on happy and unhappy marriages supports this reasoning. In a longitudinal study, Frank Fincham and Thomas Bradbury[77] studied 130 newly married couples over time and found that those couples who made dispositional attributions early in their marriages became increasingly unhappy with their spouses. In contrast, couples who made situational attributions that were forgiving of the partner's occasionally thoughtless actions became increasingly happy with their marriages. Straight talk may indeed be the royal road to consummate love.

Saul Steinberg, *Untitled drawing*, ink on paper.
Originally published in *The New Yorker*, September 10, 1960.
© The Saul Steinberg Foundation / Artists Rights Society (ARS), New York

9

Social Psychology as a Science

When I was in college, I first got interested in social psychology because it dealt with some of the most exciting aspects of being human: love, hate, prejudice, aggression, altruism, social influence, conformity, and the like. At that time, I didn't care a great deal about how this impressive body of knowledge came into existence. I simply wanted to know what was known. It wasn't until I entered graduate school that it suddenly dawned on me that I could be more than a consumer of this knowledge—I could become a producer as well. And a whole new world opened up for me—the world of scientific social psychology. I learned how to ask important questions and do the experiments to find the answers to those questions—contributing, in my own small way, to the body of knowledge that I had read about as a student. And I have been passionately involved in that activity ever since.

Reading this chapter is not going to make you into a scientist. My intention for you is a bit less ambitious but no less important. This chapter is aimed at helping to improve your ability to think scientifically about things that are happening in your own social world. I have always found this a useful thing to be able to do. But, occasionally, it can be disillusioning as well. Let me give you one example of what I mean by that statement. Not long ago, I picked up a copy of *The New Yorker* magazine, where I read an excellent, highly informative essay by James Kunen[1] about college-level educational programs in our prisons. Kunen wrote enthusiastically about their effectiveness. He then went on to decry the fact that a generally punitive congressional majority was eliminating these programs after characterizing them as wasteful and as tending to coddle criminals.

Kunen's essay contains a few vivid case histories of convicts who, while in prison, completed the college program and went on to lead productive lives after being released. The case histories are heartwarming. But, as a scientist, I wanted to know if there were any systematic data that I might use to evaluate the overall effectiveness of the program. Well, yes. Kunen reported one study published in 1991 by the New York State Department of Correctional Services, which found that 4 years after their release from prison, the recidivism rate of male inmates who had completed 1 or more years of higher education in prison was 20 percent lower than the average for all male inmates.

That sounds pretty impressive, right? Let's take a closer look. As scientists we need to ask one basic and vital question: Prior to participating in the program, were the prisoners who signed up for the program similar to those who didn't sign up? Might it not be the case that the prisoners who signed up for the program and completed a year of it were different *to begin with* (say, in motivation, ability, intelligence, prior education, mental health, or what have you) from those who did not sign up? I hasten to add that this is not simply nit-picking; if they were different at the outset from the general run of prisoners, then it is likely (or, at least, possible) that they would have had a lower rate of recidivism even without having taken the course of study. If that were the case, then it wasn't the program that caused the lower recidivism.

While I was reading Kunin's article, the liberal/humanist in me wanted to get excited by the results of this study; it would be terrific to have convincing data proving that educating prisoners pays off. But alas, the scientist in me took over—and was skeptical. Thus, looking at the social world through the eyes of a scientist can be disillusioning. But it also gives us the ability to separate the wheat from the chaff so that, as concerned citizens, we can demand that innovative programs be properly evaluated. In that way, we can determine with some degree of clarity which of thousands of possible programs are worthy of our time, effort, and money. And the truth is that, in most cases, it is not difficult to do the experiment properly—as you will see.

What Is the Scientific Method?

The scientific method—regardless of whether it is being applied in physics, chemistry, biology, or social psychology—is the best way we humans have of satisfying our hunger for knowledge and understanding. More specifically, we use the scientific method in an attempt to uncover lawful relationships among things—whether the things are chemicals, planets, or the antecedents of human prejudice or love. The first step in the scientific process is observation. In physics, a simple observation might go something like this: If there is a rubber ball in my granddaughter's wagon and she pulls the wagon forward, the ball seems to roll to the back of the wagon. (It doesn't actually roll backward; it only seems that way.) When she stops the wagon abruptly, the ball rushes to the front of the wagon. In social psychology, a simple observation might go something like this: When I am waiting on tables, if I happen to be in a good mood and smile a lot at my customers, my tips seem to be a bit larger than when I am in a foul mood and smile less frequently.

The next step is to make a guess as to why that happens; this guess is our taking a stab at uncovering the "lawful relationship" we mentioned above. The third step is to frame that guess as a testable hypothesis. The final step is to design an experiment (or a series of experiments) that will either confirm or disconfirm the hypothesis. If a series of well-designed, well-executed experiments fails to confirm that hypothesis, we give it up. As my favorite physicist, Richard Feynman,[2] once put it, "It doesn't matter how beautiful the guess is or how smart the guesser is, or how famous the guesser is; if the experiment disagrees with the guess, then the guess is wrong. That's all there is to it!" In my own opinion, this is both the essence of science and its beauty. There are no sacred truths in science.

Science and Art In my opinion, there is plenty of room for art in our science. I believe that the two processes—art and science—are different but related. Pavel Semonov, a distinguished Russian psychologist, did a pretty good job of defining the difference. According to Semonov,[3] as scientists, we look closely at our environment and try to organize the unknown in a sensible and meaningful way. As artists, we reorganize the known environment in order to create something entirely new. To this observation, I would add that the requirements of a good experiment frequently necessitate a combination of skills from both of these domains. In a very real sense, as experimenters, we use artistry to enrich our science. I believe this to be particularly true of experiments in social psychology.

Why is this blending of art and science especially true of social psychology? The full answer to this question will emerge as this chapter unfolds. For now, let me simply state that, in social psychology, we are not studying the behavior of chemicals in a beaker or of rubber balls in wagons; we are investigating the behavior of intelligent, curious, sophisticated adults who have been living in a social world for their entire lives. It goes without saying that, like the experimenters who are studying them, the people who serve as participants in our experiments have developed their own ideas and theories about what causes their feelings and behavior, as well as the feelings and behavior of the people around them. This is not the case when you are performing experiments with chemicals, with laboratory animals, or even with humans in nonsocial situations.

The fact that we are dealing with socially sophisticated human beings is part of what makes social psychology so fascinating as a topic of experimental investigation. At the same time, this situation also demands a great deal of art if the experimenter stands a chance of generating valid and reliable findings. In this chapter, I will try to communicate exactly how this happens.

From Speculation to Experimentation

In Chapter 8, we described a confusing phenomenon that we had stumbled upon several years ago: While John F. Kennedy was president, his personal popularity increased immediately after he committed a stupendously costly blunder.

Specifically, after Kennedy's tragic miscalculation known as the Bay of Pigs fiasco, a Gallup poll showed that people liked him better than they had prior to that incident. Like most people, I was dumbfounded by this event. How could we like a guy better after he screwed up so badly? As a scientist, I speculated about what could have caused that shift. My guess was that, because Kennedy previously had been perceived as such a nearly perfect person, committing a blunder might have made him seem more human, thus allowing ordinary people to feel closer to him. An interesting speculation, but was it true?

Because many things were happening at the time of the Bay of Pigs fiasco, it was impossible to be sure whether or not this speculation was accurate. How might we have tried to find out? Well, we might have simply asked people why they liked Kennedy more now than they did the prior week. That sounds simple enough. Unfortunately, it is not that easy. Over the years, we have learned that people are often unaware of why they act in certain ways or change their beliefs in one direction or another; so, in a complex situation, simply asking people to explain their behavior will usually not yield reliable results.[4] This is precisely why social psychologists perform experiments. But how could we conduct an experiment on John F. Kennedy's popularity? We couldn't. In a case like this, we would try to conduct an experiment on the underlying phenomenon, not on the specific instantiation of that phenomenon. And, indeed, it was really the underlying phenomenon—not the specific event—that held our interest: Does committing a blunder increase the popularity of a nearly perfect person?

In order to answer this more general question, it was necessary to go beyond the event that led to our speculations. My colleagues and I had to design an experiment[5] that allowed us to control for extraneous variables and test the effects of a blunder on attraction in a less complex situation—one in which we could control the exact nature of the blunder as well as the kind of person who committed it. And in that simple situation we found, as predicted, that "nearly perfect" people become *more* attractive after they commit a blunder, while "rather ordinary" people become *less* attractive after committing the identical blunder. (I have described the details of this experiment in Chapter 8.)

Designing an Experiment As suggested above, in striving for control, the experimenter must bring his or her ideas out of the helter-skelter of the real world and into the rather sterile confines of the laboratory. This typically entails concocting a situation bearing little resemblance to the real-world situation from which the idea originated. In fact, a frequent criticism is that laboratory experiments are unrealistic, contrived imitations of human interaction that don't reflect the real world at all. How accurate is this criticism?

Perhaps the best way to answer this question is to examine one laboratory experiment in great detail, considering its advantages and disadvantages, as well as an alternative, more realistic approach that might have been used to study the same issue. The initiation experiment I performed in collaboration with Judson Mills[6] suits our purpose admirably—because it contains many of the advantages and disadvantages of the laboratory. The reader may recall that Mills and I speculated that people might come to like things for which they have suffered. We then designed and conducted a laboratory experiment in which we showed that people who expended great effort (by undergoing a severe initiation) to gain membership in a group liked the group more than did people who became members with little or no effort. Here's how the experiment was performed:

> Sixty-three college women who initially volunteered to engage in several discussions on the psychology of sex were participants of the study. Each student was tested individually. At the beginning of the study, I explained that I was studying the "dynamics of the group-discussion process." I said the actual topic of the discussion was not important to me, but because most people are interested in sex, I selected that topic in order to be certain of having plenty of participants. I also explained that I had encountered a major drawback in choosing sex as the topic: Specifically, because of shyness, many people found it difficult to discuss sex in a group setting. Because any impediment to the flow of the discussion could seriously invalidate the results, I needed to know if the participants felt any hesitancy to enter a discussion about sex. When the participants heard this, each and every one indicated she would have no difficulty. These elaborate instructions were used to set the stage for the important event to follow. The reader should note how the experimenter's statements tend to make the following material believable.
>
> Up to this point, the instructions had been the same for all participants. Now it was time to give each of the people in the various experimental conditions a different experience—an experience the experimenters believed would make a difference.
>
> Participants were randomly assigned in advance to one of three conditions: (1) One-third of them would go through a severe initiation, (2) one-third would go through a mild initiation, and (3) one-third would not go through any initiation at all. For the no-initiation condition, participants were simply told they could now join the discussion group. For the severe- and mild-initiation conditions, however, I told each participant that, because it was necessary to be positive she could discuss sex openly, I had developed a screening device—a test for embarrassment—that I then asked her to take. This test constituted the initiation. For the severe-initiation condition, the test was highly embarrassing. It required the participant to recite a list of 12 obscene words and 2 detailed descriptions of sexual activity taken from contemporary novels. The mild-initiation participants had to recite only a list of words related to sex that were not obscene.

The three conditions to which participants were assigned constituted the **independent variable** in this study. Briefly, the investigator's goal in designing and conducting an experiment is to determine if what happens to participants has an effect on how they respond. *Our* goal was to determine if severity of initiation—the independent variable—*caused* systematic differences in participants' behavior. Would participants who experienced a severe initiation act differently than those who experienced a mild initiation or no initiation at all?

But act differently in what way? After the initiation, each participant was allowed to eavesdrop on a discussion being conducted by members of the group she had just joined. In order to control the content of this material, a tape recording was used; but the participants were led to believe it was a live discussion. Thus, all participants—regardless of whether they had gone through a severe initiation, a mild initiation, or no initiation—listened to the same group discussion. The group discussion was as dull and as boring as possible; it involved a halting, inarticulate analysis of the secondary sex characteristics of lower animals—changes in plumage among birds, intricacies of the mating dance of certain spiders, and the like. The tape contained long pauses, a great deal of hemming and hawing, interruptions, incomplete sentences, and so on, all designed to make it boring.

At the end of the discussion, I returned with a set of rating scales and asked the participant to rate how interesting and worthwhile the discussion had been. This is called the **dependent variable** because, quite literally, the response is assumed to be "dependent" on the particular experimental conditions the participant had been assigned to. The dependent variable is what the experimenter measures to assess the effects of the independent variable. In short, if the independent variable is the *cause*, then the dependent variable is the *effect*.

The results supported the hypothesis: Women who went through a mild initiation or no initiation at all saw the group discussion as relatively dull. But those who suffered in order to be admitted to the group thought it was really exciting. Remember, all the students were rating *exactly the same discussion.*

Designing and conducting this experiment was a laborious process. Mills and I spent hundreds of hours planning it, creating a credible situation, writing a script for the tape recording of the group discussion, rehearsing the actors who played the roles of group members, constructing the initiation procedures and the measuring instruments, recruiting volunteers to serve as participants, pilot-testing the procedure, running the participants through the experiment, and explaining the true purpose of the experiment to each participant (the reason for the deception, what it all meant, and so forth). What we found was that people who go through a severe initiation in order to join a group like that group a great deal more than people who go through a mild initiation or no initiation at all.

Surely there must be a simpler way! There is. The reader may have noticed a vague resemblance between the procedure used by Mills and me and other initiations, such as those used by primitive tribes and those used by some college fraternities and other exclusive clubs or organizations. Why, then, didn't we take advantage of the real-life situation, which is not only easier to study but also far more dramatic and realistic? Let's look at the advantages. Real-life initiations would be more severe (i.e., they would have more impact on the members); we would not have had to go to such lengths to design a group setting the participants would find convincing; the social interactions would involve real people rather than mere voices from a tape recording; we would have eliminated the ethical problem created by the use of deception and the use of a difficult and unpleasant experience in the name of science; and, finally, it could all have been accomplished in a fraction of the time the experiment consumed.

Thus, when we take a superficial look at the advantages of a natural situation, it appears that Mills and I would have had a much simpler job if we had studied existing fraternities. Here is how we might have done it. We could have rated each group's initiation for severity and interviewed the members later to determine how much they liked their group. If the members who had undergone a severe initiation liked their fraternities more than the mild- or no-initiation fraternity members, the hypothesis would be supported. Or would it? Let's take a closer look at why people bother to do experiments.

If people were asked to name the most important characteristic of a laboratory experiment, the great majority would say "control." And this *is* a major advantage. Experiments have the advantage of controlling the environment and the variables so that the effects of each variable can be precisely studied. By taking our hypothesis to the laboratory, Mills and I eliminated a lot of the extraneous variation that exists in the real world. The severe initiations were all equal in intensity; this condition would have been difficult to match if we had used several severe-initiation fraternities. Further, the group discussion was identical for all participants; in the real world, however, fraternity members would have been rating fraternities that were, in fact, different from each other. Assuming we had been able to find a difference between the severe-initiation and mild-initiation fraternities, how would we have known whether this was a function of the initiation rather than of the differential likableness that already existed in the fraternity members themselves? In the experiment, the only difference was the severity of the initiation, so we know that any difference was due to that procedure.

The Importance of Random Assignment

Control *is* an important aspect of the laboratory experiment, but it is not the major advantage. A still more important advantage is that participants can be randomly assigned to the different experimental conditions. This means each participant has an equal chance to be in any condition in the study. Indeed, the **random assignment** of participants to conditions is the crucial difference between the experimental method and nonexperimental approaches. And the great advantage of the random assignment of people to conditions is this: Any variables not thoroughly controlled are, in theory, distributed randomly across the conditions. This means it is extremely unlikely that such variables would affect results in a systematic fashion.

An example might help to clarify this point: Suppose you are a scientist and you have the hypothesis that marrying intelligent women makes men happy. How do you test this hypothesis? Let us say you proceed to find 1,000 men who are married to intelligent women and 1,000 men who are married to not-so-intelligent women, and you give them all a "happiness" questionnaire. Lo and behold, you find that the men married to intelligent women *are* happier than the men married to less intelligent women. Does this mean that being married to an intelligent woman makes a man happy? No. Perhaps happy men are sweeter, more good-humored, and easier to get along with, and that, consequently, intelligent women seek out these men and marry them. So it may be that being happy *causes* men to marry intelligent women. The problem doesn't end there. It is also possible that there is some third factor that causes *both* happiness *and* being married to an intelligent woman. One such factor could be money: It is conceivable that being rich helps make men happy and that their being rich is what attracts the intelligent women. So it is possible that neither causal sequence is true. It is possible that happiness does not cause men to marry intelligent women and that intelligent women do not cause men to be happy.

The problem is even more complicated because we usually have no idea what these third factors might be. In the case of the happiness study, it could be wealth; it could also be that a mature personality causes men to be happy and also attracts intelligent women; it could be social grace, athletic ability, power, popularity, using the right toothpaste, being a snappy dresser, or any of a thousand qualities the poor researcher does not know about and could not possibly account for. But if the researcher performs an experiment, he or she can randomly assign participants to various experimental conditions. Although this procedure does not eliminate differences due to any of these variables (money, social grace, athletic ability, and the like), it neutralizes them by distributing these characteristics randomly across various experimental conditions. That is, if participants are randomly assigned to experimental conditions, there will be approximately as many rich men in one condition as in the others, as many socially adept men in one condition as in the others, and as many athletes in one condition as in the others. Thus, if we do find a difference between conditions, it is unlikely that this would be due to individual differences in any single characteristic because all of these characteristics had an equal (or nearly equal) distribution across all of the conditions.

Admittedly, the particular example of intelligent women and their happy husbands does not easily lend itself to the confines of the experimental laboratory. But let us fantasize about how we would do it if we could. Ideally, we would take 50 men and randomly assign 25 to intelligent wives and 25 to less intelligent wives. A few months later, we could come back and administer the happiness questionnaire. If the men assigned to the intelligent wives are happier than the men assigned to the less intelligent wives, we would know what caused their happiness—we did! In short, their happiness couldn't easily be attributed to social grace, or handsomeness, or money, or power; these were randomly distributed among the experimental conditions. It almost certainly was caused by their wives' characteristics.

To repeat, this example is pure fantasy; even social psychologists must stop short of arranging marriages for scientific purposes. But this does not mean we cannot test important, meaningful, relevant events under controlled laboratory conditions. This book is loaded with such examples. Let's look at one of these examples as a way of clarifying the advantages of the experimental method. In Chapter 6, I reported a correlation between the amount of time children spend watching violence on television and their tendency to choose aggressive solutions to their problems.

Does this mean watching aggression on television causes youngsters to become aggressive? Not necessarily. It might. But it might also mean that aggressive youngsters simply like to watch aggression, and they would be just as aggressive if they watched *Sesame Street* all day long. But then, as we saw, some experimenters came along and proved that watching violence increases violence.' How? By randomly assigning some children to a situation in which they watched a video of an episode of a violent TV series—an episode in which people beat, kill, rape, bite, and slug each other for 25 minutes. As a control, the experimenters randomly assigned some other children to a situation in which they watched an athletic event for the same length of time. The crucial point: Each child stood *an equal chance* of being selected to watch the violent video as the nonviolent video; therefore, any differences in character structure among the children in this experiment were neutralized across the two experimental conditions. Thus, the finding that youngsters who watched the violent video showed more aggression afterward than those who watched the athletic event suggests quite strongly that watching violence can lead to violence.

You may recall that this was precisely the problem with the evaluation of the prison college program that we described at the beginning of this chapter: The prisoners who volunteered for the program were probably different in many ways from those who did not volunteer. So it was misleading to compare their recidivism rate with that of the nonvolunteers. Such a comparison would stack the deck, making the program appear to be more effective than it actually was. How do you solve that problem? One way would be to attract twice as many volunteers for the program as you can handle. Then you can randomly select half of the volunteers for the program and place the other half in the control condition. If the selection is truly random, comparing the recidivism rate of the two groups would give you meaningful data.

Let us return to the initiation experiment. If we conducted a survey and found that members of severe-initiation fraternities find each other more attractive than do members of mild-initiation fraternities, then we would have evidence that severity of initiation and liking for other members of the fraternity are *positively correlated.* This means that the more severe the initiation, the more a member will like his fraternity brothers. No matter how highly correlated the two variables are, however, we cannot conclude, from our survey data alone, that severe initiations *cause* liking for the group. All we can conclude from such a survey is that these two factors are associated with each other.

It is possible that the positive correlation between severe initiation and liking for other members of a fraternity exists not because severe initiations cause members to like their groups more, but for just the opposite reason. It could be that the high attractiveness of the group causes severe initiations. If group members see themselves as highly desirable, they may try to keep the situation that way by maintaining an elite group. Thus, they may require a severe initiation in order to discourage people from joining unless those people have a strong desire to do so. From our survey data alone, we cannot conclude that this explanation is false and that severe initiations really do lead to liking. The data give us no basis for making this choice because they tell us nothing about cause and effect. Moreover, as we have seen in our previous example, there could be a third variable that causes both severe initiations and liking. Who would like to give and receive a severe initiation? Why, people with strong sadomasochistic tendencies, of course. Such people may like each other not because of the initiation but because "birds of a feather" tend to like each other. Although this may sound like an outlandish explanation, it is certainly possible. What is more distressing for the researcher are the countless other explanations he or she can't even think of. The experimental method, based as it is on the technique of random assignment to experimental conditions, eliminates all of these in one fell swoop. The sadomasochists in the experiment have just as much chance of being assigned to the no-initiation condition as to the severe-initiation condition. In the real-world study, alas, most of them would most certainly assign themselves to the severe-initiation condition, thus making the results uninterpretable.

The Challenge of Experimentation in Social Psychology

Control versus Impact All is not so sunny in the world of experimentation. There are some very real problems connected with doing experiments. I mentioned that control is one of the major advantages of the experiment, yet it is impossible to exercise complete control over the environment of human participants. One of the reasons many psychologists work with rats rather than people is that researchers are able to control almost everything that happens to their participants from the time of their birth until the experiment ends—climate, diet, exercise, degree of exposure to playmates, absence of traumatic experiences, and so on. Social psychologists do not keep human participants in cages in order to control their experiences. Although this makes for a happier world for the participants, it also makes for a slightly sloppy science.

Control is further limited by the fact that individuals differ from one another in countless subtle ways. Social psychologists try to make statements about what *people* do. By this we mean, of course, what most people do most of the time under a given set of conditions. To the extent that unmeasured individual differences are present in our results, our conclusions may not be precise for all people. Differences in attitudes, values, abilities, personality characteristics, and recent experiences can affect the way people respond in an experiment. Thus, even with our ability to control the experimental situation itself, the same situation may not affect each person in exactly the same way.

Furthermore, when we do succeed in controlling the experimental setting so that it is exactly the same for every person, we run the real risk of making the situation so sterile that the participant is inclined not to take it seriously. The word *sterile* has at least two meanings: (1) germ-free and (2) ineffective or barren. The experimenter should strive to make the experimental situation as germ-free as possible without making it barren or unlifelike for the participant. If participants do not find the events of an experiment interesting and absorbing, chances are their reactions will not be spontaneous and our results, therefore, will have little meaning. Thus, in addition to control, an experiment must have an impact on the participants. They must take the experiment seriously and become involved in it, lest it not affect their behavior in a meaningful way. The difficulty for social psychologists is that these two crucial factors, impact and control, often work in opposite ways: As one increases, the other tends to decrease. The dilemma facing experimenters is how to maximize the impact on the participants without sacrificing control over the situation. Resolving this dilemma requires considerable creativity and ingenuity in the design and construction of experimental situations. This leads us to the problem of realism.

Realism Early in this chapter, I mentioned that a frequent criticism of laboratory experiments is that they are artificial and contrived imitations of the world—that they aren't "real." What do we mean by *real?* Several years ago, in writing a treatise about the experimental method, Merrill Carlsmith and I tried to pinpoint the definition of *real*.[8] We reasoned that an experiment can be realistic in two separate ways: If an experiment has an impact on the participants, forces them to take the matter seriously, and involves them in the procedures, we can say it has achieved **experimental realism.** Quite apart from this is the question of how similar the laboratory experiment is to the events that frequently happen to people in the outside world. Carlsmith and I called this **mundane realism.** Often, confusion between experimental realism and mundane realism is responsible for the criticism that experiments are artificial and worthless because they don't reflect the real world.

The difference between the two realisms can best be illustrated by providing you with an example of a study high in experimental realism but low in mundane realism. Recall the experiment by Stanley Milgram,[9] discussed in Chapter 2, in which each participant was asked to deliver shocks of increasing intensity to another person who was supposedly wired to an electrical apparatus in an adjoining room. Now, honestly, how many times in everyday life are we asked to deliver electric shocks to people? It's unrealistic—but only in the mundane sense. Did the procedure have experimental realism—that is, were the participants wrapped up in it, did they take it seriously, did it have an impact on them, was it part of their real world at that moment? Or were they merely playacting, not taking it seriously, going through the motions, ho-humming it? Milgram reports that his participants experienced a great deal of tension and discomfort. But I'll let Milgram describe, in his own words, what a typical participant looked like:

> I observed a mature and initially poised businessman enter the laboratory smiling and confident. Within 20 minutes he was reduced to a twitching, stuttering wreck, who was rapidly approaching a point of nervous collapse. He constantly pulled on his earlobe, and twisted his hands. At one point he pushed his fist onto his forehead and muttered: "Oh God, let's stop it." And yet he continued to respond to every word of the experimenter, and obeyed to the end.[10]

This hardly seems like the behavior of a person in an unrealistic situation. The things happening to Milgram's participants were *real*—even though they didn't happen to them in their everyday experience. Accordingly, it would seem safe to conclude that the results of this experiment are a reasonably accurate indication of the way people would react if a similar set of events *did* occur in the real world.

Deception The importance of experimental realism can hardly be overemphasized. The best way to achieve this essential quality is to design a setting that will be absorbing and interesting to the participants. At the same time, it is frequently necessary to disguise the true purpose of the study. Why the need for disguise?

Early in this chapter, I mentioned that just about everybody is an amateur social psychologist in the sense that we all live in a social world and are constantly forming hypotheses about things that happen to us in our social world. This includes the individuals who serve as participants in our experiments. Because they are always trying to figure things out, if they knew what we were trying to get at, they might be apt to behave in a manner consistent with their own hypotheses—instead of behaving in a way that is natural and usual for them. For this reason, we try to conceal the true nature of the experiment from the participants. Because we are almost always dealing with very intelligent adults, this is not an easy task; but it is an absolute requirement in most experiments if we are to stand a chance of obtaining valid and reliable data.

This requirement puts the social psychologist in the position of a film director who's setting the stage for action but not telling the actor what the play is all about. Such settings are called **cover stories** and are designed to increase experimental realism by producing a situation in which the participant can act naturally, without being inhibited by knowing just which aspect of behavior is being studied. For example, in the Aronson-Mills initiation study, participants were told they were taking a test for embarrassment in order to screen them for membership in a group that would be discussing the psychology of sex; this was the cover story. It was pure deception. In reality, they were being subjected to an initiation to see what effect, if any, this would have on their liking for the group. If the participants had been aware of the true purpose of the study before their participation, the results would have been totally meaningless. Researchers who have studied this issue have shown that, if participants know the true purpose of an experiment, they do not behave naturally but either try to perform in a way that puts themselves in a good light or try to "help out" the experimenter by behaving in a way that would make the experiment come out as the participants think it should. Both of these outcomes are disastrous for the experimenter. The experimenter can usually succeed in curbing the participant's desire to be helpful, but the desire to look good is more difficult to curb. Most people do not want to be thought of as weak, abnormal, conformist, unattractive, stupid, or crazy. Thus, if given a chance to figure out what the experimenter is looking for, most people will try to make themselves look good or normal. For example, in an experiment designed specifically to elucidate this phenomenon,[11] when we told participants that a particular outcome indicated they possessed a good personality trait, they exhibited the behavior necessary to produce that outcome far more often than when we told them it reflected a negative trait. Although this behavior is understandable, it does interfere with meaningful results. For this reason, experimenters find it necessary to deceive participants about the true nature of the experiment.

To illustrate, let's look again at Solomon Asch's classic experiment on conformity.[12] Recall that, in this study, a student was assigned the task of judging the relative size of a few lines. It was a simple task. But a few other students (who were actually accomplices of the experimenter) purposely stated an incorrect judgment. When faced with this situation, a sizable number of the participants yielded to the implicit group pressure and stated an incorrect judgment. This was, of course, a highly deceptive experiment. The participants thought they were participating in an experiment on perception, but, actually, their conformity was being studied. Was this deception necessary? I think so. Let's play it back without the deception: Imagine yourself being a participant in an experiment in which the experimenter said, "I am interested in studying whether or not you will conform in the face of group pressure," and then he told you what was going to happen. My guess is that you wouldn't conform. My guess is that almost *no one* would conform—because conformity is considered a weak and unattractive behavior. What could the experimenter have concluded from this? That people tend to be nonconformists? Such a conclusion would be erroneous and misleading. Such an experiment would be meaningless.

Recall Milgram's experiments on obedience. He found that around 65 percent of the average citizens in his experiment were willing to administer intense shocks to another person in obedience to the experimenter's command. Yet, each year, when I describe the experimental situation to the students in my class and ask them if *they* would obey such a command, only 1 percent indicate that they would. Does this mean my students are nicer people than Milgram's participants? I don't think so. I think it means that people, if given half a chance, will try to look good. Thus, unless Milgram had used deception, he would have come out with results that simply do not reflect the way people behave when they are led to believe they are in real situations. If we were to give people the opportunity to sit back, relax, and make a guess as to how they would behave in a certain situation, we would get a picture of how people would like to be rather than a picture of how people are.

Ethical Problems

Using deception may be the best (and perhaps the *only*) way to get useful information about the way people behave in most complex and important situations, but it *does* present the experimenter with serious ethical problems. Basically, there are three problems:

1. It is simply unethical to tell lies to people. This takes on even greater significance in the post-Watergate era, when it has been revealed that government agencies have bugged citizens illegally, that presidents tell outright lies to the people who elected them, and that all manner of dirty tricks, fake letters, forged documents, and so on have been used by people directly employed by the president. Can social scientists justify adding to the pollution of deception that currently exists?

2. Such deception frequently leads to an invasion of privacy. When participants do not know what the experimenter is really studying, they are in no position to give their informed consent. For example, in Asch's experiment, it is conceivable that some students might not have agreed to participate had they known in advance that Asch was interested in examining their tendency toward conformity rather than their perceptual judgment.

3. Experimental procedures often entail some unpleasant experiences, such as pain, boredom, anxiety, and the like.

I hasten to add that ethical problems arise even when deception is not used and when experimental procedures are not extreme. Sometimes even the most seemingly benign procedure can profoundly affect a few participants in ways that could not easily have been anticipated—even by the most sensitive and caring experimenters. Consider a series of experiments conducted by Robyn Dawes, Jeanne McTavish, and Harriet Shaklee.[13] Typically, in their investigations of "social dilemmas," participants are faced with the decision to cooperate or to "defect." If everyone cooperates, everyone benefits financially; but if one or more participants choose to defect, they receive a high payoff, and those who choose to cooperate are at a financial disadvantage. Responses are anonymous and remain so throughout the course of the study. The rules of the game are fully explained to all participants at the beginning of the experiment. And no deception is involved. This scenario seems innocuous enough.

But 24 hours after one experimental session, an elderly man telephoned the experimenter. He had been the only defector in his group and had won $190. He wanted to return his winnings and have them divided among the other participants (who had cooperated and won only $1 each). During the conversation, he revealed that he felt miserable about his greedy behavior, that he hadn't slept all night, and so on. After a similar experiment, a woman who cooperated while others defected reported that she felt gullible and had learned that people were not as trustworthy as she had earlier believed.

Despite careful planning by the investigators, the experiments had a powerful impact on participants *that could not have been easily anticipated.* I intentionally chose the experiments by Dawes, McTavish, and Shaklee because they involved no deception and were well within the bounds of ethical codes. My point is simple but important: No code of ethics can anticipate all problems, especially those created when participants discover something unpleasant about themselves or others in the course of their participation.

Social psychologists who conduct experiments are deeply concerned about ethical issues—precisely because their work is constructed on an ethical dilemma. Let me explain. This dilemma is based on two conflicting values to which most social psychologists subscribe. On the one hand, they believe in the value of free scientific inquiry. On the other hand, they believe in the dignity of humans and their right to privacy. This dilemma is a real one and cannot be dismissed either by piously defending the importance of preserving human dignity or by glibly pledging allegiance to the cause of science. And so cial psychologists must face this problem squarely, not just once, but each and every time they design and conduct an experiment—for there is no concrete and universal set of rules or guidelines capable of governing *every* experiment.

Obviously, some experimental techniques present more problems than others. In general, experiments that employ deception are cause for concern because the act of lying is, *in itself,* objectionable—even if the deception is at the service of uncovering the truth. And procedures that cause pain, embarrassment, guilt, or other intense feelings present obvious ethical problems.

More subtle but no less important ethical problems result when participants confront some aspect of themselves that is not pleasant or positive. Recall the experiences of the participants in the relatively mild experiments by Dawes, McTavish, and Shaklee. And many of Solomon Asch's[14] participants learned that they would conform in the face of group pressure; many participants in our own experiment (Aronson and Mettee)[15] learned that they were capable of cheating at a game of cards; most of Milgram's[16] participants learned that they would obey an authority even if such obedience (apparently) involved harming another person.

It could be argued that such self-discovery is of therapeutic or educational benefit to participants; indeed, many participants themselves have made this point. But this does not, in itself, justify these procedures. After all, how could an experimenter know in advance that it would be therapeutic? Morever, it is arrogant of any scientist to decide that he or she has the right or the skill to provide people with a therapeutic experience without their prior permission to do so.

Given these problems, do the ends of social psychological research justify the means? This is a debatable point. Some argue that, no matter what the goals of this science are and no matter what the accomplishments, they are not worth it if people are deceived or put through some discomfort. On the opposite end of the spectrum, others insist that social psychologists are finding things out that may have profound benefits for humankind, and accordingly, almost any price is worth paying for the results.

My own position is somewhere in between. I believe the science of social psychology is important, and I also believe that the health and welfare of experimental participants should be protected at all times. When deciding whether a particular experimental procedure is ethical or not, I believe a cost-benefit analysis is appropriate. That is, how much good will derive from doing the experiment and how much harm will be done to the experimental participants should be considered. Put another way, the benefits to science and society are compared with the costs to the participants, and this ratio is entered into the decision calculus. Unfortunately, such a comparison is difficult to make because we can never be absolutely certain of either the benefit or the harm in advance of the experiment.

Consider the obedience experiment. On the face of it, it was a difficult procedure, all right—no doubt about it. But Milgram had no way of knowing exactly *how* difficult it was until he was deeply into the experiment. In my opinion, it was also an extremely important experiment; it taught us a great deal about human behavior. In the balance, I'm glad that Milgram went ahead with it. Not everyone will agree with me. Immediately after its publication, the experiment was lambasted on ethical grounds, both by the popular press and by serious scientists. A few years after having published his results, Stanley Milgram confided in me—sadly, and with a tinge of bitterness, that he believed much of the criticism was fueled by the results he obtained rather than by the actual procedure he employed. That, in and of itself, is an interesting question: Would the criticisms of the ethics of Milgram's procedure have been less vehement if none of the participants had administered shocks beyond a moderate level of intensity? More than a decade later, Leonard Bickman and Matthew Zarantonello[17] discovered that Milgram's ruminations were on target. They did a simple little experiment in which they asked 100 people to read the procedure section of Milgram's experiment. Those people who were informed that a high proportion of Milgram's participants had been fully obedient rated the procedure as more harmful (and, therefore, less ethical) than those who were informed that hardly anyone had been fully obedient. On a more general note, I would suggest that the ethics of any experiment would seem less problematic when the results tell us something pleasant or flattering about human nature than when they tell us something we'd rather not know. That certainly doesn't mean that we should limit our research to the discovery of flattering things! Milgram's obedience experiment is an excellent case in point. I believe that, if a scientist is interested in studying the extent to which a person will harm others in blind obedience to authority, there is no way of doing it without producing some degree of discomfort.

In sum, a social psychologist's decision whether to do a particular experiment depends on an assessment of the potential costs and benefits of that specific experiment. When my students are contemplating whether or not to go forward with an experiment, I advise them to use the following 5 guidelines:

1. Procedures that cause intense pain or intense discomfort should be avoided if at all possible. Depending on the hypothesis being tested, some discomfort may be unavoidable.

2. Experimenters should provide their participants with the real option of quitting the experiment if their discomfort becomes too intense.

3. Experimenters should be alert to alternative procedures to deception. If some other viable procedure can be found, it should be used.

4. Experimenters should spend considerable time with each participant at the close of the experimental session, carefully explaining the details of the experiment, its true purpose, the reasons for the deception or discomfort, and so on. During this "debriefing" session, they should go out of their way to protect the dignity of participants, to avoid making them feel stupid or gullible about having "fallen for" the deception. They should make certain that participants leave the scene in good spirits—feeling good about themselves and their role in the experiment. This can be accomplished by any earnest experimenter who is willing to take the time and effort to repay each participant (with information and consideration) for the important role that he or she has played in the scientific enterprise.

5. Finally, experimenters should not undertake an experiment that employs deception or discomfort "just for the hell of it." Before entering the laboratory, experimenters should be certain their experiment is sound and worthwhile—that they are seeking the answer to an interesting question and doing so in a careful, well-organized manner.

Experimenters in social psychology try hard to be as sensitive as possible to the needs of their participants. Although many experiments involve procedures that cause some degree of discomfort, the vast majority of these procedures contain many safeguards for the protection of participants. Again, let us return to the obedience experiment simply because, from the perspective of the participants, it is among the most stressful procedures reported in this book. It is evident that Milgram worked hard after the experiment to turn the overall experience into a useful and exciting one for his participants. It is also clear that his efforts achieved a high degree of success: Several weeks after the experiment, 84 percent of the participants reported that they were glad to have taken part in the study; 15 percent reported neutral feelings; and only 1 percent stated that they were sorry they had participated. (We should view these findings with caution, however. The discussion of cognitive dissonance in Chapter 5 has taught us that people sometimes justify their behavior by changing their previously held attitudes.) More convincing evidence comes from a follow-up study: One year after the experimental program was completed, a university psychiatrist interviewed a random sample of the participants and found no evidence of injurious effects; rather, the typical response was that their participation was instructive and enriching.[18]

Our Debt to Participants In this chapter, I have discussed the advantages of the experimental method and have shown how complex and challenging it is to design a laboratory experiment in social psychology. In addition, I have shared some of the excitement I feel in overcoming difficulties and discussed ways of ensuring the well-being, as well as the learning, of the participants in our experiments. The knowledge, information, and insights into human social behavior described in the first eight chapters of this book are based on the techniques and procedures discussed in this chapter. They are also based on the cooperation of tens of thousands of individuals who have allowed us to study their behavior in laboratories all over the world. We owe them a lot. Ultimately, our understanding of human beings in all their complexity rests on our ingenuity in developing techniques for studying behavior that are well controlled and impactful without violating the essential dignity of those individuals who contribute to our understanding by serving as experimental participants.

What If Our Discoveries Are Misused?

There is one additional ethical consideration: the moral responsibility of the scientist for what he or she discovers. Throughout this book, I have been dealing with some powerful antecedents of persuasion. This was particularly true in Chapter 5, where I discussed techniques of inducing self-persuasion, and in some of the subsequent chapters, where I discussed applications of these techniques. Self-persuasion is a very powerful force because, in a very real sense, the persuaded never know what hit them. They come to believe that a particular thing is true, not because J. Robert Oppenheimer or T. S. Eliot or Joe "The Shoulder" convinced them it is true, but because they have convinced *themselves*. What's more, they frequently do not know why or how they came to believe it. This renders the phenomenon not only powerful but frightening as well. As long as I know why I came to believe X, I am relatively free to change my mind; but if all I know is that X is true—and that's all there is to it—I am far more likely to cling to that belief, even in the face of a barrage of disconfirming evidence.

The mechanisms I have described can be used to get people to floss their teeth, to stop bullying smaller people, to reduce pain, or to love their neighbors. Many people might consider these good outcomes, but they are manipulative just the same. Moreover, the same mechanisms can also be used to get people to buy particular brands of toothpaste and perhaps to vote for particular political candidates. In this era of political spin-doctors, propagandists, and hucksters, isn't it immoral to use powerful techniques of social influence?

As the reader of this volume must know by this time, as a real person living in the real world, I have many values—and have made no effort to conceal them; they stick out all over the place. For example, I would like to eliminate bigotry and cruelty. If I had the power, I would employ the most humane and effective methods at my disposal in order to achieve those ends. I am equally aware that, once these methods are developed, others might use them to achieve ends I might not agree with. This causes me great concern. I am also aware that you may not share my values. Therefore, if you believe these techniques are powerful, you should be concerned.

At the same time, I hasten to point out that the phenomena I have been describing on these pages are not entirely new. After all, it was not a social psychologist who got Mr. Landry hooked on Marlboros, or who invented low-balling; and it was not a social psychologist who induced Lieutenant Calley to attempt to justify the wanton killing of Vietnamese civilians. They did what they did on their own. Social psychologists are attempting to understand these phenomena and scores of others that take place in the world every day—some of which have been occurring since the first two people on earth began interacting. By understanding these phenomena, the social psychologist may be able to help people understand the processes and consequences involved and possibly refrain from performing a particular behavior when they themselves decide it is dysfunctional.

But the mere fact that we, as working social psychologists, know that the phenomena we deal with are not of our own creation does not free us from moral responsibility. Our research often crystallizes these phenomena into highly structured, easily applicable techniques. There is always the possibility that some individuals may develop these techniques and use them for their own ends. In the hands of a demagogue, these techniques could conceivably turn our society into an Orwellian nightmare. It is not my intention to preach about the responsibilities of social psychologists. What I am most cognizant of are what I believe to be my own responsibilities. Briefly, they are to educate the public about how these techniques might be used and to remain vigilant against their abuse as I continue to do research aimed at furthering our understanding of us social animals—how we think, how we behave, what makes us aggressive, and what makes us loving. Frankly, I can think of no endeavor more interesting or more important.

Glossary

actor-observer bias: the tendency to see other people's behavior as dispositionally caused while focusing on the role of situational factors when explaining one's own behavior

aggressive action: a behavior aimed at causing either physical or psychological pain

aggressive stimulus: an object that is associated with aggressive responses (e.g., a gun) and whose mere presence can increase the probability of aggression

altruism: any act that benefits another person but does not benefit the helper and often involves some personal cost to the helper

amygdala: the area in the core of the brain that is associated with aggressive behaviors

attitude: an enduring evaluation—positive or negative—of people, objects, and ideas. Attitudes have an evaluative/emotional component as well as a cognitive component

attitude accessibility: the strength of the association between an object and a person's evaluation of that object; accessibility is measured by the speed with which people can report how they feel about an issue or object

attitude heuristic: a shortcut way of making decisions by assigning objects to either a favorable or an unfavorable category

attribution theory: a description of the way in which people explain the causes of their own and other people's behavior

authenticity: when one's behavior and communication are consistent with one's feelings

availability heuristic: a mental rule of thumb whereby people base a judgment on the ease with which they can bring something to mind

benevolent sexism: Taking an attitude toward women that appears to be positive—and even chivalrous—but that is stereotypic in nature; for example believing that women need to be protected.

blaming the victim: the tendency to blame individuals (make dispositional attributions) for their victimization, typically motivated by a desire to see the world as a fair place

bystander effect: the finding that the greater the number of bystanders who witness an emergency, the less likely any one of them is to help

catharsis: the notion that "blowing off steam"—by performing an aggressive act, watching others engage in aggressive behaviors, or engaging in a fantasy of aggression—relieves built-up aggressive energies and hence reduces the likelihood of further aggressive behavior

central route to persuasion: a situation in which people elaborate on a persuasive communication, listening carefully to and thinking about the arguments; this occurs when people have both the ability and the motivation to listen carefully to a communication

cognitive dissonance: a state of tension that occurs whenever an individual simultaneously holds two cognitions (ideas, attitudes, beliefs, opinions) that are psychologically inconsistent

cognitive misers: the idea that people try to conserve cognitive energy in decision-making by taking mental shortcuts whenever they can

communal relationships: relationships in which people's primary concern is being responsive to the other person's needs

companionate love: the feelings of intimacy and affection we feel for another person when we care deeply for the person but do not necessarily experience passion or arousal in his or her presence

compliance: a response to social influence brought about by an individual's hope for reward or fear of punishment.

confirmation bias: a tendency, once we have stated a belief, to view subsequent evidence in a biased manner so as to confirm that belief if possible

conformity: change in behavior due to the real or imagined influence of other people

consummate love: according to Sternberg, the blending of intimacy, passion, and commitment

contrast effect: an object appears to be better or worse than it is, depending on the quality of objects it is compared to

correspondent inference: the tendency to attribute the cause of a person's behavior to a corresponding characteristic or trait of that person

counterattitudinal advocacy: the process of cognitive dissonance that occurs when a person states an opinion or attitude that runs counter to his or her private belief or attitude

cover story: the setting and scenario or an experiment designed to increase experimental realism by producing a situation in which the participants can behave naturally without being affected by knowing precisely which aspect of their behavior is being studied

credibility of the source: if the source of a communication is both expert and trustworthy, she or he is likely to have an impact on the beliefs of the audience

debriefing: the procedure whereby the purpose of the study and exactly what transpired is explained to participants at the end of an experiment

decoy: in consumer decision making, an alternative that is inferior to other possible selections but serves the purpose of making one of the others look good by comparison

dehumanization: the process of seeing victims as nonhumans, which lowers inhibitions against aggressive actions and makes continued aggression easier and more likely

deindividuation: a state of reduced self-awareness (usually brought about by anonymity), which results in reduced concern over social evaluation and weakened restraints against prohibited forms of behavior

dependent variable: in an experiment, the variable a researcher measures to see if it is influenced by the independent variable; the researcher hypothesizes that the dependent variable will depend on the level of the independent variable

dilution effect: the tendency for additional irrelevant information about an issue to weaken our judgment or impression of that issue

dispositional attribution: the assumption that a person's behavior is the result of his or her personality (disposition) rather than of pressures existing in the situation

egocentric thought: the tendency to perceive one's self as more central to events than it really is.

ego-defensive: Behavior aimed at maintaining a positive view of oneself at the expense of viewing the world accurately.

emotional contagion: the rapid transmission of emotions or behaviors through a crowd

empathy: the ability to put oneself in the shoes of another person—to experience events and emotions (e.g., joy, sadness) the way that person experiences them

Eros: the instinct toward life, posited by Freud

exchange relationships: relationships governed by the need for equity (i.e., for an equal ratio of rewards and costs) between the people involved

experimental realism: when an experiment has an impact on the participants, forces them to take the matter seriously, and involves them in the procedures; this can be effective even in the absence of mundane realism

external justification: a person's reason or explanation for his or her dissonant behavior that resides not in the individual but rather in the situation (e.g., a reward or a punishment)

false consensus effect: the tendency to overestimate the percentage of people who agree with us on any issue

false memory syndrome: a memory of a past traumatic experience that is objectively false but that people believe occurred

foot-in-the-door technique: a strategy to get people to comply with a large request, whereby they are presented first with a small request, to which they are likely to acquiesce, followed by a larger request

framing: in decision making, whether a proposition is presented (or framed) so as to imply the possibility of loss or of gain

frustration-aggression: frustration—the perception that you are being prevented from obtaining a goal—will increase the probability of an aggressive response

fundamental attribution error: the tendency to overestimate the extent to which people's behavior is due to internal dispositional factors and to underestimate the role of situational factors

gain-loss effect: the theory that we like people the most if we feel we have gained in their estimation of us (i.e., if they initially disliked us but now like us) and that we dislike people the most if we feel we have lost their favor (i.e., if they initially liked us but now dislike us)

groupthink: a kind of thinking in which maintaining group agreement overrides a careful consideration of the facts in a realistic manner

halo effect: a bias in which our favorable or unfavorable general impression of a person affects our inferences about and future expectations of that person

hindsight bias: once we know the outcome of an event, we have a strong tendency (usually erroneous) to believe that we could have predicted it in advance

homogeneity effect: the tendency to view greater similarity among members of an out-group than we see in members of our own group

hostile aggression: an act of aggression stemming from a feeling of anger and aimed at inflicting pain or injury

hostile sexism: Holding stereotypically negative views of women—for example, that women are less intelligent than men.

hydraulic theory: the theory that unexpressed emotions build up pressure and must be expressed to relieve that pressure

hypocrisy: an aspect of cognitive dissonance brought about by confronting individuals with the discrepancy between what they practice and what they preach

identification: a response to social influence brought about by an individual's desire to be like the influencer

illusory correlation: a tendency to see relationships or correlations between events that are actually unrelated

in group: the group with which an individual identifies and feels he or she belongs to

in-group favoritism: positive feelings and special treatment for people we have defined as being part of our in-group, and negative feelings and unfair treatment for others simply because we have defined them as being in the out-group

independent variable: the variable an experimenter changes or varies to see if it has an effect on some other variable; this is the variable the researcher predicts will cause a change in some other variable

information; as in informational social influence: the influence of other people that leads us to conform because we see them as a source of information to guide our behavior; we conform because we believe that others' interpretation of an ambiguous situation is more correct than ours

inoculation effect: the process of making people immune to attempts to change their attitudes by initially exposing them to small doses of the arguments against their position

instrumental aggression: aggression as a means to some goal other than causing pain

insufficient punishment: the dissonance aroused when individuals lack sufficient external justification for having resisted a desired activity or object, usually resulting in their devaluing that activity or object

internal justification: the reduction of dissonance by changing something about oneself (e.g., one's attitude or behavior)

internalization: a response to social influence brought about by an individual's desire to be right

jigsaw technique: a classroom structure designed to reduce prejudice and raise the self-esteem of children by placing them in small, racially mixed, cooperative groups

judgmental heuristics: mental shortcuts people use to make judgments quickly and efficiently

justification of effort: the tendency for individuals to increase their liking for something they have worked hard to attain

lowballing: an unscrupulous strategy whereby a salesperson induces a customer to agree to purchase a product at a very low cost, subsequently claims it was an error, and then raises the price; frequently the customer will agree to make the purchase at the inflated price

minimum group paradigm: the formation of meaningless groups by grouping strangers on the basis of trivial criteria; minimal group members still display in-group biases

mundane realism: the extent to which an experiment is similar to situations encountered in everyday life

opinion: that which is held to be true (without evaluation or emotion)

out-group: a group with which an individual does not identify

passionate love: the feeling of intense longing, accompanied by physiological arousal, we feel for another person; when our love is reciprocated, we feel great fulfillment and ecstasy, but when it is not, we feel sadness and despair

peripheral route to persuasion: a situation in which people do not elaborate on the arguments in a persuasive communication but are instead swayed by peripheral cues

pratfall effect: a phenomenon whereby some evidence of fallibility increases the attractiveness of a nearly perfect person

prejudice: a hostile or negative attitude toward a distinguishable group of people based solely on their membership in that group

primacy effect: under some specifiable conditions, the first argument you hear will be particularly effective

priming: a procedure based on the notion that ideas that have been recently encountered or frequently activated are more likely to come to mind and thus will be used in interpreting social events

proximity: One of the major factors determining whether we like or love someone is their physical proximity: It is more likely that we will fall in love with someone who lives in or near our town, or attend our university, that with someone who lives far away.

random assignment: the process whereby all participants have an equal chance of taking part in any condition of an experiment; through random assignment, researchers can be relatively certain that differences in their participants' personalities or backgrounds are distributed evenly across conditions

recency effect: under some specifiable conditions, the last argument you hear will be particularly effective

re-constructive memory: the process whereby memories of an event can become distorted by information encountered after the event has occurred

recovered memory phenomenon: recollections of a past event, such as sexual abuse, that had been forgotten or repressed; a great deal of controversy surrounds the accuracy of such memories

relational-aggression: A non-physical form of aggression such as gossiping, spreading false rumors, or ostracism.

relative deprivation: the perception that you (or your group) have less than you deserve, less than you have been led to expect, or less than people similar to you have

representativeness heuristic: a mental shortcut whereby people classify something according to how similar it is to a typical case

romantic love: according to Sternberg, a combination of passion and intimacy

scapegoating: the tendency for individuals, when frustrated or unhappy, to displace aggression onto groups that are disliked, visible, and relatively powerless

script: ways of behaving socially that we learn implicitly from the culture

secondary gain: after complying, an unanticipated, beneficial state of affairs that makes the compliant behavior more attractive

self-concept: the contents of the self; that is, our perception of our own thoughts, beliefs, and personality traits

self-esteem: people's evaluations of their own worth—that is, the extent to which they view themselves as good, competent, and decent

self-fulfilling prophecy: the case whereby people (1) have an expectation about what another person is like, which (2) influences how they act toward that person, which (3) causes that person to behave in a way consistent with those people's original expectations

self-justification: the tendency to justify one's actions in order to maintain one's self-esteem

self-perception theory: the theory that when our attitudes are uncertain or ambiguous, we infer what they are by observing what we do

self-schemas: organized knowledge structures about ourselves, based on our past experiences, that help us understand, explain, and predict our own behavior

self-serving bias: a tendency for individuals to make dispositional attributions for their successes and situational attributions for their failures

similarity: People tend to like and love others with similar opinions, attitudes, values, and looks.

social cognition: how people think about themselves and the social world; more specifically, how people select, interpret, remember, and use social information to make judgments and decisions

social influence: The effect that people have upon the beliefs or behavior of others.

social learning theory: the theory that we learn social behavior (e.g., aggression) by observing others and imitating them

social psychology: the scientific study of the ways in which people's thoughts, feelings, and behaviors are influenced by the real or imagined presence of other people

stereotype: the simplistic generalization about a group of people—assigning them identical characteristics consistent with one's prejudices

stereotype threat: the apprehension experienced by members of a minority group that they might behave in a manner that confirms an existing cultural stereotype. This usually results in reduced effectiveness in their performance

straight talk: a clear statement of a person's feelings and concerns without accusing, blaming, or judging the other person

testosterone: a male sex hormone associated with aggression

Thanatos: according to Freud, an instinctual drive toward death, leading to aggressive actions

triangle of love: according to Sternberg, the three components of love: passion, intimacy and commitment

ultimate attribution error: the tendency to make dispositional attributions about an entire group of people consistent with our prejudice against that group

Notes

Chapter 1   What Is Social Psychology?

1. Michener, J. (1971). *Kent State: What happened and why.* New York: Random House.

2. Clark, K., & Clark, M. (1947). Racial identification and preference in Negro children. In T. M. Newcomb & E. L. Hartley (Eds.), *Readings in social psychology* (pp. 169–178). New York: Holt.

3. Harris, J. (1970). *Hiroshima: A study in science, politics, and the ethics of war.* Menlo Park, CA: Addison-Wesley.

4. Powell, J. L. (1988). A test of the knew-it-all-along effect in the 1984 presidential and statewide elections. *Journal of Applied Social Psychology, 18,* 760–773.

5. Michener, J. (1971). *Kent State: What happened and why.* New York: Random House.

6. E. Berscheid, personal communication.

7. Zimbardo, P (1971, October 25). The psychological power and pathology of imprisonment (p. 3). Statement prepared for the U.S. House of Representatives Committee on the Judiciary, Subcommittee No. 3: Hearings on Prison Reform, San Francisco.

Chapter 2   Conformity

1. Copyright © 1933, 1961 by James Thurber. From "The day the dam broke," in *My life and hard times* (New York: Harper, 1933), pp. 41, 47. (Originally printed in *The New Yorker.*)

2. Schachter, S. (1951). Deviation, rejection, and communication. *Journal of Abnormal and Social Psychology, 46,* 190–207.

3. Kruglanski, A. W., & Webster, D. W. (1991). Group member's reaction to opinion deviates and conformists at varying degrees of proximity to decision deadline and of environmental noise. *Journal of Personality and Social Psychology, 61,* 212–225.

4. Speer, A. (1970). *Inside the Third Reich: Memoirs.* (R. Winston & C. Winston, Trans.). New York: Macmillan.

5. *Playboy,* January 1975, p. 78.

6. Kruglanski, A. W. (1986, August). Freeze-think and the Challenger. *Psychology Today*, pp. 48–49.

7. Janis, I. L. (1971, November). Groupthink. *Psychology Today*, pp. 43–46.

   Janis, I. L. (1984). Counteracting the adverse effects of concurrence-seeking in policy-planning groups. In H. Brandstatter, J. H. Davis, & G. Stocker-Kreichgauer (Eds.), *Group decision making*. New York: Academic Press.

   Kameda, T., & Sugimori, S. (1993). Psychological entrapment in group decision making: An assigned decision rule and a groupthink phenomenon. *Journal of Personality and Social Psychology, 65*, 282–292.

8. Asch, S. (1951). Effects of group pressure upon the modification and distortion of judgment. In M. H. Guetzkow (Ed.), *Groups, leadership and men* (pp. 117–190). Pittsburgh: Carnegie.

   Asch, S. (1956). Studies of independence and conformity: A minority of one against a unanimous majority. *Psychological Monographs, 70* (9, Whole No. 416).

9. Gitow, Andi & Rothenberg, Fred (Producers). Dateline NBC: Follow the leader. Distributed by NBC News. (August 10, 1997)

10. Wolosin, R., Sherman, S., & Cann, A. (1975). Predictions of own and other's conformity. *Journal of Personality, 43*, 357–378.

11. Deutsch, M., & Gerard, H. (1955). A study of normative and informational social influence upon individual judgment. *Journal of Abnormal and Social Psychology, 51*, 629–636.

    See also: Kaplowitz, S., Fink, E., D'Alessio, D., & Armstrong, G. (1983). Anonymity, strength of attitude, and the influence of public opinion polls. *Human Communication Research, 10*, 5–25.

12. Moulton, J., Blake, R., & Olmstead, J. (1956). The relationship between frequency of yielding and the disclosure of personal identity. *Journal of Personality, 24*, 339–347.

13. Argyle, M. (1957). Social pressure in public and private situations. *Journal of Abnormal and Social Psychology, 54*, 172–175.

14. Asch, S. (1955). Opinions and social pressure. *Scientific American, 193(5)*, 31–35.

    Morris, W., & Miller, R. (1975). The effects of consensus-breaking and consensus-preempting partners on reduction of conformity. *Journal of Experimental Social Psychology, 11*, 215–223.

    Boyanowsky, E., Allen, V., Bragg, B., & Lepinski, J. (1981). Generalization of independence created by social support. *Psychological Record, 31*, 475–488.

15. Allen, V., & Levine, J. (1971). Social support and conformity: The role of independent assessment of reality. *Journal of Experimental Social Psychology, 7*, 48–58.

16. Deutsch, M., & Gerard, H. (1955). A study of normative and informational social influence upon individual judgment. *Journal of Abnormal and Social Psychology, 51*, 629–636.

17. Pennington, J., & Schlenker, B. R. (1999). Accountability for consequential decisions: Justifying ethical judgments to audiences. *Personality and Social Psychology Bulletin, 25*, 1067–1981.

18. Quinn, A., & Schlenker, B. R. (2002). Can accountability produce independence? Goals as determinants of the impact of accountability on conformity. *Personality and Social Psychology Bulletin, 28*, 472–483.

19. Mausner, B. (1954). The effects of prior reinforcement of the interaction of observed pairs. *Journal of Abnormal and Social Psychology, 49,* 65–68.

    Mausner, B. (1954). The effect on one's partner's success in a relevant task on the interaction of observed pairs. *Journal of Abnormal and Social Psychology, 49,* 557–560.

    Goldberg, S., & Lubin, A. (1958). Influence as a function of perceived judgment error. *Human Relations, 11,* 275–281.

    Wiesenthal, D., Endler, N., Coward, T., & Edwards, J. (1976). Reversibility of relative competence as a determinant of conformity across different perceptual tasks. *Representative Research in Social Psychology, 7,* 35–43.

20. Bond, R., & Smith, P. (1996). Culture and conformity: A meta-analysis of studies using Asch's (1952, 1956) line judgment task. *Psychological Bulletin, 119,* 111–137.

    Frager, R. (1970). Conformity and anticonformity in Japan. *Journal of Personality and Social Psychology, 15,* 203–210.

    See also: Triandis, H. C. (1990). Cross-cultural studies of individualism and collectivism. In J. J. Berman (Ed.), *Nebraska Symposium on Motivation, 37,* 41–133.

21. Maccoby, E., & Jacklin, C. (1974). *The psychology of sex differences* (pp. 268–272). Stanford, CA: Stanford University Press.

    Cooper, H. (1979). Statistically combining independent studies: A meta-analysis of sex differences in conformity research. *Journal of Personality and Social Psychology, 37,* 131–146.

22. Eagly, A., & Carli, L. (1981). Sex of researchers and sex-typed communications as determinants of sex differences in influenceability: A meta-analysis of social influence studies. *Psychological Bulletin, 90,* 1–20.

    Javornisky, G. (1979). Task content and sex differences in conformity. *Journal of Social Psychology, 108,* 213–220.

    Feldman-Summers, S., Montano, D., Kasprzyk, D., & Wagner, B. (1980). Influence attempts when competing views are gender-related: Sex as credibility. *Psychology of Women Quarterly, 5,* 311–320.

23. Schneider, F. (1970). Conforming behavior of black and white children. *Journal of Personality and Social Psychology, 16,* 466–471.

24. Allport, G. (1954). *The nature of prejudice* (pp. 13–14). Cambridge, MA: Addison-Wesley.

25. Dittes, J., & Kelley, H. (1956). Effects of different conditions of acceptance upon conformity to group norms. *Journal of Abnormal and Social Psychology, 53,* 100–107.

26. Bushman, B. J. (1988). The effects of apparel on compliance: A field experiment with a female authority figure. *Personality and Social Psychology Bulletin, 14,* 459–467.

27. Gladwell, M. (2000) *The Tipping Point.* New York: Little Brown.

28. Festinger, L. (1954). A theory of social comparison processes. *Human Relations, 7,* 117–140.

29. Mullen, B., Cooper, C., & Driskell, J. E. (1990). Jaywalking as a function of model behavior. *Personality and Social Psychology Bulletin, 16(2),* 320–330.

30. Aronson, E., & O'Leary, M. (1982–1983). The relative effectiveness of models and prompts on energy conservation: A field experiment in a shower room. *Journal of Environmental Systems, 12,* 219–224.

31. Reno, R., Cialdini, R., & Kallgren, C. A. (1993). The trans-situational influence of social norms. *Journal of Personality and Social Psychology, 64,* 104–112.

    Cialdini, R. B., Reno, R. R., & Kallgren, C. A. (1990). A focus theory of normative conduct: Recycling the concept of norms to reduce littering in public places. *Journal of Personality and Social Psychology, 58,* 1015–1029.

32. Cialdini, R. B., Reno, R. R., & Kallgren, C. A. (1990). A focus theory of normative conduct: Recycling the concept of norms to reduce littering in public places. *Journal of Personality and Social Psychology, 58,* 1015–1029.

33. Schachter, S., & Singer, J. (1962). Cognitive, social, and physiological determinants of emotional state. *Psychological Review, 69,* 379–399.

34. James, W. (1890). *Principles of psychology.* New York: Smith.

35. Haney, C. (1984). Examining death qualification: Further analysis of the process effect. *Law and Human Behavior, 8,* 133–151.

36. Kelman, H. (1961). Processes of opinion change. *Public Opinion Quarterly, 25,* 57–78.

37. Kiesler, C., Zanna, M., & De Salvo, J. (1966). Deviation and conformity: Opinion change as a function of commitment, attraction, and presence of a deviate. *Journal of Personality and Social Psychology, 3,* 458–467.

38. Kuetner, C., Lichtenstein, E., & Mees, H. (1968). Modification of smoking behavior: A review. *Psychological Bulletin, 70,* 520–533.

39. Milgram, S. (1963). Behavioral study of obedience. *Journal of Abnormal and Social Psychology, 67,* 371–378.

    Milgram, S. (1965). Some conditions of obedience and disobedience to authority. *Human Relations, 18,* 57–76.

    Milgram, S. (1974). *Obedience to authority.* New York: Harper & Row.

40. Elms, A. C., & Milgram, S. (1966). Personality characteristics associated with obedience and defiance toward authoritative command. *Journal of Experimental Research in Personality, 1,* 282–289.

41. Kilham, W., & Mann, L. (1974). Level of destructive obedience as a function of transmitter and executant roles in the Milgram obedience paradigm. *Journal of Personality and Social Psychology, 29,* 696–702.

    Shanab, M., & Yahya, K. (1977). A behavioral study of obedience in children. *Journal of Personality and Social Psychology, 35,* 530–536.

    Miranda, F. B., Caballero, R. B., Gomez, M. G., & Zamorano, M. M. (1981). Obedience to authority. *Psiquis: Revista de Psiquiatria, Psicologia y Psicosomatica, 2,* 212–221.

    Mantell, D. (1971). The potential for violence in Germany. *Journal of Social Issues, 27,* 101–112.

    Meeus, W. H. J., & Raaijmakers, Q. A. W. (1995). Obedience in modern society: The Utrecht studies. *Journal of Social Issues, 51,* 155–176.

42. Milgram, S. (1974). *Obedience to authority.* New York: Harper & Row.

    Sheridan, C., & King, R. (1972, August). Obedience to authority with an authentic victim. Paper presented at the convention of the American Psychological Association.

    Blass, T. (1999) The Milgram Paradigm after 35 years: Some things we now know about obedience to authority. *Journal of Applied Social Psychology, 29,* 955–978.

43. Milgram, S. (1965). Liberating effects of group pressure. *Journal of Personality and Social Psychology, 1*, 127–134.

   Meeus, W. H. J., & Raaijmakers, Q. A. W. (1995). Obedience in modern society: The Utrecht studies. *Journal of Social Issues, 51*, 155–176.

44. Milgram, S. (1965). Some conditions of obedience and disobedience to authority. *Human Relations, 18*, 57–76.

45. Meeus, W. H. J., & Raaijmakers, Q. A. W. (1995). Obedience in modern society: The Utrecht studies. *Journal of Social Issues, 51*, 155–176.

46. Milgram, S. (1965). Liberating effects of group pressure. *Journal of Personality and Social Psychology, 1*, 127–134.

47. Rosenthal, A. M. (1964). *Thirty-eight witnesses*. New York: McGraw-Hill.

48. Korte, C., & Kerr, N. (1975). Response to altruistic opportunities in urban and nonurban settings. *Journal of Social Psychology, 95*, 183–184.

   Rushton, J. P. (1978). Urban density and altruism: Helping strangers in a Canadian city, suburb, and small town. *Psychological Reports, 43*, 987–990.

49. Darley, J., & Latane, B. (1968). Bystander intervention in emergencies: Diffusion of responsibility. *Journal of Personality and Social Psychology, 8*, 377–383.

   Latane, B., & Darley, J. (1968). Group inhibition of bystander intervention in emergencies. *Journal of Personality and Social Psychology, 10*, 215–221.

   Latane, B., & Rodin, J. (1969). A lady in distress: Inhibiting effects of friends and strangers on bystander intervention. *Journal of Experimental Social Psychology, 5*, 189–202.

50. Latane, B., & Nida, S. (1981). Ten years of research on group size and helping. *Psychological Bulletin, 89*, 308–324.

51. Latane, B., & Rodin, J. (1969). A lady in distress: Inhibiting effects of friends and strangers on bystander intervention. *Journal of Experimental Social Psychology, 5*, 189–202.

52. Darley, J., & Latane, B. (1968). Bystander intervention in emergencies: Diffusion of responsibility. *Journal of Personality and Social Psychology, 8*, 377–383.

53. Piliavin, I., Rodin, J., & Piliavin, J. (1969). Good samaritanism: An underground phenomenon? *Journal of Personality and Social Psychology, 13*, 289–299.

54. Bickman, L. (1971). The effect of another bystander's ability to help on bystander intervention in an emergency. *Journal of Experimental Social Psychology, 7*, 367–379.

   Bickman, L. (1972). Social influence and diffusion of responsibility in an emergency. *Journal of Experimental Social Psychology, 8*, 438–445.

55. Piliavin, J., & Piliavin, E. (1972). The effect of blood on reactions to a victim. *Journal of Personality and Social Psychology, 23*, 353–361.

56. Darley, J., & Batson, D. (1973). "From Jerusalem to Jericho": A study of situational and dispositional variables in helping behavior. *Journal of Personality and Social Psychology, 27*, 100–108.

57. Clark, R., III, & Word, L. (1972). Why don't bystanders help? Because of ambiguity? *Journal of Personality and Social Psychology, 24*, 392–400.

Solomon, L., Solomon, H., & Stone, R. (1978). Helping as a function of number of bystanders and ambiguity of emergency. *Personality and Social Psychology Bulletin, 4*, 318–321.

58. Baron, R. A. (1970). Magnitude of model's apparent pain and ability to aid the model as determinants of observer reaction time. *Psychonomic Science, 21*, 196–197.

59. Suedfeld, P., Bochner, S., & Wnek, D. (1972). Helper-sufferer similarity and a specific request for help: Bystander intervention during a peace demonstration. *Journal of Applied Social Psychology, 2*, 17–23.

Chapter 3   Mass Communication, Propaganda, and Persuasion

1. ABC to air major nuclear war film (1983, September). *Report from Ground Zero, 3* (1), 1–2.

2. Schofield, J. W., & Pavelchak, M. A. (1989). Fallout from "The Day After": The impact of a TV film on attitudes related to nuclear war. *Journal of Applied Social Psychology, 19*, 433–448.

3. *Newsweek*, June 2, 1974, p. 79.
   O'Connor, J. J. (1974, March 10). They sell all kinds of drugs on television. *The New York Times*, p. D15.

4. McCartney, J. (1997). News lite. The tendency of network newscasts to favor entertainment and tabloid stories. *American Journalism Review, 19*, 18–26.

5. Piccalo, G. (2001, September 26). *Los Angeles Times*.
   Kirtz, W. (1997). Dancy laments TV news today; former NBC reporter sees too much entertainment. *Quill 85*, 11–16.

6. Gilbert, G. M. *Nuremberg Diary*. New York: Farrar, Straus and Company, 1947 (pp. 278–279).

7. *St. Petersburg* (Florida) *Times*, October 21, 1982.
   The (Nashville) *Tennesseean*, October 31, 1982.

8. *Newsbank*, October 1982, Vol. 19, p. 1.

9. Phillips, D. P., & Carstensen, L. L. (1986). Clustering of teenage suicides after television news stories about suicide. *New England Journal of Medicine, 315*, 685–689.
   Phillips, D. P., Lesyna, K., & Paight, D. J. (1992). Suicide and the media. In R. W. Maris, A. L. Berman, J. T. Maltsberger, & R. I. Yufit (Eds.), *Assessment and prediction of suicide* (pp. 499–519). New York: Guilford Press.
   Phillips, D. P., & Carstensen, L. L. (1990). The effect of suicide stories on various demographic groups 1968–1985. In R. Surette (Ed.), *The media and criminal justice policy: Recent research and social effects* (pp. 63–72). Springfield, IL: Charles C. Thomas.
   Phillips, D. P. (1989). Recent advances in suicidology: The study of imitative suicide. In R. F. W. Diekstra, R. Maris, S. Platt, A. Schmidtke, & G. Sonneck (Eds.), *Suicide and its prevention: The role of attitude and imitation. Advances in suicidology* (Vol. 1, pp. 299–312). Leiden, the Netherlands: E. J. Brill.

10. Phillips, D. P. (1979). Suicide, motor vehicle fatalities, and the mass media: Evidence toward a theory of suggestion. *American Journal of Sociology, 84,* 1150–1174.

11. McGinness, J. (1970). *The selling of the president: 1968* (p. 160). New York: Pocket Books.

12. Regan, M. B. (1996). A deepening cesspool of politics and cash. *Business Week, 3485,* 36–38.

13. Lyle, J., & Hoffman, H. (1971). Explorations in patterns of television viewing by preschool-age children. In J. P. Murray, E. A. Robinson, & G. A. Comstock (Eds.), *Television and social behavior* (Vol. 4, pp. 257–344). Rockville, MD: National Institutes of Health.

14. Lyle, J., & Hoffman, H. (1971). Children's use of television and other media. In J. P. Murray, E. A. Robinson, and G. A. Comstock (Eds.), *Television and social behavior* (Vol. 4, pp. 129–256). Rockville, MD: National Institutes of Health.
   See also: Unnikrishnan, N., & Bajpai, S. (1996). *The impact of television advertising on children.* New Delhi: Sage.
   Kunkel, D., & Roberts, D. (1991). Young minds and marketplace values: Issues in children's television advertising. *Journal of Social Issues, 47(1),* 57–72.

15. Bem, D. (1970). *Beliefs, attitudes, and human affairs.* Belmont, CA: Brooks/Cole.

16. Zajonc, R. (1968). The attitudinal effects of mere exposure. *Journal of Personality and Social Psychology, Monograph Supplement, 9,* 1–27.

17. Grush, J., McKeough, K., & Ahlering, R. (1978). Extrapolating laboratory exposure research to actual political elections. *Journal of Personality and Social Psychology, 36,* 257–270.
   Grush, J. E. (1980). Impact of candidate expenditures, regionality, and prior outcomes on the 1976 presidential primaries. *Journal of Personality and Social Psychology, 38,* 337–347.

18. Pfau, M., Diedrich, T., Larson, K. M., & Van Winkle, K. M. (1995). Influence of communication modalities on voters' perceptions of candidates during presidential primary campaigns. *Journal of Communication, 45(1),* 122–133.
   Soley, L. C., Craig, R. L., & Cherif, S. (1988). Promotional expenditures in congressional elections: Turnout, political action committees and asymmetry effects. *Journal of Advertising, 17(3),* 36–44.

19. White, J. E. (1988, November 14). Bush's most valuable player. *Time,* pp. 20–21.

20. Rosenthal, A. (1988, October 24). Foes accuse Bush campaign of inflaming racial tension. *The New York Times,* pp. A1, B5.
   Pandora's box (1988, October). *The New Republic,* pp. 4, 45.

21. Tolchin, M. (1988, October 12). Study says 53,000 get prison furloughs in '87, and few did harm. *The New York Times,* p. A23.

22. Pratkanis, A. R., & Aronson, E. (1992). *The age of propaganda: The everyday use and abuse of persuasion.* New York: W. H. Freeman.

23. Pratkanis, A. R. (1993). Propaganda and persuasion in the 1992 U.S. presidential election: What are the implications for a democracy. *Current World Leaders, 36,* 341–361.

24. Zimbardo, P., Ebbesen, E., & Maslach, C. (1977). *Influencing attitudes and changing behavior* (2nd ed.). Reading, MA: Addison-Wesley.

25. Petty, R. E., & Cacciopo, J. T. (1986). The elaboration likelihood model of persuasion. In L. Berkowitz (Eds.) *Advances in experimental social psychology* (pp. 123–205). Hillsdale, NJ: Erlbaum.
    See also: Petty, R. E., Heesacker, M., & Hughes, J. N. (1997). The elaboration likelihood model: Implications for the practice of school psychology. *Journal of School Psychology, 35(2)*, 107–136.
    See also: Chaiken, S., Wood, W., & Eagly, A. H. (1996). Principles of persuasion. In E. T. Higgins & A. W. Kruglanski (Eds.), *Social psychology: Handbook of basic principles* (pp. 702–742). New York: Guilford Press.

26. Aristotle. (1954). Rhetoric. In W. Roberts (Trans.), *Aristotle, rhetoric and poetics* (p. 25). New York: Modern Library.

27. Hovland, C., & Weiss, W. (1951). The influence of source credibility on communication effectiveness. *Public Opinion Quarterly, 15,* 635–650.

28. Aronson, E., & Golden, B. (1962). The effect of relevant and irrelevant aspects of communicator credibility on opinion change. *Journal of Personality, 30,* 135–146.

29. Walster (Hatfield), E., Aronson, E., & Abrahams, D. (1966). On increasing the persuasiveness of a low-prestige communicator. *Journal of Experimental Social Psychology, 2,* 325–342.

30. Eagly, A., Wood, W., & Chaiken, S. (1978). Causal inferences about communicators and their effect on opinion change. *Journal of Personality and Social Psychology, 36,* 424–435.

31. *Santa Cruz Sentinel,* January 13, 1987, p. A8.

32. Walster (Hatfield), E., & Festinger, L. (1962). The effectiveness of "overheard" persuasive communications. *Journal of Abnormal and Social Psychology, 65,* 395–402.

33. Mills, J., & Aronson, E. (1965). Opinion change as a function of communicator's attractiveness and desire to influence. *Journal of Personality and Social Psychology, 1,* 173–177.

34. Eagly, A., & Chaiken, S. (1975). An attribution analysis of the effect of communicator characteristics on opinion change: The case of communicator attractiveness. *Journal of Personality and Social Psychology, 32,* 136–144.
    Eagly, A. H., Ashmore, R. D., Makhijani, M. G., & Longo, L. C. (1991). What is beautiful is good, but . . . : A meta-analytic review of research on the physical attractiveness stereotype. *Psychological Bulletin, 110(1),* 109–128.

35. Hartmann, G. (1936). A field experience on the comparative effectiveness of "emotional" and "rational" political leaflets in determining election results. *Journal of Abnormal and Social Psychology, 31,* 336–352.

36. Leventhal, H. (1970). Findings and theory in the study of fear communications. In L. Berkowitz (Ed.), *Advances in experimental social psychology* (Vol. 5, pp. 119–186). New York: Academic Press.

37. Leventhal, H., Meyer, D., & Nerenz, D. (1980). The common sense representation of illness danger. In S. Rachman (Ed.), *Contributions to medical psychology* (Vol. 2), New York: Pergamon Press.

See also: Cameron, L. D., & Leventhal, H. (1995). Vulnerability beliefs, symptom experiences, and the processing of health threat information: A self-regulatory perspective. *Journal of Applied Social Psychology, 25(21)*, 1859–1883.

38. *Time*, February 16, 1987, pp. 50–53.

39. *San Francisco Chronicle*, June 19, 1987, p. 9.

40. Leishman, K. (1987, February). Heterosexuals and AIDS. *The Atlantic Monthly*, pp. 39–58.

41. Liberman, A., & Chaiken, S. (1992). Defensive processing of personally relevant health messages. *Personality and Social Psychology B, 18*, 669–679.

42. Clark R. D., III. (1990). The impact of AIDS on gender differences in willingness to engage in casual sex. *Journal of Applied Social Psychology, 20*, 771–782.

43. Leishman, K. (1987, February). Heterosexuals and AIDS. *The Atlantic Monthly*, p. 44.

44. Williams, S. S., Kimble, D. L., Cowell, N. H., Weiss L. H., Newton, K. J., Fisher, J. D., & Fisher, W. A. (1992). College students use implicit personality theory instead of safe sex. *Journal of Applied Social Psychology, 22*, 921–933.

45. Hirschorn, M. (1987, April 29). AIDS not seen as a major threat by heterosexuals on campuses. *Chronicle of Higher Education*.
    Poppen, P. J. (1994). Adolescent contraceptive use and communication: Changes over a decade. *Adolescence, 29(115)*, 503–514.
    Poppen, P. J. (1994). Adolescent contraceptive use and communication: Changes over a decade. *Adolescence, 29*, 503–514.
    Keller, Mary L. (1993). Why don't young adults protect themselves against sexual transmission of HIV? Possible answers to a complex question. *AIDS Education and Prevention, 5*, 220–233.

46. Aronson, E. (1989). *Excuses, excuses, excuses: Why sexually active college students do not use condoms.* Invited address, meeting of the Western Psychological Association.

47. Aronson, E. (1991). *How to persuade sexually active college students to use condoms.* Invited address, meeting of the American Psychological Association, San Francisco.

48. Zimbardo, P., *Psychology Today* (2003). In Press.

49. Nisbett, R., Borgida, E., Crandall, R., & Reed, H. (1976). Popular induction: Information is not always informative. In J. S. Carroll & J. W. Payne (Eds.), *Cognition and social behavior* (pp. 227–236). Hillsdale, NJ: Erlbaum.
    Nisbett, R., & Ross, L. (1980). *Human inference: Strategies and shortcomings of social judgment.* Englewood Cliffs, NJ: Prentice-Hall.
    Hamill, R., DeCamp Wilson, T., & Nisbett, R. (1980). Insensitivity to sample bias: Generalizing from atypical cases. *Journal of Personality and Social Psychology, 39*, 578–589.
    Shelley Taylor, a cognitive social psychologist, argues that the "vividness" effect is not supported by a majority of the experimental findings. For a discussion of this issue, see Taylor, S., & Thompson, S. (1982). Stalking the elusive "vividness" effect. *Psychological Review, 89*, 155–181.

50. Gonzales, M. H., Aronson, E., & Costanzo, M. (1988). Increasing the effectiveness of energy auditors: A field experiment. *Journal of Applied Social Psychology, 18*, 1049–1066.

51. Hovland, C., Lumsdain, A., & Sheffield, F. (1949). *Experiments on mass communications.* Princeton, NJ: Princeton University Press.

52. Miller, N., & Campbell, D. (1959). Recency and primacy in persuasion as a function of the timing of speeches and measurements. *Journal of Abnormal and Social Psychology, 59,* 1–9.
    See also: Neath, I. (1993). Distinctiveness and serial position effects in recognition. *Memory and Cognition, 21,* 689–698.
    Korsnes, M. (1995). Retention intervals and serial list memory. *Perceptual and Motor Skills, 80,* 723–731.

53. Zimbardo, P. (1960). Involvement and communication discrepancy as determinants of opinion conformity. *Journal of Abnormal and Social Psychology, 60,* 86–94.

54. Whittaker, J. O. (1963). Opinion change as a function of communication-attitude discrepancy. *Psychological Reports, 13,* 763–772.

55. Hovland, C., Harvey, O. J., & Sherif, M. (1957). Assimilation and contrast effects in reaction to communication and attitude change. *Journal of Abnormal and Social Psychology, 55,* 244–252.

56. Aronson, E., Turner, J., & Carlsmith, J. M. (1963). Communication credibility and communication discrepancy as determinants of opinion change. *Journal of Abnormal and Social Psychology, 67,* 31–36.

57. Zellner, M. (1970). Self-esteem, reception, and influenceability. *Journal of Personality and Social Psychology, 15,* 87–93.
    Wood, W., & Stagner, B. (1994). Why are some people easier to influence than others? In S. Shavitt & T. Brock (Eds.), *Persuasion: Psychological insights and perspectives* (pp. 149–174). Boston: Allyn & Bacon.

58. Janis, I. J., Kaye, D., & Kirschner, P. (1965). Facilitating effects of "eating-while-reading" on responsiveness to persuasive communication. *Journal of Personality and Social Psychology, 1,* 181–186.

59. Petty, R. E., Schumann, D. W., Richman, S. A., & Strathman, A. (1993). Positive mood and persuasion: Different roles for affect under high- and low-elaboration conditions. *Journal of Personality and Social Psychology, 64(1),* 5–20.

60. Cohen, G. T., Aronson, J., Steele, C. (2000). When beliefs yield to evidence: Reducing biased evaluation by affirming the self. *Personality & Social Psychology Bulletin, 26,* 1151–1164.

61. Hass, R. G., & Grady, K. (1975). Temporal delay, type of forewarning, and resistance to influence. *Journal of Experimental Social Psychology, 11,* 459–469.

62. Freedman, J., & Sears, D. (1965). Warning, distraction, and resistance to influence. *Journal of Personality and Social Psychology, 1,* 262–266.
    Petty, R. E., & Cacioppo, J. T. (1979). Effects of forewarning of persuasive intent and involvement on cognitive responses and persuasion. *Personality and Social Psychology Bulletin, 5,* 173–176.
    Chen, H. C., Reardon, R., Rea, C., & Moore, D. J. (1992). Forewarning of content and involvement: Consequences for persuasion and resistance to persuasion. *Journal of Experimental Social Psychology, 28(6),* 523–541.

63. Brehm, J. (1966). *A theory of psychological reactance.* New York: Academic Press.

64. Bensley, L. S., & Wu, R. (1991). The role of psychological reactance in drinking following alcohol prevention messages. *Journal of Applied Social Psychology, 21,* 1111–1124.

65. Heilman, M. (1976). Oppositional behavior as a function of influence attempt intensity and retaliation threat. *Journal of Personality and Social Psychology, 33,* 574–578.

66. Petty, R., & Cacioppo, J. (1977). Forewarning, cognitive responding, and resistance to persuasion. *Journal of Personality and Social Psychology, 35,* 645–655.

67. Festinger, L., & Maccoby, J. (1964). On resistance to persuasive communications. *Journal of Abnormal and Social Psychology, 68,* 359–366.

68. McGuire, W., & Papageorgis, D. (1961). The relative efficacy of various types of prior belief-defense in producing immunity against persuasion. *Journal of Abnormal and Social Psychology, 62,* 327–337.

69. McAlister, A., Perry, C., Killen, J., Slinkard, L. A., & Maccoby, N. (1980). Pilot study of smoking, alcohol and drug abuse prevention. *American Journal of Public Health, 70,* 719–721.

70. Pryor, B., & Steinfatt, W. (1978). The effects of initial belief level on inoculation theory and its proposed mechanisms. *Human Communications Research, 4,* 217–230.

71. Aronson, E. (1972) *The social animal.* New York: W. H. Freeman.

72. Canon, L. (1964). Self-confidence and selective exposure to information. In L. Festinger (Ed.), Conflict, decision, and dissonance (pp. 83–96). Stanford, CA: Stanford University Press.

73. Robinson, J. P. (1990). I love my TV (TV viewing). *American Demographics, 12(9),* 24–28.
    Walling, A. D. (1990). Teenagers and television. *American Family Physician, 42(3),* 638–641.
    Huston, A. C., Wright, J. C., Rice, M. L., & Kerkman, D. (1990). Development of television viewing patterns in early childhood: A longitudinal investigation. *Developmental Psychology, 26(3),* 409–421.

74. TV violence for a new generation (1987). *TV Monitor* (p. 2). San Francisco: The Children's Television Resource and Education Center.

75. Statistics cited in Pratkanis, A. R., & Aronson, E. (1992). *Age of propaganda: The everyday use and abuse of persuasion.* New York: W. H. Freeman.

76. Liebert, R. (1975, July 16). Testimony before the Subcommittee on Communications of the House Committee on Interstate and Foreign Commerce.

77. Gerbner, G., Gross, L., Morgan, M., & Signorielli, N. (1986). Living with television: The dynamics of the cultivation process. In J. Bryant & D. Zillman (Eds.), *Perspectives on media effects* (pp. 17–40). Hillsdale, NJ: Erlbaum.
    Gerbner, G., Gross, L., Morgan, M., & Signorielli, N. (1993). Growing up with television: The cultivation perspective. In J. Bryant & D. Zillman (Eds.), *Media effects: Advances in theory and research.* Hillsdale, NJ: Erlbaum.
    Gerbner, G. (1996). TV violence and what to do about it. *Nieman Reports 50,* 3, 10–13.

78. Quoted in *Newsweek,* December 6, 1982, p. 140.

79. Haney, C., & Manzolati, J. (1981). Television criminology: Network illusions of criminal justice realities. In E. Granson (Ed.), *Readings about the social animal* (6th ed., pp. 120–131). San Francisco: W. H. Freeman.

    Oliver, M. B. (1994) Portrayals of crime, race, and aggression in "reality-based" police shows: A content analysis. *Journal of Broadcasting and Electronic Media, 38(2)*, 179–192.

80. Hennigan, K., Heath, L., Wharton, J. D., DelRosario, M., Cook, T., & Calder, B. (1982). Impact of the introduction of television on crime in the United States: Empirical findings and theoretical implications. *Journal of Personality and Social Psychology, 42*, 461–477.

81. Ronis, D., Baumgardner, M., Leippe, M., Cacioppo, J., & Greenwald, A. (1977). In search of reliable persuasion. *Journal of Personality and Social Psychology, 35*, 548–569.

Chapter 4   Social Cognition

1. Lippmann, W. (1922). *Public opinion.* New York: Harcourt, Brace.

2. Panati, C. (1987). *Extraordinary origins of everyday things.* New York: Harper & Row.

3. Guttmacher, S., Ward, D., & Freudenberg, N. (1997). Condom availability in New York City public high schools: Relationships to condom use and sexual behavior. *American Journal of Public Health, 87*, 1427–1433.

4. Gilovich, T. (1991). *How we know what isn't so.* New York: Free Press.

5. Bentham, J. (1876/1948). *A fragment on government and an introduction to the principles of morals and legislation.* Oxford: Blackwell.

    For a modern version of the felicific calculation, see Fishbein, M., & Ajzen, I. (1975). *Belief, attitude, intention, and behavior: An introduction to theory and research.* Reading, MA: Addison-Wesley.

6. Kelley, H. H. (1967). Attribution theory in social psychology. In D. Levine (Ed.), *Nebraska symposium on motivation* (Vol. 15, pp. 192–241). Lincoln: University of Nebraska Press.

    Kelley, H. H. (1973). The process of causal attribution. *American Psychologist, 28*, 107–128.

7. Interestingly, it has been argued that even scientists do not always think like scientists and instead fall prey to some of the biases described in this chapter. See Greenwald, A. G., Pratkanis, A. R., Leippe, M. R., & Baumgardner, M. H. (1986). Under what conditions does theory obstruct research progress? *Psychological Review, 93*, 216–229.

8. Fiske, S. T., & Taylor, S. E. (1991). *Social cognition.* New York: McGraw-Hill.

9. Oakes, P., & Reynolds, K. (1997). Asking the accuracy question: Is measurement the answer? In R. Spears, P. J. Oakes, N. Ellemers, & S. A. Haslam (Eds.), *The social psychology of stereotyping and group life* (pp. 51–71). Oxford: Blackwell.

10. Bronowski, J. (1973). *The ascent of man.* Boston: Little, Brown.

Pratkanis, A. R., & Aronson, E. (1991). *The age of propaganda: The everyday use and abuse of persuasion.* New York: W. H. Freeman.

11. Pratkanis, A. R., Farquhar, P. H., Silbert, S., & Hearst, J. (1989). *Decoys produce contrast effects and alter choice probabilities.* Unpublished study, University of California, Santa Cruz.

12. Kenrick, D. T., & Gutierres, S. E. (1980). Contrast effects in judgments of attractiveness: When beauty becomes a social problem. *Journal of Personality and Social Psychology, 38,* 131–140.

13. Marsh, H. W., Kong, C-K., & Hau, K-T. (2000). Longitudinal multilevel models of the big-fish-little-pond effect on academic self-concept: Counterbalancing contrast and reflected glory effects in Hong Kong schools. *Journal of Personality and Social Psychology, 78,* 337–349.

14. Thornton, B., & Maurice, J. (1997). Physique contrast effect: Adverse impact of idealized body images for women. *Sex Roles, 37,* 433–439.

15. Higgins, E. T., Rholes, W. S., & Jones, C. R. (1977). Category accessibility and impression formation. *Journal of Experimental Social Psychology, 13,* 141–154.

16. Bargh, J., Chen, M., & Burrows, L. (1996). Direct effects of trait construct and stereotype activation on action. *Journal of Personality and Social Psychology, 71,* 230–244.

17. Heath, L., Acklin, M., & Wiley, K. (1991). Cognitive heuristics and AIDS risk assessment among physicians. *Personality and Social Psychology Bulletin, 21,* 1859–1867.

18. Rogers, E. M., & Dearing, J. W. (1988). Agenda-setting research: Where has it been, where is it going? In J. A. Anderson (Ed.), *Communication yearbook 11* (pp. 555–594). Beverly Hills, CA: Sage.

19. McCombs, M. E., & Shaw, D. L. (1972). The agenda-setting function of mass media. *Public Opinion Quarterly, 36,* 176–187.
    McCombs, M. (1994). News influence on our pictures of the world. In J. Bryant & D. Zillmann (Eds.), *Media effects: Advances in theory and research* (pp. 1–16). Hillsdale, NJ: Erlbaum.

20. Penner, L. A., & Fritzsche, B. A. (1993). Magic Johnson and reactions to people with AIDS: A natural experiment. *Journal of Applied Social Psychology, 23(13),* 1035–1050.
    Basil, M. D. (1996). Identification as a mediator of celebrity effects. *Journal of Broadcasting and Electronic Media, 40(4),* 478–495.
    Herek, G. M., & Capitanio, J. P. (1997). AIDS stigma and contact with persons with AIDS: Effects of direct and vicarious contact. *Journal of Applied Social Psychology, 27(1),* 1–36.
    Brown, B. R., Jr., Baranowski, M. D., Kulig, J. W., & Stephenson, J. N. (1996). Searching for the Magic Johnson effect: AIDS, adolescents, and celebrity disclosure. *Adolescence, 31(122),* 253–264.

21. Iyengar, S., & Kinder, D. R. (1987). *News that matters.* Chicago: University of Chicago Press.
    Iyengar, S., Peters, M., & Kinder, D. (1991). Experimental demonstrations of the "not-so-minimal" consequences of television news programs. In D. Protess &

M. McCombs (Eds.), *Agenda setting: Readings on media, public opinion, and policy-making* (pp. 89–95). Hillsdale, NJ: Erlbaum.

22. Cited in Rogers, E. M., & Dearing, J. W. (1988). Agenda-setting research: Where has it been, where is it going? In J. A. Anderson (Ed.), *Communication Yearbook II* (pp. 555–594). Beverly Hills, CA: Sage.

23. Kahneman, D., & Tversky, A. (1984). Choices, values, and frames. *American Psychologist, 39*, 341–350.

24. Gonzales, M. H., Aronson, E., & Costanzo, M. (1988). Increasing the effectiveness of energy auditors: A field experiment. *Journal of Applied Social Psychology, 18*, 1046–1066.

25. Meyerowitz, B. E., & Chaiken, S. (1987). The effect of message framing on breast self-examination attitudes, intentions, and behavior. *Journal of Personality and Social Psychology, 52*, 500–510.

26. Asch, S. (1946). Forming impressions of personality. *Journal of Abnormal and Social Psychology, 41*, 258–290.

27. Jones, E. E., Rock, L., Shaver, K. G., Goethals, G. R., & Ward, L. M. (1968). Pattern of performance and ability attribution: An unexpected primacy effect. *Journal of Personality and Social Psychology, 10*, 317–340.

28. Aronson, J. M., & Jones, E. E. (1992). Inferring abilities after influencing performances. *Journal of Experimental Social Psychology, 28*, 277–299.

29. Zukier, H. (1982). The dilution effect: The role of the correlation and the dispersion of predictor variables in the use of nondiagnostic information. *Journal of Personality and Social Psychology, 43*, 1163–1174.
    Denhaerinck, P., Leyens, J., & Yzerbyt, V. (1989). The dilution effect and group membership: An instance of the pervasive impact of outgroup homogeniety. *European Journal of Social Psychology, 19*, 243–250.

30. Nisbett, R., & Ross, L. (1980). *Human inference: Strategies and shortcomings of social judgment.* Englewood Cliffs, NJ: Prentice-Hall.
    Sherman, S. J., & Corty, E. (1984). Cognitive heuristics. In R. S. Wyer & T. K. Srull (Eds.), *Handbook of social cognition* (Vol. 1, pp. 189–286). Hillsdale, NJ: Erlbaum.
    Tversky, A., & Kahneman, D. (1974). Judgment under uncertainty: Heuristics and biases. *Science, 185*, 1124–1131.

31. Kahneman, D., & Tversky, A. (1973). On the psychology of prediction. *Psychological Review, 80*, 237–251.

32. Comparison based on U.S. Department of Health and Human Services. (1987). *Eating to lower your high blood cholesterol.* (NIH Pub. No. 87–2920). Saturated fats such as animal fat and some vegetable fats such as coconut oil, cocoa butter, palm oil, and hydrogenated oils have been shown to raise cholesterol levels. Cereal manufacturers sometimes use such fats, especially coconut, palm, and hydrogenated oils, in their products. Many manufacturers are in the process of reformulating their cereals to remove such oils, so check the label before making a final decision.

33. "Which cereal for breakfast?" (1981, February). *Consumer Reports*, pp. 68–75.

34. Nisbett, R., & Ross, L. (1980). *Human interference: Strategies and shortcomings of social judgment.* Englewood Cliffs, NJ: Prentice-Hall.

Shweder, R. (1977). Likeness and likelihood in everyday thought: Magical thinking in judgments about personality. *Current Anthropology, 18,* 637–658.

35. Plous, S. (1993). *The psychology of judgment and decision making.* New York: McGraw-Hill.

Manis, M., Shedler, J., Jonides, J., & Nelson, T. E. (1993). Availability heuristic in judgments of set size and frequency of occurrence. *Journal of Personality and Social Psychology, 65,* 448–457.

Schwarz, N., Bless, H., Strack, F., Klumpp, G., Rittenauer-Schatka, H., Simmons, A. (1991). Ease of retrieval as information: Another look at the availability heuristic. *Journal of Personality and Social Psychology, 61,* 195–202.

Tversky, A., & Kahneman, D. (1973). Availability: A heuristic for judging frequency and probability. *Cognitive Psychology, 5,* 207–232.

36. Signorielli, N., Gerbner, G., & Morgan, M. (1995). Violence on television: The Cultural Indicators Project. *Journal of Broadcasting and Electronic Media, 39,* 278–283.

37. Pratkanis, A. R. (1989). The cognitive representation of attitudes. In A. R. Pratkanis, S. J. Breckler, & A. G. Greenwald (Eds.) *Attitude structure and function* (pp. 71–98). Hillsdale, NJ: Erlbaum.

Pratkanis, A. R., & Greenwald, A. G. (1989). A socio-cognitive model of attitude structure and function. In L. Berkowitz (Ed.), *Advances in experimental social psychology* (Vol. 22, pp. 245–285). New York: Academic Press.

38. Pratkanis, A. R. (1988). The attitude heuristic and selective fact identification. *British Journal of Social Psychology, 27,* 257–263.

39. Thistlewaite, D. (1950). Attitude and structure as factors in the distortion of reasoning. *Journal of Abnormal and Social Psychology, 45,* 442–458.

40. Stein, R. I., & Nemeroff, C. J. (1995). Moral overtones of food: Judgments of others based on what they eat. *Personality and Social Psychology Bulletin, 21(5),* 480–490.

41. Ross, L., Greene, D., & House, P. (1977). The "false-consensus effect": An egocentric bias in social perception and attribution process. *Journal of Experimental Social Psychology, 13,* 279–301.

42. Pratkanis, A. R. (1989). The cognitive representation of attitudes. In A. R. Pratkanis, S. J. Breckler, & A. G. Greenwald (Eds.), *Attitude structure and function* (pp. 71–98). Hillsdale, NJ: Erlbaum.

43. For a laboratory demonstration, see Gilovich, T. (1981). Seeing the past in the present: The effect of associations to familiar judgments and decisions. *Journal of Personality and Social Psychology, 40,* 797–808.

44. Darley, J. M., & Gross, P. H. (1983). A hypothesis-confirming bias in labeling effects. *Journal of Personality and Social Psychology, 44,* 20–33.

45. Rosenthal, R., & Jacobson, L. (1968). *Pygmalion in the classroom.* New York: Holt, Rinehart & Winston.

Rosenthal, R. (2002). The Pygmalion effect and its mediating mechanisms. In J. Aronson (Ed.), *Improving academic achievement: Impact of psychological factors on education.* San Diego: Academic Press.

46. Hamilton, D. L., & Rose, T. L. (1980). Illusory correlation and the maintenance of stereotypic beliefs. *Journal of Personality and Social Psychology, 39*, 832–845.

    Hamilton, D., Dugan, P., & Trolier, T. (1985). The formation of stereotypic beliefs: Further evidence for distinctiveness-based illusory correlations. *Journal of Personality and Social Psychology, 48*, 5–17.

47. A. R. Pratkanis, personal communication.

48. Chapman, L. J. (1967). Illusory correlation in observational report. *Journal of Verbal Learning and Verbal Behavior, 6*, 151–155.

    Chapman, L. J., & Chapman, J. P. (1967). Genesis of popular but erroneous psychodiagnostic observations. *Journal of Abnormal Psychology, 72*, 193–204.

    Chapman, L. J., & Chapman, J. P. (1969). Illusory correlation as an obstacle to the use of valid psychodiagnostic signs. *Journal of Abnormal Psychology, 74*, 271–280.

49. Park, B., & Rothbart, M. (1982). Perception of out-group homogeneity and levels of social categorization: Memory for the subordinate attributes of in-group and out-group members. *Journal of Personality and Social Psychology, 42*, 1051–1068.

50. For reviews and discussion, see Tajfel, H. (1981). *Human groups and social categories.* Cambridge: Cambridge University Press.

    Turner, J. C. (1987). *Rediscovering the social group.* New York: Basil Blackwell.

51. Greenwald, A. G. (1980). The totalitarian ego: Fabrication and revision of personal history. *American Psychologist, 35*, 603–618.

    Greenwald, A. G., & Banaji, M. R. (1989). The self as a memory system: Powerful, but ordinary. *Journal of Personality and Social Psychology, 57*, 41–54.

52. Loftus, E. F., & Loftus, G. R. (1980). On the permanence of stored information in the human brain. *American Psychologist, 35*, 409–420.

53. Loftus, E. F., & Ketchum, K. (1991). *Witness for the defense.* New York: St. Martin's Press.

54. Loftus, E. F., & Palmer, J. C. (1974). Reconstruction of automobile destruction: An example of the interaction between language and memory. *Journal of Verbal Learning and Verbal Behavior, 13*, 585–589.

55. Loftus, E. F. (1977). Shifting human color memory. *Memory and Cognition, 5*, 696–699.

56. Markus, H. (1977). Self-schemata and processing information about the self. *Journal of Personality and Social Psychology, 35*, 63–78.

    Markus, H., & Nurius, P. (1986). Possible selves. *American Psychologist, 41*, 954–969.

57. Ross, M., McFarland, C., & Fletcher, G. O. J. (1981). The effect of attitude on the recall of personal history. *Journal of Personality and Social Psychology, 40*, 627–634.

58. Loftus, E. F. (1993). The reality of repressed memories. *American Psychologist, 48*, 518–537.

59. Loftus, E. F., & Ketcham, K. (1994). *The myth of repressed memory: False memories and allegations of sexual abuse.* New York: St. Martin's Press.

    Loftus, E. F. (1993). The reality of repressed memories. *American Psychologist, 48*, 518–537.

Schacter, D. L., Norman, K. A., & Koutstaal, W. (1997). The recovered memories debate: A cognitive neuroscience perspective. In M. A. Conway (Ed.), *Recovered memories and false memories. Debates in psychology* (pp. 63–99). Oxford: Oxford University Press.

Schooler, J. W., Bendiksen, M., & Ambadar, Z. (1997). Taking the middle line: Can we accommodate both fabricated and recovered memories of sexual abuse? In M. A. Conway (Ed.), *Recovered memories and false memories. Debates in psychology* (pp. 251–292). Oxford: Oxford University Press.

Kihlstrom, J. F. (1997). Suffering from reminiscences: Exhumed memory, implicit memory, and the return of the repressed. In M. A. Conway (Ed.), *Recovered memories and false memories. Debates in psychology* (pp. 100–117). Oxford: Oxford University Press.

60. Wright, L. (1994). *Remembering Satan.* New York: Knopf.

61. Ofshe, R., & Watters, E. (1994). *Making monsters: False memories, psychotherapy, and sexual hysteria.* New York: Scribner's.
    Loftus, E. F., & Ketcham, K. (1994). *The myth of repressed memory: False memories and allegations of sexual abuse.* New York: St. Martin's Press.

62. Blume, S. E. (1990). *Secret survivors.* New York: Ballantine.

63. Davis, L. (1990). *The courage to heal workbook.* New York: Perennial.

64. Kihlstrom, J. F. (1997). Memory, abuse, and science. *American Psychologist, 52,* 994–995.

65. De Rivera, J. (1994). Impact of child abuse memories on the families of victims. *Issues in Child Abuse Accusations, 6,* 149–155.

66. Nelson, E. L., & Simpson, P. (1994). First glimpse: An invited examination of subjects who have rejected their recovered visualizations as false memories. *Issues in Child Abuse Accusations, 6,* 123–133.

67. Ofshe, R., & Watters, E. (1994). *Making monsters: False memories, psychotherapy, and sexual hysteria.* New York: Scribner's.
    Wright, L. (1994). *Remembering Satan.* New York: Knopf.

68. Wyatt, D. F., & Campbell, D. T. (1951). On the liability of stereotype or hypothesis. *Journal of Abnormal and Social Psychology, 46,* 496–500.
    Bruner, J. S., & Potter, M. C. (1964). Interference in visual recognition. *Science, 144,* 424–425.

69. Snyder, M., & Swann, W. B. (1978). Hypothesis-testing processes in social interaction. *Journal of Personality and Social Psychology, 36,* 1202–1212.

70. Fischhoff, B. (1975). Hindsight is not equal to foresight: The effect of outcome knowledge on judgment under uncertainty. *Journal of Experimental Psychology: Human Perception and Performance, 1,* 288–299.
    Fischhoff, B. (1977). Perceived informativeness of facts. *Journal of Experimental Psychology: Human Perception and Performance, 3,* 349–358.

71. Greenwald, A. G. (1980). The totalitarian ego: Fabrication and revision of personal history. *American Psychologist, 35,* 603–618.

72. LaPiere, R. (1934). Attitudes versus actions. *Social Forces, 13,* 230–237.

73. Wicker, A. W. (1969). Attitudes versus actions: The relationship of verbal and overt behavioral responses to attitude objects. *Journal of Social Issues, 25(4),* 41–78.

74. Jones, E. E. (1990). *Interpersonal perception.* New York: W. H. Freeman.

    Jones, E. E., & Davis, K. E. (1965). From acts to dispositions: The attribution process in person perception. In L. Berkowitz (Ed.), *Advances in experimental social psychology* (Vol. 2, pp. 219–266). New York: Academic Press.

75. Jones, E. E., & Harris, V. A. (1967). The attribution of attitudes. *Journal of Experimental Social Psychology, 3,* 1–24.

76. Fazio, R. H. (1986). How do attitudes guide behavior? In R. M. Sorrentino & E. T. Higgins (Eds.), *Handbook of motivation and cognition* (pp. 204–242). New York: Guilford Press.

    Fazio, R. H. (1989). On the power and functionality of attitudes: The role of attitude accessibility. In A. R. Pratkanis, S. J. Breckler, & A. G. Greenwald (Eds.), *Attitude structure and function* (pp. 153–179). Hillsdale, NJ: Erlbaum.

77. Fazio, R. H., & Williams, C. J. (1986). Attitude accessibility as a moderator of the attitude–perception and attitude–behavior relations: An investigation of the 1984 presidential election. *Journal of Personality and Social Psychology, 51,* 505–514.

    See also: Bassili, J. N. (1995). On the psychological reality of party identification: Evidence from the accessibility of voting intentions and of partisan feelings. *Political Behavior, 17,* 39–358.

78. Fazio, R. H., Chen, J., McDonel, E. C., & Sherman, S. J. (1982). Attitude accessibility, attitude–behavior consistency, and the strength of the object–evaluation association. *Journal of Experimental Social Psychology, 50,* 339–357.

    Fazio, R. H., Powell, M. C., & Herr, P. M. (1983). Toward a process model of attitude–behavior relation: Accessing one's attitude upon mere observation of the attitude object. *Journal of Personality and Social Psychology, 44,* 723–735.

    Fazio, R. H., & Zanna, M. P. (1981). Direct experience and attitude–behavior consistency. In L. Berkowitz (Ed.), *Advances in experimental social psychology* (Vol. 14, pp. 162–202). New York: Academic Press.

    Regan, D. T., & Fazio, R. H. (1977). On the consistency between attitudes and behavior: Look to the method of attitude formation. *Journal of Experimental Social Psychology, 13,* 38–45.

79. Herr, P. M. (1986). Consequences of priming: Judgment and behavior. *Journal of Personality and Social Psychology, 51,* 1106–1115.

80. Dweck, C. S. (1999). *Self-theories: Their role in motivation, personality, and development.* Philadelphia, PA: Taylor & Francis.

81. Aronson, J., Fried, C., & Good, C. (2002). Reducing the Effects of Stereotype Threat on African American College Students by shaping theories of intelligence. *Journal of Experimental Social Psychology, 38,* 113–125.

82. Ross, L. (1977). The intuitive psychologist and his shortcomings: Distortions in the attribution process. In L. Berkowitz (Ed.), *Advances in experimental social psychology* (Vol. 10, pp. 173–220). New York: Academic Press.

83. Bierbrauer, G. (1973). *Effect of set, perspective, and temporal factors in attribution.* Unpublished Ph.D. dissertation, Stanford University as described in Ross (1977).

84. Ross, L., Amabile, T. M., & Steinmetz, J. L. (1977). Social roles, social control, and biases in social-perception processes. *Journal of Personality and Social Psychology, 35,* 485–494.

85. Answers: Forbes field in Pittsburgh, Vilnius, and July 4, 1826.

86. Jones, E. E., & Nisbett, R. E. (1971). The actor and the observer: Divergent preceptions of the causes of behavior. In E. E. Jones, D. E. Kanouse, H. H. Kelley, R. E. Nisbett, S. Valins, & B. Weiner (Eds.), *Attribution: Perceiving the causes of behavior* (pp. 79–94). Morristown, NJ: General Learning Press.

87. See Jones, E. E., Rock, L., Shaver, K. G., Goethals, G. R., & Ward, L. M. (1968). Pattern of performance and ability attribution: An unexpected primacy effect. *Journal of Personality and Social Psychology, 10,* 317–349.

    McArthur, L. (1972). The how and what of why: Some determinants and consequences of causal attribution. *Journal of Personality and Social Psychology, 22,* 171–193.

    Nisbett, R. E., Caputo, C., Legant, P., & Marecek, J. (1973). Behavior as seen by the actor and as seen by the observer. *Journal of Personality and Social Psychology, 27,* 154–164.

88. Storms, M. D. (1973). Videotape and the attribution process: Reversing the perspective of actors and observers. *Journal of Personality and Social Psychology, 27,* 165–175.

89. Roberts, W., & Strayer, J. (1996). Empathy, emotional expressiveness, and prosocial behavior. *Child Development, 67(2),* 449–470.

90. James, W. (1890/1950). *The principles of psychology* (pp. 314–315). New York: Dover.

91. Greenwald, A. G. (1980). The totalitarian ego: Fabrication and revision of personal history. *American Psychologist, 35,* 603–618.

    Greenwald, A. G., & Pratkanis, A. R. (1984). The self. In R. S. Wyer & T. K. Srull (Eds.), *Handbook of social cognition* (Vol. 3, pp. 129–178). Hillsdale, NJ: Erlbaum.

92. Greenwald, A. G. (1980). The totalitarian ego: Fabrication and revision of personal history. *American Psychologist, 35,* 603–618.

93. Jervis, R. (1976). *Perception and misperception in international politics.* Princeton, NJ: Princeton University Press.

94. Maura Reynolds. *The Los Angeles Times,* Jan. 3, 2003.

95. Langer, E. J. (1975). The illusion of control. *Journal of Personality and Social Psychology, 32,* 311–329.

    Langer, E. J. (1977). The psychology of chance. *Journal for the Theory of Social Behavior, 7,* 185–208.

96. Glick, P., Gottesman, D., & Jolton, J. (1989). The fault is not in the stars: Susceptibility of skeptics and believers in astrology to the Barnum effect. *Personality and Social Psychology Bulletin, 15(4),* 572–583.

97. Petty, R. E., & Brock, T. C. (1979). Effects of "Barnum" personality assessments on cognitive behavior. *Journal of Consulting and Clinical Psychology, 47,* 201–203.

98. Markus, H. (1977). Self-schemata and processing information about the self. *Journal of Personality and Social Psychology, 35,* 63–78.

Breckler, S. J., Pratkanis, A. R., & McCann, D. (1991). The representation of self in multidimensional cognitive space. *British Journal of Social Psychology, 30,* 97–112.

Brenner, M. (1973). The next-in-line effect. *Journal of Verbal Learning and Verbal Behavior, 12,* 320–323.

Slamecka, N. J., & Graf, P. (1992). The generation effect: Delineation of a phenomenon. *Journal of Experimental Psychology: Human Learning and Memory, 4,* 592–604.

Rogers, T. B., Kuiper, N. A., & Kirker, W. S. (1977). Self-reference and the encoding of personal information. *Journal of Personality and Social Psychology, 35,* 677–688.

Klein, S. B., & Loftus, J. (1988). The nature of self-referent encoding: The contributions of elaborative and organizational processes. *Journal of Personality and Social Psychology, 55,* 5–11.

99. *San Francisco Sunday Examiner and Chronicle,* April 22, 1979, p. 35.

100. Greenberg, J., Pyszczynski, T., & Solomon, S. (1982). The self-serving attributional bias: Beyond self-presentation. *Journal of Experimental Social Psychology, 18,* 56–67.

Arkin, R. M., & Maruyama, G. M. (1979). Attribution, affect, and college exam performance. *Journal of Educational Psychology, 71,* 85–93.

Gilovich, T. (1983). Biased evaluation and persistence in gambling. *Journal of Personality and Social Psychology, 44,* 1110–1126.

Ross, M., & Sicoly, F. (1979). Egocentric biases in availability and attribution. *Journal of Personality and Social Psychology, 37,* 322–336.

Breckler, S. J., Pratkanis, A. R., & McCann, D. (1991). The representation of self in multidimensional cognitive space. *British Journal of Social Psychology, 30,* 97–112.

Johnston, W. A. (1967). Individual performance and self-evaluation in a simulated team. *Organization Behavior and Human Performance, 2,* 309–328.

Cunningham, J. D., Starr, P. A., & Kanouse, D. E. (1979). Self as actor, active observer, and passive observer: Implications for causal attribution. *Journal of Personality and Social Psychology, 37,* 1146–1152.

101. Greenwald, A. G., & Breckler, S. J. (1985). To whom is the self presented? In B. R. Schlenker (Ed.), *The self and social life* (pp. 126–145). New York: McGraw-Hill.

102. Miller, D. T., & Ross, M. (1975). Self-serving biases in the attribution of causality: Fact or fiction? *Psychological Bulletin, 82,* 213–225.

103. Weary (Bradley), G. (1978). Self-serving biases in the attribution process: A reexamination of the fact or fiction question. *Journal of Personality and Social Psychology, 36,* 56–71.

Weary, G. (1980). Examination of affect and egotism as mediators of bias in causal attributions. *Journal of Personality and Social Psychology, 38,* 348–357.

Weary, G., Harvey, J. H., Schwieger, P., Olson, C. T., Perloff, R., & Pritchard, S. (1982). Self-presentation and the moderation of self-serving attributional biases. *Social Cognition, 1,* 140–159.

104. Grove, J. R., Hanrahan, S. J., & McInman, A. (1991). Success/failure bias in attributions across involvement catagories in sport. *Personality and Social Psychology Bulletin, 17,* 93–97.

105. Taylor, S. E. (1989). *Positive illusions: Creative self-deception and the healthy mind.* New York: Basic Books.

106. Seligman, M. E. P. (1991). *Learned optimism.* New York: Alfred A. Knopf.

Chapter 5   Self-Justification

1. Prasad, J. (1950). A comparative study of rumors and reports in earthquakes. *British Journal of Psychology, 41,* 129–144.

2. Sinha, D. (1952). Behavior in a catastrophic situation: A psychological study of reports and rumours. *British Journal of Psychology, 43,* 200–209.

3. Festinger, L. (1957). *A theory of cognitive dissonance.* Stanford, CA: Stanford University Press.

4. Kassarjian, H., & Cohen, J. (1965). Cognitive dissonance and consumer behavior. *California Management Review, 8,* 55–64.

5. Tagliacozzo, R. (1979). Smokers' self-categorization and the reduction of cognitive dissonance. *Addictive Behaviors, 4,* 393–399

6. Gibbons, F. X., Eggleston, T. J., & Benthin, A. C. (1997). Cognitive reactions to smoking relapse: The reciprocal relation between dissonance and self-esteem. *Journal of Personality and Social Psychology, 72,* 184–195.

7. Goleman, D. (1982, January). Make-or-break resolutions. *Psychology Today,* p. 19.

8. Levin, M. (1997, July 18) Jury views CEO's "gummy bear" deposition. *Los Angeles Times,* p. D3.

9. *Austin American,* November 18, 1971, p. 69.

10. Hastorf, A., & Cantril, H. (1954) They saw a game: A case study. *Journal of Abnormal and Social Psychology, 49,* 129–134.

11. Bruce, L. (1966). *How to talk dirty and influence people* (pp. 232–233). Chicago: Playboy Press, and New York: Pocket Books.

12. *Time,* November 24, 1980, p. 11.

13. Jones, E., & Kohler, R. (1959). The effects of plausibility on the learning of controversial statements. *Journal of Abnormal and Social Psychology, 57,* 315–320.

14. Lord, C., Ross, L., & Lepper, M. (1979). Biased assimilation and attitude polarization: The effects of prior theories on subsequently considered evidence. *Journal of Personality and Social Psychology, 37,* 2098–2109.
    See also: Edwards, K., & Smith, E. (1996). A disconfirmation bias in the evaluation of arguments. *Journal of Personality and Social Psychology, 71,* 5–24.

15. Ehrlich, D., Guttman, I., Schonbach, P., & Mills, J. (1957). Postdecision exposure to relevant information. *Journal of Abnormal and Social Psychology, 57,* 98–102.

16. Brehm, J. (1956). Postdecision changes in the desirability of alternatives. *Journal of Abnormal and Social Psychology, 52,* 384–389.

See also: Gilovich, T., Medvec, V. H., & Chen S. (1995). Commission, omission, and dissonance reduction: Coping with regret in the "Monty Hall" problem. *Personality and Social Psychology Bulletin, 21,* 182–190.

17. Johnson, D. J., & Rusbult, C. E. (1989). Resisting temptation: Devaluation of alternative partners as a means of maintaining commitment in close relationships. *Journal of Personality and Social Psychology, 57,* 967–980.

18. Simpson, J. A., Gangestad, S. W., & Lerma, M. (1990). Perception of physical attractiveness: Mechanisms involved in the maintenance of romantic relationships. *Journal of Personality and Social Psychology, 59,* 1192–1201.

19. Wiesel, E. (1969). *Night.* New York: Avon.

20. White, R. (1971, November). Selective inattention. *Psychology Today,* pp. 47–50, 78–84.

21. Janis, I. (1972). *Victims of groupthink.* Boston: Houghton Mifflin.

22. Pentagon papers: The secret war. (1971, June 28). *Time,* p. 12.

23. Freedman, J., & Fraser, S. (1966). Compliance without pressure: The foot-in-the-door technique. *Journal of Personality and Social Psychology, 4,* 195–202.

24. Pliner, P., Hart, H., Kohl, J., & Saari, D. (1974). Compliance without pressure: Some further data on the foot-in-the-door technique. *Journal of Experimental Social Psychology, 10,* 17–22.

25. Knox, R., & Inkster, J. (1968). Postdecision dissonance at post time. *Journal of Personality and Social Psychology, 8,* 319–323.

26. Frenkel, O. J., & Doob, A. (1976). Post-decision dissonance at the polling booth. *Canadian Journal of Behavioural Science, 8,* 347–350.

27. Cialdini, R., Cacioppo, J., Bassett, R., & Miller, J. (1978). Low-ball procedure for producing compliance: Commitment then cost. *Journal of Personality and Social Psychology, 36,* 463–476.

28. Ibid.

29. Mills, J. (1958). Changes in moral attitudes following temptation. *Journal of Personality, 26,* 517–531.

30. Adams, H., Wright, L., Lohr, B. (1996). Is homophobia associated with homosexual arousal? *Journal of Abnormal Psychology, 105,* 440–445.

31. Festinger, L., & Carlsmith, J. M. (1959). Cognitive consequences of forced compliance. *Journal of Abnormal and Social Psychology, 58,* 203–210.

32. Cohen, A. R. (1962). An experiment on small rewards for discrepant compliance and attitude change. In J. W. Brehm & A. R. Cohen, *Explorations in cognitive dissonance* (pp. 73–78). New York: Wiley.

33. Leippe, M. R., & Eisenstadt, D. (1994). Generalization of dissonance reduction: Decreasing prejudice through induced compliance. *Journal of Personality and Social Psychology, 67,* 395–413.

34. Zimbardo, P., Weisenberg, M., Firestone, I., & Levy, B. (1965). Communicator effectiveness in producing public conformity and private attitude change. *Journal of Personality, 33,* 233–255.

35. Mills, J. (1958). Changes in moral attitudes following temptation. *Journal of Personality, 26,* 517–531.

36. Aronson, E. (1968). Dissonance theory: Progress and problems. In R. P. Abelson, E. Aronson, W. J. McGuire, T. M. Newcomb, M. J. Rosenberg, & P. H. Tannenbaum (Eds.), *Theories of cognitive consistency: A sourcebook* (pp. 5–27). Chicago: Rand McNally.
    Aronson, E. (1969). The theory of cognitive dissonance: A current perspective. In L. Berkowitz (Ed.), *Advances in experimental social psychology* (Vol. 4, pp. 1–34). New York: Academic Press.

37. Nel, E., Helmreich, R., & Aronson, E. (1969). Opinion change in the advocate as a function of the persuasibility of his audience: A clarification of the meaning of dissonance. *Journal of Personality and Social Psychology, 12,* 117–124.

38. Hoyt, M., Henley, M., & Collins, B. (1972). Studies in forced compliance: Confluence of choice and consequence on attitude change. *Journal of Personality and Social Psychology, 23,* 204–210.
    Schlenker, B., & Schlenker, P. (1975). Reactions following counterattitudinal behavior which produces positive consequences. *Journal of Personality and Social Psychology, 31,* 962–971.
    Riess, M., & Schlenker, B. (1977). Attitude change and responsibility avoidance as modes of dilemma resolution in forced-compliance situations. *Journal of Personality and Social Psychology, 35,* 21–30.

39. Cialdini, R., & Schroeder, D. (1976). Increasing compliance by legitimizing paltry contributions: When even a penny helps. *Journal of Personality and Social Psychology, 34,* 599–604.

40. Freedman, J. (1963). Attitudinal effects of inadequate justification. *Journal of Personality, 31,* 371–385.

41. Deci, E. (1975). *Intrinsic motivation.* New York: Plenum.
    Deci, E. (1971). Effects of externally mediated rewards on intrinsic motivation. *Journal of Personality and Social Psychology, 18,* 105–115.
    Deci, E., Nezlek, J., & Sheinman, L. (1981). Characteristics of the rewarder and intrinsic motivation of the rewardee. *Journal of Personality and Social Psychology, 40,* 1–10.
    Ryan, R. M., & Deci, E. L. (1996). When paradigms clash: Comments on Cameron and Pierce's claim that rewards do not undermine intrinsic motivation. *Review of Educational Research, 66,* 33–38.

42. Lepper, M. R., & Greene, D. (1975). Turning play into work: Effects of adult surveillance and extrinsic rewards on children's intrinsic motivation. *Journal of Personality and Social Psychology, 31,* 479–486.
    Lepper, M. R., Keavney, M., & Drake, M.. (1996). Intrinsic motivation and extrinsic rewards: A commentary on Cameron and Pierce's meta-analysis. *Review of Educational Research, 66,* 5–32.

43. Henderlong, J., & Lepper, M. R. (2002). The effects of praise on children's intrinsic motivation: A review and synthesis. *Psychological Bulletin, 128,* 774–795.

44. Dweck, C. (1999). *Self-theories: Their role in motivation, personality, and development.* Philadelphia, PA: Psychology Press.

45. Aronson, E., & Carlsmith, J. M. (1963). Effect of the severity of threat on the devaluation of forbidden behavior. *Journal of Abnormal and Social Psychology, 66,* 584–588.

46. Freedman, J. (1965). Long-term behavioral effects of cognitive dissonance. *Journal of Experimental Social Psychology, 1,* 145–155.

47. Sears, R., Whiting, J., Nowlis, V., & Sears, P. (1953). Some child-rearing antecedents of aggression and dependency in young children. *Genetic Psychology Monographs, 47,* 135–234.

    Strassberg, Z., Dodge, K., Pettit, G., & Bates, J. (1994). Spanking in the home and children's subsequent aggression toward kindergarten peers. *Development and Psychopathology, 6,* 445–461.

48. Aronson, E., & Mills, J. (1959). The effect of severity of initiation on liking for a group. *Journal of Abnormal and Social Psychology, 59,* 177–181.

49. Gerard, H., & Mathewson, G. (1966). The effects of severity on initiation on liking for a group: A replication. *Journal of Experimental Social Psychology, 2,* 278–287.

50. Cooper, J. (1980). Reducing fears and increasing assertiveness: The role of dissonance reduction. *Journal of Experimental Social Psychology, 16,* 199–213.

51. Conway, M., & Ross, M. (1984). Getting what you want by revising what you had. *Journal of Personality and Social Psychology, 47,* 738–748.

52. Michener, J. (1971). *Kent State: What happened and why.* New York: Random House.

53. Ibid.

54. Khrushchev, N. (1970). In S. Talbot (Ed. and Trans.), *Khrushchev remembers.* Boston: Little, Brown.

55. Davis, K., & Jones, E. E. (1960). Changes in interpersonal perception as a means of reducing cognitive dissonance. *Journal of Abnormal and Social Psychology, 61,* 402–410.

    See also: Gibbons, F. X., & McCoy, S. B. (1991). Self-esteem, similarity, and reactions to active versus passive downward comparison. *Journal of Personality and Social Psychology, 60(3),* 414–424.

56. Glass, D. (1964). Changes in liking as a means of reducing cognitive discrepancies between self-esteem and aggression. *Journal of Personality, 32,* 531–549.

    See also: Sorrentino, R., & Boutilier, R. (1974). Evaluation of a victim as a function of fate similarity/dissimilarity. *Journal of Experimental Social Psychology, 10,* 84–93.

    Sorrentino, R., & Hardy, J. (1974). Religiousness and derogation of an innocent victim. *Journal of Personality, 42,* 372–382.

57. Berscheid, E., Boyce, D., & Walster (Hatfield), E. (1968). Retaliation as a means of restoring equity. *Journal of Personality and Social Psychology, 10,* 370–376.

58. Jones, E., & Nisbett, R. (1971). *The actor and the observer: Divergent perceptions of the causes of behavior.* New York: General Learning Press.

59. Shaw, G. B. (1952). In D. Russel (Ed.), *Selected prose.* New York: Dodd, Mead.

60. Brehm, J. (1959). Increasing cognitive dissonance by a *fait-accompli. Journal of Abnormal and Social Psychology, 58,* 379–382.

61. Darley, J., & Berscheid, E. (1967). Increased liking as a result of the anticipation of personal contact. *Human Relations, 20,* 29–40.

62. Kay, A., Jimenez, M., & Jost, J. (2002). Sour grapes, sweet lemons, and the antici-patory rationalization of the status. *Personality and Social Psychology Bulletin, 28,* 1300–1312.

63. Lehman, D., & Taylor, S. E. (1987). Date with an earthquake: Coping with a proba-ble, unpredictable disaster. *Personality and Social Psychology Bulletin, 13,* 546–555.

64. Aronson, E., & Mettee, D., (1968). Dishonest behavior as a function of different lev-els of self-esteem. *Journal of Personality and Social Psychology, 9,* 121–127.

65. Kernis, M. H. (2001). Following the trail from narcissism to fragile self-esteem. *Psy-chological Inquiry, 12,* 223–225.

66. Baumeister, Roy F., Bushman, Brad J., Campbell, W. Keith. (2000). Self-esteem, nar-cissism, and aggression: Does violence result from low self-esteem or from threatened egotism? *Current Directions in Psychological Science, 9,* 26–29.

67. Salmivalli, C., Kaukiainen, A., Kaistaniemi, L., Lagerspetz, K. M. Self evaluated self-esteem, peer-evaluated self-esteem, and defensive egotism as predictors of ado-lescents' participation in bullying situations. *Personality & Social Psychology Bulletin 25,* 1268–1278.

68. Bem, D. J. (1967). Self-perception: An alternative interpretation of cognitive disso-nance phenomena. *Psychological Review, 74,* 183–200.

69. Fazio, R., Zanna, M., & Cooper, J. (1977). Dissonance and self-perception: An inte grative view of each theory's proper domain of application. *Journal of Experimental Social Psychology, 13,* 464–479.

70. Devine, P. G. (1998). Moving beyond attitude change in the study of dissonance-related processes. In E. Harmon-Jones & J. S. Mills (Eds.), *Cognitive dissonance theory: Revival with revisions and controversies.* Washington, D.C.: American Psycho-logical Association.

71. Pallak, M. S., & Pittman, T. S. (1972). General motivational effects of dissonance arousal. *Journal of Personality and Social Psychology, 21,* 349–358.

72. Zanna & Cooper, 1974; Fried & Aronson, 1995.

73. Zimbardo, P. (1969). *The cognitive control of motivation.* Glencoe, IL: Scott, Foresman.

74. Brehm, J. (1962). Motivational effects of cognitive dissonance. In *Nebraska Sympo-sium on Motivation,* 1962 (pp. 51–77). Lincoln: University of Nebraska Press.

75. Mountain West Research, Inc. (1979). Three Mile Island telephone survey. Prelimi-nary report on procedures and findings. Report submitted to the U.S. Nuclear Regu-latory Commission (NUREG CR-1093).

76. *Newsweek,* April 16, 1979, pp. 35, 93. CBS News–New York Times poll. The New York Times, April 10, 1979, pp. 1, 16.

77. Axsom, D., & Cooper, J. (1981). Reducing weight by reducing dissonance: The role of effort justification in inducing weight loss. In E. Aronson (Ed.), *Readings about the social animal* (pp. 181–196). San Francisco: W. H. Freeman.
    Axsom, D., & Cooper, J. (1985). Cognitive dissonance and psychotherapy: The role of effort justification in inducing weight loss. *Journal of Experimental Social Psychology, 21,* 149–160.

78. Biek, M., Wood, W., & Chaiken, S. (1996) Working knowledge, cognitive processing, and attitudes: On the determinants of bias. *Personality and Social Psychology Bulletin, 22,* 547–556.

79. Stone, J., Aronson, E., Crain, A. L., Winslow, M. P., & Fried, C. B. (1994). Inducing hypocrisy as a means of encouraging young adults to use condoms. *Personality and Social Psychology Bulletin, 20,* 116–128.

    Aronson, E. (1997) The giving away of psychology—and condoms. *APS Observer, 10,* 17–35.

    Aronson, E. (1997) The theory of cognitive dissonance: The evolution and vicissitudes of an idea. In S. Craig McGarty, & A. Haslam (Eds.), *The message of social psychology: Perspectives on mind in society* (pp. 20–35). Oxford: Blackwell.

    Aronson, E. (in press). Dissonance, hypocrisy, and the self concept. In E. Harmon-Jones & J. S. Mills (Eds.), *Cognitive dissonance theory: Revival with revisions and controversies.* Washington, D.C.: American Psychological Association Books.

80. Dickerson, C. A., Thibodeau, R., Aronson, E., & Miller, D. (1992). Using cognitive dissonance to encourage water conservation. *Journal of Applied Social Psychology, 22,* 841–854.

81. Friedman, Thomas (2002). *Longitudes and Attitudes: Exploring the World After September 11.* pp. 334–335.

82. Beauvois & Joule, 1996, 1998; Sakai, 1999.

83. Sakai, H. (1999). A multipliative power-function model of cognitive dissonance: Toward an integrated theory of cognition, emotion, and behavior after Leon Festinger. In E. Harmon-Jones & J. S. Mills (Eds.), *Cognitive dissonance: Progress on a pivotal theory in social psychology.* Washington, D.C.: American Psychological Association.

84. Johnson, L. B. (1971). *The vantage point: Perspectives of the presidency 1963–69.* New York: Holt, Rinehart and Winston.

Chapter 6 Human Aggression

1. *Newsweek,* April 28, 1986, p. 22.

2. Berkowitz, L. (1993). *Aggression.* New York: McGraw-Hill.

3. Geen, R. (1998). *Aggression and anti-social behavior.* In D. Gilbert, S. Fiske, & G. Lindzey (Eds.), *Handbook of social psychology* (4th. ed.), pp. 317–356). New York: McGraw-Hill.

4. Rousseau, J.-J. (1930). *The social contract and discourses.* New York: Dutton.

5. Freud, S. (1948). *Beyond the pleasure principle.* London: Hogarth Press and Institute of Psycho-Analysis.

6. Freud, S. (1959). Why war? (letter to Albert Einstein, 1932). In E. Jones (Ed.), *Collected papers* (Vol. 5., p. 282). New York: Basic Books.

7. Storr, A. (1970). *Human aggression.* New York: Bantam Books.

8. Kuo, Z. Y. (1961). Genesis of the cat's response to the rat. In E. Aronson (Ed.), *Instinct* (p. 24). Princeton, NJ: Van Nostrand.

9. Eibl-Eibesfeldt, I. (1963). Aggressive behavior and ritualized fighting in animals. In J. H. Masserman (Ed.), *Science and psychoanalysis, Vol. VI. Violence and war.* New York: Grune & Stratton.

10. Scott, J. P. (1958). *Aggression.* Chicago: University of Chicago Press.

11. Lorenz, K. (1966). *On aggression* (M. Wilson, Trans.). New York: Harcourt, Brace and World.

12. Lore, R. K., & Schultz, L. A. (1993). Control of human aggression. *American Psychologist, 48,* 16–25.

13. Berkowitz, L. (1993). *Aggression.* New York: McGraw-Hill.

14. Baron, R. A., & Richardson, D. R. (1994). *Human aggression* (2nd ed.). New York: Plenum.

15. Hunt, G. T. (1940). *The wars of the Iroquois.* Madison: The University of Wisconsin Press.

16. Nisbett, R. E. (1993). Violence and U.S. regional culture. *American Psychologist, 48,* 441–449.

17. Cohen, D., & Nisbett, R. E. (1994). Self-protection and the culture of honor: Explaining Southern violence. *Personality and Social Psychology Bulletin, 20,* 551–567.
    Cohen, D., Nisbett, R., Bowdle, Brian F., Schwarz, N. (1996) Insult, aggression, and the southern culture of honor: An "experimental ethnography." *Journal of Personality and Social Psychology, 70,* 945–960.

18. Cohen, D., & Nisbett, R. E. (1997). Field experiments examining the culture of honor: The role of institutions in perpetuating norms about violence. *Personality and Social Psychology Bulletin, 23,* 1188–1199.

19. Lorenz, K. (1966). *On aggression* (M. Wilson, Trans.). New York: Harcourt, Brace & World.

20. Washburn, S., & Hamburg, D. (1965). The implications of primate research In I. DeVore (Ed.), *Primate behavior: Field studies of monkeys and apes.* (pp. 607–622). New York: Holt, Rinehart and Winston.

21. Pinker, S. (1997). *How the mind works.* New York: Norton.

22. LeBoeuf, B. (1974). Male-male competition and reproductive success in elephant seals. *American Zoologist, 14,* 163–176.

23. Montagu, A. (1950). *On being human.* New York: Hawthorne Books.

24. Kropotkin, P. (1902). *Mutual aid.* New York: Doubleday.

25. Nissen, H., & Crawford, M. P. (1936). Preliminary study of food-sharing behavior in young chimpanzees. *Journal of Comparative Psychology, 22,* 383–419.

26. Leakey, R., & Lewin, R. (1978). *People of the lake.* New York: Anchor Press/Doubleday.

27. Eiseley, L. (1946). *The immense journey* (p. 140). New York: Random House.

28. Menninger, W. (1948). Recreation and mental health. *Recreation, 42,* 340–346.

29. Bushman, B. (2002). Does venting anger feed or extinguish the flame? Catharsis, rumination, distraction, anger and aggressive responding. *Personality & Social Psychology Bulletin, 28,* 724–731.

30. Patterson, A. (1974, September). Hostility catharsis: A naturalistic quasi-experiment. Paper presented at the annual convention of the American Psychological Association, New Orleans.

31. Green, R. (1981). Spectator moods at an aggressive sports event. Journal of Social Psychology, 3, 217–227.

32. Glass, D. (1964). Changes in liking as a means of reducing cognitive discrepancies between self-esteem and aggression. *Journal of Personality, 32,* 531–549.
    Davis, K. E., & Jones, E. E. (1960). Changes in interpersonal perception as a means of reducing cognitive dissonance. *Journal of Abnormal and Social Psychology, 61,* 402–410.

33. Kahn, M. (1966). The physiology of catharsis. *Journal of Personality and Social Psychology, 3,* 278–298.
    See also: Berkowitz, L., Green, J., & Macauley, J. (1962). Hostility catharsis as the reduction of emotional tension. *Psychiatry, 25,* 23–31.
    DeCharms, R., & Wilkins, E. J. (1963). Some effects of verbal expression of hostility. *Journal of Abnormal and Social Psychology, 66,* 462–470.

34. Glass, D. (1964). Changes in liking as a means of reducing cognitive discrepancies between self-esteem and aggression. *Journal of Personality, 32,* 531–549.
    Davis, K. E., & Jones, E. E. (1960). Changes in interpersonal perception as a means of reducing cognitive dissonance. *Journal of Abnormal and Social Psychology, 61,* 402–410.
    See also: Buss, A. H. (1963). Physical aggression in relation to different frustrations. *Journal of Abnormal and Social Psychology, 67,* 1–7.

35. Doob, A. N., & Wood, L. (1972). Catharsis and aggression: The effects of annoyance and retaliation on aggressive behavior. *Journal of Personality and Social Psychology, 22,* 156–162.

36. Stoff, D. M., & Cairns, R. B. (1996). *Aggression and violence: Genetic, neurobiological, and biosocial perspectives.* Mahwah, NJ: Erlbaum.

37. Moyer, K. E. (1983). The physiology of motivation: Aggression as a model. In C. J. Scheier & A. M. Rogers (Eds.), *G. Stanley Hall Lecture Series* (Vol. 3). Washington, D.C.: American Psychological Association.

38. Dabbs, J. M., Jr., Ruback, R. B., Frady, R. L., Hopper, C. H., & Sgoutas, D. S. (1988). Saliva testosterone and criminal violence among women. *Personality and Individual Differences, 18,* 627–633.
    Dabbs, J. M., Carr, T. S., Frady, R. L., & Riad, J. K. (1995). Testosterone, crime, and misbehavior among 692 male prison inmates. *Personality and Individual Differences, 7,* 269–275.

39. Banks, T., & Dabbs, James M., Jr. (1996). Salivary testosterone and cortisol in delinquent and violent urban subculture. *Journal of Social Psychology, 136(1),* 49–56.

40. Dabbs, J. M., Jr., Hargrove, M. F., & Heusel, C. (1996). Testosterone differences among college fraternities: Well-behaved vs. rambunctious. *Personality and Individual Differences, 20(2)*, 157–161.

41. Human Capital Initiative Committee (1997, October). Reducing violence. *APS Observer*, pp. 5–21.

42. Maccoby, E. E., & Jacklin, C. N. (1974). *The psychology of sex differences.* Stanford, CA: Stanford University Press.

43. Wilson, J. Q., & Hernstein, R. J. (1985). *Crime and human nature.* New York: Simon & Schuster.

44. Archer, D., & McDaniel, P. (1995). Violence and gender: Differences and similarities across societies. In R. B. Ruback & N. A. Weiner (Eds.), *Interpersonal violent behaviors: Social and cultural aspects* (pp. 63–88). New York: Springer.

45. Desmond, E. W. (1987, November 30). Out in the open. *Time*, pp. 80–90.

46. Shupe, L. M. (1954). Alcohol and crimes: A study of the urine alcohol concentration found in 882 persons arrested during or immediately after the commission of a felony. *Journal of Criminal Law and Criminology, 33*, 661–665.

47. Taylor, S. P., & Leonard, K. E. (1983). Alcohol and human physical aggression. In R. Geen & E. Donnerstein (Eds.), *Aggression: Theoretical and empirical reviews.* New York: Academic Press.

    White, H. (1997). Longitudinal perspective on alcohol use and aggression during adolescence. In M. Galanter (Ed.), *Recent developments in alcoholism* (Vol. 13, pp. 81–103). New York: Plenum Press.

    Yudko, E., Blanchard, D., Henrie, J., & Blanchard, R. (1997) Emerging themes in preclinical research on alcohol and aggression. In M. Galanter (Ed.), *Recent developments in alcoholism* (Vol. 13, pp. 123–138). New York: Plenum Press

48. Bushman, B. J. (1997). Effects of alcohol on human aggression: Validity of proposed explanations. In M. Galanter (Ed.), Recent developments in alcoholism: Vol. 13. Alcohol and violence: Epidemiology, neurobiology, psychology, family issues (pp. 227–243). New York: Plenum.

49. Azrin, N. H. (1967, May). Pain and aggression. *Psychology Today*, pp. 27–33.

    Hutchinson, R. R. (1983). The pain–aggression relationship and its expression in naturalistic settings. *Aggressive Behavior, 9*, 229–242.

50. Berkowitz, L. (1988). Frustrations, appraisals, and aversively stimulated aggression. *Aggressive Behavior, 14*, 3–11.

51. Stoff, D., & Cairns, R., (1996). *Aggression and violence: Genetic, neurobiological, and biosocial perspectives.* Mahwah, NJ: Erlbaum.

52. Carlsmith, J. M., & Anderson, C. A. (1979). Ambient temperature and the occurrence of collective violence: A new analysis. *Journal of Personality and Social Psychology, 37*, 337–344.

53. Anderson, C. A., Bushman, B. J., & Groom, R. W. (1997). Hot years and serious and deadly assault: Empirical tests of the heat hypothesis. *Journal of Personality and Social Psychology, 73*, 1213–1223.

54. Griffitt, W., & Veitch, R. (1971). Hot and crowded: Influences of population density and temperature on interpersonal affective behavior. *Journal of Personality and Social Psychology, 17,* 92–98.

    See also: Anderson, C., Anderson, B., & Deuser, W. (1996) Examining an affective aggression framework: Weapon and temperature effects on aggressive thoughts, affect, and attitudes. *Personality and Social Psychology Bulletin, 22,* 366–376.

    Bell, P. A. (1980). Effects of heat, noise, and provocation on retaliatory evaluative behavior. *Journal of Social Psychology, 110,* 97–100.

55. Reifman, A. S., Larrick, R., & Fein, S. (1988). The heat–aggression relationship in major-league baseball. Paper presented at the meeting of the American Psychological Association, San Francisco.

56. Kenrick, D. T., & MacFarlane, S. W. (1986). Ambient temperature and horn honking: A field study of the heat/aggression relationship. *Environment and Behavior, 18,* 179–191.

57. Barker, R., Dembo, T., & Lewin, K. (1941). Frustration and aggression: An experiment with young children. *University of Iowa Studies in Child Welfare, 18,* 1–314.

58. Harris, M. (1974). Mediators between frustration and aggression in a field experiment. *Journal of Experimental and Social Psychology, 10,* 561–571.

59. Kulik, J., & Brown, R. (1979). Frustration, attribution of blame, and aggression. *Journal of Experimental and Social Psychology, 15,* 183–194.

60. Tocqueville, A. de. (1981). *Democracy in America.* Westminster, MD: Random House.

61. Aronson, E. (2000). *Nobody Left to Hate: Teaching Compassion After Columbine.* New York: Worth/Freeman.

62. Twenge, Jean M.; Baumeister, Roy F.; Tice, Dianne M.; Stucke, Tanja, S. If you can't join them, beat them: Effects of social exclusion on aggressive behavior. *Journal of Personality & Social Psychology,* 1058–1069.

63. *Time,* December 20, 1999.

64. Mallick, S., & McCandless, B. (1966). A study of catharsis of aggression. *Journal of Personality and Social Psychology, 4,* 591–596.

65. Johnson, T. E., & Rule, B. G. (1986). Mitigating circumstances information, censure, and aggression. *Journal of Personality and Social Psychology, 50,* 537–542.

66. Berkowitz, L. (1965). Some aspects of observed aggression. *Journal of Personality and Social Psychology, 2,* 359–369.

67. Berkowitz, L., & Geen, R. (1966). Film violence and the cue properties of available targets. *Journal of Personality and Social Psychology, 3,* 525–530.

68. Berkowitz, L., & LePage, A. (1967). Weapons as aggression-eliciting stimuli. *Journal of Personality and Social Psychology, 7,* 202–207.

69. Berkowitz, L. (1971). *Control of aggression* (p. 68). Unpublished manuscript.

70. Zimbardo, P. (1969). The human choice: Individuation, reason, and order versus deindividuation, impulse, and chaos. In W. Arnold & D. Levine (Eds.), *Nebraska Symposium on Motivation, 17,* 237–307.

71. Mullen, B. (1986). Atrocity as a function of lynch mob composition: A self-attention perspective. *Personality and Social Psychology Bulletin, 12,* 187–197.

72. Bandura, A., Ross, D., & Ross, S. (1961). Transmission of aggression through imitation of aggressive models. *Journal of Abnormal and Social Psychology, 63,* 575–582.
    Bandura, A., Ross, D., & Ross, S. (1963). A comparative test of the status envy, social power, and secondary reinforcement theories of identificatory learning. *Journal of Abnormal and Social Psychology, 67,* 527–534.
    Bandura, A., Ross, D., & Ross, S. (1963). Vicarious reinforcement and initiative learning. *Journal of Abnormal and Social Psychology, 67,* 601–607.

73. Huston, A., & Wright, J. (1996). Television and socialization of young children. In T. M. MacBeth (Ed.), *Tuning in to young viewers: Social science perspectives on television* (pp. 37–60). Thousand Oaks, CA: Sage.

74. Seppa, N. (1997). Children's TV remains steeped in violence. *APA Monitor, 28,* 36.

75. Cantor, J. Confronting children's fright responses to mass media. In D. Zillmann, J. Bryant, & A. C. Huston (Eds.), *Media, children, and the family: Social scientific, psychodynamic, and clinical perspectives* (LEA's communication series, pp. 139–150). Hillsdale, NJ: Erlbaum.
    Kunkel, D., Wilson, B., Donnerstein, E., Blumenthal, E., & others. (1995). Measuring television violence: The importance of context. *Journal of Broadcasting and Electronic Media, 39,* 284–291.

76. Eron, L. D. (1982). Parent–child interaction, television violence, and aggression of children. *American Psychologist, 37,* 197–211.
    Eron, L. D. (1987). The development of aggressive behavior from the perspective of a developing behaviorism. *American Psychologist, 42,* 425–442.
    Eron, L. Huesmann, L., Lefkowitz, M., & Walder, L. (1996). Does television violence cause aggression? In D. Greenberg (Ed.), *Criminal careers: Vol. 2. The international library of criminology, criminal justice and penology* (pp. 311–321). Dartmouth.
    Huesmann, L. R. (1982). Television violence and aggressive behavior. In D. Pearly, L. Bouthilet, & J. Lazar (Eds.), *Television and behavior: Vol. 2. Technical reviews* (pp. 220–256). Washington, D.C.: National Institute of Mental Health.
    Turner, C. W., Hesse, B. W., & Peterson-Lewis, S. (1986). Naturalistic studies of the long-term effects of television violence. *Journal of Social Issues, 42(3),* 51–74.

77. Eron, L., Huesmann, L., Lefkowitz, M., & Walder, L. (1996). Does television violence cause aggression? In D. Greenberg (Ed.), *Criminal careers: Vol. 2. The international library of criminology, criminal justice and penology* (pp. 311–321). Dartmouth.
    Geen, R. (1994) Television and aggression: Recent developments in research and theory. In D. Zillmann, J. Bryant, & A. C. Huston (Eds.), *Media, children, and the family: Social scientific, psychodynamic, and clinical perspectives* (LEA's communication series, pp. 151–162). Hillsdale, NJ: Erlbaum.
    Geen, R. (1998). Aggression and anti-social behavior. In D. Gilbert, S. Fiske, & G. Lindzey (Eds.), *Handbook of social psychology* (4th. ed., pp. 317–356). New York: McGraw-Hill.
    Huesmann, L. R., & Miller, L. (1994). Long-term effects of repeated exposure to media violence in childhood. In: L. R. Huesmann, (Ed.) *Aggressive behavior: Current perspectives.* New York: Plenum Press, pp. 153–186.

78. Liebert, R., & Baron, R. (1972). Some immediate effects of televised violence on children's behavior. *Developmental Psychology, 6,* 469–475.

79. Josephson, W. D. (1987) Television violence and children's aggression: Testing the priming, social script, and disinhibition prediction. *Journal of Personality and Social Psychology, 53,* 882–890.

80. Parke, R., Berkowitz, L., Leyens, J., West, S., & Sebastian, R. (1977). Some effects of violent and nonviolent movies on the behavior of juvenile delinquents. In L. Berkowitz (Ed.), *Advances in experimental social psychology* (pp. 135–172). New York: Academic Press.

81. Signorelli, N., Gerber, G., & Morgan, M. (1995). Violence on television: The Cultural Indicators Project. *Journal of Broadcasting and Electronic Media, 39(2),* 278–283.

82. Johnson, Jeffrey G., Cohen, Patricia, Smailes, Elizabeth M., Karen, Stephani, Brook, Judith (2002). Television viewing and aggressive behavior during adolescence and adulthood. *Science, 295,* 2468–2471.

83. Phillips, D. P. (1986). Natural experiments on the effects of mass media violence on fatal aggression: Strengths and weaknesses of a new approach. In L. Berkowitz (Ed.), *Advances in experimental social psychology* (Vol. 19, pp. 207–250). Orlando, FL: Academic Press.

84. Cline, V. B., Croft, R. G., & Courrier, S. (1973). Desensitization of children to television violence. *Journal of Personality and Social Psychology, 27,* 360–365.

85. Thomas, M. H., Horton, R., Lippincott, E., & Drabman, R. (1977). Desensitization to portrayals of real-life aggression as a function of exposure to television violence. *Journal of Personality and Social Psychology, 35,* 450–458.

86. Thomas, M. (1982) Physiological arousal, exposure to a relatively lengthy aggressive film, and aggressive behavior. *Journal of Research in Personality, 16,* 72–81.

87. Check, J., & Malamuth, N. (1983). Can there be positive effects of participation in pornography experiments? *Journal of Sex Research, 20,* 14–31.

88. Cox News Service.

89. Roiphe, K. (1994) *The morning after: Sex, fear, and feminism.* New York: Little, Brown.
    Paglia, C. (1994). *Vamps and tramps: New essays.* New York: Vintage Books.

90. Malamuth, N. M. (1983). Factors associated with rape as predictors of laboratory aggression against women. *Journal of Personality and Social Psychology, 45,* 432–442.
    Malamuth, N. M. (1986). Predictors of naturalistic sexual aggression. *Journal of Personality and Social Psychology, 50,* 953–962.

91. Donnerstein, E. (1980). Aggressive erotica and violence against women. *Journal of Personality and Social Psychology, 39,* 269–277.

92. Malamuth, N. (1981). Rape fantasies as a function of exposure to violent sexual stimuli. *Archives of Sexual Behavior, 10,* 33–47.

93. Malamuth, N., & Check, J. (1981). The effects of mass media exposure on acceptance of violence against women: A field experiment. *Journal of Research in Personality, 15,* 436–446.

94. Malamuth, N., Haber, S., & Feshbach, S. (1980). Testing hypotheses regarding rape: Exposure to sexual violence, sex differences, and the "normality" of rapists. *Journal of Research in Personality, 14,* 121–137.

95. Check, J., & Malamuth, N. (1983). Can there be positive effects of participation in pornography experiments? *Journal of Sex Research, 20,* 14–31.

96. Linz, D., Donnerstein, E., & Penrod, S. (1988). Effects of long-term exposure to violent and sexually degrading depictions of women. *Journal of Personality and Social Psychology, 55,* 758–768.

97. Bushman, B. J., & Bonacci, A. M. (2002). Violence and sex impair memory for television ads. *Journal of Applied Psychology, 87,* 557–564.

98. Clark, K. (1971). The pathos of power: A psychological perspective. *American Psychologist, 26,* 1047–1057.

99. Aristotle (1954). Rhetoric. In W. R. Roberts (Trans.), *Aristotle, rhetoric and poetics* (p. 22). New York: Modern Library.

100. Sears, R., Maccoby, E., & Levin, H. (1957). *Patterns of child rearing.* Evanston, IL: Row, Peterson.
    Baumrind, D. (1966). Effects of authoritative parental control on child behavior. *Child Development, 37,* 887–907.
    Becker, W. (1964). Consequences of different kinds of parental discipline. In M. L. Hoffman & L. W. Hoffman (Eds.), *Review of child development research* (Vol. 1). New York: Russell Sage.
    Owens, D., & Straus, M. (1975). The social structure of violence in childhood and approval of violence as an adult. *Aggressive Behavior, 1,* 193–211.

101. Hamblin, R., Buckholt, D., Bushell, D., Ellis, D., & Ferritor, D. (1969, January). Changing the game from "get the teacher" to "learn." *Trans-Action,* pp. 20–31.

102. Haney, C. (1979). A psychologist looks at the criminal justice system. In A. Calvin (Ed.), *Challenges and alternatives to the American criminal justice system* (pp. 77–85). Ann Arbor, MI: University International Press.

103. Eichmann, C. (1966). *The impact of the Gideon decision on crime and sentencing in Florida.* Tallahassee, FL: Division of Corrections Publications.

104. Aronson, E., & Carlsmith, J. M. (1963). The effect of severity of threat on the devaluation of forbidden behavior. *Journal of Abnormal and Social Psychology, 66,* 584–588.
    Freedman, J. (1965). Long-term behavioral effects of cognitive dissonance. *Journal of Experimental and Social Psychology, 1,* 145–155.

105. Olweus, D. (1991). Bully/victim problems among school children: Basic facts and effects of a school-based intervention program. In D. Pepler & K. Rubin (Eds.), *The development and treatment of childhood aggression* (pp. 411–448). Hillsdale, NJ: Erlbaum.
    Olweus, D. (1997) Tackling peer victimization with a school-based intervention program. In D. Fry & K. Bjorkqvist (Eds.), *Cultural variation in conflict resolution: Alternatives to violence* (pp. 215–231). Mahwah, NJ: Erlbaum.
    Olweus, D. (1996). Bullying at school: Knowledge base and an effective intervention program. In C. Ferris & T. Grisso (Eds.), *Understanding aggressive behavior in*

children (Annals of the New York Academy of Sciences, Vol. 794, pp. 265–276). New York: New York Academy of Sciences.

106. U.S. President's Commission on Law Enforcement and Administration of Justice. (1967). *The challenge of crime in a free society: A report.* Washington, D.C.: U.S. Government Printing Office.

107. Bandura, A., Ross, D., & Ross, S. (1963). Imitation of film-mediated aggressive models. *Journal of Abnormal and Social Psychology, 66,* 3–11.
    Bandura, A., Ross, D., & Ross, S. (1963). Vicarious reinforcement and imitative learning. *Journal of Abnormal and Social Psychology, 67,* 601–607.

108. Brown, P., & Elliot, R. (1965). Control of aggression in a nursery school class. *Journal of Experimental Child Psychology, 2,* 103–107.

109. Davitz, J. (1952). The effects of previous training on postfrustration behavior. *Journal of Abnormal and Social Psychology, 47,* 309–315.

110. Baron, R. A., & Kepner, C. R. (1970). Model's behavior and attraction toward the model as determinants of adult aggressive behavior. *Journal of Personality and Social Psychology, 14,* 335–344.

111. Baron, R. A. (1976). The reduction of human aggression: A field study of the influence of incompatible reactions. *Journal of Applied Social Psychology, 6,* 260–274.

112. Feshbach, S. (1971). Dynamics and morality of violence and aggression: Some psychological considerations. *American Psychologist, 26,* 281–292.

113. Michener, J. (1971). *Kent State: What happened and why.* New York: Random House.

114. Feshbach, N., & Feshbach, S. (1969). The relationship between empathy and aggression in two age groups. *Developmental Psychology, 1,* 102–107.

115. Feshbach, N. (1978, March). Empathy training: A field study in affective education. Paper presented at the American Educational Research Association, Toronto, Ontario, Canada.
    Feshbach, N., & Feshbach, S. (1981, April). Empathy training and the regulation of aggression: Potentialities and limitations. Paper presented at the convention of the Western Psychological Association.

116. Hammock, G. S., & Richardson, D. R. (1992). Aggression as one response to conflict. *Journal of Applied Social Psychology, 22,* 298–311.
    See also: Richardson, D., Hammock, G., Smith, S., & Gardner, W. (1994). Empathy as a cognitive inhibitor of interpersonal aggression. *Aggressive Behavior, 20,* 275–289.
    See also: Ickes, W. (1997) *Empathic accuracy.* New York: Guilford Press.

117. Obuchi, K., Ohno, T., & Mukai, H. (1993) Empathy and aggression: Effects of self-disclosure and fearful appeal. *Journal of Social Psychology, 133,* 243–253.

Chapter 7 Prejudice

1. Poussaint, A. (1971). A Negro psychiatrist explains the Negro psyche. In *Confrontation* (pp. 183–184). New York: Random House.

2. Clark, K., & Clark, M. (1947). Racial identification and preference in Negro children. In T. M. Newcomb & E. L. Hartley (Eds.), *Readings in social psychology* (pp. 169–178). New York: Holt.

3. Goldberg, P. (1968, April). Are women prejudiced against women? *Trans-Action*, pp. 28–30.

4. Porter, J. R., & Washington, R. E. (1989, July–September). Developments in research on Black identity and self-esteem: 1979–1988. *Revue Internationale de Psychologie Sociale, 2(3)*, 339–353.

   Gopaul-McNicol, S. (1987, August). A cross-cultural study of the effects of modeling, reinforcement and color meaning word association on doll color preference of Black preschool children and White preschool children in New York and Trinidad. Dissertation Abstracts International, 48, 340–341.

   Hraba, J., & Grant, G. (1970). Black is beautiful: A reexamination of racial preference and identification. *Journal of Personality and Social Psychology, 16*, 398–402.

   Banks, C. (1976). White preference in blacks: A paradigm in search of a phenomenon. *Psychological Bulletin, 83*, 1179–1186.

5. Swim, J., Borgida, E., Maruyama, G., & Myers, D. G. (1989). Joan McKay vs. John McKay: Do gender stereotypes bias evaluations? *Psychological Bulletin, 105*, 409–429.

6. Wolpoff, C. (1996). Amid more fires, Congress acts on church burnings. Congressional Quarterly Weekly Report, 54, 17–66.

7. Fountain, J. W. (1997, May 4). No fare. Washington Post.

8. Allport, G. (1954, 1980). *The nature of prejudice* (p. 13). Reading, MA: Addison-Wesley.

9. Brewer (1988); Kunda and Oleson (1995).

10. *Newsweek*, November 25, 1974, p. 39.

11. Neugarten, B (1946). Social class and friendship among schoolchildren. *American Journal of Sociology, 51*, 305–313.

12. Bond, C. F., Jr., DiCandia, C. G., & MacKinnon, J. R. (1988). Response to violence in a psychiatric setting: The role of the patient's race. *Personality and Social Psychology Bulletin, 14*, 448–458.

13. Bodenhausen, G., & Wyer, R. (1985). Effects of stereotypes on decision making and information-processing strategies. *Journal of Personality and Social Psychology, 48*, 267–282.

14. Shaffer, D. R., & Wallace, A. (1990). Belief congruence and evaluator homophobia as determinants of the attractiveness of competent homosexual and heterosexual males. *Journal of Psychology and Human Sexuality, 3*, 67–87.

15. Steele, C. (1992, April). Race and the schooling of black Americans. *The Atlantic Monthly*, pp. 16–23.

    Steele, C. (1997). A threat in the air: How stereotypes shape intellectual identity and performance. *American Psychologist, 52*, 613–629.

16. Steele, C., & Aronson, J. (1994). Stereotype threat and the intellectual test performance of African Americans. *Journal of Personality and Social Psychology, 69(5)*, 797–811.

Aronson, J., Quinn, D., & Spencer, S. (in press). Stereotype threat and the academic underperformance of women and minorities. In J. Swim & C. Stangor (Eds.), *Stigma: The target's perspective.* New York: Academic Press.

17. Aronson, J., Lustina, M. J., Good, C., Keough, K., Steele, C. M., & Brown, J. (1999). When white men can't do math: Necessary and sufficient factors in stereotype threat. *Journal of Experimental Social Psychology, 35,* 29–46.

18. Pettigrew, T. F. (1979). The ultimate attribution error: Extending Allport's cognitive analysis of prejudice. *Personality and Social Psychology Bulletin, 5,* 461–476.

19. Ibid.

20. Deaux, K., & LaFrance, M. (1998). Gender. In D. Gilbert, S. Fiske, & G. Lindzey (Eds.), *Handbook of social psychology* (4th. ed., Vol. 1, pp. 788–829). New York: McGraw-Hill.

    Deaux, K., & Lewis, L. (1984). Structure of gender stereotypes: Interrelationships among components and gender label. *Journal of Personality and Social Psychology, 46,* 991–1004.

21. Buss, D. (1995). Evolutionary psychology: A new paradigm for psychological science. *Psychological Inquiry, 6,* 1–30.

    Buss, D. (1996). Sexual conflict: Evolutionary insights into feminism and the "battle of the sexes." In D. Buss & N. Malamuth (Eds.), *Sex, power, conflict: Evolutionary and feminist perspectives* (pp. 296–318). New York: Oxford University Press.

    Buss, D., & Kenrick, D. (1998). Evolutionary social psychology. In D. Gilbert, S. Fiske, & G. Lindzey (Eds.), *Handbook of social psychology* (4th. ed., Vol. 1, pp. 982–1026). New York: McGraw-Hill.

    Buss, D., & Schmitt, D. (1993). Sexual strategies theory: An evolutionary perspective on human mating. *Psychological Review, 100,* 204–232.

22. Eagly, A. (1995). The science and politics of comparing women and men. *American Psychologist, 50,* 145–158.

    Eagly, A. (1996). Differences between women and men: Their magnitude, practical importance, and political meaning. *American Psychologist, 51,* 158–159.

    Eagly, A., & Wood, W. (1991). Explaining sex differences in social behavior: A metaanalytic perspective. Special Issue: Meta-analysis in personality and social psychology. *Personality and Social Psychology Bulletin, 17,* 306–315.

    Swim, J. (1994) Perceived versus meta-analytic effect sizes: An assessment of the accuracy of gender stereotypes. *Journal of Personality and Social Psychology, 66,* 21–36.

23. Feldman-Summers, S., & Kiesler, S. B. (1974). Those who are number two try harder: The effect of sex on attributions of causality. *Journal of Personality and Social Psychology, 30,* 845–855.

24. Deaux, K., & Emswiller, T. (1974). Explanations of successful performance on sex-linked tasks: What is skill for the male is luck for the female. *Journal of Personality and Social Psychology, 29,* 80–85.

25. Swim, J., & Sanna, L. (1996). He's skilled, she's lucky: A meta-analysis of observers' attributions for women's and men's successes and failures. *Personality and Social Psychology Bulletin, 22,* 507–519.

26. Nicholls, J. G. (1975). Causal attributions and other achievement related cognitions: Effects of task outcome, attainment value, and sex. *Journal of Personality and Social Psychology, 31,* 379–389.

27. Stipek, D., & Gralinski, J. H. (1991). Gender differences in children's achievement-related beliefs and emotional responses to success and failure in mathematics. *Journal of Educational Psychology, 83,* 361–371.

28. Jacobs, J., & Eccles, J. (1992). The impact of mothers' gender-role stereotypic beliefs on mothers' and children's ability perceptions. *Journal of Personality and Social Psychology, 63,* 932–944.

29. Weinberg, R. S., Richardson, P. A., & Jackson, A. E. (1983). Effect of situation criticality on tennis performance of males and females. *Newsletter of the Society for the Advancement of Social Psychology, 9,* 8–9.

30. Turner, M., & Pratkanis, A. (1993). Effects of preferential and meritorious selection on performance: An examination of intuitive and self handicapping perspectives. *Personality and Social Psychology Bulletin, 19,* 47–58.

31. Lerner, M. (1980). *The justice motive.* New York: Plenum Press.
    Montada, L., & Lerner, M. (1996). *Current societal concerns about justice.* New York: Plenum Press.

32. Furnham, A., & Gunter, B. (1984). Just world beliefs and attitudes toward the poor. *British Journal of Social Psychology, 23,* 265–269.

33. Fischhoff, B., & Beyth, R. (1975). "I knew it would happen": Remembered probabilities on once-future things. *Organizational Behavior and Human Performance, 13,* 1–16.

34. Janoff-Bulman, R., Timko, C., & Carli, L. L. (1985). Cognitive bias in blaming the victim. *Journal of Experimental Social Psychology, 21,* 161–177.
    See also: LaBine, S., & LaBine, G. (1996). Determinations of negligence and the hindsight bias. *Law and Human Behavior, 20,* 501–516.

35. Gould, S. (1977). *Ever since Darwin: Reflections on natural history* (p. 243). New York: Norton.

36. Pearson, K., & Moul, M. (1925). The problem of alien immigration into Great Britain, illustrated by an example of Russian and Polish Jewish children. *Annals of Eugenics, 1,* 5–127.

37. Janis, I., & Field, P. (1959). Sex difference and personality factors related to persuasibility. In C. I. Hovland & I. L. Janis (Eds.), *Personality and persuasibility* (pp. 55–68). New Haven, CT: Yale University Press.

38. Sistrunk, F., & McDavid, J. (1971). Sex variable in conforming behavior. *Journal of Personality and Social Psychology, 17,* 202–207.

39. Word, C., Zanna, M., & Cooper, J. (1974). The nonverbal mediation of self-fulfilling prophecies in interracial interaction. *Journal of Experimental Social Psychology, 10,* 109–120.

40. Snyder, M. (1984). When belief creates reality. In L. Berkowitz (Ed.), *Advances in experimental social psychology* (Vol. 18, pp. 247–305). Orlando, FL: Academic Press.

41. Merton, R. F. (1968). The self-fulfilling prophecy. *Antioch Review, 8,* 193–210.

42. Snyder, M., & Swann, W. B., Jr. (1978). Hypothesis-testing processes in social interactions. *Journal of Personality and Social Psychology, 36,* 1202–1212.

43. Pettigrew, T. F., & Meertens, R. W. (1995). Subtle and blatant prejudice in western Europe. *European Journal of Social Psychology, 25,* 57–75.

44. Frey, D. L., & Gaertner, S. I. (1986). Helping and the avoidance of inappropriate interracial behavior: A strategy that perpetuates a nonprejudiced self-image. *Journal of Personality and Social Psychology, 50,* 1083–1090.

45. Ayers, I. (1991). Fair driving: Gender and race discrimination in retail car negotiations. *Harvard Law Review, 104,* 817–872.

46. Hebl, M. Foster, J. Bigazzi, J., Mannix, L., Dovidio, J. (2002). Formal and interpersonal discrimination: A field study of bias toward homosexual applicants. *Personality & Social Psychology Bulletin, 28(6),* 815–825.

47. Glick, P. & Fiske, S. (2002). Ambivalent responses. *American Psychology, 57,* 444–446.

48. Bem, D., & Bem, S. (1970, November). We're all nonconscious sexists. *Psychology Today,* pp. 22–26, 115–116.

49. Weitzman, L., Eifler, D., Hokada, E., & Ross, C. (1972). Sex-role socialization in picture books for preschool children. *American Journal of Sociology, 77,* 1125–1150.
    Kolbe, R., & LaVoie, J. (1981). Sex-role stereotyping in preschool children's picture books. *Social Psychology Quarterly, 44,* 369–374.

50. Hartley, R. (1960). Children's concepts of male and female roles. *Merrill-Palmer Quarterly, 6,* 83–91.

51. Lipman-Blumen, J. (1972). How ideology shapes women's lives. *Scientific American, 226(1),* 34–42.

52. Taeuber, C. M. (1996). *Statistical handbook on women in America.* Phoenix, AZ: Oryx Press.

53. Gray, S. W. (1975). Masculinity-femininity in relation to anxiety and social acceptance. *Child Development, 28,* 203–214.

54. Broverman, I. K., Vogel, S., Broverman, D., Clarkson, F., & Rosencrantz, P. (1972). Sex-role stereotypes: A current appraisal. *Journal of Social Issues, 28,* 59–78.

55. Porter, N., & Geis, F. (1981). Women and nonverbal leadership cues: When seeing is not believing. In C. Mayo & N. Henley (Eds.), *Gender and nonverbal behavior.* New York: Springer-Verlag.

56. Eagly, Alice H., Karau, Steven J. (2002). Role congruity theory of prejudice toward female leaders. *Psychological Review, 109,* 573–598.

57. Jackson, L. A., & Cash, T. F. (1985). Components of gender stereotypes: Their implications for inferences on stereotypic and nonstereotypic dimensions. *Personality and Social Psychology Bulletin, 11,* 326–344.

58. Gerbner, G. (1993). Women and minorities on television. Unpublished paper, Annenberg School for Communication, University of Pennsylvania.

Gerbner, G., Gross, L., Morgan, M., & Signorielli, N. (1993). Growing up with television: The cultivation perspective. In J. Bryant & D. Zillman (Eds.), *Media effects: Advances in theory and research*. Hillsdale, NJ: Erlbaum.

59. Thibodeau, R. (1989). From racism to tokenism: The changing face of blacks in New Yorker cartoons. *Public Opinion Quarterly, 53,* 482–494.

60. Chavez, D. (1985). Perpetuation of gender inequality: A context analysis of comic strips. *Sex Roles, 13,* 93–102.

61. Geis, F., Brown, V., Jennings (Walstedt), J., & Porter, N. (1984). TV commercials as achievement scripts for women. *Sex Roles, 10,* 513–525.

62. Buss, D., & Kenrick, D. (1998). Evolutionary social psychology. In D. Gilbert, S. Fiske, & G. Lindzey (Eds.), *Handbook of social psychology* (4th. ed., Vol. 1, pp. 982–1026). New York: McGraw-Hill.

63. Dollard, J. (1987). *Class and caste in a southern town*. New Haven, CT: Yale University Press.

64. Dollard, J. (1938). Hostility and fear in social life. *Social Forces, 17,* 15–26.

65. Roberts, E., quoted by Jacobs, P., & Landau, S. (1971). *To serve the devil* (Vol. 2, p. 71). New York: Vintage Books.

66. Crocker, C., quoted by Jacobs, P., & Landau S. (1971). *To serve the devil* (Vol. 2, p. 81). New York: Vintage Books.

67. Greeley, A., & Sheatsley, P. (1971). The acceptance of desegregation continues to advance. *Scientific American, 225(6),* 13–19.
    See also: Vanneman, R. D., & Pettigrew, T. F. (1972). Race and relative deprivation in the urban United States. *Race, 13,* 461–486.

68. Sherif, M., Harvey, O. J., White, B. J., Hood, W., & Sherif, C. (1961). *Intergroup conflict and cooperation: The Robbers Cave experiment*. Norman. University of Oklahoma Institute of Intergroup Relations.

69. Hovland, C., & Sears, R. (1940). Minor studies of aggression: Correlation of lynchings with economic indices. *Journal of Psychology, 9,* 301–310.

70. Klineberg, O. (1971). Black and white in international perspective. *American Psychologist, 26,* 119–128.
    Lamont-Brown, R. (1993). The burakumin: Japan's underclass. *Contemporary Review 263,* 136–139.

71. Speer, A. (1970). *Inside the Third Reich: Memoirs* (R. Winston & C. Winston, Trans.). New York: Macmillan.

72. Miller, N., & Bugelski, R. (1948). Minor studies in aggression: The influence of frustrations imposed by the in-group on attitudes expressed by the out-group. *Journal of Psychology, 25,* 437–442.

73. Rogers, R., & Prentice-Dunn, S. (1981). Deindividuation and anger-mediated interracial aggression: Unmasking regressive racism. *Journal of Personality and Social Psychology, 41,* 63–73.

74. Weatherly, D. (1961). Anti-semitism and the expression of fantasy aggression. *Journal of Abnormal and Social Psychology, 62,* 454–457.

75. Crocker, J., Thompson, L. L., McGraw, K. M., & Ingerman, C. (1987). Downward comparison, prejudice, and evaluations of others: Effects of self-esteem and threat. *Journal of Personality and Social Psychology, 52,* 907–916.

76. Dollard, J. (1987). *Class and caste in a southern town.* New Haven, CT: Yale University Press.

77. Bettelheim, B., & Janowitz, M. (1964). *Social change and prejudice, including dynamics of prejudice.* New York: Free Press.

78. Tumin, M., Barton, P., & Burrus, B. (1958). Education, prejudice, and discrimination: A study in readiness for desegregation. *American Sociological Review, 23,* 41–49.

79. Fein, S., & Spencer, S. J. (1997). Prejudice as self-image maintenance: Affirming the self through derogating others. *Journal of Personality and Social Psychology, 73,* 31–44.

80. Adorno, T., Frenkel-Brunswick, E., Levinson, D., & Sanford, R. N. (1950). *The authoritarian personality.* New York: Harper.

81. McFarland, S. M., Ageyev, V. S., & Abalakina-Paap, M. A. (1992). Authoritarianism in the former Soviet Union. *Journal of Personality and Social Psychology, 63,* 1004–1010.

82. Taylor, D., Sheatsley, P., & Greeley, A. (1978) Attitudes toward racial integration. *Scientific American, 238,* 42–49.

83. Pettigrew, T. F. (1959). Regional differences in anti-Negro prejudice. *Journal of Abnormal and Social Psychology, 59,* 28–36.

84. Minard, R. D. (1952). Race relations in the Pocahontas coal field. *Journal of Social Issues, 8,* 29–44.

85. Pettigrew, T. F. (1958). Personality and sociocultural factors and intergroup attitudes: A cross-national comparison. *Journal of Conflict Resolution, 2,* 29–42.

86. Watson, J. (1950). Some social and psychological situations related to change in attitude. *Human Relations, 3,* 15–56.

87. Kirkland, S. L., Greenberg, J., & Pyszczynski, T. (1987). Further evidence of the deleterious effects of overheard derogatory ethnic labels: Derogation beyond the target. *Personality and Social Psychology Bulletin, 13,* 216–227.

88. MacCrone, I. (1937). *Race attitudes in South Africa.* London: Oxford University Press.

89. Lazarsfeld, P. (1940). *Radio and the printed page.* New York: Duell, Sloan & Pearce.

90. Deutsch, M., & Collins, M. E. (1951). *Interracial housing: A psychological evaluation of a social experiment.* Minneapolis: University of Minnesota Press.
    See also: Wilner, D., Wallcley, R., & Cook, S. (1955). *Human relations in interracial housing.* Minneapolis: University of Minnesota Press.

91. Pettigrew, T. (1997). Generalized intergroup contact effects on prejudice. *Personality and Social Psychology Bulletin, 23,* 173–185.

92. Brehm, J. (1959). Increasing cognitive dissonance by a fait accompli. *Journal of Abnormal and Social Psychology, 58,* 379–382.

93. Darley, D., & Berscheid, E. (1967). Increased liking as a result of the anticipation of personal contact. *Human Relations, 20,* 29–40.

94. National Opinion Research Center (1980). *General social surveys, 1972–1980: Cumulative code book.* Storrs, CT: Roper Public Opinion Research Center, University of Connecticut.

95. Pettigrew, T. F. (1961). Social psychology and desegregation research. *American Psychologist, 16,* 105–112.

96. Clark, K. B. (1953). Desegregation: An appraisal of the evidence. *Journal of Social Issues, 9(4),* 2–76.

97. Stouffer, S., Suchman, E., DeVinney, L., Star, S., & Williams, R. (1949). *The American soldier: Adjustment during army life.* World War II). Princeton, NJ: Princeton University Press.

98. Kramer, B. (1951). Residential contact as a determinant of attitudes toward Negroes. Unpublished Ph.D. dissertation, Harvard University.
    Winder, A. (1952). White attitudes towards Negro–white interaction in an area of changing racial composition. *American Psychologist, 7,* 330–331.

99. Asher, S., & Allen, V. (1969). Racial preference and social comparison processes. *Journal of Social Issues, 25,* 157–166.
    Stephen, W., Kennedy, J. (1975). An experimental study of inter-ethnic competition in segregated schools. *Journal of School Psychology, 13,* 234–247.
    Gerard, H., & Miller, N. (1976). *School desegregation.* New York: Plenum Press.

100. Stephan, W. G. (1978). School desegregation: An evaluation of predictions made In Brown v. The Board of Education. *Psychological Bulletin, 85,* 217–238.

101. Lester, J. (1971). Beep! Beep! Bang! Umgawa! Black power! In R. Kytle (Ed.), *Confrontation: Issues of the 70s* (pp. 162–181). New York: Random House.

102. Deutsch, M., & Collins, M. E. (1951) *Interracial housing: A psychological evaluation of a social experiment.* Minneapolis: University of Minnesota Press.

103. Sherif, M., & Sherif, C. (1956). *An outline of social psychology.* New York: Harper & Bros. Sherif, M., Harvey, O. J., White, B. J., Hood, W., & Sherif, C. *Intergroup conflict and cooperation: The Robbers Cave experiment.* Norman: University of Oklahoma Institute of Intergroup Relations.

104. Deutsch, M. (1949). A theory of cooperation and competition. *Human Relations 2,* 129–152.
    Deutsch, M. (1949). An experimental study of the effects of cooperation and competition upon group process. *Human Relations, 2,* 199–232.

105. Keenan, P., & Carnevale, P. (1989). Positive effects of within-group competition on between-group negotiation. *Journal of Applied Social Psychology, 19,* 977–992.

106. Aronson, E., Stephan, C., Sikes, J., Blaney, N., & Snapp, M. (1978). *The jigsaw classroom.* Beverly Hills, CA: Sage.

Aronson, E., & Osherow, N. (1980). Cooperation, prosocial behavior, and academic performance: Experiments in the desegregated classroom. In L. Bickman (Ed.), *Applied social psychology annual* (Vol. 1, pp. 163–196). Beverly Hills, CA: Sage.

Aronson, E. (1992). Stateways can change folkways. In R. Baird & S. Rosenbaum (Eds.), *Bigotry, prejudice and hatred: Definitions, causes and solutions* (pp. 111–124). Buffalo, NY: Prometheus Books.

Aronson, E., & Patnoe, S. (1997). *Cooperation in the classroom: The jigsaw method.* New York: Longman.

107. Aronson, E., & Osherow, N. (1980). Cooperation, prosocial behavior, and academic performance: Experiments in the desegregated classroom. In L. Bickman (Ed.), *Applied social psychology annual* (Vol. 1, pp. 163–196). Beverly Hills, CA: Sage.

108. Aronson, E. (2002). Building empathy, compassion, and achievement in the jigsaw classroom. In Aronson, Joshua (Ed.), *Improving academic achievement: Impact of psychological factors on education* (pp. 209–225). San Diego, CA, US: Academic Press.

Juergen-Lohmann, Julia; Borsch, Frank; Giesen, Heinz. (2001). Cooperative learning at the university: An evaluation of jigsaw in classes of educational psychology/Kooperatives Lernen an der Hochschule. *Evaluation des Gruppenpuzzles in Seminaren der Paedagogischen Psychologie Zeitschrift fuer Paedagogische Psychologie, 15,* 74–84.

Perkins, D., & Saris, R. (2001). A "jigsaw classroom" technique for undergraduate statistics courses. *Teaching of Psychology, 28,* 111–113.

Walker, I., & Crogan, M. (1998). Academic performance, prejudice, and the Jigsaw classroom: New pieces to the puzzle. *Journal of Community & Applied Social Psychology, 8,* 381–393.

109. Desforges D. M., Lord, C. G., Ramsey, S. L., Mason, J. A., Van Leeuwen, M. D., West, S. C., & Lepper, M. R. (1991). Effects of Structured Cooperative Contact on changing negative attitudes towards stigmatized social groups. *Journal of Personality and Social Psychology, 60,* 531–544.

110. Leippe, M. R., & Eisenstadt, D. (1994). Generalization of dissonance reduction: Decreasing prejudice through induced compliance. *Journal of Personality and Social Psychology, 67,* 395–413.

111. Gaertner, S. L., Mann, J. A., Dovidio, J. F., Murrell, A. J., & Pomare, M. (1990). How does cooperation reduce intergroup bias? *Journal of Personality and Social Psychology, 59,* 692–704.

112. Bridgeman, D. (1981). Enhanced role-taking through cooperative interdependence: A field study. *Child Development, 52,* 1231–1238.

113. Slavin, R. (1996). Research on cooperative learning and achievement: What we know, what we need to know. *Contemporary Educational Psychology, 21,* 43–69.

Qin, Z., Johnson, D. W., & Johnson, R. T. (1995). Cooperative versus competitive efforts and problem solving. *Review of Educational Research, 65,* 29–143.

114. Aronson, E., & Patnoe, S. (1997). *Cooperation in the classroom: The jigsaw method.* New York: Longman.

115. McConahay, J. B. (1981). Reducing racial prejudice in desegregated schools. In W. D. Hawley (Ed.), *Elective school desegregation.* Beverly Hills, CA: Sage.

116. Aronson, E. (2000). *Nobody Left to Hate: Teaching Compassion After Columbine.* New York: Henry Holt.

117. Shipler, D. K. (1997). *A country of strangers: Blacks and whites in America.* New York: Alfred A. Knopf.

Chapter 8   Liking, Loving, and Interpersonal Sensitivity

1. Darwin, C. (1910). *The expression of emotions in man and animals.* New York: Appleton.

2. Carnegie, D. (1937). *How to win friends and influence people.* New York: Simon & Schuster.

3. Remmers, H. H., & Radler, D. H. (1958). Teenage attitudes. *Scientific American, 198(6),* 25–29.
   Adler, P. A., & Adler, P. (1995). Dynamics of inclusion and exclusion in pre-adolesent cliques. *Social Psychology Quarterly, 58,* 145–162.
   Cohen, P., Reinherz, H., & Frost, A. (1994). Self-perceptions of unpopularity in adolescence: Links to past and current adjustment. *Child and Adolescent Social Work Journal, 11,* 37–52.
   Kennedy, E. (1995). Correlates of perceived popularity among peers: A study of race and gender differences among middle school students. *Journal of Negro Education, 64,* 186–195.

4. Lemann, T., & Solomon, R. (1952). Group characteristics as revealed in sociometric patterns and personality ratings. *Sociometry, 15,* 7–90.

5. Homans, G. (1961). *Social behavior: Its elementary forms.* New York: Harcourt, Brace and World.

6. Walster (Hatfield), E., Aronson, V., Abrahams, D., & Rottman, L. (1966). Importance of physical attractiveness in dating behavior. *Journal of Personality and Social Psychology, 5,* 508–516.

7. Byrne, D. (1969). Attitudes and attraction. In L. Berkowitz (Ed.), *Advances in experimental social psychology* (Vol. 4). New York: Academic Press.
   Sprecher, S., & Duck, S. (1994). Sweet talk: The importance of perceived communication for romantic and friendship attraction experienced during a get-acquainted date. *Personality and Social Psychology Bulletin, 20(4),* 391–400.
   Pilkington, N. W., & Lydon, J. E. (1997). The relative effect of attitude similarity and attitude dissimilarity on interpersonal attraction: Investigating the moderating roles of prejudice and group membership. *Personality and Social Psychology Bulletin, 23(2),* 107–122.

8. Sherif, M. (1956). Experiments in group conflict. *Scientific American, 195,* 53–58.

9. Aronson, E., Stephan, C., Sikes, J., Blaney, N., & Snapp, M. (1978). *The jigsaw classroom.* Beverly Hills, CA: Sage.
   Aronson, E., & Osherow, N. (1980). Cooperation, prosocial behavior, and academic performance: Experiments in the desegregated classroom. In L. Bickman (Ed.), *Applied social psychology annual* (Vol. 1, pp. 163–196). Beverly Hills, CA: Sage.

10. Aronson, E., & Mills, J. (1959). The effect of severity of initiation on liking for a group. *Journal of Abnormal and Social Psychology, 59,* 177–181.

11. Aronson, E., & Darwyn, L. (1965). Gain and loss of esteem as determinants of interpersonal attractiveness. *Journal of Experimental Social Psychology, 1,* 156–171.
    Aronson, E., & Worchel, P. (1966). Similarity versus liking as determinants of interpersonal attractiveness. *Psychonomic Science, 5,* 157–158.
    Sigall, H., & Aronson, E. (1969). Liking for an evaluator as a function of her physical attractiveness and nature of the evaluations. *Journal of Experimental Social Psychology, 5,* 93–100.

12. Amabile, T. (1983). Brilliant but cruel: Perceptions of negative evaluators. *Journal of Experimental Social Psychology, 19,* 146–156.

13. Deutsch, M., & Solomon, L. (1959). Reactions to evaluations by others as influenced by self-evaluations. *Sociometry, 22,* 93–112.

14. Jones, E. E. (1964). *Ingratiation.* New York: Appleton-Century-Crofts.

15. Jennings, H. H. (1959). *Leadership and isolation* (2nd ed). New York: Longman, Green.

16. Lott, B., & Lott, A. (1960). The formation of positive attitudes toward group members. *Journal of Abnormal and Social Psychology, 61,* 297–300.

17. Brehm, J., & Cole, A. (1966). Effect of a favor which reduces freedom. *Journal of Personality and Social Psychology, 3,* 420–426.

18. Tolstoy, L. (1942). *War and peace.* New York: Simon & Schuster.

19. Bigelow, J. (Ed.). (1916). *The autobiography of Benjamin Franklin* (pp. 216–217). New York: G. P. Putnam's Sons.

20. Jecker, J., & Landy, D. (1969). Liking a person as a function of doing him a favor. *Human Relations, 22,* 371–378.

21. Lerner, M., & Simmons, C. (1966). Observer's reaction to the "innocent victim": Compassion or rejection? *Journal of Personality and Social Psychology, 4,* 203–210.

22. Lott, A. J., Lott, B. E., Reed, T., & Crow, T. (1960). Personality-trait descriptions of differentially liked persons. *Journal of Personality and Social Psychology, 16,* 284–290.

23. Bales, R. (1958). Task roles and social roles in problem solving groups. In E. E. Maccoby, T. M. Newcomb, & E. L. Hartley (Eds.), *Readings in social psychology* (3rd ed., pp. 437–447). New York: Holt.
    Bales, R., & Slater, P. (1955). Role differentiation in small decision-making groups. In T. Parsons & R. F. Bales (Eds.), *The family, socialization, and interaction process.* Glencoe, IL: Free Press.

24. Aronson, E., Willerman, B., & Floyd, J. (1966). The effect of a pratfall on increasing interpersonal attractiveness. *Psychonomic Science, 4,* 227–228.

25. Deaux, K. (1972). To err is humanizing: But sex makes a difference. *Representative Research in Social Psychology, 3,* 20–28.

26. Aronson, E., Helmreich, R., & LeFan, J. (1970). To err is humanizing—sometimes: Effects of self-esteem, competence, and a pratfall on interpersonal attraction. *Journal of Personality and Social Psychology, 16,* 259–264.

27. Tesser, A., & Brodie, M. (1971). A note on the evaluation of a "computer date." *Psychonomic Science, 23,* 300.

28. Feingold, A. (1990). Gender differences in effects of physical attractiveness on romantic attraction: A comparison across five research paradigms. *Journal of Personality and Social Psychology, 59,* 981–993.

29. Walster, E., Aronson, V., Abrahams, D., & Rottman, L. Importance of physical attractiveness in dating behavior. *Journal of Personality and Social Psychology, 5,* 508–516.

30. White, G. (1980). Physical attractiveness and courtship progress. *Journal of Personality and Social Psychology, 39,* 660–668.

31. Dion, K., Berscheid, E., & Walster (Hatfield), E. (1972). What is beautiful is good. *Journal of Personality and Social Psychology, 24,* 285–290.

32. Tan, A. S. (1979). TV beauty ads and role expectations of adolescent female viewers. *Journalism Quarterly, 56,* 283–288.

33. Dion, K., & Berscheid, E. (1971). Physical attractiveness and sociometric choice in nursery school children. Mimeographed research report.

34. Dion, K. (1972). Physical attractiveness and evaluations of children's transgressions. *Journal of Personality and Social Psychology, 24,* 207–213.
    Similar findings reported in Berkowitz, L., & Frodi, A. (1979). Reactions to a child's mistakes as affected by her/his looks and speech. *Social Psychology Quarterly, 42,* 420–425.

35. Lerner, R. M., Lerner, J. V., Hess, L. E., & Schwab, J. (1991). Physical attractiveness and psychosocial functioning among early adolescents. *Journal of Early Adolescence, 11(3),* 300–320.

36. Hunsberger, B., & Cavanagh, B. (1988). Physical attractiveness and children's expectations of potential teachers. *Psychology in the Schools, 25(1),* 70–74.

37. Frieze, I. H., Olson, J. E., & Russell, J. (1991). Attractiveness and income for men and women in management. *Journal of Applied Social Psychology, 21,* 1037–1039.

38. Sigall, H., & Aronson, E. (1969). Liking for an evaluator as a function of her physical attractiveness and nature of the evaluations. *Journal of Experimental and Social Psychology, 5,* 93–100.

39. Sigall, H., & Ostrove, N. (1975). Beautiful but dangerous: Effects of offender attractiveness and nature of the crime on juridic judgment. *Journal of Personality and Social Psychology, 31,* 410–414.

40. Downs, C. A., & Lyons, P. M. (1991). Natural observations of the links between attractiveness and initial legal judgments. *Personality and Social Psychology Bulletin, 17,* 541–547.

41. Sigall, H., & Landy, D. (1973). Radiating beauty: Effects of having a physically attractive partner on person perception. *Journal of Personality and Social Psychology, 28,* 218–224.

42. Snyder, M., Tanke, E. D., & Berscheid, E. (1977). Social perception and interpersonal behavior: On the self-fulfilling nature of social stereotypes. *Journal of Personality and Social Psychology, 35,* 656–666.

43. Byrne, D. (1969). Attitudes and attraction. In L. Berkowitz (Ed.), *Advances in experimental social psychology* (Vol. 4). New York: Academic Press.

44. Marks, G., Miller, N., & Maruyama, M. (1981). Effect of targets' physical attractiveness on assumptions of similarity. *Journal of Personality and Social Psychology, 41,* 198–206.

   Granberg, D., & King, M. (1980). Cross-lagged panel analysis of the relation between attraction and perceived similarity. *Journal of Experimental Social Psychology, 16,* 573–581.

45. Aronson, E., & Worchel, S. (1966). Similarity versus liking as determinants of interpersonal attractiveness. *Psychometric Science, 5,* 157–158.

   Condon, J. W., & Crano, W. D. (1988). Inferred evaluation and the relationship between attitude similarity and interpersonal attraction. *Journal of Personality and Social Psychology, 54,* 789–797.

46. Secord, P., & Backman, C. (1964). Interpersonal congruency, perceived similarity, and friendship. *Sociometry, 27,* 115–127.

47. Curtis, R. C., & Miller, K. (1986). Believing another likes or dislikes you: Behaviors making the beliefs come true. *Journal of Personality and Social Psychology, 51,* 284–290.

48. Walster (Hatfield), E. (1965). The effect of self-esteem on romantic liking. *Journal of Experimental and Social Psychology, 1,* 184–197.

49. Kiesler, S. B., & Baral, R. L. (1970). The search for a romantic partner: The effects of self-esteem and physical attractiveness on romantic behavior. In K. J. Gergen & D. Marlowe (Eds.), *Personality and social behavior.* Reading, MA: Addison-Wesley.

50. Baumeister, Roy F., Twenge, Jean M., Nuss, Christopher K. (2002). Effects of social exclusion on cognitive processes: Anticipated aloneness reduces intelligent thought. *Journal of Personality & Social Psychology, 83,* 817–827.

51. Twenge, Jean M., Catanese, Kathleen R., Baumeister, Roy F. (2002). Social exclusion causes self-defeating behavior. *Journal of Personality & Social Psychology, 83,* 606–615.

52. Aronson, E., & Linder, D. (1965). Gain and loss of esteem as determinants of interpersonal attractiveness. *Journal of Experimental and Social Psychology, 1,* 156–171.

   See also: Gerard, H., & Greenbaum, C. W. (1962). Attitudes toward an agent of uncertainty reduction. *Journal of Personality, 30,* 485–495.

   Mettee, D., Taylor, S. E., & Friedman, H. (1973). Affect conversion and the gain-loss like effect. *Sociometry, 36,* 505–519.

   Aronson, E., & Mettee, D. (1974). Affective reactions to appraisal from others. In *Foundations of interpersonal attraction.* New York: Academic Press.

   Clore, G. L., Wiggins, N. H., & Itkin, S. (1975). Gain and loss in attraction: Attributions from nonverbal behavior. *Journal of Personality and Social Psychology, 31,* 706–712.

   Marshall, L. L., & Kidd, R. F. (1981). Good news or bad news first? *Social Behavior and Personality, 9(2),* 223–226.

   Tzeng, O. C. S., & Gomez, M. (1992). Behavioral reinforcement paradigm of love. In O. C. S. Tzeng (Ed.), *Theories of love development, maintenance, and dissolution: Octagonal cycle and differential perspectives* (pp. 17–132). New York: Praeger/Greenwood.

   Turcotte, S. J., & Leventhal, L. (1984). Gain-loss versus reinforcement-affect ordering of student ratings of teaching: Effect of rating instructions. *Journal of Educational Psychology, 76(5),* 782–791.

53. Aronson, E., & Linder, D. (1965). Gain and loss of esteem as determinants of interpersonal attractiveness. *Journal of Experimental and Social Psychology, 1,* 156–171.

54. Spinoza, B. de (1910). The ethics. In A. Boyle (Trans.), *Spinoza's ethics and "De Intellectus Emendatione."* New York: Dutton.

55. Mettee, D. R., Taylor, S. E., & Friedman, H. (1973). Affect conversion and the gain-loss like effect. *Sociometry, 36,* 505–519.

56. Mettee, D. R., & Aronson, E. (1974). Affective reactions to appraisal from others. *Foundations of interpersonal attraction.* New York: Academic Press.

57. Clark, M. S., & Mills, J. (1979). Interpersonal attraction in exchange and communal relationships. *Journal of Personality and Social Psychology, 37,* 12–24.
    Mills, J., & Clark, M. S. (1982). Exchange and communal relationships. In L. Wheeler (Ed.), *Review of personality and social psychology* (Vol. III). Beverly Hills, CA: Sage.
    Clark, M. S. (1986). Evidence for the effectiveness of manipulations of desire for communal versus exchange relationships. *Personality and Social Psychology Bulletin, 12,* 425.

58. Walster, E., Walster, G. W., & Traupmann, J. (1979). Equity and premarital sex. In M. Cook & G. Wilson (Eds.), *Love and attraction.* New York: Pergamon Press.
    Schafer, R. B., & Keith, P. M. (1980). Equity and depression among married couples. *Social Psychology Quarterly, 43,* 430–435.

59. Clark, M. S., Mills, J. R., & Corcoran, D. M. (1989). Keeping track of needs and inputs of friends and strangers. *Personality and Social Psychology Bulletin, 15,* 533–542.

60. Berscheid, E., & Reis, H. (1998). Attraction and close relationships. Gilbert, T., Fiske, S., & Lindzey, G. (Eds.), *The handbook of social psychology,* Vol. 2 (4th ed.) (pp. 193–281). New York, NY: McGraw Hill

61. Rubin, Z. (1970). Measurement of romantic love. *Journal of Personality and Social Psychology, 16,* 265–273.

62. Rubin, Z. (1973). *Liking and loving: An invitation to social psychology.* New York: Holt, Rinehart and Winston.

63. Hatfield, E., & Rapson, R. L. (2002). Passionate love and sexual desire: Cultural and historical perspectives. In A. L. Vangelisti, & H. T. Reis (Eds.), *Stability and change in relationships across the life span* (pp. 306–324). New York: Cambridge University Press.

64. Sternberg, R. J. (1988). *The triangle of love.* New York: Basic Books.

65. Baumeister, R. (1991). *Meanings of life.* New York: Guilford Press.
    Buss, D., & Kenrick, D. (1998). Evolutionary social psychology. In D. Gilbert, S. Fiske, & G. Lindzey (Eds.), Handbook of social psychology (4th. ed., Vol. 1, pp. 982–1026). New York: McGraw Hill.

66. Duck, S. (1995). Stratagems, spoils and a serpent's tooth: On the delights and dilemmas of personal relationships. In W. R. Cupach, & B. H. Spitzberg (Eds.), *The darkside of interpersonal communication.* Hillsdale, NJ: LEA.

67. Harvey, O. J. (1962). Personality factors in resolution of conceptual incongruities. *Sociometry, 25,* 336–352.

68. Stevenson, H., Keen, R., & Knights, J. (1963). Parents and strangers as reinforcing agents for children's performance. *Journal of Abnormal and Social Psychology, 67,* 183–185.

69. Floyd, J. (1964). Effects of amount of reward and friendship status of the other on the frequency of sharing in children. Unpublished Ph.D. dissertation, University of Minnesota.

70. Cicero (46 B.C.). *De amicitia.* Libri Sapientis: Horti Novabaculae, Rome.

71. Harvey, J. H., Weber, A. L., & Orbuch, T. L. (1990). *Interpersonal accounts: A social psychological perspective.* Oxford: Blackwell.

72. Rands, M., Levinger, G., & Mellinger, G. (1981). Patterns of conflict resolution and marital satisfaction. *Journal of Family Issues, 2,* 297–321.

73. Skotko, P. K. (1981). The relation between interpersonal attraction and measures of self-disclosure. *Journal of Social Psychology, 112,* 311–312.
    Archer, R., & Burleson, J. (1980). The effects of timing of self-disclosure on attraction and reciprocity. *Journal of Personality and Social Psychology, 38,* 120–130.
    Taylor, D., Gould, R., & Brounstein, P. (1981). Effects of personalistic self-disclosure. *Personality and Social Psychology Bulletin, 7,* 437–492.

74. Aron, A., Melinat, E., Aron, E. N., & Vallone, R. D. (1997). The experimental generation of interpersonal closeness: A procedure and some preliminary findings. *Personality and Social Psychology Bulletin, 23(4),* 363–377.

75. Pennebaker, J. W. (1997). Opening up: The healing power of expressing emotions (rev. ed.). New York: Guilford Press.

76. Kahn, M. (1995). The tao of conversation. Oakland, CA: New Harbinger.

77. Fincham, Frank D., & Bradbury, Thomas N. (1993). Marital satisfaction, depression, and attributions: A longitudinal analysis. *Journal of Personality & Social Psychology, 64,* 442–452.
    Karney, Benjamin, & Bradbury, Thomas N. (2000). Attributions in marriage: State or trait? A growth curve analysis. *JPSP, 78,* 295–309.

Chapter 9 Social Psychology as a Science

1. Kunen, J. S. (1995, July 10). Teaching prisoners a lesson. *The New Yorker,* pp. 34–39.

2. *Nova,* KQED (1993, December 21). Richard Feynman: The best mind since Einstein.

3. P. Semonov, personal communication.

4. Nisbett, R., & Wilson, T. (1977). Telling more than we know: Verbal reports on mental processes. *Psychological Review, 84,* 231–259.

5. Aronson, E., Willerman, B., & Floyd, J. (1966). The effect of a pratfall on increasing interpersonal attractiveness. *Psychonomic Science, 4,* 227–228.

6. Aronson, E., & Mills, J. (1959). The effect of severity of initiation on liking for a group. *Journal of Abnormal and Social Psychology, 59,* 177–181.

7. Liebert, R., & Baron, R. (1972). Some immediate effects of televised violence on children's behavior. *Developmental Psychology, 6,* 469–475.

8. Aronson, E., & Carlsmith, J. M. (1969). Experimentation in social psychology. In G. Lindzey & E. Aronson (Eds.), *Handbook of social psychology* (2nd ed., Vol. 2, pp. 1–79). Reading, MA: Addison-Wesley.
   See also: Aronson, E., Brewer, M., & Carlsmith, J. M. (1985). Experimentation in social psychology. In G. Lindzey & E. Aronson (Eds.), *Handbook of social psychology* (3rd ed., Vol. 1, pp. 441–486). New York: Random House.

9. Milgram, S. (1963). Behavioral study of obedience. *Journal of Abnormal and Social Psychology, 67,* 371–378.

10. Ibid.

11. Aronson, E., Sigall, H., & Van Hoose, T. (1970). The cooperative subject: Myth or reality? *Journal of Experimental and Social Psychology, 6,* 1–10.

12. Asch, S. (1951). Effects of group pressure upon the modification and distortion of judgment. In M. H. Guetzkow (Ed.), *Groups, leadership, and men* (pp. 177–190). Pittsburgh: Carnegie.
   Asch, S. (1951). Studies of independence and conformity: A minority of one against a unanimous majority. *Psychological Monographs, 70* (9, Whole No. 416).

13. Dawes, R., McTavish, J., & Shaklee, H. (1977). Behavior, communication, and assumptions about other people's behavior in a common dilemma situation. *Journal of Personality and Social Psychology, 35,* 1–11.

14. Asch, S. (1951). Effects of group pressure upon the modification and distortion of judgment. In M. H. Guetzkow (Ed.), *Groups, leadership, and men* (pp. 177–190). Pittsburgh: Carnegie.

15. Aronson, E., & Mettee, D. (1968). Dishonest behavior as a function of differential levels of induced self-esteem. *Journal of Personality and Social Psychology, 9,* 121–127.

16. Milgram, S. (1963). Behavioral study of obedience. *Journal of Abnormal and Social Psychology, 67,* 371–378.

17. Bickman, L., & Zarantonello, M. (1978). The effects of deception and level of obedience on subjects' ratings of the Milgram study. *Personality and Social Psychology Bulletin, 4,* 81–85.

18. Milgram, S. (1964). Issues in the study of obedience: A reply to Baumrind. *American Psychologist, 19,* 848–852.

Name Index

Subject Index